T4-AMH-549

CCNP™ Switching

Sean Odom
Douglas Hammond

CCNP™ Switching Exam Prep

The Coriolis Group, LLC
14455 N. Hayden Road, Suite 220
Scottsdale, Arizona 85260

480/483-0192
FAX 480/483-0193
www.coriolis.com

Library of Congress Cataloging-in-Publication Data
Odom, Sean.
CCNP switching exam prep / by Sean Odom and Doug Hammond.
p. cm.
ISBN 1-57610-689-6
1. Electronic data processing personnel--Certification.
2. Telecommunication--Switching systems--Examinations--Study guides. I. Hammond, Doug, 1956- II. Title.
QA76.3. O35 2000
004.6'6--dc21 00-031675
CIP

President, CEO
Keith Weiskamp

Publisher
Steve Sayre

Acquisitions Editor
Shari Jo Hehr

Marketing Specialist
Cynthia Caldwell

Project Editor
Toni Zuccarini Ackley

Technical Reviewer
Thomas Hielsberg

Production Coordinator
Todd Halvorsen

Cover Designer
Jesse Dunn

Layout Designer
April Nielsen

CD-ROM Developer
Michelle McConnell

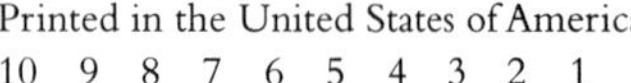
Printed in the United States of America
10 9 8 7 6 5 4 3 2 1

The Coriolis Group, LLC • 14455 North Hayden Road, Suite 220 • Scottsdale, Arizona 85260

ExamCram.com Connects You to the Ultimate Study Center!

Our goal has always been to provide you with the best study tools on the planet to help you achieve your certification in record time. Time is so valuable these days that none of us can afford to waste a second of it, especially when it comes to exam preparation.

Over the past few years, we've created an extensive line of *Exam Cram* and *Exam Prep* study guides, practice exams, and interactive training. To help you study even better, we have now created an e-learning and certification destination called **ExamCram.com**. (You can access the site at **www.examcram.com**.) Now, with every study product you purchase from us, you'll be connected to a large community of people like yourself who are actively studying for their certifications, developing their careers, seeking advice, and sharing their insights and stories.

I believe that the future is all about collaborative learning. Our **ExamCram.com** destination is our approach to creating a highly interactive, easily accessible collaborative environment, where you can take practice exams and discuss your experiences with others, sign up for features like "Questions of the Day," plan your certifications using our interactive planners, create your own personal study pages, and keep up with all of the latest study tips and techniques.

I hope that whatever study products you purchase from us—*Exam Cram* or *Exam Prep* study guides, *Personal Trainers*, *Personal Test Centers*, or one of our interactive Web courses—will make your studying fun and productive. Our commitment is to build the kind of learning tools that will allow you to study the way you want to, whenever you want to.

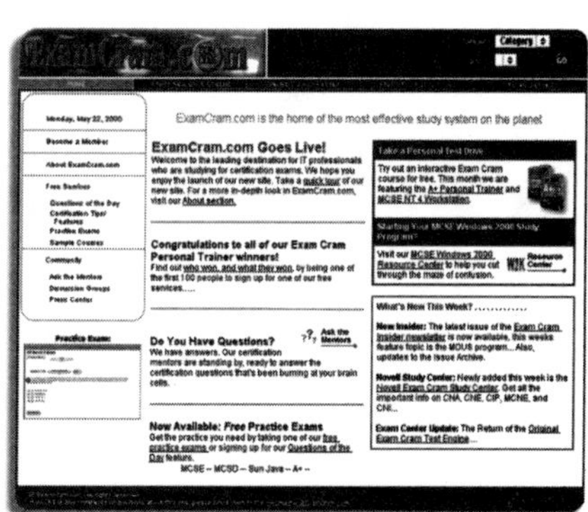

Visit ExamCram.com now to enhance your study program.

Help us continue to provide the very best certification study materials possible. Write us or email us at **learn@examcram.com** and let us know how our study products have helped you study. Tell us about new features that you'd like us to add. Send us a story about how we've helped you. We're listening!

Good luck with your certification exam and your career. Thank you for allowing us to help you achieve your goals.

Keith Weiskamp
President and CEO

This book is dedicated to all my friends and family who never saw me while I was writing this book.

—Sean Odom

❧

This book is dedicated to my friends and family who made this dream a reality.

—Douglas Hammond

❧

ABOUT THE AUTHORS

Sean Odom has been in the computer networking field for about 12 years and is currently a Systems Administrator for CH2M HILL (**www.ch2m.com**), one of the largest engineering firms in the world. Sean is also the president of the Sacramento/Placer County Cisco Users Group (**www.cisco-cert.org**) and proprietor of Certification Solutions (**www.thequestforcertification.com**), which provides classroom learning for Cisco certifications. In addition, Sean has been a consultant for many companies, such as Advanced Computer Systems, American Licorice, NCR, Wells Fargo Bank, The Money Store, and Intel. You can reach Sean at his email address **sodom@rcsis.com**.

Douglas Hammond is a Senior Network Engineer working for NEC Business Network Solutions. He has more than 14 years of networking, engineering, and consulting experience. He has a diverse range of skills, from operating systems and software to IP telephony, network management, and data networking. Doug's expertise includes large multivendor, multiprotocol networks that require systems and network integration. He has held positions from operations to management in both the public and private sectors. Doug is currently preparing for his CCIE.

ACKNOWLEDGMENTS

Throughout the last 10 years that I have been in the computer networking and support field there have been a number of people who I couldn't thank enough for helping me get to this point in my life. These individuals, without realizing it, gave me chances to prove myself and deserve recognition for helping me along the path to where I am today. These include Jace Davis, Mike Lawton—Xerox, Leif Seymour—Intel, Ev Placentia—The Money Store, Paul Cardon, Guy Mahan—Advanced Computer Systems, Hanson Nottingham—HP, Mitch Hendrickson—FTG, Adele Galus—Cavion.COM, Steve Clevenger—UCDMC, Todd Lammle, who couldn't be a nicer guy, and all those mentors at CH2M HILL, including Greg Houston, Greg Barton, Marie Ortman, Cheryl Wagner, Adam Marsh, Mike Perrego, Doug Ennis, Brett Ammerman, and Chad Gau.

I would also like to thank contributors to the book and those who made this book possible. Those include first and foremost my Acquisitions Editor, Jeff Kellum, for believing in me and giving me the opportunity of a lifetime; Toni Zuccarini Ackley, my Project Editor, who is the nicest person in the world; Deb Doorley, my Developmental Editor, for putting up with me when I knew nothing about formatting a book; Tiffany Taylor, the copyeditor, for doing an awesome job of catching all of my typos; Doug Hammond, for the long nights and endless days tapping keys; Jim Healis, for his exceptional knowledge of switch features; and last but not least Thomas Hielsberg and Gina Galbraith, for their fine technical editing skills; Todd Halvorsen, the production coordinator; Jody Winkler, the cover designer; and April Nielsen, the layout designer.

After all that, I couldn't forget friends and family who have made sacrifices in their lives while I have been in seclusion writing. Those include all the Odom family—my Dad, my Mom, Erin, Hillary, Macky, Mikayla, Chris, Andy, Jamie, Julie, Ken Gregg, The Rodonis, The Nottinghams, and the Bowlers. I can't forget Jim and Rob Marvin at Ciro's Pizza for keeping me fed at all hours of the night with the best pizza on the planet!

—Sean Odom

After spending countless hours writing this book, this is surely the most difficult part, but definitely the most rewarding. It would be impossible to do a project of this size without the help and support of many people. First and foremost, I want to thank my wife and family, Ginger, Allissa, and William, for helping me through those long nights glued to the computer. They make all my dreams possible.

I want to thank all the people at Coriolis who have played a part in this book, especially Tiffany and Toni. My powers of description cannot do justice to the level of respect I have for them. Special thanks go out to Sean Odom, for including me on this project. Sean is proof that if you have courage and desire, you can do the impossible.

I want to give special thanks to my boss, Vic Peterson. I absolutely could not have done this book without your support. I couldn't ask for a better boss. It's a lot to go through for a free book!

Last, I want to thank my mom and dad, who instilled in me a love of words from an early day. Ever since I can remember, I've had a clear mental picture of a book I wrote sitting on my father's bookcase. Here it is, dad. Enjoy.

—*Douglas Hammond*

Contents at a Glance

TABLE OF CONTENTS

Chapter 14
IP Multicast 421

Chapter 15
Policy Networking 447

Exam Insights

Welcome to *CCNP Switching Exam Prep*! This book aims to help you get ready to take—and pass—Cisco certification Exam 640-504, titled "CCNP Switching 2.0." This Exam Insights section discusses exam preparation resources, the testing situation, Cisco's certification programs in general, and how this book can help you prepare for Cisco's certification exams.

Exam Prep books help you understand and appreciate the subjects and materials you need to pass Cisco certification exams. Our aim is to make sure all key topics are clearly explained and to bring together as much information as possible about Cisco certification exams.

Nevertheless, to completely prepare yourself for any Cisco test, we recommend that you begin by taking the Self-Assessment included in this book immediately following this Exam Insights section. This tool will help you evaluate your knowledge base against the requirements for a CCNP under both ideal and real circumstances.

Based on what you learn from that exercise, you might decide to begin your studies with some classroom training or some background reading. You might decide to read The Coriolis Group's *Exam Prep* book that you have in hand first, or you might decide to start with another study approach. You may also want to refer to one of a number of study guides available from Cisco or third-party vendors.

We also strongly recommend that you install, configure, and fool around with the network equipment that you'll be tested on, because nothing beats hands-on experience and familiarity when it comes to understanding the questions you're likely to encounter on a certification test. Book learning is essential, but hands-on experience is the best teacher of all!

How to Prepare for an Exam

Preparing for any Cisco career certification test (including CCNP) requires that you obtain and study materials designed to provide comprehensive information about Cisco switch operation and the specific exam for which you are preparing. The following list of materials will help you study and prepare:

- *Instructor-led training*—There's no substitute for expert instruction and hands-on practice under professional supervision. Cisco Training Partners, such as GeoTrain Corporation, offer instructor-led training courses for all of the Cisco career certification requirements. These companies aim to help prepare network administrators to run Cisco switched internetworks and pass the Cisco tests. Although such training runs upwards of $350 per day in class, most of the individuals lucky enough to partake find them to be quite worthwhile.

- *Cisco Connection Online*—This is the name of Cisco's Web site (**www.cisco.com**), the most current and up-to-date source of Cisco information.
- *The CCPrep Web site*—This is the most well-known Cisco certification Web site in the world. You can find it at **www.ccprep.com** (formerly known as **www.CCIEprep.com**). Here, you can find exam preparation materials, practice tests, self-assessment exams, and numerous certification questions and scenarios. In addition, professional staff members are available to answer questions that you can post on the answer board.
- *Cisco training kits*—These are available only if you attend a Cisco class at a certified training facility or if a Cisco Training Partner in good standing gives you one.
- *Study guides*—Several publishers—including Certification Insider Press—offer study guides. The Certification Insider Press series includes:
  - *The Exam Cram series*—These books give you information about the material you need to know to pass the tests.
  - *The Exam Prep series*—These books provide a greater level of detail than the *Exam Cram* books and are designed to teach you everything you need to know from an exam perspective.

  Together, the two series make a perfect pair.

By far, this set of required and recommended materials represents an unparalleled collection of sources and resources for preparing for the CCNP exam. We anticipate that you'll find that this book belongs in this company. In the next section, we explain how this book works and give you some good reasons why this book counts as a member of the required and recommended materials list.

Taking a Certification Exam

Alas, testing is not free. Each computer-based exam costs between $100 and $200, and the CCIE laboratory exam costs $1,000. If you do not pass, you must pay the testing fee each time you retake the test. In the United States and Canada, computerized tests are administered by Sylvan Prometric. Sylvan

Prometric can be reached at (800) 755-3926 or (800) 204-EXAM, any time from 7:00 A.M. to 6:00 P.M., Central Time, Monday through Friday. You can also try (612) 896-7000 or (612) 820-5707. CCIE laboratory exams are administered by Cisco Systems and can be scheduled by calling the CCIE lab exam administrator for the appropriate location.

To schedule a computer-based exam, call at least one day in advance. To cancel or reschedule an exam, you must call at least 24 hours before the scheduled test time (or you may be charged regardless). When calling Sylvan Prometric, have the following information ready for the telesales staffer who handles your call:

- Your name, organization, and mailing address.
- Your Cisco Test ID. (For most U.S. citizens, this is your Social Security number. Citizens of other nations can use their taxpayer IDs or make other arrangements with the order taker.)
- The name and number of the exam you wish to take. For this book, the exam name is "CCNP Switching 2.0" and the exam number is 640-504.
- A method of payment. The most convenient approach is to supply a valid credit card number with sufficient available credit. Otherwise, Sylvan Prometric must receive check, money order, or purchase order payment before you can schedule a test. (If you're not paying by credit card, ask your order taker for more details.)

When you show up to take a test, try to arrive at least 15 minutes before the scheduled time slot.

The Exam Situation

When you arrive at the testing center where you scheduled your exam, you'll need to sign in with an exam coordinator. He or she will ask you to show two forms of identification, one of which must be a photo ID. After you've signed in and your time slot arrives, you'll be asked to deposit any books, bags, or other items you brought with you. Then, you'll be escorted into a closed room.

All exams are completely closed book. In fact, you will not be permitted to take anything with you into the testing area. However, you are furnished with a blank sheet of paper and a pen. We suggest that you immediately write down on that sheet of paper all the information you've memorized for the test. Although the amount of time you have to actually take the exam is limited, the time period does not start until you're ready, so you can spend as much time as necessary writing notes on the provided paper. If you think you will need more paper than what is provided, ask the test center administrator before entering the exam room. You must return all pages prior to exiting the testing center.

You will have some time to compose yourself, to record this information, and even to take a sample orientation exam before you begin the real thing. We suggest you take the orientation test before taking your first exam, but because they're all more or less identical in layout, behavior, and controls, you probably won't need to do this more than once.

Typically, the room will be furnished with anywhere from one to half a dozen computers, and each workstation will be separated from the others by dividers designed to keep you from seeing what's happening on someone else's computer. Most test rooms feature a wall with a large picture window. This permits the exam coordinator to monitor the room, to prevent exam-takers from talking to one another, and to observe anything out of the ordinary that might go on. The exam coordinator will have preloaded the appropriate Cisco certification exam—for this book, that's Exam 640-504—and you'll be permitted to start as soon as you're seated in front of the computer.

All Cisco certification exams allow a certain maximum amount of time in which to complete your work (this time is indicated on the exam by an on-screen counter/clock, so you can check the time remaining whenever you like). All Cisco certification exams are computer generated and most use a multiple-choice format. Although this may sound quite simple, the questions are constructed not only to check your mastery of basic facts and figures, but they also require you to evaluate one or more sets of circumstances or requirements. Often, you'll be asked to give more than one answer to a question. Likewise, you might be asked to select the best or most effective solution to a problem from a range of choices, all of which technically are correct. Taking the exam is quite an adventure, and it involves real thinking. This book shows you what to expect and how to deal with the potential problems, puzzles, and predicaments.

When you complete a Cisco certification exam, the software will tell you whether you've passed or failed. All tests are scored on a basis of 100 percent, and results are broken into several topic areas. Even if you fail, we suggest you ask for—and keep—the detailed report that the test administrator should print for you. You can use this report to help you prepare for another go-round, if needed. Once you see your score, you have the option of printing additional copies of the score report. It's a good idea to print it twice.

If you need to retake an exam, you'll have to call Sylvan Prometric, schedule a new test date, and pay another testing fee.

Note: *The first time you fail a test, you can retake the test the next day. However, if you fail a second time, you must wait 14 days before retaking that test. The 14-day waiting period remains in effect for all retakes after the second failure.*

In the next section, you'll learn more about how Cisco test questions look and how they must be answered.

Exam Layout and Design

Whichever type of test you take, questions generally belong to one of four basic types:

- Multiple-choice with a single answer
- Multiple-choice with one or more answers
- Multipart with a single answer
- Multipart with one or more answers

A few of the questions may be in a different format, such as switch simulations.

Always take the time to read a question at least twice before selecting an answer, and always look for an Exhibit button as you examine each question. Exhibits include graphics information related to a question. An exhibit is usually a screen capture of program output or GUI information that you must examine to analyze the question's contents and formulate an answer. The Exhibit button brings up graphics and charts used to help explain a question, provide additional data, or illustrate page layout or program behavior.

Not every question has only one answer; many questions require multiple answers. Therefore, it's important to read each question carefully, to determine how many answers are necessary or possible, and to look for additional hints or instructions when selecting answers. Such instructions often occur in brackets immediately following the question itself (as they do for all multiple-choice questions in which one or more answers are possible).

The following multiple-choice question requires you to select a single correct answer. Following the question is a brief summary of each potential answer and why it is either right or wrong.

Question 1

Which of the following are benefits of implementing virtual LANs?

❍ a. Efficient bandwidth utilization

❍ b. Load balancing among multiple paths

❍ c. Isolation between problem components

❍ d. All of the above

The correct answer is d. The benefits of virtual LANs include efficient bandwidth utilization, load balancing among multiple paths, and isolation between problem components.

This sample question format corresponds closely to the Cisco certification exam format—the only difference on the exam is that questions are not followed by answer keys. To select an answer, you would position the cursor over the radio button next to the answer. Then, click the mouse button to select the answer.

Let's examine a question where one or more answers are possible. This type of question provides checkboxes rather than radio buttons for marking all appropriate selections.

Question 2

A Spanning Tree Bridge ID is made up of which two components? [Choose the two best answers]

❑ a. 32-byte IP address

❑ b. 2-byte priority

❑ c. 6-byte MAC address of the switch

❑ d. None of the above

The correct answers are b and c. A Spanning Tree Bridge ID is made up of a 2-byte priority and a 6-byte MAC address. A 32-byte IP address is used in Layer 3 logical addressing for the IP protocol. Therefore, answer a is incorrect.

For this particular question, two answers are required. As far as the authors can tell (and Cisco won't comment), such questions are scored as wrong unless all the required selections are chosen. In other words, a partially correct answer does not result in partial credit when the test is scored. For Question 2, you have to check the boxes next to items b and c to obtain credit for a correct answer. Notice that picking the right answers also means knowing why the other answers are wrong!

Question-Handling Strategies

Based on exams we have taken, some interesting trends have become apparent. For those questions that take only a single answer, usually two or three of the answers will be obviously incorrect, and two of the answers will be plausible—of course, only one can be correct. Unless the answer leaps out at you (if it does, reread the question to look for a trick; sometimes those are the ones you're most likely to get wrong), begin the process of answering by eliminating those answers that are most obviously wrong.

Almost always, at least one answer out of the possible choices for a question can be eliminated immediately because it matches one of these conditions:

- The answer does not apply to the situation.
- The answer describes a nonexistent issue, an invalid option, or an imaginary state.

After you eliminate all answers that are obviously wrong, you can apply your retained knowledge to eliminate further answers. Look for items that sound correct but refer to actions, commands, or features that are not present or not available in the situation that the question describes.

If you're still faced with a blind guess among two or more potentially correct answers, reread the question. Try to picture how each of the possible remaining answers would alter the situation. Be especially sensitive to terminology; sometimes the choice of words ("remove" instead of "disable") can make the difference between a right answer and a wrong one.

Only when you've exhausted your ability to eliminate answers, but remain unclear about which of the remaining possibilities is correct, should you guess at an answer. An unanswered question offers you no points, but guessing gives you at least some chance of getting a question right; just don't be too hasty when making a blind guess.

Numerous questions assume that the default behavior of a particular utility is in effect. If you know the defaults and understand what they mean, this knowledge will help you cut through many Gordian knots.

Mastering the Inner Game

In the final analysis, knowledge breeds confidence, and confidence breeds success. If you study the materials in this book carefully and review all the practice questions at the end of each chapter, you should become aware of those areas where additional learning and study are required.

After you've worked your way through the book, take the practice exam in Chapter 17 and test yourself with some of the varying exam formats on the CD-ROM. This will provide a reality check and help you identify areas to study further. Make sure you follow up and review materials related to the questions you miss on the practice exams before scheduling a real exam. Only when you've covered that ground and feel comfortable with the whole scope of the practice exams should you set an exam appointment. Only if you score 75 percent or better should you proceed to the real thing (otherwise, obtain some additional practice tests so you can keep trying until you hit this magic number).

Armed with the information in this book and with the determination to augment your knowledge, you should be able to pass the certification exam. However, you need to work at it, or you'll spend the exam fee more than once before you finally pass. If you prepare seriously, you should do well. Good luck!

The next section covers the exam requirements for the various Cisco certifications.

The Cisco Career Certification Program

The Cisco Career Certification program is relatively new on the internetworking scene. The best place to keep tabs on it is the Cisco Training Web site, at **www.cisco.com/certifications/**. Before Cisco developed this program, Cisco Certified Internetwork Expert (CCIE) certification was the only available Cisco certification. Although CCIE certification is still the most coveted and prestigious certification that Cisco offers (possibly the most prestigious in the internetworking industry), lower-level certifications are now available as stepping stones on the road to the CCIE. The Cisco Career Certification program includes several certifications in addition to the CCIE, each with its own acronym (see Table 1). If you're a fan of alphabet soup after your name, you'll like this program:

Note: *Within the certification program, there are specific specializations. For the purposes of this book, we will focus only on the Routing and Switching track. Visit* ***www.cisco.com/warp/public/10/wwtraining/certprog/index.html*** *for information on the other specializations.*

- *Cisco Certified Design Associate (CCDA)*—The CCDA is a basic certification aimed at designers of high-level internetworks. The CCDA consists of a single exam (640-441) that covers information from the Designing Cisco Networks (DCN) course. You must obtain CCDA and CCNA certifications before you can move up to the CCDP certification.
- *Cisco Certified Network Associate (CCNA)*—The CCNA is the first career certification. It consists of a single exam (640-507) that covers information from the basic-level class, primarily Interconnecting Cisco Network Devices (ICND). You must obtain CCNA certification before you can get your CCNP and CCDP certifications.
- *Cisco Certified Network Professional (CCNP)*—The CCNP is a more advanced certification that is not easy to obtain. To earn CCNP status, you must be a CCNA in good standing. There are two routes you can take to obtain your CCNP. For the first route, you must take four exams: Routing (640-503), Switching (640-504), Remote Access (640-505), and Support (640-506). For the second route, you must take the Foundation (640-509) and Support (640-506) exams.

Table 1 Cisco Routing and Switching CCNA, CCNP, and CCIE Requirements

CCNA

Only 1 exam required	
Exam 640-507	Cisco Certified Network Associate 2.0

CCNP*

All 4 of these are required	
Exam 640-503	Routing 2.0
➤ **Exam 640-504**	Switching 2.0
Exam 640-505	Remote Access 2.0
Exam 640-506	Support 2.0

* You need to have your CCNA before you become a CCNP.

CCIE

1 written exam and 1 lab exam required	
Exam 350-001	CCIE Routing and Switching Qualification
Lab Exam	CCIE Routing and Switching Laboratory

Although it may seem more appealing on the surface, the second route is more difficult. The Foundation exam contains more than 130 questions and lasts almost 3 hours. In addition, it covers all the topics covered in the Routing, Switching, and Remote Access exams.

Whichever route you choose, there are four courses Cisco recommends that you take:

- *Building Scalable Cisco Networks (BSCN)*—This course corresponds to the Routing exam.
- *Building Cisco Multilayer Switched Networks (BCMSN)*—This course corresponds to the Switching exam.
- *Building Cisco Remote Access Networks (BCRAN)*—This course corresponds to the Remote Access exam.
- *Cisco Internetworking Troubleshooting (CIT)*—This course corresponds to the Support exam.

Once you have completed the CCNP certification, you can further your career (not to mention beef up your resume) by branching out and passing one of the CCNP specialization exams. These include:

- *Security*—Requires you to pass the Managing Cisco Network Security exam (640-422).

  - *LAN ATM*—Requires you to pass the Cisco Campus ATM Solutions exam (640-446).
  - *Voice Access*—Requires you to pass the Cisco Voice over Frame Relay, ATM, and IP exam (640-447).
  - *SNA/IP Integration*—Requires you to pass the SNA Configuration for Multiprotocol Administrators (640-445) and the SNA Foundation (640-456) exams.
  - *Network Management*—Requires you to pass either the Managing Cisco Routed Internetworks—MCRI (640-443)—or the Managing Cisco Switched Internetworks—MCSI (640-444)—exam.
- *Cisco Certified Design Professional (CCDP)*—The CCDP is another advanced certification. It's aimed at high-level internetwork designers who must understand the intricate facets of putting together a well-laid-out network. The first step in the certification process is to obtain the CCDA and CCNA certifications (yes, both). As with the CCNP, you must pass the Foundation exam or pass the Routing, Switching, and Remote Access exams individually. Once you meet those objectives, you must pass the Cisco Internetwork Design exam (640-025) to complete the certification.
- *Cisco Certified Internetwork Expert (CCIE)*—The CCIE is possibly the most influential certification in the internetworking industry today. It is famous (or infamous) for its difficulty and for how easily it holds its seekers at bay. The certification requires only one written exam (350-001); passing that exam qualifies you to schedule time at a Cisco campus to demonstrate your knowledge in a two-day practical laboratory setting. You must pass the lab with a score of at least 80 percent to become a CCIE. Recent statistics have put the passing rates at roughly 20 percent for first attempts and 35 through 50 percent overall. Once you achieve CCIE certification, you must recertify every two years by passing a written exam administered by Cisco.
- *Certified Cisco Systems Instructor (CCSI)*—To obtain status as a CCSI, you must be employed (either permanently or by contract) by a Cisco Training Partner in good standing, such as GeoTrain Corporation. That training partner must sponsor you through Cisco's Instructor Certification Program, and you must pass the two-day program that Cisco administers at a Cisco campus. You can build on CCSI certification on a class-by-class basis. Instructors must demonstrate competency with each class they are to teach by completing the written exam that goes with each class. Cisco also requires that instructors maintain a high customer satisfaction rating, or they will face decertification.

TRACKING CISCO CERTIFICATION STATUS

As soon as you pass any Cisco exam (congratulations!), you must complete a certification agreement. You can do so online at the Certification Tracking Web site (**www.galton.com/~cisco/**), or you can mail a hard copy of the agreement to Cisco's certification authority. You will not be certified until you complete a certification agreement and Cisco receives it in one of these forms.

The Certification Tracking Web site also allows you to view your certification information. Cisco will contact you via email and explain it and its use. Once you are registered into one of the career certification tracks, you will be given a login on this site, which is administered by Galton, a third-party company that has no in-depth affiliation with Cisco or its products. Galton's information comes directly from Sylvan Prometric, the exam-administration company for much of the computing industry.

Once you pass the necessary exam(s) for a particular certification and complete the certification agreement, you'll be certified. Official certification normally takes anywhere from four to six weeks, so don't expect to get your credentials overnight. When the package arrives, it will include a Welcome Kit that contains a number of elements, including:

- A Cisco certificate, suitable for framing, stating that you have completed the certification requirements, along with a laminated Cisco Career Certification identification card with your certification number on it
- Promotional items, which vary based on the certification.

Many people believe that the benefits of the Cisco career certifications go well beyond the perks that Cisco provides to newly anointed members of this elite group. There seem to be more and more job listings that request or require applicants to have a CCNA, CCDA, CCNP, CCDP, and so on, and many individuals who complete the program can qualify for increases in pay or responsibility. In fact, Cisco has started to implement requirements for its Value Added Resellers: To attain and keep silver, gold, or higher status, they must maintain a certain number of CCNA, CCDA, CCNP, CCDP, and CCIE employees on staff. There's a very high demand and low supply of Cisco talent in the industry overall. As an official recognition of hard work and broad knowledge, a Cisco career certification credential is a badge of honor in many IT organizations.

ABOUT THE BOOK

To aid you in fully understanding the concepts required for CCNP certification, there are many features in this book designed to improve its value:

- *Chapter objectives*—Each chapter in this book begins with a detailed list of the topics to be mastered within that chapter. This list provides you with a quick reference to the contents of that chapter, as well as a useful study aid.
- *Illustrations and tables*—Numerous illustrations of screenshots and components aid you in the visualization of common setup steps, theories, and concepts. In addition, many tables provide details and comparisons of both practical and theoretical information.
- *Notes, tips, and warnings*—Notes present additional helpful material related to the subject being described. Tips, from the author's experience, provide extra information about how to attack a problem, or what to do in certain real-world situations. Warnings are included to help you anticipate potential mistakes or problems so you can prevent them from happening.
- *Chapter summaries*—Each chapter's text is followed by a summary of the concepts it has introduced. These summaries provide a helpful way to recap and revisit the ideas covered in each chapter.
- *Review questions*—End-of-chapter assessment begins with a set of review questions that reinforce the ideas introduced in each chapter. These questions not only ensure that you have mastered the concepts, but are written to help prepare you for the Cisco certification examination. Answers to these questions are found in Appendix A.
- *Real-world projects*—Although it is important to understand the theory behind Cisco internetworking technology, nothing can improve upon real-world experience. To this end, along with theoretical explanations, each chapter provides numerous projects aimed at providing you with real-world implementation experience.
- *Sample tests*—Use the sample test and answer key in Chapters 17 and 18 to test yourself. Then, move on to the interactive practice exams found on the CD-ROM. The testing engine offers a variety of testing formats to choose from.

WHERE SHOULD YOU START?

This book is intended to be read in sequence, from beginning to end. Each chapter builds upon those that precede it, to provide a solid understanding of CCNP topics. After completing the chapters, you may find it useful to go back through the book and use the review questions and projects to prepare for the CCNP Switching 2.0 test (Exam 640-504). Readers are also encouraged to investigate the many pointers to online and printed sources of additional information that are cited throughout this book.

Please share your feedback on the book with us, especially if you have ideas about how we can improve it for future readers. We'll consider everything you say carefully, and we'll respond to all suggestions. Send your questions or comments to us at **learn@examcram.com**. Please remember to include the title of the book in your message; otherwise, we'll be forced to guess which book you're writing about. Also, be sure to check out the Web pages at **www.examcram.com**, where you'll find information updates, commentary, and certification information. Thanks, and enjoy the book!

Self-Assessment

The reason we included a Self-Assessment in this *Exam Prep* is to help you evaluate your readiness to tackle CCNP certification. It should also help you understand what you need to master the topic of this book—namely, Exam 640-504, "CCNP Switching 2.0." But before you tackle this Self-Assessment, let's talk about concerns you may face when pursuing a CCNP, and what an ideal CCNP candidate might look like.

CCNPs in the Real World

In the next section, we describe an ideal CCNP candidate, knowing full well that only a few real candidates will meet this ideal. In fact, the description of that ideal candidate might seem downright scary. But take heart: Although the requirements to obtain a CCNP may seem pretty formidable, they are by no means impossible to meet. However, you should be keenly aware that it does take time and require some expense and substantial effort to get through the process.

The first thing to understand is that the CCNP is an attainable goal. You can get all the real-world motivation you need from knowing that many others have gone before, so you will be able to follow in their footsteps. If you're willing to tackle the process seriously and do what it takes to obtain the necessary experience and knowledge, you can take—and pass—all the certification tests involved in obtaining an CCNP. In fact, we've designed these *Exam Preps*, and the companion *Exam Crams*, to make it as easy on you as possible to prepare for these exams. But prepare you must!

The same, of course, is true for other Cisco career certifications, including:

- CCNA, which is the first step on the road to the CCNP certification. It is a single exam that covers information from Cisco's Introduction to Cisco Router Configuration (ICRC) class and the Cisco LAN Switch Configuration (CLSC) class. Cisco also has developed a class that is geared to CCNA certification, known as Cisco Routing and LAN Switching (CRLS).

- CCDA, which is the first step on the road to the CCDP certification. It is a single exam that covers the basics of design theory. To prepare for it, you should attend the Designing Cisco Networks (DCN) class and/or the Cisco Internetwork Design (CID) class.

- CCDP, which is an advanced certification regarding internetwork design. It consists of multiple exams. There are two ways to go about attaining the CCDP. You could pass the individual exams for ACRC, CLSC, CMTD, and CIT. However, if you're not one for taking a lot of exams, you can take the Foundation Routing/Switching exam and the CIT exam. Either combination will complete the requirements.

- CCIE, which is commonly referred to as the "black belt" of internetworking. It is considered the single most difficult certification to attain in the internetworking industry. First you must take a qualification exam. Once you pass the exam, the real fun begins. You will need to schedule a two-day practical lab exam to be held at a Cisco campus, where you will undergo a "trial by fire" of sorts. Your ability to configure, document, and troubleshoot Cisco equipment will be tested to its limits. Do not underestimate this lab exam.

The Ideal CCNP Candidate

Just to give you some idea of what an ideal CCNP candidate is like, here are some relevant statistics about the background and experience such an individual might have. Don't worry if you don't meet these qualifications, or don't come that close—this is a far from ideal world, and where you fall short is simply where you'll have more work to do.

- Academic or professional training in network theory, concepts, and operations. This includes everything from networking media and transmission techniques through network operating systems, services, and applications.

- Three-plus years of professional networking experience, including experience with Ethernet, token ring, modems, and other networking media. This must include installation, configuration, upgrade, and troubleshooting experience.

- Two-plus years in a networked environment that includes hands-on experience with Cisco routers, switches, and other related equipment. A solid understanding of each system's architecture, installation, configuration, maintenance, and troubleshooting is also essential.

- A thorough understanding of key networking protocols, addressing, and name resolution, including TCP/IP, IPX/SPX, and AppleTalk.

- Familiarity with key TCP/IP-based services, including ARP, BOOTP, DNS, FTP, SMTP, SNMP, Telnet, TFTP, and other relevant services for your internetwork deployment.

Fundamentally, this boils down to a bachelor's degree in computer science, plus three years of work experience in a technical position involving network design, installation, configuration, and maintenance. We believe that well under half of all certification candidates meet these requirements; in fact, most meet less than half of these requirements—at least, when they begin the certification process. But because thousands of people have survived this ordeal, you can survive it too—especially if you heed what our Self-Assessment can tell you about what you already know and what you need to learn.

Put Yourself to the Test

The following series of questions and observations is designed to help you figure out how much work you must do to pursue Cisco career certification and what kinds of resources you should consult on your quest. Be absolutely honest in your answers, or you'll end up wasting money on exams you're not yet ready to take. There are no right or wrong answers, only steps along the path to certification. Only you can decide where you really belong in the broad spectrum of aspiring candidates.

Two things should be clear from the outset, however:

- Even a modest background in computer science will be helpful.
- Extensive hands-on experience with Cisco products and technologies is an essential ingredient to certification success.

1. Have you ever taken any computer-related classes? [Yes or No]

   If Yes, proceed to Question 2; if No, proceed to Question 4.

2. Have you taken any classes included in Cisco's curriculum? [Yes or No]

   If Yes, you will probably be able to handle Cisco's architecture and system component discussions. If you're rusty, brush up on basic switching, the IOS operating system concepts, and Cisco hardware including RAM, NVRAM, and Flash memory. You'll also want to brush up on the basics of internetworking, especially IP subnetting, access lists, and physical LAN technologies. We have tried to cover most of the prerequisites in this *Exam Prep*.

   If No, consider some extensive reading in this area. We strongly recommend instructor-led training offered by a Cisco Training Partner. However, you may want to check out a good general advanced switching technology book, such as *Cisco IOS 12.0 Switching Services* (Cisco Press, Indianapolis, IN, 1999 ISBN: 1-57870-157-0). If this title doesn't appeal to you, check out reviews for other, similar titles at your favorite online bookstore.

3. Have you taken any networking concepts or technologies classes? [Yes or No]

   If Yes, you will probably be able to handle Cisco's switching terminology, concepts, and technologies. If you're rusty, brush up on basic internetworking concepts and terminology, especially networking media, transmission types, the OSI Reference Model, and LAN networking technologies.

   If No, you might want to read one or two books in this topic area. Check out Appendix B for some suggestions, as well as online resources.

4. Have you done any reading on routing protocols and/or routed protocols (IP, IPX, AppleTalk, etc.)? [Yes or No]

   If Yes, review the requirements stated in the first paragraphs after Questions 2 and 3. If you meet those requirements, move on to the next question.

   If No, consult the recommended reading for both topics. A strong background will help you prepare for the Cisco exams better than just about anything else.

The most important key to success on all of the Cisco tests is hands-on experience with Cisco switches and related equipment. If we leave you with only one realization after taking this Self-Assessment, it should be that there's no substitute for time spent installing, configuring, and using the various Cisco products upon which you'll be tested repeatedly and in depth. It cannot be stressed enough that quality instructor-led training will benefit you greatly and give you additional hands-on configuration experience with the technologies upon which you are to be tested.

5. Have you installed, configured, and worked with switches? [Yes or No]

   If Yes, make sure you understand basic concepts as covered for the Cisco Certified Network Associates (CCNA) Exam before progressing into the materials covered here, because this book expands on the basic topics taught there.

Tip: You can download objectives and other information about Cisco exams from the company's Training and Certification page on the Web at **www.cisco.com/training/**.

   If No, you will need to find a way to get a good amount of instruction on the intricacies of configuring Cisco equipment. You need a broad background to get through any of Cisco's career certification. You will also need to have hands-on experience with the equipment and technologies on which you'll be tested.

Tip: If you have the funds, or your employer will pay your way, consider taking a class at a Cisco Training Partner (preferably one with "distinguished" status for the highest quality possible). In addition to classroom exposure to the topic of your choice, you get a good view of the technologies being widely deployed and will be able to take part in hands-on lab scenarios with those technologies.

Before you even think about taking any Cisco exam, make sure you've spent enough time with the related software to understand how it may be installed and configured, how to maintain such an installation, and how to troubleshoot that software when things go wrong. This will help you in the exam, and in real life!

Whether you attend a formal class on a specific topic to get ready for an exam or use written materials to study on your own, some preparation for the Cisco career certification exams is essential. At $100 to $200 a try (depending on the exam), pass or fail, you want to do everything you can to pass on your first try. That's where studying comes in.

6. Have you taken a practice exam on your chosen test subject? [Yes or No]

   If Yes, and you scored 75 percent or better, you're probably ready to tackle the real thing. If your score isn't above that crucial threshold, keep at it until you break that barrier.

   If No, obtain all the free and low-budget practice tests you can find and get to work. Keep at it until you can break the passing threshold comfortably.

We have included a practice exam in this book, so you can test yourself on the information and techniques you've learned. If you don't hit a score of at least 75 percent after this test, you'll want to investigate the other practice test resources we mention in this section.

For any given subject, consider taking a class if you've tackled self-study materials, taken the test, and failed anyway. The opportunity to interact with an instructor and fellow students can make all the difference in the world, if you can afford that privilege. For information about Cisco classes, visit the Training and Certification page at **www.cisco.com/training** or **www.geotrain.com** (use the "Find a Course" section).

If you can't afford to take a class, visit the Training and Certification page anyway, because it also includes pointers to additional resources and self-study tools. And even if you can't afford to spend much at all, you should still invest in some low-cost practice exams from commercial vendors, because they can help you assess your readiness to pass a test better than any other tool. The following Web sites offer some practice exams online:

- CCPrep.com at **www.ccprep.com** (requires membership)
- Network Study Guides at **www.networkstudyguides.com** (pay as you go)

Tip: When it comes to assessing your test readiness, there is no better way than to take a good-quality practice exam and pass with a score of 75 percent or better. When we're preparing ourselves, we shoot for 80-plus percent, just to leave room for the "weirdness factor" that sometimes shows up on Cisco exams.

Assessing Readiness for Exam 640-504

In addition to the general exam-readiness information in the previous section, there are several things you can do to prepare for the CCNP Switching 2.0 exam. You will find a great source of questions and related information at the CCprep Web site at **www.ccprep.com**. This is a good place to ask questions and get good answers, or simply to watch the questions that others ask (along with the answers, of course).

You should also cruise the Web looking for "braindumps" (recollections of test topics and experiences recorded by others) to help you anticipate topics you're likely to encounter on the test.

Tip: When using any braindump, it's OK to pay attention to information about questions. But you can't always be sure that a braindump's author will also be able to provide correct answers. Thus, use the questions to guide your studies, but don't rely on the answers in a braindump to lead you to the truth. Double-check everything you find in any braindump.

For switching preparation in particular, we'd also like to recommend that you check out one or more of these resources as you prepare to take Exam 640-504:

- Cisco Connection Online (CCO) Documentation (**www.cisco.com/univercd/home/home.htm**). From the CCO Documentation home page you can select a variety of topics, including but not limited to LAN switching and multilayer switching guides.
- Douglas Comer. *Internetworking with TCP/IP, Volume 1: Principles, Protocols, and Architecture*, Prentice Hall: Englewood Cliffs, NJ, 1995. ISBN: 0-13-216987-8.
- Sean Odom. *Cisco Switching Black Book,* The Coriolis Group: Scottsdale, AZ, 2000. ISBN: 1-57610-706-X.
- Radia Perlman. *Interconnections: Bridges and Routers.* Addison Wesley Publishing Company, Inc.: Reading, MA, 1992. ISBN: 0-201-56332-0.

Stop by the Cisco home page, your favorite bookstore, or an online bookseller to check out one or more of these resources.

One last note: Hopefully, it makes sense to stress the importance of hands-on experience in the context of the CCNP Switching 2.0 exam. As you review the material for that exam, you'll realize that hands-on experience with the Cisco IOS with various technologies and configurations is invaluable.

Onward, Through the Fog!

Once you've assessed your readiness, undertaken the right background studies, obtained the hands-on experience that will help you understand the products and technologies at work, and reviewed the many sources of information to help you prepare for a test, you'll be ready to take a round of practice tests. When your scores come back positive enough to get you through the exam, you're ready to go after the real thing. If you follow our assessment regime, you'll not only know what you need to study, but when you're ready to make a test date at Sylvan Prometric. Good luck!

CHAPTER ONE

THE NEED FOR SWITCHING

After completing this chapter, you will be able to:

✓ Explain how networks evolved over time

✓ Understand the restrictions of traditional network architectures

✓ Define switching

✓ Describe the reasons for switching

✓ Describe the different methods of switching

✓ Address general equipment issues

✓ Understand the challenges of internetworking

To fully understand the need for switches on a network, you must have a clear understanding of how networks have evolved from their beginnings to where they are now. This chapter will discuss this history, and will show the limitations that exist with traditional local area networks (LANs). We will also examine some of the methods that network designers used to overcome the constraints of these older network topologies. Although traditional network architectures are still being used in corporations all over the world, high-bandwidth applications such as video, voice, and the Internet have forced networks to adapt to meet today's challenges.

We will also cover the components of the network in depth in this chapter, from repeaters to hubs, routers, and switches. The advantages and disadvantages of each device will be discussed, as well as when they should be used in the network.

Last, we will show the different types of switches in use in today's networks. We will describe the various types of switching used on these devices and discuss the challenges involved with this technology.

A Bit of History

The first LANs began as a result of the introduction of PCs into the workplace. As more computers were used, a need arose for sharing resources, such as printers or files. These early networks were simple, with a handful of computers and printers and not much more. Before long, however, the increasing numbers of computers, along with applications that could take advantage of the network, pointed out the weaknesses in traditional network designs.

The limitations of traditional Ethernet technology brought forth a number of innovations to the Ethernet protocol—such as full-duplexing, Fast Ethernet, and Gigabit Ethernet—that have made possible a transition to switches from shared hubs. Because of the limitations to the way networks operated in a shared environment, alternative methods had to be designed to permit the use of bandwidth-intensive applications such as video and voice. Switches are one of these alternative methods. In many respects, switches are relatively simple devices. By design, they require very little configuration to get them up and running. To properly use these devices in your network, though, it's important to have an in-depth knowledge of the issues involved when using switches. This includes knowing the basics of Ethernet technology. To effectively do your job, you need a good grasp of the technology and how it works, as well as the constraints of each type of device you may use in the network. We will cover the basics of Ethernet technology in depth.

The types of devices you use in the network have important implications for network performance. For example, bridges and routers are both devices that network administrators use to extend the capabilities of their networks. Both of them have advantages and disadvantages. Bridges, for example, can easily solve distance limitations and increase the number of stations you can have on a network, but they can have real problems with broadcast traffic. Routers can be used to prevent this problem, but they increase the time it takes to forward the traffic.

This has been the pattern throughout the history of networking. A new product is introduced. Problems are found that limit the product's usefulness. Innovations are made to the product to make it perform better. As we will see in upcoming sections, this pattern began in the earliest days of networking and continues to this day.

Traditional Network Architectures

From the beginning of networking, designers of networks were faced with the limitations of the LAN topologies they were using. Modern-day corporate networks use LAN topologies such as Ethernet, Token Ring, and Fiber Distributed Data Interface (FDDI) to provide network connectivity. Network designers try to deploy a design that uses the fastest functionality that can be applied to the physical cabling. Although networks have been designed using all these methods, Ethernet LANs have won the battle for market share and remain the dominant type of network in most corporations.

A few years ago, many analysts saw a competing technology, Token Ring, as a technically superior product and a viable alternative to Ethernet. Many installations still have Token-Ring networks, but very few new installations are being done. This is due in part to the fact that Token Ring was basically an IBM product with little support from other vendors, and prices were substantially higher than for its Ethernet counterparts.

FDDI networks share some of the same limitations of Token Ring. Like Token Ring, it offers excellent benefits in the areas of performance and redundancy. Unfortunately, it has the same limitations of high equipment costs and limited vendor support. FDDI has been used in many organizations to provide a high-speed backbone that could withstand the problems that happen to networks. However, it was not widely embraced by the networking community due to its complexity and high costs.

Ethernet networks, by contrast, are open-standards-based, cost-effective, and have a large base of vendors supporting the products. In addition, a huge number of professionals understand how Ethernet works. Even IBM now recognizes the hold that Ethernet LANs have on the market and supports the technology.

Traditional LANs Limit Productivity

Local area networks closely tracked the PC revolution. The early networks consisted of a single LAN with a number of workstations running peer-to-peer networks and sharing files, printers, and other resources. This type of topology confined the network to a very limited area, such as a room or building.

This setup evolved into a client/server model where the server had applications and data storage that were shared by multiple workstation users. A LAN in this environment consisted of the physical wire connecting the devices. LANs enabled multiple users in a relatively small geographical area to exchange files and messages, as well as access shared resources such as file servers. Isolated LANs made communication between different offices or departments difficult, if not impossible.

Duplication of resources meant that the same hardware and software had to be supplied to each office or department, along with a separate support staff. This lack of centralized network management meant that no method of managing and troubleshooting networks existed. Wide area networks (WANs) soon developed, which interconnected LANs across normal telephone lines (and other media), thereby enabling geographically dispersed users to share resources.

A traditional LAN setup had many limitations that directly impacted the network users. Virtually anyone who has ever used a shared network has had to contend with the other users of that network and experienced impacts, such as slow response times or poor network performance. This is due to the nature of shared environments. Collisions are Ethernet's natural flow control. When collision rates increase, however, the usefulness of the bandwidth decreases. As applications begin having to resend data due to excessive collisions, the amount of bandwidth used increases and the response time for users increases. As more and more users require services from the network, the interruptions limit the benefits of the network. You see increased complaints from the users of the network regarding response times and timeouts. These are all telltale signs that you need a switched Ethernet network.

Ethernet Technology Basics

Robert M. Metcalfe invented Ethernet at the Xerox Palo Alto Research Center in the early 1970s. It was originally designed to help support research on the "office of the future." At first the speed was limited to 3Mbps. In 1980, a group of vendors consisting of Digital Equipment Corporation (DEC), Intel, and Xerox created what was known as the *DIX standard*. Ultimately, after a few modifications, it became the IEEE 802.3 standard. It is the 802.3 standard that most people associate with the term *Ethernet*.

Ethernet is a multi-access, packet-switched system with very democratic principles. The stations themselves provide access to the network, and all devices on an Ethernet LAN can access the LAN at any time. Ethernet signals are transmitted serially, one bit at a time, over a shared channel available to every attached station.

To send data, a station first "listens" to the channel; when the channel is idle the station transmits its data in the form of an Ethernet frame, or *packet*. After each frame transmission, all stations on the network contend equally for the next frame transmission. This competition allows access to the network channel in a fair manner, and ensures that no single station can lock out the other stations. Access to the shared channel is determined by the Media Access Control (MAC) mechanism on each network interface card (NIC) located in each station.

To reduce the likelihood of multiple stations transmitting at the same time, Ethernet LANs use a mechanism known as Carrier Sense Multiple Access Collision Detection (CSMA/CD) to listen to the network to see if it is in use. If a station has data to transmit, it does so and the remaining stations defer transmissions. If two stations transmit at the same time, a collision occurs. The stations are notified of this event, and they instantly reschedule their transmissions using a specially designed backoff algorithm. As part of this algorithm, each station involved chooses a random time interval to schedule the retransmission of the frame, which keeps the stations from making transmission attempts at the same time and continuing to collide.

Although CSMA/CD allows collisions to be detected, all frames on the LAN still have to be processed by every device on the network. Each of these frames on the network reduces the amount of bandwidth on the network that can be used to send information across the physical wire. CSMA/CD also forces every device on the network to analyze each individual frame and determine if the device was the intended recipient of the packet. The process of decoding and analyzing each individual packet generates additional CPU usage on each machine, which degrades each machine's performance.

As networks grew in popularity they also began to grow in size and complexity. For the most part, networks began as small, isolated islands of computers. In many of the early environments, the network was installed over a weekend. When you came in on Monday, a fat orange cable was threaded throughout the organization connecting all the devices. A method of connecting these segments had to be derived. In the next section, we look at a number of approaches in which networks can be connected, including repeaters, hubs, bridges, and routers, and demonstrate the benefits and drawbacks to each approach.

Repeaters

The first LANs were designed using thick coaxial cables, with each station physically tapping into the cable. In order to extend the distance and overcome other limitations on this type of installation, a device known as a *repeater* is used. Essentially, a repeater consists of a pair of back-to-back transceivers. The transmit wire on one transceiver is hooked to the receive wire on the other, so that bits received by one transceiver are immediately transmitted by the other.

Repeaters work by regenerating the signals from one segment to another and allowing networks to overcome distance and other factors. These devices do not create separate networks—they simply extend an existing one. A standard rule of thumb is that no more than three repeaters may be located between any two stations. This is also commonly referred to as the 5-4-3 rule, which states that no more than 5 segments may be attached by no more than 4 repeaters, with no more than 3 segments populated with workstations. This limit prevents *propagation delay*—which is the time it takes for a packet to go from the beginning of the link to the opposite end—from getting out of hand, because you seldom know how much cable is really buried in the walls and ceilings.

A typical cabling arrangement would be to string a cable vertically from floor to floor in a building's utility closets and place a repeater on each floor to connect to individual segments. This is known as a *backbone cable*; it requires only two repeaters between any pair of interfaces, with a potentially large number of repeaters being used.

As you can imagine, in the early LANs this method resulted in a host of performance and fault-isolation problems. As LANs multiplied, a more structured approach, called *10BaseT*, was introduced. This method consists of attaching all the devices to a hub in the wiring closet. All stations are connected in a point-to-point configuration between the station and the hub.

Hubs

A *hub* is, in effect, a group of repeaters. Similar to repeaters, hubs are Open System Interconnection (OSI) physical layer devices that operate at the OSI Layer 1 and simply retransmit bits. (For more about OSI layers, see Chapter 2.) They are also known as *concentrators*. Hubs are used to connect multiple cable runs in a star-wired network topology into a single network. This design is similar to the spokes of a wheel converging on the center of the wheel.

There are many types of hubs:

- *Intelligent hubs*—Contain logic circuits that shut down a port if the traffic indicates that malformed frames are the rule rather than the exception.

- *Managed hubs*—Have application-layer software installed so that they can be remote-controlled. Network management software is very popular in organizations that have staff responsible for a network spread over many buildings.
- *Stackable hubs*—Have a cable to connect hubs that are in the same location without requiring the data to pass through multiple hubs.

Hubs can be connected in a variety of ways. *Backbone hubs* can collect other hubs into a single collection point; this is also known as a *multi-tiered design*. In a typical setup, servers and other critical devices are on high-speed Fast Ethernet or Gigabit uplinks. This setup creates a very fast connection to the servers that lower-speed networks can use; it helps prevent the server or the path to the server from being a bottleneck.

Many benefits derive from this type of setup:

- It provides interdepartmental connections between hubs.
- It extends the maximum distance between any pair of nodes on the network.
- It improves the ability to isolate problems from the rest of the network.

In all of these types of hub setups, one crucial problem exists: All stations share the bandwidth, and they all remain in the same collision domain. This means that whenever two or more stations transmit simultaneously on any hub, there is a strong likelihood of a collision occurring. These collisions will lead to congestion during high-traffic loads. As the number of stations increases, each station gets a smaller portion of the LAN bandwidth.

Bridges

The term *bridging* refers to a technology in which a device (known as a *bridge*) connects two or more LAN segments. Bridges are OSI link layer (Layer 2) devices that were originally designed to connect two network segments. *Multiport bridges* were introduced later to connect two or more network segments, and are still in use in many networks today. These devices analyze the frames as they come in and make forwarding decisions based on information in the frames themselves.

A bridge is a relatively simple device consisting of a pair of interfaces with some packet buffers and simple logic. The bridge receives a packet on one interface, stores it in a buffer, and immediately queues it for transmission by the other interface. The two cables each experience collisions, but collisions on one cable do not cause collisions on the other. The cables are in separate *collision domains*.

To do their job effectively, bridges rely on two functions:

- Filtering the frames to determine if the frame should be forwarded
- Forwarding the frames to the proper interface to send the packet

Bridges learn the location of the network stations without any intervention from a network administrator or any manual configuration of the bridge software. This is commonly referred to as "self-learning." When a bridge is turned on and begins to operate, it examines the MAC addresses of the traffic that passes through it to build a table of known destinations. The *MAC address* is the physical encoded number or address on a Network Interface Adapter.

In this table, an entry exists that contains the MAC address of each node and the bridge interface that it resides on. If the bridge knows that the destination is on the same segment as the source, it drops the packet because there is no need to transmit it. If the bridge knows that the destination is on another segment, it transmits the packet on that segment only. If the bridge does not know the destination segment, the bridge transmits the copies of the packet to all network segments except the source segment, using a technique known as *flooding*. For each packet an interface receives, the bridge stores into its table the following information:

- The frame's source address
- The interface the frame arrived on
- The time it was received into its table

Figure 1.1 illustrates how a bridge works.

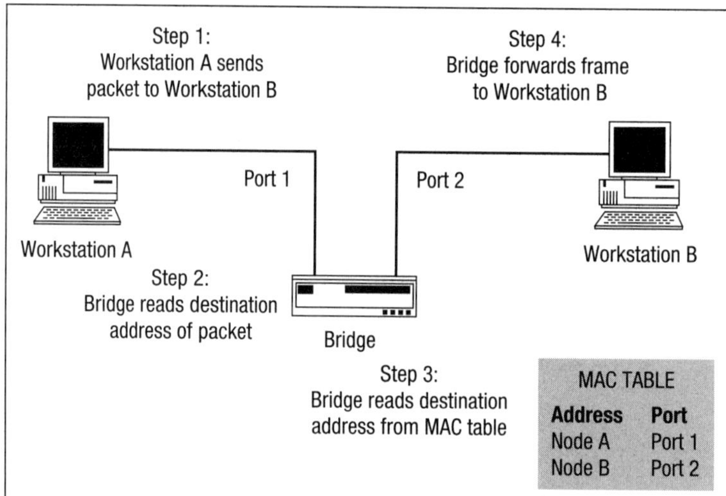

Figure 1.1 How a bridge works.

There are four kinds of bridges:

- *Transparent bridges*—Primarily used in Ethernet environments. They are called transparent bridges because their presence and operation are transparent to network hosts. Transparent bridges learn and forward packets in the manner described earlier.
- *Source-route bridges*—Primarily used in Token Ring environments. They are called source-route bridges because they assume that the complete source-to-destination route is placed in frames sent by the source.
- *Translational bridges*—Translates between different media types (usually Ethernet and Token Ring).
- *Source-route transparent bridges*—Combines transparent bridging and source-route bridging to enable communication in mixed Ethernet/Token Ring environments.

The Problem with Broadcasts

Broadcasts are the biggest problem with bridges. Bridges help reduce network traffic by filtering packets and allowing them to be forwarded only if needed; but bridges also forward broadcasts to devices on all segments of the network. As networks grow, so does broadcast traffic. Instead of frames being broadcast through a limited number of devices, there are now often hundreds of devices on multiple segments communicating with other devices; as a result, all devices on all segments of the network are now processing data intended for one device. Excessive broadcasts reduce the amount of bandwidth available to end users. This causes bandwidth problems called *network broadcast storms*. Broadcast storms occur when broadcasts throughout the LAN use up all available bandwidth on a LAN, thus grinding the network to a halt.

The types of broadcast traffic that most often affect network performance are inquiries about the availability of a device, advertisements for a component status on the network, and inquiries from one device trying to locate another device. The typical types of network broadcasts are those from Address Resolution Protocol (ARP), Internetwork Packet Exchange (IPX) Get Nearest Server (GNS) requests, IPX Service Advertising Protocol (SAP), multicast traffic broadcasts, and NetBIOS name requests. These broadcasts are built into the network protocols and are essential to the operation of the network operating systems.

Latency

Due to the overhead involved in forwarding packets, bridges also introduce a delay in forwarding traffic. This delay is known as *latency*. Latency delay is measured from the moment a packet enters the input port on the switch until the time that the bridge forwards the packet out the exit port. Bridges can introduce 20 to 30 percent loss of throughput for some applications. Latency is a big problem with some timing-dependent technologies, such as mainframe connectivity, video, or voice.

High levels of latency can result in loss of connections and noticeable video and voice degradation. The inherent problems of bridging over multiple segments with Layer 2 devices became a problem to network administrators. To overcome these issues, a device called a *router*, operating at the network layer (OSI Layer 3), was introduced.

Routers

Routers are devices that connect several Ethernet segments (with or without bridging). Routers perform the same functions as bridges and also forward information and filter broadcasts between multiple segments (see Figure 1.2). Using an OSI network Layer 3 solution, routers logically segment traffic into subnets.

Routers were originally introduced to connect dissimilar networks as well as to provide a means to route traffic, filter broadcasts across multiple segments, and improve overall performance. This approach eliminated broadcasts over multiple segments by filtering broadcasts; but routers became a bottleneck in some networks, and also resulted in a loss of throughput for some types of traffic.

When connecting large networks, or when connecting networks to a WAN, routers are very important. Routers will perform media conversion, adjusting the data link protocol as necessary; thus, you could connect an Ethernet network and a Token Ring network via a router.

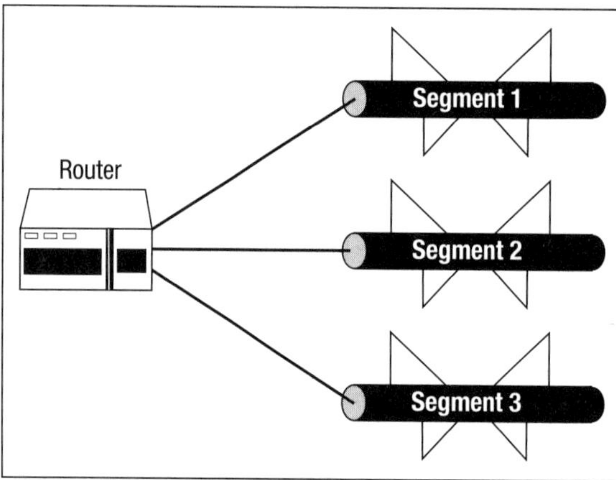

Figure 1.2 Routers connecting multiple segments.

However, routers have several disadvantages:

- The cost of routers is very high and is an expensive way to segment networks. If protocol routing is necessary, you must pay this cost; otherwise, other solutions may work better.
- Routers are difficult to configure and maintain, meaning that administrators will have a difficult time keeping the network up and running. Knowledgeable workers who understand routing can be expensive.
- Routers are somewhat limited in their performance, especially in the areas of latency and forwarding rates.

These disadvantages force network administrators to look elsewhere when designing many large network installations.

SWITCHING

A new option had to be developed to overcome the problems associated with bridges and routers. These devices are called *switches*. The term *switching* was originally applied to packet-switch technologies, such as Link Access Procedure, Balanced (LAPB), Frame Relay, Switched Multimegabit Data Service (SMDS), and X.25. Today, switching is more commonly associated with LAN switching and refers to a technology that is similar to a bridge in many ways.

Benefits of Switches

Switches allow fast data transfers without introducing the latency typically associated with bridging. They create a one-to-one dedicated network segment for each device on the network. These segments are interconnected by using an extremely fast high-capacity infrastructure, commonly referred to as a *backplane*, that provides optimal transport of data on a LAN. This setup reduces competition for bandwidth on the network, allows maximum utilization of the network, and increases flexibility for network designers and implementers.

Ethernet switches provide a number of enhancements over shared networks. The ability to divide networks into smaller and faster segments at *wire-speed*—that is, at the stated speed of the network—without delay is the most important.

To succeed in improving network performance, switches must address three issues:

- They must stop unneeded traffic from crossing network segments.
- They must allow multiple communication paths between segments.
- They must not introduce performance degradation.

To improve performance, routers are typically attached to switches to connect multiple LAN segments. A switch forwards the traffic to the port on the switch the destination device is connected to, which in turn reduces the traffic to the other devices on the network. Information from the sending device is routed directly to the receiving device. No device other than the router, switch, and end nodes sees or processes the information.

The network now becomes less saturated, more secure, and more efficient at processing information, and precious processor time is freed up on the local devices. Routers today are typically placed at the edge of the network and used to connect WANs, filter traffic, and provide security. See Figure 1.3.

Like bridges, switches perform at the OSI Layer 2 level by examining the packets and building a forwarding table based on what they hear. Switches differ from bridges by helping to meet the following needs for network designers and administrators:

- Deterministic paths
- Ability to relieve network bottlenecks
- Deterministic failover
- Capability for scalable network growth
- Fast convergence
- Means to centralize applications
- Capacity to reduce latency

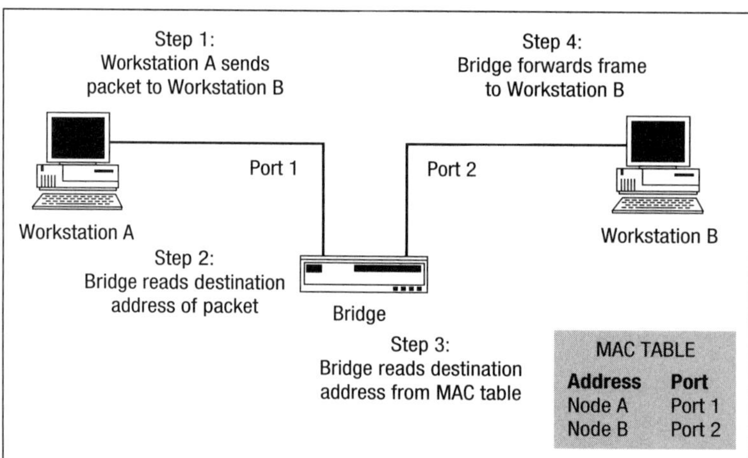

Figure 1.3 Routers and switches.

The 80/20 Rule

Traditionally, network administrators and designers strived to design networks using the *80/20 rule*. Using this rule, a network designer would try to design a network in which 80 percent of the traffic stayed on local segments and 20 percent of the traffic went on the network backbone.

This was an effective design during the early days of networking, when the majority of LANs were departmental and most of the traffic was destined for data that resided on the local servers. However, it is not a good design in today's environment, where the majority of traffic is destined for enterprise servers or the Internet.

A switch's ability to create multiple data paths and provide swift, low-latency connections allows network administrators to permit up to 80 percent of the traffic on the backbone without causing a massive overload of the network. This ability allows for the introduction of many bandwidth-intensive uses such as network video, video conferencing, and voice communications.

Multimedia and video applications can demand as much as 1.5Mbps or more of continuous bandwidth. In a typical environment, users can rarely obtain this bandwidth if they share an average 10Mbps network with dozens of other people. The video will also look jerky if the data rate is not sustained. In order to support this application, a means of providing greater throughput is needed. The ability of switches to provide dedicated bandwidth at wire-speed will meet this need.

Switched Ethernet Innovations

Although many other vendors had devices popular at the time known as *intelligent multiport bridges*, the first known usage of the term *switch* was the Etherswitch by Kalpana in 1990. At that time, these devices were used mainly to connect multiple segments and usually did very little to improve performance other than the inherent benefits bridges provide, such as filtering and broadcast suppression.

Kalpana changed that by positioning its devices as performance enhancers. The Kalpana switches had a number of important features that made them popular, such as using multiple transmission paths for network stations and cut-through switching.

Cut-through switching reduced the delay problems associated with standard bridges. By providing the means to have multiple transmission paths to network devices, each device could have its own data path to the switch and not have to be in a shared environment.

Kalpana was able to do this by dedicating one pair of the station wiring to transmitting data and one pair to receiving data. This allowed the Kalpana designers to ignore the constraints of collision detection and carrier sense, because the cables were dedicated to one station. Kalpana continued its history of innovation with the introduction in 1993 of full duplex Ethernet.

Full Duplex Ethernet

Prior to the introduction of full duplex Ethernet, Ethernet stations could either transmit or receive data; they could not do both at the same time because there was no way to ensure a collision-free environment. This is known as half duplex (HDX) operation.

Full duplex (FDX) has been a feature of WAN networks for years, but only the advent of advances in LAN switching technology made it practical to now consider FDX on the LAN. In FDX operation, both the transmission and reception paths can be used simultaneously. Because FDX operation uses a dedicated link, there are no collisions, which greatly simplifies the MAC protocol. Some slight modifications in the way the packet header is formatted enable FDX to maintain compatibility with HDX Ethernet.

You don't need to replace the wiring in a 10BaseT network, because FDX operation runs on the same two-pair wiring used by 10BaseT. It simultaneously uses one pair for transmission and another pair for reception. A switched connection has only two stations: the station itself and the switch port. This setup makes simultaneous transmission possible and has the net effect of doubling a 10Mbps LAN.

This last point is an important one. In theory, FDX operation can provide double the bandwidth of HDX operation, giving 10Mbps speeds in each direction. However, achieving this speed would require that the two stations have a constant flow of data and that the applications themselves would benefit from a two-way data flow. FDX links are extremely beneficial in connecting switches to each other. If there were servers on both sides of the link between switches, the traffic between switches would tend to be more symmetrical.

Fast Ethernet

Another early innovation in the switching industry was the development of Fast Ethernet. Ethernet as a technology has been around since the early 1970s, but by the early '90s its popularity began to wane. Competing technologies such as FDDI running at 100Mbps showed signs of overtaking Ethernet as a de facto standard, especially as high-speed backbones.

Grand Junction, a company founded by many of the early Ethernet pioneers, proposed a new Ethernet technology that would run at 10 times the 10Mbps speed of Ethernet. It was joined by most of the top networking companies—with the exception of Hewlett-Packard (HP), which had a competing product. HP's product, known as 100Mbps VG/AnyLAN, was in most respects far superior to the product proposed by Grand Junction. It had a fatal flaw, though: It was incompatible with existing Ethernet standards and was not backward compatible to most of the equipment in use at the time. While the standards bodies debated the merits of each of the camps, the marketplace decided for them. Fast Ethernet is the overwhelming winner, so much so that even HP sells Fast Ethernet on almost all its products.

Note: *In 1995, Cisco purchased both Kalpana and Grand Junction and incorporated their innovations into its hardware. These devices became the Catalyst line of Cisco products.*

Gigabit Ethernet

In order to implement Gigabit Ethernet (GE), the CSMA/CD method was changed slightly to maintain a 200-meter collision diameter at gigabit-per-second data rates. This slight modification prevented the situation that could occur when Ethernet packets would complete transmission before the transmitting station sensed a collision, which would violate the CSMA/CD rule.

GE maintains a packet length of 64 bytes, but provides additional modifications to the Ethernet specification. The minimum CSMA/CD carrier time and the Ethernet slot time have been extended from 64 bytes to 512 bytes. Also, packets smaller than 512 bytes have an extra carrier extension added to them. These changes, which can impact the performance of small packets, have been offset by implementing a feature called *packet bursting*, which allows servers, switches, and other devices to deliver bursts of small packets in order to utilize the available bandwidth.

Because it follows the same form, fit, and function as its 10- and 100Mbps predecessors, Gigabit Ethernet can be seamlessly integrated into existing Ethernet and Fast Ethernet networks using LAN switches or routers to adapt between the different physical line speeds. Because GE is Ethernet, only faster, network managers will find the migration from Fast Ethernet to Gigabit Ethernet to be as smooth as the migration from Ethernet to Fast Ethernet.

Switching Methods

Switches can use more than one switching method, and some switches use three. Cisco switches use three different switching methods:

- Store-and-forward
- Cut-through
- Fragment-free

Store-and-Forward Switching

Store-and-forward switching pulls the entire packet received into its onboard buffers, reads the entire packet, and calculates its cyclic redundancy check (CRC). It then determines if the packet is good or bad. If the CRC calculated on the packet matches the CRC calculated by the switch, the destination address is read and the packet is forwarded out the correct port on the switch. If it does not match the packet, the packet is discarded. Because this type of switching waits for the entire packet before forwarding, latency times can become quite high, which can result in some delay of network traffic.

Cut-Through Switching

Cut-through switching, sometimes referred to as *realtime switching* or *FastForward switching*, was developed to reduce the latency involved in processing frames as they arrive at the switch and are forwarded on to the destination port. The switch begins by pulling the frame header into its network interface card buffer. As soon as the destination MAC address is known (usually within the first 13 bytes), the switch then forwards the frame out of the correct port.

This type of switching reduces latency inside the switch; however, if the frame is corrupt because of a late collision or wire interference, the switch will still forward the bad frame. The destination receives the bad frame, checks its CRC, and discards it, forcing the source to resend the frame. This process will certainly waste bandwidth; if it occurs too often, major impacts can occur on the network.

In addition, cut-through switching is limited by its inability to bridge different media speeds. In particular, some network protocols (including NetWare 4.1 and some IP networks) use windowing technology, where multiple frames may be sent without a response. In this situation, the latency across a switch is much less noticeable, so the on-the-fly switch loses its main competitive edge. In addition, the lack of error checking poses a problem for large networks. That said, there is still a place for the fast cut-through switch for smaller parts of large networks.

Fragment-Free Switching

Fragment-free switching, also known as *runtless switching*, was developed to solve the late-collision problem. These switches perform a modified version of cut-through switching. Because most corruption in a packet occurs within the first 64 bytes, instead of just reading the first 13 bytes to get the destination MAC address, the switch looks at the first 64 bytes. The minimum valid size for an Ethernet frame is 64 bytes. By verifying the first 64 bytes of the frame, the switch then determines if the frame is good or if a collision occurred during transit.

Adaptive Switching

To resolve the problems associated with the switching methods discussed so far, another method was developed. Some switches—such as the Catalyst 1900, 2820, and 3000 series—begin with either cut-through or fragment-free switching. As frames are received and forwarded, the switch also checks the frame's CRC. Although the CRC might not match the frame itself, the frame is still forwarded before the CRC check and after the MAC address is reached.

The switch performs this task so that if too many bad frames are forwarded, the switch can take a proactive role, changing from cut-through mode to store-and-forward mode. This method, in addition to the development of high-speed processors, has reduced many of the problems associated with switching.

Only the Catalyst 1900, 2820, and 3000 series switches support cut-through and fragment-free switching. One might ponder the reasoning behind the faster Catalyst series switches not supporting this seemingly faster method of switching. Well, store-and-forward switching is not necessarily slower than cut-through switching. When switches were first introduced, the two modes were quite different. With better processors and integrated-circuit technology, store-and-forward switching can perform at the physical wire limitations. This method allows the end user to see no difference in the switching methods.

Types of Switching

The following types of switching are in use today:

- *Ethernet switching*—This method is based on the IEEE 802.3 standard but doesn't rely on the CSMA/CD technology. It includes 10Mbps LANs, as well as Fast Ethernet and Gigabit Ethernet.
- *Token-Ring switching*—Although not as popular as Ethernet switching, Token-Ring switching can also be used to improve LAN performance.
- *FDDI switching*—This method is rarely used, chiefly due to the high expense of FDDI equipment.
- *Port switching*—This type of switching takes place in the backplane of a shared hub. For instance, ports 1, 2, and 3 could be connected to backplane 1, whereas ports 4, 5, and 6 could be connected to backplane 2. This method is typically used to form a collapsed backbone and to provide some improvements in the network.
- *Cell switching*—This method uses Asynchronous Transfer Mode (ATM) as the underlying technology. Switch paths can be either permanent virtual circuits (PVC) that never go away, or switched virtual circuits that are built up, used, and torn down when you're finished.

Migrating Legacy Equipment

Although dedicated switch connections provide the maximum benefits for network users, sometimes you don't want to fork-lift your equipment and exchange it for the bigger, better, faster equipment. It may sometimes be necessary to support legacy equipment.

Fortunately, Ethernet switches can provide connectivity in a number of ways. You can attach shared hubs to any port on the switch in the same manner that you connect end stations.

Generally, users migrate toward single-station segments as bandwidth demands increase. This migration will provide them with the increased bandwidth they need without wholesale replacement of existing equipment or cabling. In this scenario, a backbone switch is created in which each port on the switch is attached to a shared (multiple-station) segment. This switch would replace existing connections to routers or bridges and provide communication between each of the shared segments.

Internetworking Challenges

Regardless of the type of LAN topology in use, sending data effectively through the network is a challenge for network designers and administrators. The first data processing environments consisted mostly of time-sharing networks that used mainframes and attached terminals. Communications between devices were proprietary and dependent on what vendor your equipment came from. Both IBM's System Network Architecture (SNA) and Digital's network architecture implemented such environments.

Today, high-speed LANs and switched internetworks are universally used, owing largely to the fact that they operate at very high speeds and support such high-bandwidth applications as voice and video conferencing. Internetworking evolved as a solution to three key problems: isolated LANs, duplication of resources, and a lack of network management.

Implementing a functional internetwork is no simple task. You must face many challenges, especially in the areas of connectivity, reliability, network management, and flexibility. Each area is key in establishing an efficient and effective internetwork. The challenge when connecting various systems is to support communication between disparate technologies. Different sites, for example, might use different types of media, or they might operate at varying speeds.

Another essential consideration—reliable service—must be maintained in any internetwork. Individual users and entire organizations depend on consistent, reliable access to network resources. Network management must provide centralized support and troubleshooting capabilities. Configuration, security, performance, and other issues must be adequately addressed for the internetwork to function smoothly. Flexibility, the final concern, is necessary for network expansion and new applications and services, among other factors.

The Roles of Routers, Switches, and Bridges

In today's networks, the trend is to replace hubs and bridges with switches. This approach reduces the number of routers connecting the LAN segments while speeding the flow of data in the network. A smart network administrator uses switches to inexpensively increase network bandwidth and ease network administration.

A switch is a low-cost solution to provide more bandwidth, reduce collisions, filter traffic, and contain broadcasts. But, switches don't solve all network routing problems. Routers provide a means of connecting multiple physical topologies, restricting broadcasts, and providing network security. Using switches and routers together, you can integrate large networks and provide a high level of performance without sacrificing the benefits of either technology.

Chapter Summary

In this chapter, we covered early network architectures (where the need for switching originated) and, most importantly, the methods used in switching. Some of the key concepts to remember are:

- *Carrier Sense Multiple Access Collision Detection (CSMA/CD)* is used to "listen" to the network to see if it is in use. If it is clear, data is transmitted. If a collision occurs, both stations will re-transmit their data.
- Innovations in Ethernet, such as full-duplexing and Fast Ethernet, made advances in switching possible.
- The *backbone* is a high-capacity infrastructure system that provides optimal transport of data on a LAN. Typically in a LAN, the data running from router to router is transported through a faster physical topology than the local area or virtual LAN devices. The physical cable is called the backbone.
- The *backplane* is similar to the motherboard in a PC. It interconnects all the modules inside the switch chassis.
- *Bridges* are Layer 2 devices that connect multiple physical segments using identical protocols. An incoming frame is filtered or forwarded based on the MAC address of the frame.
- *Latency delay* is measured from the moment a packet enters the input port on the switch until the time that the switch forwards the packet out the output port.

- The *MAC address* is the physical encoded number or address on a Network Interface Adapter.
- *Network broadcast storms* occur when broadcasts throughout the LAN use up all available bandwidth on a LAN, thus grinding the network to a halt.
- A *repeater* is a device that regenerates and retransmits data over the physical network. Typically, repeaters are used to overcome the distance limitation of the physical cabling.
- A *router* is a device that resides at the network Layer 3 and controls the flow of data between multiple physical segments.

You should also make sure that you have a clear understanding of and can identify the different LAN switching methods:

- *Store-and-forward*—The switch waits for the entire packet to arrive before checking the CRC; it then forwards or discards the packet. This type of switching has the highest latency.
- *Cut-through*—Begins forwarding the frame as soon as the first 13 bytes and the MAC address are received. It relies on the receiving device to discard the frame if there is corruption.
- *Fragment-free*—Reads the first 13 bytes and MAC address and begins to forward the frame. It then reads up to 64 bytes to verify that there is no corruption of the packet. If there is corruption, a preset maximum of errors changes the switching type from cut-through switching to store-and-forward switching.

Later in this book, we will devote many chapters to configuring and troubleshooting each type of switch and each switching method. In Chapter 4, you will also learn what each Cisco switch chassis supports for switching methods.

Review Questions

1. What is not one of the three methods of switching?
    a. Store-and-forward
    b. Cut-through
    c. Fragment-free
    d. Fast
2. Which is the best answer to describe the difference between full and half duplex?
    a. Full duplex is only used on WAN circuits.
    b. Full duplex uses both the transmission and receive pairs of wires, whereas half duplex uses only the transmission pairs.

c. Half duplex uses a dedicated link.

d. Full duplex uses both transmission and receive pairs of wires at the same time.

3. Bridges operate at what OSI layer?

   a. Layer 1—physical

   b. Layer 2—data link

   c. Layer 3—network

   d. All of the above

4. Routers operate at what OSI layer?

   a. Layer 1—physical

   b. Layer 2—data link

   c. Layer 3—network

   d. All of the above

5. What method is used to reduce the likelihood of two stations transmitting at the same time?

   a. IEEE 802.3

   b. Carrier Sense Multiple Access Collision Detection (CSMA/CD)

   c. Full duplexing

   d. Fragment-free switching

6. Switches were designed to help reduce what problems? [Choose the three best answers]

   a. Network bottlenecks

   b. Lack of scalable growth

   c. Increased latency

   d. Broadcast suppression

   e. Reduced bandwidth

7. What term more accurately describes latency?

   a. The delay introduced because of excessive collisions on a network

   b. The delay on a network due to broadcast storms

   c. The delay in forwarding packets due to network errors

   d. The delay in forwarding caused by bridge overhead

8. What is a problem associated with cut-through switching? [Choose the two best answers]
   a. Decreased network traffic
   b. Increased network traffic
   c. Broadcast suppression
   d. Retransmissions
9. What is a network broadcast storm?
   a. When network broadcasts use up all bandwidth
   b. When video is running on the network
   c. When one station transmits to all other stations
   d. When no one is doing anything on the network
10. Which switches support both cut-through and fragment-free switching? [Choose the three best answers]
    a. Catalyst 5500
    b. Catalyst 1900
    c. Catalyst 6500
    d. Catalyst 2820
    e. Catalyst 3000
11. An increase in the time it takes to examine a frame is the main disadvantage of what type of switching?
    a. Fragment-free
    b. Cut-through
    c. Store-and-forward
    d. Fast
12. What is a backbone?
    a. Where all workstations connect to the network
    b. The strongest point in the network
    c. An extremely fast high-capacity infrastructure that connects other segments
    d. A set of stackable hubs that look like one device
13. What is a sign that you may need to move to a switched environment? [Choose the two best answers]
    a. You have high rates of utilization.
    b. You are getting frequent complaints about network response times.

c. Excessive collisions are occurring on your network.

d. The network is slow.

14. What standard is commonly referred to as Ethernet?

a. IEEE 802.5

b. IEEE 802.3

c. IEEE 802.2

d. IEEE 802.4

15. What are the two innovations to Ethernet that helped foster switching?

a. Faster speed

b. Full duplexing

c. Half duplexing

d. Cut-through switching

16. A repeater is used to overcome distance limitations on the physical cabling.

a. True

b. False

17. What type of bridge knows the entire network path from source to destination?

a. Transparent

b. Source route

c. Translational

d. DEC

18. What is the term used when a bridge transmits a packet to all network segments except the source segment?

a. Broadcasting

b. Self-learning

c. Filtering

d. Flooding

19. What term is used to describe the delay in traffic caused by the overhead of bridging?

a. Latency

b. Filtering

c. Forwarding

d. Throughput

20. Which technology is the dominant type of networking protocol?
    a. Token-Ring
    b. FDDI
    c. ATM
    d. Ethernet
21. What term is used to describe the data a network station transmits?
    a. Bucket
    b. Message
    c. Frame
    d. Channel
22. A hub that connects other hubs in a multi-tier design to form a common network is known by what term?
    a. Intelligent
    b. Departmental
    c. Dumb
    d. Backbone
23. What is the biggest problem associated with hubs?
    a. All stations share the same bandwidth.
    b. They are slow.
    c. They have no management ability.
    d. They can't connect to high-speed uplinks.
24. What are the two main functions of bridges?
    a. Framing
    b. Filtering
    c. Flagging
    d. Forwarding
25. Which of the following is not a purpose of routers?
    a. Filtering broadcasts
    b. Routing traffic
    c. Media conversion
    d. Improve throughput

CHAPTER TWO

2 ELEMENTS OF CAMPUS DESIGN

After completing this chapter, you will be able to:

- ✓ Identify the factors that influence network design
- ✓ Understand the network performance issues that exist on networks
- ✓ Describe the principles of hierarchical networks
- ✓ Identify the components of Cisco's Switched Campus Model
- ✓ Describe the elements of the OSI Model
- ✓ Explain the functions of Layers 2, 3, and 4, and multilayer switching
- ✓ Define and describe network building blocks
- ✓ Address backbone routing options

This chapter discusses the network design issues that need to be considered when designing (or modifying) a network. One of the most important parts of any networking project is the design phase. Networks that begin without a good design are seldom successful at achieving their goals. The ability to successfully deploy network technology depends on a number of factors: your knowledge of network fundamentals, a firm understanding of your company's existing infrastructure and business needs, and your grasp of the fundamental concepts of design.

Although this book is not a network design book itself, several concepts of network design are important to understand in order to provide a good solution. We will present the concept of hierarchical network models and how they aid in understanding the structure of networks and can be used to help the performance issues of a network. The Open Systems Interconnection (OSI) Model will be explained in depth. The topic of switching at the OSI layers will be covered, with a full explanation of Layer 2, 3, and 4 switching. We will show how using a network building block approach can help you decide what devices to use in your network. Lastly, we show some options for backbone routing to consider.

We begin with a discussion about some of the network design issues we all face.

Network Design Issues

The major issues for network users and administrators are providing maximum availability for the networks while maintaining high levels of performance. As we mentioned in Chapter 1, traditional LANs had a host of problems associated with them, such as broadcast control, network segmentation, and latency. In order to provide an acceptable level of performance, network designers began implementing segmented networks using routers or virtual LANs (VLANs) to parse the network.

As long as a majority of the data traffic stayed local to the subnet, this type of design worked fine. However, at the same time switches began to stake their claim on the network infrastructure, other technologies also began to make their appearance—notably, massive data farms that the entire enterprise could access, and intranets to deliver corporate data.

With these technical developments, a trend began that changed the way traffic flowed in the networks. Where previously a network designer would try to model his network on the fact that 80 percent of the traffic was local and 20 percent was remote (the 80/20 rule), these developments reversed the situation, such that now 20 percent of the traffic is local and 80 percent is remote. As a result, routers increasingly became the bottleneck for network traffic. One idea to remedy this issue is to move the applications or servers closer to the users, but doing so defeats the benefits of providing enterprise-wide resources. Therefore, we must consider new ways of designing networks to provide better performance. This process involves designing networks into forms that can perform well in today's networks.

Basic Design Principles

Everyone has a different way of approaching network design, but we all follow many of the same basic concepts. One of the principle issues involved is to thoroughly understand the business needs that drive the project. The business climate in today's marketplace has made it important to review the impact on the bottom line for any project, and networking technology is no different. If your primary responsibility is day-to-day network administration and operations, you're probably more concerned with making your network run more efficiently than in business concepts like return on investment (ROI). However, when you first approach a network design, you should always consider why you are being asked to do the project. A good network designer has these goals in mind:

- Understanding the needs of the customer
- Developing a design that meets those needs
- Testing and deploying the design

Design Factors

The process of designing a network is a balancing act of conflicting needs and desires. For example, you might wish to have your network fully redundant and capable of withstanding any natural or manmade event. However, this setup will cost dearly. Also, in an effort to fully protect everything on your network, you may make the network too cumbersome to work on. It is vital that you gain an understanding of the purposes for which the network is planned. Although you can take into account a wide variety of factors when designing a network, the following components should be considered during network design:

- *Scalability*—How much growth the network design supports. A solid network design should be able to support the anticipated increases in network usage as new users, sites, or functions are added to it.
- *Availability*—The amount of time a network is operational. Availability concerns itself with two main areas: redundancy and reliability of the network resources. *Redundancy* is met by providing duplicate links or devices to a network to avoid downtime. *Reliability* is measured in a number of ways, such as accuracy in the data, error rates, stability, and the mean time between failures.

- *Performance*—Throughput is measured in the amount of data traffic that can flow through the network, the accuracy of the data, efficiency of the network, the delay in sending data traffic, and the application response times.
- *Security*—Includes two components. A good design will provide assurances that a business's data is protected against theft, damage, or loss. However, a proper security design will not impede the company's ability to do its job. To protect network resources, it is critical that the company identify what it wants to protect and what the impact on the company would be if those resources were lost. Only then can reasonable trade-offs be made to protect them.
- *Management*—Management of the different aspects of a network. The International Organization for Standardization (ISO) uses a model called Fault, Configuration, Accounting, Performance, and Security (FCAPS). It is important to determine the extent network management plays in the network you are designing. Some network administrators want to measure every aspect of the network and prepare daily, weekly, and monthly reports, accounting for every second of time and billing accordingly, whereas others do little in the way of management.
- *Adaptability*—The critical ability to respond rapidly to a change in the network as it grows. This includes the capability of the network to converge after part of the network changes.

Hierarchical Network Models

Hierarchical models use the concept of layering to provide a logical framework to understand and discuss complex topics. In this manner, you can discuss a specific, well-defined component of the overall structure. In a layered architecture, each layer implements a specific functionality or service. Each layer provides its own functionality by performing certain actions within that layer and using the services of the layer below it.

This concept is particularly beneficial when changing a layer's function. As long as the layer provides the same functions to the layer above it that it previously did, and it uses the same services from the layer below, you don't have to change your entire model to reflect that level's change in functionality.

In a hierarchical network, each layer is responsible for performing a given set of tasks. These are:

- *Error control*—Provides a more reliable channel between the two layers
- *Flow control*—Prevents one layer from overwhelming another layer

- *Segmentation and reassembly*—Divides large chunks up into smaller, more manageable ones
- *Multiplexing*—Allows multiple connections to a single layer
- *Connection setup*—Provides handshaking between two layers

Campus Models

An excellent example of using a hierarchical model to break down a complex idea into more manageable areas is Cisco's hierarchical internetworking model. Although mostly associated with Cisco, this model has been widely deployed, with the telephone system being the best example. This model is designed to provide the maximum bandwidth to the users of the network while also filtering the data in an efficient manner.

The idea behind this network model is that most networks fail due to their creating unstable network links or routing loops. When a failure inevitably occurs in such a network, it does not converge in time to prevent a major problem.

Cisco defines a *campus* as a group of buildings connected into an enterprise network of many LANs. It has a fixed geographical location and is owned and controlled by the organization. In general, campus networks use LAN technologies, such as Ethernet, to connect these LANs.

Designing a network using a campus model helps prevent a network failure by providing logical points to aggregate and summarize network traffic. This setup prevents a failure in one part of the network from affecting the entire enterprise network. This model divides the network into three distinct layers:

- *Core network layer*—Forwards traffic at high speeds
- *Distribution network layer*—Summarizes traffic and combines routes
- *Access layer*—Passes traffic to the network

This three-tiered model is depicted in Figure 2.1.

Core Network Layer

The core network layer is designed for one thing, and one thing only: switching packets at the fastest possible speed. It is the final aggregation point for the entire network, so devices at this level must be fast and reliable. They should be configured with the fastest processors possible and a sizeable amount of memory. Connections at this level must be of the highest possible bandwidth. Some of the attributes of this layer are as follows:

- *No decision making*—At the core network layer, no decisions about packet filtering or policy routing should take place. There are two basic reasons for

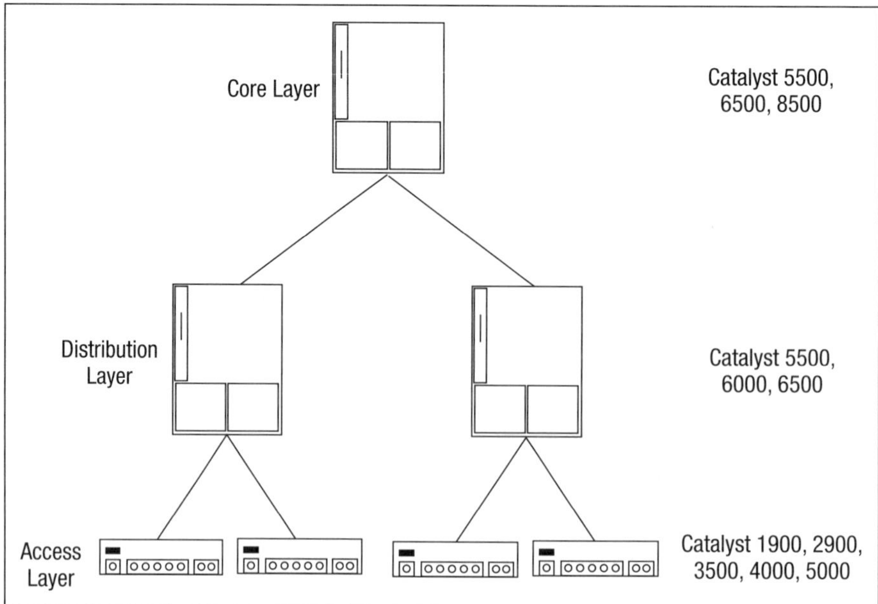

Figure 2.1 A hierarchical network design.

this. First, any filtering or policy decisions at this layer will add to the processing requirements of the system and will inevitably introduce a delay in forwarding packets. Second, any mistakes at this level will severely impact the rest of the network.

- *Reachability*—The devices placed in the network core should be able to reach any device in the network. This doesn't mean that they have to have a connection to each device. It just means they need to be reachable in the routing table. To prevent these devices from having a path to every device in their routing tables, you should use network route summarization. Because traffic is very heavy at this layer, poorly designed architectures can place very heavy demands on the network and could lead to an unstable network.

  A good example is the global Internet. You would be extremely unlikely to find a device that could carry a path to each device connected to the Internet, because such a device would have to have routes to millions of devices. The Internet works chiefly due to the fact that each Network Access Point (NAP) to the Internet is required to summarize all the addresses in its control and all the NAPs have the full routing table to all the other NAPs' devices.

Switch devices that are commonly found at this level are the Cisco 6500 and 8500. These devices have wire-speed capabilities and provide robust multicast routing features that make them a good fit for the core of a network. We will cover these models extensively in later chapters.

Distribution Network Layer

The distribution network layer is the demarcation point between the access and core layers. This level terminates the traffic that originates in the access layer connections and summarizes the traffic before passing it along to the core layer. It can be described best as the layer that provides policy-based connectivity.

The main focus of the distribution layer is to define the boundaries for the network and to provide packet manipulation of the network traffic. It provides isolation from topology changes, manages the size of the routing table, and aggregates network traffic. As such it has the following functions:

- Aggregating network addresses
- Providing access to departments and workgroups
- Defining broadcast or multicast boundaries
- Routing VLANs
- Translating media types
- Providing security

In addition, the distribution layer is where interdomain traffic is redistributed and is the point at which static and dynamic route redistribution occurs. This layer is also commonly used as the point at which remote sites connect to the network.

Common devices at this level are the 2926G and Catalyst 5000 family. The Catalyst 5000 can be configured with a router processor board that provides Layer 3 functionality, or it can work with an external router to provide these routing functions.

Access Layer

The access layer is the starting point for most traffic on the network. The access or workgroup layer connects users. Some important functions of this layer are shared bandwidth, switched bandwidth, MAC-layer filtering, and microsegmentation.

This layer has two goals: to pass traffic to the network for valid network users and to filter traffic that is passed along. The access layer is the point at which end users are connected to the network; it provides the means to connect to the devices located on the distribution layer. It provides connections to both local and remote devices. Because the access layer is the entry point to the network, security and policy decisions are made here. This is also the logical termination point for virtual private networks (VPN).

Devices found at this level are shared hubs; the 1600, 2500, 2600 family of routers; and switch devices, including the Catalyst 1900 or 2820 for small to medium networks, the Catalyst 2900 for medium-size networks with fewer than 50 users, and the Catalyst 4000 series for high-performance networks of fewer than 96 users. In a large network, the Catalyst 5000 series is a good fit.

OSI Model

Perhaps the most well-known hierarchical model is the Open Systems Interconnection (OSI) Model. This being a network book, it is almost mandatory to have coverage of the OSI Model. As you can see from Figure 2.2, the OSI Model divides the problem of moving information between computers over a network medium into seven smaller and more manageable services.

The OSI Model is not a network implementation. Instead, it describes the functions each layer should perform. It is similar to the plans for building a house. The house still needs to be built after plans to build it have been completed, but any number of builders can do the actual work. The same is true in the networking industry; multiple network vendors can build a protocol implementation from a protocol specification and will differ from each other in relatively minor ways.

The OSI Model describes how information makes its way from application programs (such as spreadsheets) through a network medium (such as wires) to another application program in another computer. As the information to be sent descends through the layers of a given system, it looks less and less like human language and more and more like the ones and zeros that a computer understands.

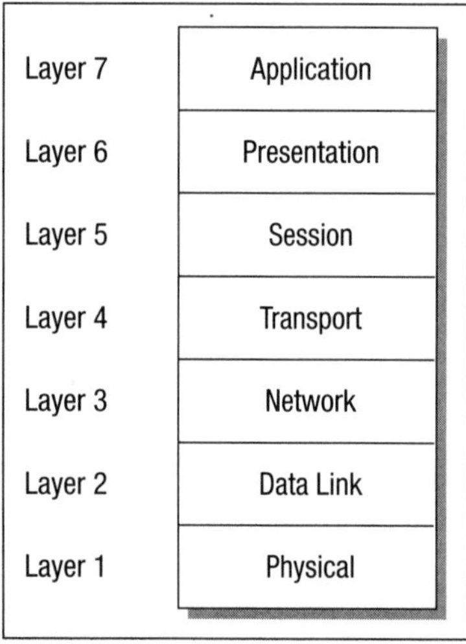

Figure 2.2 The OSI Network Model.

The seven layers of the OSI Model can be divided into upper and lower layers. The upper layers concern themselves with application issues and generally are implemented only in software. The lower layers of the OSI Model handle data transport issues.

Most network devices implement all seven layers. To streamline operations, however, some network implementations skip one or more layers. The physical layer and data link layer are implemented in hardware and software. The other layers are generally implemented in software only. The lowest layer—the physical layer—is closest to the physical network medium (the network cabling, for example) and is responsible for actually placing information on the medium.

Application Layer

The application layer is the OSI layer closest to the user. This layer provides the user with the applications needed to communicate through the network. It differs from the other layers in that it does not provide services to any other OSI layer. Instead, it provides services to other applications not included in the OSI model.

The application layer identifies and establishes the availability of intended communication partners, synchronizes cooperating applications, and establishes agreement on procedures for error recovery and control of data integrity. The application layer also determines whether sufficient resources exist for the intended communication. Examples of such application processes include:

- *Netscape*—To browse the Internet (HTTP/TCP port 80)
- *FTP*—To transfer files (FTP/TCP ports 20 and 21)
- *Eudora*—To send and receive email (SMTP/TCP port 25)

Presentation Layer

The presentation layer ensures that information sent by the application layer of one system will be readable by the application layer of another system. The presentation layer concerns itself not only with the format and representation of user data, but also with data structures used by programs. Therefore, in addition to actual data format transformation, the presentation layer negotiates data transfer syntax for the application layer.

Other functions that may correspond to the presentation layer are data encryption and decryption and compression/decompression.

Session Layer

As its name implies, the session layer establishes, manages, and terminates sessions between applications. *Sessions* consist of dialogue between two or more presentation entities. A *dialogue* is a formal conversation in which two nodes agree to exchange data. The communications can take place in one of three modes: simplex, half duplex, or full duplex. The session layer synchronizes dialogue between the presentation layer entities and manages their data exchange.

The session layer enables nodes to communicate in an organized manner. Each session has three phases:

- Connection establishment
- Data transfer
- Connection release

In addition to basic regulation of conversations (sessions), the session layer offers provisions for data expedition, class of service, and exception reporting of session-layer, presentation-layer, and application-layer problems.

Transport Layer

The transport layer forms the boundary between application-layer protocols and lower-layer protocols. Whereas the application, presentation, and session layers are concerned with application issues, the lower four layers are concerned with data transport issues.

The transport layer attempts to provide a data transport service that shields the upper layers from transport implementation details. Specifically, the transport layer is concerned with issues such as how reliable transport over an internetwork can be accomplished.

In providing reliable service, the transport layer provides mechanisms for the establishment, maintenance, and orderly termination of virtual circuits; transport fault detection and recovery; and information flow control (to prevent one system from overrunning another with data). One of these functions is to divide messages into fragments that fit within the size limitations established by the network. Ethernet, for example, limits the size of the data field to 1500 bytes.

Network Layer

The network layer is a complex layer that provides connectivity and path selection between two end systems that may be located on geographically diverse subnets. A *subnet*, in this instance, is essentially a single network cable (sometimes called a *segment*).

Because substantial geographic distance and many subnets can separate two end systems desiring communication, the network layer is the domain of routing. Routing protocols select optimal paths through the series of interconnected subnets. Traditional network-layer protocols then move information along these paths.

Data Link Layer

The data link layer (also known as the link layer) provides reliable transit of data across a physical link. In so doing, the link layer is concerned with physical (as opposed to network, or logical) addressing, network topology, line discipline (how end systems will use the network link), error notification, ordered delivery of frames, and flow control.

The data link layer is responsible for providing node-to-node communication on a single, local network. To provide this service, the data link layer must perform two functions:

- It must provide an address mechanism that enables messages to be delivered to the correct nodes.
- It must translate messages from upper layers into bits that the physical layer can transmit.

The data link layer is commonly associated with two sublayers:

- Logical Link Control (LLC)
- Media Access Control (MAC)

The LLC sublayer was designed by the Institute of Electrical and Electronics Engineers (IEEE) to add more functionality to the data link layer. The LLC is part of the IEEE 802.2 standard. Some of the more popular 802 specifications are listed in Table 2.1.

At the MAC sublayer, an address is assigned that uniquely identifies a device on the network; this is called a *MAC address*. The first three octets of the MAC

Table 2.1 IEEE 802 standards.

Specification	Description
802.1	802 specification overview
802.2	Logical Link Control
802.3	Bus networks using CSMA/CD—Ethernet
802.4	Token bus
802.5	Token Ring
802.6	Metropolitan area network (MAN)
802.7	Broadband technology
802.8	Fiber-optic technology
802.9	Voice/Data integration on LANs
802.10	Interoperable LAN security
802.11	Wireless networks
802.12	100BaseVG/AnyLAN

address identify the manufacturer of the network interface card (NIC). This is known as the Organizationally Unique Identifier (OUI). MAC addresses are critical to the operation of bridges, switches, and routers, because this is the mechanism by which they identify workstations on the network.

Physical Layer

The physical layer defines the electrical, mechanical, procedural, and functional specifications for activating, maintaining, and deactivating the physical link between end systems. Such characteristics as voltage levels, timing of voltage changes, physical data rates, maximum transmission distances, physical connectors, and other, similar attributes are defined by physical layer specifications.

How Communication Occurs between Layers

The OSI model's layering doesn't permit direct communication between peer layers in different systems. Each layer in one system must rely on services provided by the adjacent system's layers to help achieve communication with its peer. Each Layer *N* communicates with its peers by using the services provided by a Layer *N*-1 entity via a service access point (SAP). The relationship between adjacent layers in a single system is shown in Figure 2.3.

If System A has data from a software application to send to System B, the data is passed to the application layer. The application layer in System A adds a header to the data that is passed to the presentation layer. The presentation layer adds its own header that contains the information intended for the presentation layer in System B.

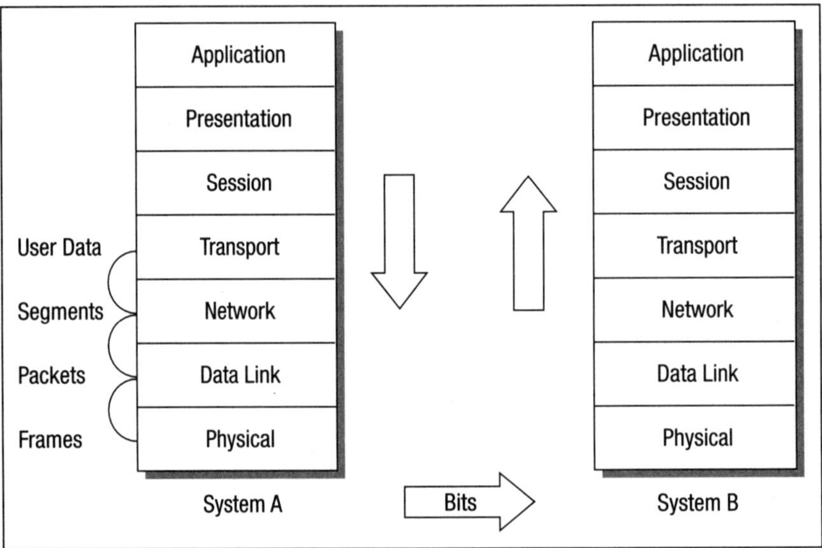

Figure 2.3 Relationship between adjacent layers.

Each layer in the source system adds control information to the data, and each layer in the destination system analyzes and removes the control information from that data. The information unit grows in size as each layer adds its own header (and in some cases a trailer) that contains control information to be used by its peer layer in System B. At the physical layer, the entire information unit is placed onto the network medium.

The physical layer in System B receives the information and passes it up its data link layer. The data link layer in System B then reads the control information contained in the header added by the data link layer in System A. The header is removed, and the remainder of the information unit is passed to the network layer.

Each layer performs the same actions: The layer reads the header from its peer layer, strips it off, and passes the remaining information unit to the next highest layer. After the application layer performs these actions, the data is passed to the software application in System B, in exactly the form in which it was transmitted by the application in System A.

Protocols

The OSI model provides a conceptual framework for communication between computers, but the model itself is not a method of communication. Actual communication is made possible only by using communication protocols. A protocol is a set of rules that govern how computers exchange information. A protocol makes use of the functions of one or more of the OSI layers. The most common types of communication protocols are:

- *LAN protocols*—Define communication over LAN media. They function at the physical and data link layers.
- *WAN protocols*—Define communication over WAN. They function at the physical, data link, and network layers.
- *Network protocols*—Define upper-layer functions, such as TCP/IP or IPX.
- *Routing protocols*—Define network layer functions. They are responsible for path determination and traffic switching.

Protocol Data Units

Protocol data units (PDUs) are the terms used to define the network data units used by the protocols. Each PDU is associated with one and only one protocol. There is some disagreement among the network vendors as to the names of the data units, but the most common definitions are as follows:

- The application layer data stream units are called *messages*.
- The transport layer data stream units are known as *segments*.

- The network layer data units are called *datagrams* (or, in some instances, *packets*).
- The data link layer data units are most commonly called *frames*.
- The physical layer data units are known as *bits*.

Switching at the OSI Layers

Switching is a term that has been applied to so many parts of the network landscape, it has become very difficult to define. We have switching hubs, multilayer switches, netflow switching, Layer 2 switches, Layer 3 switches, Layer 4 switches, routing switches, MFT switches, and so on. This section will try to make sense of the different terms you may hear.

Layer 2 Switching

Layer 2 switches are, in effect, self-learning bridges. Of course, we don't use the term *bridges* anymore, because that term is considered old-fashioned these days. However, just like bridges, Layer 2 switches work by discovering the topology that surrounds them, keeping track of the Layer 2 Media Access Control (MAC) addresses that identify them. Also, just like a bridge, when a switch receives a packet with a familiar destination MAC address, it simply forwards it to the right port. Because this occurs in hardware, it is very quick and efficient and doesn't involve the software processing steps that bog down a router.

Layer 2 switches differ from bridges in one critical area: They provide multiple simultaneous wire-speed connections between ports. In addition, they increase traffic flow by terminating Ethernet's collision detection protocol (CSMA/CD) on each port, which reduces the number of potential collisions that occur. In this manner, each switch port represents a different network segment.

By providing dedicated bandwidth to each switch port, the main benefit of using a Layer 2 switch is increased bandwidth. For this reason, most large companies have deployed Layer 2 switching in their networks for the simple reason that it offers a low-cost, easy-to-implement performance boost. Another big benefit to using Layer 2 switches is the ability to group individual ports into switched logical groupings called virtual local area networks (VLANs).

VLANs

VLANs improve performance by confining the broadcast domain to the VLAN ports. By breaking a single large broadcast domain into multiple broadcast domains, VLANs help address the scalability problems present in large networks.

VLANs help simplify life by offering easier moves and changes in a network and provide a fundamental change in how LANs are designed, administered, and managed.

VLANs use OSI Layer 2 bridging and multiplexing mechanisms, such as IEEE 802.10, LAN Emulation (LANE), and Inter-Switch Link (ISL). These mechanisms allow the networks to have multiple broadcast groups on a single network infrastructure.

Benefits of Routing

Even though a great deal of performance improvement was gained in converting routed and shared networks to Layer 2 switching, it became apparent that some level of network partitioning was still required. This task fell to the traditional routers. Routers provide the following benefits:

- Control of broadcast and multicast traffic
- Route determination
- Packet filtering
- Logical network addressing
- Security

This movement of traffic from local LANs to the routed network led to bottlenecks and pointed out the weaknesses of the traditional switch/router design. A method to provide Layer 3 functionality without losing the performance improvements of switching had to be devised.

Layer 3 Switching

The term *Layer 3 switching* has been very popular of late. In contrast to *Layer 2 switching*, which was simply a redefinition of multiport bridging, *Layer 3 switching* has been applied to a wide array of uses, from Layer 2 VLAN switching to full-fledged routing. Perhaps the most consistent definition is "products that bridge packets but use forwarding information to enhance the forwarding decisions."

As the routers increasingly became bottlenecks, high-bandwidth applications such as video became harder to deploy. At the same time, the movement from 10Mbps LANs to 100Mbps drew increased attention to the routers being a choke point in the network. Layer 3 switching provides router functionality within a switch and allows LAN-based routing at near-switching speeds. It does this by placing the "routing" decisions in silicon rather than in software.

Benefits of Layer 3 Switching

Compared to standard routers, Layer 3 switching routers process more packets more quickly by using hardware instead of software. Some of the benefits of Layer 3 switching are:

- Hardware-based traffic forwarding
- High packet speed rates
- Low latency rates
- Lower costs
- Security
- Quality of Service

Types of Layer 3 Switching

Layer 3 switching products fall into two basic types: packet-by-packet routing and flow-based routing.

Packet-by-packet routing does a complete routing operation for the packets that need to be routed and then forwards them to their destination. Every incoming packet is forwarded on to its destination based on its Layer 3 or network layer (such as Internet Protocol [IP] or Internetwork Packet Exchange [IPX]) destination address. Routing protocols, such as Open Shortest Path First (OSPF), Enhanced Interior Gateway Routing Protocol (EIGRP), or Routing Information Protocol (RIP), can be used to provide fast network convergence in the event of network changes. Traditional router services such as security filtering, broadcast containment, and IP multicast may be included.

Flow-based routing examines the first packet, determines its destination, and then switches the remaining packets to that same destination at Layer 2 speeds, without further routing control. After the flow has been determined, any further packets have the same rights as the first packet. This method minimizes the latency typical of most routed environments.

Layer 4 Switching

Layer 4 switching is Layer 3 switching that considers the application in use. Layer 4 switches consider the same criteria as Layer 2 switches (MAC addresses) and Layer 3 switches (source and destination addresses). In addition to these characteristics, Layer 4 switches are able to make forwarding decisions based upon the Transmission Control Protocol (TCP) or User Datagram Protocol (UDP) port. This ability enables Layer 4 switches to consider what type of information is being carried in the packets when forwarding packets.

Using the Layer 4 information to determine the traffic filtering provides the ability for switches to:

- Prioritize traffic based on application
- Provide quality of service to network users
- Account for traffic flows

Layer 4 switching is particularly useful with high-bandwidth applications such as video, or applications such as voice that are sensitive to timing delays.

Multilayer Switching

This switching method, also known as *netflow switching*, combines all the previous layers of switching. It uses the *route once, switch many* concept. This method forwards traffic at wire speed on LANs; but because its forwarding decisions are based in hardware, it removes the constraints of traditional Layer 3 routers.

These devices can function as both Layer 3 and 4 switches. When used as a Layer 3 switch, a multilayer switch uses only MAC address information and IP addresses to make its decision as to where to forward traffic. When used as a Layer 4 switch, it uses both source and destination address information, as well as source and destination port information to make its decision.

Network Building Blocks

In conjunction with the concept of using hierarchical networks, networks can be designed using a building block approach. Cisco's approach, known as *CiscoFusion Architecture*, is a set of network building blocks:

- The building block
- The core block
- The file-server block
- The switch block
- The WAN/dial block

You need to consider each of these areas and evaluate the possible effects on each building block to achieve a good network design. For the purposes of this book, however, we'll cover only the portions that concern the switch block and the core block.

Switch Block

This block consists of a combination of Layer 2 and Layer 3 devices. The Layer 2 functions are provided by switches located in the wiring closets to provide a connection point for all the devices on the network. These devices are typically members of the Catalyst 1900, 2800, or 2900 families. The Layer 3 devices provide the user with network layer services and will help prevent problems that originate in other networks from impacting local users and vice-versa. Devices at this level should be able to provide the following functions:

- High-speed uplinks to core devices
- Fast convergence times in the event of network topology changes
- Redundant links

Core Block

The core block is responsible for transferring data as quickly as possible without doing any processor-intensive operations. The types of technology used can be Fast Ethernet, Asynchronous Transfer Mode (ATM), or Gigabit Ethernet switching. Because all inter-campus traffic must pass through the core level, this level must be able to move traffic quickly. Although there are no firm requirements for multiple switches at the core level, it is highly desirable to have multiple devices to eliminate a single point of failure on the network.

Core networks can be configured in two ways. *Collapsed cores* are networks in which the core and distribution layer functions are provided in one device. Note that all the functions are still provided—they just occur in a single box. The other type is a *dual core*, in which multiple switch blocks are present and multiple redundant links are a requirement.

Devices found at this level are Catalyst 5500 (with router functionality), Catalyst 6500, and Catalyst 8500 in LAN environments. In an ATM environment, you might find IGX 8400 series, BPX 8600 series, MGX 8800 series, and 12000 GSR series switches.

Network Services

It is important to consider the flow of traffic in a network when designing one. In the past, once a network reached a certain size you simply segmented the network and continued on. These days, proper server placement and application traffic can dramatically impact the network. It is vital to understand the different types of network services. There are three categories:

- *Local services*—A service is local when the device supplying the services and the device that wants to use them are on the same physical subnet or VLAN. In this case, no traffic has to pass through a router or cross the backbone. Placement of the switches in this instance is at the edge of the network, connecting the servers and the users into a single workgroup.

- *Remote services*—Remote services require the network traffic to cross router boundaries. The device supplying the service is on a separate subnet from the devices wishing to use those services. The traffic may or may not pass through the core layer of the network.
- *Enterprise services*—Enterprise services supply services to all users of the network, no matter where they are located. Common examples of enterprise services are email and Internet access. These services are on a separate subnet from any other devices and require a Layer 3 device to access them. Because these types of services are accessed by a large number of users, they require high-speed access to prevent bottlenecks from occurring.

Backbone Routing Options

It is the dream of every network administrator to have one robust, multifeature protocol running on the network. It would be flexible enough to handle any demand, yet capable of utilizing any form of media. This protocol would be bulletproof and resilient from errors, yet accommodating enough to handle any future technology. In reality, there is no such protocol. Sorry to burst your bubble. Today, many different types of protocols may be running on your network, ranging from the most simple to the highly complex.

Networks, by their very nature, have swelled as much as they have grown. In the early days, peer-to-peer networks sharing printers and files made up the majority of networks. As more networks came into existence, they were typically built on the fly with whatever happened to be in fashion at the time. This means that on today's networks you may simultaneously have IPX (multiple versions), AppleTalk, NT, System Network Architecture (SNA), and a host of other protocols.

Network backbones can be RIP, Interior Gateway Routing Protocol (IGRP), EIGRP, OSPF, Border Gateway Protocol (BGP), or a wide variety of combinations. A method of integrating these protocols into a single campus network is a fact of network life. In their native mode, other than sharing the same physical media, most LAN network protocols typically have nothing to do with each other. They studiously ignore the presence of everything not under their control.

This concept, also known as *ships in the night*, can be applied to network routing protocols by using a different routing protocol for each LAN protocol. For example, you might use RIP to route IPX traffic, and OSPF to route IP traffic. Each of the routing protocols uses its own method to determine the best way to route traffic in its control, and unless the protocols are redistributed into each other, they will not communicate with the other routing processes.

This arrangement can be awkward to configure and troubleshoot, and will lead to increased processing demands due to the extra overhead of multiple routing processes. If multiple protocols are to be passed over the internetwork, unsupported protocols must be encapsulated within the supported protocol or the routing nodes will ignore them.

So, why do this?

The ability of network staffs to support multiple protocols is a big reason. Increased overhead due to the talkative nature of some protocols is another. IPX and AppleTalk, for instance, are well known for impacting low-speed wide-area links. In these cases, a policy of allowing the use of IPX or AppleTalk on the LAN, but only IP on the wide-area links, may be the best idea.

That said, however, encapsulation does add overhead to traffic on the network. If multiple protocols are supported widely throughout a large internetwork, a multiprotocol backbone approach is likely to work better.

Chapter Summary

Network design is an area that affects anyone who uses a computer network. A good, solid design will help support your existing requirements and allow you to move forward in the future with relative ease.

During this chapter we touched on many areas of network design. The goals of a good network design are to provide maximum availability while providing high performance. Network designs need to consider the principles of understanding the customer's needs and developing a network that meets those needs. Items to consider during a network design are scalability, availability, performance, security, management, and adaptability.

Hierarchical models use the concept of layering to assist in the understanding of how networks work and to provide models to design networks. Layering also helps because a change in one layer will affect only that layer without having to redesign the whole model.

Campus models are used to help prevent network issues from disrupting your network by providing logical points to aggregate traffic and providing isolation points from the rest of the network. Cisco uses a hierarchical internetworking model, called the Cisco Switched Campus Model, consisting of core, distribution, and access layers to serve as a guideline for how to design a stable, high-performance network.

The OSI Model is one that every network professional needs to be aware of. Although few protocols adhere strictly to the OSI model, it is used extensively as a tool to understand how networks function. The upper layers of the OSI chart deal mainly with application issues, whereas the lower layers deal with data transport issues.

Switching can occur at OSI Layers 2, 3, 4, or a combination of all three. Layer 2 switching is bridging with the addition of VLANs. Layer 3 switching is Layer 2 switching plus some routing functions. Layer 4 switching is Layer 3 switching with some knowledge of the application being used.

Network building blocks are another hierarchical network model used to design networks. It uses the concepts of a switch block and a core block to isolate traffic from each layer. Devices found in the switch block are Catalyst 1900, 2800, or 2900. Devices found in the core block are Catalyst 5500, Catalyst 6500, and Catalyst 8500.

Network services can be characterized as local if the device wanting the service and the device supplying the service are on the same subnet, remote if traffic crosses a router, or enterprise if traffic crosses the backbone.

We addressed several important terms in this chapter. Let's review some of them and note their significance:

- *Scalability*—Refers to how much growth a network can accommodate. This is one of the factors of network design and deals with the anticipated increases in network usage. A properly designed network must be able to grow as the network grows.
- *Availability*—Refers to how much of the time the network is operational. This is another factor of network design. It concerns itself with the redundancy and reliability of the network resources. An example of providing network availability is having duplicate links to a resource.
- *Performance*—Refers to the throughput, accuracy, and efficiency of a network. The performance of the network is one of the most important design factors when designing a network. If a network cannot meet the demands of the users, it will not be successful.
- *Security*—An area of network design that considers how well a network is protected from theft and damage. Providing security on a network is a tradeoff of securing the data from prying eyes but not impacting performance too much.
- *Management*—Refers to network management in the areas of fault, capacity, accounting, performance, and security. Not every organization will manage all these areas, but it is a good idea to review these topics to see if they are needed in your organization.

- *Hierarchical Internetworking Model*—A framework to develop networks. Hierarchical networks allow a logical grouping of network resources to provide segmentation, fault isolation, and performance in the network.
- *Campus*—A group of buildings in a fixed geographical location, owned and controlled by the organization. The idea behind using a campus model is that most networks fail due to their creating unstable network links or routing loops. Designing a network using this model prevents a failure in one part of the network from affecting the entire enterprise network.
- *Core layer*—The final aggregation point for the entire network. Core network devices are concerned with switching packets at the fastest possible speed. This is the layer where you put the biggest, fastest switches possible.
- *Distribution layer*—The demarcation point for the core and access layers. This layer's primary duty is to provide policy-based connectivity. At this level, you put in devices with more port density, fast uplinks, and a lot of management functionality than is required at the access layer, but not necessarily the top-of-the-line switches found at the core layer.
- *Access layer*—The starting point for network devices. This is the point at which most end users are connected to the network. It provides the means to connect to the devices located on the distribution layer. Access layer devices are the workhorses of this layer.
- *Protocols*—A set of rules that govern network communications. A protocol makes use of the functionality of one or more of the OSI layers. The most common types of communication protocols are LAN, WAN, routing, and routed protocols.
- *Packet*—Data units used by protocol layers. Each layer has its own type of associated unit. These units are messages, segments (transport layer), datagrams (network layer), frames (data link layer), and bits (physical layer).
- *Layer 2 switches*—Bridges with some VLAN capability. Similar to bridges, they learn what devices are on each port and build a table of addresses to use. Unlike bridges, they provide dedicated, multiple simultaneous wire-speed connections. Most large companies have deployed Layer 2 switching in their networks for the simple reason that it offers a low-cost, easy-to-implement performance boost.
- *Layer 3 switches*—Layer 2 switches with some routing capability. Layer 3 switching is a term that has been associated with a wide variety of devices. Perhaps the best definition is that it is a device that switches packets but can make forwarding decisions based on what is in the packet header.

- *Layer 4 switches*—Layer 3 switches with some knowledge of the application being used. Using the Layer 4 information in a packet allows network administrators to control the flow of data in the network. This ability is useful for providing high quality of service to timing-dependent protocols. An example would be giving priority to voice or video traffic.
- *Multilayer switches*—A combination of Layer 2, 3, and 4 switches that use the concept of route once, switch many. These devices work as both Layer 3 and Layer 4 devices. By doing this, the devices can forward traffic at wire speed on LANs; but because their forwarding decisions are based in hardware, they can forward much more quickly than traditional Layer 3 devices.
- *Switch block*—A device located in the wiring closet that requires high-speed uplinks and redundancy. Layer 2 devices are used at this layer to provide access to the network for end users. Layer 3 devices are used to provide network layer functions for these devices. These devices are typically members of the Catalyst 1900, 2800, or 2900 families.
- *Core block*—An end point for networks that requires fast access and no policy implementation. This layer is responsible for moving data quickly. Devices found at this level are Catalyst 5500 (with router functionality), Catalyst 6500, and Catalyst 8500 in LAN environments.
- *Local services*—Services where the device supplying the services resides on the same subnet as the device requesting the services.
- *Remote services*—Services where the device supplying the services resides on a separate subnet than the device requesting the services.
- *Enterprise services*—Services that involve crossing the backbone to access a device. These services are typically located on a separate subnet than the rest of the network devices.

Review Questions

1. Which basic design factor deals with the concerns of network growth?
   a. Availability
   b. Performance
   c. Scalability
   d. Management
   e. Security

2. In the Cisco campus model, which layer is responsible for summarizing traffic and combining switching routes?
   a. Access layer
   b. Distribution layer
   c. Session layer
   d. Core layer
3. In the Cisco campus model relating to Catalyst switches, in which layer would you typically find the 8500 Series switch?
   a. Access layer
   b. Distribution layer
   c. Session layer
   d. Core layer
4. In the Cisco campus model, which Catalyst switch would you typically find in the access layer?
   a. 5500 Series
   b. 6000 Series
   c. 4000 Series
   d. 2900 Series
5. Bridges are typically associated with which layer of the OSI Model?
   a. Core layer
   b. Physical layer
   c. Data link layer
   d. Session layer
6. What type of protocols function at the OSI's physical and data link layers?
   a. Routing protocols
   b. WAN protocols
   c. Network protocols
   d. LAN protocols
7. What types of protocols are used in path determination?
   a. Routing protocols
   b. WAN protocols
   c. Network protocols
   d. LAN protocols

8. Which OSI layer is responsible for routing packets between segments?
   a. Physical layer
   b. Data link layer
   c. Network layer
   d. Transport layer
9. Which is not a benefit of Layer 2 switching?
   a. Control of broadcast traffic
   b. Route determination
   c. Accessing the Internet
   d. Routing determined by switching modes
10. Which is not a benefit of Layer 3 switching?
    a. Quality of service
    b. Hardware-based traffic forwarding
    c. Sending a print job to a local printer in your collision domain
    d. Security
11. Which is not a benefit of Layer 4 switching?
    a. Switching based on TCP or UDP port
    b. Traffic forwarding based on source and destination addresses
    c. Particularly useful for high-bandwidth applications such as video
    d. Forwarding based on TCP/IP address
12. Which is not a basic design factor category?
    a. Availability
    b. Performance
    c. Scalability
    d. Management
    e. Printers
13. IEEE 802.5 does not cover which method of switching?
    a. SRB
    b. SRT
    c. TB
    d. SR/TRB

14. Early network designers tried to design networks around which rule?
    a. 60/30 rule
    b. 80/20 rule
    c. 50/50 rule
    d. 40/60 rule
15. A good network designer keeps what basic goals in mind?
    a. Satisfying the needs of the customer
    b. Satisfying the needs of the paycheck
    c. Satisfying the needs of the company
    d. Testing and deployment of the design
16. In a hierarchical network, each layer is responsible for providing which given tasks?
    a. Handshaking between two layers
    b. Flow control
    c. Segmentation and reassembly
    d. Error control
17. Which layer of the Cisco Switched Campus Model provides high-speed transferring of data and makes no filtering and queuing decisions?
    a. Transport layer
    b. Core layer
    c. Access layer
    d. Distribution layer
18. The users' point of access to the network takes place at which layer of the Cisco Switched Campus Model?
    a. Transport layer
    b. Core layer
    c. Access layer
    d. Distribution layer
19. Which IEEE standard deals with bus networks utilizing CSMA/CD.
    a. 802.10
    b. 802.3
    c. 802.5
    d. 802.12

20. In the OSI Model, communication to peer layers is handled by what entity?
    a. Interactive Communication Protocol (ICP)
    b. Service Access Point (SAP)
    c. Service Advertising Protocol (SAP)
    d. Ethernet

CHAPTER THREE

COMPONENTS OF SWITCHES

After completing this chapter, you will be able to:

- ✓ Describe how to connect to a switch and enter commands
- ✓ Explain the types of switching modes used
- ✓ Understand the functions of ASICs and how they work
- ✓ Describe the internal workings of the switch BUS
- ✓ Depict the types of switch architectures in use
- ✓ Explain the features available in second generation switches

This chapter will provide you with an overview of the internal workings of Cisco switches. You will learn in great detail about the different types of electronic components that make the switch function and the hardware that enables switches to forward data frames and packets faster than a typical CPU. The features that are available on the second generation of switches are also covered in great detail.

You will learn from this chapter the different bridging modes that are available for not just Ethernet, but Token Ring and Fiber Distributed Data Interface (FDDI) as well. Pay close attention to the terminology covered in this chapter: A clear understanding of the different terms used will help you when we cover items in more depth in later chapters.

Methods to connect to the console port are also covered in this chapter. When you get to the section covering the use of Cisco Express Forwarding (CEF) Application-Specific Integrated Circuits (ASIC), study this section well, including the commands that are given. CEF and dCEF are Cisco's newest ASICs. Your knowledge of them will be tested well, as will your knowledge of their two main components: the Forwarding Information Base (FIB) and the adjacency table.

SWITCH BASICS

Your first impression when looking at a switch is that it appears pretty basic. Just like a PC, it has a case or chassis, a motherboard that on some switches allows you to add additional modules and additional components, and a power supply or two. That's about where the similarities end. This is a very powerful device, and it can be one of the most important devices in your network. Unlike a PC, you won't find a port to plug in a keyboard and mouse. You won't find a place to plug in that SuperVGA monitor with 13 million colors, either. What you will find on every switch is a console port.

Connecting to the Console

You enter instructions for the switch through the console port. The console comes preconfigured and ready to use. You gain access to the console port in a couple of ways, as shown in Figure 3.1. You can use a dumb terminal or you can use the more popular way—a third-party program such as HyperTerminal. You can also use Telnet after you have configured port access on some switches. Let's take a look at the current types of Cisco switch console ports.

On the 1900, 2800, and 2900XL Series switches, you will find an Ethernet RJ-45 console port that allows you to connect a serial port to the switch. When connecting to the console port, Cisco recommends that you use a straight-through

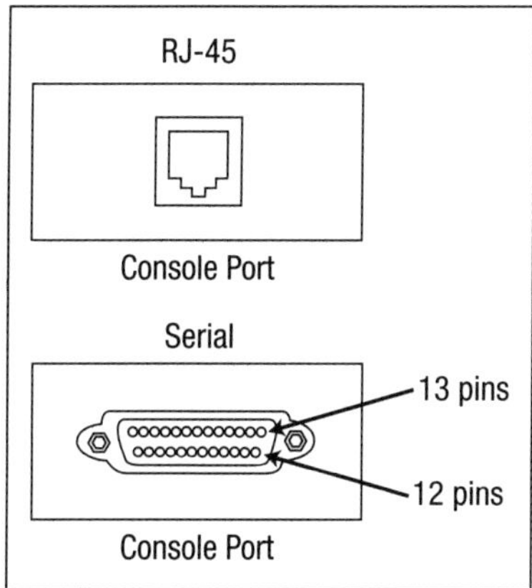

Figure 3.1 The two different console ports: RJ-45 and serial.

Category 5 cable wired for 10BaseT. For a 100BaseT connection, Cisco recommends that you use just a straight-through Category 5 cable. On the terminal or PC side, you will need to plug that RJ-45 Category 5 cable into one of three supplied adapters:

- *For a PC*—Use the Data Terminal Equipment (DTE) adapter that has RJ-45 to DB-9 female connection ends.
- *For a Unix workstation*—Use the DTE adapter that converts an RJ-45 connector to a DB-25 female connector.
- *For a modem connection*—Use the adapter similar to the Unix workstation adapter, but with a DB-25 male end.

Warning: Remember: Never connect a live ISDN line or telephone line directly into the back of your switch. If you do, you might have to get a new switch or replace the console port. Always use the supplied RJ-45 to RJ-45 adapter to connect the console to another device.

The Catalyst 5000 uses a Supervisor Engine. To connect to the Supervisor Engine console port, use the RJ-45 to RJ-45 rollover cable that came with the switch. To connect a PC to the console port, attach the RJ-45 to DB-9 female DTE adapter to one of the serial ports of the PC. To attach to a Unix workstation, use the RJ-45 to D-subminiature female adapter. To connect a modem, use the RJ-45 to D-subminiature male adapter.

You can add other components and modules to the switch to increase its functionality and scalability. We will cover those in more advanced topics later in the book.

TYPES OF SWITCHES

The first switches introduced were Layer 2-only switches. In functionality, they were identical to the smart bridges in use at the time. These switches were divided into two types:

- *Processor-based switches*—These were Reduced Instruction Set Computing (RISC)-based processor switches. These switches had a great deal of functionality but were typically slow and very expensive.
- *ASIC*—Modified versions of ASIC switching are still used in the switches of today. This first generation was typically faster than a processor but the functionality was limited. Their downfall was that they typically offered no filtering, had limited bridging modes, limited the number of virtual local area networks, and had very limited management features.

A second generation of switches was introduced in 1997. These switches kept the ASIC-based switching but had dramatically increased functionality. In the next section, we'll take a look at the major functions of the ASICs involved in today's Cisco Catalyst switching line. Keep in mind that there are many ASICs, both Cisco proprietary and those from other vendors.

FUNCTIONS OF ASICs

All switches use a central processing unit (CPU), an ASIC, or a combination of both. These hardware components process and forward the frames that are received to the switch. The CPU and ASIC add the destination Media Access Control (MAC) address of the network interface card to the switching table so the switch can make intelligent forwarding decisions. The speed of the switch depends entirely on the amount of traffic flowing into the switch and the speed of the processor.

ASICs are designed to switch frames to the limits of the physical LAN topology. They are not as functional as a CPU but cost quite a bit less. They can, however, be implemented in such a way that they can provide faster switching decisions and update the switching table more quickly than a CPU. They may be great in some ways, but like everything else, there is a drawback. Occasionally you can do a firmware upgrade, but most of the time you have to replace the motherboard or upgrade to another switch to get the processing power you need.

In the current generation of switches, a combination of ASICs and CPUs work together. The CPUs handle such things as management, spanning tree, and other network management protocols, whereas the ASICs take care of the actual processing and forwarding of data in and out of the switch.

Let's take a look at the some of Cisco's ASICs and their features in the newer line of Catalyst switches.

Enhanced Address Recognition Logic

The Enhanced Address Recognition Logic (EARL) ASIC performs the same basic function as the Content Addressable Memory (CAM). The CAM is used in bridges to make filtering and forwarding decisions. The EARL is an ASIC that connects to the data switching bus and allows the bus to see every frame that crosses the bus. This ability is important for the roles in which the EARL ASICs participate. The EARL ASIC's components are shown in Figure 3.2. Components such as the Line Module Communication Processor (LCP) and Network Management Processor (NMP) work with the EARL ASIC. Each is explained in more detail in later chapters.

The EARL is responsible for looking at all frames as they arrive on the bus. It then makes a switching decision based on the destination MAC address after determining what virtual local area network (VLAN) the frame arrived from. The originating VLAN is referred to as the *color*.

When the frame is placed on the bus, all the ports on the switch pull the frame into the switch's output buffer. It's essentially the responsibility of the EARL to make the forwarding and filtering decisions and to notify the index/control bus that carries out the decisions.

The Local Target Logic (LTL) ASIC is located on each line module of the switch. The LTL assists the EARL in finding the destination ports for which the frame will be forwarded.

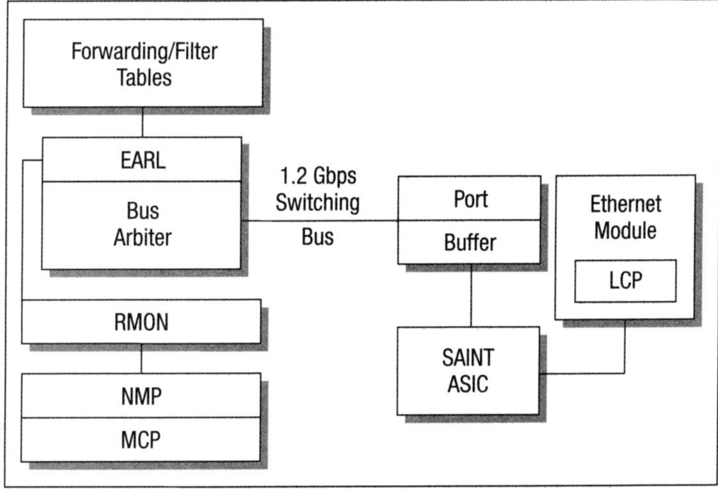

Figure 3.2 The EARL ASIC's components.

The Color Blocking Logic (CBL) ASIC helps the EARL make forwarding decisions. It ensures that a frame that comes from a particular VLAN does not leave through a port belonging to a different VLAN. CBL also helps Spanning Tree Protocol (STP) place ports in blocking, learning, listening, or forwarding mode.

The EARL ASIC is also responsible for building the address-switching table stored in memory. The address-switching table is dynamic (as opposed to static) and can hold up to 128,000 MAC addresses. The table stores each machine's MAC address, the VLAN associated with the MAC address, and the port in which the frame should exist to reach the MAC address.

EARL adds entries into the address-switching table when it finds a MAC in a frame whose address is not currently stored in the table. It removes the address from the table after the address's time to live (TTL) has expired. The default TTL at which entries are removed is 300 seconds, or 5 minutes. The TTL can be set from 1 minute to a maximum of 20 minutes. If the EARL detects a MAC address already in the table, the MAC address's timer is reset. This step allows a machine that is moved (such as a laptop) to be redetected, should it change VLANs, while at the same time keeping frequently used addresses in the table.

Another EARL function is to tag frames when they arrive at the switch before they enter the buffer. EARL encapsulates the Ethernet frame by adding the source port's identity and VLAN. It then adds a checksum to the end of the Ethernet frame. This encapsulation is not the same as the Inter-Switch Link (ISL) encapsulation performed on trunk ports. It is used only to help the EARL make intelligent forwarding decisions. The outgoing port removes the encapsulation prior to forwarding the frame.

EARL+ is an enhancement to the Supervisor III Engine that allows EARL to support the Token Ring Line Module. This ability lets the EARL make switching decisions for Token Ring frames, including the Routing Information Field (RIF) information used in Source Route Bridging (SRB). EARL+ forwards the RIF and SRB frames to Fast Ethernet ISL trunks. Ethernet and Token Ring frames use different bit-ordering. The EARL+ transparently differentiates between the two types of addresses.

Synergy Advanced Multipurpose Bus Arbiter

The Synergy Advanced Multipurpose Bus Arbiter (SAMBA) and the EARL work together to allow port access to the bus, thereby letting frames be forwarded correctly. The bus is the path used by electrical signals to travel between the CPU and the attached hardware. SAMBA is responsible for access to the bus.

The Supervisor Engine and the line modules all have this ASIC. The SAMBA ASIC is connected to the switch bus in a master and a slave mode. SAMBA supports up to 13 line modules in master mode. In master mode, it is responsible for arbitrating access to the switch bus. Access to a port's bus is based on its priority. There are three priorities: normal, high, and critical. In master mode, SAMBA makes its final decision regarding the interval in which ports access the switch bus.

To access the bus, each port posts a request to the slave SAMBA ASIC on its line module. The slave is responsible for negotiating its local ports and for forwarding all arbitration requests to the Supervisor Engine's master SAMBA ASIC. The Supervisor Engine also has a slave SAMBA for the 2 uplink ports as well as support for up to 48 ports on any line modules. The slave also has the responsibility to implement broadcast suppression, and it gathers bus-related priority statistics.

Synergy Advanced Interface and Network Termination

The Synergy Advanced Interface And Network Termination (SAINT) ASIC is responsible for half-duplex and full-duplex Ethernet support. There are two configurable priority levels for ISL Ethernet trunk ports. (*Trunk ports* are special connections between two switches that carry traffic for more than one VLAN.) SAINT is responsible for Ethernet encapsulations, de-encapsulations, port monitoring, and gathering statistics for Ethernet trunk ports.

All of the processing performed by SAINT takes place in the hardware ASICs. It therefore never uses any CPU cycles from the main processor. This fact enables the ASIC to provide zero latency to the switch, allowing the switching process to occur faster than the frame is clocked on the physical LAN topology.

Synergy Advanced Gate-Array Engine

The Synergy Advanced Gate-Array Engine (SAGE) ASIC performs the same functions as SAINT. It also adds some features, such as gaining access to the token in FDDI or Token Ring. Again, as in SAINT, the processing performed by SAGE takes place in the hardware ASICs, requires no CPU cycles, and adds no additional latency to the switch.

Phoenix ASIC

The Phoenix ASIC is a special component of the Supervisor III Engine. This ASIC provides a gigabit bridge between each of the buses. From the perspective of the EARL and the SAMBA, the Phoenix ASIC appears as another port on the box. It has a 384K buffer for handling traffic as it travels between buses.

It is important to note that some line modules do not have access to all three buses. In the case of the Catalyst 5500 13-slot chassis, slots 1 through 5 are connected to bus A, slots 1 through 9 are connected to bus B, and slots 1 through 5 and 10 through 12 are connected to bus C. The placement of line modules in the chassis becomes important. You will learn more about this in the following chapter, as well as later in the book.

Cisco Express Forwarding ASIC

The Cisco Express Forwarding (CEF) ASIC and Distributed Cisco Express Forwarding (dCEF) ASIC are Cisco's newest ASICs for routers and switches. Not only are they the newest, but they are also among the most functional and most efficient ASICs for the higher-end Cisco product line. This section is rather large, covering not only what CEF and dCEF are but also how to configure them. You will find CEF in the new 12.0 IOS and used on the 8500 series switches, as well as the 12000 series Gigabit Switch Routers (GSRs).

The CEF is a miniature CPU used to ensure that all packets have equal access into internal memory. It performs lookups via the CEFA search engine, verifying that each lookup is done fairly by arbitration. You will find the CEFA micro-controller local to four ports on the Catalyst 8500 line module. CEFA uses a round-robin approach, giving fair access to data traffic on each port as well as cycling data between each port and processing requests as needed.

The CEF microprocessor forwards system messages back to the centralized CPU. CEF forwards such data as spanning tree Bridge Protocol Data Units (BPDUs), routing advertisements, Address Resolution Protocol (ARP) frames, Cisco Discovery Protocol (CDP) packets, and other control message types. Some of CEF's main attributes are its ability to optimize large network scalability, superb performance, and efficient traffic patterns. It is an excellent choice for large networks using Web-based applications as well as bandwidth-intensive applications such as voice over IP, multicast, unicast, and other critical applications.

Functions of the CEF

CEF is a very complex function that is less CPU-intensive than fast-switching route caching. This attribute allows more processing ability for other Layer 3 services such as QoS queuing, and higher level encryption and decryption process applications. It offers a high level of consistency and stability in very large networks. The Forwarding Information Base (FIB), which contains all the known routes to a destination, allows the switch to eliminate the route cache maintenance and fast switch or process switch that doesn't scale well to large network routing changes.

The routing table is created first, and information from the routing table is forwarded to the FIB. The FIB is a highly optimized routing lookup algorithm. Through the use of prefix matching of the destination address, the FIB makes the process of looking up the destination in a large routing table occur much more quickly than the line-by-line lookup of the traditional routing table.

The FIB maintains a copy of the forwarding information contained in the IP routing table based on the next-hop address. The IP table is updated if there are routing or topology changes. Those changes are then recorded in the FIB, and the next-hop is then recomputed based on those changes. This process eliminates the need for fast or optimum switching in previous versions of the Internetwork Operating System (IOS).

The Adjacency Table

The adjacency table maintains a one-to-one correspondence to the FIB. All entries in the FIB are maintained in the adjacency table. CEF uses the adjacency table to apply Layer 2 address information. The adjacency table provides the Layer 2 information necessary to switch the packet to its next point destination; the table is updated as adjacencies are discovered. The following are some commands to display the adjacency table:

- To view the adjacency table, use this command:

  ```
  show adjacency
  ```

- To get a more detailed view, including Layer 2 information, use this command:

  ```
  show adjacency detail
  ```

- To clear the adjacency table, use this command:

  ```
  clear adjacency
  ```

All entries will be repopulated with the latest information as soon as this command is through executing. This allows the CEF to recalculate all next-hop values.

The adjacency tables contain MAC address for routers that remap Layer 2 addresses to Layer 3 addresses. It uses the IP Address Resolution Protocol (ARP) to populate neighbors gleaned from Internet Protocol (IP) and Internetwork Packet Exchange (IPX) updates, indexed by interface and address. For each computed path, a pointer is added for the adjacency corresponding to the next-hop. This mechanism is used for load balancing where there is more than one path to a destination.

Other Adjacency Tables

In host-route adjacencies, a few other types of adjacencies are used to expedite switching in certain conditions:

- *Null adjacency*—Refers to packets destined for a Null0 interface that are dropped. This is an effective form of access filtering.

- *Glean adjacency*—A node is connected directly to more than one host. In this situation, the router or switch maintains a prefix for the subnet instead of the individual host. If a packet needs to reach a specific host, the adjacency table is gleaned for the information specific to that node.
- *Punt adjacency*—Occurs when switching paths are sent to the next switching layer for handling. This is done when a packet needs special handling, or when the packets need to be forwarded to a higher switching layer or level.
- *Discard adjacency*—Packets are discarded only. You will find this type of adjacency only on a Cisco 12000 Series.
- *Drop adjacency*—Packets are dropped but the prefix is checked.

After a data packet is forwarded to the CEF search engine, it uses the content addressable memory (CAM) table to perform lookups. It can hold either 16,000 or 64,000 entries, depending on the options supported by the CAM table.

CEF Search Engine

The CEF search engine can make either Layer 2-based or Layer 3-based switching decisions. With Layer 3 FIB, incoming packets are placed into the internal memory. The CEF ASIC microcontroller is designed to handle traffic to each port in an equal access manner. It provides equal access to the internal memory and lookups by using the CEF search engine.

The switch reads the first 64 bytes of the frame, then the microcode sends the search engine the relevant source MAC address, destination MAC address, or the network of destination. The search engine then conducts a lookup of the CAM table for the corresponding information. CEF uses the search engine to find the MAC address or the longest match on the destination network address. It does this very quickly and responds with the corresponding rewrite information; it then stores this information in the CAM table. The CAM table then forwards the information to the first-in/first-out (FIFO) of the control interface.

Finally, the CEF now knows the port-of-exit for the packet, based either on its MAC address or on the Layer 3 IP or IPX network numbers. The packet is then transferred across the switching fabric to its point of destination. The fabric interface prepares the packet prior to exiting the switch. You'll learn more about the fabric interface in Chapter 4 when we discuss the 8500 Series switches.

3

Fabric Interface FIFOs

In the final stages of packet switching within the Cisco Catalyst 8500, the switching CEFA knows the port from which the packet will exit, based on information such as its MAC address or Layer 3 protocol address. The packet is then transferred across the switching fabric to the port of destination. The fabric interface prepares the packet before it is forwarded through the switching fabric.

The fabric interface contains only two components: the frame FIFO and the control FIFO. The CEFA and the search engine use an internal memory connection into the frame FIFO. Before the control FIFO performs a lookup, the packet moves from internal memory into the frame FIFO. The search engine then returns to the control FIFO all relevant rewrite and QoS information.

At this point, the fabric interface rewrites the packet with the appropriate information, recalculates the checksum, and edits the internal routing tag containing the port of exit, the QoS priority, and the drop priority. After the fabric interface edits the packet, a frame scheduler is signaled to forward the frame back to the fabric and out the destination port. This process takes care of identifying the output port of exit, rewriting the frame tag, and error checking the frame.

CEF supports Ethernet, FDDI, Point-to-Point Protocol (PPP), High-Level Data Link Control (HDLC), Asynchronous Transfer Mode (ATM)/AAL5snap, ATM/AAL5mux, ATM/AAL5nlpid, and tunnels. Figure 3.3 shows the CEF components.

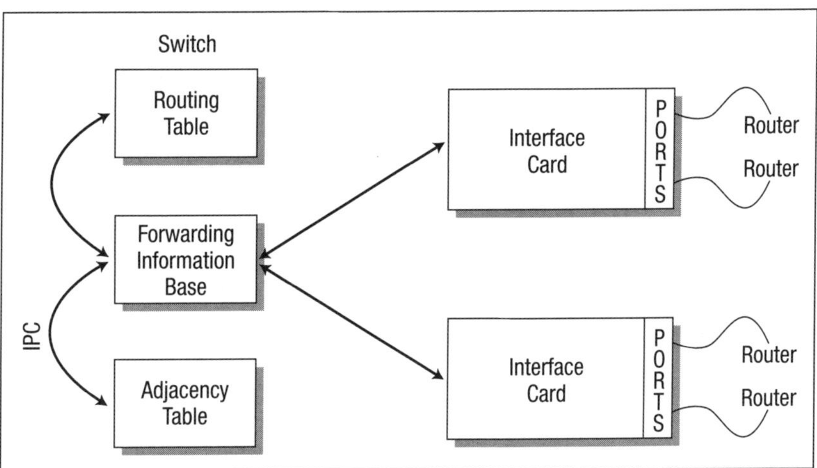

Figure 3.3 Cisco Express Forwarding ASIC components: The entry port and exit port in the interfaces use identical physical media types.

Distributed CEF

The Distributed Cisco Express Forwarding (dCEF) ASIC is a mode that can be enabled on line cards; this mode uses interprocess communication (IPC) to synchronize a copy of the FIB. This synchronization enables identical copies of the FIB and adjacency tables to be stored on one of the line cards contained on the switch backplane. The line cards can then express forward between port adapters. This process relieves the Route/Switch Processor (RSP) of its involvement. The Cisco 12000 GSRs have dCEF enabled by default. This is valuable knowledge when troubleshooting the 12000 GSR because it does not list that dCEF is enabled when viewing the configuration. See Figure 3.4.

Configuring Cisco Express Forwarding

Even if you have already taken the CLSC course or have configured Cisco switches, commands are probably new to you. To enable or disable the Cisco Express Forwarding ASIC, you must be in Global Configuration Mode.

To enable standard CEF, use this command:

```
ip cef
```

To disable standard CEF, use this command:

```
no ip cef
```

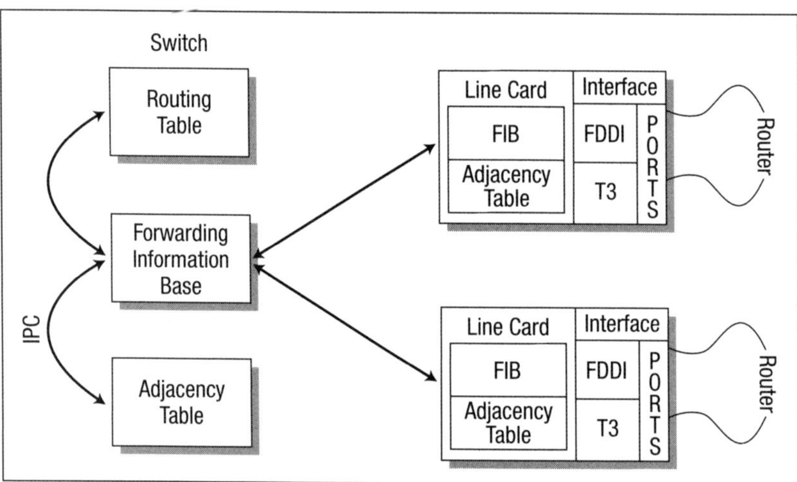

Figure 3.4 Distributed Cisco Express Forwarding ASIC components. Notice that the main difference between CEF and dCEF is that the interface cards for dCEF support the use of different physical media types.

To enable dCEF operation, use this command:

```
ip cef distributed
```

To disable dCEF operation, use this command:

```
no ip cef distributed
```

By enabling or disabling CEF or dCEF in Global Configuration Mode, all supported interfaces that support CEF or dCEF are affected. Some features on interfaces do not support CEF, such as policy routing. In that case, you will need to disable CEF on that interface. To disable CEF on an interface, use this command:

```
no ip route-cache cef
```

Warning: Never disable dCEF on a Cisco 12000 GSR Series because an active ASIC needs to remain active on the switch, and CEF is not a valid configuration option.

CEF allows you to optimize the resources on your switch by using multiple paths to load-balance traffic. You can configure per-destination or per-packet load balancing on the outbound interface of the switch. Per-destination load balancing is enabled by default when you enable CEF. It allows multiple paths to be used for load sharing. Packets destined for a given destination or source host are guaranteed to take the same path, although multiple paths are available.

If you want to use per-packet load balancing, you need to disable per-destination load balancing. To do so, use this command:

```
no ip load-sharing per-destination
```

Per-packet load balancing uses a round-robin approach to determine what path individual packets will take over the network. Per-packet load balancing is a way to ensure balancing when multiple paths are available to a given destination. This method allows packets for a given destination to take different paths. However, per-packet load balancing does not work well with data such as voice over IP and video. These types of data packets need a guarantee that they will arrive at the destination in the same sequence in which they were sent.

To enable per-packet load balancing, use this command:

```
ip load-sharing per-packet.
```

To disable per-packet sharing, use this command:

```
no ip load-sharing per-packet
```

Network Accounting for CEF ASIC

CEF has an accounting feature that allows you to collect forwarding statistics to analyze the traffic patterns of your network. *Network Accounting for CEF* allows you to collect information such as the number of packets and bytes switched to or through certain destinations.

To configure Network Accounting for CEF to collect the numbers of packets and bytes forwarded to a destination, use this command:

```
ip cef accounting per-prefix
```

To set Network Accounting for CEF to collect the numbers of packets express-forwarded through a destination, use this command:

```
ip cef accounting non-recursive
```

The information collected by Network Accounting for CEF is collected at the route processor. Distributed CEF information is collected by the line cards, not the route processor.

To view the information collected, use this command:

```
show ip cef
```

To view the number of packets dropped from each line card, use this command:

```
show cef drop
```

To view what packets went to a path other than CEF, use this command:

```
show cef not-cef-switched
```

The Bus and Component Operations

When a port accesses the bus, it involves two phases. First, all ports on the local line module send their bus access requests to the slave SAMBA ASIC. It is the slave ASIC that is responsible for setting port priorities and allocating separate queues for each priority level on the local line module. The slave SAMBA ASIC then forwards requests at the appropriate priority level to the Supervisor Engine's master SAMBA ASIC.

Hierarchical, Two-Tier Design

After the slave ASICs in the chassis forward requests to the master ASIC, the master ASIC uses a round-robin scheme within each priority level to grant access to the data-switching bus. Higher priority queues are always processed first by the master services in hierarchical fashion: critical priority first, high priority second, and normal priority last. The master ASIC typically processes the high priority queue for five frames and the normal priority queue for only one frame.

It is every line module's responsibility to police its local priority tables. It then becomes the Supervisor Engine's responsibility to enforce equal access to the bus for each individual line module. An understanding of the switching architecture will help you in understanding the different bus and queuing components.

Switching Architecture

Since Kalpana introduced the switch that became Cisco's 3000 Series switch, switches have evolved from simple bridges to complex feature-laden devices with an incredible number of ports. However, the principles and architecture have not changed too dramatically.

Bus Architecture

A data bus is required in every switch in order for the switch to forward data arriving from one port to another port. The bus performs the main function of the switch: forwarding frames across the switch's backplane. Because more than one port is always connected to the bus, there must be some type of control that allows only one port to access the bus at a time. Shared Ethernet provides a good analogy: If two Ethernet cards try to use the same wire simultaneously, a collision occurs. To solve this problem, an arbiter is used to guarantee that the bus receives only one frame at a time.

When there is only a single data bus, arbitration is fairly simple. Single-bus architecture has a drawback, though: Its very limited bandwidth can cause blocking. *Blocking* occurs when the throughput of the ports exceeds the capacity of the bus. This means that more information needs to be moved across the bus than the bus can process. To resolve blocking, you can use buffering and create a storage area for data that is waiting to be processed.

Crossbar Matrix

A crossbar matrix has a multiple-bus architecture. It can be used to control blocking problems and increase throughput. The increased bus capacity allows for less buffering and latency to be placed on the switch. This architecture uses multiple buses for data switching to ensure that every port is connected to every other port. The crossbar matrix also allows for multiple packets on the backplane, allowing for more congestion control.

Frame Flow through the Switch

Because the Cisco Catalyst 5000 Series switch is used as a distribution and core layer switch in different switched environments, it is a good device to aid in providing you with a basic understanding of how data frames interact with the switch hardware components.

Suppose that data has just arrived at a port on our switch. Here is where the process begins. Immediately after the data arrives, the port's ASIC checks the frame's Cyclical Redundancy Check (CRC). If the frame's CRC does not match, the ASIC determines that the frame is bad and discards the frame.

If the CRC matches, it then encapsulates or tags the frame with a source-port identifier, VLAN identifier, unique identifier, or checksum. The ASIC then places the frame in the input buffer. Once the frame is in the buffer, the ASIC posts a bus access request to the slave SAMBA ASIC.

The slave SAMBA ASIC places priorities on the request and forwards it to the index/control bus on the Supervisor Engine's master SAMBA. The master SAMBA reprioritizes the request according to other requests it has received from the other line modules. The master SAMBA relays access to the slave SAMBA when it becomes the requested port's turn. At this point, the slave SAMBA forwards the reply to the port's ASIC. The frame is then forwarded to the exit port.

Prior to the frame flowing out the desired port on the switch, the tagging information is removed. When the frame flows from switch to router and back to be routed to a different VLAN, the switch retags the frame with new identifiers.

By using multilayer switching or net flow switching hardware, you can use different network interfaces for different VLANs to communicate after viewing only the route processor and port configuration. This allows communication from port to port on a switch, eliminating the need for frames to travel from the switch to router and back to the switch again for inter-VLAN routing. You will learn more about this subject in Chapters 8 and 10.

Buffering Architecture

Every switch employs a queuing mechanism to solve problems associated with blocking. If a frame from an Ethernet segment arrives on a port when the port does not have access to the bus, the port must have some type of buffering space to store the data until it can be processed. Otherwise, the data will have to be discarded, resulting in data loss. The port stores the frame in the buffer while the port waits its turn to forward the frame across the bus.

Input Queuing

Input queuing buffers a frame as it arrives at the switch. It is a simple and inexpensive solution for resolving blocking problems from the port to the bus.

As with other resolutions, input queuing also has a drawback: You run the possibility of head-of-line blocking. Frames that are placed in the buffer are eventually placed on the bus. The bus assumes that the exit port can handle the frame when it is forwarded from the bus. However, if the outbound port is busy it creates head-of-line blocking. This blocking can dramatically limit the throughput of the switch.

Output Queuing

To resolve the problem of head-of-line blocking, output queuing is used with input queuing. Each port on the switch is armed with an output queue as well as an input queue. The disadvantage of this approach is that it makes for some very expensive switches—and head-of-line blocking will still occasionally occur during large frame bursts. It seems to occur more frequently if the port is connected to a shared Ethernet segment on which many collisions occur. Even with the increase in cost, most current switches employ an architecture using a combination of input and output queuing to resolve blocking problems.

Shared Buffering

Shared buffering is an alternative to output queuing. Shared buffering allows ports to use a larger, shared output buffer instead of individual smaller buffering spaces. This approach eliminates head-of-line blocking and increases throughput. With shared buffering, each port has access to one large shared memory space. As frames arrive at the switch, the frame is placed in the buffering area. There the frame is tagged for an outgoing port or ports. When the outbound ports become available, the tag is removed and the frame is forwarded out the exit port.

Second Generation Features

The second generation of switches is much faster and more affordable than earlier switches. The new generation switches include many new features:

- Dedicated Token Ring (DTR) on all ports
- High-speed links
- Remote Network Monitoring (RMON)
- Broadcast control
- Filtering

Dedicated Token Ring

Dedicated Token Ring (DTR) is similar to full-duplexing with two-way communication. DTR enables an end station to send and receive at the same time. Although typical Token Ring networks use a token in a half-duplex or one-way, single-wire virtual circle, this type of switching uses two individually crossed wires. One is used for sending and one is used for receiving. This approach doubles the bandwidth, because information can be sent and received at the same time; it also eliminates the need to get a token to send the information in a one-way fashion through the network. Because DTR is so fast, it is the ideal way to send information from switch to switch, router to switch, or file server to switch.

High-Speed Links

Second generation switches now include switches that support links of 100Mbps to OC-3c (155.52Mbps). Switches now support ATM line speeds of up to OC-12c (622.08Mbps).

Remote Network Monitoring

Remote Network Monitoring (RMON) is an industry-standard method used to provide monitor statistics on a network. With Cisco switches, it reports usage to a management station running Simple Network Management Protocol (SNMP). RMON allows a network administrator to obtain information about a switch from Layer 1 and Layer 2 environments, which can't be obtained by using the console port of the switch.

RMON also collects information about connection problems, performance, and configuration statistics. RMON can monitor continuously, even when communication with the management station is not possible. It can also notify the management station when an error condition occurs.

With other types of SNMP monitoring, the management station running SNMP continuously polls the switch acting as the SNMP agent for connection information on performance and configuration of the switch. Because the client must constantly send network traffic to poll the client, it uses constant network bandwidth and causes increased traffic through the network.

With RMON, you can have the switch monitor a particular statistic internally. There is no contact with the SNMP management station unless the statistic reaches a predefined threshold. When the switch reaches the predetermined threshold, it will send a trap message to the management station. This monitoring method reduces traffic between the SNMP management station and the switch.

Nine groups can provide RMON information. In order to see all nine groups, you must use the Switched Port Analyzer (SPAN). Cisco Catalyst switches support RMON information from the following four groups:

- *Statistics Group*—Monitors such things as collisions, oversized packets, runt or undersized packets, network jabber, fragmented packets, multicast, and unicast bandwidth utilization. Its basic function is to maintain utilization and error statistics on the switch ports it monitors.

- *History Group*—Contains periodical statistical information such as bandwidth utilization, frame counts, and error counts and stores it for later use.
- *Alarm Group*—Allows you to set thresholds and intervals for alarms. You can set thresholds and intervals for such things as port utilization, frame counts, and errors. Any monitored event can be set to alarm the management station with a Trap message at any absolute or relative value or threshold.
- *Event Group*—Allows you to monitor logging events on the switches. It sends trap messages to the management station with the time and date of the logged event. This process allows the management station to create customized reports based on the Alarm Group's predetermined thresholds. Reports can be printed or logged for future use.

Token-Ring Extensions

RMON provides support for the following groups of the Token Ring extensions:

- *MAC-layer Statistics Group*—A collection of statistics from the MAC sublayer of the data link layer, kept for each Token Ring interface. This group collects information such as the total number of MAC layer packets received and the number of times the port entered a beaconing error state.
- *Promiscuous Statistics Group*—A collection of promiscuous statistics kept for non-MAC packets on each Token Ring interface. This group collects information such as the total number of good non-MAC frames received that were directed to a Logical Link Control (LLC) broadcast address.
- *Ring Station Group*—A collection of statistics and status information associated with each Token Ring station on the local ring. This group also provides status information for each ring being monitored.
- *Ring Station Order Group*—A listing order of stations on the monitored Token Ring network's rings.

RMON Commands

RMON works in conjunction with SNMP and requires a protocol analyzer or probe to use its full features. To use SNMP-based monitoring, you need to verify that SNMP is running on your IOS-based switch.

To verify that SNMP is running, use the following command in User or Exec Mode:

```
show snmp
```

To enable SNMP and allow read-only access to hosts using the public SNMP string, use this command in Configuration Mode:

```
snmp-server community public
```

After enabling SNMP, you need to define a host IP address to send SNMP trap messages. Here is an example:

```
snmp-server host 130.77.40.05 public
```

After identifying the SNMP community and the SNMP trap host address for messages, enable SNMP on the switch with the following command:

```
set snmp enable
```

To verify that RMON is running, use the following command in Exec Mode:

```
show rmon
```

To configure RMON on a Set/Clear command-based swiitch, use the following commands.

To enable SNMP and allow read-only access to hosts using the public SNMP string, use the following command in Configuration Mode:

```
set snmp read-only public
```

Note: *There are several other command options that can be used in lieu of read-only. Use the* ***set snmp ?*** *command to view these options.*

After enabling SNMP, you need to define a host IP address to send the SNMP trap messages:

```
set snmp trap 130.77.40.05 public
```

To verify that RMON is running, use the following command in Exec Mode:

```
show rmon
```

To show RMON statistics, use the following command. It shows statistics for the number of packets, octets, broadcast packets, and multicast packets received as well as errors detected and packet lengths received:

```
show rmon statistics
```

Broadcast Control

Parallel backbones are a way of designing source-routed networks. With source routing, traffic is typically distributed between two backbone physical connections. This distribution enables a backup and load distribution. Second generation Token Ring switches support reduction of explorer-type traffic. This is called

All Routes Explorer (ARE) reduction or broadcast control. ARE reduction verifies that the number of ARE exploring frames do not overwhelm the network bandwidth. The IEEE 802.1d standard specifies two ways of reducing ARE frames. Both of these involve the examination of the entire RIF to determine where the frame has been to verify that the frame has not encompassed the entire network more than once:

3

- *Method 1*—This method is based on whether the frame on any ring attached to the bridge prior to this examination. It examines the RIF and determines whether it had been on the ring by matching the LAN ID in the frame with any LAN IDs associated with rings attached to the bridge.
- *Method 2*—This method is less restrictive than the first. It checks to see whether the frame has been on the bridge before by examining the RIF of the received frame for a ring-bridge-ring combination. If the combination matches the bridge's number, this method discards the frame. Catalyst switches use this method, which is the simpler of the two.

Filtering

Many bridged networks today employ filtering to reduce broadcast traffic, block protocols, and provide simple security. Switches provide filtering capabilities for the same purpose. You can filter frames based on the following:

- *MAC address (source address, destination address)*—MAC address filters and broadcast filters can be applied only at input ports.
- *Destination Service Access Point (DSAP) and Source Service Access Point (SSAP)*—These can be applied to input ports and output ports for filtering. The DSAP indicates the destination field in a packet and the SSAP indicates the source field of a packet. A bit pattern 0xAA is used to indicate the presence of a Subnetwork Access Protocol (SNAP), which is used to transfer certain data for which there is no specific SAP value assigned within an 802.2 frame.
- *Subnetwork Access Protocol (SNAP)*—This protocol specifies a standard method of encapsulating IP datagrams and ARP messages. It operates between two network interfaces and performs three functions: data transfer, connection management, and QoS.

Bridging vs. Routing

In the 1980s, IBM developed a non-routable protocol called NetBIOS as part of its implementation strategy. NetBIOS joined a few other non-routable protocols in wide use, such as SNA and LAT. IBM also developed a physical network topology called Token Ring. With Token Ring came the first of two chief bridging technologies: Source Route Bridging (SRB).

The SRB algorithm for Token-Ring LAN bridging became the IEEE 802.5 Token Ring LAN specification. Token Ring has various combinations, which will be discussed in more detail in the next chapter. These include:

- Source Route Bridging (SRB)
- Source Route Transparent Bridging (SRT)
- Source Route Translational Bridging (SR/TRB)

The second chief bridging technology that was developed primarily for DEC is Transparent Bridging (TB). Although it was developed for DEC, it is the primary bridging algorithm used in today's switches and routers. It maintains a routing table, building tables composed of destination addresses. It has the ability to switch network packets based upon a match of the destination address, such as those used with IP, IPX, and AppleTalk.

Transparent Bridging tables are built differently than routing tables. Whereas routing tables rely heavily on routing protocols to learn about foreign networks, Transparent Bridging tables learn the location of each MAC address by logging the port that the frame arrived from. Thus, assuming that the network the frame arrived from is attached to the port of entry, TB then logs the information along with a maximum age or time to live (TTL). When this maximum is reached, TB removes the entry from the table.

Transparent Bridging is so named because the interfaces or domains connected to each port are unaware of the existence of the bridge. No additional software or protocols are required for the end interfaces to function; nor are special packets such as Explorer Frames used. Source Route Bridging uses Explorer Frames, which will be explained in the next section.

Cisco has some specific routing and bridging solutions such as Remote Source Route Bridging (RSRB). RSRB takes the idea of virtual rings to a new level. It forwards Token Ring frames through the interface out to an IP cloud, providing an additional Source Route Bridging WAN solution. RSRB essentially creates encapsulated bridging from Token Ring over an IP backbone. SRB frames are sent over the RSRB tunnel without modifying the RIF. (For a little history, IBM had nothing comparable when Cisco announced RSRB. IBM's solution was a data link layer device known as a half-bridge.)

Another Cisco-specific routing and bridging solution is Concurrent Routing and Bridging (CRB). CRB allows for certain specific protocols to be routed out specific interfaces and then bridged out other interfaces. Integrated Routing and Bridging (IRB) takes CRB one step further, allowing the same network layer protocols to exist together on the same interface. IRB creates a Bridged Virtual Interface (BVI), allowing the merger of bridged and routed domains so that data can flow between the two domains.

Data Link Switch Plus (DLSw; RFC-1795) was created by IBM in response to Cisco's RSRB. Cisco then created Data Link Switching Plus (DLSW+), primarily to provide support for SNA over an IP backbone. DLSW+ is compatible with RSRB but has improvements in functionality. It performs the functions of RSRB but adds support for interconnection of TB, SRT, SR/TLB, and SDLLCover on an IP backbone. Using Switch to Switch Protocol (SSP) messages to set up a circuit over a WAN to two remote segments, DLSW+ can connect the following types of segments:

- Ethernet to Ethernet
- Token Ring to Token Ring
- Token Ring to Ethernet
- QLLC to Token Ring
- QLLC to Ethernet
- SDLC to Token Ring

DLSW+ conforms to all of the elements of DLSW as well as adding support for multiple encapsulation types. Where DLSW offers only TCP/IP, DLSW+ adds FST/IP; non-TCP/IP encapsulation types; DLSW+ Lite, which is direct encapsulation for point-to-point connections; as well as LLC2 encapsulation for Frame Relay.

Source Route Bridging

Source Route Bridging (SRB) is a method of bridging used to connect Token Ring segments. The SRB makes all forwarding decisions based upon data in the Routing Information Field (RIF). It cannot acquire or look up MAC addresses. Therefore, SRB frames without a corresponding RIF are not forwarded.

With SRB, every port on the switch is assigned a ring number. The switch itself is assigned one or more bridge numbers. SRB then uses this information to build the RIF. It then searches the RIF to determine where to forward incoming frames.

SRB modifies frames when they arrive using Explorer Frames. Explorer Frames are typically one of two types: All Routes Explorer (ARE) or Spanning-Tree Explorer (STE). SRB bridges copy ARE and STE frames and modify the RIF with their own routing information.

Transparent Bridging

Transparent bridges are so named because they are invisible to all the networks they provide services for. Transparent bridges acquire knowledge of the network by looking at the source address of all incoming frames from all the attached interfaces or nodes. The bridge then creates an internal table based on the information from the frames it receives. For example, if host A sends a frame and it arrives from port 3 on the switch, the bridge assumes that host A is attached to port 3.

At the same time, if host B sends a frame and it arrives on port 1, the bridge would assume that host B is connected to port 1. If host A again tries to send a frame to host address B, the bridge would immediately forward that frame to port 1, because the switch now assumes that line 1 has host B attached to it.

Now, what would happen if a frame is received for host C and no host C frames have been received? In this situation, the bridge would flood the frame received out all the line ports except the port it was received on. Broadcasts and multicasts are also flooded in the same fashion.

Transparent bridges do a good job of isolating traffic from segment to segment. This isolation reduces traffic on each individual segment, freeing bandwidth for intrasegment functions. The traffic reduced depends on the amount or volume of traffic being sent between individual segments.

Source Route Translational Bridging

Source Route Translational Bridging (SR/TLB) has a Token Ring attached to one port of the bridge and another media-type topology (such as FDDI or Ethernet) attached to another port. SR/TLB's main function is to make the two media types transparent to one another. The bridge receives the token, converts the data to a readable format for the Ethernet segment, and then forwards the data out the Ethernet to the receiving host address. All this takes place transparently to both hosts on the network—the Ethernet host believes that the Token Ring host is on Ethernet, and vice versa.

Source Route Transparent Bridging

Source Route Transparent Bridging (SRT) is a combination of Source Route Bridging and Transparent Bridging. SRT bridges make forwarding decisions based on either the RIF for the destination or the MAC address in the frames.

Some protocols attempt to establish a connection using a frame without using a RIF. Some applications send a test frame to see if the destination is on the same ring as the source. If no response is received from this test frame, then an All Routes Explorer (ARE) test frame with a RIF is sent. If the destination receives the ARE, it responds, and the spanning-tree path through the bridge is used.

If the network is configured with parallel full-duplex backbones, this detected path may be very undesirable. If the spanning-tree path is used, then only one of the backbones will carry the traffic.

Source Route Switching

Source Route Switching (SRS) was created to overcome the disadvantages of standard Transparent Bridging. Transparent Bridging does not support source-routing information. SRS forwards frames that do not contain routing information based on the MAC address the same way that Transparent Bridging does. All the rings that are source-route switched have the same ring number, and the switch learns the MAC addresses of adapters on these rings.

SRS also learns the route descriptors. A *route descriptor* is a portion of a RIF that indicates a single hop. It defines a ring number, a bridge number, and the hop closest to the switch. Future frames received from other ports with the same next-hop route descriptor are forwarded to that port.

If you have a Token Ring switch that has reached the limitation of ring stations on the current ring, SRS is your best choice for bridging. Unlike SRB, SRS looks at the RIF; it never makes the changes to the RIF. Using Source Route Switching, the switch does not need to obtain the MAC addresses of the devices. This method reduces the number of MAC addresses that the switch must learn and maintain.

Catalyst Processors

We have discussed the ASICs and their association with the on-board processors. Together, ASICs and processors provide the work and intelligence behind the frame-switching process. Now let's take a look at the different processors you will find in Catalyst switches:

- Line Module Communication Processor (LCP)
- Network Management Processor (NMP)
- Master Communication Processor (MCP)

Line Module Communication Processor

The Line Module Communication Processor (LCP) is located on each line module. It is the responsibility of the LCP to provide communications for the Master Communication Processor (MCP) located on the Supervisor Engine.

The LCP boots from ROM using an 8051 processor. It then forwards an information package called Resetack to the Master Communication Processor. Resetack includes information regarding boot diagnostics and module information. This information is then forwarded from the MCP to the NMP.

Master Communication Processor

The Master Communication Processor (MCP), also known as the Management Control Processor, uses the serial management bus to communicate between the NMP on the Supervisor module and the LCP on the individual line cards located in the chassis.

The MCP also handles the testing and configuration of local ports, control of local ports, downloading of runtime code, and the diagnostics. Diagnostics cover the usage of onboard chips including memory, ASICs, Local Target Logic (LTL), and Color Blocking Logic (CBL).

Network Management Processor

The Network Management Processor (NMP) controls the system hardware, configuration, network management, Spanning Tree Protocol, and diagnostic functions.

Units of Logic

Units of logic or *logic units* are used in switching and provide forwarding logic based on VLAN, MAC address, or port assignment. The devices discussed in this section are the Arbiter, Local Target Logic, Color Blocking Logic, and the ROM monitor.

Arbiter

The Arbiter (ARB) in the Catalyst System uses a two-tier method of arbitration in the switching process. The Local Bus Arbiter is located on each module and assigns priorities for queuing. It also controls all traffic on all ports of the module. This process then uses the Central Bus Arbiter, which is located on the Supervisor module, to obtain permission to transmit frames to the switching engine.

The Central Bus Arbiter uses a round-robin process, with special handling for high-priority frames. This process allows priority levels to be set by the administrator for time-sensitive traffic, such as voice and video.

Local Target Logic

Local Target Logic (LTL) works in association with the EARL ASIC to determine whether a frame is switched to a single port or multiple ports. It also helps to identify the port or ports on the switch to which the frame needs to be forwarded. LTL differentiates between unicast, multicast, and broadcast forwarding. LTL uses index values provided by the EARL ASIC to select the port or ports to forward the frame on the line module.

Color Blocking Logic

Color Blocking Logic (CBL) works by blocking traffic from entering or leaving a port that is not part of the VLAN. CBL also takes part in the spanning-tree process to block ports, preventing bridging loops. Each port is associated with a single VLAN, assuming it is not a trunk port. As frames flow through the switch, each incoming frame is tagged with an identifier for the VLAN noting its color within the switch. For example, a frame coming from a blue VLAN port would be blocked from exiting a red VLAN port.

ROM Monitor

The ROM monitor is a ROM-based program that executes upon boot up, upon reset, upon a fatal exception error, if the switch fails to find a valid system image, if the nonvolatile RAM (NVRAM) configuration is corrupt, or if the configuration register is manually set to enter ROM monitor mode.

The ROM monitor command-line interface (CLI) is present only on the Supervisor Engine III and the Catalyst 4000 and 2948G Series switch Supervisor Engine modules. The Supervisor Engine and Supervisor Engine II modules do not have a ROM monitor interface. The ROM monitor mode allows you to load a system image manually from flash memory, network server file, or the bootflash.

To enter ROM monitor mode, restart the switch and press the Break key during the first 60 seconds of startup. (The Break key is only enabled for the first 60 seconds after rebooting the system; it cannot be disabled in the configuration register settings.) You can also access the ROM monitor through a terminal server. To do this, escape to the Telnet prompt and enter the break command for the terminal emulation program you are using.

You will know you have entered ROM monitor mode when you see the prompt **rommon#>**. To see the available commands, use the **?** command. Table 3.1 lists the ROM command-line interface commands and a brief description of each.

Trivial File Transfer Protocol (TFTP) boot is not supported on the Supervisor Engine III or on the Catalyst 4000 Series and the 2948G switch Supervisor Engine modules.

To load an image from the network, use one of the following three commands:

```
copy file-ld tftp
copy file-ld flash
copy file-ld
```

Table 3.1 ROM monitor command-line interface commands.

Command	Description
alias	Configures and displays aliases
boot	Boots up an external process
confreg	Configures the configuration register utility
dev	Shows device IDs available on a platform
dir	Shows files of the named device
history	Shows the last 16 commands
meminfo	Shows switch memory information
repeat	Repeats a specified command
reset	Performs a switch reboot/reset
set	Shows monitor variable names with their values
sync	Saves the ROM monitor configuration
unalias	Deletes the alias name and associated value from the alias list
unset=varname	Deletes a variable name from the variable list
varname=value	Assigns a value to a variable

To boot from a flash device, use the following command:

```
boot [-xv] [device][imagename]
```

If you do not specify a file name, the system defaults to the first valid file in the device. Remember that file names are case sensitive.

Chapter Summary

In this chapter, we covered early network architectures, where the need for switching originated; the different ASICs, CPUs, and architectures; and, most important, the methods used in switching. We also described the way to connect to a switch and enter commands using the command-line interface. This chapter contains many important terms that you need to remember. Here is a short overview and quick definition of each. Make sure you go over these, because you may see them one day on a test:

- *Adjacency Table*—Works with FIB and the CEF ASIC to keep a table of nodes that are adjacent or within a single hop from the switch. CEF uses the adjacency table to prepend Layer 2 addressing table information.
- *Application-Specific Integrated Circuit (ASIC)*—A feature of many LAN controllers. ASICs are internal to the switch. They work in conjunction with the internal processor to make Layer 2 forwarding decisions. However, they lack the ability to make flexible software-implemented forwarding decisions. Their ability to perform small tasks quickly and inexpensively makes them a key in the switching process.

- *Color Blocking Logic (CBL)*—A feature of the SAMBA ASIC, used to help the EARL make forwarding decisions. It also makes sure that a tagged frame that comes from a particular VLAN does not exit through a port belonging to another VLAN. CBL also assists in placing ports in one of four different modes for Spanning Tree Protocol: blocking, learning, listening, and forwarding.
- *Content Addressable Memory (CAM)*—A table used by a bridge to make forwarding and filtering decisions. The CAM table contains MAC addresses with port addresses leading to the physical interfaces. The CAM table uses a specialized interface that is faster than RAM to make forwarding and filtering decisions. The CAM table updates information by examining frames it receives from a segment and then updating the table with the source MAC address from the frame.
- *Forwarding Information Base (FIB) Switching*—A mirror image of the routing information of the IP routing table, similar to a routing table or information base. It updates routing information when routing or topology changes occur in the network and recalculates the next-hop information. FIB maintains a list of all known routes and eliminates the need for route cache maintenance associated with fast switching or optimum switching. FIB is used with the CEF ASIC.
- *Line Module Communication Processor (LCP)*—Located on each line module. It is the responsibility of the LCP to provide communications for the MCP located on the Supervisor Engine.
- *Local Target Logic (LTL)*—A feature of some line modules that assist the EARL in making forwarding decisions.
- *Master Communication Processor (MCP)*—A feature of the Supervisor Engine that takes commands from the Network Management Processor (NMP) and forwards them to the correct Line Module Communication Processor (LCP). MCP is also responsible for testing the local ports, configuring the local ports, and controlling the ports using LTL and CBL. It also performs diagnostics on the memory, SAINT ASICs, LTL, and CBL. MCP also is responsible for downloading software to the line modules.
- *Network Management Processor (NMP)*—A feature of the Supervisor Engine that is responsible for general control of the switch. The major responsibilities of NMP are to execute system configuration changes from the command-line interface (CLI), run boot diagnostics at boot or when a new module is added, as well as the handling of STP for each VLAN.
- *Remote Network Monitoring (RMON)*—An Internet Engineering Task Force Standard (IETF) that defines how devices gather and share their network monitoring information. RMON is used to send gathered information to

an SNMP Management Station. RMON gathers Layer 2 information concerning bandwidth use, collisions, and errors. Catalyst switches can gather four of the nine different information types: the Statistics, History, Alarms, and Event types. The other five groups can be monitored using a SPAN port and attached protocol analyzer or probe.

Later in this book, you will learn how to configure and troubleshoot each type of switch and each switching method. You will also learn what each Cisco switch chassis supports for switching methods.

REVIEW QUESTIONS

1. What ASIC uses FIB and the adjacency table to make forwarding decisions?
    a. Phoenix ASIC
    b. SAMBA
    c. SAINT
    d. CEFA
    e. SAGE
2. Why would you use Source Route Translational Bridging (SR/TLB)?
    a. You have a 2900 Series switch supporting only Ethernet connections.
    b. You have a Token Ring and need to convert to another media type.
    c. You need to allow 53-byte ATM compatibility.
    d. You need FDDI-to-Ethernet conversion.
3. Source Route Switching (SRS) combines which two types of bridging modes?
    a. SRT and SRB
    b. SRS and SR/TLB
    c. FIB and ARE
    d. SRT and SRS
4. What type of bridging should you use if you need to add more ring stations because you have reached your ring limitations?
    a. SRT
    b. SR/TLB
    c. SRB
    d. SRS
    e. TB

5. Which of the following bridging types will you find in both Ethernet and Token Ring? [Choose the two best answers]
   a. SRT
   b. SR/TLB
   c. SRB
   d. SRS
   e. TB

6. Which field is marked in an All Routes Explorer (ARE) packet?
   a. Port
   b. Distance
   c. Hop Count
   d. RIF

7. Which bridging mode combines SRB and TB for different methods of Token Ring addressing?
   a. SRT
   b. SR/TLB
   c. SRB
   d. SRS
   e. TB

8. Which cable should you plug into the Ethernet console port of the switch when connecting to a serial port on your PC?
   a. A live ISDN line
   b. A live PSTN Line
   c. An RJ-45 to RJ-45 straight-through cable that came with the switch
   d. A 120V plug that came with the switch

9. Which ASIC is a special component of the Supervisor III Engine that provides gigabit bridging between buses?
   a. Phoenix ASIC
   b. SAMBA
   c. SAINT
   d. CEFA
   e. SAGE

10. What does the adjacency table maintain one-to-one correspondence with?
    a. CEFA
    b. RIF
    c. FIB
    d. ARE
11. How many entries can the Content Addressable Memory (CAM) table hold, depending on the configuration? [Choose the two best answers]
    a. 45,000
    b. 16,000
    c. 64,000
    d. 128,000
12. If you want to collect forwarding statistics in Cisco Express Forwarding ASIC, what feature of CEF will you use?
    a. Remote Network Monitor (RMON)
    b. Network Accounting for CEF
    c. Simple Network Management Protocol (SNMP)
    d. Forwarding Information Base (FIB)
13. RMON is a standard created by which standards organization?
    a. ANSI
    b. The ATM Forum
    c. IETF
    d. IEEE
14. Which group is not a Token Ring extension supported by RMON.
    a. MAC-layer Statistics Group
    b. Promiscuous Statistics Group
    c. Ring Station Group
    d. Data Link Layer Group
15. Which unit of logic included in the SAMBA ASIC aids the EARL ASIC in making forwarding decisions?
    a. Color Blocking Logic (CBL)
    b. Line module
    c. Backplane
    d. RMON

CHAPTER FOUR

4

CHOOSING A CISCO SWITCH

After completing this chapter, you will be able to:

- ✓ Identify switches found at each campus layer
- ✓ Describe the key features that are available on Cisco switches
- ✓ Describe the products that make up the Catalyst switch line
- ✓ Understand the types of add-ons and modules available for each switch

Cisco's product line includes a wide variety of switches, from the simple, entry-level workgroup switches to robust, enterprise-level backbone switches. The ability of Cisco's line of switches to meet the demands of the customer while providing high performance and manageability is a strong selling point of this product line.

These features and others will be covered in depth in this chapter. We will describe each of the Cisco products that make up the current line of switches. Finally, we will detail the features of these switches and describe key components, add-ons, and modules.

Chapter Terms

Throughout this chapter, we will refer to several switch features. The specifications for these features will be presented in a tabular form. To help you understand the features and the performance of each switch, you should be familiar with the following terms:

- *Backplane*—A series of electric traces located on the back of the chassis on which data is run. The traces are the electrical connection between the processor, data bus, and power supply.
- *Switching fabric*—The "highway" the data takes to get from the port of entry to the exit port.
- *Over-subscription*—Occurs when the total bandwidth of the ports is greater than the capacity of the switching fabric. For example, a switch may be able to handle 100Mbps of traffic, but contain 18 10Mbps ports. The total data coming in could total up to 360Mbps, if the ports are using full-duplex.
- *Non-blocking*—The ideal solution. It is the opposite of over-subscription. The switching fabric contains more bandwidth than the sum total of all the ports combined. For example, a switch may have eight 100Mbps ports but be able to handle 1Gbps (1000Mbps).
- *Forwarding rate*—The rate at which packets are moved per second from the entry point to the exit point.
- *pps*—Packets per second.

Switch Features

Cisco's Internetwork Operating System (IOS) software has been written to work on all Cisco switches. It provides features that enhance the switching environment. Some of these enhancements include:

- Increased reliability and fault tolerance with Fast EtherChannel technology. Using the Port Aggregation Protocol (PAgP) allows Fast EtherChannel groups to be created automatically. This automation provides the mechanism for aggregating traffic and allows links of up to 400Mbps between switches, routers, and servers.
- Improved security via the Terminal Area Security Access Control (TACACS) protocol. This protocol provides a method to use usernames and passwords to authenticate and authorize access to the switch.
- Enhanced support for controlling multicast traffic through the use of the Cisco Group Management Protocol (CGMP). CGMP allows a switch to filter IP multicasts and forward them to targeted multimedia end stations.
- Improved manageability via GUI-based, command-line interface (CLI)-based, and Web-based management.
- Embedded Remote Network Monitoring (RMON) capability of the History, Statistics, Alarms, and Events groups. Using a Switched Port Analyzer (SPAN) port and an external RMON probe can provide full RMON support.
- Support for Cisco Discovery Protocol (CDP). CDP is a media- and protocol-independent advertisement protocol developed by Cisco; it runs on all Cisco devices. CDP allows the switch to be managed via CiscoWorks software.
- In-depth support for Simple Network Management Protocol (SNMP) and remote management capabilities.
- Increased availability due to enhanced Spanning Tree Protocol (STP) features.

Core Layer Catalyst Switches

The core layer is designed to switch packets at the fastest possible speed. It is the final aggregation point for the entire network, so devices at this level must be fast and reliable. They should be configured with the fastest processors possible and a sizeable amount of memory. No policy decisions are made at this level, and connections at this level must be of the highest possible bandwidth. Switch devices that are commonly found at this level are:

- Cisco Catalyst 5500 Series
- Cisco Catalyst 6500 Series
- Cisco Catalyst 8500 Series

Distribution Layer Catalyst Switches

The distribution layer is the demarcation point between the access and core layers. This level terminates the traffic that originates in the access layer connections and summarizes the traffic before passing it along to the core layer. It can best be described as the layer that provides policy-based connectivity. The switches found at this layer are:

- Cisco Catalyst 4000 Series
- Cisco Catalyst 5500 Series
- Cisco Catalyst 6000 Series

Note: *The Cisco Catalyst 4000 Series can be configured to perform functions for the access and distribution layers.*

Access Layer Catalyst Switches

The access layer is the access point for the end-user interfaces into the network. The access (or workgroup) layer connects users. Some important functions of this layer are shared bandwidth, switched bandwidth, Media Access Control (MAC) layer filtering, and micro-segmentation. Switches found at this layer are:

- Cisco Catalyst 1900 Series
- Cisco Catalyst 2820 Series
- Cisco Catalyst 2900G Series including the new 2980G Series
- Cisco Catalyst 2900 Series XL
- Cisco Catalyst 3000 Series
- Cisco Catalyst 3500 Series XL
- Cisco Catalyst 4000 Series
- Cisco Catalyst 5000 Series

Switch Descriptions and Features

If every switch suited every function in the network, there would only be a need for one model. Each Cisco Catalyst series and individual switch model has its own functions, abilities, compatibilities, and add-on modules, and is designed to be implemented in a certain layer of the network. In the following sections we will take a look at those features, beginning with the most powerful core layer switches. Throughout the rest of this book you will learn how to configure these switches and their many additional interfaces and modules.

Cisco Catalyst 8500 Series

The Cisco Catalyst 8500 is a core layer switch that meets the core layer definition by providing high-performance switching. The Catalyst 8500 is built from the ground up to utilize the full features of the Cisco IOS. The switch enables the Cisco IOS to use multiple layers of protocols including Internet Protocol (IP), Internetwork Packet Exchange (IPX), IP multicast, bridging, Asynchronous Transfer Mode (ATM) switching, and CiscoAssure policy-enabled Quality of Service (QoS) implemented in the Application-Specific Integrated Circuits (ASICs).

The 8500 Series switch/routers come in two versions, which are changeable based on the switch and route processors installed:

- *Campus Switch Router (CSR) version*—Provides complete Layer 3 routing capabilities over Fast and Gigabit Ethernet, OC-3, OC-12, ATM, and Packet over SONET (PoS) uplinks.
- *Multiservice ATM Switch Router (MSR) version*—Provides ATM switching capabilities with link speeds from T1 up to OC-48. The MSR edition also provides the same functionality as the CSR edition. The integrated ATM switching capabilities of the Catalyst 8500 make it one of the industry's best campus backbone platforms. It's capable of data, voice, and video traffic in ATM LAN emulation (LANE), Multiprotocol Over ATM (MPOA), and Multiprotocol Label Switching (MPLS) networks.

Architecture Features

The Cisco Catalyst 8500 switch/router architecture features are based on some of these key elements:

- Flexible wire-speed ASICs on the line cards that make the packet forwarding and policy-based decisions.
- A non-blocking switching fabric with one of the lowest latencies of any networking device.
- A powerful MultiChannel Interface Processor (MIP) architecture-based CPU running the Cisco IOS software.
- Interface modules that provide access to many types of media such as Ethernet, Fast Ethernet, Gigabit Ethernet, ATM, and PoS.
- Powerful ASICs, allowing scalable control and forwarding.
- Routing protocol support for Enhanced Interior Gateway Routing Protocol (EIGRP), Interior Gateway Routing Protocol (IGRP), Open Shortest Path First (OSPF), Border Gateway Protocol version 4 (BGPv4), Private Network-to-Network Interface (PNNI), and the Cisco Express Forwarding (CEF) ASIC Forwarding Information Base (FIB).

- Redundancy and failover support for protocols such as Hot Standby Routing Protocol (HSRP) and Simple Server Redundancy Protocol (SSRP).
- Redundant power supply modules (offered in both the 8510 and 8540 switches). The Catalyst 8510 utilizes the same power supplies used on the Catalyst 5000 and the LightStream 1010 switches. The Catalyst 8540 uses the same power supplies found on the Catalyst 5500 Series switches.
- Low latency times, from 18 to 25 microseconds.

Let's take a look at both the Cisco Catalyst 8510 and the Cisco Catalyst 8540 in Figure 4.1. The key features for both of these switches are shown in Table 4.1.

The modular slots for the Cisco Catalyst 8510 and the Catalyst 8540 are shown in Figures 4.2 and 4.3, respectively.

Supported Multiservice and Layer 3 Line Cards

The line card types supported on the Catalyst 8510 are listed in Table 4.2.

Table 4.1 The key features of the Cisco Catalyst 8510 and 8540.

Feature	8510	8540
Modular slots	5	13
Forwarding rate	6,000,000pps	24,000,000pps
Backplane	10Gbps	40Gbps

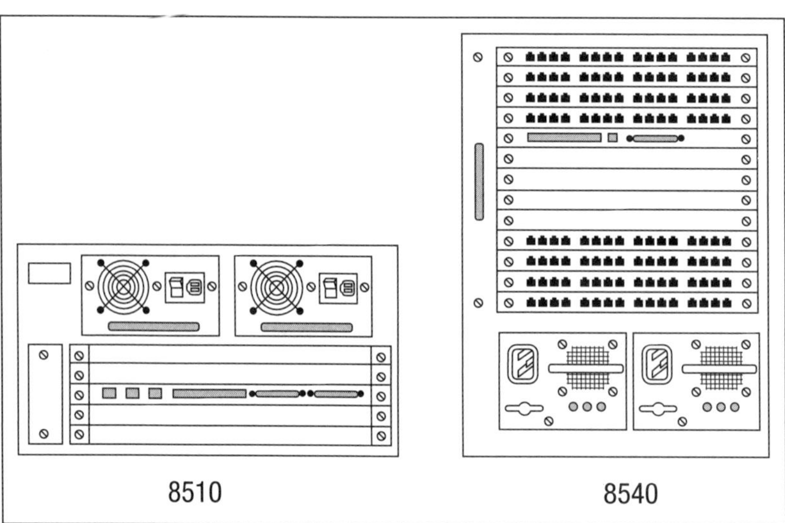

Figure 4.1 The Cisco Catalyst 8510 on the left, and the Cisco 8540 on the right.

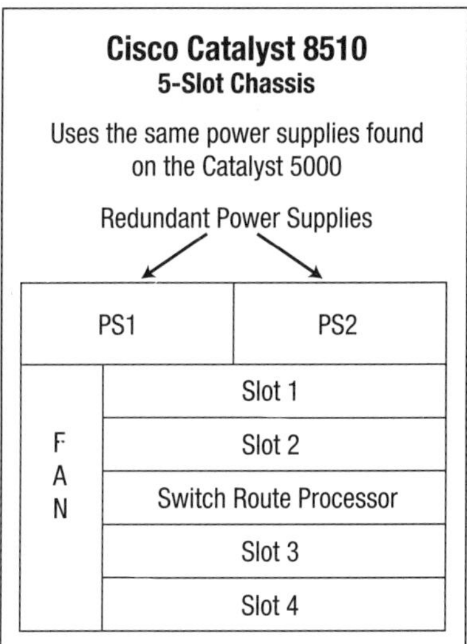

Figure 4.2 The modular slots for a Cisco Catalyst 8510.

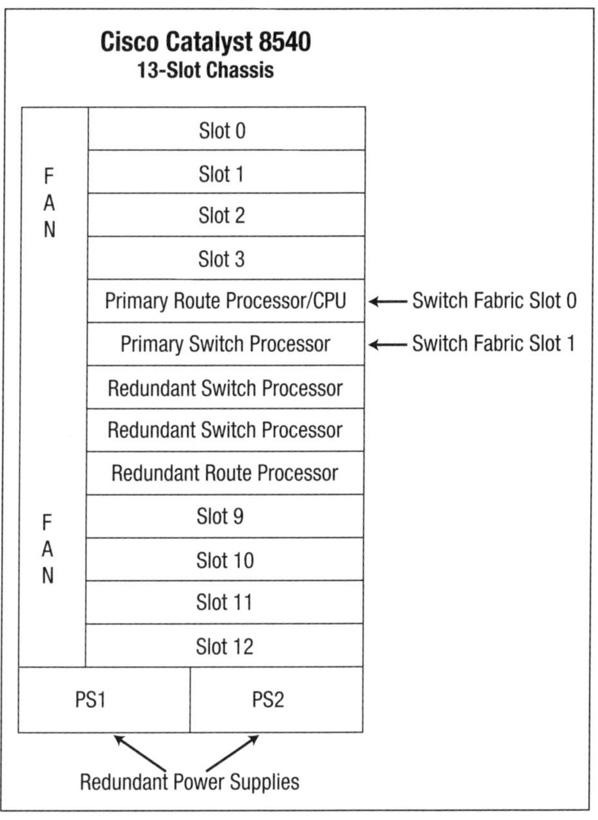

Figure 4.3 The modular slots for a Cisco Catalyst 8540.

Table 4.2 The number of ports on each multiservice line card and the maximum available for each switch.

Line Card Type	Interface Ports	8510 Max Ports	8540 Max Ports
10/100	8/16	32	128
GE	1/2	4	16
25 ATM	12	96	N/A
OC-3	4/16	32	128
OC-12c	1	8	32
OC-48	1	N/A	8
DS3 ATM	4	32	64
E3 ATM	4	32	64
T1/E1 ATM	4	32	64
T1/E1 CES	4	32	64

Cisco Catalyst 6000 Series

The Catalyst 6000 Series switches are designed to address the need for gigabit port density, high availability, and multilayer switching for the core layer backbone and server-aggregation environments. The 6000 Series is designed to support the high-speed processing of gigabit traffic. It also provides the means necessary to effectively and efficiently manage core layer network traffic.

The Catalyst 6000 family of switches uses the Cisco IOS to utilize the high speeds of the ASICs. This utilization, in turn, aids in the delivery of wire-speed traffic management services end to end. The Catalyst 6000 Series also offers a range of WAN/MAN protocols and media, as well as future scalability for direct analog and digital connectivity. The switch also allows existing voice infrastructures, to allow easy migration from existing networks to high-speed converged LAN/WAN/MAN networks with Voice over IP (VoIP) architectures.

Both the Catalyst 6000 and 6500 Series switches use a modular chassis. This chassis offers slot densities of six slots for the 6000 Series and nine slots for the 6500 Series. Both switch series support the same suite of Supervisor Engines, interface line cards, and common equipment. (For configuration information on the line cards and route processor cards, see Chapter 10.) Both the chassis for the Catalyst 6006 and the 6506 are identical, as is the chassis for the 6009 and the 6509, as shown in Figure 4.4. The key features for the Catalyst 6000 and 6500 Series are shown in Table 4.3.

Architecture Features

The key benefits of the 6000 family of switches are as follows:

- Support for a wide range of interface types and densities, including support for up to 384 10/100 Ethernet ports, up to 192 100FX Fast Ethernet ports, and up to 130 Gigabit Ethernet ports.

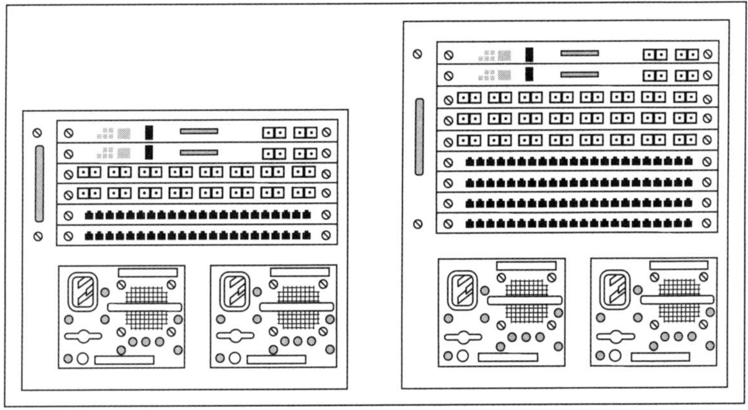

Figure 4.4 On the left, the chassis for the 6006 and the 6506. On the right, the chassis for the 6009 and the 6509. The 6509 is also available in a vertical slot version, which is not depicted.

Table 4.3 The key features of the Cisco Catalyst 6000 family.

Feature	6006	6009	6506	6509
Backplane	32Gbps	32Gbps	256Gbps	256Gbps
Forwarding rate	15,000,000pps	15,000,000pps	150,000,000pps	150,000,000pps
Modular slots	6	9	6	9
Max gigabit ports	130	130	130	130
Max 100FX ports	192	192	130	130
Max 10/100 ports	240	384	240	384
Max 10BaseFL	192	192	192	192
Max ATM	8	8	8	8
Max VLANs	1,000	1,000	1,000	1,000

- Support for Multilayer Switch Feature Card (MSFC), which is available for wire-rate IP, IPX, and IP-multicast routing support; AppleTalk; DecNet; and VINES.
- Support for up to 8 physical links, which can be bundled for Fast EtherChannel (FEC); or up to 16 Gigabit Ethernet and 4 Gigabit EtherChannels, for logical connections up to 16Gbps.
- Support for CiscoWorks2000 and Cisco Resource Essentials.
- Support for Protocol Independent Multicast (PIM), Internet Group Management Protocol (IGMP), CGMP, and GARP Multicast Registration Protocol (GMRP).

- Platforms offer up to 32Gbps of switching capacity and a multilayer switching forwarding rate of up to 30 million pps on the 6000 Series. The 6500 Series can provide up to 256Gbps and a multilayer switching forwarding rate of up to 150 million pps.
- Extensive QoS support for Layers 2 through 4. This feature utilizes information such as precedence bits from IP, Resource Reservation Protocol (RSVP), Inter-Switch Link (ISL), and 802.1p frames or Transmission Control Protocol (TCP) port numbers.
- Support for Dynamic Host Configuration Protocol (DHCP), Domain Name Service (DNS), and dynamic virtual LANs (VLANs).
- Redundant Supervisor Engines.
- Redundant load-sharing power supplies.
- Redundant load-sharing fans.
- Redundant system clocks.
- Redundant uplinks.
- Redundant switch fabrics (Catalyst 6500 Series only).

Supported Cards and Modules

The following are the available cards and modules for the Catalyst 6000 family:

- *48-Port 10/100 Ethernet Module*—Provides 48 ports of RJ-45 Ethernet or Fast Ethernet. This card is also available in a 10/100 TELCO or RJ-21 version.
- *24-Port 100FX Ethernet Module*—Provides 24 fiber-supported ports for 100Mbps support.
- *8-Port Gigabit Ethernet Module*—Provides eight ports of Gigabit Ethernet per module.
- *Multilayer Switch Module (MSM)*—Works with a Supervisor Engine card to provides multiprotocol routing for the Catalyst 6000 Ethernet interfaces.
- *Policy Feature Card (PFC)*—Offers multilayer services using interchangeable line cards as an integral part of the CiscoAssure end-to-end QoS and policy-based security solution.
- *Multilayer Switch Feature Card (MSFC)*—A route switch processor card that can work in combination with the PFC to provide a forwarding rate of 15 million pps performance for IP, IPX, and IP Multicast traffic.
- *FlexWAN Module*—Cisco's newest module. Accepts up to two Cisco 7200/7500 Series WAN port adapters, which support asynchronous and synchronous serial interfaces at speeds from 56Kbps to 155Mbps.

Note: *The FlexWAN Module does not support modules for Ethernet, Token Ring, Fiber Distributed Data Interface (FDDI), channel port adapters, encryption service modules, compression service modules, and double-wide port adapters.*

The Supervisor Engine card and MSM must be placed in certain slots in the rear of the chassis. The other slots can contain any configuration of additional cards or modules that are compatible with the Cisco Catalyst 6000 family. The 6500 Series is an exception to the rule, however—when more than one MSM is used, the last slot cannot contain an 8-Port Gigabit Ethernet Module. Figure 4.5 shows the 6006 and 6506 chassis with slot numbers and the internal interface assignments. Figure 4.6 shows the 6009 and 6509 chassis with the slot numbers. Both figures list the slots in which the Supervisor Engine cards and MSM cards should be placed.

Cisco Catalyst 5000 Series

The Catalyst 5000 family of switches consists of two different series: the 5000 Series, which fits nicely into the distribution layer; and the 5500 Series, which is an ideal backbone solution residing in the core layer of the campus network.

This switch family is one of the most feature-laden of all the Cisco Catalyst switching lines, with the most additional components, add-on cards, and modules available. The Catalyst 5000 family of switches includes the 5000, 5002, 5500, 5505, and 5509, which feature modular chassis in 2-, 5-, 9-, and 13-slot versions. All five chassis share the same set of interface modules and software features, providing scalability while maintaining interoperability and investment protection.

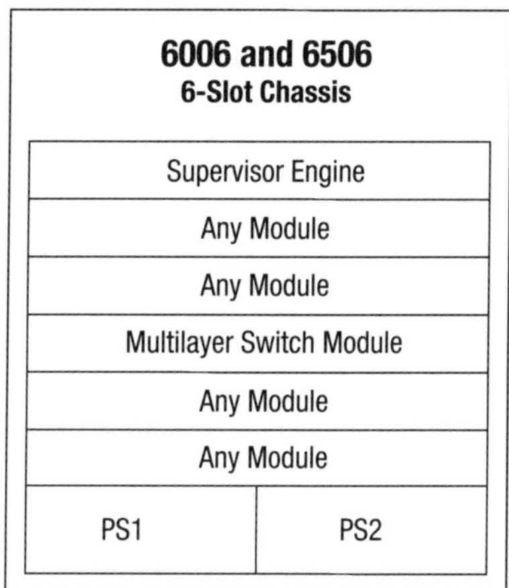

Figure 4.5 The Catalyst 6006 and 6506 chassis with slot numbers, internal interface addresses, and placement of the Supervisor Engine and MSM cards.

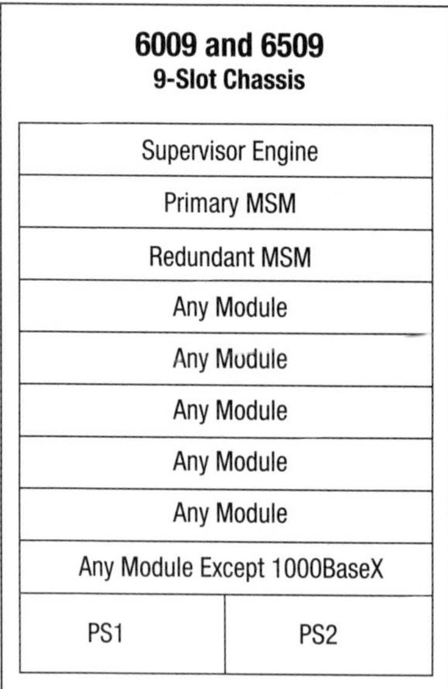

Figure 4.6 The Catalyst 6009 and 6509 chassis with slot numbers and placement of the Supervisor Engine and MSM cards.

Figure 4.7 shows the 13-slot Catalyst 5500 and the 9-slot Catalyst 5509. Figure 4.8 shows the 5-slot Catalyst 5000/5505, both of which use the same chassis, and the 2-slot Catalyst 5002 chassis.

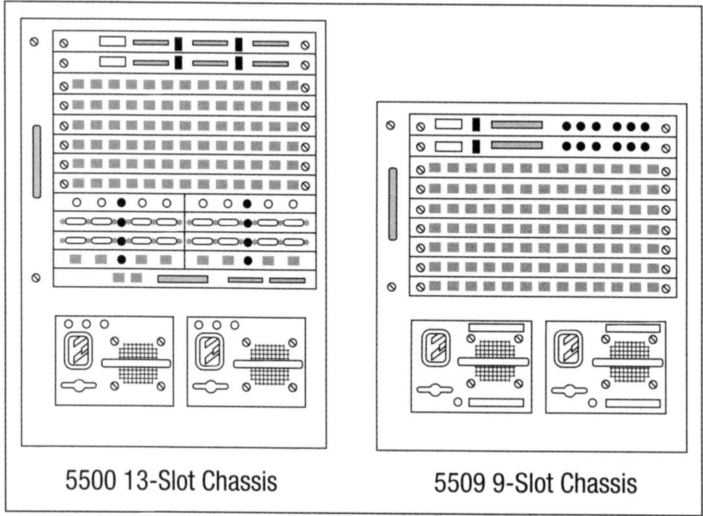

Figure 4.7 The Cisco Catalyst 5500 and 5509 chassis. The Supervisor Engine must be placed in Slot 0. If there is a redundant Supervisor Engine, it is placed in Slot 1 of either switch.

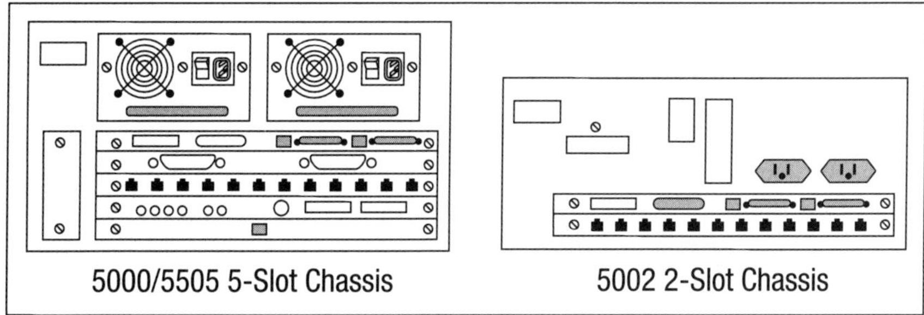

Figure 4.8 The Cisco Catalyst 5000/5505 and 5002 chassis.

Architecture Features

The key features for the Cisco Catalyst 5000 Series are as follows:

- High-speed connectivity using standard Fast Ethernet, FDDI, or ATM interfaces
- Fast EtherChannel supported on Supervisor Engine II ports and Fast Ethernet line cards, providing up to 800Mbps of load-sharing, redundant point-to-point connections
- Support for all Supervisor Engines (including I, II, and III) that provide switching, network management, and uplink ports, including the NetFlow Switching feature on Supervisor Engine II, which scales to multimillion pps forwarding across campus
- Dual redundant switching engines, dual redundant power supplies, and a passive backplane design that ensure full system redundancy for mission-critical environments
- Cisco's Virtual Trunking Protocol (VTP), which supports dynamic VLANs and dynamic trunk configuration across all switches
- Support for all advanced switching features of Cisco IOS software
- Support for advanced multicasting with CGMP

Table 4.4 shows the key features of the Catalyst 5000 Series of switches.

Table 4.4 The key features of the Catalyst 5000 family of switches.

Feature	5000	5002	5500	5505	5509
Modular slots	5	2	13	5	9
Backplane	1.2Gbps	1.2Gbps	3.6Gbps	3.6Gbps	3.6Gbps
Forwarding rate	1,000,000pps	3,000,000pps	25,000,000pps	25,000,000pps	25,000,000pps
Max VLANs	1,000	1,000	1,000	1,000	1,000

Supported Modules

The Catalyst 5000 Series has many switching modules available for high-density wiring closets and data center connectivity. These switching modules provide the ability to have a high port density for connectivity to the desktop, in addition to a high-speed uplink. Table 4.5 shows the switching modules, the ports available for each module, and the maximum allowable ports on each switch chassis.

The Catalyst 5000 family switching modules are as follows:

- Token Ring Module
- Group-Switched 10BaseT Ethernet
- Switched 10BaseT Ethernet (RJ-21)
- Switched 10BaseT Ethernet (RJ-45)
- Switched 10BaseFL Ethernet
- Group-Switched 100BaseTX Ethernet
- Switched 10/100BaseTX Fast Ethernet
- Switched 100BaseFX Fast Ethernet
- ATM LAN Emulation (OC-3 or OC-12)
- Copper Distributed Data Interface (CDDI)/FDDI
- ATM OC-3, 155Mbps Multimode Fiber
- ATM OC-3, 155Mbps Single-Mode Fiber

Table 4.5 Catalyst 5000 family port densities for each switch chassis.

Switching Module	Ports Supported Per Module	Max Ports Per Chassis 5002	5000	5505	5509	5500
Gigabit Ethernet	2/3/9	3	20	20	38	32
Group-Switched	48	48	192	192	384	528
10BaseT Ethernet	24/48	48	192	192	384	528
Switched 10BaseT	24/48	24	96	96	192	264
Switched 10BaseFL	12	12	48	48	96	132
Group-Switched	24	24	96	96	192	264
Switched10/100BaseTX	12/24	26	98	98	194	266
Switched 10/100BaseTX	24	26	98	98	194	266
Switched 100BaseFX	12	12	50	50	98	134
ATM Uplink	1 (dual-PHY)	1	4	4	7	7
CDDI/FDDI	1	1	4	4	8	11

- ATM OC-3, 155Mbps Unshielded Twisted-Pair (UTP), Category 5 (UTP-5)
- ATM OC-12, 622Mbps Single-Mode Fiber
- DS3
- E-3
- T1/E1 ATM Trunk
- T1/E1 Circuit Emulation
- 25Mbps ATM

Cisco Catalyst 4000 Series

The Catalyst 4000 Series provides intelligent Layer 2 services. This series of switches can be found in the core layer of the network as well as the distribution layer. It has a powerful bandwidth architecture, scaling from 22 to 64Gbps. It supports 10Mbps, 100Mbps, and 1000Mbps Ethernet switching.

The Catalyst 4000 family contains two different series: a 4000 Series, which provides support for 10Mbps and 100Mbps ports; and a 4900G Series, which provides 1Gbps Gigabit Interface Converter (GBIC) ports. These two Series provide advanced, very efficient, high-performance solutions for enterprise and branch office wiring closets.

Architecture Features

Key features of the Catalyst 4000 family include:

- Switching solutions that scale bandwidth as you add ports. The Catalyst 4000 Series is powered by high-speed ASICs for wire-speed Layer 2 and Layer 3 10Mbps to 1000Mbps switching.
- Capable of up to 240 Fast Ethernet ports in a chassis.
- Catalyst 4000 system can easily upgrade all system ports to higher-layer switching by adding additional fabric engine modules.
- Catalyst 4006 chassis backplane and Supervisor Engine connectors are designed to support future Supervisor Engine upgrades.
- Support for PIM Dense and Sparse mode, IGMP, and CGMP, which support standards-based and Cisco-enhanced multimedia networking.
- Shared-memory architecture with no head-of-line blocking and very low latency.
- Support for the enhanced Web-based GUI- and CLI-based management alternatives.

- Support for enterprise-wide policy creation features with CiscoAssure support and network-wide QoS for both Layer 2 cost of service (CoS) and Layer 3 type of service (ToS), for a guarantee of application performance.
- Catalyst 4000 Series delivers self-healing network intelligence that is fast enough to recover from port, device, and link failures without noticeable delays to an end user.

Table 4.6 shows the key features of the Cisco Catalyst 4000 family of switches. Figure 4.9 shows the Catalyst 4003 and 4006 chassis. Figure 4.10 shows the Catalyst 4008G and 4912G chassis.

Catalyst 4000 Series Ethernet switches are available in a chassis-based form, with modular configurations providing a range of port densities for 10/100 to 1000Mbps speeds.

The following are features available for the Catalyst 4003:

- A flexible, three-slot modular chassis, with one slot reserved for a Supervisor Engine and two slots for switched port modules
- Two power-supply bays that support redundant (optional), load-sharing, fault-tolerant AC power supplies
- One hot-swappable fan tray bay

Table 4.6 The key features of the Catalyst 4000 family of switches.

Feature	4003	4006	4908G	4912G
Slots	3	6	None	None
Max ports	96	240	8	12
Backplane	24Gbps	60Gbps	22Gbps	24Gbps
Forwarding rate	18,000pps	18,000pps	18,000,000pps	18,000,000pps
Max VLANs	1,024	1,024	1,024	1,024
Max MAC addresses	16,000	16,000	16,000	16,000

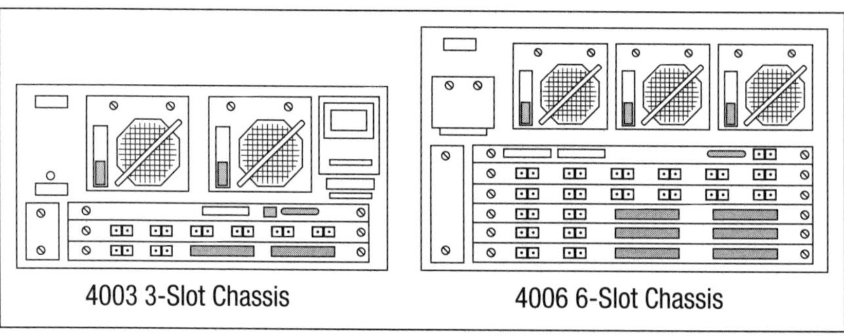

Figure 4.9 The Catalyst 4003 and 4006 chassis.

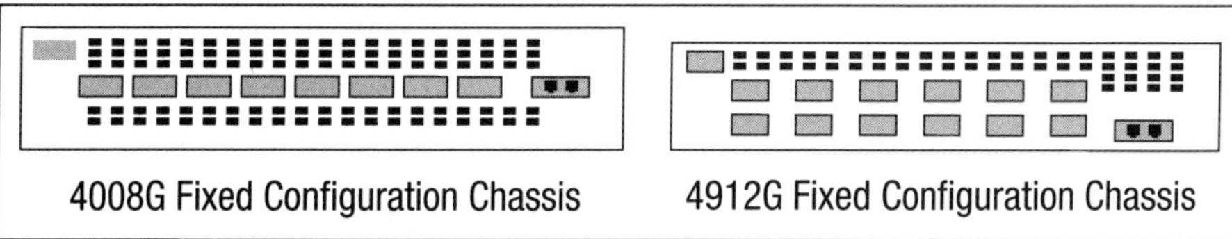

Figure 4.10 The Catalyst 4008G and the 4912G fixed configuration chassis.

Note: *The Catalyst 4006 chassis has the same features but provides a six-slot modular chassis, with one slot reserved for a Supervisor Engine and five slots for switched port modules.*

Using Gigabit Ethernet on the Catalyst 4008G is easy because of the modular chassis and the variety of modules. Up to 96 10/100 Fast Ethernet ports, or up to 36 Gigabit Ethernet ports, can be installed into one chassis.

The following are key features of the Cisco Catalyst 4008G switch:

- Fixed configuration Layer 3 Ethernet switch
- Ideal for backbone deployment in mid-sized networks that require wire-speed Layer 3 performance but do not require the Gigabit Ethernet densities offered in the Catalyst 6000 and Catalyst 8500 Series of switches

Tip: A fixed configuration switch does not contain slots to add cards or modules.

- Eight ports of 1000BaseX Gigabit Ethernet with GBIC support; all ports have Layer 3 switching capability at wire speed
- High performance switching with over 11 million pps Layer 3 switching and routing of IP, IPX, and IP Multicast traffic
- High performance CPU with Cisco IOS system software
- QoS via multiple queues with Weighted Round Robin (WRR) scheduling
- Comprehensive management tools based on standard CiscoWorks2000 applications
- Access list support on all ports

The following are key features of the Cisco Catalyst 4912G switch:

- Fixed configuration Layer 2 Ethernet switch
- Contains 12 Gigabit Ethernet ports
- Designed to handle demanding network bandwidth situations with Ether-Channel technology that scales to 8Gbps

Supported Modules and Cards

The following Catalyst 4003 and 4006 modules and cards are available:

- 48-port 10BaseT/100BaseTX autosensing Fast EtherChannel (RJ-45) line card
- 48-port 10BaseT/100BaseTX autosensing Fast EtherChannel (RJ-21) line card
- 24-port 100BaseTX Fast Ethernet (MT-RJ) line card
- 32-port 10BaseT/100BaseTX autosensing Fast EtherChannel (RJ-45), plus 2-port 1000BaseX (GBIC) line card
- 6-port 1000BaseX Gigabit EtherChannel (GBIC) line card
- 4-port 100BaseT Fast Ethernet Ports, MT-RJ interface
- 18-port server switching 1000BaseX Gigabit Ethernet (GBIC)

Cisco Catalyst 3900 Series

Even though the Cisco 5000 Series provides a Token Ring module, the Catalyst 3900 and 3920 are Cisco's primary low-cost solutions for Token Ring users to migrate to a switched environment. The 3900 can be stacked back-to-back with up to eight 3900 or 3920 Series switches using the Cisco Catalyst Switch Matrix, shown in Figures 4.11 and 4.12.

The Catalyst 3900 provides an ISL module for connections between wiring closets. This module consists of two ports, either fiber or copper. Two feature cards can be used in the 3900. This link can provide up to 100Mbps uplink connectivity. Also supported is an ATM module that provides Token Ring users

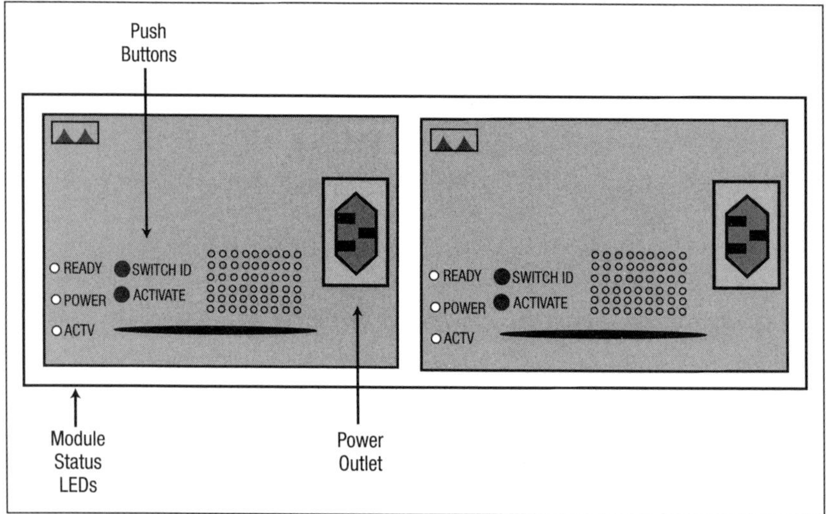

Figure 4.11 The Cisco Catalyst Switch Matrix front view.

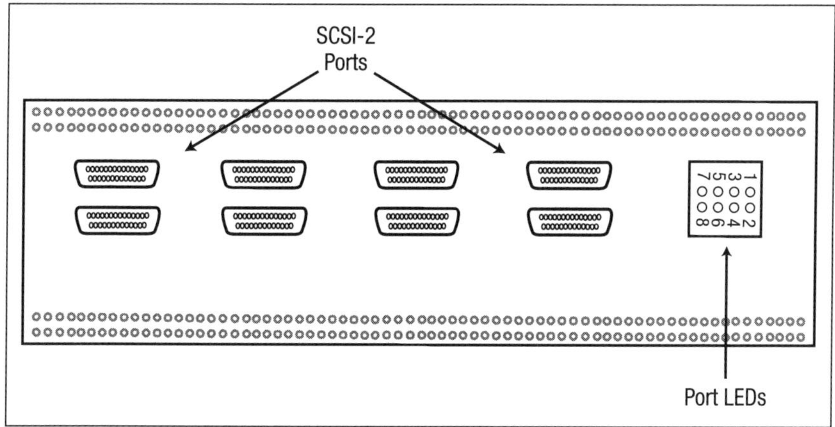

Figure 4.12 The Cisco Catalyst Switch Matrix rear view.

with ATM access to campus backbones. The module provides a single 155Mbps connection with a multimode fiber interface. In addition, optional four-port Token Ring modules can be added to the expansion ports in the Catalyst 3900. These cards allow for expansion to up to 28 Token Ring ports. Up to eight units can be stacked using the optional stack port module and the Catalyst Matrix, for a total of 224 Token Ring ports. The four-port fiber module supports IEEE 802.5J standard for ring-in/ring-out (RI/RO) and the fiber lobe attachment of end stations.

Catalyst Matrix for the Cisco 3900 Series

The Catalyst Switch Matrix is an eight-port interface that connects up to eight Catalyst 3900 Series switches. A Cisco Catalyst 3900 has the ability to detect if it is connected to a Catalyst 3900 switch that is connected to a Catalyst Matrix. The connected Catalyst 3900 Series switch then connects in the switch block to make a stack that logically appears to be one switch.

One of the great features of the Catalyst Matrix in the 3900 Series is the switch's ability to connect any combination of up to eight Catalyst 3900 switches or remove any one switch without the need to have the power cycled or turned off.

A Cisco Systems proprietary shielded cable 1 meter in length, with a 50-pin connector at each end, is used to connect the switches participating in the switch stack. The cable uses crossover wiring so either end can be used for both sides of the connection. The cable plugs into a stack port I/O connector on the back of each Catalyst Matrix. The other end is plugged into a Catalyst stack port module interface card that is installed in an expansion slot on another Catalyst 3900 Series switch.

The 3900 Series supports three types of bridging:

- Source Route Bridging
- Source Route Transparent Bridging
- Source Route Switched Bridging

Architecture Features

The Catalyst 3900 has the following features:

- Twenty shielded Token Ring ports for 150-ohm shielded twisted-pair (STP) or 100-ohm UTP connectivity
- FlexSlot accommodating two expansion modules or one double-wide module for future expansion
- Nine-pin EIA/TIA-232 interface for local console or modem connectivity
- Automatic 4Mbps, 16Mbps, and 32Mbps speed adaptation
- TokenChannel switch interconnect
- MAC address and protocol (DSAP/SNAP) filters
- IEEE and IBM Spanning-Tree Protocol

The Catalyst 3920 provides the following features:

- Twenty-four shielded Token Ring ports for 150-ohm STP or 100-ohm UTP connectivity
- Nine-pin EIA/TIA-232 interface for local console or modem connectivity
- Automatic 4Mbps, 16Mbps, and 32Mbps speeds
- TokenChannel switch interconnect
- MAC address and protocol (DSAP/SNAP) filters
- IEEE and IBM Spanning-Tree Protocol

Figure 4.13 shows Cisco Catalyst 3900 and 3920 switch chassis. Table 4.7 shows key features of the Catalyst 3900 Series.

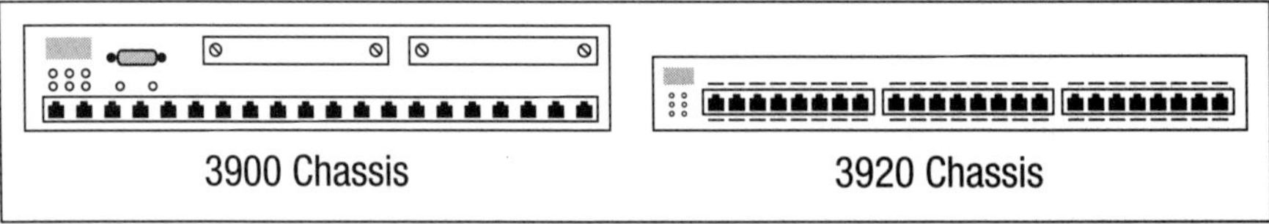

Figure 4.13 The Cisco Catalyst 3900 chassis on the left and the 3920 chassis on the right.

Table 4.7 The key features of the Cisco Catalyst 3900 Series.

Feature	3900	3920
Ports	20/24/28	24
Stack slot	1	1
FlexSlots	1	None
Backplane	520Mbps	520Mbps
Processor	Intel 960SA	Intel 960SA
DRAM	Up to 8MB	Up to 8MB
Stackable	Yes	Yes

Two Catalyst 3900 or 3920 switches can be connected using any of the ports on each switch to form a TokenChannel. A TokenChannel is two to eight parallel links that connect Catalyst 3900 or 3920 switches. TokenChannels provide a capacity between the two Catalyst 3900 or 3920 switches of up to 128Mbps in half-duplex (HDX) mode, and up to 256Mbps if all ports in the TokenChannel are operating in full-duplex (FDX) mode.

To aid in network management, the Catalyst 3900 or 3920 also maintains status information and a variety of statistics. Status information is available for each port and for each TokenChannel, if defined. Statistics are kept by port, by VLAN, and for the switch as a whole.

Network management can be performed in a number of ways. The Catalyst 3900 and 3920 support RMON, SNMP, SPAN Port, CiscoView, Traffic Director, VlanDirector, CDP, and VTP.

Tip: If you need to upgrade the Catalyst 3900 or 3920 software, you can do so through the same serial port used for configuration. The code can be downloaded from a customer-supplied programmable workstation using the X-modem protocol. Code upgrades can also be accomplished using Trivial File Transfer Protocol (TFTP).

Cisco Catalyst 3500 Series XL

The Cisco Catalyst 3500 Series XL line of stackable 10/100/1000Mbps switches provides high performance and investment protection for companies that are expanding their switched networks.

This series of switches can be used in a number of applications, such as in the enterprise wiring closet; in a branch office, where they can provide a LAN backbone and desktop connectivity; and in a multilayer network, where they can be deployed with a Layer 3 switch for a low-cost solution.

Each Catalyst 3500 XL comes with two Gigabit Ethernet interfaces that have 12, 24, or 48 auto-sensing 10BaseT/100BaseTX ports. The 3508G XL provides 8 Gigabit Ethernet ports for GBIC Ethernet aggregation.

Architecture Features

Some of the key features of the Catalyst 3500 Series switches are as follows:

- The switch engine supports the switching fabric. This feature manages transactions between a central 4MB shared-memory buffer and any number of satellites.
- All incoming traffic passes through the switch via the memory buffer. A shared-memory buffer design eliminates head-of-line blocking problems associated with bus architectures that have limited dedicated input buffers for each port.
- Features store/receive channels that can exist between the switch and a satellite to provide 200Mbps bandwidth each way, for a total channel capacity of 400Mbps between the switch fabric and each satellite.
- Architecture designed to run with the Cisco IOS software for full interoperability with Cisco routers and switches. Cisco IOS software delivers network services and enables networked applications.
- Catalyst clustering technology that allows up to 16 switches, regardless of their geographic proximity or their interconnecting media, to be managed through a single IP address.
- Support for Cisco Visual Switch Manager (CVSM), which provides a GUI to enable quick execution of many network management tasks. CVSM is launched from the switch itself through a Web browser such as Netscape Navigator or Microsoft Internet Explorer, allowing network and device-level management including port configuration, VLAN configuration, network views, and port monitoring.

In addition, the 3500 Series supports many of the features of the 1900 and 2900 Series, such as DNS and DHCP. The series is offered in both Standard and Enterprise Editions. Table 4.8 shows the features of the Catalyst 3500 Series. Figure 4.14 shows the 3512 XL and the 3524 XL chassis. Figure 4.15 shows the 3508G XL and the 3548 XL chassis.

Table 4.8 The Cisco 3500 Series key switching features.

Feature	3512 XL	3524 XL	3508G XL	3548 XL
10/100 ports	12	24	None	48
GBIC ports	2	2	8	2
Backplane	10Gbps	10Gbps	10Gbps	10Gbps
Stackable	Yes	Yes	Yes	Yes
Forwarding rate	4,800,000pps	6,500,000pps	7,400,000pps	8,800,000pps
Max VLANs	250	250	250	250
Max MAC addr.	8,192	8,192	8,192	8,192

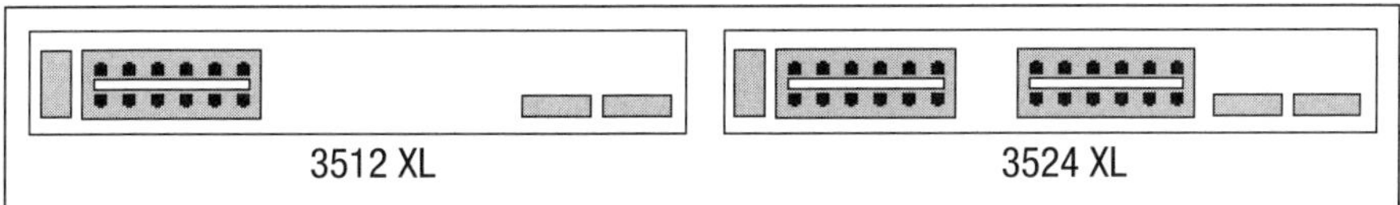

Figure 4.14 The 3512 XL and 3524 XL chassis.

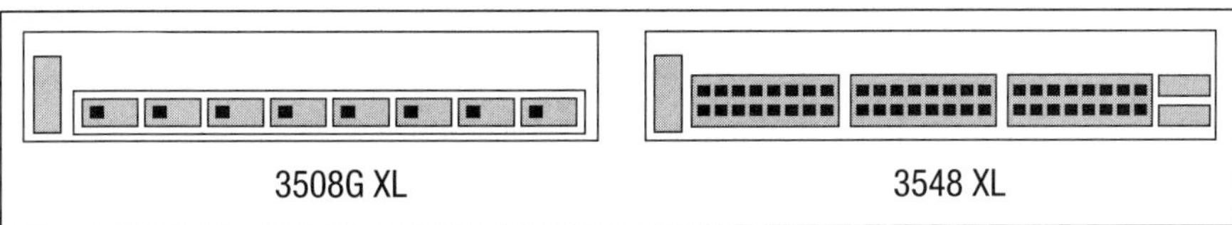

Figure 4.15 The 3508G XL and 3548 XL chassis.

Cisco Catalyst 3000 Series

The Cisco Catalyst 3000 Series has a completely different architecture and IOS than any other Cisco switch. However, this series of switches received an End-of-Life notice from Cisco (meaning that Cisco will no longer be manufacturing the switch or provide new features), so we will provide only a basic overview in this chapter.

The Catalyst 3000 Series provides the following features:

- Stacked switch platforms that are manageable as if they were a single logical entity. These switches automatically configure themselves as new switches are added or removed.
- Cut-through switching technology delivering wire-speed, low-latency switching. It also has the ability to use fragment-free or runtless switching, which automatically switches to store-and-forward when an error rate has been exceeded.
- Optional modules that can provide interfaces for additional Ethernet ports, Fast Ethernet ports, ATM ports, and WAN connectivity.
- User definable per-port and secure-mode filtering that provide access control for sensitive information resources.
- Support for up to 64 VLANs using Cisco's LANE-based ATM, and ISL-based Fast Ethernet VLANs to extend switched VLANs throughout the enterprise.
- STP implemented by VLAN for data loop detection.
- Optional stack port interface module that connects one 3000 Series switch to another. This Catalyst Matrix delivers 280Mbps per switch of bandwidth for unrestricted traffic flow.

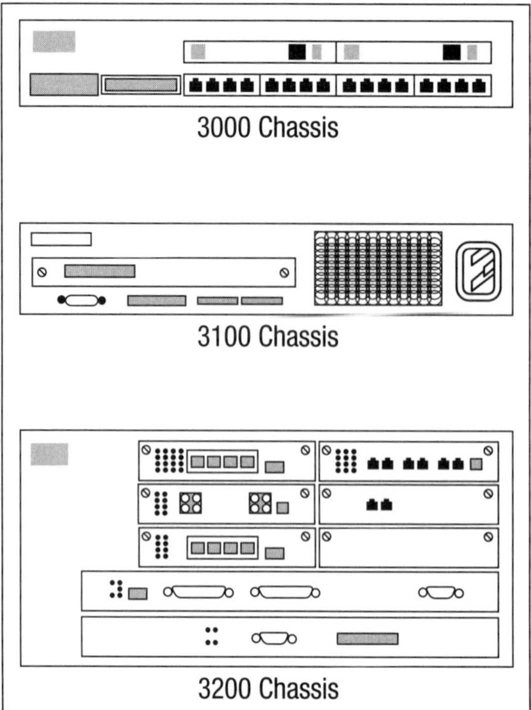

Figure 4.16 The Cisco Catalyst 3000, 3100, and 3200 series chassis.

Table 4.9 The key features of the Cisco Catalyst 3000 Series switches.

Feature	3000	3100	3200
10BaseT ports	16	24	0
Flex slots	0	1	1
Modular slots	0	1	7
Max VLANs	1,700	1,700	1,700

Some of the basic hardware features of the Cisco Catalyst 3000 Series of switches are listed in Table 4.9. Figure 4.16 shows the Catalyst 3000, 3100, and 3200 Series switch chassis.

Cisco Catalyst 2900 Series

Two significantly different architectures are found in the Catalyst 2900 series of switches: the 2900 Series switches and the XL version of the 2900 Series switches. About the only relation between these series is their low cost. When you compare the Catalyst 2900 family of switches' performance and features to other Cisco Catalyst switches, this series is one of the best values for your money.

The 2900 Series includes the 2901, 2902, 2926G, 2948G, and the new 2980G. This series of switches uses an architecture similar to that of the Cisco Catalyst 5002 Series switch. You will find the Set/Clear command-based CLI on the 2900 Series switches, which allows the switch to support advanced features such as ISL.

Note: *The Cisco Catalyst 2901 and 2902 received an End-of-Life notice some time ago, so they will not be covered in this chapter.*

The 2900 XL Series was introduced long after Cisco released its prized Catalyst 5000 Series of switches. One of the most noticeable differences is that the XL series uses the true Cisco IOS, which is almost identical to that of Cisco routers. It also allows for 10/100 half-duplex and full-duplex auto-negotiation. Auto-negotiation allows the switch port to negotiate the switch port speed and duplex based on the type of traffic being sent to the port by the sending interface. The models available in this series are the 2908 XL, 2912 XL, 2916 XL, and 2924 XL.

The 2900 Series XL supports some comprehensive management features, including a built-in HTTP server for the Web-based Cisco Visual Switch Manager, SNMP, auto-configuration, Cisco Discovery Protocol, CiscoWorks for Switched Internetworks, and embedded agent support for four groups of RMON.

Architecture Features

The Cisco Catalyst 2926G, 2948G, and 2980G are similar to the architecture of the Cisco Catalyst 5000 Series. These are store-and-forward mode switches with many high-end features:

- Users can configure each port with higher-priority levels to accommodate time-sensitive applications such as voice and video.
- Support of FEC uplink bundles for up to 400Mbps on the Catalyst 2926T and 2926F. The Catalyst 2926GS and the 2926GL each support uplinks of up to 800Mbps. (More on these versions a little later in this section.) These FEC ports can be configured between two switches, two routers, or a switch and a router. Special configurations and NIC cards also allow a server to be configured with FEC uplinks to a router or switch, providing for a very efficient high-speed backbone and data center uplinks with automatic load balancing and failover for port failures.
- Support for RMON statistics that provide good visibility of network activity for the statistics, history, events, and alarms groups.
- Support for VLAN load-balancing and spanning-tree on multiple parallel Fast Ethernet ISL trunks to increase capacity and fault tolerance between switches.

- Support for ISL, Dynamic Inter-Switch Link (DISL), CDP, VTP, VLAN Membership Policy Server (VMPS), Dynamic VLANs, and port security based on the MAC address.
- Support for complete SNMP management for Ethernet Management Information Base (MIB), bridge MIB, MIB II, and VTP.
- Support for management with CiscoWorks for Switched Internetworks (CWSI), CiscoView, TrafficDirector, and VlanDirector.
- 2948G support for advanced scalability for Fast EtherChannel, Dynamic VLANs, and 802.1Q trunking.
- 2948G support for bandwidth control using QoS features such as protocol filtering, link load balancing, per-port security, TACACS+ authentication, and IP permit lists.

The four different versions of the Cisco Catalyst 2926 switch are listed here:

- *2926T*—A fixed switch with 24 RJ-45 10/100MB ports and two 100BaseTX ports.
- *2926F*—A fixed switch with 24 RJ-45 10/100MB ports and two 100BaseFX ports.

Investment Protection

Cisco continuously provides enhancements to the Cisco IOS—the Catalyst system software—and provides different IOS platforms for different switches. (New platforms are usually released when Cisco purchases a switch vendor.) The IOS delivers one of the most important investment protection features. Three different types of IOS are primarily found in Cisco switches:

- *Legacy menu-driven IOS*—Found in the older legacy Cisco Catalyst 1900 Series, 2820 Series, and 3000 Series switches.
- *Cisco IOS command-line interface*—Found in many of the Cisco Catalyst switches, switch route processors, and routers.
- *Cisco Set/Clear-based command-line interface*—Found in the newer, higher-end switches such as the Cisco Catalyst 5000, 5500, 6000, and 6500 Series. This is the most comprehensive and feature-laden IOS of the three.

The IOSs and switching hardware are constantly upgraded, and new features are added almost weekly. The Cisco Connection Online (CCO) Web site (**www.cisco.com**) is your best resource for the new upgrades, features, and hardware available for Cisco Catalyst switches.

- *2926GS*—A fixed switch with 24 RJ-45 10/100MB ports and two 1000BaseSX ports.
- *2926GL*—A fixed switch with 24 RJ-45 10/100MB ports and two 1000BaseLX/LH ports.

***Note:** As we were writing this book, Cisco announced an End-of-Life notice for each of the Cisco Catalyst 2926G Series switches. A new switch—the Cisco 2980G Series—was announced.*

The key features of the 2900 Series XL switches are shown in Table 4.10. Figure 4.17 shows the models available for the Cisco Catalyst 2900 Series XL.

The hardware features available for the Cisco Catalyst 2900 Series switches are listed in Table 4.11. Figure 4.18 shows the Cisco Catalyst 2926G and 2948G models. Figure 4.19 shows the Cisco Catalyst 2980G switch.

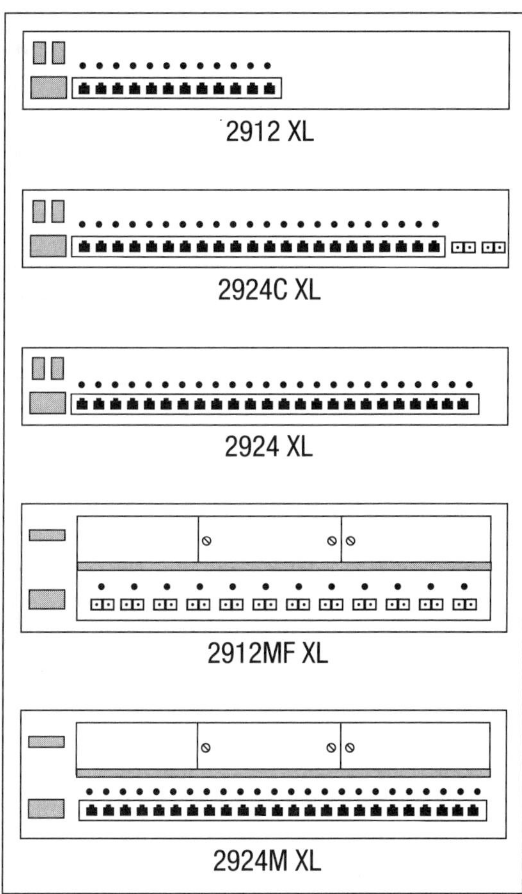

Figure 4.17 The 2900 XL Series switch chassis.

Table 4.10 Models and features for the standard version of each Cisco Catalyst 2900 Series XL switch.

Feature	2908 XL	2912MF XL	2916 XL	2924M XL	2924 XL/ 2924C XL
10/100 ports	8	0	16	24	22
100BaseFX ports	0	12	0	0	2
Modular slots	0	2	0	2	0
Enterprise Edition	Yes	Yes	Yes	Yes	Yes
Standard Edition	Yes	No	Yes	Yes	Yes
Backplane	3.2Gbps	3.2Gbps	3.2Gbps	3.2Gbps	3.2Gbps
Forwarding rate	3,000,000pps	3,000,000pps	3,000,000pps	3,000,000pps	3,000,000pps
Max MAC addr.	2,048	8,192	2,048	8,192	2,048
Max VLANs	64	64	64	64	64

Table 4.11 The models and key features for the standard versions of Cisco Catalyst 2926G, 2948G, and 2980G switches.

Feature	2926T/F	2926GS/GL	2948	2980G
10/100 ports	24	24	48	80
100MB Forwarding Engines	2	0	0	0
Gb ports	0	2	2	2
Expansion slots	0	0	2	0
Enterprise Edition	Yes	Yes	Yes	Yes
Standard Edition	No	No	No	No
Backplane	1.2Gbps	1.2Gbps	1.2Gbps	24Gbps
Forwarding rate	1,000,000pps	1,000,000pps	1,000,000pps	18,000,000pps
Max MAC addr.	16,000	16,000	16,000	N/A
Max VLANs	1,000	1,000	1,024	N/A

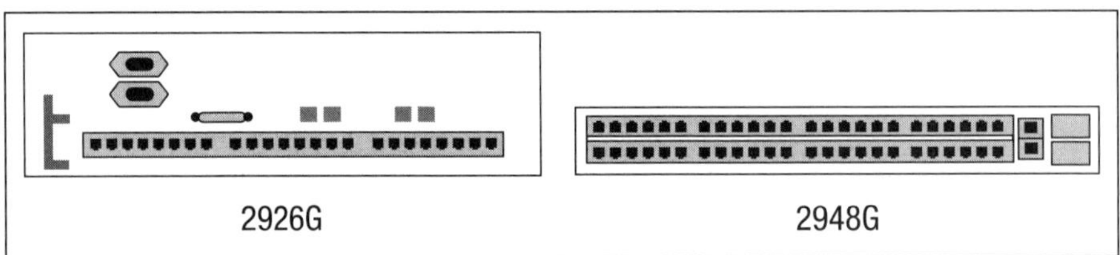

Figure 4.18 The Cisco Catalyst 2926G on the left, and the Cisco 2948G on the right.

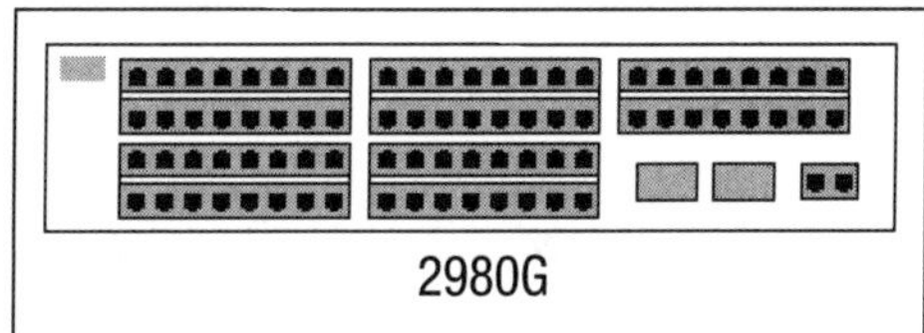

Figure 4.19 The Cisco Catalyst 2980G switch.

Supported Modules and Cards

Each Catalyst 2924M XL and 2912MF XL switch contains two versatile module slots. Following are the features of the modules available:

- *4-port 10BaseT/100BaseTX Switch Module*—Supports autosensing, is IEEE 802.3u 100BaseT compatible for use with 100BaseTX and 100BaseFX cabling, uses RJ-45 connectors, and supports two-pair Category 5 UTP wiring.
- *2-port or 4-port 100BaseFX Switch Module*—A 100BaseFX-compatible card that uses SC connectors with support for 50/125 and 62.5/125-micron multimode fiber. This allows a maximum cable distance up to 6,558 feet (2 kilometers).
- *1-port 1000BaseX GBIC-Based Module*—Based on the IEEE 802.3z standard. It uses either shortwave (SX) multimode fiber with a maximum cable distance of 1,804 feet and longwave/long-haul (LX/LH) single-mode fiber with a maximum cable distance of 32,790 feet.
- *1-port ATM Modules*—Four different ATM modules support the media types of UTP, Multimode Fiber (MMF), Single-Mode Fiber-Medium Range (SMF-MR), and Single-Mode Fiber-Long Range (SMF-LR). The maximum cable distance for SMF-MR is 32,790 feet and for SMF-LR 131,160 feet.

Modules available for the Cisco Catalyst 2948G are as follows:

- 1000BaseSX GBIC module
- 1000BaseLX/LH GBIC module
- 1000BaseZX GBIC module

Cisco Catalyst 2820 Series

The Cisco Catalyst 2820 Series is a great solution for the access layer network that needs high-speed links to the wiring closet for 20 or so users. The switch is perfect for smaller wiring closets where it is not economical to purchase a high-end solution such as a Cisco Catalyst 5000 Series switch.

The Catalyst 2820 Series switch's architecture is virtually identical to that of the Cisco Catalyst 1900 Series switches. The switch comes in a Standard Edition and an Enterprise Edition. The switch is different because of its height and uplink bays: Two uplink bays allow for high-speed uplink options such as FDDI, CDDI, 100Mbps, and ATM modules.

Two models are available for the 2820 Series: the Cisco Catalyst 2822 and the Cisco Catalyst 2828. On both switches, you will find 24 10BaseT Ethernet ports and 1 10Mbps AUI port. All the features listed for the Catalyst 1924 are the same for the Catalyst 2822 and the Catalyst 2828, with the exception of the number of allowable MAC addresses (see Table 4.12). Figure 4.20 shows the Cisco 2820 Series switch.

Note: *Cisco has issued an End-of-Life notice for the Cisco Catalyst 2822.*

Cisco Catalyst 1900

The Catalyst 1900 is the entry point for Cisco's switch line. There are two types of Catalyst 1900: the Standard Edition (SE) and the Enterprise Edition (EE).

The Standard Edition is a low-cost alternative for companies migrating from a shared hub environment or smaller scale installations. These switches are designed to be plug-and-play right out of the box, with no configuration needed. The Catalyst 1900 SE has 12 fixed 10BaseT ports with 2 high-speed 100BaseT (or one 100BaseT and one 100BaseFX) ports for connecting to corporate backbones. This switch can be configured via a Web-browser interface or by the Cisco Visual Switch Manager. Support for DNS and DHCP is included to help in ease of use. The Standard Edition can be upgraded via Flash to an Enterprise Edition version.

Table 4.12 The two models available for the Cisco Catalyst 2820 Series switches.

Feature	2822	2828
Ports	24	24
Backplane	1Gbps	1Gbps
Processor	80486 CPU	80486 CPU
Forwarding rate	370pps	370pps
Max MAC addr.	2,048	8,192

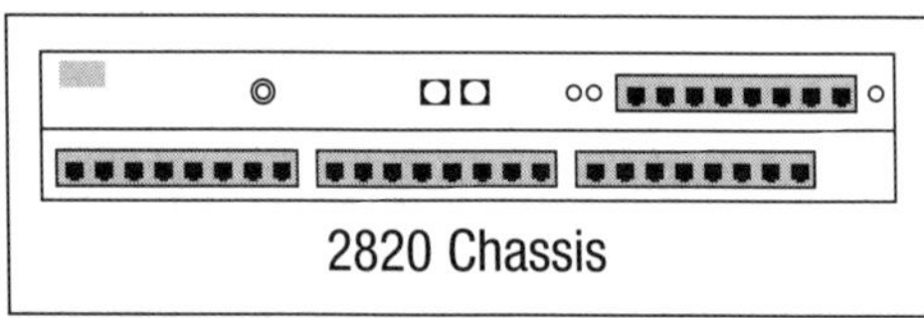

Figure 4.20 The Cisco 2820 Series switch.

The Enterprise Edition contains all the features of the Standard Edition but provides several high-end solutions. These solutions include Fast EtherChannel, support for ISL, an IOS CLI, and support for CGMP.

Two different models are available in the 1900 Series: the Cisco Catalyst 1912 and the Cisco Catalyst 1924. Each is identified by the number of standard ports. Table 4.13 shows the features of each switch. Figure 4.21 shows the Catalyst 1912 and 1924 chassis.

4

Chapter Summary

In this chapter, we covered the most important features of the Cisco Catalyst switches available for today's networks. Some of the switches have been issued an End-of-Life notice from Cisco, but that does not mean you won't see the information on a test or encounter these switches in real life. Cisco hasn't sold thousands of switches just to have them immediately be replaced the moment the company issues an End-of-Life notice.

This chapter contains a lot of information that you need to remember. On the test, you will find questions regarding the number of slots found on a particular switch. These questions are directed primarily toward the 2900 through 5500 Series, with most relating to the 5000 and 5500 Series.

Knowledge of the daughtercards that work with the Supervisor Engines, line cards, and route processor cards available on each switch will also aid you in passing this section of the test. Knowing which switches can use route processor cards and NetFlow Feature Cards is important. Paying close attention to which

Table 4.13 The features available for the Cisco Catalyst 1912 and the Catalyst 1924.

Feature	1912	1924
Ports	12	24
Backplane	1Gbps	1Gbps
Processor	80486 CPU	80486 CPU
Forwarding rate	370pps	370pps
Max MAC addr.	1,024	2,048

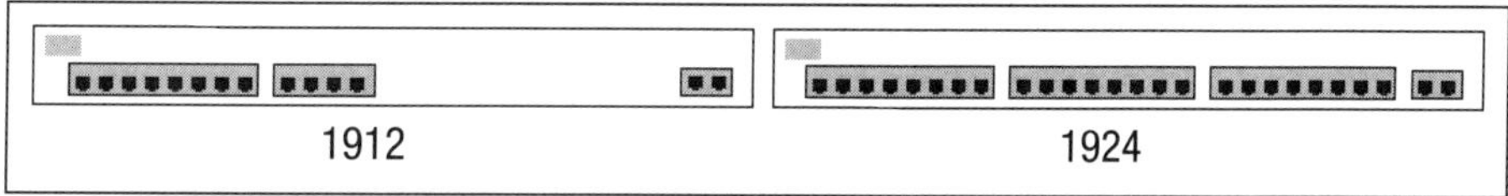

Figure 4.21 The Catalyst 1912 chassis on the left, and the 1924 chassis on the right.

switches can use a Route Switch Module (RSM), Route Switch Feature Card (RSFC), MSM, NetFlow Feature Card (NFFC), NFFC II, and the MSFC will greatly enhance your chances of passing this section of the test.

Note: *The RSM, RSFC, MSM, NFFC, and NFFC II are covered in detail in Chapter 10.*

Cisco continuously changes the feature sets available with each switch. Almost weekly, you will find an announcement of an upgraded IOS, an upgraded hardware component, new line cards, new switches, and new routers that work with switches, adding Layer 3 and Layer 4 support.

Just during the few weeks of writing this chapter, three major announcements occurred from Cisco: the announcement of the FlexWAN card offering high-end Layer 3 routing abilities for the Catalyst 6000 Series, the End-of-Life announcement for the Catalyst 2926G Series, and the addition of the 2980G switch. The best way to keep up on changes is to get a handle on what equipment and software features are available now; then, once a week, take time to visit Cisco's CCO Web site and read the weekly announcements. If you want to really stay on top of things (and you have a lot of time), sort the new articles posted on the CCO Web site by date and read the last seven days' article and technical sheets.

Review Questions

1. Which of the following switches would work best in the core layer of the network?
    a. Cisco Catalyst 1924
    b. Cisco Catalyst 2822
    c. Cisco Catalyst 5509
    d. Cisco Catalyst 3200
2. Switches without modular ports are called which of the following?
    a. Non-modular
    b. Fixed configuration
    c. Modularless
    d. None of the above
3. Which of the following series of Cisco switches provide support for Token Ring? [Choose the two best answers]
    a. 1900 Series
    b. 4000 Series

c. 3900 Series

d. 5000 Series

4. The Catalyst Switch Matrix can used to stack up to eight of which of the following switch series? [Choose the two best answers]

   a. 3000 Series

   b. 4000 Series

   c. 3900 Series

   d. 5000 Series

5. Which of the following are route processors that can provide Layer 3 routing in Cisco Catalyst switches?

   a. Route Switch Module (RSM)

   b. Multilayer Switch Module (MSM)

   c. Route Switch Feature Card (RSFC)

   d. All of the above

6. An engineering company has only 14 employees but will double in size within the next few years. The users transfer large CAD drawings to local servers. What is the most appropriate device for the access layer?

   a. Catalyst 5500 with a Route Switch Module (RSM)

   b. Catalyst 6000 with a Multilayer Switch Module (MSM)

   c. Catalyst 2924 XL with 10/100 ports

   d. Catalyst 4000 Series with Layer 3 routing features

7. A large book publishing company has experienced greater than 400 percent growth in the past two years and has installed different Ethernet media types throughout the campus. The campus has gigabit requirements due to multimedia implementations. Which of the following switches would work best in the distribution layer?

   a. Catalyst 4000 with a 6-port Gigabit Ethernet Module

   b. Catalyst 5500 Series with a Route Switch Module (RSM)

   c. Catalyst 6000 Series with a 16-port Gigabit Ethernet Module

   d. Catalyst 3920 Series with a Catalyst Switch Matrix

8. Which of the following best describes over-subscription?

   a. Leaving adequate ports for future expansion.

   b. The total bandwidth of the ports is greater than the capacity of the switching fabric.

c. The switching fabric contains more bandwidth than the sum total of all the ports combined.

d. The rate at which packets are moved per second from the entry point to the exit point.

9. Which of the following switches supports the FlexWAN Module?

a. Catalyst 2980G

b. Catalyst 4000 Series

c. Catalyst 6000 Series

d. Catalyst 8500 Series

10. Which of the following terms best describes the switching fabric?

a. A series of electric traces located on the back of the chassis on which data is run

b. The "highway" the data takes to get from the port of entry to the exit port

c. The ability to process more bandwidth than the sum total of all the ports combined

d. The rate at which packets are moved per second from the entry point to the exit point

11. Which of the following would work best in the access layer of the network?

a. Cisco Catalyst 1924

b. Cisco Catalyst 5002

c. Cisco Catalyst 5509

d. Cisco Catalyst 6506

12. Which of the following terms best describes a backplane?

a. A series of electric traces located on the back of the chassis on which data is run

b. The "highway" the data takes to get from the port of entry to the exit port

c. The ability to process more bandwidth than the sum total of all the ports combined

d. The rate at which packets are moved per second from the entry point to the exit point

13. Which of the following uses a menu-driven interface?
    a. Catalyst 6000 Series
    b. Route Switch Module
    c. Catalyst 3000 Series
    d. Catalyst 2926G

14. Which switch does not use a Cisco IOS using the Set/Clear command set?
    a. Catalyst 2924 XL
    b. Catalyst 5002
    c. Catalyst 5505
    d. Catalyst 6509

15. All 12 ports on a Catalyst 1912 can be configured to use 100BaseT.
    a. True
    b. False

16. On a Cisco 5000 series switch, the primary Supervisor Engine card should be placed in which slot on the back of the chassis?
    a. Slot 1
    b. Slot 2
    c. Slot 3
    d. Slot 4

17. How many slots can be found on the chassis of a Cisco Catalyst 5500?
    a. 5
    b. 9
    c. 13
    d. 2

18. The Catalyst 5000 family of switches supports which of the following Supervisor Engines?
    a. Supervisor Engine I
    b. Supervisor Engine II
    c. Supervisor Engine III
    d. All of the above
    e. None of the above

19. Without using a Switch Probe Analyzer, which of the following groups is not a supported RMON group on a Cisco Catalyst switch?
    a. Event Group
    b. Alarm Group
    c. Policy Group
    d. Statistics Group
    e. History Group
20. Which of the following series of switches has not received an end-of-life notice?
    a. Catalyst 3000
    b. Catalyst 3900
    c. Catalyst 2820
    d. None of the above

Real-World Projects

Let's meet Joe Snow, CCIE. He is our imaginary technical guru, who will walk you through his work assignments in the "Real-World Projects" section found at the end of each chapter throughout the rest of this book.

Joe works for an imaginary Cisco Systems consulting company that supports and creates somc of the largest imaginary networks in the world—including the network of the publishers of this book, The Coriolis Group.

Today, Joe will be involved in designing three networks of different sizes for a large hospital. The main hospital network is large, consisting of about 1,000 users. The second is a medium-size network of about 500 users, for the hospital's medical billing office. The third network will consist of about 22 users in the hospital administration building; these users provide computer desktop and server support for the entire network.

Each building houses a different number of users and a different type of user and requires a different networking solution. In the next three projects, Joe will decide the best routing and switching solution for each network.

Take a look at a diagram of what the networks will look like when Joe is finished. Figure 4.22 diagrams each building and the campus switching layers that must contain the correct networking equipment for the job that they must perform. Joe needs to create a small network, a medium-size network, and a very large network, and then mesh them together to communicate successfully without network bottlenecks.

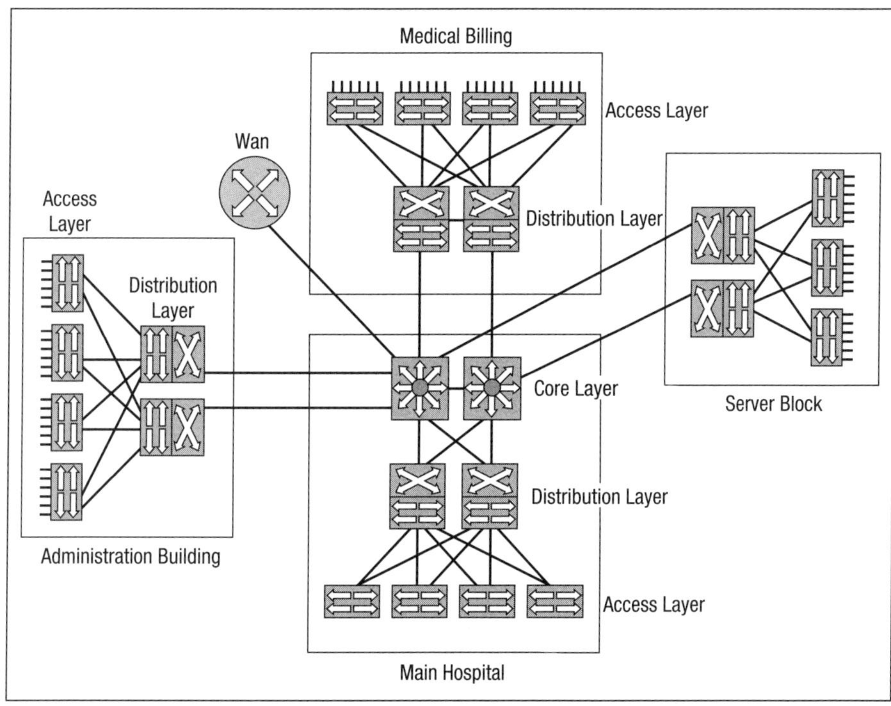

Figure 4.22 The main hospital building, administration building, server block, and medical billing building, and the campus switching layers at which data is switched.

4

Project 4.1

To place the correct switches at each layer of the main hospital building, Joe performed the following:

1. Joe needs to determine the type of traffic being used at the access layer. After some querying, he has determined that there are no high-end users in this building. The building's users are mainly doctors and nurses entering text patient information, using Microsoft Office products, Microsoft Exchange email, and some Internet applications. However, the customer has requested that Joe's company provide for future expansion via 100Mbps links to the desktops and printers, as well as expansion for up to 100 more users.
2. Joe needs to determine what types of policy routing to use and whether Layer 3 solutions are needed at the distribution layer. At this point, he must assess whether the hospital needs inter-VLAN routing, Internet access, and access to other buildings, in determining which types of switches are required. Joe will add two identical switches for redundancy at this layer. He has decided to divide the network into small broadcast domains and assign port-based

static VLANs to separate the users in different departments such as the Emergency Room, Pediatrics, Adult Medicine, and so on. As a result, he must use a switch with a route processor to provide Layer 3 routing ability.

3. The core layer will reside in the main building on the campus. Therefore, a very powerful Catalyst switch must reside here.

Joe made the following switch decisions for this location of the campus:

- Two Catalyst 8500 Series switches at the core layer
- Two Cisco Catalyst 6500 Series switches equipped with two 8-port Gigabit Switching Modules and a Multilayer Switch Module (MSM) for the distribution layer
- Fourteen Catalyst 2980G switches at the access layer, providing 1,120 10/100 ports and a gigabit link between each access layer switch and each distribution layer switch

Project 4.2

To place the correct switches at the server block in the main hospital building, Joe performed the following:

1. Joe must assess the number of servers needing access to the network at the access layer. He has determined that 12 Compaq 3500 servers provide services to the rest of the network. Each uses a 100BaseT Ethernet NIC at full-duplex. In order to keep from producing bottlenecks between the access layer switch and the distribution layer switch, Joe needs to provide gigabit trunk links between the servers. (Trunk links are covered in depth in Chapters 8 through 10.)

2. Joe must assess the needs of the distribution layer. Because he is already using VLANs, Ethernet, and switching between sites, this assessment becomes easier.

In the access layer, Joe chose to place two Catalyst 2926GS switches, each containing twenty-four 10/100 ports and two gigabit uplink ports. In the distribution layer, he chose two Cisco Catalyst 5000 Series switches with an RSM and two 2-port Gigabit Ethernet Modules for trunk ports to the core layer and the access layer switches.

Project 4.3

To place the correct switches in the medical billing office building, Joe performed the following:

1. Joe must assess the needs of the users at the access layer of the network. These are low-end users utilizing some company database applications, Microsoft Office products, and email.
2. In the distribution layer, the same theories apply here as for the main hospital building, with the exception that there are about half as many users.

Joe decided that at the access layer he will use 1900 Series switches, because there was no request to use anything other than 10Mbps and this environment has no high-end usage. These switches will yield a great per-port cost savings to the company, as well. In the distribution layer, he has decided to install a Catalyst 5000 Series switch with an RSM and 10/100 uplinks to the access layer switches and gigabit uplinks to the core layer switches.

Project 4.4

To place the correct switches in the administration office building, Joe performed the following:

1. Joe's evaluation for the access layer from the staff is that this site has only 22 employees, but they do considerable multimedia training. They would like to have the ability to utilize 100Mbps speeds and have separate VLANs for their server support and desktop support decisions.
2. Joe's decisions in this building are easy again. VLANs are implemented, and the users are considered high-end because of their needs.

Joe's decision is to place two Catalyst 4000G Series switches (one for redundancy) at the distribution layer to provide gigabit uplinks to the core layer. For the access layer, Joe has decided to use two Catalyst 2924 XLs, to provide forty-eight 10/100 ports.

CHAPTER FIVE

5

CONFIGURING A CISCO SWITCH

After completing this chapter, you will be able to:

- ✓ Identify the different media types that connect to a Cisco switch
- ✓ Identify the limitations of the media types
- ✓ Understand the differences between Ethernet, Fast Ethernet, and Gigabit Ethernet
- ✓ Explain where the different media types are commonly deployed
- ✓ Connect to a switch console
- ✓ Understand how to configure port settings for speed and duplexing
- ✓ Use the command-line interface to perform basic configuration

Here is the chapter you've been waiting for—how to configure a Cisco switch and plug devices into it. This chapter discusses the basic configuration steps that need to be considered when you initially set up a Cisco switch. In later chapters we will get into more advanced topics, but for now, we will cover the initial steps in configuring a Cisco switch.

As a result of Cisco's acquisition of several switching vendors (Kalpana, Crescendo, and others), Cisco switches have a variety of command-line interfaces you need to be familiar with to set up and maintain the devices. The most common, found on the Catalyst 5000/5500 line of switches, as well as the 2926, 2926G, 2948G, 4000, and 6000 Series, is the original Crescendo interface. This interface is often termed the Set/Clear interface, because these switches are limited to Set, Clear, and Show commands.

A second type of interface is found on more recent models of the 1900/2820 and the 2900 XL. The Enterprise Edition Software of these switches uses the standard Cisco IOS found on Cisco's line of routers.

A third type of interface is found on the Cisco Catalyst 1900/2820 and 3000 Series of switches. These devices have a menu-driven interface that you use to enter commands. The menu selections are pretty intuitive, so you don't have to memorize a lot of commands to work with the switches.

Regardless of the type of interface used, you'll need to perform certain common tasks on any switch. On most switches, you will need to connect to the console port and begin the initial configuration of the device.

In this stage, you can assign the switch a unique hostname to identify it. For security reasons, you should change the default password and add an enable password. You will probably want to assign an IP address, subnet mask, and default route for management purposes.

Once the switch has been configured, you can connect it to the rest of the network. There are many options for the type of physical medium to use. In this chapter we will discuss using the Ethernet, Fast Ethernet, and Gigabit Ethernet media types and we will explain the benefits and limitations of each. In addition, we will discuss where these different technologies could or should be used.

There are two types of connections to a switch: the connection to the switch console where you configure the switch or monitor the network and an Ethernet port on the switch. That is where we will begin our discussion for this chapter.

Connecting to the Switch Block

Among the high-speed LAN technologies available today, there is near-universal acceptance of the 10BaseT Ethernet standard. Building on this success, Fast Ethernet technology provides a smooth, non-disruptive evolution to better performance.

The growing use of 100BaseT connections to servers and desktops, however, has created a clear need for an even higher-speed network technology at the backbone and server level. Ideally, this technology should also provide a smooth upgrade path, be cost effective, and not require retraining. One appropriate solution is Gigabit Ethernet.

Gigabit Ethernet provides 1Gbps bandwidth for campus networks while still retaining the simplicity of Ethernet. It also allows organizations to leverage their existing infrastructure and network knowledge and training.

This section will examine the different methods used to connect to the switch block and illustrate where it is feasible to use these technologies.

Media Types

As the demand for network bandwidth has increased, so has the need to find better ways to use the network. Ethernet technology has become an essential media type owing mostly to its ability to adapt to new requirements, its relative simplicity, and the huge core of engineers who understand it.

Many other technologies have been advocated as more suitable replacements, such as Asynchronous Transfer Mode (ATM) or Fiber Distributed Data Interface (FDDI). Ethernet and its derivatives are by far the most widely used solutions for a wide range of network requirements.

To resolve Ethernet's limitations, engineers and standards organizations have tweaked the original Ethernet 802.3 technology to create larger network pipes. This is not your daddy's Ethernet! In this section, we will discuss the different media types that can connect to a Cisco switch and their benefits and limitations.

Ethernet

Ethernet has been around since the early 1970s. It was originally designed to run in environments that had fairly low demands with the occasional burst of heavy traffic. It was not really designed to function in today's high-demand, heavy-bandwidth traffic. As a Carrier Sense Multiple Access Collision Detection (CSMA/CD) environment, Ethernet allows any station on the network to transmit whenever the network is quiet. As has been mentioned previously, this freedom can cause significant performance issues. However, for smaller environments, this type of technology may be a good fit. There are several Ethernet media types.

10BaseT (twisted pair) is the most prevalent type of Ethernet. It is also the most economical cable type, because it is probably already installed in most companies, and it is quite easy to manipulate. 10BaseT segments support a maximum of two devices: the switch port and the device. These segments are limited to a maximum of 100 meters (328 feet). Particular attention must be given to patch panel connections common in many organizations. In these environments, a patch panel cable up to 5 meters in length is used on each end, so the cable run should be no longer than 90 meters.

The specifications allow the use of Category 3 or 4 Unshielded Twisted Pair (UTP) cable, but Category 5 is a better cable to use because it also supports 100BaseT (Fast Ethernet) and will help prevent re-cabling if you move to the faster technologies. 10BaseT is not recommended for installations with high levels of electromagnetic interference (EMI) or radio frequency interference (RFI), commonly referred to as EMI/RFI. This interference can disrupt the flow of data on the wire and result in retransmissions and wasted bandwidth.

For these types of environments, 10BaseFL is a better use. Fiber cable transmits data as light pulses rather than electrical charges, so EMI/RFI interference is not an issue. 10BaseFL segments can be a maximum length of 2000 meters (6561 feet).

Ethernet 10BaseT or 10BaseFL is used for providing connectivity from an end workstation to a switch port located at the access layer. It is generally not used on a distribution or core layer.

Fast Ethernet

Fast Ethernet (100BaseT) is an extension of the IEEE 802.3 Ethernet standard. It is a high-speed LAN technology that provides increased bandwidth for the devices on the network. A benefit of 100BaseT is that it retains the characteristics of the existing LAN technologies. It is easily integrated into existing 10Mbps Ethernet LANs, so re-cabling is not needed and applications don't need to be rewritten. It's also backed by a wide array of equipment manufacturers in the networking industry.

Fast Ethernet supports a broad range of cabling options. There are three standards for Fast Ethernet:

- 100BaseTX
- 100BaseT4
- 100BaseFL

Table 5.1 Fast Ethernet features.

Features	100BaseTX	100BaseT4	100BaseFL
Cable type	Category 5 UTP	Category 3, 4, or 5 UTP	62.5/125-micron multimode fiber
Cable pairs or strands	2 pairs	2 or 4 pairs	2 strands
Connector type	RJ-45	RJ-45	Duplex SC MIC ST
Maximum length	100 meters	100 meters	400 meters
Maximum diameter	205 meters	200 meters	400 meters

The characteristics of each of these technologies are summed up in Table 5.1.

Because 100BaseT and 10BaseT use the same IEEE 802.3 MAC access and collision detection methods, they also retain the same frame format and length requirements. In fact, the chief difference between the two, other than the tenfold increase in speed, is a reduction in the network diameter. The maximum network diameter for a 100BaseTX network is 205 meters, which is approximately 10 times less than 10BaseFL (2000 meters).

This change is due to the collision-detection scheme used by both technologies, which requires a station to know within the first 64 bytes of transmission that a collision has taken place with another station. Because the actual medium is not changed, a station transmitting 10 times faster must have a maximum distance that is 10 times less.

Fast Ethernet is used on all layers of the campus model. It is used on the access layer, typically to provide connectivity for high-end workstations. It is also used on the distribution layer to provide connectivity between the access layer and the distribution layer, between the distribution layer and the core layer, and between servers on the core layer.

Gigabit Ethernet

Like Fast Ethernet, Gigabit Ethernet is an extension of the IEEE 802.3 Ethernet standard. Gigabit Ethernet builds on the Ethernet protocol but increases speed tenfold over Fast Ethernet, to 1000Mbps (1Gbps). This standard is rapidly becoming a proven method to provide high-speed LAN backbones. As in Fast Ethernet, Gigabit Ethernet is able to take advantage of the existing network infrastructure and knowledge base.

As in Fast Ethernet, Gigabit Ethernet looks identical to Ethernet from the data link layer upward, and compromises were made to provide the boost in speed from 100Mbps to 1Gbps. In order to make the data link layer look similar to those of Ethernet and Fast Ethernet, two standards were merged: IEEE 802.3 Ethernet and ANSI X3T11 fiber channel. Merging these two technologies allowed the standard to take advantage of the existing high-speed physical interface technology of fiber channel and still retain backward compatibility to the IEEE 802.3 frame format.

However, Gigabit Ethernet differs from its predecessors in several ways that affect its deployment and network design. For one thing, Gigabit Ethernet relies on a modified MAC layer, which affects network size and utilization. For another, it uses frame bursting. And, its cabling requirements are very different.

Let's take the MAC layer modifications first. If you recall our discussions about the implementation of Fast Ethernet, it maintained the Ethernet framing format and raised the speed to100Mbps. This increase shrank the network diameter from 2 kilometers for 10BaseFL to 200 meters for 100BaseT.

If we applied the same reasoning to Gigabit Ethernet, that would result in a network diameter of 20 meters—not a particularly useful distance. In order to provide the same network diameter of 200 meters, a mechanism known as *carrier extension* was used. Carrier extension adds bits to the frame until the frame meets the minimum time for Ethernet MAC to handle collisions (known as *slot time*). As a result, smaller packet sizes can meet the minimum slot time and allow seamless operation with current Ethernet CSMA/CD.

Another change to the Ethernet specification is the addition of frame bursting. *Frame bursting* is a method that allows an end station to transmit a burst of frames over the wire without having to relinquish control, as long as there is no idle time on the wire. The transmitting station that is bursting onto the wire fills the interframe interval with extension bits so that the wire never appears free to any other end station.

Cabling is another key way that Gigabit Ethernet differs from its predecessors. Gigabit Ethernet is supported over two types of multimode fiber: 62.5-micron and 50-micron diameter fibers. The 62.5-micron fiber is typically seen in vertical campus and building cable plants and has been used for Ethernet, Fast Ethernet, and FDDI backbone traffic.

This type of fiber, however, has a lower *modal bandwidth* (the ability of the cable to transmit light), especially with short-wave lasers. This means that short-wave lasers over 62.5-micron fibers are able to transverse shorter distances than long-wave lasers. The 50-micron fiber has significantly better modal bandwidth characteristics and can go over longer distances with short-wave lasers relative to 62.5-micron fiber. The distance limitations are shown in Table 5.2.

The most likely applications for Gigabit Ethernet are for campuses or buildings that require greater bandwidth between routers, switches, hubs, repeaters, and servers on the distribution and core layers of the campus model. These types of

Table 5.2 Distance limitations that apply to Gigabit Ethernet.

Standard	Fiber Type	Diameter (in Microns)	Distance (in Meters)
1000BaseSX	MM	62.5	2 to 220
	MM	62.5	2 to 275
	MM	50	2 to 500
	MM	50	2 to 550
1000BaseLX	MM	62.5	2 to 550
	MM	50	2 to 550
	MM	50	2 to 550
	SM	9	2 to 5000
1000BaseCX	n/a		25
1000BaseT	n/a		100

connections can include switch-to-router, switch-to-switch, and switch-to-server connections. Gigabit Ethernet is not likely to be widely deployed to the desktop, although it may be used in certain high-performance environments.

Connecting to the Console Port

Instructions to the switch are entered via the console port. The console comes pre-configured and ready to use. You gain access to the console port in a couple of ways, as shown in Figure 5.1.

If the console port is an RJ-45 port, you can plug a rolled RJ-45 cable straight into the port. If it is a DB-25 style, you will need to use an RJ-45 to DB-25 connector to connect to it.

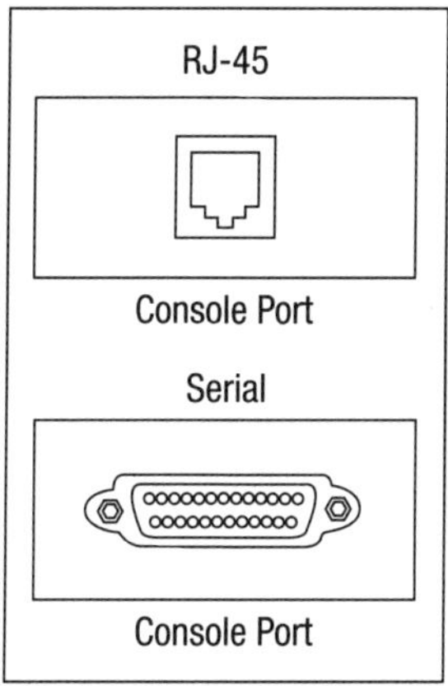

Figure 5.1 The different types of consoles.

Whatever the type of console port in use on the switch, you will need to connect an RJ-45 cable from the console port or connector to a dumb terminal. You can also use the more popular method of a third-party program, such as HyperTerminal, to gain access. After a switch has been configured with an IP address, you can also use Telnet to gain access to the switch.

Types of RJ-45 Cabling

There are two types of RJ-45 cabling: straight and rolled. You can tell what type of cable it is by holding the two ends of an RJ-45 cable side by side. You will see eight colored strips, or pins, at each end. If the order of the colored pins matches at both ends, then it is a straight-through cable. If the colors are reversed, then you have a rolled cable. Cisco switches will include the appropriate type of console cable with each purchase. Cisco switches, with the exception of the Cisco Catalyst 6500 line, use the rolled type of cable.

Types of RJ-45 to DB-25 Connectors

Cisco uses two types of RJ-45 to DB-25 connectors. One is the Data Communications Equipment (DCE) style that is used for modem connections, and the other is the Data Terminal Equipment (DTE) style used to connect to terminals or PCs.

Cable Pinouts

RS232 communication involves using control signals between a DTE device and a DCE device. The following control signals implement most of the important functions of an R232 DTE to DCE link:

- *Request to send (RTS)*—A signal from the DTE to the DCE. RTS tells the DCE that the DTE wishes to transmit data.
- *Clear to send (CTS)*—A signal from the DCE to the DTE. It is used to show that the DCE is ready to receive data from the DTE.
- *Data set ready (DSR)*—A signal from the DCE to the DTE. It is used to indicate that the DCE is able to receive from the DTE. DSR indicates that the device is switched on and is in its normal functioning mode.
- *Data terminal ready (DTR)*—A signal from the DTE to the DCE. DTR indicates that the DTE is ready to accept data from the DCE. This signal is used to keep the channel open and maintain the connection. If DTR is not present, the communication path is broken.

Other important terms used in serial communication are *TXD*, which is the term used to indicate the connector that data is transmitted on, and *RXD*, which is used to indicate the connector that data is received on.

Table 5.3 shows the pinouts for RJ-45 console and AUX ports. Table 5.4 shows the pinouts for RJ-45 to DB-25 connectors. Table 5.5 shows DB-25 to DB-9 adapter pinouts.

Connecting the Console to a PC

For connections to a personal computer, you will need to use the DTE adapter that has RJ-45 to DB-9 female connection ends. For a Unix

Table 5.3 RJ-45 console cable pinouts for RJ-45 to DB-9 connection.

Pin	Signal	Input/Output
1	RTS	Out
2	DTR	Out
3	TXD	Out
4	GND	n/a
5	GND	n/a
6	RXD	In
7	DSR	In
8	CTS	In

Table 5.4 RJ-45 to DB-25 connectors.

RJ-45	DTE	DCE
1	4	5
2	20	8
3	2	3
4	7	7
5	7	7
6	3	2
7	6	20
8	5	4

Table 5.5 DB-25 to DB-9 adapter pinouts.

DB-25	Signal	DB-9
2	TXD	3
3	RXD	2
4	RTS	7
5	CTS	8
6	DSR	6
7	GND	5
8	DCD	1
20	DTR	4

workstation, you should use the RJ-45 to DB-25 female adapter. If you are connecting with a modem, choose the adapter similar to the Unix workstation adapter, but with a DB-25 male end.

Warning: Remember—never connect an active network cable, ISDN line, or telephone line directly into your switch! It might do serious harm to the switch. Only use the supplied console cable that came with your switch or a suitably configured cable to connect the console to another device.

Now that we've shown the different combinations of connectors and adapters that can exist, let's take a look at what types of console ports are on the Cisco switches.

Types of Console Ports

On the 1900, 2800, and 2900 XL Series switches, you will find an RJ-45 console port. When connecting to the console port, Cisco recommends you use a straight-through Category 5 cable. The Catalyst 3000 uses a DB-9 type connector to access the console port. The Catalyst 5000 line uses a Supervisor Engine. To connect to a console on a Supervisor Engine I or II, you use a DB-25 connection. If the switch uses a Supervisor Engine III, you use the RJ-45 to RJ-45 rollover cable.

The Catalyst 6000 family also uses a Supervisor Engine with an RJ-45 style of connector. To access this console port, you use the RJ-45 to RJ-45 straight-through cable.

Note: *Console port settings by default are 9600 baud, 8 data bits, 1 stop bit, and no parity.*

Configuring the Switch

Three types of Cisco operating systems are in use. They are summarized as follows:

- *Cisco IOS-based command line*—Found on Catalyst 1900/2820, 2900 XL, and 8500 Series models. The commands used in this interface are similar to the ones used on the Cisco IOS-based routers.
- *Set/Clear interface*—Found on models of the Catalyst 2926, 2926G, 2948G, 4000, 5000, 5500, 6000, and 6500 Series of switches. They are termed Set/Clear because these commands (and Show) are the only commands on this type of device.
- *Menu-driven*—Found exclusively on the Catalyst 3000 family.

Default Configuration

You have to do very little in order to get a Cisco switch to work. The switches are designed to be plug-and-play devices: Basically, you turn the switches on, plug devices into the ports, and away you go. By default, Cisco switches have the following default attributes:

- The prompt name is set to **Console>**.
- No hostname for the switch is defined.
- No passwords are set (just press Enter and you're in).
- All ports are in VLAN1.
- The console interface is in VLAN1 and has no IP information.
- No contact name or location information is defined.
- Remote Network Monitoring (RMON) is disabled.
- Simple Network Management Protocol (SNMP) traps are disabled. SNMP community strings are *public* for read-only, *private* for read-write, and *secret* for read-write-all access.
- Virtual Trunk Protocol (VTP) mode is set to Server. No VTP domain, password, or pruning information is configured.
- All VLANs are eligible for trunking. Inter-Switch Link (ISL) is set to Auto.

Switch Setup Tasks

On any switch, you should perform a few tasks regardless of the command-line interface in use. Although these tasks are not mandatory, they will help you immensely to better manage the switch. These tasks are:

- Set login and enable passwords for security.
- Change the console prompt to something meaningful.
- Enter contact name and location information.
- Configure an IP address and netmask for a management interface. Doing so will enable you to Telnet into the switch later.
- Set up a default route and gateway.
- Set up speed and duplex port settings.
- Define port names for descriptive purposes.
- Enable SNMP to report to a Network Management System.

Basic Configuration Tasks for Set/Clear Devices

The command-line interface (CLI) of a Set/Clear interface is based on Unix, so certain c-shell commands can be issued to recall commands issued previously. The switch by default stores the previous 20 commands in its buffer. Unlike the Cisco IOS routers or switches, the up arrows do not work. However, you can use the key sequences shown in Table 5.6 to recall or modify commands.

Logging On to a Switch

To begin configuring your switch, connect the console cable or connector to a terminal or PC. If the device is not powered up, turn it on now. The switch will then go through its initial Power-On Self-Test (POST) routines. It will run tests that check for the reliability of the switch components, including ports, line modules, backplane, and other electronic components. Once it has successfully (we hope!) completed these tasks, you will see a prompt that says:

```
Enter Password:
```

Because no password has been set, just press the Enter key to continue. This switch will respond with a **Console>** prompt, because it has not been configured with a host name by default.

Cisco switches have two levels of access by default: User Mode and Privileged Mode. User Mode will allow you to do some basic tasks, such as showing port or VLAN information. In order to see the configuration or modify it, you need to be in Privileged Mode. Enter Privileged Mode in the following manner:

```
Console> enable
Enter password:
```

Table 5.6 Command recall key sequences.

Key Sequence	Action
!!	Repeat the last command
!-*nn*	Repeat the *nn*th number of commands
!*n*	Repeat command *n* in list
!zzz	Repeat the command that starts with the zzz string
!?zzz	Repeat the command containing the zzz string
^*yyy*^zzz	Replace the string *yyy* with zzz in the previous command
!!zzz	Add the string zzz to the previous command
!*n* zzz	Add the string zzz to command *n*
!*yyy* zzz	Add the string zzz to the end of the command that begins with *yyy*
!?*yyy* zzz	Add the string zzz to the end of the command containing *yyy*

Once again, because no Privileged password has been set up, just pressing Enter will put you into Privileged Mode. The console will respond with this prompt to indicate that it is in Privileged Mode:

```
Console> (enable)
```

At this point you are in Privileged Mode and can begin entering commands. We will now step through the process of setting up a basic configuration on a Catalyst switch.

Task 1: Set Up Login and Enable Passwords

As you can see from the previous sequence, Cisco switches are shipped without a User or Privileged Mode password. Although this is fine for initially gaining access to a switch, it is a gigantic security hole to leave open. You should also set up passwords to prevent unauthorized access to your switch. To set a password for user access, do the following (in Privileged Mode):

```
Console> (enable)  set password
Enter old password:  Press Enter
Enter new password: newone
Retype new password: newone
Password changed.
```

Warning: Configuration changes are executed and saved to memory immediately.

As you can see, the system will prompt you for the old password. Because this is a new setup, press Enter to continue; the system will then ask you to enter the new password. Enter the password of your choice. For security purposes, the password will be masked. The system will then ask you to re-enter the password. This sequence changes the user password. To change the Privileged Mode password, enter the following:

```
Console> (enable) set enablepass
Enter old password: Press Enter
Enter new password: newone
Retype new password: newone
Password changed.
```

Notice that **enablepass** is all one word.

Tip: Some of the commands can be difficult to remember. Note that at any time you can type "?" or "help" to access the CLI help facility. For help on specific commands, you can enter the command followed by a question mark; for example, **set ?** or **set help**.

Task 2: Change the System Prompt

You may have noticed in the preceding examples that the switch console is by default **Console>**. Because you may have many switches in your environment, it is a good idea to uniquely name the switch in such a way that you can readily identify it. (It can be pretty embarrassing to shut down the wrong switch in the middle of the day!) To change your switch host name, use the following command:

```
Console> (enable) set prompt IS-Catalyst
IS-Catalyst> (enable)
```

Notice the change in the switch prompt.

Task 3: Define System Information

SNMP management stations and Cisco Discovery Protocol (CDP) use the system information you enter to identify the switch. It is a good idea to set the correct data and time so error or log messages will be easier to understand. To make changes to the system information, use commands like the following:

```
Console> (enable) set system contact Al Begone
Console> (enable) set system location Wiring Closet 2
Console> (enable) set system name IS-Catalyst
Console> (enable) set time Mon 02/07/00 23:59:00
```

Task 4: Configure IP Information for Console Port

Before you can Telnet, ping, or otherwise manage the switch remotely, you need to define an IP address and netmask for the console port and assign it to a VLAN. By default, the switch console is in VLAN1. The syntax for setting up a console interface is:

```
Console> (enable) set interface sc0 [vlan] [ip address] [subnet mask]
[broadcast address]
```

For example, to set up a console address with the IP address 192.168.1.1 and a netmask of 255.255.255.0 in VLAN2, you would enter the following command:

```
Console> (enable) set interface sc0 2 192.168.1.1 255.255.255.0
Interface sc0 vlan set, IP address and netmask set.
```

Note: *It is only necessary to enter the broadcast address if it is something other than a class A, B, or C address.*

Serial Line Internet Protocol (SLIP) access can also be set up for the console port. SLIP is an older method of connecting to network devices. When you configure the SLIP (sl0) interface, you can open a point-to-point connection to the switch through the console port from a workstation. The command syntax for configuring a SLIP interface is:

```
Console> (enable) set interface sl0 slip_addr dest_addr
```

To configure a SLIP interface, enter the following:

```
Console> (enable) set interface sl0 192.168.1.1 192.168.1.2
Interface sl0 slip and destination address set.
Console> (enable) slip attach
Port now running SLIP.
```


Warning: The console port must be used for the SLIP connection. If you use the console port to access the switch when you enter the **slip attach** command, you will lose the console port connection. When the SLIP connection is enabled and SLIP is attached on the console port, an EIA/TIA-232 terminal cannot connect through the console port.

To see the interface IP information you have entered, enter the following command:

```
Console> (enable) show interface
sl0: flags=51<UP,POINTOPOINT,RUNNING>
    slip 192.168.1.1 dest 192.168.1.2
sc0: flags=63<UP,BROADCAST,RUNNING>
    vlan 1 inet 192.168.1.1 netmask 255.255.255.0 broadcast 192.168.1.1
Console> (enable)
```

Task 5: Set Up a Default IP Route and Gateway

You can define up to three default IP gateways on a switch. Use the **primary** keyword to make a gateway the primary gateway. If a primary default gateway is not defined, the first gateway configured is the primary gateway. If multiple gateways are defined, the last primary gateway configured is the primary default gateway.

All network traffic for destinations outside the current subnet of the console port is sent to the primary default gateway. If the primary gateway is lost, the switch attempts to use the backup gateways in the order they were configured. The switch sends periodic ping messages to determine whether each default gateway is up or down. If connectivity to the primary gateway is restored, the switch resumes sending traffic to the primary. The following commands show how to set up default IP routes:

```
Console> (enable) set ip route default 192.168.1.3
Route added.
```

```
Console> (enable) set ip route default 192.168.1.2
Route added.
Console> (enable) set ip route default 192.168.1.1 primary
Route added.
```

To see the default routes, enter the following command:

```
Console> (enable) show ip route
Fragmentation   Redirect   Unreachable
-------------   --------   -----------
enabled         enabled    enabled

The primary gateway: 192.168.1.1
Destination    Gateway        RouteMask    Flags   Use     Interface
-----------    -------        ---------    -----   ---     ---------
default        192.168.1.1     0x0          UG     100          sc0
default        192.168.1.2     0x0          G        0          sc0
default        192.168.1.3     0x0          G        0          sc0
```

Task 6: Set Up Port Speed and Duplex Settings

You can manually set the speed for 10/100 ports. You will sometimes need to do so if the devices cannot autonegotiate the speed correctly. This is a frequent occurrence in environments that have several different kinds of devices and NIC cards (isn't that everybody?). The syntax of the command is:

```
Set port speed module_number/port_number 10|100|auto
```

For example, to configure the second port on module 3 to auto, use the following command:

```
Console> (enable) set port speed 3/2 auto
Port 3/2 set to auto-sensing mode.
```

Note: *Setting a port speed to auto also enables auto duplexing.*

You can also enter multiple ports. You can specify a range of ports or multiple ports separated by commas. For example, to configure ports 3, 4, and 5 on module 3 to be 10Mbps, use the following command:

```
Console> (enable) set port speed 3/3-5 10
Port 3/3-5 set to 10Mbps
```

To manually set a port for full or half duplex, use the following command:

```
Console> (enable) set port duplex 3/2 half
Port 3/2 set to half-duplex.
```

Task 7: Enable SNMP

SNMP is used by Network Management Stations (NMS) to monitor and control your network. SNMP can be configured to generate traps when changes or problems occur on a switch. SNMP has three components:

- Managed devices (such as a switch)
- Management agents that run on managed devices—referred to as Management Information Base (MIBs)
- Management applications, such as HP Openview or CiscoWorks2000, that communicate with agents to get statistics and alerts from the managed devices

5

There are three levels of access for SNMP. The levels of access are dependent on the type of community string the device accessing the switch has configured. The community strings for a Catalyst switch are:

- *Read-Only*—Allows the management station to read the SNMP information and nothing more.
- *Read-Write*—Allows a management station to set any SNMP parameter on the switch except the community strings themselves.
- *Read-Write-All*—Allows full access and control to the SNMP information and community strings.

The following example commands set up the SNMP community strings and define which management stations receive the information:

```
Console> (enable) set snmp community read-only kings
SNMP read-only community string set to 'kings'.
Console> (enable) set snmp community read-write lakers
SNMP read-write community string set to 'lakers'.
Console> (enable) set snmp community read-write-all celtics
SNMP read-write-all community string set to 'celtics'.
Console> (enable) set snmp trap 192.168.1.1 read-write
SNMP trap receiver added.
Console> (enable) set snmp trap 192.168.1.2 read-write-all
SNMP trap receiver added.
Console> (enable) set snmp trap enable all
All SNMP traps enabled.
```

Basic Configuration Tasks for IOS-Based Devices

The CLI of IOS-based switches is similar to the IOS-based routers. Commands can be recalled by using the up or down arrows or using a combination of control or escape sequences to do certain editing functions to the command-line history buffers. Table 5.7 summarizes the editing commands on an IOS-based switch.

Table 5.7 Command editing keys and functions.

Key	Function
Tab	Completes a partial command name
Delete	Erases the character to the left of the cursor
Enter	Performs a command
Space	Scrolls down a page
Left arrow	Moves a character to the left
Right arrow	Moves a character to the right
Up arrow	Recalls commands in the history buffer
Down arrow	Returns to more recent commands
Ctrl+A	Moves to the beginning of the line
Ctrl+B	Moves back one character
Ctrl+D	Deletes a character
Ctrl+E	Moves to the end of the command line
Ctrl+F	Moves forward one character
Ctrl+K	Deletes all characters to the end of the line
Ctrl+L	Redisplays the system prompt and command line
Ctrl+T	Transposes the character to the left of the cursor with the character at the cursor
Ctrl+U	Deletes all characters to the beginning of the command
Ctrl+V	Indicates that the next keystroke is a command
Ctrl+W	Deletes to the left of the cursor
Ctrl+Y	Recalls the most recently deleted command
Ctrl+Z	Ends Configuration Mode and returns you to EXEC Mode

On an IOS-based switch, you can access many commands modes to enter commands. The following detail some of the more important modes:

- *EXEC Mode*—When you log in to a switch, you are automatically in user EXEC command mode. The EXEC commands are a subset of those available at the Privileged level. In general, EXEC commands allow you to test connectivity, perform basic tests, and list system information.
- *Privileged EXEC Mode*—The Privileged command set includes those commands contained in user EXEC Mode, as well as the **configure** command, through which you can access the remaining command modes. Privileged EXEC Mode also includes high-level testing commands, such as **debug**.
- *Global Configuration Mode*—Global Configuration commands apply to features that affect the system as a whole. Use the **configure** Privileged EXEC command to enter Global Configuration Mode.

- *Interface Configuration Mode*—Many features are enabled on a per-interface basis. Interface Configuration commands modify the operation of an interface such as an Ethernet port or a VLAN.

We will now step through the process of setting up a basic configuration on a Catalyst switch that's IOS-based.

Task 1: Set Up Login and Enable Passwords

Just like the Set/Clear devices, by default the Cisco IOS-based switches have no password when they are shipped. On these switches, you can set levels of authority for console access. Two levels are defined on these switches: Privilege level 1 is User EXEC Mode, and privilege level 15 is Privileged EXEC Mode. To set up the user level and enable passwords on a Cisco IOS-based switch, enter the following commands:

```
Switch>  enable
Switch# configure terminal
Switch (config)  enable password level 1  letmein
Switch (config)  enable password level 15 power
```

Notice the change from the > to the #. This change indicates that the switch is now in Privileged EXEC Mode. Also notice the **(config)** prompt, which indicates that you are in Global Configuration Mode.

Task 2: Change the System Prompt

On a Cisco IOS-based switch, use the following command in Global Configuration Mode:

```
Switch (config) hostname IS-Catalyst
IS-Catalyst>
```

Note: *As soon as a command is entered in Global Configuration Mode, it takes effect. Be careful!*

Task 3: Define System Information

On Cisco IOS-based switches, no fields exist to enter contact information with the exception of SNMP information. Interfaces can be configured with description fields to describe their purpose or you can use some other method, but no overall description field is available. To set the system clock on an IOS-based switch and to put it in the PST time zone, use a command like the following:

```
Switch (config)  clock set 23:59:00 29 Feb 00
Switch (config)  clock timezone PST -8
```

Task 4: Set Up a Default IP Route and Gateway

To set up an IP address on a Cisco IOS-based switch, enter the following commands in Global Configuration Mode:

```
Switch (config) interface vlan 1
Switch (config-int) ip address 192.168.1.1 255.255.255.0
Switch (config-int) exit
Switch (config) ip default-gateway 192.168.1.2
Switch (config) end
```

This sequence demonstrates a couple of issues. Notice the change in prompts as you move from Global Configuration Mode to Interface Configuration Mode. Also notice the **exit** to return to Global Mode, and the **end** to get out of Configuration Mode entirely. No matter where you are, **end** will get you completely out of Configuration Mode.

Task 5: Set Up Port Speed and Duplex Settings

To connect to a remote 100BaseT device that does not autonegotiate, do not configure the duplex setting to be AUTO on the local device. Autonegotiation of the port speed works correctly even if the attached device does not autonegotiate. To configure port speed and duplex settings, enter the following commands in Global Configuration Mode:

```
Switch (config) interface FastEthernet 0/1
Switch (config-int) speed 100
Switch (config-int) duplex full
```

Task 6: Enable SNMP

You can set the system contact, location, and serial number of the SNMP agent so that these descriptions can be accessed through the configuration file. To do so, use one or more commands like the following in Global Configuration Mode:

```
Switch (config) snmp-server contact Ima Hurting
Switch (config) snmp-server location 3rd floor data center
Switch (config) snmp-server chassis-id 123456789
Switch (config) snmp-server community moe rw
Switch (config) snmp-server community larry ro
Switch (config) snmp-server community curly rwa
```

Chapter Summary

For those of you who are new to Cisco switches, this is one of the most important chapters in this book. This chapter probably answers many of your questions and lets you take a Cisco Catalyst switch out of the box and do something more than stare at the new paperweight.

During the first four chapters we didn't cover many of the media types and their properties that connect the parts of the network. One of the most important pieces of knowledge in networking is the distance limitations of the physical media between the patch panel and the end workstation. If you have an end user or network segment in your building next door and that building is 600 meters away from the closest patch panel, chances are there won't be a place for a repeater in the middle, and you'll have to use another type of physical media.

In this chapter we covered the most important aspects of basic switch configuration. It is important to have a basic understanding of switching technology, even if you plan to take some official training courses provided by Cisco Training Partners. When you pay to attend any certification course, one of the prerequisites is that you know the basics of switch configuration—they don't teach it. Therefore, this chapter is a blessing in disguise.

We aligned the basic switch configuration into six different tasks for an IOS command-based switch and another set for a Set/Clear command-based switch. We did this to make the steps easy to identify and find in the event that you are setting up a switch. Each task shows the different commands used to configure the switch for the assigned task. Here's what we showed in each task:

- *Task 1*—Setting up the login and enable passwords
- *Task 2*—Changing the system prompt
- *Task 3*—Defining the system information
- *Task 4*—Configuring IP information for the console port
- *Task 5*—Setting up a default IP route and a primary gateway
- *Task 6*—Configuring the port speed and duplex settings on the switch
- *Task 7*—Configuring Simple Network Management Protocol

Also remember the operating systems associated with each series of Cisco Catalyst switches:

- *Cisco IOS-based command line*—Found on Catalyst 1900/2820, 2900 XL, and 8500 Series models. The commands used in this interface are similar to the ones used on the Cisco IOS-based routers.
- *Set/Clear interface*—Found on models of the Catalyst 2926, 2926G, 2948G, 4000, 5000, 5500, 6000, and 6500 Series of switches. They are termed Set/Clear because these commands (and Show) are the only commands on this type of device.
- *Menu-driven*—Found exclusively on the Catalyst 3000 family.

The following is a list of important terms to remember from this chapter:

- *Fast Ethernet*—IEEE 802.3 specification for data transfers of up to 100Mbps.
- *Fiber Distributed Data Interface (FDDI)*—A high-speed data-transfer technology designed to extend the capabilities of existing local area networks using a dual-rotating ring technology similar to Token Ring.
- *Gigabit Ethernet*—IEEE specification for transfer rates up to one gigabit per second.
- *Unshielded twisted-pair (UTP)*—A type of cable that uses multiple twisted pairs of copper wire in a casing that does not provide much protection from EMI. The most common network cable in Ethernet networks, it is rated in five categories.

Review Questions

1. What is the maximum length of an Ethernet 10BaseT segment from the hub to another device interface?
   a. 100 meters
   b. 200 meters
   c. 2000 meters
   d. 20 feet
2. 400 meters is the maximum distance data can travel between two devices for what physical medium?
   a. Slow Ethernet
   b. Fast Ethernet (100BaseFX)
   c. Ethernet (10BaseT)
   d. 100BaseTX
3. What physical media types would you be more likely to find on the backbone of larger networks? [Choose the two best answers]
   a. FDDI
   b. Gigabit Ethernet
   c. 4MB Token Ring
   d. 10BaseT Ethernet

4. What standards emerged to create Gigabit Ethernet? [Choose the two best answers]
   a. ANSI X3T11
   b. IEEE 802.3
   c. IEEE 802.10
   d. ANSI Ethernet
5. Gigabit Ethernet supports what types of multimode fiber? [Choose the two best answers]
   a. 45.5-micron fiber
   b. 50-micron fiber
   c. 62.5-micron fiber
   d. 100-micron fiber
6. What type of media would you use in an environment with heavy electrical magnetic interference?
   a. Fast Ethernet
   b. Category 5 cable
   c. FDDI
   d. UTP
7. What are the types of RJ-45 cabling? [Choose the two best answers]
   a. Snipped
   b. Straight
   c. Cuffed
   d. Rolled
8. What are the types of RJ-45 to DB-25 connectors used by Cisco switches? [Choose the two best answers]
   a. STE
   b. MMF
   c. DCE
   d. DTE
9. Which series of switches do not use an IOS-based command-line interface? [Choose the two best answers]
   a. 5000 Series Catalyst switches
   b. 2820 Catalyst switch
   c. 4000 Series Catalyst switches
   d. 8500 Series Catalyst switches

10. Which is not part of a default configuration of a Cisco switch?
    a. The prompt name is set to **Console>**.
    b. No password is set.
    c. All VLANs are assigned to VLAN10.
    d. RMON is disabled.
11. Which command allows you to set a password at the Privileged Mode prompt of a Set/Clear-based switch?
    a. **set priv password**
    b. **set enable password**
    c. **set password**
    d. **set # password**
12. Which command allows you to set the system location to Coriolis in Privileged Mode on a Set/Clear-based switch?
    a. **set loc Coriolis**
    b. **set system location Coriolis**
    c. **set system name Coriolis**
    d. **set my system to Coriolis**
13. On an IOS-based CLI, when you immediately log in to the switch, what mode are you in?
    a. EXEC Mode
    b. Global Configuration Mode
    c. Privileged EXEC Mode
    d. Interface Configuration Mode
14. Which command would allow you assign a password for Privileged EXEC Mode on an IOS command-based switch?
    a. **set enable password**
    b. **enable password level 1**
    c. **enable password level 15**
    d. **enable my password**
15. What is the maximum length of 10BaseFL?
    a. 200 meters
    b. 2000 meters
    c. 100 meters
    d. 1000 meters

16. What key sequence will display the last command entered on a Cisco IOS-based switch?
    a. !!
    b. !1
    c. ??
    d. @1

17. What is the default password on Cisco switches?
    a. **cisco**
    b. **password**
    c. There is no default password
    d. **open**

18. On a Set/Clear interface, what command is used to configure the default gateway?
    a. **set ip route 192.168.1.2**
    b. **set gateway 192.168.1.2**
    c. **set ip route default 192.168.1.2**
    d. **set ip default gateway 192.168.1.2**

19. Which protocol is used to set up a PPP connection to a console port?
    a. PPP
    b. SLIP
    c. SLURP
    d. sc0

20. What is the command to set the default route on an IOS-based switch?
    a. **set ip route 0.0.0.0 0.0.0.0 192.168.1.2**
    b. **set ip route default 192.168.1.2**
    c. **ip route 0.0.0.0 0.0.0.0 192.168.1.2**
    d. **ip route default 192.168.1.2**

Real-World Projects

Let's meet Joe Snow. He is a computer consultant/technician with about eight years of experience, and he loves his job as a Cisco consultant. He is a mild-mannered technician who likes to set out with goals and resolve conflicts in switched Cisco networks. He uses a step-by-step approach.

Today, he has just gotten back from lunch to learn that UPS delivered a new Cisco Catalyst 5500 Series switch and a 2900 XL Series switch, both destined for The Coriolis Group. Before another technician takes the switches and installs them at the customer's site, the basic configuration needs to be done.

Joe's boss handed him a list of requirements from the sales person to aid in his configuration efforts.

Project 5.1

After reviewing the information from the sales consultant, Joe determined the following configuration tasks need to be performed on the Cisco Catalyst 5500:

- Set the user enable password to book1234
- Set the Privileged EXEC enable password to book4321
- Change the console prompt to **Coriolis5500**
- Enter the contact name as Joe Snow
- Enter the location information as Coriolis
- Enter the system time
- Configure the IP address 38.187.128.26 for the console port
- Configure an IP address to 38.187.128.25 and the subnet mask to 255.0.0.0
- Set up a default primary route and gateway to 38.187.128.1
- Assign the secondary route and gateway to 38.187.128.2

Knowing that the Catalyst 5500 Series switch is a Set/Clear command-line interface switch, take the following steps:

1. To begin configuring the switch, connect the console cable or connector to a terminal or PC. If the device is not powered up, do so now. The switch will then go through its initial Power-On Self-Test (POST) routines. After the switch has completed the initial POST, it should come to this prompt:

   ```
   Enter Password:
   ```

2. Because no password has been set, press the Enter key to continue.
3. In order to see the configuration or modify it, you need to be in Privileged Mode. Enter the **enable** command to enter Privileged Mode in the following manner:

```
Console> enable
Enter password:
```

Simply press the Enter key. The console will respond with this prompt to indicate that it is in Privileged Mode:

```
Console> (enable)
```

4. To set a password for user access, enter the following commands (in Privileged Mode):

```
Console> (enable)     set password
Enter old password:   Press Enter
Enter new password:   book1234
Retype new password: book1234
Password changed.
```

5. To change the Privileged Mode password, enter the following:

```
Console> (enable)     set enablepass
Enter old password:   Press Enter
Enter new password:   book4321
Retype new password: book4321
Password changed.
```

6. To change your switch host name, use the following command:

```
Console> (enable) set prompt coriolis5500
Coriolis5500(enable)
```

7. To make changes to the system information, use the following commands:

```
Coriolis5500(enable) set system contact Joe Snow-Technical Consulting
Coriolis5500(enable) set system location Coriolis Group
Coriolis5500(enable) set time Mon 06/05/00 23:59:00
```

8. To set up a console address with the IP address 38.187.128.26 and a netmask of 255.0.0.0 in VLAN2, enter the following command:

```
Coriolis5500(enable) set interface sc0 2 38.187.128.26 255.0.0.0
Interface sc0 vlan set, IP address and netmask set.
```

9. To set up default IP routes, use the following commands:

```
Coriolis5500(enable) set ip route default 38.187.128.2
Route added.
Coriolis5500(enable) set ip route default 192.168.1.1 primary
Route added.
```

10. To see the default routes, enter the following command:

```
Coriolis5500(enable) show ip route
Fragmentation   Redirect   Unreachable
-------------   --------   -----------
enabled         enabled    enabled

The primary gateway: 192.168.1.1
Destination     Gateway          RouteMask    Flags    Use    Interface
-----------     -------          ---------    -----    ---    ---------
default         38.187.128.1       0x0           UG    100          sc0
default         38.187.128.2       0x0           G       0          sc0
```

Project 5.2

After reviewing the information from the sales consultant, Joe determined that the following configuration tasks need to be performed on the Cisco Catalyst 2900:

- Set the user enable password to book1234
- Set the Privileged EXEC enable password to book4321
- Change the console prompt to **Coriolis2900**
- Enter the system time
- Enter the contact name as Joe Snow
- Enter the location information as Coriolis
- Configure the IP address 38.187.128.27 for interface VLAN1
- Set up a default primary route and gateway to 38.187.128.3

Notice in the following steps that the commands are much closer to your standard router IOS commands, because this switch uses an IOS command-line interface:

1. To set up user mode and enable passwords on a Cisco IOS-based switch, enter the following commands:

```
Switch>  enable
Switch# Configure terminal
Switch (config)  enable password level 1 book1234
Switch (config)  enable password level 15 book4321
```

2. Use the following command in Global Configuration Mode to configure the name for the switch prompt:

```
Switch (config)  hostname coriolis2900
Coriolis2900>
```


3. To set the system clock on an IOS-based switch and to put it in the PST time zone, use the following commands:

```
Switch (config)  clock set 23:59:00 05 jun 00
Switch (config)  clock timezone PST -8
```

4. To set up an IP address on a Cisco IOS-based switch, enter the following commands in Global Configuration Mode:

```
Switch (config) interface vlan 1
Switch (config-int) ip address 38.187.128.27 255.0.0.0
Switch (config-int) exit
Switch (config) ip default-gateway 38.187.128.3
Switch (config) end
```

CHAPTER SIX

6

ADVANCED SWITCH CONFIGURATION

After completing this chapter, you will be able to:

✓ Back up or restore a switch configuration

✓ Identify methods to upgrade system software

✓ Understand logging information for a file or server

✓ Implement the Network Time Protocol

✓ Configure Domain Name Services

✓ Connect a modem to your switch

✓ Strengthen security on a Catalyst switch

✓ Recover a lost password

In Chapter 5, we covered the basics of how to configure a Cisco switch using either the Set/Clear interface or the Cisco IOS-based command set. This chapter delves into more advanced topics to help you better manage your switch and network.

On any type of network device, you should perform certain tasks to maintain the integrity of the system. Other tasks will allow your network to function in the event a disaster occurs. Still other tasks simply make life easier for hard-working network professionals.

One of the most important tasks we will cover in this chapter is strengthening security on your switch and network. On a Cisco switch, you can increase security on a global scale or on a per-port basis. We will show you how to lock down a switch to avoid unauthorized use. We will also cover the Terminal Access Controller Access Control System (TACACS) software and how you can use it to implement your security policies.

Another important area we will address is system administration tasks that you should perform on a regular basis to ensure that your switch runs properly. We will cover tasks such as upgrading the system software, downloading new images to the switch, and backing up and restoring system configurations.

In addition, we will show you some tasks that will make life a little easier for you, such as setting up a logging server to store console messages, implementing the Network Time Protocol so you can keep a consistent time clock in your network, and configuring Domain Name Services (DNS) so that you can use names instead of network addresses to connect to remote resources.

As we did with the last chapter, we will be dividing this chapter into two sections: One section will cover the advanced configuration tasks for a Set/Clear switch, and the other will cover the same tasks from a Cisco-IOS view.

Configuration Tasks for Set/Clear Devices

In this section, we will cover the commands you need to set up advanced features using the Catalyst 5000 Set/Clear command set. Although none of these tasks are mandatory, some of them will really come in handy if something happens to your switch or the configuration gets messed up by mistake. The following list details the tasks we will explain in this section:

- Backing up and restoring a switch configuration
- Upgrading a switch to a newer version
- Setting up logging on a switch
- Configuring the Network Time Protocol

- Setting up Domain Name Services
- Connecting a modem to your switch
- Strengthening security on a Catalyst switch

Backing Up and Restoring a Switch's Configuration

On a device with a Set/Clear interface, the switch commands are automatically stored in the configuration file once they are entered. So, it is not necessary to write the configuration to memory, as it is on routers or IOS-based switches.

However, it is always a wise precaution to store the configuration file in an alternate location in case something unforseen renders the switch nonfunctional, or in the event that someone changes the configuration and it no longer does what you think it should.

There are a number of methods for making a copy of a configuration file. The easiest, but certainly not the quickest, is to cut and paste the configuration into a text file using a terminal emulation package, such as HyperTerminal. Two other popular methods for copying a configuration file are as follows:

- Copy the configuration file to a file on Flash memory.
- Copy the file to a server using Trivial File Transfer Protocol (TFTP).

Copying a File to Flash Memory

If you have a Supervisor Engine IIG or IIIG, a limited Flash file system was implemented in software release 5.2. It can contain up to two configuration files, which are named cfg1 and cfg2. Each configuration file can be up to 256K in size.

Use the following procedure to copy the configuration file to Flash memory:

```
Console> (enable) copy config cfg1
Upload configuration to flash cfg1 (y/n) [n]? y
<lines deleted>
...
Erasing flash sector...done.
Programming flash sector...done.

Configuration has been copied successfully.
Console> (enable)
```

Note: *The ... in the display indicates that the file transfer is taking place.*

To restore the cfg1 file to the working configuration, use the following command:

```
Console> (enable) copy cfg1 config
Configure using flash cfg1 (y/n) [n]? y

Finished network download.  (8712 bytes)
>>
<lines deleted>
Console> (enable)
```

To see the cfg1 file on the Flash device, use the following command:

```
Console> (enable) show file cfg1
```

Copying Files Using TFTP

Copying configuration files using the Trivial File Transfer Protocol (TFTP) involves two components. The first part is a TFTP client, which in this case will be the switch. The second part is a TFTP server.

A TFTP server can be either a PC running TFTP software (copies of which are available on the Cisco Web site) or a Unix workstation with TFTP services running. If the TFTP server is on a Unix workstation, the file must exist on the server before it can be downloaded. In addition, you must make sure you have permission to write to the directory where the file is located.

To copy a file to a TFTP server, use the following commands:

```
Console> (enable) write network
IP address or name of remote host? 192.168.1.1
Name of configuration file? cat5_config.cfg
Upload configuration to cat5002_config.cfg on 192.168.1.1 (y/n) [n]? y
.....
..........
..........
..
Finished network upload.  (8534 bytes)
Console> (enable)
```

To restore the configuration file from the TFTP server, use the following commands:

```
Console> (enable) configure network 192.168.1.1 cat5_config.cfg
Configure using cat5_config.cfg from 192.168.1.1 (y/n)? y
<lines deleted>
Done. Finished Network Download (8534 bytes)
```

Upgrading a Switch to a Newer Version of Software

The system software of a Catalyst switch can also be loaded using TFTP. You may need to do this to gain additional hardware or software functionality that comes with a new image. You also may need to do this to downgrade to a lower software version if incompatible bugs are found in a newer image.

If no network access is available, an image can also be downloaded via the console terminal using a file transfer package called Kermit. This process may be necessary if a system image becomes corrupted during the file transfer process and leaves the system with an unusable software image. These file transfers are slow—the maximum transfer rate is 38,400bps—and may take a while to load.

Two types of images can be downloaded to a switch: the Supervisor Engine software image and the Intelligent Module software images for specific modules in the switch.

On a Catalyst 5000 class switch with a Supervisor Engine II or IIIG, the Supervisor image is stored on the Supervisor Engine Flash memory; this memory can contain only one version. On the Catalyst 5000 family Supervisor Engine III and IIIF, you can store multiple images on the Supervisor Engine; you can store additional images on the Flash PC card.

If you have redundant Supervisor Engines, it is not possible to download a system image directly from a TFTP server to the Flash memory on the standby Supervisor Engine. If you load the system image to the active Supervisor Engine, however, the active Supervisor Engine will synchronize with the passive Supervisor Engine.

To see what version of system software is located on your switch, issue the following command:

```
Console> (enable) show version 1
Mod   Port   Model      Serial #    Versions
---   ----   -----      --------    --------
1     2      WS-X5509   007486003   Hw : 2.3
                                    Fw : 3.1(2)
                                    Fw1: 3.1(1)
                                    Sw : 4.1(2)
```

Downloading a New Software Version Using TFTP

As with uploading and downloading configuration files, before using TFTP to download a system image, you should verify that you have connectivity to the TFTP server and that you have proper file permissions for the file and directory you are going to download. Before downloading a new system image, it is always a good idea to have a current backup of your configuration and a current software image in case something happens to the network or power or the download has unexpected results.

To download a new system image using TFTP, use the following procedure:

```
Console> (enable) download 192.168.1.1 cat5000-supg.5-2-1.bin
Download image cat5000-supg.5-2-1.bin from 192.168.1.1 to module 1 FLASH
(y/n) [n]? y
Finished network single module download. (4104180 bytes)
Erasing flash sector...done.
Programming flash sector...done.
Verifying Flash Image ...
The system needs to be reset to run the new image.
Console> (enable) reset
This command will reset the system.
Do you want to continue (y/n) [n]? y
%SYS-5-SYS_RESET:System reset from Console//
```

Note: *Notice how the system requires a reset of the switch after a new image has been downloaded. This reset is not needed after an Intelligent Module image has been applied. In that case, you can just issue the* ***reset module*** *command.*

When the upgraded switch or module comes up, it is a good idea to enter the **show version 1** command to check the version of the code on the switch.

Downloading a New Software Version Using Kermit

Before you can use Kermit to download a new image, you should verify these items:

- Make sure you are directly connected from the console port to a serial port on your PC or Unix workstation.
- Make sure Kermit is installed on your machine, or that the terminal emulation package supports it. HyperTerminal supports Kermit and is included with Windows, so the following procedure will use it as an example.
- Console ports can support up to 38,400bps, but Cisco recommends you use 19,200bps to help prevent communication problems.

To download a new system image using HyperTerminal's Kermit protocol, use the following procedure:

1. Connect to the console port of the switch using HyperTerminal.
2. Begin the download process on the switch by entering the following commands:

```
Console> enable
Console> (enable) download serial
Download CBI image via console port (y/n) [n]? y
```

3. Begin the file transfer on your PC. In HyperTerminal, select Transfer|Send File.
4. Enter the file name of the system image.
5. Select Kermit as the protocol.

A dialog box will appear to inform you of the file transfer process. The switch will download the image file, erase the current contents in Flash memory on the Supervisor Engine (or the appropriate module), and reprogram the Flash memory with the downloaded Flash code. The switch dialog will look like this:


```
Finished network download.  (1136844 bytes)
Flash erase in progress ... Erase done
Programming Flash:  Flash Programming Complete
<lines deleted>
The system needs to be reset to run the new image.

Cisco Systems Console
Enter password:
Mon Aug 07, 2000, 14:35:08
Console>
```

Setting Up Logging on a Switch

Cisco switches include logging software that you can use to monitor your switch. This software can save system messages in either a log file located on the switch or a file located on some other device. Normally, the switch sends these messages to the system console and to an internal file. In this file, up to 1,024 messages can be stored.

Messages can be filtered based on the type of facility, as shown in Table 6.1, or based on severity, as shown in Table 6.2.

Logging messages appear as

```
mm/dd/yyy:hh/mm/ss:facility-severity-MNEMONIC:description
```

where:

- ***mm/dd/yyy:hh/mm/ss*** indicates the date and time.
- ***facility*** indicates one of the facilities shown in Table 6.1.
- ***severity*** is one of the severity levels shown in Table 6.2.
- ***MNEMONIC*** is a unique text string that identifies the message.
- ***description*** is the detailed description.

Table 6.1 Types of facilities the system logging feature supports.

Facility	Description
CDP	Cisco Discovery Protocol
DTP	Dynamic Trunking Protocol
DRIP	Dual Ring Protocol
DVLAN	Dynamic VLAN
EARL	Enhanced Address Recognition Logic
FDDI	Fiber Distributed Data Interface
Filesys	Flash file system
IP	IP permit list
Kernel	Kernel
Mgmt	Management messages
Mcast	Multicast messages
PAgP	Port Aggregation Protocol
Protfilt	Protocol filtering
Pruning	VTP pruning
RMON	Remote monitoring
SNMP	Simple Network Management Protocol
Spantree	Spanning Tree Protocol
Sys	System
Tac	TACACS+
TCP	Transmission Control Protocol
Telnet	Terminal emulation protocol in the TCP/IP protocol stack
TFTP	Trivial File Transfer Protocol
VMPS	VLAN membership policy server
VTP	VLAN Trunking Protocol
Security	Port security

Table 6.2 Severity levels of the system log.

Severity Level	Keyword	Description
0	Emergencies	System unusable
1	Alerts	Immediate action required
2	Critical	Critical condition
3	Errors	Error conditions
4	Warnings	Warning conditions
5	Notifications	Normal but significant condition
6	Informational	Informational messages
7	Debugging	Debugging messages

To show what logging is enabled, use the following command:

```
Console> (enable) show logging
Logging console:enabled
Logging server:disabled
```

In this example, the logging is enabled for the console, but a logging server is disabled. To enable a logging server, you must first configure a syslog server on a computer to receive the messages. Typically this is a Unix workstation, but it can also be a Windows platform. To add a syslog server, you need to tell the switch where it is located, enable the server, and set the facility and logging levels for the server.

For example, to add a syslog server located at the IP address 192.168.1.1 to the logging system and send notifications of modules going online, use the following commands:

```
Console> (enable) set logging server 192.168.1.1
Console> (enable) set logging server enable
Console> (enable) set logging level sys 5
```

You can set a maximum of three syslog servers at a time. To clear a syslog server, use the following command:

```
Console> (enable)  clear logging server 192.168.1.1
```

Configuring the Network Time Protocol

The Network Time Protocol (NTP) is used to synchronize time between designated time servers and clients on a network. An NTP network usually gets its time from an authoritative time source, such as a radio clock or an atomic clock attached to a time server. NTP will then distribute this time across the network. NTP time is always in coordinated universal time (UTC), which is equivalent to Greenwich mean time.

NTP uses a stratum to describe how far a machine is from an authoritative time source. The distance is measured by NTP in terms of hops. Stratum 1 time servers have a radio or atomic clock directly attached, Stratum 2 time servers get the time from a Stratum 1 time server, etc. A machine running NTP will automatically choose as its time source the machine with the lowest stratum number. This strategy effectively builds a self-organizing tree of NTP speakers.

NTP devices can be either servers or clients. Cisco switches can only be configured as clients; an NTP server must be accessible by the switch NTP client. A client can be configured in broadcast-client mode if an NTP broadcast server, such as a router, regularly broadcasts time-of-day information on the network. Cisco does not support Stratum 1 NTP servers, so the company recommends getting the time from a public NTP site on the Internet. After the correct time has been obtained, the other devices can synchronize to that device.

To set up NTP, you need to do three tasks, as follows:

- Configure the NTP server address
- Configure the client mode
- Configure time zone information, if needed

You do so with the following commands:

```
Console> (enable) set ntp server 192.168.1.2
Console> (enable) set ntp broadcastclient enable
NTP Broadcast Client mode enabled
```

Use the **show ntp** command to see how NTP is configured:

```
Console> (enable) show ntp
Current time: Fri Aug 04 2000, 20:25:43
Timezone: '', offset from UTC is 0 hours
Summertime: '', disabled
Last NTP update:
Broadcast client mode: enabled
Broadcast delay: 3000 microseconds
Client mode: disabled

NTP-Server
----------
Console> (enable)
```

As you can see from this display, the time is in UTC time. This is probably not the time format you are used to on a day-to-day basis. To change the time to something familiar, such as pacific standard time (PST), you need to set the time zone and the offset from GMT time. For example, PST is 8 time zones to the left (to the west) of GMT time, so it is a -8 offset from GMT. The command for setting up this time zone is as follows:

```
Console> (enable) set timezone Pacific -8
Timezone set to 'Pacific', offset from UTC is -8 hours
```

You can also set the switch to recognize daylight saving time:

```
Console> (enable) set summertime enable Pacific
Summertime is enabled and set to 'Pacific'
```

If you do, the switch will advance the clock one hour on the first Sunday in April at 2:00 A.M. and move the clock back one hour on the last Sunday in October at 2:00 A.M. Of course, you can always come in at 2 A.M. and do it manually!

Setting Up Domain Name Services

DNS is a protocol that is used to map hostnames to IP addresses. A DNS server that maintains the database of these translations must be available on your network. When you configure DNS on the switch, you can substitute the hostname for the IP address with all IP commands, such as **ping** or **telnet**.

A primary DNS name server and two backup DNS servers may be configured on a switch. The first server entered is considered the primary DNS server unless you tell the switch otherwise. In operation, the switch will send DNS queries to the primary server. If these initial queries fail, the switch will query the backup servers. To configure a switch to use DNS, follow these instructions:

1. Configure the address of the primary DNS server:

```
Console> (enable) set ip dns server 192.168.1.2 primary
192.168.1.2 added to DNS server table as primary server.
```

2. Configure the address of the secondary DNS server:

```
Console> (enable) set ip dns server 192.168.1.3
192.168.1.3 added to DNS server table as backup server.
```

3. Set up the domain name you want to use:

```
Console> (enable) set ip dns domain mydomain.com
Default DNS domain name set to mydomain.com
```

4. Enable the DNS process:

```
Console> (enable) set ip dns enable
DNS is enabled
```

5. To see how DNS is configured on your system, use the following command:

```
Console> (enable) show ip dns
DNS is currently enabled.
```

```
The default DNS domain name is: mydomain.com

DNS name server                    status
---------------                    ------
dns2
dns1                               primary
```

Connecting a Modem to Your Switch

Connecting a modem to a Catalyst 5000 switch is not as easy as you might think. Unfortunately, the switch was never designed to support remote access via a modem. It was designed to be used as a Data Communications Equipment (DCE) device to connect to a Data Terminal Equipment (DTE) terminal or PC. This design introduces an interesting problem with dial-up connections. When a call is made to connect to the switch, the DCE setup in the switch keeps the Data Set Ready (DSR) signal high, not the carrier detect (CD) that modems require. As a result, once the Catalyst accepts a dial-in connection, the Catalyst cannot hang up the phone call. The call can only be terminated by the caller.

In addition, the fact that the Catalyst 5000 is a DCE device makes cabling to a modem, which is also a DCE device, an issue. The "standard" null-modem cable used by the switches is designed to connect a DTE device to another DTE device, not a DCE to a DCE. This cable ties two of the cable pins together, which can overdrive the voltage and cause harm to the Universal Asynchronous Receiver/Transmitter (UART) chip of one of the devices. Cisco's recommended cable pinout for making a modem appear to be a DTE device is shown in Table 6.3.

Note: *The RJ-45/DB-25 connector included in the Cisco Console kit will make these conversions for you.*

Table 6.3 Pinouts for a Catalyst 5000 modem connection.

	Cat5000 console (DB-25 DCE)		Standard DB-25 DCE	
Direction	**Pin**	**Signal**	**Pin**	**Signal**
In	2	TxD	3	RxD
Out	3	RxD	2	TxD
In	4	RTS	5	CTS
Out	5	CTS	4	RTS
	7	GND	7	GND
Out	8	CD	20	DTR
In	20	DTR	6	DSR

The next steps in this process will make the modem look even more DTE-like. You need to perform the following actions on the modem to accomplish this:

1. Set the modem to ignore DTR.
2. Set the modem to auto-answer.
3. Lock the speed to 9600 if possible.
4. Suppress the local echo.
5. Suppress result codes.
6. Suppress error codes if possible.
7. Set the flow control to hardware (RTS/CTS).
8. Use the **set system modem enable** command to enable RTS/CTS hardware flow control on the Catalyst 5000.

Strengthening Security on a Catalyst Switch

One of the more important tasks you may want to perform is to secure your system from unauthorized use. Such use could involve people from the outside trying to gain access to your network or internal personnel trying to get into areas they are not authorized to access. Cisco offers two popular methods of authentication:

- Local authentication
- TACACS+ authentication

By default, the switch uses local authentication. This method uses locally configured login and enable passwords to authenticate login attempts. The login and enable passwords are local to each switch and are not mapped to individual usernames. If TACACS+ authentication is enabled, you can disable local authentication. If TACACS+ is disabled, the system will once again default to local authentication. You can enable local authentication and TACACS+ authentication at the same time. In this case, local authentication is used only if TACACS+ authentication fails.

Here are a few guidelines to follow when you configure authentication on the switch:

- Authentication applies to console access and Telnet connections unless the keyword **console** or **telnet** is used to specify the connection type individually.

- If you configure a TACACS+ key on the switch, it must agree with the key on the TACACS+ server.
- A TACACS+ server must be configured before you configure TACACS+ on the switch.
- The first TACACS+ server configured is considered the primary server, and authentication requests are sent to this server first. If you want a particular server to be the primary, you need to use the keyword **primary**.
- Only one Privileged Mode can be configured.

Configuring Local Authentication

By default, a switch is set up for local authentication for both console and Telnet access. However, you can use a mix of authentication methods—for example, local authentication on the console and TACACS+ authentication for Telnet access. This would be an effective configuration, because it would ensure access to the console in the event of network issues preventing access to your TACACS+ server.

To enable local authentication for login access on the console port, enter this command:

```
Console> (enable) set authentication login local enable console
```

To enable local authentication for enable access on the console port, enter this command:

```
Console> (enable) set authentication enable local enable console
```

Once you've done this, set the passwords the same as you would normally. Use the **set password** and **set enablepass** commands as shown here:

```
Console> (enable) set password
Enter old password: <old_password>
Enter new password: <new_password>
Retype new password: <new_password>
Password changed.

Console> (enable) set enablepass
Enter old password: <old_password>
Enter new password: <new_password>
Retype new password: <new_password>
Password changed.
```

If you have set up TACACS+ for authentication, you may want to disable local authentication. You do so with the following command:

```
Console> (enable) set authentication login local disable both
```

Warning: Be sure that you have a TACACS+ server available before issuing this command. Otherwise, you may have to practice the break-in techniques covered in the next section!

Configuring TACACS+ Authentication

TACACS+ authentication can be configured for either login or enable access to the switch or both. You should enable at least one TACACS+ server before you enable TACACS+ authentication on the switch. The first server you add is the primary; any others added will be secondary servers. To set up a TACACS+ server, enter the following commands:

```
Console> (enable) set tacacs server 192.168.1.2
192.168.1.2 added to TACACS server table as primary server.
Console> (enable) set tacacs server 192.168.1.3
192.168.1.3 added to TACACS server table as backup server
```

Verify the operation by using the following command:

```
Console> (enable) show tacacs

Login Authentication:   Console Session   Telnet Session
---------------------   ---------------   --------------
tacacs                  disabled          disabled
local                   enabled(primary)  enabled(primary)

Enable Authentication:  Console Session   Telnet Session
---------------------   ---------------   --------------
tacacs                  disabled          disabled
local                   enabled(primary)  enabled(primary)
Tacacs key:
Tacacs login attempts: 3
Tacacs timeout: 5 seconds
Tacacs direct request: disabled

Tacacs-Server                              Status
-------------                              ------
192.168.1.3
192.168.1.2                                primary
```

The next step is to enable TACACS+ authentication for login and enable access to the switch. Use the following commands to do this:

```
Console> (enable) set authentication login tacacs enable both
tacacs login authentication set to enable for console and
telnet session.

Console> (enable) set authentication enable tacacs enable
tacacs enable authentication set to enable for console
and telnet session.
```

Verify the operation with the following command:

```
Console> (enable) show authentication

Login Authentication:  Console Session   Telnet Session
---------------------  ---------------   --------------
tacacs                 enabled(primary)  enabled(primary)
local                  enabled           enabled

Enable Authentication: Console Session   Telnet Session
---------------------  ---------------   --------------
tacacs                 enabled(primary)  enabled(primary)
local                  enabled           enabled
```

To disable TACACS+ authentication, use this command:

```
Console (enable) set authentication login tacacs disable both
```

Configuration Tasks for Cisco IOS-Based Switches

In this section, we will cover the commands needed to set up advanced functions using the Catalyst IOS-based command set. As in the previous section, we will be covering the following tasks:

- Backing up and restoring a switch configuration
- Upgrading a switch to a newer version
- Setting up logging on a switch
- Configuring the Network Time Protocol
- Setting up Domain Name Services
- Connecting a modem to your switch

- Strengthening security on a Catalyst switch
- Recovering a lost password

Backing Up and Restoring a Switch's Configuration

The Cisco IOS-based switches use the same IOS-based command-line interface. As such, the commands are the same. When you start a session on the router, you begin in User Mode, often called EXEC Mode. Only a limited subset of the commands is available in EXEC Mode. In order to have access to all commands, you must enter Privileged EXEC Mode. Normally, you must enter a password to enter Privileged EXEC Mode. From Privileged Mode, you can enter any EXEC command or enter Global Configuration Mode. The configuration modes allow you to make changes to the running configuration. In order to save these changes, you must save the configuration.

There are two types of configuration files. *Startup configuration files* are used during system startup to configure the software. *Running configuration files* contain the current configuration of the software. The two configuration files do not always agree. Sometimes you might need to make a short-term, temporary change in the configuration rather than changing it permanently. In this case, you would change the running configuration instead of the startup configuration.

To make a change to the running configuration files, issue the command **configure terminal** and make whatever changes you need to make. When you are done making changes, copy the running configurations to the startup configurations. This process is shown in the following example:

```
Switch> enable
Switch# configure terminal
Enter configuration commands, one per line. End with CNTL/Z.
switch(config)# hostname Switch1
Switch1 (config) end
Switch1# copy running-config startup-config
```

To copy a running configuration file to a TFTP server, use the following command:

```
Switch# copy system:running-config tftp://192.168.1.2/switch-confg
Write file switch-confg on host 192.168.1.2? [confirm] y
```

Upgrading a Switch to a Newer Version of Software

Follow these steps to upgrade the switch software by using a TFTP transfer. This procedure copies the system image files as well as the HTML files used by the Cisco Visual Switch Manager (CVSM):

1. Copy the file to a TFTP server to which you have access. In this case, we will be upgrading from the switch image c3500XL-c3h2s-mz-112.8.2-SA6.bin to c3500XL-c3h2s-120.5-XP.bin.

2. Telnet to the switch or connect to the switch console port.

3. Enter Privileged EXEC Mode:

```
switch> enable
switch#
```

4. Display the name of the running (default) image file. The image name is the part following the **flash**:

```
switch# show boot
BOOT path-list:    flash:c3500XL-c3h2s-mz-112.8.2-SA6.bin
Config file:       flash:config.text
Enable Break:      1
Manual Boot:       no
HELPER path-list:
NVRAM/Config file
buffer size: 32768
```

5. If no file is defined in the BOOT path-list, enter **dir flash:** to display the contents of Flash memory.

6. Rename the existing switch image to match the name of the new system image you downloaded—but use a .bin extension. For example, if the file you downloaded was named c3500XL-c3h2s-mz-112.8.2-SA6.tar, rename the switch image to c3500XL-c3h2s-mz-112.8.2-SA6.bin:

```
switch# rename flash:c3500XL-c3h2s-mz-112.8.2-SA6.bin
flash:c3500XL-c3h2s-mz-120.5-XP.bin
Source filename [c3500XL-c3h2s-mz-112.8.2-SA6.bin]?
Destination filename [c3500XL-c3h2s-mz-120.5-XP.bin]?
```

7. Display the contents of Flash memory to verify the renaming of the file:

```
switch# dir flash:
Directory of flash:
-rwx   1557283   Aug 17 1999 23:47:28   c3500XL-c3h2s-mz-120.5-XP.bin
-rwx   82475     Aug 17 1999 03:10:38   c3500XL-diag-mz-120.5-XP
-drwx  14144     Aug 17 1999 00:04:14   html
```

```
-rwx   2047      Mar 01 1993 18:46:01   config.text
-rwx   43        Jan 01 1970 00:00:34   env_vars

3612672 bytes total (1224704 bytes free)
```

8. Enter Global Configuration Mode and disable access to the switch HTML pages:

```
switch# config terminal
Enter configuration commands, one per line. End with CNTL/Z.
switch(config)# no IP http server
switch(config)# end
switch#
```


9. Remove the CVSM HTML files:

```
switch# delete flash:html/*
Press Enter to confirm the deletion of each file. Do not press any
other keys during this process.
```

10. Copy the new image and HTML files to the switch's Flash memory (note the use of the URL-based file system convention):

```
switch# tar /x tftp://192.168.1.2/c3500XL-c3h2s-mz-112.0.66-SA6.tar
flash:
Loading /path/filename.tar from server_ip_address (via VLAN1):!)
extracting info (110 bytes)
extracting c3500XL-c3h2s-mz-112.0.66-SA6.bin (1271095 bytes)!!!!!!!!!!
html/ (directory)
extracting html/Detective.html.gz (1139 bytes)!
extracting html/ieGraph.html.gz (553 bytes)
extracting html/DrawGraph.html.gz (787 bytes)
extracting html/GraphFrame.html.gz (802 bytes)!
...
```

11. Enter Global Configuration Mode and re-enable switch HTTP pages:

```
switch# config terminal
Enter configuration commands, one per line. End with CNTL/Z.
switch(config)# ip http server
switch(config)# end
switch#
```

12. Reload the new software with the following command:

```
switch# reload
System configuration has been modified. Save? [yes/no]:y
Proceed with reload? [confirm]
Press Return to confirm the reload.
```

Note: *Your Telnet session ends when the switch resets.*

The running configuration is normally contained in config.text on the Flash card, but you can make a copy for backup purposes by using the following command:

```
Switch# copy running-config flash:config.bak
```

Setting Up Logging on a Switch

The logging process on Cisco IOS-based devices is very similar to the logging process on Set/Clear devices. Just like the Set/Clear devices, Cisco IOS-based devices send system error messages to a logging process. This process controls the distribution of logging messages to various destinations, such as a logging buffer, terminal lines, or a syslog server, as well as to the system console. IOS-based devices use the same concept of severity levels, as shown earlier in Table 6.2. They differ from the Set/Clear devices in the facility levels they support, as shown in Table 6.4.

Table 6.4 Logging facilities supported on Cisco IOS-based switches.

Facility	Description
Auth	Authorization system
Cron	The cron facility
Daemon	System daemon
Kern	Kernel
Local0-7	Reserved for locally defined messages
Lpr	Line printer system
Mail	Mail system
News	USENET news
Sys9	System use
Sys10	System use
Sys11	System use
Sys12	System use
Sys13	System use
Sys14	System use
Syslog	The system log
User	User process
UUCP	Unix-to-Unix copy system

To enable message logging on a Cisco IOS-based switch, enter the following command in Global Configuration Mode:

```
Switch#  (config) logging on
```

Once logging is enabled, you can send messages to other locations, in addition to the console. For example, you can send the messages to an internal buffer. You can specify how large you want the buffer to be by including the size at the end of the command. The buffer is circular, so older messages are overwritten by the new messages after the buffer has filled. To display the messages that are logged in the buffer, use the **show logging** EXEC command. The first message displayed is the oldest message in the buffer.

To enable the logging messages to be sent to a buffer, use the following Privileged EXEC command:

```
Switch# (config) logging buffered 100
```

To clear the current contents of the buffer, use the following Privileged EXEC command:

```
Switch# (config) clear logging
```

If you Telnet into a switch and want to see the logging messages as they appear, use the following command:

```
Switch# (config) terminal monitor
```

Switches can be configured to synchronize unsolicited messages and debug command output with solicited device output and prompts for a specific line. When a switch is configured to do this, unsolicited device output is displayed on the console after the solicited device output has been displayed. Then, the prompt for user input is returned.

This feature is a wonderful tool to use during debugging sessions or troubleshooting, because it reduces the clutter that can come from debug output being merged with system prompts and the results of commands you've input. Once the unsolicited messages are displayed, the console displays the user prompt again. When using this feature, you will need to specify which line you want the messages to be synchronized on—for example, **vty 0 4** for Telnet sessions or **console** for console sessions.

To enable this feature, use the following commands:

```
Switch# (config) line vty 0 4
Switch# (config) terminal logging synchronous
```

```
Switch# (config) exit
Switch# (config) line console 0
Switch# (config) terminal logging synchronous
Switch# (config) end
```

To set up logging messages to be forwarded to a syslog server, enter the following command:

```
Switch# (config) logging 192.168.1.2
```

Configuring the Network Time Protocol

As with the Set/Clear IOS interface, Cisco IOS-based switches can be set up as NTP clients to synchronize time for the switches. There are a few differences between the types of devices. On Cisco IOS-based switches, you can enter the IP addresses of up to 10 NTP servers.

You can also ensure the validity of information received from NTP servers by authenticating NTP messages with public-key encryption. This procedure must be coordinated with the administrator of the NTP servers. The servers must match the same information. In order to set up NTP, you need to perform the following tasks:

- Configure the NTP server or peer address
- Configure the client mode
- Configure time zone information, if needed
- Configure NTP authentication, if desired

To form an NTP association with another system, use the following commands:

```
Switch# (config) ntp server 192.168.1.3
Switch# (config) ntp peer ip-address 192.168.1.2
Switch# (config) ntp broadcast client
```

To set up time zone information, enter the following commands:

```
Switch# (config) clock timezone PST -8
Switch# (config) clock summer-time PDT recurring
```

To authenticate the associations with other systems for security purposes, you need to do three tasks:

- Enable the NTP authentication feature.
- Define each of the authentication keys. Each key has a key number, a type, and a value. Currently, the only key type supported is MD5.
- Define the authentication keys.

Enter the following commands to set up NTP authentication:

```
Switch# (config) ntp authenticate
Switch# (config) ntp authentication-key 1 md5 cisco
```

Setting Up Domain Name Services

As we covered in the section on Set/Clear devices, IP defines a naming scheme that allows a device to be identified by its location in the IP. This is a hierarchical naming scheme that provides for domains. To keep track of domain names, IP has defined the concept of a *name server*, whose job is to maintain a database of names mapped to IP addresses. To map domain names to IP addresses, you must first identify the hostnames, specify a name server, and then enable the Domain Name System (DNS)—the Internet's global naming scheme that uniquely identifies network devices. These tasks are described next.

You can specify a default domain name that the Cisco IOS software will use to complete domain name requests. You can specify either a single domain name or a list of domain names. Any IP hostname that does not contain a domain name will have the domain name you specify appended to it before being added to the host table. The command is as follows:

```
Switch# (config) ip domain-name myname.com
```

To specify one or more hosts (up to six) that can function as a name server to supply name information for the DNS, use the following command in Global Configuration Mode:

```
Switch# (config) ip name-server 192.168.1.2
```

By default, the DNS lookup is enabled. If the DNS has been disabled, you may re-enable it by performing the following task in Global Configuration Mode:

```
Switch# (config)  ip domain-lookup
```

Connecting a Modem to Your Switch

Compared to the difficulties in connecting a modem on the Catalyst 5000 line, it is much easier to configure an IOS-based switch to use a modem. With a few exceptions, the majority of these devices use an RJ-45 connector to the switch. Whether it is connected to a terminal or a modem, a Catalyst switch must be configured to the same baud rate and character format as the terminal or modem. The only real difference is that you need to use a standard modem cable with an RJ-45 to DB-25 male DCE adapter labeled *Modem* to connect to the modem.

Some devices require additional attention. To connect a modem to a Catalyst 6500 family switch's Supervisor Engine 1 console port, plug the RJ-45 to RJ-45 rollover cable into the console port jack. Use a paper clip or other small, pointed object to access the port mode switch located next to the console port. Use the paper clip to put the button in Position Mode 1 (the button is pressed). Use the console cable and RJ-45 to DB-25 male DCE adapter labeled *Modem* that shipped with the switch.

On the Catalyst 2600, use the DB-9 to RJ-45 female adapter to plug into the switch and standard PC connector.

Configure the baud rate and character format of the management station or modem and the console port on the switch so that they match. The following are the default physical characteristics of the console port on the switch: 9600 baud, 8 data bits, 1 stop bit, no parity, no flow control.

Strengthening Security on a Catalyst Switch

As mentioned earlier, TACACS+ is an access-control protocol that allows a switch to authenticate all login attempts through a central authentication server. The network administrator configures the switch with the address of the TACACS+ server, and the switch and the server exchange messages to authenticate each user before allowing access to the management console.

TACACS+ consists of three services:

- *Authentication*—Determines whom the user is and if he or she is allowed access
- *Authorization*—Determines what the user is allowed to do on the system
- *Accounting*—Collects data related to the user's resource usage

To enable TACACS+ on a Cisco IOS-based router, perform the following tasks:

1. Enable authentication for login:

```
Switch# (config) aaa authentication login default tacacs+ local
```

2. Provide a local authentication username for login in case the TACACS+ server is unavailable:

```
Switch# (config) username curly password moe
```

3. Enable TACACS+ authentication for enable mode:

```
Switch# (config) aaa authentication enable default tacacs+ enable
```

4. Provide an enable password in the event the TACACS+ server is unavailable:

```
Switch# (config) enable password Cisco
```

5. Provide a key to use for encryption:

```
Switch# (config) tacacs-server key sekure
```

6. Configure the TACACS+ server location:

```
Switch# (config) tacacs-server host 192.168.1.3
```


Recovering a Lost Password

If you're extremely lucky, you will never change your password and forget what it is after you've changed it. Sometimes, though, funny things happen—and what you thought you entered doesn't agree with what the switch thinks. Unfortunately, the switch always wins this fight.

Catalyst 1200, 2900, 2926, and 5000 Password Recovery

To recover a lost password on Catalyst 1200, Catalyst 2900, Catalyst 2926, and Catalyst 5000 Series switches, perform the following tasks:

1. Connect to the console port.
2. Reset the switch.
3. Press Enter when the password prompt appears (there is no password for 30 seconds).
4. At the console prompt, enter "Enable".
5. When the password prompt appears, press Enter (there is no password for 30 seconds).
6. Enter the new password.

Catalyst 1600 Password Recovery

To recover a lost password on the Catalyst 1600, push and hold the reset button on the switch until the LCD displays "erasing mgmt passwd". Stop holding the button, and the switch will reset. It will restart without a password.

Catalyst 1700, 1900, 2100, 2800, and 2820 Password Recovery

Losing the password on one of these Catalyst switches requires a call to the Cisco Technical Assistance Center (TAC). Provide the TAC with the switch serial number or MAC address, and the engineer will supply a new password.

Catalyst 1800 Password Recovery

To reset a password on the Catalyst 1800, first let the box boot normally. When the box has booted up and asks for the password, press the NMI switch five times. Doing so will reload the switch and reset the password to its default value of "public".

Catalyst 2600 Password Recovery

Click on the System Request button to access the System Request menu, and then choose Clear NVRAM. Doing so will clear the password—but in addition, it will reset any configuration parameters to their default values. As a result, you will lose all options you have previously configured on the switch.

Catalyst 2900 XL Password Recovery

To recover a lost password on a Catalyst 2900 XL switch, perform the following tasks:

1. Unplug the power cord from the back of the switch.
2. Hold down the Mode button (located on the far-left corner of the switch) and reconnect the power cord to the switch. After the LED above Port 1 turns off, wait a second or so and release the Mode button.
3. Enter the **flash_init** command.
4. Enter the **load_helper** command.
5. Enter the **dir flash:** command.
6. Enter the **rename flash:config.text flash:config.old** command.
7. Enter the **boot** command.
8. Enter "N" at the prompt to start the Setup program.
9. Enter "N" at the Continue with the configuration prompt.
10. Enter "en" at the switch prompt.
11. Enter the **rename flash:config.old flash:config.text** command.
12. Enter the **copy flash:config.text system:running-config** command.
13. Press Enter in response to the two confirmation prompts.
14. The configuration file is now loaded, and you can configure a new password normally.
15. Enter the **config terminal** command.
16. Enter the **enable password newpassword** command.

17. Write the running configuration to the configuration file using the **copy running-config startup-config** command.

Catalyst 3000, 3100, and 3200 Password Recovery

To recover a lost password on a Catalyst 3000, 3100, or 3200 switch, perform the following tasks:

1. Click on the System Request button.
2. Clear NVRAM.
3. Press the Enter key.
4. The box will now reboot with no password required.

Catalyst 3900 Password Recovery

To recover a lost password on a Catalyst 3900 switch, perform the following tasks:

1. Click on the System Request button to access the System Request menu.
2. Select Clear The System Password. Doing so will clear only the system password. All the other configuration parameters saved in NVRAM will be retained.

Warning: If you press the System Request button for more than five seconds, you'll force a download of the main image.

Chapter Summary

In our last chapter, we covered the basics of configuring a Cisco switch. We covered the most common tasks people perform on a switch, such as connecting media to it or connecting to the console. In this chapter, we continued that process with a focus on the more advanced topics that help with the administration of the switch.

You may never have to perform some of these tasks, but nonetheless, they can help you to more effectively manage your switch. For example, tasks such as implementing DNS or NTP services on your switch aren't required, but it sure makes life easier to use real names instead of addresses. Similarly, troubleshooting is a little easier when your network contains a dependable time source that all devices in the network use to agree to the same time. You probably should routinely perform other tasks we covered in this chapter. These tasks may determine whether your network will continue to operate normally after problems occur or if the network will be down for an extended period of time while you rebuild the system from the ground up.

One of the more important areas we covered in this chapter was how to make copies of your switch configuration to an alternate location. These copies are important safeguards in case you have to restore the configuration in the event of an emergency or if a change you make to the switch does not have the effect you're looking for. We discussed how to use **copy** commands to make copies on a Flash card and how to use TFTP to make copies on a network server.

In a similar vein, we covered the procedures you can use to upgrade (or downgrade) the system image that runs on your switch. You may need to do this for a wide variety of reasons—for example, if you add modules that are not supported by your existing image. You may want to upgrade to a different image to get more features; for instance, you might upgrade from a standard edition to an enterprise edition of the 2900 switch. We discussed how to upgrade a switch via a TFTP download, which is the best way to upgrade an image. We also covered how to do it via the console port, in case something happens to the network that makes a TFTP download impossible.

Another area we covered was how to send logging information about events that occur on your switch to a file or to a server located on your network. This is a good practice in larger environments, because you can create a central point for system and network error messages. This process can help eliminate problems before they escalate into worse problems and can reduce the frequency with which you have to log in to see what error messages are in the log. In addition, we also discussed how to filter out any unwanted messages by setting the level or severity of the messages as they are logged.

We also covered the steps needed to implement the Network Time Protocol on your switch to maintain a consistent time clock in your network. NTP can be especially useful if you have set up a logging server for multiple network devices, because it can be quite confusing if none of the devices agree about the time.

We talked about implementing Domain Name Services on your switches. This is another useful protocol to configure, because it is a lot easier to ping something by name than it is to remember IP addresses. By default, domain lookup is enabled; so, if you don't want to use DNS, it is best to turn it off to avoid waiting for the switch to discover that you have not implemented it.

We covered the procedure for connecting modems to your switches. In most devices, connecting a modem is simple: You use the modem connector that shipped with your switch, connect a modem cable to it, and plug an RJ-45 to DB-25 connector into your modem. On Catalyst switches, this process is a little more involved. You must take care to avoid damaging your switch port or your modem.

Perhaps the most important area we discussed is strengthening security on a switch. Catalyst switches support both local authentication and authentication using the TACACS+ protocol. On Set/Clear type switches, only one level of authentication is supported. In addition to authorizing a user, TACACS+ can support multiple levels of access, so you can tailor a user's authentication to his or her needs.

Our final area of discussion was how to recover a lost password. A wide variety of ways exist to recover passwords—almost as many as there are switches. However, finding the appropriate procedure when you're in the middle of a problem can be a chore that is less than fun. Of course, maybe you'll be the lucky one and never forget a password!

Review Questions

1. A Catalyst 5000 with a Supervisor Engine III can contain how many configuration files?
    a. 16
    b. 3
    c. 2
    d. 1
2. What is the maximum size for a configuration file on a Catalyst 5000?
    a. 1024 bytes
    b. 256K
    c. 4K
    d. 256 bytes
3. Which types of images can you use on a Set/Clear device? [Choose the two best answers]
    a. Supervisor Engine
    b. Intelligent Module
    c. Line module
    d. Switch module
4. Which command is the correct one to copy a configuration file to Flash memory on a Set/Clear switch?
    a. **copy config cfg1**
    b. **write config**
    c. **copy config flash**
    d. **copy cfg1 config**

5. Which command copies a configuration file to a network TFTP server on a Set/Clear switch?
    a. **write network**
    b. **copy network**
    c. **copy flash net**
    d. **copy cfg1 net**
6. What is the maximum number of messages that a Catalyst 5000 can hold in its log file?
    a. 256
    b. 1,024
    c. 512
    d. 10
7. What is the maximum number of log servers that can be configured on a Set/Clear switch?
    a. 2
    b. 1
    c. 3
    d. 6
8. Severity level 0 refers to what level of messages on a Cisco switch?
    a. Emergency
    b. Errors
    c. Debug messages
    d. Warnings
9. What time zone is used by default when you configure NTP?
    a. Pacific standard time
    b. Coordinated universal time
    c. Greenwich green time
    d. The system clock
10. Which command sets up the pacific standard time time zone on a Set/Clear switch?
    a. **set timezone Pacific Standard Time**
    b. **set timezone Pacific -8**
    c. **set timezone Pacific +8**
    d. **set timezone PST -8**

11. Which command is used to configure a switch to use a primary DNS server on IP address 192.168.1.2?
    a. **set ip dns server 192.168.1.2**
    b. **set ip dns 192.168.1.2**
    c. **set ip dns server 192.168.1.2 secondary**
    d. **set ip dns primary 192.168.1.2**

12. How is hardware flow enabled on a Catalyst 5000?
    a. **set system modem enable**
    b. **set system RTS/CTS enable**
    c. **set modem RTS/CTS enable**
    d. **set line RTS/CTS**

13. What is the default authentication method used on a Catalyst switch?
    a. Local
    b. Remote
    c. TACACS+
    d. Password

14. How do you enable TACACS+ authorization to IP address 192.168.1.2 on a Set/Clear switch?
    a. **set tacacs server 192.168.1.2**
    b. **set tacacs 192.168.1.2**
    c. **set tacacs+ server 192.168.1.2**
    d. **set tacacs enable 192.168.1.2**

15. On a Cisco IOS-based switch, which configuration file has the current configuration of the switch?
    a. Startup configuration
    b. Running configuration
    c. Current configuration
    d. cfg1

16. Which command do you use to make a copy of the current configuration to a TFTP server located on IP address 192.168.1.2?
    a. **copy running-config tftp**
    b. **copy running-config 192.168.1.2**
    c. **copy system:running-config net**
    d. **copy system:running-config tftp://192.168.1.2/running-config.txt**

17. Which command is used on an IOS-based switch to show the current system image?
    a. **show system**
    b. **show boot**
    c. **show image**
    d. **show flash**

18. Which command is used to see logging messages as they appear on an IOS-based switch?
    a. **show log**
    b. **show messages**
    c. **term monitor**
    d. **monitor log**

19. How would you forward logging messages to a syslog server located at IP address 192.168.1.2?
    a. **set logging 192.168.1.2**
    b. **logging 192.168.1.2**
    c. **logging enable 192.168.1.2**
    d. **log messages 192.168.1.2**

20. Which command will set up an NTP connection with an NTP server located at 192.168.1.2 on an IOS-based switch?
    a. **ntp server 192.168.1.2**
    b. **ntp peer 192.168.1.2**
    c. **set ntp 192.168.1.2**
    d. **ntp client 192.168.1.2**

21. How would you configure an IOS-based switch to use pacific standard time?
    a. **set time pst**
    b. **set timezone pacific -8**
    c. **clock set timezone PST -8**
    d. **clock timezone PST -8**

22. Which type of encryption is used for NTP authentication?
    a. DES
    b. Triple-DES
    c. MD5
    d. Triple-SEC

23. What is the maximum number of DNS servers you can configure on an IOS-based switch?
    a. 2
    b. 4
    c. 6
    d. 1

24. Which command is used to configure a DNS server located at IP address 192.168.1.2 on an IOS-based switch?
    a. **set dns server 192.168.1.2**
    b. **set name-server 192.168.1.2**
    c. **set ip name-server 192.168.1.2**
    d. **ip name-server 192.168.1.2**

25. Which type of connector is used on a modem port?
    a. RJ-45 to DB-25 DCE male
    b. RJ-45 to DB-25 DCE female
    c. RJ-45 to DB-25 DTE male
    d. RJ-45 to DB-25 DTE female

26. Which command sets up TACACS+ authentication on an IOS-based switch?
    a. **aaa authentication login default tacacs+ login**
    b. **aaa auth login default tacacs+ login**
    c. **aaa authorization default tacacs+ login**
    d. **set authorization tacacs+**

Real-World Projects

When we last met Joe Snow, he had just completed configuring a Catalyst 5500 switch and a Catalyst 2900 XL switch in record time. He boxed up the switches with instructions on how to rack-mount them and make connections to them. Inside the packages, he left a note saying how much he had enjoyed working with Coriolis and said the company should feel free to call on him with any other questions.

When he returned to his desk on Monday, he found a note from his boss asking him to come and talk about doing some more work on the switches.

"The customer loved your work," Joe's boss said, "but he would like some more work done." He went on to add that Coriolis had just purchased a state-of-the-art Network Management System with all the best software on it. The company would like to have each of the switches set up so that any logging messages would be forwarded to this workstation. Because many different systems would be sending messages to this workstation, Coriolis would be implementing an NTP server from which the switches should get their time.

In addition, the company would like to store backup configurations of the switches on the workstation as well as the software images that were running. Doing so would help in the event of an emergency. Also, one of the packages Coriolis was adding was CiscoSecure, which supports the TACACS+ protocol. The company would like to have the switches set up to authenticate against this package.

As Joe left the office, his mental checklist was already built. He needed to perform the following tasks:

- Back up the configurations and images
- Set up NTP
- Configure logging
- Implement TACACS+
- Call his wife to let her know he'd be working late

Project 6.1

The Catalyst 5500 is based on the original Catalyst switch software, so Joe used the Set/Clear interface to enter his commands. He proceeded to the tasks at hand.

To back up the system configurations and images to the network TFTP server located at IP address 192.168.1.2 on the corporate backbone, do the following:

1. Copy the existing system configurations with the following commands:

```
Coriolis> (enable) write network
IP address or name of remote host? 192.168.1.2
Name of configuration file? cat5_config.cfg
Upload configuration to cat5002_config.cfg on 192.168.1.2 (y/n) [n]? y
.....
..........
..........
..
Finished network upload.  (8534 bytes)
Coriolis> (enable)
```

2. For safety's sake, make a copy of the configuration on the Flash card by entering the following commands:

```
Console> (enable) copy config cfg1
Upload configuration to flash cfg1 (y/n) [n]? y
<lines deleted>
...
Erasing flash sector...done.
Programming flash sector...done.

Configuration has been copied successfully.
Console> (enable)
```


Fortunately, a project last year required Joe to purchase a time server that gets the time from an atomic clock at a big government facility.

To configure NTP on the switch, perform the following:

1. Synchronize your switch to that device:

```
Coriolis> (enable) set ntp server 192.168.1.2
Coriolis> (enable) set ntp broadcastclient enable
NTP Broadcast Client mode enabled
```

2. Because Joe lives in California, he wants the time in his local time zone instead of eight hours ahead. Enter the following commands:

```
Console> (enable) set timezone Pacific -8
Timezone set to 'Pacific', offset from UTC is -8 hours
```

3. Because Joe isn't fond of coming in to work at 2 A.M. if he can help it, he sets the switch for daylight savings time:

```
Coriolis> (enable) set summertime enable Pacific recurring
```

To configure the switch to send any logging messages to a syslog server your system administrator has set up, perform the following:

1. Enter these commands to send any messages of severity level 5 or below to the log file—that is, all notification messages, as well as any of the lower levels of messages:

```
Coriolis> (enable) set logging server 192.168.1.2
Coriolis> (enable) set logging server enable
Coriolis> (enable) set logging level sys 5
```

It's time for Joe to configure the switch to use the TACACS+ component of CiscoSecure to authenticate login access to the switch. Doing so will provide a central device to maintain usernames and passwords, as well as a log of who accesses what device.

To configure TACACS+ authentication, perform the following:

1. Point the switch to the TACACS+ server:

```
Coriolis> (enable) set tacacs server 192.168.1.2
192.168.1.2 added to TACACS server table as primary server.
```

2. Set up the switch to use TACACS+ for login access and enable access:

```
Coriolis> (enable) set authentication login tacacs enable  both
```

Project 6.2

Having completed the first tasks on the Catalyst 5500, Joe turns his attention to the Catalyst 2900 XL. Because this switch is running the Enterprise Edition of the switch software, it has an IOS-based command set like that seen on Cisco routers.

To begin backing up your configuration files to your TFTP server and to the Flash card, use these commands:

```
Coriolis# copy system:running-config tftp://192.168.1.2/switch-confg
Write file switch-confg on host 192.168.1.2? [confirm] y

Coriolis# copy running-config flash:
```

To configure NTP on the switch, perform the following:

1. Synchronize the switch to the same server described earlier:

```
Switch# (config) ntp server 192.168.1.2
Switch# (config) ntp peer ip-address 192.168.1.2
Switch# (config) ntp broadcast client
```

2. Set up the time zone information:

```
Switch# (config) clock timezone PST -8
Switch# (config) clock summer-time PDT recurring
```

To set up logging messages to go to the syslog server, use these commands:

```
Switch# (config) logging on
Switch# (config) logging 192.168.1.2
```

To set up TACACS+ as your authentication method, use these commands:

```
Switch# (config) tacacs-server host 192.168.1.3
Switch# (config) aaa authentication enable default tacacs+ enable
```


That's it—time to go home!

CHAPTER SEVEN

THE STANDARD EDITION IOS

After completing this chapter, you will be able to:

- ✓ Identify the features of the Standard Edition IOS
- ✓ Identify the menus used on the Catalyst 1900 Series
- ✓ Identify the menus used on the Catalyst 2820 Series
- ✓ Configure the network settings on the 1900 and 2820 Series
- ✓ Configure broadcast storm control on switch ports
- ✓ Configure SNMP on the 1900 and 2820 Series
- ✓ Identify the port status messages on the switch ports
- ✓ Configure port monitoring on the Standard Edition IOS
- ✓ Configure VLANs on the Standard Edition IOS
- ✓ Upgrade the switch software with a TFTP server or client
- ✓ Upgrade the switch software with a modem
- ✓ Get reports from the Standard Edition IOS

Cisco designed two switches specifically to replace the 1700 and the 2100 Series switches: the 2820 and 1900 Series, which are architecturally the same as the 3000 Series. These switches, which are found in the access layer, have two unique Internetwork Operating Systems (IOSs) that we will cover in this chapter. The Cisco 2820 and 1900 Series switches come with either a Standard or an Enterprise version of the IOS. The Standard version is a character-select IOS, and the Enterprise version is similar to the IOS on the routers that we all know and love. In this chapter, we will cover the setup of each switch's Standard Edition IOS in detail.

The Cisco 3000 Series switches have a unique IOS all to themselves. They use an IOS that has a graphical user interface (GUI) to configure the switch. However, the Cisco Catalyst 3000 received an End-of-Life notice some time ago and will not be covered in this book.

The 1900 and 2820 Standard Editions

When I teach CCNA classes, it's fun to instruct students to use a 1900 Series switch. The students are given a Catalyst 1924 and two Cisco 2514 routers to use during the class labs for their CCNA instruction. The routers are always on, and the switches are left off. When the class comes in, I ask them to press the power button on the switch. A few minutes later, when I can't keep myself from laughing any longer, I calmly ask them to go ahead and plug in the switch. You see, the Cisco Catalyst 1900 has no power switch—you simply plug it in and go. It's the switch without a switch! (You can pull some other fun tricks in class, such as using the **debug** command on your neighbor's router; but this book is not called *The Administrators' Guide to Practical Jokes*, so I will stop right there.)

The Cisco Catalyst 1900 and 2820 Standard Edition IOS switches are Cisco's low-end switches; they closely resemble a managed hub in many ways. These are typically the workhorses of the access layer, used to provide up to 2 100BaseT or 100BaseFX uplink ports and up to 24 10BaseT ports.

The Catalyst 1900 is the entry point for Cisco's switch line. There are two types of Catalyst 1900: the Standard Edition (SE) and the Enterprise Edition (EE). The Standard Edition is a low-cost alternative for those migrating from a shared hub environment to a smaller workgroup environment. These switches were specifically designed to be plug-and-play right out of the box with no manual configuration. The Catalyst 1900 SE has 12 or 24 fixed 10BaseT ports with 2 high-speed 100BaseT ports or 1 100BaseT port and 1 100BaseFX port. This switch can be configured by the console port, the TTY line, the Web-browser interface, or the Cisco Visual Switch Manager. Support for Domain Name Service (DNS) and Dynamic Host Configuration Protocol (DHCP) is included to help in ease of use. The Standard Edition can be upgraded via Flash to an Enterprise Edition version, which is typical in the 1900 Series of today. The first screen of the Enterprise Edition has an additional option to use a command-line interface, as shown here:

```
PCA Number:             73-3122-04
PCA Serial Number:      FAB0347250K
Model Number:           WS-C1912-A
System Serial Number:   FAB0339U01U
Power Supply S/N:       PHI031803JK
PCB Serial Number:      FAB0337240K,73-3222-04
------------------------------------------------

1 user(s) now active on Management Console.

        User Interface Menu

     [M] Menus
     [K] Command Line
     [I] IP Configuration

Enter Selection:
```

The Enterprise Edition contains all the features of the Standard Edition but provides several high-end solutions, including an IOS that is similar to the Cisco router IOS, if you select the Command Line option from the User Interface menu. These additional features include Fast EtherChannel, support for Inter-Switch Link (ISL), an IOS command-line interface (CLI), and support for Cisco Group Management Protocol (CGMP).

The Cisco 2820 Series, which includes the 2822 and 2828, is designed for an environment that needs 10BaseT links to the wiring closet for 20 or so users. This switch is perfect for smaller wiring closets where it is not economical to purchase a high-end solution such as a Cisco Catalyst 5000 Series switch. On both switches, you will find 24 10BaseT Ethernet ports and 1 10Mbps AUI port.

The Catalyst 2820 Series switch architecture is virtually identical to that of the Cisco Catalyst 1900 Series switches. The switch is different because of its height and uplink bays, which allow for high-speed uplink options such as Fiber Distributed Data Interface (FDDI), Copper Distributed Data Interface (CDDI), 100Mbps, and Asynchronous Transfer Mode (ATM) modules. In this chapter, we are going to concentrate more on the configuration of the Standard Edition IOS than the switch specifications for the 1900 and 2820 Series, which were covered in Chapter 4.

Unfortunately for the Catalyst 2820 Series, Cisco issued an End-of-Life notice, which means this switch will no longer be manufactured. You still need to know how to configure and support this switch in the real world, however—thousands of these switches are still sitting in the access layers of networks. As luck would have it, you'll probably find one that you will have to support!

In the next sections, we'll take a look at the menu-driven interface and how to configure the basics on the Standard Edition IOS found on the Cisco Catalyst 1900 and 2820 Series.

Cisco Catalyst 1900 and 2820 Standard Edition Basic Configuration

When you first turn on the Catalyst 1900 switch, you will be presented with a screen that looks similar to this:

```
Catalyst 1900 Management Console
Copyright (c) Cisco Systems, Inc.1993-1999
All rights reserved.

Standard Edition Software
Ethernet address:      00-E0-1E-40-AA-B2

     PCA Number: 73-2239-01
     PCA Serial Number: SAD01203451
     Model Number: WS-C1924-A
     System Serial Number: FAA01205461
     ------------------------------------

     User Interface Menu

     [M] Menus
     [I] IP Address
     [P] Console Password

Enter Selection:
```

The following list shows the three options and a description of each:

- *[M] Menus*—Displays the switch's Main menu.
- *[I] IP Address*—Available at logon if a password is not configured for the switch.
- *[P] Console Password*—Allows you to enter an unencrypted Privileged-level password to the switch management interface. This option is available at logon only if the switch does not have a password. The password must be at least four characters long and no more than eight.

Both the 1900 and the 2820 Series switches' menus look virtually identical, with the exception of the different model numbers listed above each menu. When logging on to the 1900 or 2820 Series switch, you are presented with a Main menu that looks similar to this:

```
Catalyst 2820 - Main Menu

     [C] Console Password
     [S] System
     [N] Network Management
     [P] Port Configuration
     [A] Port Addressing
     [D] Port Statistics Detail
     [M] Monitor
     [V] Virtual LAN
     [R] Multicast Registration
     [F] Firmware
     [I] RS-232 Interface
     [U] Usage Summaries
     [H] Help

     [X] Exit Management Console

Enter Selection:
```

Let's look at the menu options in more detail.

[C] Console Password

By typing the letter associated with each command, you enter that configuration screen. We will begin configuring the basic system settings by choosing C to reach the Console Settings menu on the Cisco Catalyst 1900 Series:

```
Catalyst 1900 - Console Settings

     ----------Settings----------
     [P] Password intrusion threshold               3 attempt(s)
     [S] Silent time upon intrusion detection       None
     [T] Management Console inactivity timeout      None
     [D] Default mode of status LED                 Port Status

     ----------Actions----------
     [M] Modify password
     [E] Modify secret password

     [X] Exit to Main Menu

Enter Selection:
```

The Console Settings menu on the Cisco Catalyst 1900 Series switch offers these options:

- *[P] Password Intrusion Threshold*—Configures the number of failed password attempts before the port is placed in silent time. The default is three attempts.
- *[S] Silent Time Upon Intrusion Detection*—Sets the number of minutes the management console is unavailable because of an excessive number of failed login attempts. The configurable range of minutes is 0 to 65,500. The default is 0 minutes.
- *[T] Management Console Inactivity Timeout*—Sets the number of seconds the management console can wait without activity before it times out. After timeout, you must reenter the password. The configurable range is 30 to 65,500 seconds. The default is 0, which means the console session does not time out.
- *[D] Default Mode Of Status LED*—Selects the default mode of the port LEDs. The switch returns to this mode 30 seconds after you release the Mode button shown in Figure 7.1. You can select [1] Port Status, [2] Utilization, or [3] Duplex Status. The default is [1] Port Status.
- *[M] Modify Password*—Configures an unencrypted Privileged-level password for the switch management interfaces. The password can be four to eight characters and is not case-sensitive.

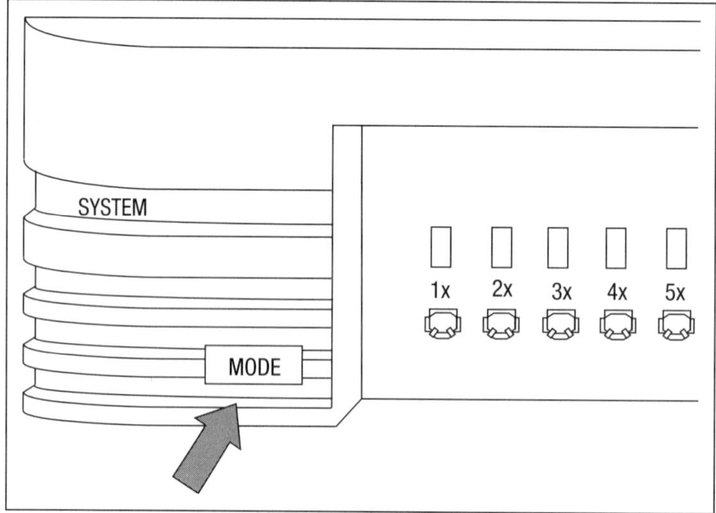

Figure 7.1 The Mode button on the Cisco Catalyst 1900 switch.

- *[E] Modify Secret Password*—Allows the encrypted secret Privileged-level password for the switch management interfaces. This password can be 1 to 25 characters and is case-sensitive.
- *[X] Exit To The Main Menu*—Returns you to the Main menu.

[S] System

Choose S from the Main Menu to reach the following System Configuration menu:

```
Catalyst 2820 - System Configuration
         System Revision: 0      Address Capacity: 2048
         System Last Reset:    Mon Aug 21 11:13:03 2000
     ---------Settings---------
     [N] Name of system                            Coriolis Editings 2820
     [C] Contact Name                              Joe Snow (888)555-9700
     [L] Location                                  Editor staff closet
     [D] Date/time                                 Mon Aug 7 12:52:23 2000
     [S] Switching Mode                            FragmentFree
     [U] Use of store-and-forward for multicast Disabled
     [A] Action upon address violation             Disable
     [G] General alert on address violation        Disabled
     [M] Management Console inactivity timeout  65500 second(s)
     [I] Address aging time                        10 second(s)
     [P] Network Port                              None
     ---------Actions---------
     [R] Reset system                    [F] Reset to factory defaults
     ---------Related Menus---------
     [B] Broadcast storm control         [X] Exit to Main Menu
```

Let's take a look at the System Configuration commands. Each is listed here with a brief explanation:

- *[N] Name Of System*—In multiple switch environments, this aids in determining which switch you are currently configuring. You can use up to 255 characters in the switch name, including spaces.
- *[C] Contact Name*—Defines a contact name in case problems occur with the switch. This field can also contain up to 255 characters. You may find it helpful to include a pager number or home contact information.
- *[L] Location*—Contains up to 255 characters of additional information about where the switch physically resides.
- *[D] Date/time*—Configures the current date and time.
- *[S] Switching Mode*—Allows the switch to be configured for all three switching modes. The three configuration choices are [1] Store-and-Forward, [2] FragmentFree, and [3] FastForward.

- *[U] Use Of Store-and-Forward For Multicast*—Allows you to determine which method to use for multicast frames. The switch will always use store-and-forward for broadcasts. You can choose two options: E (enabled) allows the switch to use store-and-forward for multicast frames, and D (disabled) uses the method defined in the Switching Mode option from the System Configuration Method. The default is D.
- *[A] Action Upon Address Violation*—Gives you three options to inform the switch what to do when an address violation occurs. The option S (suspend) stops the port from forwarding frames of the violation. Option D (disabled) turns off the port until an administrator disables it. Option I (ignore) indicates that no action will be taken.
- *[G] General Alert On Address Violation*—Indicates whether Simple Network Management Protocol (SNMP) trap messages are sent when an address violation occurs.
- *[M] Management Console Inactivity Timeout*—Defines the valid timeout setting available from the console. If no keystrokes are received to the console port during this configured amount of time, the user logged in to the console port is logged out. The valid time period is 30 to 65,500 seconds. A setting of 0 indicates the timeout is disabled.
- *[I] Address Aging Time*—Defines the number of seconds that dynamic entries into the Media Access Control (MAC) address table will remain. The valid settings are 10 to 1,000,000 seconds. The default is 300 seconds.
- *[P] Network Port*—Specifies the port to which all unknown unicasts are forwarded. You can specify a port in the range of port numbers on the switch: A indicates port 25, B indicates port 26, AUI indicates the AUI port, and N indicates none.
- *[R] Reset System*—Recycles the power on the switch.
- *[F] Reset To Factory Defaults*—Clears all configuration settings back to the factory defaults.

Warning: If you apply the [F] Reset To Factory Defaults option, all manual configuration settings will be lost.

- *[B] Broadcast Storm Control*—Launches the Broadcast Storm Control menu, which includes five options discussed in the next section.
- *[X] Exit To Main Menu*—Exits to the Main menu.

The 1900 and 2820 Series switches use one configuration for the entire switch. Other switches in the Catalyst Series use individual settings for each port. The following is a listing of the Broadcast Storm Control menu:

```
Catalyst 2820 - Broadcast Storm Control

     ------------------Settings------------------
     [A] Action upon exceeding broadcast threshold     Block
     [G] Generate alert when threshold exceeded        Enabled
     [T] Broadcast Threshold (BC's received / sec)     1000
     [R] Broadcast re-enable threshold                 300

     [X] Exit to previous menu

Enter Selection:
```


This menu allows you to control the propagation of broadcasts to each port. The following list gives a brief breakdown of each setting:

- *[A] Action Upon Exceeding Broadcast Threshold*—Indicates what action will be taken in the event that the broadcast number threshold is exceeded. Option I ignores broadcasts, and option B blocks them until the number of broadcasts becomes lower than the threshold setting.
- *[G] Generate Alert When Threshold Exceeded*—Controls whether an SNMP trap message is sent when the broadcast threshold has been exceeded. Two options are available: E (enable) and D (disable).
- *[T] Broadcast Threshold (BC's Received / sec)*—Sets the broadcast threshold in broadcasts per second. The possible settings are 10 to 14,400; the default is 500 per second.
- *[R] Broadcast Re-enable Threshold*—Indicates the number of broadcasts per second at which the port will re-enable after an instance in which the threshold maximum disabled the port. The possible settings are 10 to 14,400; the default is 500 per second.
- *[X] Exit To Previous Menu*—Returns you to the System Configuration menu.

[N] Network Management

By pressing N from the Main menu, you can configure the Network Management menu. This menu can be used to define an IP address for the system, SNMP, Spanning Tree Protocol (STP), Cisco Discovery Protocol (CDP), and Cisco Group Management Protocol (CGMP).

The following displays the Network Management menu:

```
Catalyst 2820 - Network Management

     [I] IP Configuration
     [S] SNMP Management
     [B] Bridge - Spanning Tree
     [C] Cisco Discover Protocol
     [G] Cisco Group Management Protocol

     [X] Exit to Main Menu

Enter Selection:
```

Choosing [I] IP Configuration from the Network Management menu brings up a menu that looks similar to the following:

```
Catalyst 2820 - IP Configuration

          Ethernet Address:   00-D3-1F-11-B1-05

     ----------Settings----------
     [I] IP address                              38.187.128.254
     [S] Subnet mask                             255.255.255.0
     [G] Default gateway                         38.187.128.1
     [V] Management VLAN                         1

     [X] Exit to previous menu

Enter selection:
```

In order to use Telnet or SNMP to manage the switch, an IP address must be assigned to the switch. The following are the settings from the IP Configuration menu.

- *[I] IP Address*—Configures the IP address on the switch.
- *[S] Subnet Mask*—Configures the switch's subnet mask.
- *[G] Default Gateway*—Configures the destination address for the route processor to which the switch will forward unknown or out-of-subnet addresses.
- *[V] Management VLAN*—Allows you to set the virtual LAN (VLAN) in which you will configure your switch. Cisco recommends that you choose a VLAN other than 1, because all ports are in VLAN1 by default. On the

Standard Edition of the IOS software, the available VLANs are 1 through 4. The Enterprise Edition has 64 available VLANs.

- *[X] Exit To Previous Menu*—Exits back to the Network Management menu.

Tip: When you change the IP address, the change takes effect immediately. However, all other options from this menu require the power to be recycled. Configuration changes on the 1900 and 2820 Series are automatically saved, but changes require up to 30 seconds to take effect.

To make changes to SNMP, choose S from the Network Management menu. The following shows the SNMP Configuration menu options:

```
Catalyst 2820 - Network Management (SNMP) Configuration

    ----------Settings----------
    [R] READ  community string
    [W] WRITE community string
    [1] 1st WRITE manager IP address              0.0.0.0
    [2] 2nd WRITE manager IP address              0.0.0.0
    [3] 3rd WRITE manager IP address              0.0.0.0
    [4] 4th WRITE manager IP address              0.0.0.0

    [F] First TRAP community string               0.0.0.0
    [A] First TRAP manager IP address             0.0.0.0
    [S] Second TRAP community string              0.0.0.0
    [B] Second TRAP manager IP address            0.0.0.0
    [T] Third TRAP community string               0.0.0.0
    [C] Third TRAP manager IP address             0.0.0.0
    [U] Authentication Trap generation            Disabled
    [L] LinkUp/LinkDown trap generation           Disabled
    ----------Actions----------
    [X] Exit to previous Menu

Enter selection:
```

The following list shows the options available from the SNMP Configuration menu:

- *[R] READ Community String*—Identifies the community that is assigned to the management stations. Those management stations assigned to this community can read the trap messages sent from the switch. You can define a name up to 32 characters long; the default is *public*.

Note: *When VLANs are implemented, the VLAN needs to be included in the string. For example, public in VLAN2 would be public2.*

- *[W] WRITE Community String*—Identifies the community that is assigned to the management stations. Those management stations assigned to this community can read or set SNMP configurations on the switch. You can define a name up to 32 characters long; the default is *private*.
- *WRITE Manager IP Address*—Allows you to define up to four SNMP management stations that can set SNMP configuration parameters on the switch.
- *TRAP Messages*—Allows you to define which SNMP management stations can receive trap messages on the switch.
- *[U] Authentication Trap Generation*—Allows you to enable or disable authentication trap message generation.
- *[L] LinkUp/LinkDown Trap Generation*—Informs the switch of the actions to take when the port changes its state to suspended, down, or up from STP; an address violation; a link error; or a manual configuration.
- *[X] Exit To Previous Menu*—Returns you to the Network Management menu.

SNMP Default Trap Messages

By default, the Cisco Catalyst 1900 and the Cisco Catalyst 2820 Series switches send certain trap messages. The following trap messages are sent by default:

- Port security violations
- Power recycling (powering on and off)
- Logon authentication failures
- STP port changes
- STP bridge assignments
- Broadcast threshold problems
- Power supply problems

By selecting [B] Bridge - Spanning Tree from the Network Management menu, you will reach the following menu:

```
Catalyst 2820 - VLAN 1 Spanning Tree Configuration
       Bridge ID:  0002 00-D3-1F-11-B1-05
```

```
----------Information---------
Designated root 0001 00-D3-1F-13-A3-11
Number of member ports     27     Root port               3
Max age (sec)              20     Root path cost       1000
Forward Delay (sec)        15     Hello Time (sec)       10
Topology changes            0     Last TopChange 235d08h12m22s

----------Settings---------
[S] Spanning Tree Algorithm & Protocol         Enabled
[B] Bridge priority                            32,768 (8000 Hex)
[M] Max age when operating as root             20 second(s)
[H] Hello time when operating as root          10 second(s)
[F] Forward delay when operating as the root   15 second(s)

----------Actions---------
[N] Next VLAN bridge              [G] Goto VLAN bridge
[P] Previous VLAN bridge          [X] Exit to previous menu

Enter Selection:
```

Note: *Spanning Tree Protocol and its defaults are covered in detail in Chapter 9.*

Choosing [C] Cisco Discover Protocol from the Network Management menu will bring up the following menu:

```
Catalyst 2820 - CDP Configuration/Status

     CDP enabled on: 1-24, AUI, A, B

     ----------Settings---------
     [H] Hold Time (secs)                          180
     [T] Transmission Interval (secs)               60

     ----------Actions---------
     [E] Enable CDP on Port(s)
     [D] Disable CDP on Port(s)
     [S] Show Neighbor
     [X] Exit to previous menu

Enter Selection:
```

The following list shows the commands from the CDP Configuration/ Status menu:

- *[H] Hold Time (Secs)*—Indicates how long a CDP multicast will remain in the CDP table. The valid entries are from 5 to 255 seconds; the default is 180 seconds.

- *[T] Transmission Interval (Secs)*—Defines the interval in which the switch will send CDP multicast messages.
- *[E] Enable CDP On Port(s)*—Identifies one or more ports to enable CDP. You can use the All setting to enable all ports. Or, you can identify blocks of ports such as 1 through 10 by using a hyphen, like this: "1-10". Use spaces to separate the variables; for example, if you also want 12-15, use "1-10 12-15".
- *[D] Disable CDP On Port(s)*—Identifies one or more ports on which to disable CDP.
- *[S] Show Neighbor*—Displays a list of neighboring Cisco devices with their device ID, MAC address, port, and capabilities, and identifies the device platform. The possible capabilities are indicated by letters: R indicates a router, T indicates a trans bridge, B indicates a route bridge, S indicates a switch, P indicates a repeater, H indicates a host, and I indicates Internet Group Management Protocol (IGMP).
- *[X] Exit To Previous Menu*—Returns you to the Network Configuration menu.

Configuring CGMP by choosing [G] Cisco Group Management Protocol is the last configuration option on the Network Management menu. CGMP is a protocol that likes all the ports on the switch to reside in the same VLAN in order to function properly. CGMP allows an intelligent means of limiting multicast flooding to specific ports.

The following shows the menu on a Catalyst 2820 when you use the G command from the Network Management menu:

```
Catalyst 2820 - Cisco Group Management Protocol (CGMP) Configuration

     ----------Settings----------
     [H] Router hold time (secs)                  300
     [C] CGMP                                     Enabled

     ------------Actions------------
     [L] List IP multicast addresses

     [X] Return to previous menu
```

The following list shows the commands and descriptions for the CGMP Configuration menu:

- *[H] Router Hold Time (Secs)*—Indicates the amount of time that the switch will keep CGMP multicast information. When the CGMP router fails or the power is recycled, the switch will flood multicast broadcasts out all the ports. The valid range is from 5 to 900 seconds; the default is 5 seconds.

- *[C] CGMP*—Enables or disables CGMP on the switch. There are two valid options: E (enabled) and D (disabled); the default is disabled.
- *[L] List IP Multicast Addresses*—Lists all multicast addresses learned by CGMP along with the VLAN, source MAC address, and the port of the source address.
- *[X] Return To Previous Menu*—Returns you to the Network Management menu.

[P] Port Configuration

By choosing P from the Main menu, you can configure each port's settings by using the Port Configuration menu. You must specify a port from the list in Table 7.1.

7

The Port Configuration menu looks like this:

```
    [A] Port addressing                [V] View port settings
    [N] Next port                      [G] Goto port
    [P] Previous port                  [X] Exit to Main Menu

Enter Selection:
```

The following list shows the options and a description of each item on the Port Configuration menu:

- *[D] Description/name Of Port*—Allows you to change the port name to a name with 60 characters or less, such as *Port to Sean Odom's PC.*
- *[S] Status Of Port*—Has two configurable options: E (enabled) or D (disabled). The default setting places all ports in the enabled mode.

Table 7.1 The available configurable ports on a Catalyst 2820 from the Port Configuration menu.

Syntax	Port
A1	Identifies port 25
B1	Identifies port 26
AUI	Identifies the AUI port
1 through 24	Identifies an individual port on the switch

Port Status

Although the administrator has only two configurable settings under the [S] Status Of Port option, the port can be in any of the following statuses:

- *Enabled*—The port is available to send and receive data frames.
- *Disabled-mgmt*—The port has been manually disabled.
- *Suspended-linkbeat*—The port cannot detect a link at the other end of the cable. Possibly the cable has become unplugged, the device on the other end is turned off, or the port is not configured on the far-end device.
- *Suspended-jabber*—The port is temporarily disabled because of excessive jabber or indecipherable data frames.
- *Suspended-violation*—The port has been temporarily disabled because of an address violation. The port is automatically re-enabled once it discontinues receiving the invalid source address information.
- *Suspended-ring down*—The port is using FDDI links and cannot detect an attached FDDI ring.
- *Suspended-Spanning-Tree-Protocol*—The port is not participating in any STP forwarding state.
- *Suspended-not-present*—A module in an expansion slot cannot be detected (on the 2820 Series only).
- *Suspended-not-recognized*—The switch cannot detect the switch port or a module in the expansion slot (on the 2820 Series only).
- *Disabled-self-test*—This indicates that the port is disabled because the port failed its self-test.
- *Disabled-violation*—This indicates that the port is disabled due to an invalid source-address violation.
- *Reset*—This indicates that the port is currently in the reset state.

- *[A] Port Addressing*—Accesses the Port Addressing menu.
- *[V] View Port Settings*—Displays individual port statistics.
- *[N] Next Port*—Forwards to the next configurable port.
- *[G] Goto Port*—Configures any identified port.
- *[P] Previous Port*—Configures the previous configurable port.
- *[X] Exit To Main Menu*—Returns you to the Main menu.

Let's take a look at the options available on the 2820 using a FDDI Module on port A1:

```
Catalyst 2820 - Port A1 Configuration (Left Slot)

     Module Name: FDDI (Fiber SAS Model). Version 00
     Description: Single Attached Station
     Ring Status: Not operational
     802.1d STP State: Blocking      Forwarding:  0
     ----------Settings----------
     [D] Description/name of port
     ----------Module Settings----------
     [M] Module status                       Suspended-ring-down
     [I] Port priority (spanning tree)       128 (80 hex)
     [C] Path cost (spanning tree)           100
     [H] Port fast mode (spanning tree)      Disabled
     [L] Novell SNAP frame translation       Automatic
     [U] Unmatched SNAP frame destination    All
     ----------Actions----------
     [R] Reset module                   [F] Reset to factory defaults
     ----------Related Menus----------
     [1] Basic FDDI settings            [2] Secondary FDDI settings
     [A] Port addressing                [V] View port settings
     [N] Next port                      [G] Goto port
     [P] Previous port                  [X] Exit to Main Menu

Enter Selection:
```

The following list shows the menu options and an explanation of each:

- *[M] Module Status*—Has three options: S for the status of the module, E to enable the module, or D to disable it.
- *[I] Port Priority*—Sets the port priority for the STP root port. The lower the priority number, the higher the port priority. The valid range is 0 to 255; the default is 128.
- *[C] Path Cost*—Sets the path cost used to choose the STP root port. For more information on port cost defaults, see Table 9.1 in Chapter 9.
- *[H] Port Fast Mode*—Allows a port using STP to immediately go into forwarding mode. This option is explained in detail in Chapter 9. This selection offers two options: E (enabled) and D (disabled).
- *[L] Novell SNAP Frame Translation*—Determines whether manual or automatic frame translation is used by Internetwork Packet Exchange (IPX).
- *[U] Unmatched SNAP Frame Destination*—Identifies the translation of frames for which the frame type cannot be determined. To use this option, set option [L] Novell SNAP Frame Translation to automatic.

7

- *[R] Reset Module*—Resets the expansion module.
- *[F] Reset To Factory Defaults*—Resets the expansion module's configuration to the factory defaults.
- *[1] Basic FDDI Settings*—Allows you to see the first expansion module's status and current configuration.
- *[2] Secondary FDDI Settings*—Displays the second screen of the expansion module's status and current configuration.
- *[A] Port Addressing*—Accesses the Port Addressing menu.
- *[V] View Port Settings*—Displays individual port statistics.
- *[N] Next Port*—Forwards to the next configurable port.
- *[G] Goto Port*—Configures any identified port.
- *[P] Previous Port*—Configures the previous configurable port.
- *[X] Exit To Main Menu*—Returns you to the Main menu.

[A] Port Addressing

The Port Addressing menu allows you to set up security and to add static MAC addresses to a port. When entering this option, you must first identify a port to configure from the list in Table 7.2.

The following is the Port Addressing configuration menu:

```
Catalyst 2820 - Port 2 Addressing

     Address:  Static    00-00-D3-1F-11-34
     ----------Settings----------
     [T] Address table size                          Unrestricted
     [S] Addressing security                         Disabled
     [U] Flood unknown unicast                       Enabled
     [M] Flood unregistered multicast                Enabled
     ----------Actions----------
     [A] Add a static address
     [D] Define restricted static address
     [L] List addresses
     [E] Erase an address
     [R] Remove all addresses
     ----------Related Menus----------
     [C] Configure port                [V] View port statistics
     [N] Next port                     [G] Goto port
     [P] Previous Port                 [X] Return to Main Menu

Enter selection:
```

Table 7.2 The available configurable ports on a Catalyst 2820 from the Port Addressing menu.

Syntax	Port
A	Identifies port 25
AUI	Identifies the AUI port
1 through 24	Identifies an individual port on the switch

When the port is a secured port, its MAC address is 00-00-00-00-00-00. The following is the list of options and parameters for the Port Addressing menu:

- *[T] Address Table Size*—Defines the number of allowable MAC addresses if the port is secure-port enabled. The range can be any value from 1 to 132. The default is 132, and this default cannot be changed if the port is not secure-port enabled.
- *[S] Addressing Security*—Allows you to enable or disable a secure port; also known as addressing security.
- *[U] Flood Unknown Unicast*—Allows you to enable or disable whether unknown unicasts are flooded out all the ports.
- *[M] Flood Unregistered Multicast*—Allows you to enable or disable whether unregistered multicasts are flooded out all the ports.
- *[A] Add A Static Address*—Allows you to add a static unicast hexadecimal MAC address to the table, if the table is not full.
- *[D] Define Restricted Static Address*—Allows a source MAC address to be identified, allowing only the device using that MAC address to use the port.
- *[L] List Addresses*—Displays all the static and dynamic MAC addresses that the switch has learned are attached to the port. The screen displays the first 15 entries beginning with those that have been statically configured.
- *[E] Erase An Address*—Allows you to remove a statically or dynamically configured MAC address associated with the port.
- *[R] Remove All Addresses*—Allows you to remove all statically or dynamically configured MAC addresses associated with the port.
- *[C] Configure Port*—Provides a shortcut to the Port Configuration menu.
- *[A] Port Addressing*—Accesses the Port Addressing menu.
- *[V] View Port Settings*—Displays individual port statistics.
- *[N] Next Port*—Forwards to the next configurable port.
- *[G] Goto Port*—Configures any identified port.

- *[P] Previous Port*—Configures the previous configurable port.
- *[X] Exit To Main Menu*—Returns you to the Main menu.

[D] Port Statistics Detail

The Port Statistics Detail displays the receive and transmit statistics for the port you select. This page can be used to help you identify performance or connectivity problems.

The options available from the Port Statistics Detail menu are as follows:

- *[A] Port Addressing*—Displays the Port Addressing menu.
- *[C] Configure Port*—Displays the Port Configuration menu.
- *[R] Reset Port Statistics*—Allows you to clear the port statistics. Enter [Y] (yes) to clear the port statistics.
- *[N] Next Port*—Displays the detailed port statistics for the next sequentially numbered Port on the switch.
- *[G] Go To Port*—Displays the detailed port statistics for a manually specified port.

[M] Monitor

When you choose M from the Main menu, you should see the following Monitoring Configuration menu:

```
Catalyst 1900 - Monitoring Configuration

    ----------Settings----------
    [C] Capturing frames to the Monitor                  Disabled
    [M] Monitor port assignment                          None
    Current capture list: 1-24, AUI

    ----------Actions----------
    [A] Add ports to capture list
    [D] Delete ports from capture list

    [X] Exit to Main Menu

Enter Selection:
```

The following list shows the Monitoring Configuration menu options and a description of each:

- *[C] Capturing Frames To The Monitor*—Allows you to enable or disable port monitoring on the switch.
- *[M] Monitor Port Assignment*—Lets you enter the port to which captured frames are sent. The default is none.
- *[A] Add Ports To Capture List*—Allows the addition of ports you want to monitor. You can enter "all" for all ports.
- *[D] Delete Ports From Capture List*—Allows the addition of ports you want to remove from monitoring. You can enter "all" for all ports.
- *[X] Exit To Main Menu*—Displays the Main menu.

[V] Virtual LAN

To implement VLANs (covered in Chapters 8 and 10), use the V command from the Main menu. Because the Standard Edition software does not support ISL and other high-end VLAN protocols, the VLAN menu is quite simple. The following shows the Virtual LAN Configuration menu:

```
Catalyst 2820 - Virtual LAN Configuration

     VLAN   Name                         Member Ports
     ----   -----------------------      ----------------
        1   VLAN 1                       1-24, AUI, A, B

     ----------Action----------
     [C] Configure VLAN
     [X] Exit to Main Menu

Enter Selection:
```

This menu only gives two options. You can use C to enter another menu that allows you to configure a VLAN name and move member ports to another VLAN, or you can exit back to the Main menu.

[R] Multicast Registration

The 1900 Series and 2820 Series switches, by default, forward all multicast packets to all ports on the switch. To reduce the amount of multicast flooding on the switch, you can register multicast addresses and list the ports to which these packets are to be forwarded.

To display the Multicast Registration menu, enter the R option from the Main Menu. The following is a Multicast Registration menu from the Catalyst 2820:

```
Catalyst 2820 - Multicast Registration

     Registered multicast addresses: 1

     ----------Actions----------
     [R] Register a multicast address
     [L] List all multicast addresses
     [U] Unregister a multicast address
     [E] Erase all multicast addresses

     [X] Exit to Main Menu

Enter Selection:
```

The first line of the menu displays the number of registered multicast addresses. The menu options are as follows:

- *[R] Register A Multicast Address*—Allows the addition of multicast addresses and ports to which multicasts can be forwarded. Invalid multicasts—such as unicasts, broadcasts, and reserved multicasts—are automatically rejected. The switch supports up to 64 IP multicast group registrations.
- *[L] List All Multicast Addresses*—Displays all registered multicast addresses that exist in the switch.
- *[U] Unregister A Multicast Address*—Removes registered multicast addresses.
- *[E] Erase All Multicast Addresses*—Removes all registered multicast addresses from the switch's address table.
- *[X] Exit To Main Menu*—Displays the Management Console Main menu.

[F] Firmware

Loading an upgraded version of the system software is fairly simple. When you download the firmware to Flash memory, the switch does not respond to commands for approximately one minute. You should not turn off the switch until after the switch resets and begins using the new firmware.

Note: *Cisco periodically provides new firmware to implement enhancements and maintenance releases. New firmware releases can be downloaded from Cisco Connection Online (CCO), Cisco Systems' customer Web site, at* ***www.cisco.com***.

When you enter the Firmware Configuration menu, your display will look similar to this:

```
Catalyst 1900 - Firmware Configuration

     ----------System Information----------
     FLASH: 1024K bytes
     V9.00.00 Standard Edition
     Upgrade status:
     No upgrade currently in progress.

     ----------Settings----------
     [S] TFTP Server name or IP address
     [F] Filename for firmware upgrades
     [A] Accept upgrade transfer from other hosts    Disabled

     ----------Actions----------
     [U]System XMODEM upgrade      [D]Download test subsystem (XMODEM)
     [T]System TFTP upgrade        [X]Exit to Main Menu

Enter Selection:
```


The switch firmware version and the amount of Flash memory are displayed in the System Information area of the Firmware Configuration menu. The following list displays each option and a description of each:

- *[S] TFTP Server Name Or IP Address*—Allows you to enter the server name or the IP address of the Trivial File Transfer Protocol (TFTP) server where the upgrade file is located.
- *[F] Filename For Firmware Upgrades*—Lets you enter the name of the firmware upgrade file to be downloaded.
- *[A] Accept Upgrade Transfer From Other Hosts*—Allows you to enable or disable an upgrade from another host on the network. To prevent any unauthorized upgrades, disable this option after you upgrade your firmware.
- *[U] System XMODEM Upgrade*—Allows you to begin the upgrade using the XMODEM protocol.
- *[T] System TFTP Upgrade*—Allows you to begin the upgrade from a TFTP server. The address of the server and the name of the file must already be configured with options S and F.
- *[D] Download Test Subsystem (XMODEM)*—Available for Cisco personnel only. This option is not available during a Telnet session.
- *[X] Exit To Main Menu*—Returns to the Main menu.

[I] RS-232 Interface

The I option, available from the Main menu, configures the RS-232 interface on the switch. The following is the RS-232 Interface Configuration menu:

```
Catalyst 1900 - RS-232 Interface Configuration

     ----------Group Settings----------
     [B] Baud rate                                  9600 baud
     [D] Data bits                                  8 bit(s)
     [S] Stop bits                                  1 bit(s)
     [P] Parity setting                             None

     ----------Settings----------
     [M] Match remote baud rate (auto baud)         Enabled
     [A] Auto answer                                Enabled
     [N] Number for dial-out connection
     [T] Time delay between dial attempts           300
     [I] Initialization string for modem

     ----------Actions----------
     [C] Cancel and restore previous group settings
     [G] Activate group settings

     [X] Exit to Main Menu

Enter Selection:
```

The following list explains the options available from the RS-232 Interface Configuration menu:

- *[B] Baud Rate*—Enters the baud rate. The possible settings are 2400, 9600, 19200, 38400, or 57600 for the console port. The default baud rate is 9600.
- *[D] Data Bits*—Allows the configuration of data bits for the console port. The possible options are 7 and 8. The default is 8.
- *[S] Stop Bits*—Allows the configuration of the stop bit value for the console port. The default is 1.
- *[P] Parity Settings*—Changes the parity settings for the console port. The default is None.
- *[M] Match Remote Baud Rate (Auto Baud)*—Allows you to enable or disable the console port from automatically matching the baud rate of an incoming call. The switch only matches a baud rate lower than its configured baud rate.
- *[A] Auto Answer*—Allows you to enable or disable the switch for automatically answering incoming calls.

- *[N] Number For Dial-out Connection*—Lets you enter the phone number the switch is configured to use when dialing out. This number is dialed when the switch is configured to communicate with a remote terminal upon power-up or power recycling.
- *[T] Time Delay Between Dial Attempts*—Configures the number of seconds between dial-out attempts. A value of 0 (zero) disables all retries. The default is 300 seconds.
- *[I] Initialization String For Modem*—Allows you to change the initialization string to match your modem requirements.
- *[C] Cancel And Restore Previous Group Settings*—Allows you to undo any new values entered for the baud rate, data bits, stop bits, and parity settings.
- *[G] Activate Group Settings*—Allows you to activate the settings you have entered for baud rate, data bits, stops bits, and parity.
- *[X] Exit To Main Menu*—Returns you to the Main menu.

[U] Usage Summaries

The Usage Summaries menu allows you to receive usage and summary reports. You can receive five types of reports based on the following options:

```
Catalyst 1900 - Usage Summaries

     [P] Port Status Report
     [A] Port Addressing Report
     [E] Exception Statistics Report
     [U] Utilization Statistics Report
     [B] Bandwidth Usage Report

     [X] Exit to Main Menu

Enter Selection:
```

The following list explains the options from the Usage Summaries menu:

- *[P] Port Status Report*—Displays the Port Status Report, which lists the current connection status of ports.
- *[A] Port Addressing Report*—Displays the Port Addressing Report, which lists the number of MAC addresses and the MAC addresses assigned to a port.
- *[E] Exception Statistics Report*—Displays the Exception Statistics Report, which gives a summary of errors on a port.
- *[U] Utilization Statistics Report*—Displays the Utilization Statistics Report, which indicates the utilization of each port.

- *[B] Bandwidth Usage Report*—Displays the Bandwidth Usage Report, which gives a port-by-port bandwidth usage report for each port.
- *[X] Exit*—Returns you to the Main menu.

Chapter Summary

This chapter focuses on the configuration, menus, and options available for the Standard Edition of the IOS on the Cisco 1900 and 2820 Series of switches. The following switches can be configured with the menu-driven Standard Edition of the Cisco IOS:

- Cisco Catalyst 1912
- Cisco Catalyst 1924
- Cisco Catalyst 2822
- Cisco Catalyst 2828

Cisco designed the 1900 and 2820 Series switches specifically to replace the 1700 and the 2100 Series switches. The 2820 and 1900 Series are architecturally the same. The 2820 series allows for additional modules such as Fiber Distributed Data Interface (FDDI), Copper Distributed Data Interface (CDDI), 100Mbps, and Asynchronous Transfer Mode (ATM).

The Cisco 2820 and 1900 Series switches come with either a Standard or an Enterprise version of the IOS. The Standard version is a character-select IOS, and the Enterprise version is similar to the IOS on the routers.

In this chapter, we took a look at each individual menu associated with the Main menu and covered how to perform the following tasks in the Standard Edition of the Cisco IOS for the 1900 and 2820 Series:

- Identify the menus
- Configure the network settings
- Configure broadcast storm control
- Configure SNMP
- Identify the port status messages
- Configure port monitoring
- Configure VLANs
- Upgrade the switch software with a TFTP server or client

- Upgrade the switch software with a modem
- Create switch reports

The Cisco Catalyst 3000 Series also has a menu-driven IOS, but we did not cover it in this chapter because the switch is no longer being manufactured.

Review Questions

1. Which button on the front of the switch allows for switch diagnostics?

   a. Reset button

   b. Power button

   c. Mode button

   d. All of the above

2. Which report shows the errors on a port?

   a. Bandwidth Usage Report

   b. Exception Statistics Report

   c. Utilization Statistics Report

   d. Port Status Report

3. Which of the following cannot be configured from the System Configuration menu?

   a. Address Aging Time

   b. Reset System

   c. Location

   d. Modify Password

4. How can you upgrade the firmware on a Cisco Catalyst 1900 or 2820 Series switch? [Choose the three best answers]

   a. TFTP client

   b. Kermit

   c. TFTP server

   d. XMODEM

5. Which of the following identifies the first port of an expansion module?
   a. 1
   b. A1
   c. 26
   d. AUX
6. Under which selection from the Main menu can you configure an IP address on the switch?
   a. [S] System
   b. [N] Network Management
   c. [P] Port Configuration
   d. [A] Port Addressing
7. Which option allows you to activate changes made to the RS-232 Console port?
   a. A
   b. C
   c. G
   d. I
8. The switch automatically saves each configuration change.
   a. True
   b. False
9. The IP address on the IP Configuration menu requires a reboot to take effect.
   a. True
   b. False
10. Which port status indicates that the switch cannot detect a link at the other end of the cable?
    a. Suspended-jabber
    b. Suspended-ring-down
    c. Suspended-not-present
    d. Disabled-violation

11. Which port status indicates that the switch has received multiple undecipherable frames?

    a. Suspended-jabber

    b. Suspended-ring-down

    c. Suspended-not-present

    d. Disabled-violation

12. You cannot assign a description or name to a port.

    a. True

    b. False

13. The address table on a Cisco 1900 or Cisco 2820 Series switch can contain an unlimited number of MAC addresses.

    a. True

    b. False

14. Which baud rate is the default on the RS-232 interface on the Cisco Catalyst 1900 or 2820 Series of switches?

    a. 2400

    b. 9600

    c. 19200

    d. 36000

15. Which baud rate is not valid on the RS-232 interface on the Cisco Catalyst 1900 or 2820 Series of switches?

    a. 2400

    b. 9600

    c. 19200

    d. 36000

16. The Standard Edition IOS 1900 and 2820 Series switches can use a Cisco command-line interface.

    a. True

    b. False

17. Which of the following is not found on Cisco 1900 Series switches?
    a. Token Ring ports
    b. 10BaseT Ethernet ports
    c. Console port
    d. Two uplink ports
18. The 1900 Series switch has a power switch for cycling the power.
    a. True
    b. False
19. Which of the following are not found on the Standard Edition User Interface menu when first cycling the power on the switch?
    a. Menus
    b. Port Configuration
    c. Console Password
    d. IP Address
20. Which of the following allows STP to immediately enter forwarding mode?
    a. HSRP
    b. CGMP
    c. PortFast
    d. UplinkFast

Real-World Projects

When Joe Snow got to work, he scanned his work assignment tickets and found that he was to upgrade system software in the access layer switches at The Coriolis Group. This layer contained a number of Cisco Catalyst 2820 switches and one Cisco Catalyst 1900 Series switch, located offsite.

Joe pondered what he was about to take on and made a mental note of what he needed to do:

- Download version 9 of the system software from the Cisco Web site
- Upgrade the system software on the Catalyst 2820 switches at Coriolis
- Upgrade the system software on the Catalyst 1900 Series switch located offsite through a modem using Procomm

Project 7.1

To download the switch software from a TFTP server and install it on the Cisco Catalyst 2820, perform the following:

1. Download the upgrade file from the Cisco Web site using CCO login information. Place the file into the download menu on the TFTP server.
2. Open the Firmware Configuration menu on the Cisco Catalyst 2820 switch. Use the [S] TFTP Server Name Or IP Address option and enter the IP address of the TFTP server where the new switch software file is located.

Warning: You can only use the server name if the switch is connected to a network in which this host's IP address is defined within a DNS server.

3. Enter the name of the new switch software file on the TFTP server using the [F] Filename For Firmware Upgrades option from the Firmware Configuration menu.
4. Use the [T] System TFTP Upgrade option from the menu to initiate the TFTP download.
5. When the download has been completed, verify that the firmware validates the file, the new image is transferred into Flash memory (which may take a minute or so), the switch resets, and the new firmware begins to execute.

Now, you need to repeat all these steps—with the exception of Step 1—on the remaining Cisco Catalyst switches.

Project 7.2

To install the new switch software using the XMODEM Protocol, perform the following:

1. Enter the same baud rate that is configured on the console port on the switch using a management station running the XMODEM emulation software program Procomm.
2. Using the Firmware Configuration menu, choose the [U] System XMODEM Upgrade option to use the XMODEM protocol to download the new switch software file.
3. Enter "Y" (yes) to start the download.
4. Verify that the upgrade is in progress by checking the Upgrade Status field in the System Information area of the menu. If the upgrade is in progress, the field reads *in-progress*.

Warning: If you stop the download before it is complete, you may corrupt the software on the switch.

5. When the upload has been completed, verify that the firmware validates the file, the new image is transferred into Flash memory (this may take a minute or so, and the switch may become unresponsive), the switch resets, and the new firmware begins to execute.

Chapter Eight

8

Virtual Local Area Networks

After completing this chapter, you will be able to:

- ✓ Enable a single physical connection to carry multiple VLANs
- ✓ Ensure broadcast integrity by establishing VLANs in the switch block
- ✓ Identify the different VTP modes
- ✓ Configure basic VTP trunks
- ✓ Maintain VLAN configuration consistency using VTP domains
- ✓ Configure VTP pruning
- ✓ Configure trunk links as well as know the variables

As we progress through this book, things seem to be getting increasingly technical. The topic we are covering in this chapter may be one of the most important we have covered so far, and is one of the most important for the aspiring network professional to understand. More than half the questions on the CCNP Switching exam deal in some form with virtual local area networks (VLANs). Pay close attention to this and the next two chapters. In fact, before you take the test, it would be a good idea to reread Chapters 8, 9, and 10 from beginning to end.

In this chapter we will introduce you to VLANs. Some of the topics we will present include the basics of how to configure VLANs on Cisco switches. We will show how VLANs can be used to ensure that broadcasts are suppressed. A great deal of information will be provided about the topic of virtual trunking and how it can be used in your network to carry multiple VLANs over a single connection.

Last, we will cover the technologies used in designing VLANs and the configuration of VLANs. When you finish reading this chapter, you should understand these concepts and be able to identify and deploy basic VLANs on a switch.

Introduction to VLANs

As noted in our previous chapters, VLANs have been widely implemented in today's networks to address many of the problems associated with Layer 2 campus networks. In a typical non-switched Ethernet network, also known as a *flat network*, certain problems have made themselves apparent, such as broadcast control and latency issues. The ability to create multiple, logical subnets and provide dedicated data paths to each switch port is the chief reason VLAN technology has achieved such success. VLANs provide many other features. These include:

- Control over broadcast activity
- The ability to centrally administer networks
- The ability to provide workgroup and network security
- The simplification of moves, adds, and changes of workstations and servers in the network

Cisco's VLAN Trunking Protocol (VTP), also known as Virtual Trunking Protocol, is one of the most powerful features provided by Cisco switches. Among other attributes, it permits you to define a single logical link for multiple physical connections. One of the chief benefits to using Cisco's VTP is the ability to substantially reduce the process of setting up and administering VLANs.

This ability is especially helpful in large networks with multiple segmented networks because it lets you automate the setup and distribution of each VLAN across the network. VTP helps eliminate configuration errors and the potentially complex diagnostics required to track these errors. Moreover, VTP substantially decreases the time required by network managers to add new VLANs and reduces the complexity of mapping between different technologies.

Before continuing this chapter, you should understand the differences between a trunk link and an access link. An *access link* is the connection between the switch port and the end-user interface or other non-switch or router interface. All additional headers containing VLAN information are removed before data exits an access port to the destination interface. A *trunk link* is a link between two switches or a router and a switch. Frames on a trunk link can contain additional headers identifying the VLAN, as we will discuss later in this chapter.

To understand how VLANs work and the advantages of VLANs, we need to first discuss scalability issues; security issues such as man-in-the-middle attacks; and the addition of headers, sometimes referred to as *frame tagging*. Several different protocols are related to frame tagging. We will be discussing all of them and going into great detail on a few. Those relating to Fiber Distributed Data Interface (FDDI) and Asynchronous Transfer Mode (ATM) will be discussed in further detail in later chapters.

Scalability Issues

One of the biggest problems associated with flat networks is scalability of the network. A flat network topology allows broadcasts and collisions to eat up the available bandwidth of the physical cabling and affect the entire network. It forces every interface on the network to process every packet floating around the network to see if the interface looking at the packet is the intended recipient. This task uses considerable processing time on each interface.

In addition, when a collision occurs between two stations, the sending station's interface detects the collision or the loss of the packet. It then resends the data at a random interval. This behavior results in unneeded retransmissions of the same data.

As networks become larger, and new, more bandwidth-intensive uses of the network—such as video and voice—are introduced, network utilization increases and collisions tend to happen more frequently. To make matters worse, we have a whole new generation of users who dislike waiting for anything. A slow network is frustrating and is a large source of complaints.

VLANs also can be used to provide security firewalls, restrict individual user access, flag any unwanted intrusion to the network, and control the size and composition of your broadcast domains. You can increase security by segmenting the network into distinct broadcast groups. Doing so enables you to restrict the number of users in each VLAN while preventing another user from joining a VLAN without first receiving approval from the network administrator.

Tip: A port can be configured by static VLAN assignment, where the connected host is a member of the port-assigned VLAN, or dynamically, where the MAC address determines the VLAN assignments. In this book we cover only static VLAN assignments because dynamic assignments by CiscoWorks for Switched Internetworks is not covered on the exam.

Security Issues: Man-in-the-Middle Attacks

Another issue is security on the network. This type of problem is sometimes referred to as the *man-in-the-middle attack*, because someone between the communicating interfaces views—and in some cases has the ability to change—the data and resend it to the recipient transparently.

For example, let's say that a manager sends a termination form for Joe Snow over the network to HR. Now let's say that Joe Snow intercepts the form, modifies it to give himself a big raise, and resends it to the receiver in HR. All this happens transparently to both the sender and the receiver. The receiving party in HR opens the document and, believing the document to be authentic, reads the document and acts on it. Joe Snow just got a nice raise—not exactly the desired result.

In addition, how would leaking sensitive information about the company, such as the purchase of another company, affect the price of the company stock? If the wrong party recovered a document alluding to such a purchase, the result could be a big problem. What if someone really works for a competitor and is working for your company only in order to gain access to your information? This scenario may seem a little far fetched, but it happens every day.

This is the basic nature of flat networks; everyone on the network segment can view all data packets. If you have 1 router and 300 users, you can see all 300 people's data. It is actually quite simple to do so, and the necessary software is included in most operating systems (including Windows NT) or available for next to nothing on the Internet.

Frame Tagging and Encapsulation Methods

Frame tagging is used to uniquely assign a VLAN identification or color to each frame passing through the switch fabric. The switch fabric is the highway that data takes from the input access switch port to the outbound access switch port. VLAN technology has developed this frame tagging procedure to tag frames through the switch fabric and then remove the tag prior to sending the frame to the end-user interface. This process provides the network administrator with more control over the flow of data in the network.

Frame tagging places a unique identifier into each frame as a header. Each switch in the switch fabric can view this header information to learn the VLAN information of the frame. Each switch can then make appropriate decisions for forwarding the frame or transmitting the frame to ports assigned to the same VLAN, as is the case with a broadcast.

In the case of a trunk link, which is a connection between two switches or a switch and a router, the switch will continue to allow the added frame tag to remain in the header of the frame. However, when the frame reaches its final destination switch, the frame tag is removed from the frame and the frame exits out of the access link port to the end user.

The end-user interface never knows what happened to the frame—it merely knows that the frame came from someone located on the physical media attached to the interface. Different types of frame tagging exist for different types of physical media. The different types of frame tagging are:

- IEEE 802.1Q
- IEEE 802.10
- Inter-Switch Link
- LAN emulation

IEEE 802.1Q

IEEE 802.1Q is a method used for identifying VLANs. The IEEE 802.1Q standard protocol inserts a frame tag VLAN identifier in the frame header. There is no encapsulation, and it is used for Ethernet physical media.

As a frame enters the switch fabric, it is tagged with additional information regarding the VLAN properties. The tag remains in the frame as it is forwarded from switch to switch and is removed prior to exiting the access link to the destination interface. This process is completely transparent to the end user, and the destination sees the frame intact as though no changes or additions had occurred to the frame. We will cover this topic in more detail later in this chapter.

IEEE 802.10

IEEE 802.10 is another Cisco proprietary protocol that will be discussed later in this chapter. You will find this protocol used primarily in FDDI backbones to transport VLAN information and data.

Inter-Switch Link

Inter-Switch Link (ISL) is a Cisco proprietary encapsulation protocol that is supported in both Cisco Catalyst switches and routers. It uses an external tagging process. In ISL external tagging, the original frame is not altered. It is encapsulated with a new 26-byte ISL header, sometimes referred to as a *tag*, and a new, extra 4-byte frame check sequence (FCS) is appended at the end of the frame, as shown in Figure 8.1.

Only ISL-aware devices are capable of interpreting frames with an ISL frame tag. Using ISL frame encapsulation means that the frame can violate the normal Ethernet maximum transmission unit size of 1518 bytes. No tags are inserted into the frame, and it is used for Ethernet physical media.

ISL adds VLAN IDs only to frames exiting a port connected to another switch or router. The link between two ports from router to switch (or switch to switch) is referred to as a *trunk link*. When the frame is finally sent out an access link, the switch removes the ISL header, making the whole process of adding and subtracting an ISL header transparent to the end user.

The ISL header, as shown in Figure 8.2, is entered into the frame. The ISL header contains the following:

- A destination address (DA), which is a 40-bit multicast address set to 01-00-0c-00-00. This address signals the receiver that this packet is in ISL format.
- A frame type field indicating the media type the frame is supporting. The possible options are 0000 for Ethernet, 0001 for Token Ring, 0010 for FDDI, and 0011 for ATM.
- A 4-byte user field that identifies one of four priorities of the frame. The four possible priorities are XX00 for normal, XX01 for priority 1, XX02 for priority 2, and XX11 for the highest priority.

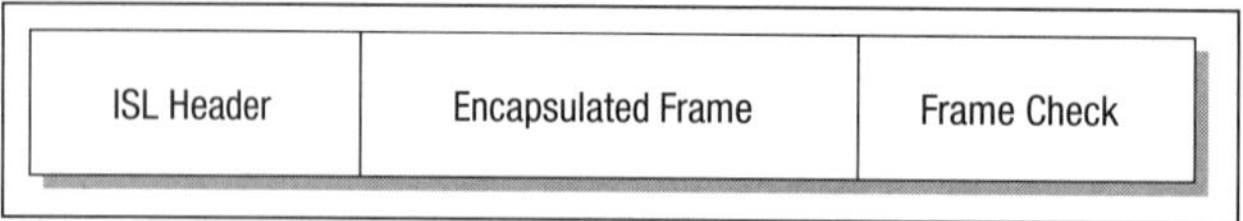

Figure 8.1 A typical ISL frame.

DA	Media Type	Frame Priority	SA	Frame Length	AAAA03	HSA	VLAN	BPDU	Index	Reserve

Figure 8.2 The ISL header inserted into an ISL encapsulated packet.

- The source MAC address (SA). This address is set to the sending switch port's IEEE 802.3 MAC address. Some receiving devices ignore the SA field.
- A 16-bit LEN field shows the length of the packet in bytes minus the excluded fields. The excluded fields are the CRC, DA, Type, User, Source Address, and the LEN field itself. The total of the excluded fields is 18 bytes. Therefore, the LEN field would contain the total packet size minus 18 bytes from the excluded fields.
- The 802.2 LLC header AAAA03.
- The high bit of source address (HSA), which is the 3-byte manufacturer's portion of the SA field or vendor field of the source port's MAC address.
- A 15-bit descriptor, of which 10 bits are used to indicate the source port. This field is used to distinguish the frame from other VLANs or colors.
- A Bridge Protocol Data Units (BPDU) bit used to indicate Spanning Tree Protocol (STP) or Cisco Discovery Protocol (CDP) topology information.
- A 16-bit index value, used to indicate the port address. This index can be set to any value and may be used for diagnostic purposes only.
- A reserved field is used only by FDDI and Token Ring. In Token Ring, the Frame Control (FC) and Token Ring AC bits (AC) fields are placed in the header. You can specify whether the address-recognized (A) bit and the frame-copied (C) bit should be set unconditionally on repeated source-routed Logical Link Control (LLC). For FDDI, the FC is placed in the reserved field. For Ethernet, the field includes all zeros.

LAN Emulation

LAN Emulation (LANE) is an IEEE standard for transporting VLANs over networks utilizing Asynchronous Transfer Mode (ATM). It uses no encapsulation or tagging. ATM is covered in great detail later in this book.

VLAN Components and Standards

With so many ideas for the implementation of virtual LANs, Cisco found it essential to set up certain standards. Cisco chose to submit its standardization to the body of the IEEE Internetworking Subcommittee.

A *standard* is a basis that participating vendors use to maintain functionality and compatibility between different vendors' products on a network. For example, when you get a 100BaseT network interface card (NIC) from one vendor and you purchase a second card from another vendor, standards ensure that they will work with each other in your network.

Besides the IEEE, other standards have been created for VLANs by the Internet Engineering Task Force (IETF). Other standards related to the use of ATM and LANE have been designated by the ATM forum. This section will focus mainly on the standards created by the IEEE, IETF, and ATM forums. The main focus will be on those standards created and submitted for standardization by Cisco to enhance VLANs in their route processors and other switching products.

Organizations install high-speed switched networks to create a network that can efficiently handle the growing demands of software and hardware applications. These installations can cause some unexpected problems in the network. Some of the standards discussed in this section relate to monitoring and managing VLAN networks and resources. This management enables organizations to reduce problems in their networks and to increase functionality and compatibility of different vendor products on the networks.

IEEE 802.1 Internetworking Subcommittee

In 1996, the IEEE 802.1 Internetworking Subcommittee completed its initial investigation in developing VLAN standardization. It came up with three standards that are used today. Those VLAN standards cover multiple devices when more than one vendor is involved, the establishment of a frame format for frame tagging, and a standardized architectural approach to VLANs.

The committee was made up of representatives from all the major switch vendors, such as Cisco, IBM, Bay Networks, 3Com, and Alentec/FORE Systems. These companies agreed unanimously to implement the new standards as outlined.

IEEE 802.1D

The 802.1D standard is officially known by the IEEE as *Media Access Control (MAC) Bridges: Traffic Class Expediting and Dynamic Multicast Filtering*. However, today we call it Spanning Tree Protocol (STP).

The STP is essentially an algorithm to prevent loops in networks with redundant links. In other words, suppose a network has more than one path from point A to point B. STP ensures that there will be no loops of data continuously traversing the network. If the network contained a loop, then bridges—or switches, for that matter—might forward traffic indefinitely. This forwarding would result in increased traffic and severely degrade your network's performance. You wouldn't want too many of those loops to go undetected in your network.

IEEE 802.1P

The IEEE 802.1P standard is officially known as the *Standard for Local and Metropolitan Area Networks (MAN)*. It extends the concept of filtering services introduced in the STP 802.1D standard. This standard also defines additional capabilities for use on VLANs, including filtering capabilities and the use of dynamic group MAC addresses.

Another part of this standard deals with associating group properties and characteristics. Group properties are the forwarding and filtering behaviors of a VLAN or bridge with respect to the frame destined for members of a certain VLAN group.

The main service differences between 802.1D and 802.1P are:

- Filtering
- Quality of service
- MAC service to end stations
- Preservation of the MAC service
- Internal sublayer service support and specified MAC procedures

The IEEE 802.1P standard allows for frame order changes, which introduce the capability of allowing for user priority. It actually introduces the delay and queuing mechanisms. Filtering allows the switch to learn which port a MAC address is located on by reading the packet header to determine the source address. The switch assumes that the source is located on the port that the frame arrived from. 802.1P also allows frames (such as broadcasts destined for a group) to be filtered and delivered only to other members with the same VLAN of assignment.

All filtering services in bridged LANs rely on pre-established parameters that are configured manually. To change any type of filtering requires manual intervention by an administrator.

There are two types of filtering: dynamic unicast and static. Both dynamic and static filtering must use a filtering database to filter incoming frames. If no filtering information exists, the switch merely broadcasts the information to all the ports assigned to the VLAN from which the frame arrived, with the exception of the port on which the frame was received.

IEEE 802.1Q

In 1996, Cisco also agreed to the 802.1Q standard, despite its widespread adoption of IEEE 802.10. The official name for the IEEE 802.1Q protocol is the *Standard for Virtual Bridged Local Area Networks*. 802.1Q is a standard for tagging the frame header in switched VLAN frames. The main function of the 802.1Q standard is to identify, encode, and interpret VLAN control information. It also defines the rules that govern the insertion or deletion of VLAN control information and the protocols and algorithms involved in providing those particular services. It does this by inserting a special identifier that is placed in the header of the frame and that identifies the VLAN information. This process is called *tagging*.

Prior to frame tagging, each frame's MAC was placed in a filter table. Each time the switch received a frame, it checked the frame's MAC address against the filter table to determine the destination or fate of the particular frame. Tagging of data frames with IEEE 802.1 header information allows the frame to carry VLAN header identification and user priority information over media types that ordinarily would not support priority information. This process allows Token Ring (IEEE 802.5) data to be transmitted over non-IEEE 802.5–standard physical media.

In the frame, the tag header is placed immediately following the destination and source MAC addresses of the original frame. The header includes the user information as well as the VLAN to which the user belongs.

The frame tag is a 4-byte header placed in the front of the frame containing a tag protocol identifier (TPID) and the tag control information (TCI). The TPID contains 2 bytes with a fixed value of 0x8100 indicating that it has an IEEE 802.1Q tag and an IEEE 802.1P tag. The TCI includes a 12-bit VLAN identifier (VID) to identify the VLAN the frame originated from, a 3-bit user priority, and a 1-bit canonical format indicator (CFI).

If the destination address is located on a different VLAN, the frame is forwarded to a router or router switching module (RSM). If the source and destination media differ, tagging the frame may involve a translation or encapsulation of the rest of the frame. The frame is then recomputed and given a new frame check sequence (FCS).

IEEE 802.1Q tag headers have the unfortunate effect of increasing the size of an Ethernet frame past the maximum of 1518 to 1522 bytes. Cisco calls this frame a *baby giant frame*. Cisco switches will forward this frame, but doing so may result in the switch recording an Ethernet error.

Currently, Cisco uses 802.1Q to map multiple VLANs that require a trunking protocol.

IEEE 802.10

The IEEE 802.10 protocol provides connectivity between VLANs. It was originally developed to address the growing need for security within shared LAN and MAN environments, and it incorporates authentication and encryption techniques to ensure data confidentiality and integrity throughout the network. This protocol functions at Layer 2 and is well suited to high throughput, low-latency switched environments. The IEEE 802.10 protocol can run over any LAN or HDLC serial interface.

Like IEEE 802.1Q, IEEE 802.10 incorporates a way whereby switched traffic can be tagged with a VLAN identifier for FDDI links. This tagging provides the

LAN switching environment the ability to selectively switch packets with this VLAN identifier.

The IEEE 802.10 protocol can extend VLANs by multiplexing switched packets over a FDDI or Copper Distributed Data Interface (CDDI) VLAN interface. This multiplexing allows Catalyst-series switches such as the 5000 Series FDDI/CDDI interface links to operate as interswitch trunks, providing broadcast control between the configured VLANs.

IEEE 802.10 enables the linking of a FDDI and Ethernet or Token Ring trunk and the creation of a consistent broadcast domain. Figure 8.3 shows two Ethernet LANs connected by a FDDI backbone. After creating a VLAN across two different types of physical media, the protocol requires that you manually map the FDDI VLANs to the Ethernet or Token Ring VLANs. VLAN Trunking Protocol (VTP), discussed later in this chapter, allows mappings to emulated LANs created by ATM LANE.

The creation of the IEEE 802.10 protocol was never intended to create VLANs—it was originally intended to provide security and authentication features for metropolitan area networks (MANs). These were multiple LANs in the same geographical area that shared a FDDI backbone.

IEEE 802.10 allows for implementation to take place at the data link layer of the OSI Model, so it takes place in hardware versus software. This implementation greatly improves performance and reduces latency while providing security.

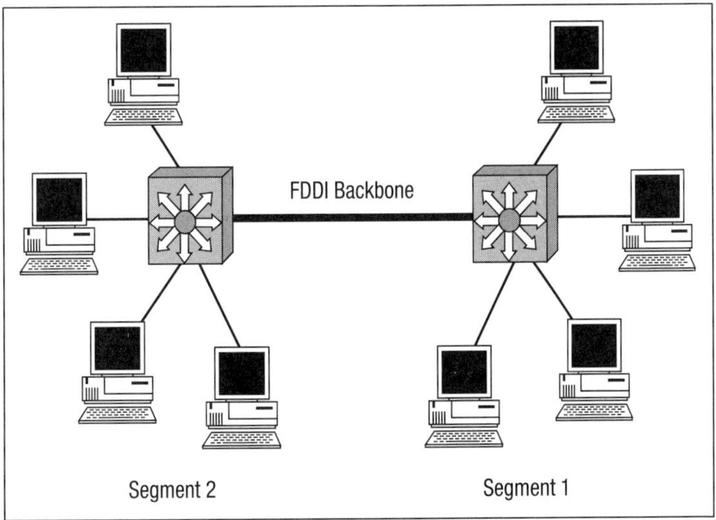

Figure 8.3 A FDDI backbone connecting two Ethernet LANs.

IEEE 802.10 Header

The IEEE 802.10 inserts a header between the MAC header and the frame's data. The header includes a Protocol Data Unit (PDU) called a Security Data Exchange (SDE). The SDE, along with another PDU called the Secure Association Identifier (SAID), creates a 7-byte addition to the header, as shown in Figure 8.4.

The protocol requires that frames be encapsulated with a VLAN identifier and packet data according to the IEEE 802.10 specification. FDDI/CDDI interfaces that support 802.10 make selective forwarding decisions within a network domain based upon the VLAN identifier.

The VLAN identifier is a user-configurable 4-byte SAID. The SAID allows for up to 4.29 billion individual VLANs and identifies traffic as belonging to a particular VLAN. It also determines to which VLAN each packet is switched. The SAID is one of three values that make up a clear header on the FDDI frame type (the other two are an LSAP and a user-definable Management Defined Field [MDF]). It is used for security for the clear header.

The SDE, sometimes referred to as the *clear header*, duplicates the MAC header contained in the original FDDI frame. This header and the data are encrypted to guard against tampering. The destination FDDI interface then compares the clear-text MAC with the protected header and determines if the frame has been tampered with. To do this, the FDDI interface uses an integrity check value (ICV), which is a Cyclical Redundancy Check (CRC)-type checksum, to verify the validity of the frame.

Dynamic Trunk Protocol

The Dynamic Trunk Protocol (DTP) allows trunk links to carry the data and VLAN information across multiple switches or routers. DTP manages trunk negotiation in the Catalyst Supervisor Engine software releases 4.2 and later.

In prior versions of the Catalyst Supervisor Engine software, trunk negotiation was managed by the Dynamic Inter-Switch Link (DISL) protocol. In version 4.1,

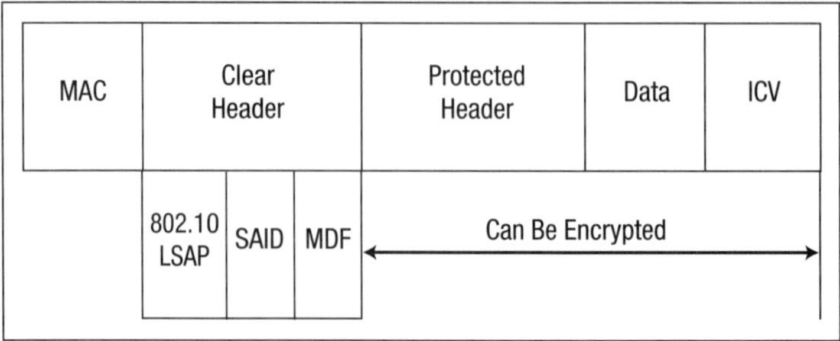

Figure 8.4 A FDDI frame with an 802.10 header inserted into it.

DISL covers auto-negotiation of ISL trunks only. You could manually configure DISL to auto-negotiate IEEE 802.1Q trunks.

In versions 4.2 and later, DTP supports and manages IEEE 802.1Q and ISL trunk links. Sometimes, other non-DTP internetworking devices might forward DTP frames improperly.

If you have non-DTP–compatible networking devices on the network, you might want to disable this feature. (See the section "Configuring Trunks" to learn how to do so.) When you disable DTP, the link can still become a trunk, but DTP frames are not generated.

VLAN Trunking Protocol

VLAN Trunking Protocol (VTP) maintains consistent VLAN configurations of the network. It creates a mapping scheme of the network across different physical media types. VTP provides for plug-and-play type connections when you add more VLANs. It also provides tracking, monitoring, and reporting of VLANs in the network.

8

VTP is a Layer 2 messaging protocol using trunk frames to manage changes in the network. Changes in the network can be additions, deletions, and the renaming of VLANs throughout the network. VTP uses centralized management to communicate changes to other switches on the network.

Security violations can occur when VLANs cross-connect, allowing duplicate names on the network. This duplication results in a disconnection, particularly when VLANs are connected from one physical media type to another.

With the default configuration of VTP, switches are configured in non-secure mode. To ensure that other switches do not join your domain without your knowledge—and to avoid security violations that can occur when inconsistencies in the network cross-connect VLANs, allowing duplicate names on the network—you need to configure a secure mode password for your VTP management domain. The management domain name can be up to 32 characters long, and your secure mode password can be from 8 to 64 characters long.

Each switch can participate in only one VTP management domain, which must be created. All the switches in the VTP management domain share VLAN information through the use of VTP advertisement messages. There are three types of advertisement messages: an advertisement request, a summary advertisement, and a subset advertisement:

- *Advertisement request*—Occurs when clients request VLAN information for the current network. The VTP server then responds with the appropriate summary and subset advertisements. The advertisement frame includes a version field, code field, reserved field, management domain name field (up to 32 bytes), and start value field.

- *Summary advertisement*—Sent automatically every 5 minutes or 300 seconds to all the switches on the network. A summary advertisement can also be sent when there is a topology change to the network, such as a switch drop or addition. The summary advertisement frame contains the version field, the code field, a followers field, a management domain name field, a configuration revision number field, the updater's identity, the updater's timestamp, and the MD5 digest field.
- *Subset advertisement*—Contains very detailed information about the network, including the version, code, sequence number, management domain name, configuration revision number, and VLAN information fields.

VTP advertisements can contain the following information:

- *802.10 SAID values*—For FDDI physical media.
- *Configuration revision number*—The higher the number, the more updated the information.
- *Emulated LAN names*—Used for ATM LANE.
- *Frame format*—Information about the format and content of the frame.
- *Management domain name*—The name of the VTP management domain. If the switch is configured for one name and receives a frame with another name, the information is ignored.
- *MD5 digest*—Used when a password is used throughout the domain. The key must match the key on the given destination or the update information is ignored.
- *Updater identity*—The identity of the switch that forwarded the summary advertisement to the switch.
- *VLAN configuration*—Includes known VLAN information, specific parameters, and a maximum transmission unit size (MTU) for each VLAN in the VTP management domain.
- *VLAN identification*—The ISL or 802.1Q information.

The advertisement frames are sent to a multicast address so all the VTP devices in the same management domain can receive the frames. The frames are not forwarded using normal bridging controls. All VTP management domain clients and servers update their databases on all deletions and additions on the network. Therefore, only the VTP client operating in server mode needs to be updated with any added or deleted VLANs to allow all the members of the VTP management domain to update their databases.

There are two types of VTP management domain advertisements:

- Server-originating advertisements
- Request advertisements from clients needing VLAN information upon power cycling or bootup

Each advertisement has a revision number. Every time a server sends out an updated advertisement, it increases the revision number by one. If a client switch receives two advertisements simultaneously, it knows that the advertisement with the highest revision number is the most updated information.

Warning: Access link ports should not be configured as VTP trunks. When configuring VTP on access links, the VLAN tag is not removed. The end-user interface does not understand the VLAN tag.

VTP Version 1 vs. Version 2

The differences between VTP version 1 and VTP version 2 are few but significant. The two versions are not compatible and will not work together. Version 1 is the default on Cisco Catalyst switches. All switches used in a version 2 VTP management domain must be configured as VTP version 2 switches. If all the switches in the network support VTP version 2, then only one switch needs to have version 2 enabled to enable version 2 on all other switches.

You must configure switches to version 2 if you need any of the following additional features:

- Consistency checks
- Token Ring support
- Unrecognized type length value support
- Transparent Mode change support

Consistency checks are performed when new information is entered through the command-line interface (CLI) or through Simple Network Management Protocol (SNMP). Normally, no consistency checks are performed when information for each switch is obtained through a VTP advertising message or read from Non-Volatile RAM (NVRAM).

Token-Ring support is provided only in VTP version 2. This support includes Token Ring LAN switching and VLANs.

When a VTP version 2 server or client receives a configuration change with an unrecognizable type length value (TLV) for its other trunks, it is saved to NVRAM.

In version 1, the Transparent Mode switches look at advertisement messages for the domain name and the version number before forwarding the frame. With VTP version 2, Transparent Mode switches merely look at the domain name.

VTP Switch Modes

Each switch must be configured to participate in VTP. Switches must be assigned as being in Client Mode, Server Mode, or Transparent Mode.

In Client Mode, the switch has the same functions as Server Mode with the exception that it cannot change any VLAN information. A Client Mode switch cannot create, modify, or delete VLANs on any VTP client or switch. It can, however, advertise its VLAN configuration, synchronize the VLAN information with other switches on the network, specify VTP configuration information such as VTP version, and participate in VTP pruning (discussed later in this section). Client Mode switches receive their information from other VTP servers in the VTP management domain. Global VLAN information is lost when the switch power is cycled.

Server Mode, which is configured by default, allows you to create, modify, and delete VLANs for the management domain. Configuration changes are then sent to all other participating members of the VTP domain. There should be at least one VTP server in the VTP management domain. Two or more switches can be configured as servers for redundancy. When a server's power is cycled, the switch configured as a server maintains its global VLAN information.

In Transparent Mode, switches can be configured not to accept VTP information. Transparent Mode switches will still send VTP information and advertisements, but will not update their databases or send out information on VLAN or topology changes. In this mode, switches do not participate in any VTP functions, such as sending VTP advertisements or synchronizing VLAN information. Version 2 does allow for the switch to forward the advertisements it receives out any configured trunk ports, to allow other switches participating in VTP to obtain the advertisements.

Tip: All the switches in a management domain can operate in Secure Mode by configuring the same password on all the switches in the domain.

VTP Pruning

VLAN Trunk Protocol *pruning* increases network bandwidth by reducing network traffic across switch trunk links. It filters network traffic such as broadcasts, multicasts, and unicasts on trunk links that connect switches that contain no VLAN ports in the particular VLAN the data is destined for.

When VTP pruning is enabled on a VTP server, the information is propagated to all other Client and Server Mode switches in the VTP management domain. This step automatically enables VTP pruning on these switches. By default, VLANs 2 through 1000 are eligible for VTP pruning, and VLAN 1 is always ineligible. VTP pruning usually takes several seconds to propagate to the other VTP management domain clients.

Methods for VLAN Identification

To logically identify which packets belong to which VLAN or VLAN group, Cisco Catalyst switches support many trunking protocols to put a header on frames. The headers identify the VLAN associated with the frame; each switch in the switch block removes the header before the frame exits the access link port or ports belonging to the identified VLAN.

The identification methods are ISL, LANE, the IEEE 802.1Q specification, and the IEEE 802.10 specification.

Single and Multi-VLAN Configuration

All ports on the switch are configured as static access ports to VLAN 1 by default. VLAN 1 is also assigned as the default management VLAN. You can change the VLAN port information using the console, Cisco Visual Switch Manager (CVSM), or SNMP. This section will cover the basics of VLAN configuration as well as assigning multi-VLAN memberships, and how to view the configuration on each type of switch. It will cover configuring VLANs on a Set/Clear command-based switch as well as a CLI-based switch.

Now, let's say that we have just pulled a brand new Cisco Catalyst 5000 family out of the box, connected the power, and are at the point in the configuration at which we would like to change our VLANs. A Catalyst 5000 Series uses the Crescendo user interface. It is commonly referred to as a Set/Clear command-based switch, because the only commands available on this type of switch are Set, Show, and Clear.

Based on the requirements of the users, we have determined the logical grouping that is needed. On module 1, ports 3 through 6 are four accounting department employees whom we are taking off our old flat network and putting into their own separate VLAN or broadcast domain. For the purposes of this demonstration, we are going to add the accounting department to VLAN 7. In order to begin configuring the VLANs, we need to be in Privileged Mode on our switch. To configure the four ports individually use these commands:

```
set vlan 7 1/3
set vlan 7 1/4
```

```
set vlan 7 1/5
set vlan 7 1/6
```

You could also use a shortcut and configure all the ports at once using this command:

```
set vlan 7 1/3-6
```

Warning: Using a space between the numbers creates an error. The switch views the number following the space as a new command argument.

You should see output that looks similar to this:

```
VLAN 7 modified.
VLAN 1 modified.
VLAN        Mod/Port
7           1/3-6
```

Remember, all VLANs belong to VLAN 1 by default, so a change in the ports to VLAN 7 removes the ports from VLAN 1. The change is noted in the configuration output.

To verify the configured VLAN information, at the Privileged EXEC Mode prompt, you can use the command:

```
show vlan
```

To remove a VLAN configured on a port, at the Privileged EXEC Mode prompt, you can use the following command (the VLAN being removed is VLAN 3, affecting all ports with VLAN 3 configured):

```
clear vlan 3
```

Note: *When you clear a VLAN that has ports assigned to it, by default those ports revert to VLAN 1. Every port must be assigned to a VLAN.*

Sometimes it is easier to track the different VLANs by assigning each one a name. For example, let's say that VLAN 4 is assigned to the accounting department and VLAN 5 is assigned to shipping. To assign a name to these VLANs, use the following commands in Privileged Mode:

```
Set vlan 4 name accounting
Set vlan 5 name shipping
```

Configuring Trunks

Trunk connections using VTP are very special VLAN connections. The devices on both ends must understand frame tags. Because Ethernet and Token Ring do not understand the frame tags, the frames must be cleared of all tags before receipt. Whereas the end-user access link carries only the data of one VLAN, a trunk carries the data of all the VLANs.

VLAN trunks can be configured between two switches or between a switch and a router. The problem with creating a trunk to a router is the introduction of latency. This latency will not be noticeable on small data files, but it will be very noticeable when you're using voice or video.

In some special circumstances, a file server has an ISL- or 802.1Q-aware NIC card that understands VLAN tagging. As a result, you can create a trunk between the switch and the file server, allowing end users to bypass the Layer 3 routing and send the frame much faster in the Layer 2 environment.

To create a trunk, you must understand some of the main pieces of the trunk subvariables. You must know whether the trunking method to be used is 802.1Q, 802.10, ISL, LANE, or negotiate.

For Fast Ethernet or Gigabit Ethernet, you set the trunking mode for each port as well as the protocol to use. Table 8.1 explains each variable for the different trunking modes. Table 8.2 explains each possible variable for each protocol.

Table 8.1 Fast Ethernet and Gigabit Ethernet modes for configuring VLAN trunks.

Mode	Description
auto	This trunking mode is used if the port uses DISL to initiate trunking. This is the default mode for Fast Ethernet and mimics plug-and-play. You cannot configure a trunk when both ends' switch ports are configured for **auto** mode. One switch must be set to **on** or **desirable** mode.
desirable	This trunking mode, if using DISL, actively tries to configure itself as a trunk link. The other end of the trunk link must be configured to **on** or **desirable** to complete the trunk initiation.
off	This option disables the port from becoming a trunk. It is typically used when the device on the other end does not support ISL or IEEE 802.1Q. The port on the other end might be a 10Mbps Ether port or FDDI interface.
on	This option basically makes the port a trunk port whether the other end is configured to be a trunk or not. Use this option when the port on the other end does not understand DTP, such as a third-party adapter.
nonegotiate	Use this option when DISL negotiation that takes place on ISL trunks is not supported. When using **dot1q** as the final parameter, **nonegotiate** tells the switch that ISL will not be used for trunking the ports.

Table 8.2 The different protocol variables that can be used when configuring VLAN trunks.

Variable	Description
isl	Applies ISL protocol encapsulation to an Ethernet trunk.
dot1q	Used for Ethernet trunks using the IEEE 802.1Q standard.
dot10	Used when assigning a FDDI trunk link to the port.
lane	Used when applying ATM to a trunk link port.
negotiate	Puts the port into permanent trunking mode. It disallows the port from generating DTP frames. Typically this command is used with switch-to-router trunks.

Now that we have covered the different variables associated with the VTP trunking command, let's take a look at the command itself. If this is the first switch in the network, you must assign it to a management domain. If other switches exist, you will probably be joining a domain. If the domain is a secure domain, you will also need to assign the switch a password that matches the other switches configured in the domain.

To configure the domain name and set the password on the switch, use the following command in Privileged Mode (the name *coriolis* refers to the switch domain name and the password is set to book1234):

```
set vtp domain coriolis passwd book1234
```

Note: *The domain can be from 1 to 32 characters long and the password can be 8 to 64 characters long.*

To see the VTP domain information, use the following **show** command from the Privileged Mode prompt:

```
Show vtp domain
```

The output should look similar to this:

```
Domain Name  Domain Index  VTP Version  Local Mode  Password
-----------  ------------  -----------  ----------  --------
Coriolis     1             2            server        -

Vlan-count  Max-vlan-storage  Config Revision  Notifications
----------  ----------------  ---------------  -------------
12          1023              8                disabled

Last Updater   V2 Mode   Pruning   PruneEligible on Vlans
------------   -------   -------   ----------------------
130.77.20.134  disabled  disabled  2-1000
```

To set the VTP mode to either Server, Client, or Transparent Mode, use the following Privileged Mode command (*coriolis* refers to the domain that the switch will join):

```
set vtp coriolis mode server
```

You can combine the last two commands by using the command:

```
set vtp domain coriolis passwd book1234 server
```

To change the VTP version number to 2, add the following parameter to the previous command. By default the switch uses version 1:

```
set vtp domain coriolis passwd book1234 server v2 enable
```


On a Set/Clear command-based switch, you use the following command to configure a trunk port (note that the port being configured is on module 2, port 1 and the VLAN range is VLANs 2 through 30):

```
set trunk 2/1 desirable 2-30 isl
```

When configuring Fast Ethernet ports, the default is ISL; so, you can use a shortened command (again, the port is port 1 on module 2 and the VLAN range is 2 through 30):

```
set trunk 2/1 on 2-30
```

When using IEEE 802.1Q on the same ports as previously, use the following command in Privileged Mode:

```
set trunk 2/1 nonegotiate dot1q
```

To remove a trunk, use the following Privileged Mode command (in this demonstration, the module number is 2 and the port number is 2; the VLAN being removed is 13):

```
Clear trunk 2/2 13
```

For more than one VLAN, such as VLANs 13 through 200, issue the following Privileged Mode command:

```
Clear trunk 2/2 13-200
```

To display all the trunks configured on the switch, use the following command in Privileged Mode:

```
switch (enable) show trunk
```

The output should look similar to this:

```
Port     Mode         Encapsulation   Status      Native vlan
----     ----         -------------   ------      -----------
1/1      desirable    isl             trunking    1
2/1      desirable    isl             trunking    1
2/2      desirable    isl             trunking    1
2/3      desirable    isl             trunking    1
3/1      desirable    isl             trunking    1

Port          Vlans allowed on trunk
----          ----------------------
1/1           1-100,1003-1005
2/1           1-100,1003-1005
2/2           1-100,1003-1005
2/3           1-100,1003-1005
3/1           1-100,1003-1005

Port          Vlans allowed and active in management domain
----          ---------------------------------------------
1/1           1,6-9,1003-1005
2/1           1,6-9,1003-1005
2/2           1,6-9,1003-1005
2/3           1,6-9,1003-1005
3/1           1,6-9,1003-1005

Port          Vlans in spanning tree forwarding state and not pruned
----          ------------------------------------------------------
1/1           1,1003-1005
2/1           1,1003-1005
2/2           1,1003-1005
2/3           1,1003-1005
3/1           1,1003-1005
```

In order to get a statistical view of the VTP traffic, use the following command:

```
set vtp statistics
```

Configuring Pruning

Pruning is a feature introduced in Network Management Protocol (NMP) version 2.3. It allows the switch to make intelligent decisions when forwarding broadcast and multicast traffic over trunk ports. VTP pruning is disabled by default on the switch and must be manually configured. Typically, it is used when a switch on the other end of a trunk port contains no ports assigned to the VLANs for which the traffic is destined.

VTP pruning solves the problem of sending data over a trunk port when there is no destination port for the information. The switch dynamically discovers which VLANs it has in common with the switches connected by trunk ports and prunes the information to allow only traffic that has a destination VLAN to pass. This process enhances network performance by terminating unnecessary broadcast and other traffic throughout the network.

VTP pruning requires all switches to be set to Server Mode and that the same common VTP domain be established. To enable pruning on a Set/Clear-based switch, use this command in Privileged Mode:


```
set vtp pruning enable
```

To disable VTP pruning, use the command:

```
set vtp pruning disable
```

Note that this command will affect all VLANs on the switch. When you enable VTP, the default behavior of the switch is to enable pruning on all VLANs. If you want to enable VTP pruning only on certain VLANs, first clear the VLAN prune-eligible list using the following command for all VLANs:

```
clear vtp pruneeligible 2-1000
```

Next, set the VLANs for which you wish to enable pruning:

```
Set vtp pruneeligible 2-30
```

***Note:** VTP pruning cannot be enabled on VLAN1, and every switch participating in VTP pruning must be configured as a VTP server. Enabling VTP pruning on one server enables VTP pruning on all of the servers in the management domain. By default, VLANs 2 through 1000 are eligible for pruning. VTP pruning will not take place on VLANs that are pruning ineligible.*

Chapter Summary

In this chapter, we covered a lot of information about the basics ofVLANs. We also covered the VLAN tunneling protocol, VTP. VTP pruning is used to enable a single physical connection to carry multiple VLANs, ensuring broadcast integrity by establishing VLANs in the switch block.

We also discussed the different VTP modes: Server, Client, and Transparent. We covered ways to configure basic VTP trunks, to maintain VLAN configuration consistency using VTP domains, and to configure VTP pruning trunk links. At this point, you should know the differences between a trunk link and an access link.

Here are some of the terms that you should review:

- *Color*—The coloring of data traffic across a FDDI backbone is done by inserting a 16-byte header between the source MAC address and the Link Service Access Point (LSAP) of frames leaving a switch. The 4-byte header is called the VLAN ID or "color." When the switch receives a frame with the header, it then removes the header and forwards the frame to ports that are using the same VLAN color.
- *IEEE 802.10*—Another Cisco proprietary protocol used primarily to transport VLAN information over FDDI. This protocol is used primarily in FDDI backbones to transport VLAN information and data.
- *IEEE 802.1Q*—The standard protocol for inserting a frame tag VLAN identifier in the frame header. As a frame enters the switch fabric it is tagged with additional information regarding the VLAN properties. The tag remains in the frame as it is forwarded between switches and is removed prior to exiting the access link to the destination interface. This process is completely transparent to the end user.
- *Inter-Switch Link (ISL)*—A special Cisco proprietary Ethernet protocol that assigns a 26-byte header and a 4-byte checksum, sometimes referred to as the FCS or the CRC, to an encapsulated frame header.
- *Link Service Access Point (LSAP)*—This is an 802.2 address that appears in a Logical Link Control header, intended to identify a source or destination of a flow of data.
- *Network Management Processor (NMP)*—A feature of the Catalyst Supervisor Engine that is responsible for general control and some management functions of the switch. It is responsible for executing the system's configuration changes, the CLI, and running diagnostics on boot components as well as on new components.

- *Security Association Identifier (SAID)*—One of the three values that make up a clear header on the FDDI frame type. It is used for security for the clear header. The clear header contains an SAID, LSAP, and a user-definable Management Defined Field (MDF).
- *Trunk*—A special type of VLAN connection. Unlike a user port, trunk links expect the device at the other end of the connection to understand the inserted frame tags.
- *VLAN*—Allows a network administrator to divide a bridged network into several broadcast domains. Each VLAN is considered its own separate subnet, and Layer 3 routing is still required between VLANs. VLANs can be based on the port identifier of the switch, the MAC address, Layer 3 addressing, directory information, or application information. VLANs can be implemented on different media types such as Ethernet, FDDI, Token Ring, or ATM. The benefits of VLANs are limiting broadcast domains, added security, and redundancy.
- *VLAN Trunking Protocol (VTP)*—A protocol used to enhance and configure the extension of broadcast domains across multiple switches. VTP dynamically reports the addition of VLANs throughout the switched network, in turn creating a consistent switched network.

Review Questions

1. Which is a true definition of a native VLAN?
   a. A native VLAN is the VLAN a port would be assigned to if it were not participating in a trunk.
   b. A native VLAN is assigned to an access switch port.
   c. A native VLAN is a VLAN to two servers.
   d. A native VLAN is a VLAN assigned to Token Ring only.
2. Which of the following answers are true about Inter-Switch Link protocol? [Choose the two best answers]
   a. Runs only on a single VLAN access link
   b. Uses a two-level tagging scheme with a 26-byte header and a 4-byte checksum
   c. Implemented in the hardware ASICs to provide wire-speed performance
   d. Cannot be used with Spanning Tree Protocol

3. What issues have VLANs been introduced to address? [Choose the two best answers]
   a. Making WAN communication possible
   b. Adding Layer 3 network management
   c. Scalability problems of a flat network
   d. Issuing IP addresses
4. Which VTP mode would you configure your switch to become if it was not necessary to add, delete, or modify VLANs?
   a. VTP Transparent Mode
   b. VTP Server Mode
   c. VTP Client Mode
   d. VTP Forwarding Mode
5. Which of the following are ways of configuring VLANs? [Choose the three best answers]
   a. By the hostname
   b. By port
   c. By a user-defined value
   d. By protocol
6. What is the purpose of the VTP protocol?
   a. To map access ports together
   b. To perform cut-through switching
   c. To perform switch diagnostics
   d. To map trunked ports on a switch together
7. Which command allows you to assign port 3 on module 2 to VLAN 20?
   a. **set my vlan to 20 port 3**
   b. **set vlan 2/20 2**
   c. **set vlan 20 2/3**
   d. **set vlan 20 2-3**
8. Which command allows you to set the switch VTP domain name to coriolis?
   a. **set domain coriolis**
   b. **set vtp domain coriolis**
   c. **set coriolis to domain VTP**
   d. **set vtp host coriolis**

9. Which layer of the OSI Model do VLANs using Spanning Tree Protocol operate on?
   a. Presentation layer
   b. Network layer
   c. Host layer
   d. Data link layer
10. Which of the following are characteristics of VLANs? [Choose the three best answers]
   a. VLANs are used to police the Internet.
   b. All devices in a VLAN are part of the same broadcast domain.
   c. A VLAN is a logical segment.
   d. VLANs can be defined by port or protocol, or they can be user defined.
11. When a VTP message for another VTP domain is received, what does the switch do?
   a. Act on the message
   b. Ignore the message
   c. Place the message in its database
   d. Perform the modifications ordered in the message
12. Which factors should determine the number of VLANs in a switch block?
   a. Data traffic patterns of the network
   b. Application types that are running on the network
   c. Network management needs of the network
   d. Group commonalities among users of the network
   e. All of the above
13. What are the basic types of VLAN boundaries? [Choose the two best answers]
   a. End-to-end VLANs
   b. Local VLANs
   c. Off-site VLANs
   d. Huge VLANs
14. All the switches in a VTP management domain can operate in Secure Mode by configuring which of the following?
   a. A hostname
   b. An IP address
   c. A password
   d. None of the above

15. What reason best describes why access link ports should not be configured as VTP trunks?
    a. VLAN tags are not removed when tagged frames are sent out trunk ports.
    b. Trunk ports send packets faster than the end-user interface can receive them.
    c. Trunk ports only send VLAN information for other VLANs than that assigned to the port.
    d. None of the above.

Real-World Projects

Our faithful technician, Joe Snow, received a nice raise at the beginning of the chapter. As he arrives at work, his supervisor explains that the on-call technician from the previous evening was sent out to a customer site and determined that the Cisco Catalyst 5000 Series switch had a power failure. Another Cisco Catalyst 5000 Series switch arrived from the company warehouse at another location and needs to be configured at the customer's site early this morning.

Another technician explains that he has been working on the new switch and has a list of things that still need to be configured at the customer's site after the switch is on the network there.

The technician then explains that no setup configuration was documented at the site. Therefore, restoring the configuration for the switch will take a great deal of time. When Joe is finished configuring the switch, the technician would like to get the configuration for the switch to keep in the customer's file to safeguard against future configuration problems.

Project 8.1

The following is a list of things that need to be configured to the switch:

- Set the system name to CORIOLIS5000
- Set the switch name and prompt to CORIOLIS5000
- Set the location to CORIOLIS ACQUISITIONS SWITCH
- Set the contact name for the switch to Joe Snow
- Set the enable prompt to CORIOLIS5000
- Set port 5/1 to VLAN 10
- Set ports 5/6 and 5/7 to VLAN 50
- Keep ports 5/2-5 and 5/8-12 in VLAN 1

- Set trunk ports 2/1-3, 5/2-5, and 5/8-12 to autonegotiate with ISL
- Set trunks 1/1-2, 5/1, and 5/6-7 to On with ISL
- Add a banner that warns, "Certification Insider Press, Authorized Use Only!"
- Assign the VTP domain name as Coriolis
- Set VTP to Server Mode

Follow these steps:

1. Configure the message-of-the-day banner using the following command:

```
set banner motd Certification Insider Press, Authorized Use Only!
```

2. Configure the system name by using the following command:

```
set system name CORIOLIS5000
```

3. Configure the command prompt name using the following command:

```
set prompt CORIOLIS5000
```

4. Configure the system location name with the following command:

```
set system location Coriolis Acquisitions Switch
```

5. Configure the contact name for the switch with the following command:

```
set system contact  Joe Snow
```

6. Configure the VTP domain for the switch using the following command:

```
set vtp domain Coriolis
```

7. Configure the VTP mode for the switch using the following command:

```
set vtp mode server
```

8. Configure the VLANs using the following commands:

```
set vlan 10 5/1
set vlan 50 5/6-7
```

***Note:** By default, all VLANs are in VLAN 1.*

9. Configure the trunks using the following commands:

```
set trunk 2/1-3 auto
set trunk 1/1-2 on isl
set trunk 5/1 on isl
set trunk 5/2-5 auto isl
set trunk 5/6-7 on isl
set trunk 5/8-12 auto isl
```

Project 8.2

To safeguard against future configuration problems, we need to be just like a doctor: We need to keep a chart.

Follow these steps:

1. Use the terminal emulation program of your choice to log in to the switch.
2. Use the **show configuration** command from the Privileged EXEC Mode prompt as shown in Listing 8.1. Listing 8.1 shows the entire configuration when Joe is finished.

Listing 8.1 The complete listing of a Cisco Catalyst 5000 configuration.

```
CORIOLIS5000 (enable) sh conf
..........
begin
set password coriolis
set enablepass corenable
set prompt CORIOLIS5000
set length 24 default
set logout 20
set banner motd ^ Certification Insider Press, Authorized Use Only!"^C
!
#system
set system baud  9600
set system modem disable
set system name  CORIOLIS5000
set system location Coriolis Acquisitions Switch
set system contact  Joe Snow
!
#snmp
set snmp community read-only      public
set snmp community read-write     private
set snmp community read-write-all secret
```

```
set snmp rmon enable
set snmp trap disable module
set snmp trap disable chassis
set snmp trap disable bridge
set snmp trap disable repeater
set snmp trap disable vtp
set snmp trap disable auth
set snmp trap disable ippermit
set snmp trap disable vmps
set snmp trap disable entity
set snmp trap disable config
set snmp trap disable stpx
set snmp extendedrmon vlanmode disable
set snmp extendedrmon vlanagent disable
set snmp extendedrmon enable
!
#ip
set interface sc0 1 38.187.127.4 255.240.0.0 38.186.20.15
set interface sc0 up
set interface sl0 0.0.0.0 0.0.0.0
set interface sl0 up
set arp agingtime 1200
set ip redirect   enable
set ip unreachable   enable
set ip fragmentation enable
set ip route 0.0.0.0         38.187.128.3    1
set ip alias default         0.0.0.0
!
#Command alias
!
#vmps
set vmps server retry 3
set vmps server reconfirminterval 60
set vmps tftpserver 0.0.0.0 vmps-config-database.1
set vmps state disable
!
#dns
set ip dns server 38.187.128.67 primary
set ip dns server 38.187.128.68
set ip dns enable
set ip dns domain coriolis.com
!
#tacacs+
set tacacs attempts 3
set tacacs directedrequest disable
set tacacs timeout 5
```

```
set authentication login tacacs disable
set authentication login local enable
set authentication enable tacacs disable
set authentication enable local enable
!
#bridge
set bridge ipx snaptoether   8023raw
set bridge ipx 8022toether   8023
set bridge ipx 8023rawtofddi snap
!
#vtp
set vtp domain coriolis
set vtp mode server
set vtp v2 disable
set vtp pruning disable
set vtp pruneeligible 2-1000
clear vtp pruneeligible 1001-1005
set vlan 1 name default type ethernet mtu 1500 said 100001 state active
set vlan 2 name VLAN2 type ethernet mtu 1500 said 100002 state active
set vlan 3 name VLAN3 type ethernet mtu 1500 said 100003 state active
set vlan 4 name VLAN4 type ethernet mtu 1500 said 100004 state active
set vlan 5 name VLAN5 type ethernet mtu 1500 said 100005 state active
set vlan 10 name VLAN10 type ethernet mtu 1500 said 100010 state active
set vlan 20 name ATlk20 type ethernet mtu 1500 said 100020 state active
set vlan 30 name ATlk30 type ethernet mtu 1500 said 100030 state active
set vlan 40 name ATlk40 type ethernet mtu 1500 said 100040 state active
set vlan 50 name test type ethernet mtu 1500 said 100050 state active
set vlan 1002 name fddi1 type fddi mtu 1500 said 101002 state active
set vlan 1004 name fnet1 type net2 mtu 1500 said 101004 state active
     bridge 0x0 stp ieee
set vlan 1005 name trnet-default type trbrf mtu 1500 said 101005 state
     active bridge 0x0 stp ieee
set vlan 1003 name token-ring-default type trcrf mtu 1500 said 101003
      state active parent 0 ring 0x0 mode srb aremaxhop 0 stemaxhop 0
!
#spantree
#uplinkfast groups
set spantree uplinkfast disable
#backbonefast
set spantree backbonefast disable
set spantree enable  all
#vlan 1
set spantree fwddelay 15    1
set spantree hello    2     1
set spantree maxage   20    1
set spantree priority 32768 1
```

```
#vlan 2
set spantree fwddelay 15     2
set spantree hello    2      2
set spantree maxage   20     2
set spantree priority 32768 2
#vlan 3
set spantree fwddelay 15     3
set spantree hello    2      3
set spantree maxage   20     3
set spantree priority 32768 3
#vlan 4
set spantree fwddelay 15     4
set spantree hello    2      4
set spantree maxage   20     4
set spantree priority 32768 4
#vlan 5
set spantree fwddelay 15     5
set spantree hello    2      5
set spantree maxage   20     5
set spantree priority 32768 5
#vlan 10
set spantree fwddelay 15     10
set spantree hello    2      10
set spantree maxage   20     10
set spantree priority 32768 10
#vlan 20
set spantree fwddelay 15     20
set spantree hello    2      20
set spantree maxage   20     20
set spantree priority 32768 20
#vlan 30
set spantree fwddelay 15     30
set spantree hello    2      30
set spantree maxage   20     30
set spantree priority 32768 30
#vlan 40
set spantree fwddelay 15     40
set spantree hello    2      40
set spantree maxage   20     40
set spantree priority 32768 40
#vlan 50
set spantree fwddelay 15     50
set spantree hello    2      50
set spantree maxage   20     50
set spantree priority 32768 50
```

```
#vlan 1003
set spantree fwddelay 4     1003
set spantree hello    2     1003
set spantree maxage   10    1003
set spantree priority 32768 1003
set spantree portstate 1003 block 0
set spantree portcost 1003 62
set spantree portpri  1003 4
set spantree portfast 1003 disable
#vlan 1005
set spantree fwddelay 15    1005
set spantree hello    2     1005
set spantree maxage   20    1005
set spantree priority 32768 1005
set spantree multicast-address 1005 ieee
!
#cgmp
set cgmp disable
set cgmp leave disable
!
#syslog
set logging console enable
set logging server disable
set logging level cdp 2 default
set logging level mcast 2 default
set logging level dtp 5 default
set logging level dvlan 2 default
set logging level earl 2 default
set logging level fddi 2 default
set logging level ip 2 default
set logging level pruning 2 default
set logging level snmp 2 default
set logging level spantree 2 default
set logging level sys 5 default
set logging level tac 2 default
set logging level tcp 2 default
set logging level telnet 2 default
set logging level tftp 2 default
set logging level vtp 2 default
set logging level vmps 2 default
set logging level kernel 2 default
set logging level filesys 2 default
set logging level drip 2 default
set logging level pagp 5 default
set logging level mgmt 5 default
set logging level mls 5 default
```

```
set logging level protfilt 2 default
set logging level security 2 default
!
#ntp
set ntp broadcastclient disable
set ntp broadcastdelay 3000
set ntp client disable
clear timezone
set summertime disable
!
#set boot command
set boot config-register 0x102

set boot system flash bootflash:cat5000-sup3.4-1-2.bin
!
#permit list
set ip permit disable
!
#drip
set tokenring reduction enable
set tokenring distrib-crf disable
!
#igmp
set igmp disable
!
#protocolfilter
set protocolfilter disable
!
#mls
set mls enable
set mls flow destination
set mls agingtime 256
set mls agingtime fast 0 0
set mls nde disable
!
#standby ports
set standbyports enable
!
#module 1 : 2-port 10/100BaseTX Supervisor
set module name    1
set vlan 1    1/1-2
set port channel 1/1-2 off
set port channel 1/1-2 on
set port enable     1/1-2
set port level      1/1-2  normal
set port speed      1/1-2  100
```

8

```
set port duplex     1/1-2  full
set port trap       1/1-2  disable
set port name       1/1-2
set port security   1/1-2  disable
set port broadcast  1/1-2  100%
set port membership 1/1-2  static
set port protocol   1/1-2 ip on
set port protocol   1/1-2 ipx auto
set cdp enable      1/1-2
set cdp interval    1/1-2 60
set trunk 1/1  on isl 1-1005
set trunk 1/2  on isl 1-1005
set spantree portfast     1/1-2 disable
set spantree portcost     1/1-2  19
set spantree portpri      1/1-2  32
set spantree portvlanpri  1/1  0
set spantree portvlanpri  1/2  0
set spantree portvlancost 1/1  cost 18
set spantree portvlancost 1/2  cost 18
!
#module 2 : 3-port 1000BaseX Ethernet
set module name    2
set module enable  2
set vlan 1          2/1-3
set port enable     2/1-3
set port level      2/1-3  normal
set port duplex     2/1-3  full
set port trap       2/1-3  disable
set port name       2/1-3
set port security   2/1-3  disable
set port broadcast  2/1-3  100%
set port membership 2/1-3  static
set port protocol   2/1-3 ip on
set port protocol   2/1-3 ipx auto
set port negotiation 2/1-3 enable
set port flowcontrol send    2/1-3 desired
set port flowcontrol receive 2/1-3 off
set cdp enable   2/1-3
set cdp interval 2/1-3 60
set trunk 2/1  auto negotiate 1-1005
set trunk 2/2  auto negotiate 1-1005
set trunk 2/3  auto negotiate 1-1005
set spantree portfast    2/1-3 disable
set spantree portcost    2/1-3  4
set spantree portpri     2/1-3  32
set spantree portvlanpri 2/1  0
```

```
set spantree portvlanpri 2/2  0
set spantree portvlanpri 2/3  0
set spantree portvlancost 2/1  cost 3
set spantree portvlancost 2/2  cost 3
set spantree portvlancost 2/3  cost 3
!
#module 3 : 1-port Route Switch
set module name    3
set port level      3/1  normal
set port trap       3/1  disable
set port name       3/1
set cdp enable   3/1
set cdp interval 3/1 60
set trunk 3/1  on isl 1-1005
set spantree portcost    3/1  2
set spantree portpri     3/1  32
set spantree portvlanpri 3/1  0
set spantree portvlancost 3/1  cost 4
!
#module 4 : 2-port MM OC-3 Dual-Phy ATM
set module name    4
set port level      4/1  normal
set port name       4/1-2
set cdp enable   4/1
set cdp interval 4/1 60
set trunk 4/1  on lane 1-1005
set spantree portcost    4/1  14
set spantree portpri     4/1  32
set spantree portvlanpri 4/1  0
set spantree portvlancost 4/1  cost 13
!
#module 5 : 12-port 10/100BaseTX Ethernet
set module name    5
set module enable  5
set vlan 1    5/2-5,5/8-12
set vlan 10   5/1
set vlan 50   5/6-7
set port enable     5/1-12
set port level      5/1-12  normal
set port speed      5/2-12  auto
set port speed      5/1  100
set port duplex     5/1  full
set port trap       5/1-12  disable
set port name       5/1-12
set port security   5/1-12  disable
set port broadcast  5/1-12  0
```

8

```
set port membership 5/1-12  static
set port protocol 5/1-12 ip on
set port protocol 5/1-12 ipx auto
set cdp enable   5/1-12
set cdp interval 5/1-12 60
set trunk 5/1  on isl 1-1005
set trunk 5/2  auto isl 1-1005
set trunk 5/3  auto isl 1-1005
set trunk 5/4  auto isl 1-1005
set trunk 5/5  auto isl 1-1005
set trunk 5/6  on isl 1-1005
set trunk 5/7  on isl 1-1005
set trunk 5/8  auto isl 1-1005
set trunk 5/9  auto isl 1-1005
set trunk 5/10 auto isl 1-1005
set trunk 5/11 auto isl 1-1005
set trunk 5/12 auto isl 1-1005
set spantree portfast    5/1-12 disable
set spantree portcost    5/1,5/3-4,5/6-7,5/11-12  19
set spantree portcost    5/2,5/5,5/8-10  100
set spantree portpri     5/1-12  32
set spantree portvlanpri 5/1  0
set spantree portvlanpri 5/2  0
set spantree portvlanpri 5/3  0
set spantree portvlanpri 5/4  0
set spantree portvlanpri 5/5  0
set spantree portvlanpri 5/6  0
set spantree portvlanpri 5/7  0
set spantree portvlanpri 5/8  0
set spantree portvlanpri 5/9  0
set spantree portvlanpri 5/10 0
set spantree portvlanpri 5/11 0
set spantree portvlanpri 5/12 0
set spantree portvlancost 5/1  cost 18
set spantree portvlancost 5/2  cost 99
set spantree portvlancost 5/3  cost 18
set spantree portvlancost 5/4  cost 18
set spantree portvlancost 5/5  cost 99
set spantree portvlancost 5/6  cost 18
set spantree portvlancost 5/7  cost 18
set spantree portvlancost 5/8  cost 99
set spantree portvlancost 5/9  cost 99
set spantree portvlancost 5/10 cost 99
set spantree portvlancost 5/11 cost 18
set spantree portvlancost 5/12 cost 18
!
```

```
#switch port analyzer
!set span 1 1/1 both inpkts disable
set span disable
!
#cam
set cam agingtime 1-5,10,20,30,40,50,1003,1005 300
end
CORIOLIS5000 (enable)
```

3. Use either the print option, if it is available in the terminal emulation program you are using, or cut and paste the configuration into a text editor such as Microsoft Notepad or Word. From there you can save the file or print it.

CHAPTER NINE

9

REDUNDANT LINK MANAGEMENT

After completing this chapter, you will be able to:

- ✓ Explain the reasoning behind the IEEE 802.1D protocol standard
- ✓ Describe how root bridge assignments are handled
- ✓ List the qualities of a transparent bridge
- ✓ Explain the Bridge Protocol Data Units (BPDUs) frame
- ✓ Identify how a root bridge is selected
- ✓ Modify Bridge Protocol Data Timers
- ✓ Give the definition of a switch diameter
- ✓ Describe the convergence time calculations
- ✓ List the five switch port states
- ✓ Configure Spanning Tree Protocol (STP)
- ✓ View the Spanning Tree Protocol settings
- ✓ Configure Per-VLAN Spanning Tree (PVST)
- ✓ Configure Per-VLAN Spanning Tree Plus (PVST+)
- ✓ Configure Port Aggregation Protocol (PAgP)
- ✓ Configure EtherChannel
- ✓ Configure UplinkFast
- ✓ Configure BackboneFast

In today's networks, the ability to provide secondary paths for redundancy is vital. Companies can no longer rely on just one connection to their critical resources. Network designers in today's network climate try to add not only device redundancy but link redundancy, as well. Whether you are employed by a Cisco reseller or have a job supporting switches, one of the most common types of support calls involves the components you will learn about in this chapter.

Redundancy is the ability to provide an immediate backup solution to a fault in the network that might otherwise cause a network or component service outage. This chapter will focus on link redundancy using the Spanning Tree Protocol (STP) and the IEEE 802.1D algorithm used to support STP.

Note: *When building a redundant network, network designers keep redundancy for power, component, link, and other critical areas in mind.*

Let's look at a real-world example to help explain redundancy. I live in a suburb of Sacramento, California. More than one path exists to just about any destination in Sacramento. To get from my house to downtown, I can take the freeway at 65 miles per hour and get there in about 20 minutes. That would be my primary optimal path. However, if an accident blocks the freeway, I can take a secondary path and use surface streets. This route takes about an hour, but I still get to my destination. This secondary path is my redundant link to downtown.

The concept is the same with networks. You have a primary high-speed path that you want to use exclusively when it is available, but you should also have a second, usually lower-speed, redundant link in case your main path is blocked. Sometimes your redundant paths are equal, and you have more than one freeway to your destination. This chapter will explain how Spanning Tree Protocol decides which paths to take and which paths to block.

As we showed in earlier chapters, the routing protocols in Layer 3 devices is responsible for handling load balancing, path determination, and notification, should a link's service be disrupted. STP is a protocol designed to allow a faster way of handling those same services, but at the data link layer—Layer 2 of the OSI Model.

This chapter will cover the history of STP from its beginnings at DEC to when it became an IEEE 802 specification of the IEEE protocol standards. We will also discuss the components, configuration, the assignment of port costs, priorities, bridge IDs, and commands associated with STP.

As we progress through the chapter, you will also learn the properties of a transparent frame and the processes used in configuring STP through multiple switches. We will also cover InterVLAN routing, BackboneFast, UplinkFast, and many other solutions to solve STP problems.

Finally, you will learn how some of Cisco's approaches differ from those associated with the IEEE 802 specifications for STP. Cisco has created some proprietary protocols to increase larger network stability and scalability as well as other protocols to allow for faster convergence and transparent use with the IEEE specifications.

SPANNING TREE ALGORITHM

The Spanning Tree Algorithm (STA) was presented to the IEEE committee by Digital Equipment Corporation (DEC). The protocol was intended to prevent the occurrence of bridged data loops and the problems they caused. It was revised by the IEEE 802 committee into what is now known as the IEEE 802.1D algorithm. The revised algorithm is different enough from DEC's algorithm that the two are incompatible.

The STA designates a Layer 2 link management algorithm to configure a loop-free network by putting redundant path ports into a standby or blocked state. If these ports remained in an active state, they would create a loop for data to continuously encircle the network. The blocked bridge ports can be activated in the event of a link failure of the primary path, thereby providing a new path through the network.

A loop is created when multiple paths exist in the network. Data flowing from one interface on the network returns on a second or redundant path through the network, creating a loop as shown in Figure 9.1. The data moves in a continuous circle unless some protocol or algorithm is in place to stop the data or a maximum time to live is assigned.

Without STP, no switch would be aware of another. Each switch would continually forward frames in a circle, and the loop could conceivably go on forever. Some of the time, the information the switch obtains will allow the frame to make it to the destination. Other times, the switch will be incorrect about the destination of its frame and will send the frame in the wrong direction.

STP forces certain redundant data paths into a standby mode or a blocked state. By blocking the paths to destinations other than the given root path, it creates only one path through the network. Should any of the forwarding paths through one of the network segments in the spanning tree become unreachable, the STA will then reconfigure the spanning-tree topology and re-establish communication with the destination interface by activating the standby path.

Spanning Tree Protocol executes the Spanning Tree Algorithm—they are two separate entities. In order to find the redundant links, the STA chooses a reference point in the network and calculates the redundant paths to that reference point.

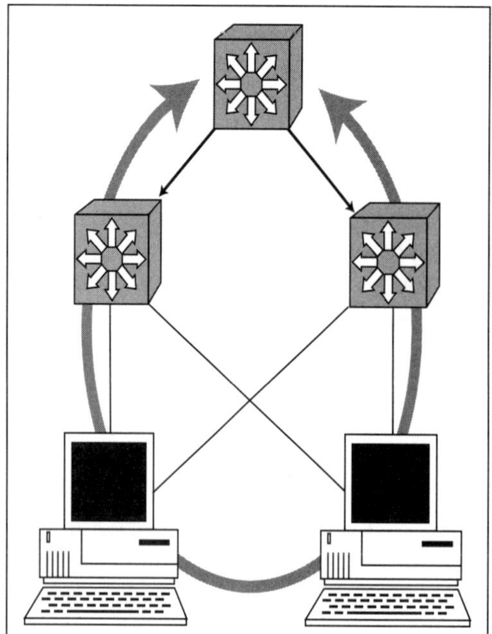

Figure 9.1 Data on a redundant path encircling the network.

If the STA finds a redundant path, it will choose one path to forward and the redundant paths to block. This process effectively severs all of the redundant links within the network.

If you fail to stop routing loops, the problem could grow much worse than the original loop itself. The properties of transparent bridging allow the behavior of always retransmitting a broadcast and never marking the frame. As a result, the bridges will actually create broadcasts in an expanding fashion when a bridge loop occurs. This process of creating new broadcasts will not stop until the loop is shut down. Eventually, the bridging loop will effectively bring down the entire network through multiple broadcasts. This process is referred to as a *broadcast storm.*

STA and Graph Theory

The STA uses conclusions obtained by a graph theory, developed by Edsger Dijkstra, to construct a loop-free subset of the network's topology. Graph theory states that for a connected graph consisting of interfaces and edges connecting pairs of interfaces, a spanning tree of the edges maintains the connectivity of the graph while containing no loops.

This theory is sometimes referred to as the *Shortest Path Algorithm*. Its simplicity and efficiency make it useful for many of today's protocols. Some of those protocols include the Spanning Tree Protocol and other link state protocols, including Open Shortest Path First (OSPF).

The algorithm provides a directed graph consisting of vertices and weighted edges. In STP, each link represents a cost. The weighted edges, which usually have more hops in the link than the straight-through points, are assigned higher values. Each link in the path has a value, and the total of the values to a given point or destination is the total weighted value of the path. The lowest total weighted value represents the most efficient path to the destination.

Each bridge in the network is assigned a unique identifier. The identifier is one of the bridge's Media Access Control (MAC) addresses, as well as an assigned priority, which is explained in more detail later in the chapter. After STA assigns each bridge a unique identifier, it then assigns each port in every bridge a unique identifier. This identifier is typically the port's own individual interface's MAC address. Each bridge port is then associated with a *path cost*. This path cost represents the cost of transmitting a frame onto the network through the port. Path costs are assigned by default, but can be assigned manually by a network administrator.

Root Bridge Assignment

One of the first actions of the STA computation is selecting a root bridge. The *root bridge* is the bridge with the lowest-value bridge identifier. After the root bridge is selected, the *root ports* on all other bridges are determined. Figure 9.2 shows the root bridge connecting to other bridges. Notice the numbers associated

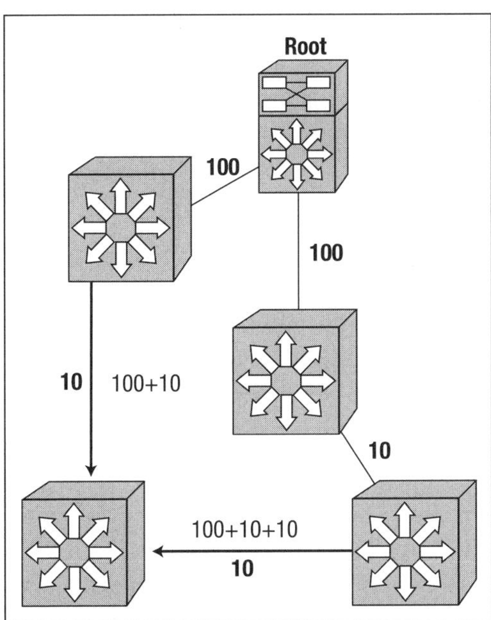

Figure 9.2 The root bridge connecting to other bridges or switches in the network.

with the root bridge's path to each individual destination. The path with the lowest number has the highest priority. The higher the number between each individual segment, the higher the cost of transmitting a frame between those two segments. The port through which the root bridge can be reached with the least amount of hops or cost determines a bridge's root port; this is referred to as the *least* path cost.

A switch immediately assumes at startup that it is the root bridge and configures its bridge ID equal to the root ID in the BPDU. The bridge ID is actually made up of two components, as follows:

- *2-byte priority set by the switch*—By default, this number is the same for all Cisco switches and is set to a priority 0x8000 or 32,768.
- *6-byte Media Access Control (MAC) address*—The MAC address of the switch or bridge.

These two fields combined yield a value that will be compared with other switches' values to determine which switch will become the root bridge. When the switches exchange BPDUs, the switches determine which switch will become the root bridge. If all the switches have the same priority, the bridge with the lowest MAC address becomes the root bridge.

Each switch will form an association with the root bridge shortly after the root bridge has been elected. Each switch listens to BPDUs as they arrive on all ports. When a switch receives BPDUs on more than one port, this is an indication that the switch has more than one path to the root bridge. The switch will determine which port will be forwarding data and which ports will be blocked from sending data. It does this by analyzing two components in the BPDU: the path cost and port ID fields.

The switch looks at the path cost first to determine which port owns the lowest-cost path to the root switch. Calculation of the path cost is based on the link speed and the number of links that the BPDU went through. If the port has the lowest port cost, the port is placed in forwarding mode. All other ports that are receiving BPDUs are placed in blocking mode. If the path cost is equal, as in the case of identical links, the bridge looks at the port ID as a tie-breaker. The port with the lowest port ID forwards, and all other ports are blocked.

When the spanning tree topology is calculated using the default parameters, there may be instances where the calculated path between the source and the destination interfaces in the network might not be the ideal path. For example if there are multiple high-speed links to a destination, the links may total more than the cost of a very slow link. Even though the straight path has the fewest hops, it may not be the most efficient path. You can manually change lower-speed links on a port to reflect a higher path cost, forcing a change in the root port selection. The goal is to make changes to the network so that the fastest, most efficient route to the root port is used. The fastest links should always have the lowest port costs.

Here is another example. In Figure 9.3, let's assume that one port on Switch A is connected to Switch C using a FDDI link. The redundant link routes to Switch B, which uses Unshielded Twisted Pair (UTP) at the wire speed of 10Mbps. Traffic would be more efficient over the high-speed FDDI link. Manually changing the spanning tree port cost on the FDDI port to a lower numerical value lowers the port cost, thus assigning it a higher priority. The FDDI port becomes the new root port, and the other port is blocked for use only in the event of a network change or loss of the FDDI connection. This arrangement prevents loops from being created and provides the second port as a redundant or backup link.

Designated Ports and Bridges

A *designated bridge* is the bridge on each LAN that provides the shortest route with the least path cost. The designated bridge is the only bridge that is allowed to forward frames to and from the other bridges. A *designated port* on the switch is the port that connects the switch to the physical interface of the designated bridge.

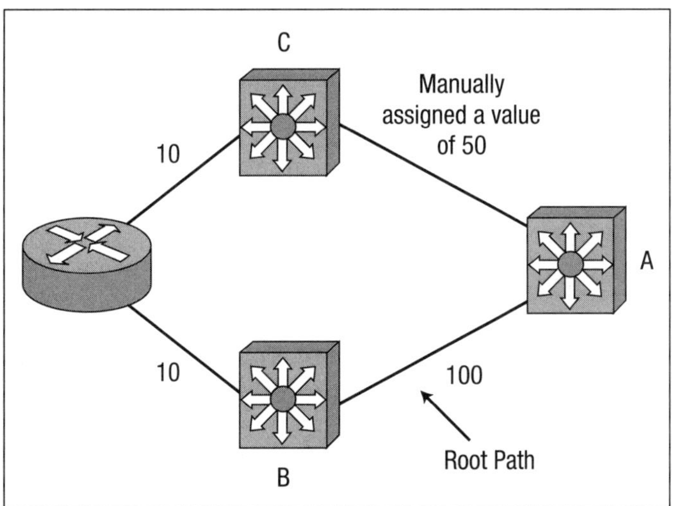

Figure 9.3 The lower number on the FDDI link creates a higher priority.

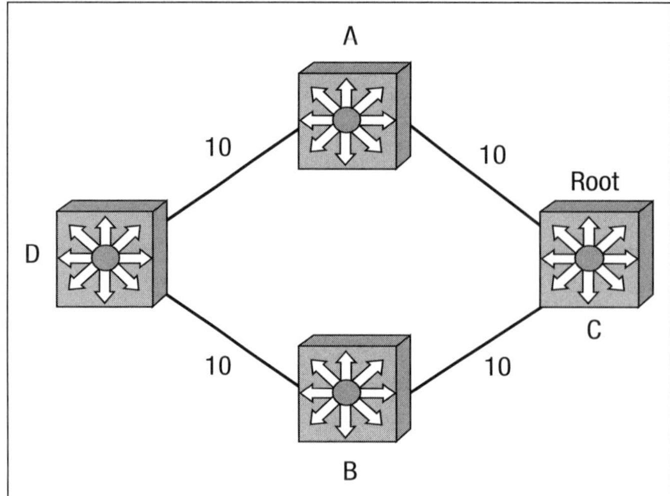

Figure 9.4 Two ports with equal path costs through the network.

Equal Path Costs

When two or more links have the same root path cost, the STA has a problem choosing a designated port or a root path through the network using the lowest path cost. For example, in Figure 9.4, Switch C acting as the root bridge can reach Switch D with two paths equaling the same path cost.

In this situation, the path cost can be manually assigned. You assign lower numbers to the faster physical media, and you assign slower media a higher path cost. If the path costs remain equal and unchanged, in the case of identical physical links, the switch or bridge uses the port ID as the tiebreaker. The port ID containing the lowest value wins, and the other ports are blocked. The range of numbers that can be assigned to the port costs are 1 through 65,535. Typically, the path cost is determined by dividing 1000 by the physical wire speed in megabits per second (Mbps), as shown in Table 9.1.

Using this process, all but one of the ports directly connected to each switch are eliminated, thereby removing all the loops in the LAN. The STA also eliminates loops involving more than two LANs, while still preserving connectivity.

Table 9.1 Examples of path cost calculations.

Physical Wire Speed	Path Cost
10Mbps	100
100Mbps	10
155Mbps	6
1000Mbps	1

Transparent Bridging

The basic function of a switch is identical to that of a transparent bridge. In order to understand the Spanning Tree Protocol, we will first look at the behavior of a transparent bridge without STP.

Transparent bridging by definition has to be transparent to the devices on the network. The developers of transparent bridging wanted to make sure that end-user interfaces did not have to be modified to support the process of bridging.

The bridge learns of the interfaces connected to it by looking at the frames it receives through each port for the source address of a device; this process is sometimes referred to as *listening*. When a frame with a source address comes from a specific port, the bridge automatically assumes that the source address can be found through that port.

Note: *A transparent bridge does not modify frames that it receives.*

The bridge next builds a table indicating that the source address it just received can be reached through the port from which the frame arrived. This process is referred to as *learning*. A bridge is always listening to and learning from what it receives through each port. A bridge will forward each broadcast it receives out all the ports connected to it *except* the port that initially received the broadcast.

An Unknown Unicast is sent when a destination address is unknown. Again, in this case, the bridge forwards the frame out all ports except the port on which it arrived.

Transparent bridging works very well when it remains simple and the network environment contains no redundant links. Transparent bridging begins to have problems when a redundant path is added to the bridged network. STP was created to overcome the problems of transparent bridging in redundant multilink networks. It was designed to avoid and eliminate loops in the network by providing a loop-free path through the network. STP determines where there are loops in the network and shuts down links that are redundant. It ensures that there will be only one path to each destination and that a bridging loop can never occur. In case of a link failure, the bridge knows what redundant links exist and will activate a link that was previously blocked.

As shown in Figure 9.5, some ports need to be disabled or put into a non-forwarding mode. Doing so creates only one path through the network. The ports remain aware of the topology of the network and can be enabled if the link that is forwarding data ever fails.

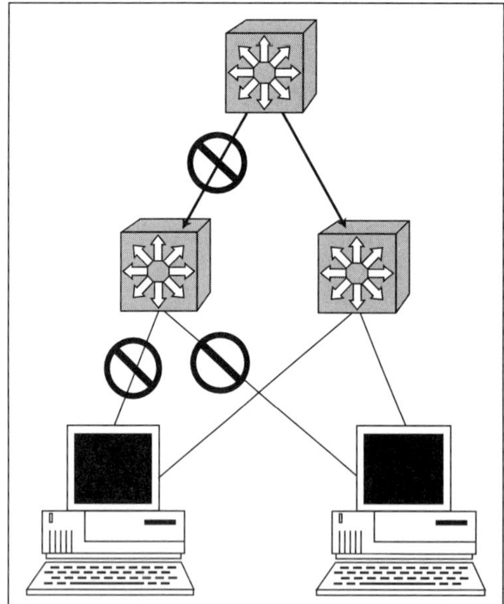

Figure 9.5 Redundant paths are disabled, creating only one path through the network.

An STA recalculation occurs whenever the bridge is powered up or when a topology change is detected in the network. This calculation requires communication between the spanning tree bridges, which is accomplished through configuration messages called *Bridge Protocol Data Units (BPDUs)*.

A BPDU message contains information that identifies the bridge presumed to be the root bridge by using a root identifier. The message also contains the distance from the sending bridge to the root bridge with the calculated root path cost. And, each configuration message contains the bridge and port identifiers of the sending bridge, as well as the age of the information contained in the message.

Bridges exchange configuration messages at regular intervals—usually every one to four seconds. If one bridge fails or there is a topology change, the neighboring bridges will detect the lack of configuration messages and initiate an immediate spanning tree recalculation. All transparent bridge topology decisions are made locally on each switch, and the configuration messages are then exchanged between the neighboring bridges. No central authority or administration exists in the network topology.

Bridge Protocol Data Units

The Bridge Protocol Data Units are responsible for electing a root bridge, blocking redundant links to prevent loops in the network, notifying other switches of topology changes, and monitoring the state of the spanning tree. All switches in

Protocol ID 2 Bytes	Version 1 Byte	Message Type 1 Byte	Flag 1 Byte	Root ID 8 Bytes	Root Path Cost 4 Bytes	Bridge ID 8 Bytes	Port ID 2 Bytes	Message Age 2 Bytes	Max Age 2 Bytes	Hello Time 2 Bytes	Fwd Delay 2 Bytes

Figure 9.6 The 12-part IEEE 802.1D transparent bridge configuration message BPDU format.

an extended LAN participating in Spanning Tree Protocol gather information on other switches in the network through an exchange of BPDU data messages. The BPDU frame is shown in Figure 9.6.

The fields of the transparent bridge configuration message or BPDU are as follows:

- *Protocol Identifier*—Contains 2 bytes and a value of zero.
- *Version*—Contains 1 byte and a value of zero.
- *Message Type*—Contains 1 byte and a value of zero.
- *Flag*—Contains 1 byte; only the first 2 bits are used. The topology change (TC) bit signals that there has been a topology change. The topology change acknowledgment (TCA) bit is then set to acknowledge receipt of a configuration message with the TC signal bit set.
- *Root ID*—Contains 8 bytes that identify the root bridge by listing a 2-byte priority followed by a 6-byte ID.
- *Root Path Cost*—Contains 4 bytes specifying the cost of the path from the bridge sending the configuration message to the root bridge.
- *Bridge ID*—Contains 8 bytes identifying the priority and ID of the bridge sending the message.
- *Port ID*—Contains 2 bytes identifying the port from which the configuration message was sent. This field allows loops created by multiple attached bridges to be detected immediately by STP.
- *Message Age*—Contains 2 bytes specifying the amount of time since the root sent the configuration message on which the current configuration message is based.
- *MaxAge*—Contains 2 bytes indicating when the current configuration message should be discarded.
- *Hello Time*—Contains 2 bytes providing the time period between root bridge configuration messages.

- *FwdDelay*—Contains 2 bytes providing the length of time that the bridge should wait before transitioning to a new state following a topology change in the network. If a bridge transitions too soon, not all network links might be ready to change their state, and loops can result.

By default, BPDUs are sent out every two seconds on every port to ensure a stable topology without data loops.

BPDU Timers

Timers are used to prevent bridging loops and to determine how long it will take STP to converge after a failure or loss of a link. When BPDUs travel through the switched network, these units face propagation delays. Propagation delays occur due to such things as bandwidth utilization, packet length, switch processing, or any other port-to-port delay encountered as a frame traverses the network. A possible result of propagation delays is a change in the topology that can take place at different times and at different locations within the network. When a switch port converts from a blocked state to a forwarding state, the port can inadvertently create temporary data loops, because the port may not have complete information about the network topology.

Spanning Tree Protocol uses timers to force the ports to wait for the correct topology information. The timers are set by default on the switch. Table 9.2 shows the three different STP timers and the default timer settings based on a default setting of 2 for the **Hello Time** and 7 for the switch diameter, discussed in the next section. Based on these assumptions, the network should always form a stable topology.

Switch Diameter

The switch diameter is a unit of measurement between the root switch and child switches. The root bridge counts as the first switch. Each subsequent child switch out from the root bridge is added to come up with the diameter number.

Table 9.2 Default STP timers and their default settings.

STP Timer Variable	Default	Description
Hello Time	2 seconds	Determines how often the switch will broadcast hello messages to other switches
Maximum Time/MaxAge	20 seconds	Determines how long protocol information received on a port is stored by the switch
FwdDelay	15 seconds	Determines how long listening and learning will last before the port begins forwarding

A parent switch brings you closer to the root bridge and a child switch takes you away from the root bridge.

The root bridge can be configured with a diameter from a minimum of two switches to a maximum of seven switches. By modifying the diameter, you will subsequently change the timer values that are advertised by the root to reflect a more accurate network diameter. For example, a diameter of 2 yields a **MaxAge** of 10 seconds and a **FwdDelay** of 7 seconds. Cisco recommends that you change the diameter to correctly reflect your network rather than manually changing the timers.

Timer Operations Using Default Values

During periods of network instability, you may want to modify spanning tree timers. During these periods, the timers should be increased to give the network a chance to stabilize. Using Cisco management software, you can modify each of these states. When the Spanning Tree Protocol is enabled, every switch in the VLAN goes through the blocking state and then transitions to the state of listening and then learning at startup, as discussed in the next section.

You can modify STP convergence time to affect the performance and operation of the bridge. Figure 9.7 shows the timing defaults of the four different states indicated in the graphic. The Forward Delay (**FwdDelay**) parameter default

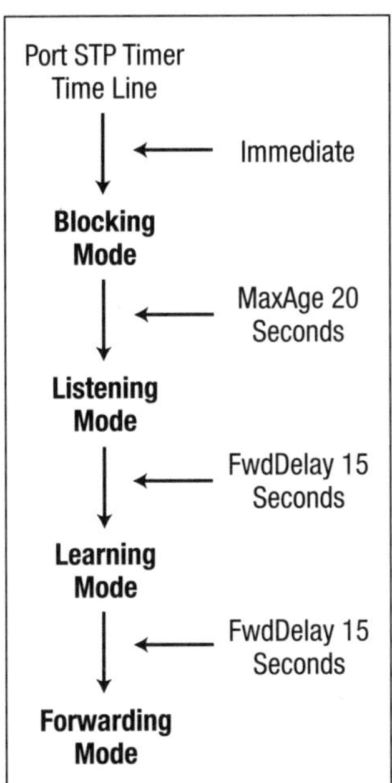

Figure 9.7 The convergence times of the port states in Spanning Tree Protocol.

value is 15 seconds. It can be set to a minimum value of four seconds. The switch is able to detect a change in the physical topology of the network and may change a port from a blocked state to a forwarding state in eight seconds. The listening and learning states are transitional states implemented by STP to force the port to wait for all BPDUs from other switches.

Convergence Time Calculation for STP

By default, **MaxAge** is 20 seconds and the **FwdDelay** is 30 seconds (because **FwdDelay** is used by both the listening and learning states). The values have meaning only at a root bridge. You can adjust **FwdDelay** and **MaxAge**; however, doing so may cause a data loop temporarily for very complex networks. Using the following example, the downtime could be as high as 50 seconds:

```
2 * FwdDelay + MaxAge = Down Time
```

For example, using the defaults:

```
2 * 15 + 20 = 50 seconds
```

STP Port States

Spanning Tree Protocol transitions each port through the four port states in a designated order before the port can forward frames. These states are blocking, listening, learning, and forwarding. A fifth state—disabled—can be manually configured.

From the switch's initialization or startup, it goes to a blocking state; it then progresses from a blocking state to a listening state, from a listening state to a learning state, and from a learning state to a forwarding state. The manually disabled or system-disabled port state can override a listening, learning, or forwarding state.

As we discussed in the previous section, propagation delays can occur when protocol information passes through a switched LAN. As a result, topology changes can take place at different times and at different places in a switched network. When a switch port transitions a directly blocked state in the stable topology to a forwarding state in the topology, it can create temporary data loops. Ports must wait for new topology information to propagate through the switched LAN before beginning to forward frames. They must wait for the lifetime to expire for frames that have been forwarded using the old topology information.

Each port state can be manually modified using management software. If properly configured, the ports should create a stable network and transition the ports of each switch to either a forwarding or blocking state.

When the STA places a port in the forwarding state, the port continues to listen for protocol information that suggests it should go to a blocking state. The port waits for the expiration of a protocol timer that allows the port to transition to a learning state. While in the learning state, the port continues to block frame forwarding as it learns information about the network. Station location information is added to the address table. The expiration of a protocol timer moves the port into the forwarding state, where both learning and forwarding are then enabled. Figure 9.8 shows the order in which ports are placed in different states.

Blocking State

A port in the blocking state does not participate in frame forwarding after initialization until a BPDU is sent to each port in the switch. A switch initially assumes it is the root until it exchanges BPDUs with other switches. This exchange establishes which switch in the network is really the root. If only one switch resides in the network, no exchange occurs, the forward delay timer expires, and the ports move to the listening state. A switch always enters the blocking state following switch initialization.

A port in the blocking state discards frames received from the attached segment and frames switched from another port for forwarding. There is absolutely no learning at this point, so there is no address database update. However, the port does receive BPDUs and direct them to the system module. Although it receives BPDUs, a port in a blocking state does not transmit BPDUs received from the system module. It does receive and respond to network management messages.

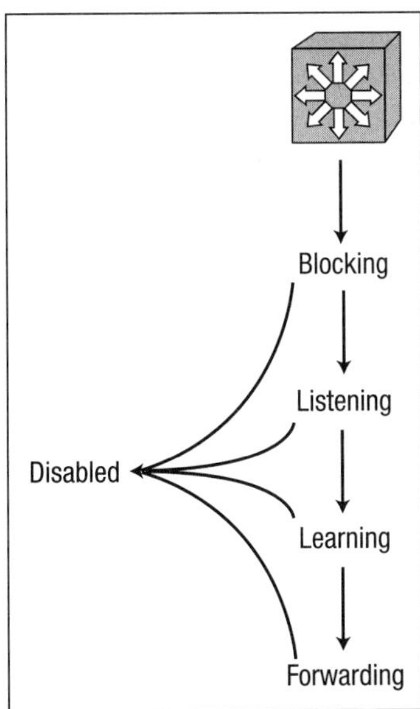

Figure 9.8 Spanning Tree Protocol port initialization order.

Listening State

A port enters the listening state after the blocking state. The port enters this state when STP determines that the port should participate in frame forwarding.

A port in the listening state discards frames received from the attached segment and frames switched from another port for forwarding. There is absolutely no learning at this point, so there is no address database update. However, the port does receive BPDUs and direct them to the system module. In the listening state, the port does not transmit BPDUs it receives from the system module. It does receive and respond to network management messages.

Learning State

The learning state is the second transition after the blocking state. This state prepares the port to participate in frame forwarding. The port enters the learning state from the listening state. In this state, the port continues to discard frames received from the attached segment and frames switched from another port for forwarding. However, the port begins to incorporate information from frames and BPDUs into the address table. Just as in the forwarding and listening states, the port continues to receive BPDUs and direct them to the system module. However, it begins to receive, process, and transmit BPDUs received from the system module. It also continues to receive and respond to network management messages.

Forwarding State

The forwarding state is the final transitional state after the blocking state. A port in the forwarding state forwards frames received from the attached segment and frames switched from another port for forwarding, and incorporates station location information into its address database. The port receives BPDUs and directs them to the system module. It also processes BPDUs received from the system module and receives and responds to network management messages.

Warning: You can use PortFast on switch ports connected to individual workstations to allow these ports to transition directly to the forwarding state, instead of going through the entire spanning tree initialization process. PortFast will be covered later in this chapter. To prevent illegal topologies, however, STP can be enabled on ports connected to switches or other devices that forward messages.

Disabled State

A port in the disabled state does not participate in any frame forwarding or STP. Disabled ports discard frames received from the attached segment and frames switched from another port for forwarding. The port does not incorporate station location into its address database. There is absolutely no learning in this state. The port does receive BPDUs, but it does not direct them to the system module.

It does not receive or process BPDUs for transmission from the system module. The only function of the port is to receive and respond to network management messages.

Topology Changes in the Network

When topology changes occur with one or more links in a network running Spanning Tree Protocol, certain steps occur using the Spanning Tree Algorithm. First, when a bridge or switch notices that a change has occurred to a link in the network, the bridge or switch sends a topology change BPDU out the root port destined for the root bridge. The topology change BPDU indicates a change with a 1-byte flag of the BPDU.

The originating bridge or switch will continue to send out the topology change BPDUs until the designated destination bridge or switch responds with a topology change acknowledgement, which is also a 1-byte flag. The designated bridge or switch also sends a topology change BPDU out its root port destined for either another designated parent bridge, a parent switch, or the root bridge.

After the root bridge receives the topology change message, it will change its configuration message to indicate that a topology change has occurred. The root bridge sets the topology change in the configuration for a period of time equal to the sum of the **FwdDelay** and **MaxAge** parameters.

Child bridges or switches receiving the topology change configuration message from the root bridge use the **FwdDelay** timer to age out entries located in their address table. By doing this, the device can age out entries more quickly than the default of 300 seconds or 5 minutes.

If an entry in the Content Addressable Memory (CAM) table is not heard from for 300 seconds, the CAM table flushes the entry from the device. Stations that are no longer available due to the change in the topology will be aged out more quickly. The child bridges and switches each continue this process until they no longer receive topology change configuration messages from the root bridge.

Configuring Spanning Tree Protocol

There are two types of command-line switches. One of these mimics the Cisco IOS-based interface that is found on all Cisco routers. The other type is based on the Set/Clear command interface found on switches like the Catalyst 5000 Series. So, you really have to learn the commands for Spanning Tree Protocol twice.

Although the commands are similar in some ways, the similarity doesn't make learning them easier. In fact, in our opinion it makes it more confusing. However, previous experience with Cisco routers and the Cisco IOS can make this process a little easier.

In this section, we will show you how to enable STP on both types of switches as well as how to disable STP. Pay close attention to the modes that you are in on each individual switch.

This section will also cover some of the basic commands for viewing and verifying the current STP configuration. Because some of the configuration information you will see on your screen is confusing, this section will cover the definition of each field when viewing the configuration on an IOS-based switch.

Set/Clear Command-Based Switch Configuration

On a Set/Clear command-based switch, you can enable and disable STP on a per-port basis. By default, STP is enabled for every port on the switch. If STP has been disabled, you can re-enable it at the Privileged Mode prompt.

Cisco has recommended that STP remain enabled on the switch. It is important that it remain enabled on any uplink port where the possibility exists of a bridging loop in the network.

To re-enable STP on a Set/Clear-based switch, use the following Privileged Mode command:

```
set spantree enable command
```

To selectively enable specific ports on the switch, use the following Privileged Mode command (1/1 represents module 1 on port 1):

```
set spantree enable 1/1
```

To selectively disable specific ports on the switch, use this Privileged Mode command (1/1 represents module 1 on port 1):

```
set spantree disable 1/1
```

To enable STP on allVLANs, use the following command in Privileged Mode:

```
set spantree enable all
```

You should see a display similar to the following if you entered the command correctly:

```
spantree enabled
```

To view the current configuration of STP on your switch, use this Privileged Mode command (12 refers to the VLAN number):

```
Show spantree 12
```

The output should look similar to this:

```
Spanning tree enabled
Spanning tree type           ieee
Designated Root              00--ad--13--18--d0--12
Designated Root Priority     8192
Designated Root Cost         0
Designated Root Port         1/0
Root Max Age 10 Sec          Hello Time 2 sec    Forward Delay 7 sec
Bridge ID MAC ADDR           00--ad--13--18--d0--12
Bridge ID Priority           8192
Bridge Max Age 20 Sec        Hello Time 2 sec    Forward Delay 15 sec

Port  vlan  Port-State  Cost  Priority  Fast-start  Group-Method
----  ----  ----------  ----  --------  ----------  ------------
3/1   3     forwarding  19    32        disabled
3/2   3     forwarding  19    32        disabled
3/3   3     blocking    19    32        disabled
3/4   3     blocking    19    32        disabled
```

Some of the description fields may contain misleading information. Here is a brief description of the fields.

- *Spanning tree enabled*—Shows that STP is in use.
- *Spanning tree type*—Typically IEEE standard.
- *Designated Root*—The 6-byte MAC address for the designated root bridge.
- *Designated Root Priority*—A 2-byte priority setting for the root bridge. By default, the priority for a secondary root bridge or switch should be 32,768; the priority for the root bridge or switch should be 8,192.
- *Designated Root Cost*—Total cost to get to the root bridge from this switch. If the root cost equals 0, this switch is the root bridge or switch.
- *Designated Root Port*—The port used to get to the root bridge.
- *Root timers*—Timer values of the root bridge or switch.
- *Bridge ID MAC ADDR*—A 6-byte address that the switch uses for its bridge ID.

- *Bridge ID Priority*—The 2-byte priority of this bridge. This number is formed from a combination of the bridge ID priority and bridge ID MAC address. If the Bridge ID Priority is identical to the Designated Root value, this bridge is the root bridge.
- *Bridge Max Age*—The maximum values from the root bridge.

The list at the bottom shows the ports in use in the spanning tree. It states the port, port-state, and priority, as well as whether Fast-Start (PortFast) is enabled.

STP Configuration on CLI- and IOS-Based Switches

To enable the Spanning Tree Protocol on Cisco IOS command-based switches, use the Global Configuration Mode and enter the following command (9 is the VLAN number and is considered a VLAN-list field; you can list up to 10 VLANs in the list):

```
spantree 9
```

To disable STP on a VLAN, in Global Configuration Mode use this command (9 is the VLAN number and is considered a VLAN-list field):

```
no spantree 9
```

For the 1900/2800/2900 XL Series, the output looks somewhat different, but it gives you the same general information.

To view the configuration, you use the same command that you would in the Set/Clear command-based switches. However, you will receive a much different output. Use this command:

```
show spantree
```

The output should look similar to this on your console:

```
VLAN1 is executing the IEEE compatible Spanning Tree Protocol
Bridge Identifier has priority 8192, address 001F.100A.E100
Configured hello time 2, max age 20, forward delay 15
Current root has priority 8192, address 001F.100A.E100
Root port is FastEthernet 1/1, cost of root path is 0
Topology change flag not set, detected flag not set
Topology changes 21, last topology change occurred 1d3h19m59s ago
Times: hold 1, topology change 9211
hello 2, max age 20, forward delay 15
Timers: hello 2, topology change 35, notification 2
Port Ethernet 0/5 of VLAN1 is Forwarding
```

```
Port path cost 0, Port priority 100
Designated root has priority 8192, address 001F.100A.E100
Designated bridge has priority 8192, address 001F.100A.E100
Designated port is Ethernet 0/5, path cost 10
Timers: message age 20, forward delay 15, hold 1
```

Redundant Link Management and Scaling

In this section, we will cover the major differences between switches and transparent bridges, paying particular attention to VLANs. Cisco has several proprietary approaches to implementing and reconciling Spanning Tree Protocol in VLANs, such as Common Spanning Tree (CST), Per-VLAN Spanning Tree (PVST), and Per-VLAN Spanning Tree Plus (PVST+).

This section will also discuss and demonstrate the scaling of STP, Fast EtherChannel, configuring STP, determining the root path, manipulating the root cost, verifying the port cost, setting the VLAN priority, modifying the VLAN timers, load distribution over links, PAgP, creating an EtherChannel bundle, PortFast, UplinkFast, and BackboneFast.

And you thought switches were simple pieces of equipment! Don't put the book down now, though. It's easier than you think, and we will try to show all the commands you will need to configure each of these items.

Switch and Transparent Bridge Differences

There are some major differences between Cisco switches and transparent bridges. Some of the main differences are Cisco's approach to the implementation of VLANs on a switch. Cisco and the IEEE 802.1Q committee approach the spanning tree and VLANs in very different ways.

Some of the major methods for reconciling STP and VLANs are:

- *Common Spanning Tree (CST)*—The IEEE 802.1Q solution to VLANs and spanning tree. CST defines a single instance of spanning tree for all the VLANs in a LAN, sending the BPDU information on VLAN 1 by default.
- *Per-VLAN Spanning Tree (PVST)*—A Cisco proprietary implementation on VLANs. PVST runs a separate instance of STP for every VLAN.
- *PVST+*—A Cisco proprietary implementation that allows CST information to be transferred to PVST.

Common Spanning Tree Protocol

Common Spanning Tree, also known as Mono-Spanning Tree, uses the IEEE 802.1Q standard specification. This specification allows STP to run only on VLAN 1, by default. All the switches in the network elect a single root bridge and form an association with that switch. In this situation using a single root bridge, the root bridge is optimized for a single VLAN; but in networks with multiple VLANs, data may take a less-than-optimal path to get to file servers and other interfaces on the network.

A CST approach does not allow for optimization of the root bridge placement for each VLAN in the network. BPDUs are sent through the first VLAN, VLAN 1 by default.

CST has some major disadvantages in larger-scale networks. One of these disadvantages is the inability of all switches in the network to send data through the most optimum path for all devices in the network. Another disadvantage is in the spanning tree topology. When the topology increases in size to encompass all ports in the switch fabric, greater convergence times and more frequent reconfiguration may result.

CST has some advantages over PVST (discussed in the next section). There are fewer BPDUs consuming bandwidth, and each switch requires less processing overhead. Although there are some advantages to CST, a single spanning tree is not an optimal solution for scalability or stability in larger networks.

Per-VLAN Spanning Tree

To create a fault-tolerant large internetwork, continuous loop-free paths must exist between all interfaces in the network. The STA calculates the least cost, loop-free path throughout the switched network. Per-VLAN Spanning Tree (PVST) is a Cisco proprietary solution to the scaling and stability problems associated with CST in large-scale spanning tree networks. PVST creates a separate instance of PVST on each VLAN in the switch block. This setup gives each VLAN a unique STP topology containing its own port cost, path cost, priority, and root switch.

Each VLAN is considered a logical LAN segment; a single instance of STP maintains a loop-free topology for each VLAN. The Cisco Catalyst 1900 and Catalyst 2820 switches support a maximum of 1005 VLANs. On the 1900 and 2820, you can enable STP on only 64 of the 1005 VLANs at any given time. By default, STP is enabled on VLANs 1 through 64. Although the two switches support more than 64 VLANs, any number of VLANs over 64 must have STP disabled.

Separate instances of PVST on each VLAN reduce the convergence time for STP recalculation and increase reliability of the network. By implementing PVST, the overall size of the spanning tree topology is reduced significantly. PVST also improves scalability and decreases convergence time, providing faster recovery in the event of network faults. It also allows control of forwarding paths on a per-subnet basis while providing a simple technique for Layer 2 redundancy.

PVST does have some disadvantages in the spanning tree. PVST uses more processing power and consumes more bandwidth to support spanning tree maintenance and BPDUs for each VLAN. Inter-Switch Link (ISL) uses one spanning tree per VLAN, using PVST over ISL trunks. PVST implementation requires the use of Cisco ISL encapsulation in order to function.

Per-VLAN Spanning Tree Plus

Not only is PVST+ a new objective, there also isn't much documentation from Cisco on this Cisco proprietary protocol. IEEE 802.1Q uses PVST+ to map multiple spanning trees to the spanning tree of authentic IEEE 802.1Q switches.

You will find PVST+ available in Catalyst software versions 4.1 or newer. Cisco Catalyst switches configured with version 4.1 or later are considered Cisco PVST+ switches. A really great feature of PVST+ is its compatibility and interoperability with legacy type Mono Spanning Tree (MST) and PVST switches without any user intervention of any kind. This gives PVST+ a type of plug-and-play functionality.

To provide support for the IEEE 802.1Q standard, Cisco's existing PVST has been modified with additional features, enabling it to support a link across the IEEE 802.1Q Common Spanning Tree region.

PVST+ performs many useful functions, such as:

- Tunnels PVST BPDUs through the 802.1Q VLAN region as multicast data.
- Adds mechanisms to ensure there is no unknown configuration.
- Eliminates inconsistencies related to port trunking or VLAN identification across the switches.
- Provides compatibility with IEEE 802.1Q's CST and Cisco's PVST protocols.
- Interoperates with 802.1Q-compliant switches using CST through 802.1Q trunking. A CST BPDU is transmitted or received with an IEEE standard bridge group MAC address.
- Transmits or receives a BPDU with Cisco's Shared STP (SSTP) address for each VLAN on a trunk. For VLANs equal to the PVID (native port VLAN), the BPDU is not tagged; however, for all other VLANs, BPDUs are tagged.
- Checks for port and VLAN inconsistencies.
- Blocks ports that receive inconsistent BPDUs in order to prevent forwarding loops. PVST+ also notifies users about all inconsistencies via syslog messages.

Scaling Spanning Tree Protocol

Creating a scalable STP network requires several provisions and technologies. By creating the most optimal topology and properly placing the root bridge in the network, you can provide efficient paths through the network.

PortFast provides efficient end-user access to the switches. It allows ports running STP to almost immediately transition to a forwarding state upon startup of the switch.

In this section we'll cover two technologies: PortVlanPri and Fast EtherChannel. They provide load balancing for redundant links through STP-enabled ports.

One of the most important scaling problems is convergence time. Improving the convergence time of spanning tree during a network reconfiguration and keeping the spanning tree up to date and running are very important features. We'll discuss two convergence time-reducing technologies in this section: BackboneFast and UplinkFast.

Root Bridge Location

In setting the location of your root bridge, certain commands can help determine which device will become the root bridge. The decision of which switch or switches in the spanning trees become root bridges is one that should not be taken lightly. The proper placement of the root bridge(s) optimizes the paths that is chosen by the STP. It also provides for deterministic paths for data.

Sometimes, you must manually configure the bridge that should be the root bridge to get the most optimal paths through the network. It may also be necessary to configure the secondary root bridge, as well. The function of the secondary root bridge is to become the root bridge, should the original root bridge fail.

The Cisco switch software is used to configure the STP configuration parameters. You need to give careful consideration to switching paths before changing the root bridge configuration. The placement of the root bridge in the spanning tree should be close to the center of the network. Typically, most root bridges are distribution layer switches, not access layer switches. The root bridge should never be a core layer switch, because the core layer's responsibility is to move traffic as quickly as possible.

Let's take a look at the commands needed to configure the spanning tree to allow a switch to become the root switch on a Set/Clear command-based switch.

To configure the switch to become the root bridge, enter the following command in Privileged Mode:

```
set spantree root 2 dia 3 hello 2
```

Table 9.4 Root and secondary bridge configuration command parameters.

Command Parameter	Definition
root	Designates the root switch. The default priority of the root bridge is 8,192.
secondary	Designates the switch as a secondary root switch if the root bridge fails. The default priority of the secondary bridge is 16,384. (optional)
n	Specifies the VLAN. If you do not specify the VLAN, VLAN 1 is used. The valid value range is 1 through 1005. (optional)
dia *n*	Specifies the diameter value discussed earlier in the chapter. It is essentially the number of bridges between any two points. The diameter should be measured starting from the root bridge. Valid values are 2 through 7. (optional)
hello *n*	Specifies in seconds how often configuration messages should be generated by the root switch. The valid values are 1 through 10. (optional)

Table 9.4 explains the different parameters used in this command. To configure the switch to become the secondary root bridge, enter the following Privileged Mode command:

```
set spantree secondary 2 dia 3 hello 2
```

To set the primary root switch for more than one VLAN on a Set/Clear-based switch, use the Privileged Mode command to change configuration to a root bridge. The priority automatically changes to 8,192, which is the default when the command is used to configure the switch as the root bridge. The default STP port settings are shown in Table 9.5. The following command specifies the root bridge for VLANs 1 through 5:

```
set spantree root 1-5 dia 2
```

Table 9.5 The default port settings for STP.

Variable	Default
Port priority	128
Port cost	62
Bridge priority	32,768
Secondary root bridge priority	16,384
Root bridge priority	8,192

When the root bridge is configured correctly, the output on the console should be similar to this:

```
VLANs 1-5 bridge priority set to 8192
VLANs 1-5 bridge max aging time set to 10 seconds.
VLANS 1-5 bridge bello time set to 2 seconds.
VLANS 1-5 bridge forward delay set to 7 seconds.
Switch is now the root switch for active VLANs 1-5.
```

Assigning Port Costs

After the root bridge has been elected, all the switches determine the best loop-free path to the root switch. STP uses several different costs, with the port priority as the tiebreaker. The sum of all the port costs to a destination through all the ports the frames must travel makes up the path cost.

As the BPDU leaves a port, the BPDU applies the port cost. The sum of all of the port costs is the path cost. The spanning tree looks first at the path cost and decides which ports should forward and which ports should be blocked. If the path costs are equal for more than one port, then the spanning tree looks at the port ID. The port with the lower port ID has priority, making that port the forwarding port. If the path cost and the port ID are the same, then the STP will use the port priority as the tiebreaker.

To manually change the port cost on a Set/Clear-based switch, use the following Privileged Mode command (1 is the module number, 3 is the port number, and 10 is the configured port cost):

```
set spantree portcost 1/3 10
```

To manually change the port cost on a Cisco IOS-based switch, use this Interface Configuration command (10 is the port cost):

```
spantree cost 10
```

For both the IOS-based and Set/Clear command-based switches, you should assign lower numbers to ports attached to faster media, such as FDDI, and higher numbers to ports attached to slower media, such as UTP. The possible value range is 1 to 65,535. The default differs for different media. The path cost is typically 1000 divided by the physical wire speed in Mbps.

To verify the port cost on the port configured previously, use the following Privileged Mode command:

```
show spantree 1/3
```

The output on the console should look similar to this:

```
Port   Vlan   Port-State    Cost   Priority   Fast-Start   Group-method
----   ----   ----------    ----   --------   ----------   ------------
1/3    1      forwarding    10     32         disabled
1/3    6      forwarding    10     32         disabled
1/3    8      forwarding    10     32         disabled
1/3    9      blocked       10     32         disabled
```

Configuring Port Priority

The Spanning Tree Protocol port priority parameter can be modified to influence the links that are forwarding or blocking. The port with the lowest priority value forwards frames for all VLANs. In the event that all ports have the same priority value, the port with the lowest port number will forward the frames. The possible port priority value range is from 0 to 63. The default value is 32. To change a port's priority, enter the following Privileged Mode command (1 is the module number, 3 is the port number, and 10 is the port priority):

9

```
set spantree portpri 1/3 10
```

To verify the proper port priority setting, use this command (only the module and port numbers are required):

```
show spantree 1/3
```

The output should look similar to this:

```
Port   Vlan   Port-State    Cost   Priority   Fast-Start   Group-method
----   ----   ----------    ----   --------   ----------   ------------
1/3    1      forwarding    10     10         disabled
1/3    6      forwarding    10     10         disabled
1/3    8      forwarding    10     10         disabled
1/3    9      blocked       10     10         disabled
```

On a Cisco IOS command-based switch, the priority value is a numerical value from 0 to 255. To set the port priority on a Cisco IOS command-based switch, enter the following Interface Configuration Mode command (100 is the priority value):

```
spantree priority 100
```

Use the **show spantree** command to verify port priority by VLAN.

To return the value of the port priority to the default value, enter this Interface Configuration Mode command:

```
no spantree
```

Setting VLAN Port Priority

Instead of setting the priority by port, you can set the priority on a VLAN basis. Configuring each port with each VLAN's own priority allows load sharing on links by allowing VLANs to individually determine which links to forward and which to block.

Just as with the port priority setting, the lowest priority value gets to forward the frames. However, in this case STP goes one step further and decides the value for each specific VLAN. If more than one or all the ports have the same priority value for a particular VLAN, the port with the lowest port number gets to forward the frames for that VLAN.

Configuring the port priority by VLAN is useful for distributing data across parallel paths. If a parallel connection exists between two devices, STP will block one of the links. Traffic from all VLANs will travel on one link, and one link will be used only as a backup. However, by changing the port priority for a specific group of VLANs, VLAN frames can be distributed across both of the links.

To change the port VLAN priority for a port on a Set command-based switch, use the following Privileged Mode command (1 represents the module, 3 represents the port, 10 represents the priority, and 1-5 represents the range of VLANs):

```
set spantree 1/3 10 1-5
```

To set another range of ports to a different priority on the same module and port number, enter the same command again with another range of VLANs and a different priority (in this example module 1, port 3 has a priority of 14 for VLANs 6-10):

```
set spantree 1/3 14 6-10
```

To verify the port's VLAN priority settings, enter the following command in Privileged Mode (only the module and port number are required):

```
show spantree 1/3
```

Default Timers

Cisco recommends that you modify the default timers used during spanning tree instability to influence the convergence times for different port states. The timers are included in STP to prevent bridging loops from occurring in the network. Having timers in place gives the network enough time to get all of the correct information about the topology and to determine if any unknown redundant links exist.

However, the timers could take up to 50 seconds after a link failure for the link's redundant backup to take over. The length of time that the spanning tree takes to converge when a link fails can be too much for most protocols and applications, resulting in lost connections, session timeouts, and lost data.

You can configure three different timing parameters related to the timers on port states: **MaxAge**, **Hello Time**, and **FwdDelay**. Table 9.6 shows a brief description of each parameter with the default setting information.

Table 9.6 A brief description and the IEEE, DEC, and IBM default settings for each port state timer.

Field	Description	IEEE	DEC	IBM
MaxAge	Sets the number of seconds a switch waits without receiving STP configuration messages before it attempts a reconfiguration. The maximum age parameter states the lifetime of a BPDU; the BPDU is valid on a port for the number of seconds configured in the **MaxAge** value. If a new BPDU is not received in that amount of time, the old BPDU is discarded. The value range is from 6 to 200 seconds.	20 seconds	15 seconds	10 seconds
Hello Time	Sets the number of seconds between STP configuration messages. This parameter is the interval between the transmissions of BPDUs from the root switch. The value range is from 1 to 10 seconds.	2 seconds	1 second	2 seconds
FwdDelay	Sets the number of seconds a port waits before it transitions from the learning and listening states to the forwarding state. This delay time is necessary to ensure that no loop is formed before the switch forwards a frame. The value range is from 4 to 200.	15 seconds	30 seconds	4 seconds

To change the **FwdDelay** default setting, use the following Privileged Mode command (4 indicates a 4-second delay and 1 indicates the VLAN):

```
set spantree fwddelay 4 1
```

To change the default **Hello Time** on the bridge, use this Privileged Mode command (4 indicates a 4-second interval):

```
set spantree hello 4
```

To change the default **MaxAge** time for a particular VLAN, use this Privileged Mode command (5 refers to the **MaxAge** time and 1 refers to the VLAN):

```
spantree maxage 5 1
```

EtherChannel

Fast EtherChannel and Gigabit EtherChannel allow high-speed redundant links in a spanning tree environment by allowing dual parallel links to be treated as though they were only one link. Cisco Fast EtherChannel technology uses the standards-based 802.3 full-duplex Fast Ethernet to provide a reliable high-speed solution for the campus network backbone. Let's look at some of the features of Fast EtherChannel:

- Load balancing with management of the distribution of traffic across each individual link
- Redundancy over Fast EtherChannel bundles
- Fast convergence times in the event of failure
- Automatic creation of EtherChannel bundles using Port Aggregation Protocol (PAgP)
- Scaled bandwidth within the campus, providing full-duplex bandwidth at wire speed for up to eight bundled links

Let's take a look at some of these features in more detail.

Load Balancing

Fast EtherChannel uses load distribution to share a group of links called a *bundle*; the bundle is managed by the Fast EtherChannel process. Should one link in the bundle fail, the Ethernet Bundle Controller (EBC) informs the Enhanced Address Recognition Logic (EARL) ASIC of the failure, and the EARL in turn ages out all addresses learned on that link. The EBC and the EARL then recalculate in the hardware, sending queries to the other switches and learning the destination link based on the responses. Broadcast traffic, as well as unicast and multicast traffic, is distributed equally across all the links in the channel or bundle.

Redundancy and Link Failure

Fast EtherChannel also provides redundancy in the event of a link failure. If a link is lost in a Fast EtherChannel, traffic is immediately rerouted on one of the other links in just a few milliseconds, making the convergence transparent to the user.

The *convergence time* is the time it takes for the new address to be relearned. (Convergence time is sometimes referred to as the *failover time*.) Now, assuming that one packet to the destination results in an instant response, convergence can occur in as soon as 10 microseconds. This process may take longer because of the windowing that the particular application uses. In this situation, relearning should not take more than a couple of milliseconds, so there is no timeout, and the user is never aware of the link failure.

Port Aggregation Protocol

Port Aggregation Protocol (PAgP) manages the Fast EtherChannel bundles and aids in the automatic creation of Fast EtherChannel links. PAgP packets are sent between Fast EtherChannel-capable ports. PAgP learns of the neighbors and their group capabilities dynamically and then informs its neighbors of the local group capabilities. After the protocol determines all the paired, point-to-point, or bi-directional links, the protocol groups into a single channel those ports that have the same neighbor device ID and neighbor group capability. Then the channel is added to spanning tree as a bridge port.

Some features have been deliberately removed from PAgP. Because dynamic VLAN ports can force a VLAN change, PAgP will not form a bundle on ports that are configured for dynamic VLANs. PAgP also requires that all ports in the channel belong to the same VLAN or are configured as trunk ports.

When there is an existing bundle and a VLAN of a port is modified, all ports in the bundle are modified to match the VLAN configuration. PAgP will not group ports running at different speeds or duplex. PAgP will change the port speed and duplex for all ports in the bundle.

You should assign all ports in a Fast EtherChannel to the same VLAN, or configure them as trunk ports. Configuring the same trunk mode on all the ports in the channel must be done on both ends of the link.

Broadcast limits can be configured on the ports. You should, however, configure the broadcast limit as a percentage limit versus by packets-per-second. Packets-per-second allows unicast packets to be dropped when the broadcast limit is exceeded.

Channels that are composed of trunk ports must be configured with the same allowed VLAN range on all ports. When VLAN ranges are not configured the same for both ends of all trunks, the data traffic for the missing VLAN is not allowed and the frames for that VLAN will be dropped. At the same time, ports on which the VLAN is allowed will transmit the traffic but the ports do not form a channel when set to **auto** or **desirable** mode with the **set port channel** command.

You might also verify that port security is disabled on channeled ports. By enabling port security, the port shuts down when it receives packets containing a source address that doesn't match the secure address of the port.

All ports in a channel must be enabled. Any disabled ports are considered link failures, and traffic for those ports is transferred to any remaining ports.

Warning: On the Catalyst 5000 Series switches the hardware controlling channeling prevents certain ports or groups of ports from forming channels.

Configuring Fast EtherChannel

To configure EtherChannel on a Set/Clear-based switch, use the following command in Privileged Mode to verify that a line card is capable of being channeled on a set command-based switch (1 is the module number and 8 is the port number):

```
Show port capabilities 1/8
```

To create a channel on two or more desired ports on a Set/Clear-based switch, enter the following Privileged Mode command (1 is the module number and 8-9 represents the port numbers on the switch):

```
Set port channel 1/8-9 auto
```

Table 9.7 explains the last option to configure the mode in which the ports will operate. They can be either **on**, **off**, **auto**, or **desirable**.

Table 9.7 The four mode options for configuring an EtherChannel bundle on a switch.

EtherChannel Mode Option	Mode Description
on	Enables the port to channel without any negotiation.
off	Disables the port from channeling.
auto	Enables a port to negotiate the state in which the port will respond to PAgP packets it receives. The syntax does not, however, initiate PAgP packet negotiation. This is the default setting.
desirable	Enables a port to actively negotiate the port state in which the port initiates negotiations with other ports. It does this by sending PAgP packets.

To verify the EtherChannel configuration on a Set/Clear-based switch, use this command:

```
Show port channel
```

The **auto** and **desirable** modes allow ports to automatically negotiate connected ports to determine if they can form a channel. Channel ports can be in different channel modes as long as the modes are compatible. As an example, when a port is in **desirable** mode, it can form a channel successfully with another port that is in **desirable** or **auto** mode and vice versa. When a link in a channel fails, traffic carried over the failed link automatically switches to the remaining link within the channel. An SNMP trap message is sent upon a failure identifying the switch, the channel, and the failed link.

To configure EtherChannel on an IOS command-based switch use this Global Configuration command:

```
Port-channel auto
```

To verify the configuration on an IOS-based switch, use the Privileged Mode command:

```
Show interface
```

PortFast

As we've mentioned before, when a switch operating STP is powered up, the port running STP goes through four states before forwarding frames through each port: blocking, listening, learning, and then forwarding. To get to the forwarding state, the Spanning Tree Algorithm makes each port wait up to 50 seconds before data is allowed to be forwarded on a port. This delay may cause problems with certain protocols and applications.

For ports where there is a single server or workstation connected, PortFast can be configured to allow the port to enter the forwarding state almost immediately. PortFast dramatically decreases the time of the listening and learning states. You can use PortFast on switch ports that connect to a single workstation or server to allow those devices to connect to the network immediately, rather than waiting for STP timers to provide for convergence.

To enable PortFast on a Set/Clear command-based switch port, use the following Privileged Mode command (1 is the module number and 3 is the port number):

```
Set spantree portfast 1/3 enable
```

To verify the PortFast setting on a Set/Clear command-based switch, enter the following Privileged Mode command (1 is the module number and 3 is the port number):

```
Show spantree 1/3
```

To enable PortFast on a Cisco IOS command-based switch, use this Interface Configuration Mode command:

```
Spantree start-forwarding
```

UplinkFast

In an STP-implemented network, the convergence time to a loop-free topology can be time-consuming. By implementing UplinkFast, you can reduce this time by optimizing convergence times and ensuring that a loop-free topology is maintained even during link faults or topology changes.

When a topology change occurs, because of the convergence time of STP, some end stations become inaccessible depending on the current state of each switch port. By decreasing convergence time, you reduce the length of the disruption.

UplinkFast allows a port in a blocked state on a switch to almost immediately begin forwarding when the switch detects a link failure or a topology change. However, UplinkFast must have direct knowledge of the link failure in order to move a blocked port into a forwarding state.

An Uplink Group is a root port that is in a forwarding state and a set of blocked ports that does not include self-looping ports. The Uplink Group is the alternate path when the currently forwarding link fails.

UplinkFast should be placed only on access-layer switches. UplinkFast is not designed for use within network cores and is not available on the 8500 Series switches. In order to utilize UplinkFast, several criteria must be met. First, UplinkFast must be enabled on the switch. In addition, the switch must have at least one blocked port and the failure must be on the root port.

Figure 9.9 shows the access switch with two uplinks to the distribution layer. One link connects the access switch to the distribution switch elected as the root bridge. The other link connecting both switches is blocked and acting as secondary root bridge.

When a link fault occurs on the primary root link, UplinkFast transitions the blocked port to a forwarding state. UplinkFast changes the port, bypassing the listening and learning phases. This occurs in about three to four seconds, allowing convergence to begin immediately without waiting for the **MaxAge** timer to expire.

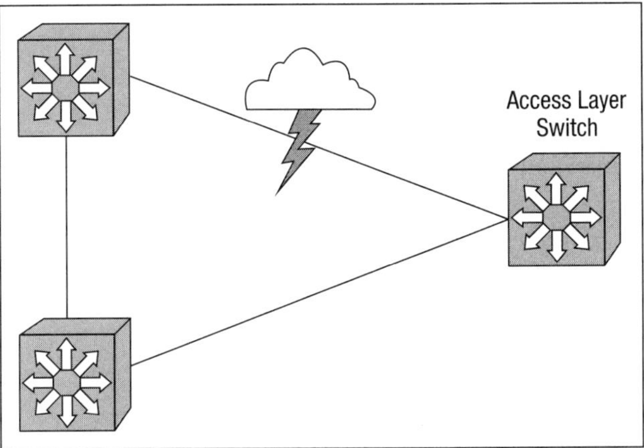

Figure 9.9 A primary and a secondary link from the access switch to the distribution switch with a link fault on the primary link.

If UplinkFast is not being used, you should use the Catalyst default settings. UplinkFast is global on the switch. It affects all VLANs on the switch and cannot be applied on just one individual VLAN. When you enable UplinkFast it automatically increases the path cost, making it unlikely that the switch will become the root switch.

To enable UplinkFast on a Set/Clear command-based switch, use the following Privileged Mode command:

```
set spantree uplink fast enable
```

There are some other options to this command, such as adding a rate station update rate or adding the **on** or **off** syntax for all protocols. The station update rate value is the number of multicast packets transmitted per 100 milliseconds (by default it is set to 15 packets per millisecond). For more information on how to execute a change in the rate station update rate, use the Help command on the console.

To verify the UplinkFast configuration on a Set/Clear command-based switch, you can use the following Privileged Mode command:

```
show spantree uplinkfast
```

You should get output similar to the following—notice that the VLANs followed by a comma, module number, and port number are forwarding to 1/1:

```
station update rate set to 15 packets/100ms.
uplinkfast all-protocol field set to off.
```

```
VLAN        port list
----        ---------
1           1/1(fwd)
2           1/2(fwd),1/1
4           1/2(fwd),1/1
10          1/1(fwd),1/1
```

To enable UplinkFast on a Cisco IOS command-based switch, in Global Configuration Mode use this command:

```
uplink-fast
```

To view the UplinkFast configuration on an IOS command-based switch, enter the following Privileged Mode command:

```
show uplink-fast
```

To view UplinkFast statistics, use this Privileged Mode command:

```
show uplink-fast statistics
```

BackboneFast

When the root port or a blocked port on a switch receives an inferior BPDU from its designated bridge, this event in turn triggers a root Link Query with the use of BackboneFast. The switch will try to determine if it has an alternate path to the root bridge. With BackboneFast however, if the inferior BPDU arrives on a blocked port, the root port and other blocked ports on the switch become alternate paths to the root bridge.

If the inferior BPDU arrives on the root port, all blocked ports become alternate paths to the root bridge. Should there be no blocked ports, the switch automatically assumes that it has lost connectivity to the root bridge, causes the maximum aging time on the root to expire, and becomes the root switch. BackboneFast must be enabled on all switches in the network to function properly—with the exception of Token Ring, which is not supported.

An inferior BPDU identifies one switch as both the root bridge and the designated bridge. When a switch receives an inferior BPDU, it indicates that a link to which the switch is not directly connected has lost its connection to the root bridge, forgoing the standard **MaxAge** time.

A new kind of BPDU called the root Link Query PDU is transmitted when more than one line exists to the root bridge. The switch will send a root Link Query PDU out all the available alternate paths to the root bridge.

To enable BackboneFast on a Set/Clear command-based switch, enter the following Privileged Mode command:

```
set spantree backbonefast
```

To view the configuration on a Set/Clear command-based switch, use the following Privileged Mode command:

```
Show spantree backbonefast
```

Chapter Summary

In this chapter, we looked at the various protocols and services related to the Spanning Tree Protocol. We covered a lot, and you may see much of this material on a test. Here are some of the key points and features that you should pay particular attention to:

- The Spanning Tree Algorithm (STA) and the Spanning Tree Protocol (STP) are bridge-to-bridge link management protocols providing path redundancy while preventing loops in the network.
- STA is responsible for performing STP topology recalculations when a switch is powered up and when a topology change occurs.
- STP communicates topology changes from switch to switch with the use of Bridge Protocol Data Units (BPDUs).
- BPDUs are never forwarded to another switch, but receipt of a topology change BPDU will cause a switch to generate a new BPDU and forward a topology change BPDU to another switch.
- PVST and PVST+ allow a single instance of STP to run on each VLAN.
- CST allows for only one instance of STP for all VLANs on the switch. BPDUs are forwarded on VLAN 1.
- The *diameter* is a unit of measurement between the root switch and child switches. The measurement is calculated from the root bridge with the root bridge counting as the first switch. Each subsequent child switch out from the root bridge is added to come up with the diameter number.
- Fast and Gigabit EtherChannel allow high-speed redundant links in a spanning tree environment by allowing dual parallel links to be treated as though they were one link.
- Port Aggregation Protocol (PAgP) manages the Fast EtherChannel bundles and aids in the automatic creation of Fast EtherChannel links.

- PortFast forces an STP port to enter the forwarding state immediately after startup for a single workstation or server connected to a switch port.
- UplinkFast provides fast convergence after an STP topology change and achieves load balancing between redundant links.
- BackboneFast is initiated when a root port or blocked port receives an inferior BPDU from its designated bridge. It allows the secondary or backup port to immediately begin forwarding after a link fault with the root link. It bypasses the **MaxAge** timer.

When STP is enabled, a port is always in one of the following five states:

- *Blocking state*—The port is not forwarding frames or learning new addresses. All ports start in blocking mode to prevent the bridge from creating a bridging loop.
- *Listening state*—The state a port enters after the blocking state. The port enters this state when STP determines that the port should participate in frame forwarding.
- *Learning state*—The port is not forwarding frames but is learning addresses and putting addresses in the address table.
- *Forwarding state*—The port forwards frames received from the attached segment and frames switched from another port for forwarding, and incorporates station location information into its address database.
- *Disabled*—The port does not participate in any frame forwarding or STP.

Review Questions

1. With Spanning Tree Protocol, if there is more than one path to a given destination (such as a primary path and a secondary path), the second path is referred to as:
   a. A cheaper path
   b. A redundant path
   c. A forced path
   d. A helper path
2. Spanning Tree Protocol was created to overcome the problems associated with what type of bridging?
   a. Source route bridging
   b. Shorter path bridging

c. Transparent bridging

d. UplinkFast bridging

3. Bridge Protocol Data Units (BPDUs) are responsible for providing information for which services in a spanning tree? [Choose the four best answers]

   a. Determining the locations of data loops

   b. Electing a root bridge

   c. Monitoring the spanning tree

   d. Deciding the manufacturer's MAC address on a physical interface

   e. Notifying other switches of network changes

4. Common Spanning Tree (CST) defines a single spanning tree for all VLANs on a network. Which VLAN are Bridge Protocol Data Units sent on by default?

   a. VLAN 64

   b. VLAN 1005

   c. VLAN 1

   d. VLAN 10

5. Which Cisco Systems proprietary protocol provides for a separate instance of Spanning Tree Protocol for every VLAN?

   a. Common Spanning Tree (CST)

   b. Spanning Tree Algorithm (STA)

   c. Port Aggregation Protocol (PAgP)

   d. Per-VLAN Spanning Tree (PVST)

6. To configure a Spanning Tree Protocol backup root bridge on a Set/Clear command-based switch, what command would be used?

   a. **set spanning tree backup**

   b. **set spantree backup**

   c. **set spantree secondary**

   d. **spanning tree 2**

7. The Catalyst 1900 and 2820 switches support 1005 VLANs, of which how many can be configured to support Spanning Tree Protocol?

   a. 1005

   b. 10

   c. 512

   d. 64

8. What is the command to change the VLAN port priority on an IOS command-based switch to a value of 16?
   a. **set spantree priority 16**
   b. **spantree priority 16**
   c. **config spantree priority 16**
   d. **change spantree pri 16**
9. The Ethernet Bundle Controller (EBC) notifies which ASIC of link bundle failures?
   a. EARL ASIC
   b. SAMBA ASIC
   c. SAGE ASIC
   d. SAINT ASIC
10. The VLAN port priority is a numerical value between what two numbers?
    a. 1 and 64
    b. 1 and 1005
    c. 0 and 63
    d. 1 and 10
11. Which types of ports will Port Aggregation Protocol (PAgP) use to form a bundle?
    a. Two ports, each using different duplex types
    b. Two dynamically assigned VLAN ports
    c. One dynamically and one statically assigned VLAN port
    d. Two statically assigned VLAN ports
12. PortFast is used on Spanning Tree Protocol ports to allow for ports to enter which state immediately following startup?
    a. Blocked
    b. Disabled
    c. Forwarding
    d. Listening
13. If the port costs are equal on a switch using Spanning Tree Protocol, STP refers to which value to make its forwarding decision?
    a. Port ID
    b. MAC address
    c. Bridge name
    d. Hello Timer

14. What is the default bridge priority value of a bridge designated as the secondary root bridge?
    a. 8,192
    b. 16,384
    c. 32,768
    d. 1

15. Fast EtherChannel provides line speeds of up to how many megabits per second if configured to use full duplex?
    a. 800Mbps
    b. 155Mbps
    c. 1000Mbps
    d. 100Mbps

Real-World Projects

Our fictional Cisco guru, Joe Snow, has just arrived at work to find out what his work load will consist of before lunch. Apparently, a new 2948 XL switch must be configured for the editorial department at Coriolis. The switch has several Ethernet interfaces that need to be configured using EtherChannel.

Joe's work list for the morning is as follows:

- On the 2948 XL switch, assign a channel to an EtherChannel interface.
- On the 2948 XL switch, assign a port channel to an Ethernet interface.
- On the 2948 XL switch, assign the Ethernet interfaces to an EtherChannel group.

Earlier in the chapter, we covered configuring EtherChannel on a Set/Clear- and IOS-based switch. Projects 9.1 to 9.3 demonstrate how to configure EtherChannel on a 2948 XL-L3, which supports Fast EtherChannel (FEC) and Gigabit EtherChannel (GEC).

Project 9.1

The EtherChannel interface can consist of up to four Ethernet interfaces. The four Ethernet interfaces can be treated as a single interface, called a *port-channel*. Joe must configure EtherChannel on the EtherChannel interface rather than on the individual Ethernet interfaces. The ISL VLAN Trunking Protocol can carry multiple VLANs across an EtherChannel, and routers attached to EtherChannel links can provide full multiprotocol routing and support for the Hot Standby Routing Protocol (HSRP), which is discussed in Chapter 12.

You can configure up to 16 different Fast EtherChannels. For Gigabit EtherChannel you can configure only one channel.

To create an EtherChannel Interface for Fast EtherChannel or Gigabit EtherChannel, perform the following:

1. To create an EtherChannel interface, use this command:

```
Switch1(config)# interface port-channel 1
```

2. Assign an IP or IPX address and subnet mask to the Fast EtherChannel interface:

```
Switch1(config-if)# ip address 130.77.20.8 255.255.254.0
```

   For demonstration purposes, an IP address is used here. For IPX, use the, **ipx network *network-number*** command.

Project 9.2

To assign a port channel for EtherChannel to an Ethernet interface, use the following steps:

1. To create an EtherChannel or port-channel 1 virtual interface, use this Global Configuration command:

```
Switch 1(config)# interface port-channel 1
```

2. Exit Global Configuration Mode:

```
Switch1(config-if)# exit
```

3. Enter Interface Configuration Mode for the interface you are adding to the port channel:

```
Switch1(config)# interface f1
```

4. Add the interface to port-channel 1:

```
Switch1(config-if)# channel-group 1
```

5. Save the configuration:

```
Switch1# copy running-config startup-config
```

Project 9.3

In order to have more than one Ethernet interface assigned to EtherChannel you must assign the Ethernet interfaces to an EtherChannel Group.

To assign Ethernet interfaces to an EtherChannel Group, perform the following:

1. Enter Ethernet Interface Configuration Mode to configure the Fast Ethernet interface:

```
Switch1(config)# interface f1
```

2. You must disable the IP address before you can continue. If an IP address is assigned, EtherChannel tries to use the IP address assigned to the interface:

```
Switch1(config-if)# no ip address
```

3. Assign the Fast Ethernet or Gigabit Ethernet interfaces to the EtherChannel using the channel number assigned in Project 9.2:

```
Switch1(config-if)# channel-group 1
```

4. Use the **End** command to exit:

```
Switch1(config-if)# end
```

5. Save the configuration:

```
Switch1# copy running-config startup-config
```

You can repeat Steps 1 through 4 to add up to four Fast Ethernet or two Gigabit Ethernet interfaces. Do not enable Layer 3 addresses on the physical Fast Ethernet or Gigabit Ethernet interfaces or assign bridge groups on the physical Fast Ethernet or Gigabit Ethernet interfaces, to avoid creating loops.

CHAPTER TEN

10

IMPLEMENTING A SWITCHED NETWORK DESIGN

After completing this chapter, you will be able to:

- ✓ Explain why VLANs limit collision and broadcast domains
- ✓ Understand why switches and VLANs are necessary in larger networks
- ✓ Determine the differences between broadcast and collision domains
- ✓ Explain the differences between end-to-end and local VLANs
- ✓ Describe the differences between demand nodes and resource nodes
- ✓ Understand how demand nodes and resource nodes affect network performance
- ✓ Explain the differences between dynamic and static VLAN ports
- ✓ Understand the differences between internal and external route processing
- ✓ Determine the benefits of adding Layer 3 routing ability to switches
- ✓ Describe the different route processor modules and daughter cards
- ✓ Explain the benefits of a NetFlow Feature Card
- ✓ Understand flat network topology packet loss and utilization measurements
- ✓ Understand when to upgrade to a switched network to increase throughput
- ✓ Configure a route processor to route VLANs
- ✓ Configure protocol filtering

Quite a few factors contribute to a need to redesign or upgrade your network. It may be a requirement for more nodes on the network or it may be a reaction to poor network response or lengthy file transfers.

As an administrator, you may not even realize when it is time to convert your company to a switched network and implement VLANs. You also may not be aware of the benefits that can occur from replacing your Layer 2 hubs and bridges with switches, or how adding some modules in your switches to implement routing and filtering abilities can improve your network's performance. This chapter covers many of the types of traffic that affect network performance and the different ways of routing traffic after your collision domains have been broken into smaller broadcast domains.

Flat Network Topology

When your flat network topology begins to slow due to traffic, collisions, and other bottlenecks, you must investigate the problems. Your first reaction should be to find out what types of data are flowing through your network. If you are in command of the network Sniffer, or other such device, you may begin to find over-utilization errors on the Sniffer occurring when the Ethernet network utilization rises above 40 percent.

Why would such errors occur at such a low utilization percentage on the network? Peak efficiency on a flat topology Ethernet network is about 40 percent utilization. A higher sustained level is a strong indicator that you should upgrade the physical network into a switched environment.

When users begin to notice that their state-of-the-art Pentiums are performing poorly, many network administrators don't realize that the problem may be due in part to the hundreds of other computers on their flat hub and bridged networks. In this type of environment, every data packet is sent to every machine, and each station has to process every frame on the network.

The processors in the PCs handle this task, taking away from the processing power needed for other tasks. Every day, we visit users and networks with this problem. When we upgrade them to a switched network, it is typically a weekend job. When the users leave on Friday, their high-powered Pentiums stacked with RAM are acting like 486s. But when they come back on Monday morning, we hear comments about how their computers boot up more quickly and run faster, and how Internet pages come up instantly.

In many cases, slow Internet access times are blamed on WAN connections. The problem isn't the WAN connection—it's the local area network saturated to a grinding halt with frames from every interface on the network.

When network performance gets this bad, it's time to either call in a Cisco consultant or learn how to implement switching. Either way, you are reading this book because you are very interested in switching or becoming Cisco certified. Consider yourself a network hero in training.

To fix the immediate problems on your 10BaseT network with Category 3 or 4 cabling, you might need to upgrade to Category 5 cabling and implement a Fast Ethernet network. Then you need to ask yourself the following questions:

- Is this only a temporary solution for my network, or will it stand the test of time?
- What types of new technologies are we considering?
- Are we going to be upgrading to Windows 2000?
- Will we be looking at using Web services or implementing Voice Over IP?
- Do we have any requirements for using multicast, unicast, video conferencing, or CAD applications?

The list goes on.

In many cases, network administrators don't realize that implementing a switched network will allow their networks to run at almost wire speed. Upgrading the backbone (not the wiring), eliminating the data collisions, making the network segments smaller, and getting those users off hubs and bridges is the answer. In terms of per-port costs, this is usually a much cheaper solution. It's also a solution you can grow with. Of course, a 100Mbps network never hurts—but even a switched 10BaseT network that has been correctly implemented can have almost the same effect of providing your network with the performance you need.

Network Performance

Network performance is usually measured by throughput. *Throughput* is the overall amount of data traffic that can be carried by the physical lines through the network. It is the maximum amount of data that can pass through any point in your network without suffering packet loss or collisions.

Packet loss is the total number of packets transmitted at the speed of the physical wire minus the number that arrive correctly at their destination. When you have a large percentage of packet losses, your network is not functioning the way it would without the multiple collisions.

The forwarding rate is another consideration in network throughput. The *forwarding rate* is the number of packets per second that can be transmitted on the physical wire. For example, if you are sending 64-byte packets on a 10BaseT Ethernet network, you can transmit a maximum of about 14,880 packets per second.

In this chapter, we will talk about the hierarchy of the network. We'll look at node types such as those found in resource nodes and demand nodes. We will then look at how VLANs create not only collision domains but how they intermingle with broadcast domains as well. There are two types of VLANs that can be made—local or point-to-point—and we will look at the boundaries of each.

In searching for the right networking technology to solve your network-related problems, implementing a properly formulated network plan is vitally important. In this situation, routing VLANs correctly after switches have been implemented in the network is just as important as having switches in the network. Poorly implemented switched networks can have awful effects.

When you implement switching, you need to consider which types of switching modules to use. If Layer 3 or Layer 4 routing is a requirement, you need to take a look at the issues involved in VLAN routing as well as some switched network rules of thumb. We will cover these issues relating to interVLAN routing and implementation in depth.

As long as we are looking at issues relating to why you should implement VLANs, we also need to look at the problems that VLANs cause and the solutions available. The following section will provide you with a complete picture of the problems involved in this task and how to resolve them.

Switched Network Design 101

When designing your network, you need to keep some basic rules in mind. The primary reason to segment your network is to relieve network congestion and increase bandwidth. Segmenting is often necessary to satisfy the bandwidth requirements of a new application or type of information the network needs to support. At other times, you may need to segment the network due to the increased traffic on the segment or subnet, or because of increased network usage or a planned increase in network population.

Some areas you need to consider are:

- Types of nodes
- User groups
- Security needs
- Population of the network
- Applications used
- Network needs for all the interfaces on the network

When designing your network, you should create it in a hierarchical manner. Doing so provides you with the ability to easily add to your network. Another important consideration is how data flows in the network.

For example, let's say your users are intermingled with your servers in the same geographical location. If you design a switched network in which the user's data must be switched through a number of links to another geographical area and then back again to create a connection between the users and file servers, you have not created the most efficient path.

We call this a *connection* between demand nodes and resource nodes. A *demand node* is an interface on the network that makes requests or queries to the resource nodes. These devices can be workstations, terminals, or even client applications.

A *resource node* is a node on an interface attached to a device that provides resources to the network. Such nodes can include printers, servers, mainframes, and even WAN routers. Network conversations occur when resource nodes and demand nodes send series of requests and responses out through the network.

Single points of failure need to be analyzed, as well. Every large network user has suffered through his or her share of network outages and downtime. By analyzing all the possible areas of failure, you can implement redundancy in the network and avoid many network outages. Redundancy is one of the reasons for the creation of Spanning Tree Protocol and the many protocols discussed in the previous chapter. In the event of a network failure, the alternate paths can be used to continue forwarding data throughout the network.

In addition to providing redundant links, you should consider other areas. Because you'll have invested all those precious budget dollars in redundant links, wouldn't it be natural to use those links not only for a redundant path, but also to load-balance data and forward data across those multiple links? You can do so by implementing a separate spanning tree on each VLAN.

The last principle that you should consider when designing your network is the behavior of the different protocols. The actual switching point for data does not have to be the physical wire level. Your data can be rerouted at the data link and network layers, as well. Protocols operating at Layer 2 can encapsulate or tag frames to create a Layer 3-like environment. This allows the implementation of Layer 3 switching while providing security and queuing (QoS) through the use of Application-Specific Integrated Circuits (ASICs) instead of the CPU on the switch at Layer 2. This arrangement uses less processing time and forwards data with less latency and more efficiency to the end destinations.

Collision Domains vs. Broadcast Domains

A Cisco Catalyst switch can be considered a high-speed multiport bridge that allows almost maximum wire-speed transfers. Dividing the local geographical network into smaller segments reduces the number of interfaces in each segment. This reduction will increase the amount of bandwidth available to all the interfaces. Each smaller segment is considered a collision domain.

In the case of switching, each port on the switch is its own collision domain. The most optimal switching configuration places only one interface on each port of a switch, making the collision domain two nodes. The two nodes would be the switch port interface and the interface of the end machine.

However, if another Layer 2 device—such as a 24-port hub—is connected to the port, and 24 interfaces are connected to the hub, you have 25 interfaces in the collision domain: the switch interface and the 24 interfaces connecting to the hub. Those interfaces place data on the physical segment that can collide. Data arriving to the hub is sent out every port for every interface to view. Figure 10.1 shows a small collision domain consisting of two PCs and a server. Notice that if data is sent at the same time, a collision will occur on the physical wire.

When a switch is set up and each port is assigned to a VLAN, a broadcast sent in VLAN 1 is seen only by those ports assigned to VLAN 1. Although the nodes on each port are in the collision domain, in the case of VLANs, the broadcast

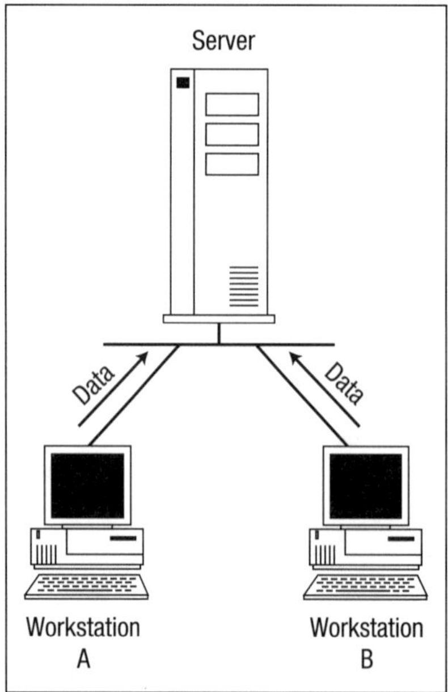

Figure 10.1 A small collision domain consisting of two PCs and a server.

domain is all the ports that are assigned to a particular VLAN. The switch segments the other users connected to other ports, preventing data collisions. When traffic remains local to the segment or workgroup, each user has more bandwidth available than if all the nodes were in one segment.

A switch with only one interface connected to each port can send local data at virtually the physical wire speed minus the latency between the input port and the output port of the switch. Physical wire limitations are close to 100 percent utilization without any network problems. In this situation, collisions are virtually eliminated.

Network administrators vary on the utilization percentage values for normal usage of the network. Table 10.1 shows the average utilization that should be seen on each of the listed utilization types. Going above these averages of network utilization on the physical wire is a sign either that the network has a problem or that you need to upgrade the network. You can use a network monitor such as a Sniffer to monitor your utilization and the type of traffic flowing through your network. You can use devices such as WAN probes to monitor the traffic on a WAN.

Just to recap, in switched environments, broadcast domains are all the ports or collision domains belonging to a VLAN. In a flat network topology, your broadcast domain is all the interfaces in your segment or subnet. If there are no devices such as switches or routers to divide your network, you have only one broadcast domain. On some switches, an almost limitless number of broadcast domains or VLANs can be configured.

Figure 10.2 shows an example of a properly switched network. Notice that you don't need high-speed links to every workstation to create an efficient network. In the figure, you see 10Mbps links to each workstation, a Fast Ethernet trunk to the switch containing the servers, and 100Mbps links to each server. This way,

Table 10.1 Average limits in terms of utilization percentage and type.

Utilization (%)	Type of Utilization
100	Full duplex
90 to 100	FDDI rings
90 to 100	Switched LAN segments
75	Cisco router and switch
70	Token Ring segments
70	WAN links
40	Non-switch Ethernet segments or subnets (flat network)
20	Broadcasts/multicasts
5-7	Collisions on the wire

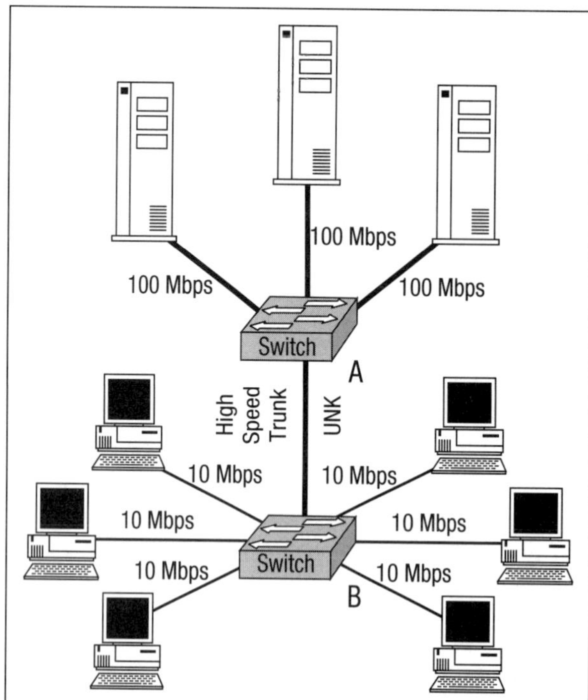

Figure 10.2 A small but properly switched network.

the amount of bandwidth entering from the 10Mbps switch will not overwhelm all the server links, and you create an efficiently switched network without bottlenecks.

Note: *Switching technology complements routing technology, and both have their place in the network. The value of having routing technology is most noticeable when you get to larger networks utilizing WAN solutions in the network environment.*

Flat Network Topology Forwarding

A small, flat network often contains multiple segments connected with hubs, bridges, and repeaters. This is a Layer 2 network and can actually be connected to a router for access to a WAN connection. In this topology, every network node sees the conversations of every other network node.

In terms of scalability, this setup has some major limitations, especially with the tech-nologies that companies must utilize to stay ahead in their particular fields. No Quality of Service, prioritizing of data, redundant links, or data security can be implemented here, other than encryption. Every node sees every packet on the network. The hubs merely forward the data they receive out every port causing collisions. You can see this topology in Figure 10.3.

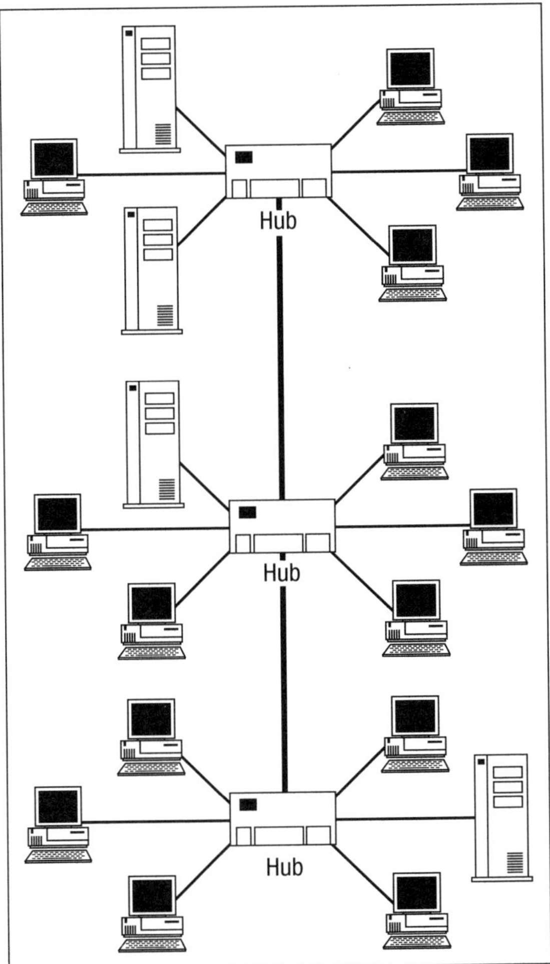

Figure 10.3 A flat network topology.

Switched Network Topology Forwarding

Switches operate at Layer 2 and forward traffic based on the destination Media Access Control (MAC) address contained in the packet's header. The switch then begins to forward the packet to the destination port as the packet is being received. Before the packet has been fully received by the source switch, the destination interface may begin receiving the packet. This strategy tends to create very low latency times and very high forwarding rates. As we mentioned in Chapter 1, there are three switching modes on switches.

The *cut-through switching* method sends packets, as just described, in real time, reading only the first part of the header to gain the destination information and then immediately forwarding the data to the destination port. The *store-and-forward switching* method, as the name implies, stores the packet in buffers, applies filters, and then forwards the packet. The last type of switching mode, *fragment-free*, is a combination of the other two. The switch receives and buffers the first 64K, makes sure that there was no collision and that the packet is not corrupted, and then forwards the packet.

Switched Network Bottlenecks

Before we inject a route processor into the equation, let's look at a simple way of understanding how switching technology increases the speed and efficiency of your network. Bear in mind, however, that increasing the speed and efficiency of the demand nodes in your network increases the throughput to the resource nodes. This increase in traffic to the resource nodes may create a *bottleneck*, which is a point in the network at which data is slowed due to collisions and too much traffic directed to one resource, such as a server.

To better illustrate this problem, let's look at Figure 10.4, which shows a switched network that has only two servers. All the demand nodes send traffic back and forth to the two servers on a 10BaseT Ethernet Category 5 physical cable. We can't draw 40 PCs, but if the total throughput for each of those 40 PCs is 10Mbps on our physical link, then even if we divided the load between the two servers, the links to the servers would need to carry 200Mbps to allow data to be efficiently processed at wire speeds. In theory, this is the case. Probably you would never have that much use of all 40 of your PCs in the network at once. Imagine,

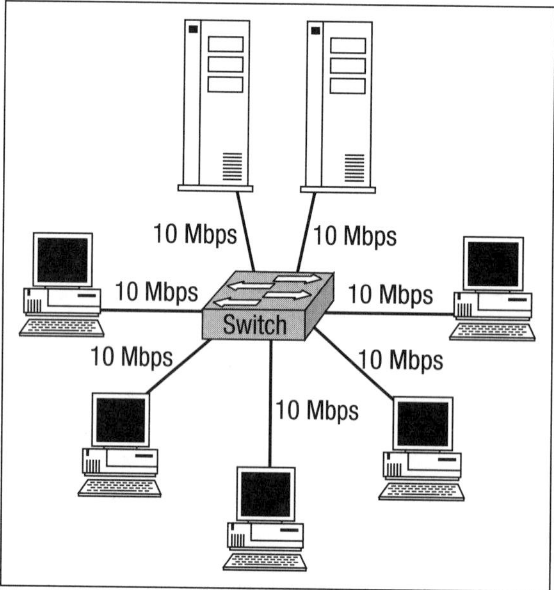

Figure 10.4 A switched network that has only two servers.

though, if you had 100 PCs in your network. Then 40 PCs sending data to your servers is much more realistic. The sheer number of clients sending data to the servers can overwhelm the trunk, create a bottleneck, and slow traffic.

When the resource node's buffer starts to drop frames sent to it because its buffers are full, it will send a message to the demand node that will tell it to slow its traffic. Thus, your bottleneck has just slowed your network. It could be moving much more quickly. How can you resolve this problem?

You can apply many types of media to this concept. In this demonstration, we will utilize Ethernet 10BaseT and 100BaseT, which are the most common media in today's networks.

Let's make a slight correction and alleviate the bottleneck on the physical link from the switch to the resource nodes (servers). By upgrading this particular link to 100BaseT, as shown in Figure 10.5, we can successfully eliminate this bottleneck.

Now, let's take a look at a more complex model, in which the demand nodes are connected to one switch and the resource nodes are connected to another switch. We'll add a couple hundred more users to switch 1 and find out where our bottleneck is. As you can see from Figure 10.6, there is now a bottleneck on our trunk link between the two switches. Even if all the switches have a VLAN assigned to each port, remember that a trunk link without pruning enabled will send all of the VLANs to the next switch.

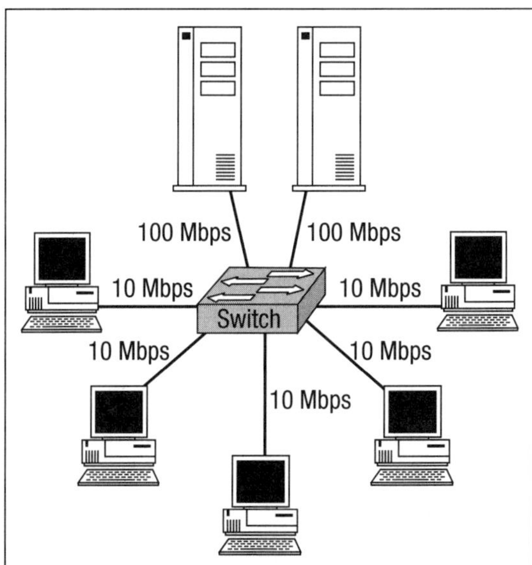

Figure 10.5 The addition of FastEthernet 100BaseT on the physical link between the switch and the servers.

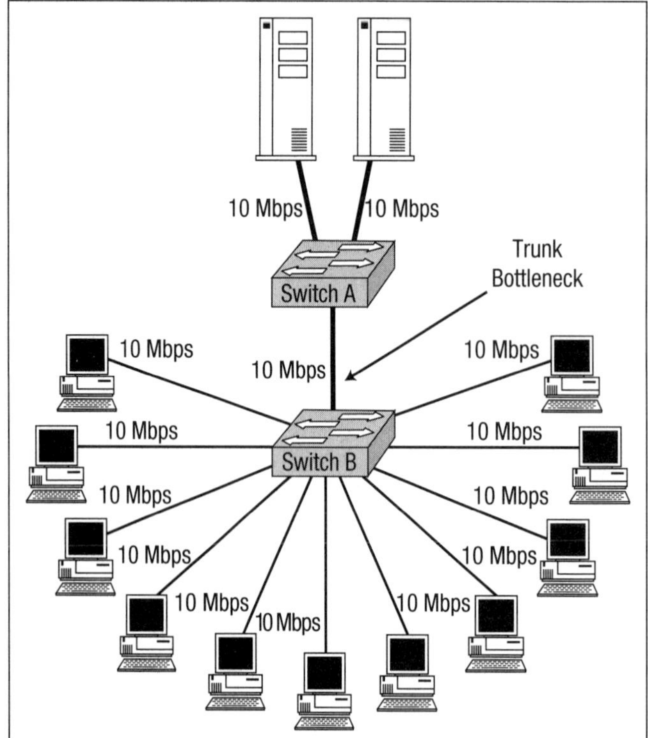

Figure 10.6 A new bottleneck between the trunk link on the two switches.

To resolve this issue, we could implement two faster connections: a faster connection on the trunk link between the two switches and a faster connection on the links between the switch and each server. In Figure 10.7 we have done this, making the links 100BaseT. The trunk link could be FDDI, Gigabit Ethernet, or any other connection faster than 10Mbps, as long as the link usage will average far below the utilization maximums for the type of link. This setup would resolve the issue and eliminate our bottleneck.

In this case, let's get even more complex and introduce another solution by implementing two physical links between the two switches and using full-duplexing technology. Full-duplexing essentially means that you have two physical wires from each port, and that data is sent on one port and received on another. This arrangement not only guarantees a collision-free connection, but also can increase your network traffic to almost 100 percent on each link.

You now have 200 percent throughput by utilizing both links. If you had a 10Mbps network on the wire, by implementing full-duplexing you now have 20Mbps flowing through the wires. The same is true with a 100BaseT network—instead of 100Mbps, you now have a 200Mbps link.

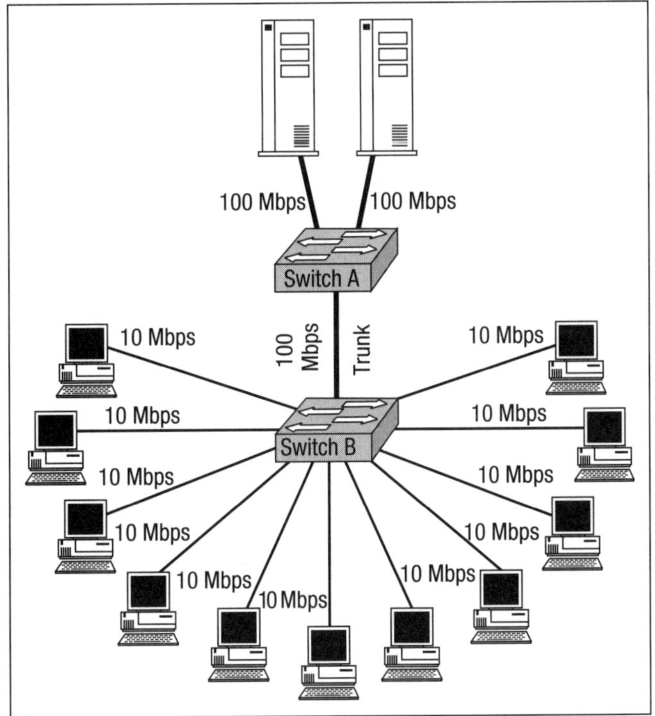

Figure 10.7 An upgrade of the trunk link and the links between the servers and the switches to 100Mbps links.

Note: If the interfaces on your resource nodes can implement full-duplexing, this may also be a secondary solution for your servers.

Blocking Switch vs. Non-Blocking Switch

This is a good time to explain the differences between blocking and non-blocking switches. We call a switch a *blocking switch* when the switch bus or components cannot handle the theoretical maximum throughput of all the input ports combined. There is a heavy debate over whether every switch should be designed as a non-blocking switch; but for now, doing so is only a dream, considering the current pricing of switches.

For example, let's consider a 24-port 10/100 switch. In full-duplex mode, the theoretical maximum of each port is 200Mbps. At full capacity, the switch would need to process 4.8GB per second, which is not likely with today's networks. The ports on the switches will likely never exceed one-third of that capacity, and the likelihood of every switch port sending that much data at the same time in the network is even less.

Almost every Cisco switch has an acceptable throughput level and will work well in its own layer of the campus layered model or its designed specification. Implementing VLANs has become a popular solution for breaking down a segment into smaller collision domains.

You can implement two types of VLANs into a switched network: end-to-end or local. Most commonly, these VLANs are used for networks that do not have centralized resources throughout the campus. In an end-to-end VLAN, the switch ports assigned to the VLAN are independent of the physical location. No matter where the user moves in the campus network, the VLAN number of the user remains the same. Each VLAN maintains its own set of common security requirements. VLANs try to group users based on common clusters such as departments or workgroups and can be configured by server usage. This type of VLAN can span multiple buildings, floors, and switch blocks.

Local VLANs are more suited for networks that have centralized resources. This type of VLAN can span a single building or just a single individual switch. Most VLANs in today's networks use local VLANs, due to the centralized and strategic placement of resource nodes on the network.

The two types of VLANs utilize either static or dynamically assigned VLAN ports. A static port is assigned to a certain VLAN, and any user who connects to the port is a member of the VLAN assigned to the port. A dynamically assigned VLAN is assigned to the MAC address of the particular interface through either CiscoWorks2000 or CiscoWorks for Switched Internetworks (CWSI). The switch queries a database to assign a VLAN number to a port.

Dynamic VLANs are beyond the scope of this book, and the Switching test will not have any questions regarding dynamic VLANs other than what is covered in the last paragraph. If you would like to learn more about dynamic VLANs, they are covered in the Cisco course titled, "Managing Cisco Switched Internetworks."

Routing between VLANs can be a challenging problem to overcome. In the next section, we'll discuss the common components used in Cisco switches to route VLAN information using either an external route processor or an internal route processor. An external route processor uses an external router to route data from one VLAN to another VLAN. An internal route processor uses internal modules and cards located on the same device to implement the routing between VLANs.

Components of Routing VLANs

Switches occupy the same place in the network as hubs. However, unlike hubs, switches examine the packet and process it accordingly. Also unlike a hub, which simply repeats the data to every single port, a switch filters the data and forwards it directly to the destination port. If data arrives on a port assigned to a VLAN and the destination is unknown, the switch repeats the signal only to the port or ports assigned to the VLAN, except for the port of arrival.

The switch can regenerate packets, enabling the data to be forwarded even greater distances than a simple hub can achieve. Devices dedicated only to data regeneration are called *repeaters*. They allow data to be forwarded over greater distances, allowing the data to overcome regular data distance limitations for the type of physical media being used.

By filtering packets and regenerating forwarded packets, the switch can split the network into many separate collision domains. This splitting allows for greater distances, dramatically lower collision rates, and higher numbers of nodes on the network. Each VLAN in the network is its own broadcast domain, and each port is its own collision domain. In a shared or flat network, every node is part of the same collision and broadcast domain.

Switches can't forward frames based on Layer 3 addresses nor can they forward data from one VLAN to another. So what happens when data from one VLAN must be forwarded to another VLAN? What does the switch do when the data needs to be routed to another network based on a Layer 3 address?

The rest of this chapter will explain the processes and network devices the switch uses to forward information from one VLAN to another. It will also explain how the switch handles Layer 3 data that must be routed to other networks or segments.

Switch Route Processors

When a switch receives a packet from a port on one VLAN destined for the port of another VLAN, the switch must find a path on which to send the frame. Because switches are designed to isolate traffic to broadcast domains or subnets, they cannot by default forward data to another VLAN or network without some other device's intervention to route the data and create routing tables of other networks and devices.

Route processors can be used to route data between foreign VLANs and other logically segmented parts of the network, such as subnets. They also route data to remote WAN segments, networks, or the Internet.

Quite a few types of route processors are available for Catalyst switches. They include:

- NetFlow Feature Card and NetFlow Feature Card II
- Route Switch Module
- Route Switch Feature Card
- MultiLayer Switch Module

NetFlow Feature Card and NetFlow Feature Card II

The NetFlow Feature Card (NFFC) and the NetFlow Feature Card II (NFFC II) are feature cards that work primarily with a Route Switch Module or another high-end router. Both are daughter cards of the Supervisor Engine III module on the Catalyst 5000 family of switches running version 11.3.4 or higher of the Cisco IOS. This Cisco solution provides frame and packet filtering at wire speeds, utilizing ASICs instead of processors, therefore allowing the switch to scale forwarding rates up from millions of packets per second to gigabit wire speeds.

Both cards provide protocol-filtering support for Ethernet VLANs and on non-trunked Ethernet, Fast Ethernet, and Gigabit Ethernet ports. By default, the protocol filtering feature is disabled on all Ethernet VLANs.

In addition to assigning a VLAN to a port, you can configure the port to be a member of one or more groups based on a common protocol.

Note: *Because trunk ports and links are members of all VLANs, no filtering can be done on trunk links. Dynamic ports and ports that have port security enabled are members of all protocol groups.*

The NFFC card's primary functions are to enable multilayer switching, NetFlow accounting, NetFlow data exporting, filtering by protocol, enhanced multicast packet replication, filtering by application, and Internet Group Management Protocol (IGMP) snooping. It is also a QoS enhancement for Cisco's CiscoAssure end-to-end solutions.

The cards have the ability to filter based not only on Layer 3 IP or VLANs but by Layer 4 application port addresses as well. This ability adds a layer of security with the ability to prevent unauthorized applications on the network. This type of filtering is critical in today's networks, especially those needing the ability to forward Voice Over IP traffic or video conferencing.

The Route Switch Module or another external switch running Multilayer Switching Protocol (MLSP) must still provide the routing functionality. Routers that can run MLSP and utilize the features of the NFFCs are the 4500, 4700, 7200, and 7500 Series routers. MLSP is also used to flush cache entries when a topology change occurs and to make modifications to the access lists used for filtering.

NFFCs populate their Layer 3 and 4 switching cache dynamically by observing and learning from the flow of data. They parse data using NetFlow Data Export to collect and export detailed information about data flows. This parsing is accomplished without introducing any additional latency into the switching or routing process.

NetFlow Data Export provides a look into all Layer 2 port traffic, as well as Layer 3 statistics. It records the statistics into User Datagram Protocol (UDP) and exports them to any RMON2-compliant network analysis package such as CWSI TrafficDirector.

Some of the information that NetFlow Data Export provides is as follows:

- Source address
- Destination address
- Traffic type
- Byte count
- Packet count
- Timestamp

NFFC also provides protocol filtering to allow segmentation by VLANs. It can provide per-port filtering of data in four different groups:

- IP
- IPX
- AppleTalk, DECnet, and Banyan Vines
- Other Group

By default, the IP group is on, but can be turned off for the other groups listed.

Note: *NFFC and NFFC II do not process Token Ring packets.*

For example, a port where a server resides that is configured for IP can be turned off for other protocols such as IPX and AppleTalk. No broadcasts from these protocols will reach the server or end-user interface, because the NFFC will filter them.

IGMP Snooping is another feature of the NFFC II. Spawned by multicast applications such as video conferencing, it provides advanced features that help keep multicast traffic from flooding all the ports and degrading network performance. Using this feature, Catalyst 5500 switches are able to intelligently forward multicast to the correct destination. IGMP Snooping reads IGMP messages from the end-user's interface and learns their port location. This process allows the NFFC II card to forward multicast data streams out the port attached to the destination interface.

Both cards can also provide broadcast and unicast flood traffic filtering based on the port's membership to the different protocol groups in addition to the port's assigned VLAN. The NFFC II also has the ability to become a multicast forwarder. The ASICs on the NFFC II card replicate multicast packets to allow wire-speed multicast forwarding.

Route Switch Module

The Route Switch Module enhances the Catalyst 5000 switch family by letting the switch provide some of the same Layer 3 switching capabilities as a router. As a result, a switch that normally forwards only Layer 2 broadcast and VLAN traffic and relies on a router to forward traffic to other segments can now route the traffic itself without relying on a router.

The RSM contains a MIPS R47000 processor, 32MB DRAM expandable to 128MB, a 16MB Flash card expandable to 40MB, 1.5MB high-speed RAM for the backplane interface, and 8MB of Flash memory.

The RSM connects directly into the backplane of the switch. It adds to the Cisco IOS such features as multiprotocol routing for the Ethernet interfaces, security control, multicast control, interVLAN routing, and some basic QoS features.

Routing protocols supported by the RSM are as follows:

- AppleTalk
- Enhanced Interior Gateway Routing Protocol (EIGRP)
- Hot Standby Routing Protocol (HSRP)
- NetWare Link Services Protocol (NLSP)
- Interior Gateway Routing Protocol (IGRP)
- Internet Protocol (IP)
- Internetwork Packet Exchange (IPX)
- Open Shortest Path First (OSPF)
- Routing Information Protocol (RIP)
- Routing Table Maintenance Protocol for AppleTalk (RTMP)

A Catalyst 5500 has 13 slots available for additional modules. Slots 1 and 2 are reserved for the Supervisor Engine and a redundant Supervisor Engine. If there is no redundant Supervisor Engine card, up to seven RSMs can be installed in the switch in slots 2 through 12.

The RSM interface to the Catalyst 5000 Series backplane is through VLAN 0 mapped to channel 0 and VLAN 1 mapped to channel 1. The switch uses VLAN 0 to communicate with the RSM. By default, VLAN 1 is the switch default, but the default can be changed and mapped to a specific channel to load balance the channels.

VLAN 0's MAC address is the address assigned to the programmable ROM (PROM) on the line communication processor (LCP) located on the RSM. This

MAC address can be used for diagnostic purposes and to identify the RSM's lot number.

***Note:** The user cannot access VLAN 0.*

All other VLANs are assigned a base MAC address from the RSM PROM, which is preprogrammed with 512 MAC addresses. The RSM can route up to 256 VLANs.

Route Switch Feature Card

The Route Switch Feature Card (RSFC) is another daughter card of the Supervisor Engine IIG or the Supervisor Engine IIIG. This card basically transforms your switch into a Layer 3 router with a whole bunch of ports.

Two great features of this card are Web browser support that provides a graphical navigation tool through the command-line interface (CLI) and the integration of NetFlow Switching services, which include those services built into the NetFlow Feature Card. Included in these features are security services, QoS, Cisco Group Management Protocol (CGMP), Protocol Independent Multicast (PIM), and queuing.

These cards build on the Route Switch Processor (RSP) found in the Cisco 7200 Series router providing exceptional performance in the routing process for the Catalyst 5000 family of switches. The card uses an R4700 150 MHz processor, 128MB of DRAM memory, 32MB of Flash memory, 2MB of high-speed packet memory, and 6MB of high-speed RAM for the Catalyst switching bus interface.

This feature card, like the others, uses a Cisco IOS that supports a wide array of protocols and provides a wide array of services. The following protocols are supported by the IOS:

- AppleTalk
- DECnet
- IP
- IPX
- Vines
- XNS

MultiLayer Switch Module

The MultiLayer Switch Module (MSM) is the interVLAN routing solution for the Catalyst 6000 family Supervisor Engine software version 5.2(1)CSX or later. It uses the Cisco IOS and plugs directly into interfaces to the switch backplane to provide Layer 3 switching.

The MSM connects directly to the switch with four full-duplex Gigabit Ethernet interfaces. The Catalyst switch sees the MSM as an external route processor not connected to the switch itself. You can group the four Gigabit interfaces into a single Gigabit EtherChannel or configure them as independent interface links. The MSM supports channeling trunks for use with 802.1Q or ISL.

The port-channel interface on the MSM is configured with one subinterface for every VLAN on the switch, providing interVLAN routing with EtherChannel and trunk ports. Each of the four Gigabit interfaces can be independently configured as a separate VLAN trunk or non-trunked routed interface.

The MSM supports the following routing protocols:

- Enhanced Interior Gateway Routing Protocol (EIGRP)
- Interior Gateway Routing Protocol (IGRP)
- Open Shortest Path First (OSPF)
- Routing Information Protocol (RIP)

Even though the focus of the test is not routing protocols, let's take a look at the routing protocols the MSM supports.

- *Enhanced Interior Gateway Routing Protocol*—EIGRP is an enhanced version of IGRP that combines the advantages of the link-state routing protocols with distance vector protocols. EIGRP uses the Diffusing Update Algorithm (DUAL) and includes features such as variable-length subnet masks, fast convergence, and multiple network layer support. When a network topology change occurs, EIGRP checks its topology table for a suitable new route to the destination. If a route exists in the table, EIGRP updates the routing table with the new route and purges the old route from the table. One of the main features of EIGRP saves WAN-link bandwidth by sending routing updates only when routing information changes, unlike other routing protocols. It also takes into effect the available bandwidth between the paths to determine the rate at which it transmits updates.
- *Interior Gateway Routing Protocol*—IGRP is a Cisco-developed distance vector protocol. A distance vector routing protocol sends all or a portion of its routing table in the form of routing update messages at regular intervals to each neighboring router. As routing information proliferates through the network, routers can calculate the distance to all the nodes in the network. IGRP uses a combination of metrics such as internetwork delay, bandwidth, reliability, and load factors to make routing decisions.
- *Open Shortest Path First*—OSPF is an IP-based link-state routing protocol designed to overcome the limitations of Routing Information Protocol (RIP).

It sends link-state advertisements (LSAs) to all other routers within the network. Information is included in the LSAs for the interfaces OSPF is running on and the metrics used. As routers collect the link-state information, they use the Shortest Path First (SPF) algorithm to calculate the shortest path to each node.

- *Routing Information Protocol*—RIP is another distance-vector routing protocol. RIP works well in small networks. However, in larger, more complex internetworks RIP has many limitations, such as a maximum hop count of 15, lack of support for variable-length subnet masks (VLSMs), slow convergence, and inefficient use of bandwidth.

Now that we have covered the cards and modules used in interVLAN routing, in the next section we'll take a look at configuring them. Because the MSM, RSFC, and RSM use identical commands, we'll only focus on configuring the RSM and the NFFC and NFFC II.

INTERVLAN ROUTING CONFIGURATION

In the preceding sections, we talked about the Route Switch Module and its different features. Several switches—such as the Catalyst 4000 and 5000 Series—are multimodule switches.

To view the modules installed on the switch, use the following Privileged Mode command:

```
Coriolis5000(enable) show module

Mod Module-Name Ports  Module-Type            Model     Serial-Num  Status
--- ----------- -----  -----------            -----     ----------  ------
1                0     Supervisor III         WS-X5530  010854649   ok
2                24    10/100baseTX Ethernet  WS-X5225R 012453433   ok
3                1     Route Switch           M-X5302   007673460   ok

Mod MAC-Address(es)                        Hw     Fw      Sw
--- --------------                         --     --      --
1   00-40-0b-80-54-00 to 00-40-0b-80-57-fi 2.0    3.1.2   4.3(la)
2   00-40-0b-03-5d-58 to 00-40-0b-03-5d-6f 3.1    4.3(l)  4.3(la)
3   00-43-0d-91-45-66 to 00-43-0d-91-dc-67 5.0    20.14   11.3(6)WAA4(9)

Mod Sub-Type Sub-Model Sub-Serial Sub-Hw
--- -------- --------- ---------- ------
1   NFFC     WS-F5521  0010954641 1.1
```

Switches with Non-Removable Cards

The Catalyst 2926G, 2948G, and 4912G do not have internal cards. Instead, they are built-in and are considered logically modular switches or fixed configuration switches. For instance, the Catalyst 2926G has 24 ports of 10/100 Fast Ethernet built in. The ports are logically considered to be located on module 2, although it cannot be removed like an add-on card from the switch.

Notice that there is a Supervisor Engine III installed as module 1, a 24-port 10/100 Ethernet module installed as module 2, and a Route Switch Module installed as module 3. From here, you can get the information needed to configure each module.

As we progress through the rest of this chapter, you will learn how to configure an internal route processor such as the RSM, RSFC, or MSM.

Configuring the Route Switch Module

In the last example, we showed how to find out what modules are installed on a switch and the assigned module number. Now we will go through the basic steps to configure the Route Switch Module.

Note: *The commands for configuring the RSM, RSFC, and MSM are the same. The Cisco course focuses on configuring the RSM, so we will primarily focus on the RSM configuration.*

In the previous example we used a **show module** command, which showed that the RSM was installed as module 3. To make modifications to the RSM, you need to activate a session and make modifications directly to the module. To open a session from the console port, use the following command:

```
Coriolis5000> session 3
```

Note: *The* ***3*** *refers to the module number assigned to the module on the switch. When the RSM shows a >, it is in EXEC Mode; when the RSM shows a #, it is in Privileged EXEC Mode.*

If a password has been configured, you need to enter the password to continue. Either way, you will come to a new prompt. If the hostname has not been configured you will come to a prompt that looks similar to this:

```
Router>
```

For security and identity purposes, you will want to configure a password and a hostname for the module. However, before you can change the hostname, you must access Global Configuration Mode. To do this use the following commands:

```
Router> enable
Router# configure terminal
```

Warning: When you make changes in this mode, they must be saved to NVRAM. Otherwise, the next time you recycle the switch, the changes will be lost. The command to do this is **copy running-config startup-config**.

The RSM needs a unique name, so we will call it Coriolis5000RSM. To config-ure the hostname, use the following command:

```
Router>(config)# hostname Coriolis5000RSM
Coriolis5000RSM>(config)#
```

Note: *The hostname can be up to 255 characters, using alphanumeric characters only. Although in this example we used uppercase to identify the hostname, in some instances when you connect to the switch with different software, the hostname may appear in lowercase.*

To clear the hostname, use the following command:

```
Coriolis5000RSM>(config)# no hostname
Router>(config)#
```

If you have not configured a password for the RSM, this is the time to do so. A password is necessary if you plan to Telnet to the RSM. You will need to enter one of the line configuration modes, either the console mode or vty mode. You can enter those modes by using either the **line console 0** command or the **line vty 0 4** command. The **0 4** indicates that you want to configure all five vty lines, which will then allow you to Telnet into the RSM from the network instead of having to use the console port access.

Once you enter either the console or vty mode, you can use the following command to configure the password. In this example, we will use the password book1234:

```
password book1234
```

After you have configured these items, you may want to go in and view the running configuration. To do so, use the following command:

```
Coriolis5000RSM# show running-config
Building configuration...

Current configuration:
!
version 11.2
no service udp-small-servers
no service tcp-small-servers
!
hostname Coriolis5000RSM
!
enable book1234
!
!
interface Vlan1
 ip address 130.77.20.15 255.255.254.0
!
interface Vlan2
 ip address 130.77.20.15 255.255.254.0
!
interface Vlan3
ip address 130.77.20.16 255.255.254.0
 shutdown
!
router eigrp 100
network 130.77.0.0
no auto-summary
!
ip default-gateway 130.77.20.254
no ip classless
snmp-server community public RO
snmp-server community private RW
!
line con 0
line aux 0
line vty 0 4
password book1234
login
!
end

Coriolis5000RSM#
```

Warning: In order to keep new changes when the switch is cycled, don't forget to save the configuration to the NVRAM.

Route Protocol Assignment

All devices communicate with each other through a path or route. If the destination interface does not reside in the same network segments as the sender, a route to the destination must be entered. The route either can be a programmed static route or it can be dynamically calculated using any number of protocols available for route determination.

To use a dynamic protocol, first you must assign a routing protocol to the route processor being configured. Earlier, in the section explaining the RSM, we explained the different routing protocols. In this example configuration, we will use IGRP as our routing protocol.

To assign a routing protocol to the route processor, use the following commands in Global Configuration Mode:

```
Coriolis5000RSM(config)#ip routing
Coriolis5000RSM(config)#router igrp
```

Once the network routing protocol has been determined, the route processor on the particular module that you are configuring needs to know the network that it is physically connected to and participating in. When you configure the network address, the switch can learn what interfaces are participating and begin sending and receiving routing updates.

In this example, our switch will be participating in a Class B IP with a network ID of 130.77.0.0. Use the following command to configure the route processor with the network address:

```
Coriolis5000RSM(config-router)#network 130.77.0.0
```

Assigning VLAN IP Addresses

At this point, we have configured the route processor for the network and for the routing protocol. If you have not assigned an IP address and subnet mask to each virtual VLAN interface, you need to assign one. Even though VLANs are created with the IOS on the switch itself when a route processor is installed, VLANs are controlled at that level.

To assign an IP address, you need to select the VLAN to configure in Global Configuration Mode. In this example, we will configure VLAN 3. The interface name is that of the VLAN number created:

```
Coriolis5000RSM(config)#interface vlan3
```

Now that you have selected the interface, you are in Interface Configuration Mode. You next need to assign the interface an IP address and a subnet mask. To do this, use the following command:

```
Coriolis5000RSM(config-if)#ip address 130.77.20.16 255.255.254.0
Coriolis5000RSM(config-if)#exit
```

Let's take a look at a short excerpt of the running configuration to see our changes. Remember to save the running configuration to the startup configuration before cycling the switch, or you will lose your changes. If you are configuring the interface for the first time, it will remain shut down until the **no shutdown** command is used. Here are our configuration changes:

```
Coriolis5000RSM# show running-config
Building configuration...

Current configuration:
!
version 11.2
no service udp-small-servers
no service tcp-small-servers
!
hostname Coriolis5000RSM
!
enable book1234
!
!
interface Vlan1
 ip address 130.77.20.15 255.255.254.0
!
interface Vlan2
 ip address 130.77.20.15 255.255.254.0
!
interface Vlan3
 ip address 130.77.20.16 255.255.254.0
```

Although different IP addresses can be assigned to the virtual VLAN interfaces on the device, all of them utilize the same global MAC address. However, specifying an individual MAC address to each interface does have benefits in some situations. Assigning an individual MAC address to each interface offers these three main benefits:

- It allows the best use of Fast EtherChannel for load distribution by using a portion of the MAC address for load distribution.

- It enhances management with the use of the Multilayer Switching (MLS) cache.
- On the Catalyst 1900, it avoids operational problems with the use of the Content Addressable Memory (CAM) table.

While in Interface Configuration Mode, you can assign a MAC address to the interface by using the following command. Use the 48-bit IEEE MAC address written as a dotted triplet of four-digit hexadecimal numbers:

```
Coriolis5000RSM(config-if)#mac-address 0040.0b03.5d6f
Coriolis5000RSM(config-if)#exit
```

To see the MAC address assigned to each VLAN, use the following command:

```
CoriolisRSM5000> (enable) show cam dynamic
* = Static Entry. + = Permanent Entry. # = System Entry.
R = Router Entry. X = Port Security Entry

VLAN  Dest MAC/Route Des [CoS]  Destination Ports or VCs
----  ------------------------  ------------------------
1     00-40-19-43-4c-70         1/1
1     00-40-94-c5-2e-43         1/1
1     00-00-0c-03-f4-78         1/1
1     00-40-94-c8-b1-80         1/1
1     00-d0-38-a4-28-0e         2/1
1     00-40-67-6b-12-3b         2/1
1     00-40-64-be-55-80         2/1

Total Matching CAM Entries Displayed = 7
```

10

External Route Processor Configuration

On the MSM and an external route processor or router, each interface can be divided into many subinterfaces. Doing so creates a flexible solution for routing streams of multiple data types through one interface. On each interface on the switch connecting to a router or external processor, you need to identify the VLAN encapsulation method and assign an IP address and subnet mask to the interface.

First, you need to identify the subinterface to be configured. In order to enter Interface Configuration Mode for Ethernet on the subinterface that needs to be configured, enter the following command in Global Configuration Mode (3 indicates the module number/slot number, 1 indicates the port number, and 2 indicates the number of the subinterfaces to be configured):

```
Coriolis5000RSM(config)#interface ethernet 3/1.2
```

Here is another example configuring a subinterface for FastEthernet. This time, the module number is 4, the port number is 2, and the subinterface is 1:

```
Coriolis5000RSM(config)#interface fastethernet 4/2.1
```

***Note:** No changes take effect until the **no shutdown** command is used.*

Once in Interface Configuration Mode, you can configure the port for the encapsulation type and identify the VLAN number that will be carried by the port. The most common encapsulation type is ISL; this will be the encapsulation type configured in the following example. (For more information on the encapsulation types, refer to Chapter 8.) We are configuring the interface for VLAN 2. Each VLAN packet destined for a non-local network is tagged with a VLAN ID within the packet header, to help identify the VLAN to the subinterface:

```
Coriolis5000RSM(config-if)#encapsulation isl 2
```

Once you have identified the subinterface, assigned an encapsulation method, and identified the VLAN, you need to assign the subinterface its own unique IP address and subnet mask. To do this, use the following commands followed by a **no shutdown** command to apply the changes and exit:

```
Coriolis5000RSM(config-if)#ip address 130.77.20.18 255.255.254.0
Coriolis5000RSM(config-if)#no shutdown
Coriolis5000RSM(config-if)#exit
```

Configuring a Default Gateway

Before routing can occur, the sending device must know the routers that are connected to the local network to forward data for destinations outside the local network. Just as an end-user interface needs to have a defined default gateway, so does a switch to know where it can route information not located on the local network.

To define the gateway, in Global Configuration Mode use the following command combined with the route processor or router IP address that is acting as the default gateway for the network:

```
Coriolis5000RSM(config)#ip default-gateway 130.77.20.1
```

You can also set a default route through the network for a certain address. This route is configured on the switch itself. In Privileged Mode on a Set/Clear command-based switch, use the following command. You're creating an IP address for the route of 130.77.16.4; the gateway is 130.77.20.1. You can configure an optional metric at the end to indicate whether the address is local or remote.

The number 0 indicates that the address is local, and 1 indicates the address is remote:

```
Coriolis5000(enable) set ip route 130.77.16.4 130.77.20.1 1
```

Instead of indicating an IP address to route, you can use the **default** command in its place to indicate the default route for all non-local address destinations not configured for another default path. The command is shown here:

```
Coriolis5000(enable) set ip route default 130.77.20.1
```

You can verify the IP configuration on the switch by using the following command:

```
Coriolis5000#show ip
IP Address: 130.77.20.15
Subnet Mask: 255.255.254.0
Default Gateway: 130.77.20.1
Management VLAN: 1
Domain name: coriolis.com
Nam server 1: 130.77.17.190
Name server 2: 130.77.16.191
HM server : Enabled
HTTP port : 80
RIP : enabled
```

You can also use the following Privileged Mode command to verify the default route configuration:

```
Coriolis5000(enable) show ip route
```

Protocol Filtering Configuration

Protocol filtering is supported only on nontrunking Ethernet, Fast Ethernet, and Gigabit Ethernet ports. Trunking ports are members of all the protocol groups, so they cannot be configured to provide protocol filtering.

Note: *Protocol filtering is supported on Catalyst 2926G, 2948G, 4000, and 5000 Series switches. However, VINES protocol is not supported on the Catalyst 2948G and the Catalyst 4000.*

In order to configure protocol filtering on the Ethernet, Fast Ethernet, or Gigabit Ethernet ports, you must first enable protocol filtering on the switch. To do so, use the following command in Privileged Mode:

```
Coriolis5000RSM>(enable) set protocolfilter enable
```

10

***Note:** To disable protocol filtering, replace **enable** with **disable**.*

After enabling protocol filtering, you need to set the protocol membership of the desired ports. Using the **set port protocol** command, you must identify three things:

- The module number and the port on the module
- The protocol, which can have a value of **IP**, **IPX**, or **group** (**group** identifies either the AppleTalk, DECnet, or VINES protocol)
- One of three modes for the particular protocol (**on**, **off**, or **auto)**

When the configuration is set to **on**, the port receives all the traffic for the particular protocol. When the configuration is set to **off**, the port does not receive traffic for that protocol. When the port configuration is set to **auto**, the port is added to the group only after receiving packets of the specific protocol. Table 10.2 shows the defaults for each protocol configuration when using the **set protocol** command.

Warning: You can configure an IP port to **auto** only if the port has an IP client connected to the port. Also, the Catalyst 2948G is a fixed configuration switch. Therefore, all ports are located on module 2.

Let's look at several sample configurations. The first example shows port 1 on module 6 being configured with the IP protocol set to auto-configure. Remember that in order to configure the port to **auto** for IP, a client configured with IP must be attached to the port:

```
Coriolis5000>(enable) set port protocol 6/1 ip auto
IP protocol set to auto mode on module 6/1.
Coriolis5000>(enable)
```

Table 10.2 Defaults associated with the **set protocol** command.

Description	Default Port Action
All ports	Set to **on** for the IP protocol by default
Ports set to IPX	Set to **auto** by default
Inactive ports	Set to **auto** if no packets are received after 60 minutes. Ports configured for **auto** are removed from the protocol group.
Link down	Dropped when the Supervisor Engine detects a link down

In the following example, port 1 is being configured on module 3. The IPX protocol is being turned off:

```
Coriolis5000>(enable) set port protocol 3/1 ipx off
IPX protocol disabled on port 3/1.
Coriolis5000>(enable)
```

To view the port filtering configuration for port 1 on module 5, use the following Privileged Mode command:

```
Coriolis5000>(enable) show port protocol 5/1
```

Chapter Summary

In the first part of this chapter, we covered the differences between collision and broadcast domains and why VLANs are a necessity in today's larger networks. We also provided a method you can use to tell when you should segment your network into smaller collision domains by implementing VLANs.

Demand nodes and resource nodes were covered, with an explanation of their performance issues and the most efficient placement of those resources in the network. We also discussed collecting throughput and utilization measurements to make accurate decisions on how and when to segment your network.

In addition, you learned the differences between internal and external route processing. A router is an external processor, and a routing module (such as the RSM located on the switch backplane) is an internal processor. In talking about processors, we also covered the benefits of adding Layer 3 and Layer 4 routing functions to the Catalyst switches by using certain daughter cards.

Daughter cards rely upon another card for management. For instance, the RSFC is a daughter card of the Supervisor III Engine. We described the features that you get from these daughter cards, and covered the benefits of NetFlow. NetFlow adds filtering at Layer 3 logical addresses, filtering by protocol, filtering by application port number, security, priority queuing, multicast, and many other features found in the high-end routers to the distribution layer switches.

NetFlow can be found on the NetFlow Feature Card, NetFlow Feature Card II, and the Route Switch Feature Card used with the Cisco Catalyst 5000 family of switches. On the Cisco Catalyst Series 6000, you can find the NetFlow features on the MultiLayer Switch Module.

In this chapter, you learned about the features of each external route processor card and the NetFlow feature of the different cards. The second part of this chapter covered interVLAN routing using those cards. Once you have segmented your network into VLANs, you still need to provide a means to communicate between them.

In the last section, we discussed the basic configuration for the different internal route processors. TCP/IP is one of the most common protocols in use today and is the standard protocol used to route data packets through the Internet. We also explained how to configure subinterfaces associated with a particular VLAN with an IP address, how to configure a gateway for interVLAN routing, and how to configure the encapsulation for the internal route processors.

Some of the terms learned in this chapter are as follows:

- *Broadcast domain*—In a non-switched network, all the devices that can receive a broadcast from one machine in the network sent on the physical wire. A segment not separated by a Layer 2 or Layer 3 device that can filter broadcasts is the broadcast domain. On a switched network using VLANs, your broadcast domain is all the ports or collision domains that belong to the same VLAN.

- *Collision domain*—All the interfaces on a single segment that can send data on the same physical wire. In a hub, all the interfaces connected to all the hub ports are in their own collision domain. In the case of a switch, all the nodes connected to each individual port are in their own collision domain.

- *Demand node*—Any end user or interface that requests and accesses network resources, such as servers or printers.

- *Dynamic VLAN port*—A VLAN number dynamically assigned to a certain MAC address. The node attaching to any dynamic port on the switch is a member of the VLAN assigned to the MAC address. Dynamically assigned VLANs are configured using CiscoWorks 2000 or CiscoWorks for Switched Internetworks software.

- *End-to-end VLAN*—A VLAN in which users (or groups of users) who utilize a common set of security requirements are grouped independent of the physical location. The port becomes a member of the VLAN assigned to the user or to the MAC address of the user's machine. This type of VLAN is beneficial for networks whose resource nodes are not centralized in one common area. Users moving around the campus network remain in the same VLAN.

- *Local VLAN*—Beneficial for networks whose resources are centralized and in one geographical location. The VLAN can span one switch or many switches within the same floor or building.

- *NetFlow switching*—A feature incorporated into the MSM, NFFC, and NFFC II, and which was originally instituted and developed for Cisco's Enterprise Routers. NetFlow allows for transparent switching in hardware while incorporating QoS features including security, multicast forwarding, multilayer switching, NetFlow data exporting, and packet filtering at Layer 3 and Layer 4 application ports.
- *Resource node*—Any interface on the network that provides a service for a demand node. Resource nodes can be such things as servers and printers. Incorrect placement of your resource nodes can have terrible effects on your network.
- *Static VLAN port*—A port on a switch that is manually assigned a VLAN number. Any node or interface connected to the port automatically becomes a member of the assigned VLAN.

Review Questions

1. What best describes the term *throughput*?
   a. The largest packet size you can use on a network
   b. The maximum amount of data you can put through a network without packet loss or collisions
   c. The maximum amount of data you can put through a network without introducing latency
   d. How fast a network is at top speed
2. What term is used to describe the maximum number of packets that can be transmitted?
   a. Forwarding rate
   b. Filtering rate
   c. Throughput
   d. Utilization
3. A device that provides resources to the network is known as what type of node?
   a. Demand node
   b. Supply node
   c. Server node
   d. Resource node

4. A device that makes requests of resource nodes is what type of node?
   a. Network node
   b. Demand node
   c. Work node
   d. Server node
5. What defines a collision domain?
   a. All the switches and routers in a network
   b. All the nodes on a switch
   c. All the nodes on a VLAN
   d. All the nodes on a port of a bridge or switch
6. What defines a broadcast domain?
   a. All the switches and routers in a network
   b. All the nodes on a switch
   c. All the nodes on a VLAN
   d. All the nodes on a port of a bridge or switch
7. What percentage of traffic is considered average on a shared hub?
   a. 5 to 10 percent
   b. 100 percent
   c. 35 to 40 percent
   d. Over 50 percent
8. What best describes a blocking switch?
   a. When too many collisions are occurring
   b. When the switch is not passing traffic
   c. When the switch is unable to handle the throughput of all the connected devices
   d. When the switch can handle the traffic load of all the combined devices
9. Which device provides Layer 3 routing on a Catalyst 5000?
   a. Network Node Manager
   b. Router Module
   c. Route Switch Module
   d. Switch Route Module

10. Which mechanism helps control multicast traffic?
    a. ICMP
    b. IRGP
    c. IGMP
    d. IMP
11. Which command do you use to list the modules installed on a switch?
    a. **list modules**
    b. **show hardware**
    c. **show module**
    d. **show devices**
12. Which command would you use to access an RSM located on module 3?
    a. **connect RSM**
    b. **session 3**
    c. **connect module 3**
    d. **telnet 3**

13. On which device would you set a password to allow Telnet access?
    a. Console port
    b. Auxiliary port
    c. VTY line
    d. Line card
14. Which type of port does not support protocol filtering?
    a. Fast Ethernet
    b. Gigabit Ethernet
    c. ISL trunk
    d. Ethernet
15. Network performance is always measured by throughput.
    a. True
    b. False
16. Which Route Switch Processor provides the ability to filter based on Layer 4 information?
    a. NetFlow Feature Cards I and II
    b. Route Switch Module
    c. NetFlow Data Export
    d. External route processor

17. Which device enables a switch to achieve wire-speed capabilities?
    a. NetFlow Feature Card I
    b. NetFlow Feature Card II
    c. ASIC
    d. Route Switch Module
18. A NetFlow Feature Card does not require a router to provide Layer 3 or 4 functions.
    a. True
    b. False
19. How many slots are available on a Catalyst 5500?
    a. 5
    b. 10
    c. 13
    d. 15
20. A Supervisor Engine must go into what slot on a Catalyst switch?
    a. Slot 1 only
    b. Slot 1 or 2
    c. Slot 13
    d. There is no specific slot requirement.
21. A Route Switch Module can support how many VLANs?
    a. 512
    b. 1,024
    c. 2
    d. 256
22. Which of the following is not considered a modular switch?
    a. Catalyst 2926
    b. Catalyst 2926G
    c. Catalyst 4000
    d. Catalyst 4912G
23. Which command displays the working configuration of a Catalyst 5000 RSM?
    a. **show configuration**
    b. **show running-config**
    c. **show start**
    d. **show module**

24. Which command do you use to make a VLAN interface active on an RSM?
    a. **no shutdown**
    b. **set vlan active**
    c. **set vlan on**
    d. **set int vlan up**
25. The VINES protocol is not supported on which platform? [Choose the two best answers]
    a. Catalyst 5000
    b. Catalyst 2948
    c. Catalyst 4000
    d. Catalyst 2948G

Real-World Projects

It's once again time to call upon our fictional Cisco Catalyst switching expert, Joe Snow. In our fictitious scenario (which is taken from the real world), the sales consultants have just finished a consultation with The Coriolis Group. The sales consultants were contacted to resolve some issues in Coriolis's switched network.

Recently, the routers at The Coriolis Group have experienced latency issues due to the number of packets being switched and the Quality of Service features the company has configured on its routers. The processors in the routers are currently running at 90 to 100 percent and the buffers are dropping packets continuously. Coriolis decided to investigate its options for upgrading the switches or routers to reduce the problems.

After being contacted by Coriolis, the sales consultants went to work to find the most economical and efficient options available for the situation. After reviewing the options and costs put forth by the sales consultants, The Coriolis Group decided that its best option would be to upgrade the current Cisco 5000s and 5500s at the distribution layer with an RSM and a NetFlow Feature Card II.

Several cards have already been installed by another technician on a Cisco Catalyst 5000, while waiting for Joe's arrival to configure the switch. The technician knows nothing about Cisco switches except how to remove the cards from the box and insert them into the back of the switch. The following items were included in the box:

- Catalyst 5000 24-port 10/100BaseTX backbone Fast EtherChannel Switching Module

- Catalyst 5000 Route Switch Module
- NetFlow Feature Card II

The Supervisor Engine III card has already been running in the switch since its initial configuration. Joe assesses the situation and creates a list of the following tasks that need to be performed on the first switch:

- Determine whether the switch is detecting the recently installed cards.
- Determine the module number assigned to the card and start a configuration session.
- Enter Privileged Mode on the switch.
- Assign the switch a unique name and password. Call it *RSMOne* and assign it the password *bookmark*.
- Configure the RIP routing protocol on the RSM.
- Configure VLANs 2 and 3 with IP addresses. Use the same port number assigned to the VLAN numbers.
- Assign a default gateway and subnet mask to the RSM.
- Because module 2 has all the ports, be sure to enable protocol filtering and set ports 2 and 3 to accept only the IP protocol-based traffic.

Project 10.1

Determine the module number, start a configuration session, and assign a hostname and password in the following manner:

1. On the switch console, enter the command **enable** and enter the password to enter Privileged Mode:

```
Coriolis5000# enable
Password: ********

Coriolis5000>(enable)
```

2. Enter the **show module** command to determine what cards are present:

```
Coriolis5000>(enable) show module

Mod  Module-Name Ports Module-Type           Model    Serial-Num Status
---  ----------- ----- -----------           -----    ---------- ------
1                0     Supervisor III        WS-X5530  010854649  ok
2                24    10/100baseTX Ethernet WS-X5225R 012453433  ok
3                1     Route Switch          M-X5302   007673460  ok
```

```
Mod MAC-Address(es)                               Hw    Fw     Sw
--- ---------------                               --    --     --
1   00-40-0b-80-54-00 to 00-40-0b-80-57-fi   2.0   3.1.2  4.3(1a)
2   00-40-0b-03-5d-58 to 00-40-0b-03-5d-6f   3.1   4.3(1) 4.3(1a)
3   00-43-0d-91-45-66 to 00-43-0d-91-dc-67   5.0   20.14  11.3(6)WAA4(9)

Mod  Sub-Type  Sub-Model  Sub-Serial  Sub-Hw
---  --------  ---------  ----------  ------
1    NFFC II    WS-F5531  0036457641
```

3. To open a session from the console port for the RSM, use the following command:

```
Coriolis5000> session 3
```

The prompt will look like this if it is the initial configuration:

```
Router>
```


4. Enter Global Configuration Mode with the following commands:

```
Router> enable
Router# configure terminal
```

5. Assign the RSM a unique hostname with the following command. Call it RSMOne:

```
Router>(config)# hostname RSMOne
RSMOne>(config)#
```

6. Assign the RSM Privileged Mode password. In this example, use the password *bookmark*:

```
password bookmark
```

Project 10.2

To assign an IP routing protocol and network number, perform the following:

1. Assign a routing protocol (RIP) to the RSM. To do this, use the following commands in Global Configuration Mode:

```
RSMOne(config)#ip routing
RSMOne(config)#router rip
```

2. Assign a network number to the route processor on the RSM:

```
RSMOne(config-router)#network 38.187.0.0 255.255.0.0
```

Project 10.3

To assign an IP address to both VLANs 2 and 3, do the following:

1. Select the interface to configure, using the following commands in Global Configuration Mode:

```
RSMOne(config)#interface vlan2
RSMOne(config-if)#
```

2. Assign an IP address to VLAN 2 and exit Configuration Mode:

```
RSMOne(config-if)#ip address 38.187.128.10 255.255.0.0
RSMOne(config-if)#exit
```

3. Do the same for VLAN 3:

```
RSMOne(config)#interface vlan3
RSMOne(config-if)#
RSMOne(config-if)#ip address 38.187.128.11 255.255.0.0
RSMOne(config-if)#exit
Coriolis5000RSM(config)#
```

4. Use the **no shutdown** command to initiate the changes without recycling the switch power.

Project 10.4

To assign a default gateway and verify the configuration, perform the following:

1. To define the gateway, in Global Configuration Mode use the following command combined with the route processor or router IP address that is acting as the default gateway for the network:

```
RSMOne(config)#ip default-gateway 38.187.120.254
```

2. To verify the IP configuration on the switch, use the following command:

```
Coriolis5000#show ip
IP Address: 38.187.120.4
Subnet Mask: 255.255.0.0
```

```
Default Gateway: 38.187.120.254
Management VLAN: 1
Domain name:
Name server 1: 0.0.0.0
Name server 2: 0.0.0.0
HM server : Enabled
HTTP port : 80
RIP : enabled
```

Project 10.5

To configure protocol filtering for IP only, do the following:

1. To configure protocol filtering on the Ethernet, Fast Ethernet, or Gigabit Ethernet ports, you must first enable protocol filtering on the switch. To enable protocol filtering, do the following in Privileged Mode on the RSM:

   ```
   RSMOne(enable) set protocolfilter enable
   ```

2. Configure port 2 on module 2 to **on** to filter all traffic unless it is IP-based:

   ```
   RSMOne(enable) set port protocol 2/2 ip on
   IP protocol set to on mode on module 2/2.
   Coriolis5000>(enable)
   ```

3. Do the same for port 3 on module 2:

   ```
   RSMOne(enable) set port protocol 2/3 ip on
   IP protocol set to on mode on module 2/3.
   Coriolis5000>(enable)
   ```

Chapter Eleven

Multilayer Switching

After completing this chapter, you will be able to:

✓ Understand Multilayer Switching (MLS) fundamentals

✓ Describe MLS components

✓ Explain how MLS works

✓ Configure MLS

✓ Apply flow masks

✓ Configure the MLS Engine

✓ Monitor MLS

Not so long ago, internetworking devices fit nicely within the confines of the Open System Interconnection (OSI) layer at which they operated and stayed within the tidy categories of bridges, routers, and switches. Bridges and switches operate at OSI Layer 2 to forward traffic to multiple segments at high speeds, and routers perform routing duties based on Layer 3 address information.

Lately, products have emerged that have blurred these distinctions. They are known by various names: multilayer switches, Layer 3 switches, routing switches, switching routers, and wire-speed routers. At the heart of the matter, these devices are simply a combination of Layer 2 switching with Layer 3 protocol routing.

Multilayer Switching (MLS) is a method for increasing the performance of IP routing by implementing routing functionality in advanced-design modules instead of the processor. This approach enables switch hardware to handle the routing functions previously performed by Layer 3 routers.

MLS is an important emerging technology that combines the functions of switching and routing and offers increased levels of performance and scalability to campus and enterprise networks. A significant area that separates MLS from traditional switching is its ability to detect network traffic conversations between network sources and destinations.

This chapter will discuss the MLS technology and how it relates to Cisco's implementation. We will describe the various components that are required to perform MLS on Catalyst switches. In addition, we will cover the mechanics of how to configure MLS. Let's begin with a discussion of what MLS is and how it can help your network's performance.

Overview of Multilayer Switching

Multilayer Switching (MLS) provides the same Layer 3 functionality that traditional routers have provided; but the actual Layer 3 switching functions occur on an Application-Specific Integrated Circuits (ASIC) module rather than the processor. MLS identifies network flows from a network source to a network destination by using the network and transport layer information in the packet headers, and then forwards the packets.

Multilayer switches have very high routing capacities and low latencies. They support the same routing protocols as do full-fledged routers such as Open Shortest Path First (OSPF), Routing Information Protocol (RIP), and Border Gateway Protocol (BGP), as well as features such as Internet Group Management Protocol (IGMP), Protocol Independent Multicast (PIM), and Distance Vector Multicast Routing Protocol (DVMRP).

You might ask, if multilayer switches offer all the benefits and features commonly associated with routing, why don't we just call them *routers*? There are a few good reasons.

First, multilayer switches are usually much faster and a lot less expensive than routers. In addition, some multilayer switches are simple, stackable workgroup switches that fall well short of the flexibility, port density, and features you find on most enterprise routers.

Protocol support on multilayer switches is also scant, with IP and (as of Cisco IOS version 12.1) Internetwork Packet Exchange (IPX) being the only protocols that support MLS. Finally, most switches—with the exception of the Catalyst 6000 family—offer little support for WAN interfaces commonly associated with traditional routers.

MLS Hardware and Software Requirements

Implementing MLS on a Catalyst switch requires a combination of functionalities that are implemented on hardware and software. At the core of Cisco's implementation of MLS is the NetFlow Feature Card (NFFC) functionality used with the Catalyst 5000 and Catalyst 6000 Series of switches.

In order to use the NFFC, you must have either a Supervisor Engine III with the NFFC daughter card (which also comes with the Policy Feature Card for Quality of Service [QoS] services); or the Supervisor IIG or IIIG card, which has the NFFC functionality incorporated into it and does not require a daughter card. Newer Catalyst models, such as the Catalyst 4908G-L3 or 2948G-L3 switch, also support the MLS functionality.

MLS also requires that you have either an internal Router Switch Module (RSM) blade or a Route Switch Feature Card (RSFC) with the Supervisor IIG or IIIG blade on the Catalyst 5000 Series of switches. On the Catalyst 6000 switches, you will need a Multilayer Switch Feature Card (MSFC) or Multilayer Switch Module (MSM).

You can also use suitable external routers that support the router component of MLS, including most of the models of larger size and capability such as the Cisco 7500, 7200, 4700, 4500, or 3600 Series. These devices must be equipped with an IOS image that is MLS-capable: IOS version 12.0(7)XE or later. The Catalyst 4908G-L3 or 2948G-L3 switch will always be shipped with an IOS version that supports MLS.

Types of Components

MLS is implemented by Cisco using three types of components:

- *MLS Switching Engine (MLS-SE)*—Moves and rewrites the data packets. It can be a Catalyst 2948G-L3 switch, a 4908G-L3 switch, or a Catalyst 5000 or 6000 Series switch with an NFFC or NFFC II. The MLS-SE provides Layer 3 LAN-switching services.

- *MLS Route Processor (MLS-RP)*—A Layer 3 device that is able to send MLS configurations and updates to Catalyst switches. This device can be an internal router, such as an RSM or RSFC in a Catalyst 5000, or an MSM or MSFC in a Catalyst 6000. The MLS-RP can also be an external router that supports MLS.
- *Multilayer Switching Protocol (MLSP)*—The protocol that runs between the MLS-SE and MLS-RP to enable MLS.

How MLS Works

Traditional Layer 3 protocols, such as IP or IPX, are connectionless in nature. They deliver every packet in a "best-effort" manner independent of any other packets. In real-life networks, however, network traffic is made up of a series of end-to-end conversations, or *flows*, between users or applications.

A flow is a sequence of packets that occurs in one direction between a particular source and destination that share the same protocol and transport-layer information. For instance, a host that is downloading data from a site and also browsing a Web page on the same site has two separate flows to that site. By identifying the unique flows between hosts, MLS can identify the user applications and classify traffic with the appropriate priority level.

Note: *For a flow to exist, the MLS-SE must know the paths to both the source and destination hosts.*

The goal in identifying the individual network flows is to provide more predictable network services by supplying dedicated bandwidth to those applications that need it. For instance, mission-critical enterprise resource planning (ERP) application traffic could be identified as high priority and receive more network bandwidth than File Transfer Protocol (FTP) transfers, which could be lower priority and receive less network usage.

To understand the MLS process better, let's examine how the data packets are forwarded in an MLS environment.

MLS Traffic Flow

When an MLS-RP starts up, it begins the MLSP operation by sending out a multicast hello message every 15 seconds to all switches in the network, informing them that it is an MLS-capable router. MLSP uses the Cisco Group Management Protocol (CGMP) multicast address, so all switches enabled for CGMP will hear it. To distinguish between normal CGMP messages and the MLS messages, the MLS-RP uses a different protocol type in the hello message.

The MLSP hello message contains information about the Media Access Control (MAC) addresses of the router, the router's virtual LAN (VLAN) information, and any changes to the router's routing information. If a switch has an MLS-SE component, it processes the hello message and records the MAC address of the MLS-RP in the MLS-SE's Content Addressable Memory (CAM) table. If multiple MLS-RPs exist in the network, the MLS-SE assigns a unique identifier—called an XTAG—to distinguish the network flows of each MLS-RP.

When a host on the network initiates a network flow that is destined for another VLAN, it sends the first packet to the MLS-RP. The MLS-SE will recognize this packet as a *candidate packet* for Layer 3 switching, because the MLS-SE has already learned the MLS-RP's destination MAC address and VLAN through MLSP and has an entry in its MLS cache.

The MLS-SE extracts the Layer 3 information for the flow, including the destination address, source address, and protocol port numbers, and forwards the first packet to the MLS-RP. Because this is the first packet, no cache entry exists; a partial MLS entry for this Layer 3 flow is created in the MLS cache.

When the MLS-RP receives the packet, it looks at its route table to determine the destination of the packet and applies any applicable access control lists or class of service (COS) policy for which the packet may be eligible. The MLS-RP rewrites the MAC header, adding a new destination MAC address (that of the destination host) and using its own MAC address as the source address. The MLS-RP routes the packet back to the MLS-SE.

Based on the entries the switch has in its CAM table, the switch knows the port to which to forward the packet. The MLS-SE also determines that the MAC address is that of the MLS-RP and that the packet's flow information matches a candidate entry in its MLS cache. The MLS-SE regards this as an *enabler packet* and completes the entry in the MLS cache begun by the candidate packet.

Note: *The maximum MLS cache size is 128K. However, when an MLS cache is larger than 32K, the probability increases that a flow will not be switched by the MLS-SE and will be forwarded to the router.*

Once the entry for the flow has been completed in the MLS cache, any further packets that are identified as belonging to the same flow are Layer 3 switched based on the cached information. The MLS-SE rewrites the headers, recomputes the checksums, and forwards the packets without their having to go through the router.

Note: *The MLS-SE rewrites the packets to look just as if they had been forwarded by a router.*

The MLS cache maintains flow information for all active flows. The state and identity of the flows are maintained as long as packet traffic for that flow is active.

When traffic for a flow is stopped, the MLS cache entry ages out. If an entry is not used for the specified period of time, the entry ages out, and statistics for that flow can be exported to a flow collector application.

MLS Flow Masks

Flow mask modes are used by the MLS-SE to determine how the network flows are compared to the MLS cache entries. The flow mask mode used is determined by the access lists that are configured on the MLS-RP. The MLS-SE is given this information via the MLSP messages from each MLS-RP for which the MLS-SE performs Layer 3 switching. Only one flow mask—the most specific one—is used for all MLS-SEs. If a different flow mask is detected, the MLS-SE changes its flow mask to the most specific flow mask detected. When the Policy Feature Card (PFC) flow mask changes, the entire MLS cache is purged.

The MLS-SE supports these three flow masks for IP MLS:

- *Destination-IP*—This is the least-specific, default flow mask. The MLS-SE will maintain one MLS entry for each destination IP address. Any flows that go to a given destination IP address will use this MLS entry.
- *Source-destination-IP*—The MLS-SE maintains one MLS entry for each source and destination IP address pair. All flows between a given source and destination use this MLS entry regardless of which IP protocol interfaces are in use. If a standard access list is used on an MLS-RP, this flow mode is used.
- *IP-flow*—This is the most specific flow mask. The MLS-SE creates a separate MLS cache entry for all IP flows. The IP-flow entry contains the source IP address, destination IP address, protocol, and protocol interfaces.

The flow mask mode you choose impacts the screen output of the **show mls ip** command. In Destination Mode, the destination IP address of the switched flows is displayed, along with the packet rewrite information.

Effect of IP Features on MLS

Some Cisco IOS commands affect how MLS operates. Any command that involves the router examining each packet to perform an action will disable MLS on an interface. Some examples of such commands are:

- **clear ip route**—Clears all MLS cache entries for all the switches that are acting as layer switches for this MLS-RP.
- **ip tcp header-compression**—Disables MLS on the interface.
- **ip tcp compression-connection**—Also disables MLS on the interface.
- **no ip routing**—Purges all MLS caches and disables MLS on the interface.
- **ip security**—All forms of this command disable MLS on the interface.

Some IP features also have a negative impact on MLS, including the following:

- *Data encryption*—When data encryption is configured on the interface, MLS will not work.
- *Policy route map*—Policy route maps disable MLS.
- *Network Address Translation (NAT)*—MLS is disabled on an interface when NAT is configured on the interface.
- *Committed access rate (CAR)*—CAR will disable MLS on the interface.
- *IP accounting*—This feature will not work if MLS is enabled on the interface.

IP Access Lists and MLS Interaction

Any interface that has an input access list applied to it cannot be used for MLS. However, you can apply an output access list on an interface, and it will not affect MLS negatively. In fact, with MLS enabled, standard and extended access lists are handled at wire speed; any modifications or changes to the access lists that are applied to the MLS-RP take effect immediately on the MLS-SE. This is true for access list changes on either internal or external routers.

To illustrate this concept, suppose that a host wishes to communicate with another host. It first sends a packet to the MLS-RP. If an access list is configured on the MLS-RP to deny access from the first host to the second, the MLS-RP receives the packet, checks the access list to see whether any of the access list's conditions are met, and, if so, discards the packet based on the access list. Because the first packet for the flow never returns from the MLS-RP, the MLS cache entry is not completed by the MLS-SE.

If a flow has been established by the MLS-SE and a new access list is created on the MLS-RP, the MLS-SE learns of the change through MLSP, immediately enforcing the access list's conditions for the flow. As a result, the MLS-SE purges the cache entry from the MLS cache. Any new flows are created based on the access list.

Configuring MLS

Setting up MLS in your network requires the following steps:

- Configuring the MLS route processor
- Configuring the MLS switch engine

We will discuss these steps in the following sections.

Configure the MLS Route Processor

To configure the MLS-RP for MLS involves the following tasks:

- Enabling MLSP
- Adding the VLAN ID to the router interface
- Adding the MLS interface to the Virtual Trunking Protocol (VTP) domain
- Enabling MLS on the router interface
- Specifying the management interface

Let's examine each of these tasks.

Enable the MLSP on the MLS-RP

The first step in configuring MLS in the network is to enable the MLSP that runs between the MLS-SE and the MLS-RP. To enable MLSP on an MLS-RP, enter the following command in Global Mode:

```
Router(config) mls rp ip
```

As of Cisco IOS 12.0, you can also enable MLSP to multilayer-switch IPX packets. To do so, enter the following command:

```
Router(config) mls rp ipx
```

To display the IP MLS route process configuration of the switch, enter the following command:

```
Router# show mls rp
ip multilayer switching is globally enabled
ipx multilayer switching is globally enabled
ipx mls inbound acl override is globally disabled
mls id is 0040.0bd0.11e0
mls ip address 192.168.1.1
mls ip flow mask is destination
mls ipx flow mask is unknown
number of domains configured for mls 0
```

To see which MLS-RPs are configured for a switch, use the following command:

```
Console> (enable) show mls include
Included MLS-RP
---------------
192.168.1.2
192.168.2.1
Console> (enable)
```

To display MLS information for a specific MLS-RP on a switch, enter the following:

```
Console> (enable) show mls rp 192.168.1.2
MLS-RP IP      MLS-RP ID      Xtag   MLS-RP              MAC-Vlans
---------      ---------      ----   ------              ---------
192.168.1.2    0000808cece0   2      00-00-80-8c-ec-e0   1-20
```

Assign a VLAN ID to the MLS-RP

MLS requires inter-VLAN routing, because the packet-forwarding decisions are based on which VLANs have been configured on the ports. Because internal route processors such as the MSM, MSFC, RSM, or RSFC by design use VLAN IDs to identify their interfaces, it is not necessary to configure a VLAN ID for them.

On the other hand, external route processors have no knowledge about VLANs, because they are configured using subnets; therefore, you must assign them a VLAN ID. The interface must be either Ethernet or Fast Ethernet, and it cannot be a subinterface. To configure a VLAN ID for an external router, enter the following command:

```
Router(config) interface fastethernet 1/1
Router(config) mls rp vlan-id 2
```

11

Add an MLS Interface to a VTP Domain

The next step in configuring MLS is to determine which of the MLS-RP interfaces will be MLS interfaces and to add them to the VTP domain of which your switch is a member. A switch can be a member of only one domain, and the MLS interface must be part of that domain. Enter the following commands to add an interface to a VTP domain:

```
Router(config) interface fastethernet 1/1
Router(config) mls rp vtp-domain coriolis
```

Warning: This step must be performed before any other MLS interface commands are entered on the MLS interface. Otherwise, the interface will be placed in the NULL domain and will be unable to perform MLS for that interface.

To display the MLS VTP domain information, enter the following command:

```
Router# show mls rp vtp-domain coriolis
vlan domain name: coriolis
   current flow mask: ip-flow
   current sequence number: 80709115
```

```
current/maximum retry count: 0/10
current domain state: no-change
current/next global purge: false/false
current/next purge count: 0/0
domain uptime: 13:07:36
keepalive timer expires in 8 seconds
retry timer not running
change timer not running
fcp subblock count = 7

1 management interface(s) currently defined:
   fastethernet 1/1 on Vlan2

1 mac-vlan(s) configured for multi-layer switching:

   mac 00e0.fefc.6000
      vlan id(s)
      2

router currently aware of following 1 switch(es):
   switch id 0010.1192.b5ff
```

To see MLS information about specific interfaces, enter the following command:

```
Router# show mls rp interface vlan 2
mls active on Vlan2, domain coriolis
```

Enable MLS on an Interface

Each interface that is to participate in MLS must have MLS enabled on it after it has been placed into a VTP domain. To enable MLS on an interface, perform this task in Interface Configuration Mode:

```
Router(config)interface fastethernet 1/1
Router(config-if)#mls rp ip
```

Assign an MLS Management Interface

MLSP sends hello messages, advertises route changes, and advertises VLAN and MAC addresses through a management interface. You must specify one of the MLS-RP's interfaces as a management interface, or MLSP packets will not be sent or received. The management interface can be any MLS interface connected to the Catalyst switch. Multiple management interfaces can be configured, but doing so is unnecessary and only adds to the management overhead for the MLS-RP.

To enable an interface to be a management interface, use the following command:

```
Router#(config)interface fastethernet 1/1
Router(config)mls rp management-interface
```

Configure the MLS Switch Engine

By default, MLS is enabled on all Catalyst switches that support Layer 3 switching. You need to enable it only if you have disabled it at some point with a **no mls ip** command. To re-enable MLS on a Catalyst 6000, use the following commands:

```
Switch(config)interface vlan 10
Switch(config)mls ip
```

To re-enable MLS on a Catalyst 5000, use the following command:

```
Switch(enable) set mls enable
```

Configure an MLS Route Processor

If the MLS-RP is an external router, the IP address of the MLS-RP must be configured in order for the switch to participate in MLS. If an external router has not been configured as an MLS-RP, the MLS-SE cannot process MLSP.

You do not need to configure an internal routing module as an MLS-RP, because such modules participate in MLS automatically. If you physically remove an internal MLS-RP or disable MLS on the MLS-RP, the MLS-RP entry is removed from the MLS-RP list.

On the Catalyst 2926G-L3, 4908G-L3, or 2948G-L3 switch, at least one MLS-RP must be configured. Multiple MLS-RPs can be configured in a single line; up to 16 MLS-RPs can participate in MLS.

To configure an MLS-RP, use the following command:

```
Console> (enable) set mls include 192.168.1.2 192.168.2.1
Multilayer switching is enabled for router 192.168.1.2 192.168.2.1
```

Configure the MLS Cache

The MLS cache maintains flow information for all active flows and is limited to a maximum size of 128K. Because of this size limitation, MLS entries are periodically dropped from the cache. This can occur if no enabler packet is seen within five seconds of a candidate packet. It also occurs if no traffic takes place in a network flow for 256 seconds. Of course, routing changes or other network conditions can also purge these entries from the cache.

You can change the amount of time the MLS cache keeps an entry in its table to a setting other than the 256 seconds by using the **agingtime** command. The aging time can be configured from 8 to 2,032 seconds (in 8-second increments). At the end of the aging time interval, if no further packets are seen in a network flow, the entry will be deleted from the MLS cache. An example of this command is shown here:

```
Console>(enable) set mls agingtime 512
Multilayer switching aging time set to 512
```

You can also make sure entries are not kept in your cache longer than necessary by using the **agingtime fast** command. This command is useful for eliminating entries in the cache that are short lived, or that make a connection to something and then terminate. Domain Name Service (DNS) lookups are an example.

After the host has received the information, it does not need to maintain an entry in the MLS cache for further flows, because there will be no successive packets. Detecting and aging out these entries saves a lot of MLS cache space for real data traffic.

Tip: Cisco recommends that the number of MLS cache entries be kept below 32K. To do this, set the initial aging time value to 128 seconds. If the number of cache entries continues to go over 32K, decrease the aging time setting and adjust it as necessary. If cache entries continue to go over 32K, decrease the normal aging time in increments of 64 seconds from the 256-second default until the cache remains below 32K.

The **agingtime fast** command has two parameters:

- **fastaging time**—The amount of time an entry remains in the cache. The default for **fastaging time** is 0, which means no fast aging occurs. This value can be configured for 32, 64, 96, or 128 seconds (values were picked for efficient aging).
- **pkt_threshold**—The number of packets that must be detected in the cache time. The default parameter value is 0. You can configure it to 0, 1, 3, 7, 15, 31, or 63 (again, values were picked for efficient aging). If fast aging time is not configured to one of the values indicated, it adjusts to the closest value. An example of how to use this command is as follows:

```
Console>(enable) set mls agingtime fast 32 0
Multilayer switching fast aging time set to 32 seconds for entries
with no more than 0 packets switched.
```

On the Catalyst 6000, the configuration of MLS aging is a little different. It is configured on the switch using the **mls aging** command, which has three parameters:

- **normal**—Configures the wait before aging out and deleting shortcut entries in the Layer 3 table. The **normal** parameter can be in the range of 32 to 4,092 seconds.
- **fast aging**—Similar to the Catalyst 5000 process to age out entries created for flows that use a few packets and then are never used again. The **fast aging** parameter uses the **time** value to see if the **threshold** keyword number of packets has been switched on the flow. If the specified number of packets hasn't been flowed in the allotted time, the entry is flushed. Both the **fast aging threshold** and **time** parameters can be in the range of 1 to 128 seconds.
- **long**—Flushes out entries that have been in use for the specified value even if the Layer 3 entry is still in use. This parameter is used to prevent inaccurate statistics. The **long** parameter is in the range of 64 to 900 seconds.

An example of configuring MLS aging is as follows:

```
Router#configure terminal
Enter configuration commands, one per line. End with CNTL/Z.
Router(config)#mls aging fast threshold 64 time 30 long 900 normal 300
```

11

To see the MLS aging time configuration, enter the following command:

```
Router# show mls aging
enable          timeout   packet   threshold
------          -------   ------   ---------
normal aging    false      300      N/A
fast aging      false      32       100
long aging      false      900      N/A
```

Monitoring MLS

The **show mls** command illustrates how to display MLS information on the MLS-SE:

```
Console> (enable) show mls
Multilayer switching enabled
Multilayer switching aging time = 256 seconds
Multilayer switching fast aging time = 0 seconds, packet threshold = 1
```

```
Destination-ip flow
Total packets switched = 101892
Active entries = 2153
Netflow data export enabled
Netflow data export configured for port 8010 on host 10.0.2.15
Total packets exported = 20

MLS-RP IP      MLS-RP ID     Xtag   MLS-RP MAC-Vlans
---------      ---------     ----   ----------------
192.168.1.2    0000808cece0   2     00-00-80-8c-ec-e0 1
192.168.2.1    0000808c1214   3     00-00-80-8c-12-14 2
```

This command gives you a lot of information about MLS, including:

- Whether MLS is enabled
- The aging time for an MLS cache entry
- The fast aging time and the threshold for a flow
- The type of flow mask being used
- How many packets have been switched
- How many entries are in the MLS cache
- Whether NetFlow has been enabled, and on which port
- Total number of packets exported
- What MLS-RPs have been configured, their MAC addresses, their XTAG values, and the VLANs they support

On the Catalyst 6000, you can get information similar to that provided by the previous command by entering the following:

```
Console> (enable) show mls ip
Total Active MLS entries = 0
Total packets switched = 0
IP Multilayer switching enabled
IP Multilayer switching aging time = 256 seconds
IP Multilayer switching fast aging time = 0 seconds,
packet threshold = 0
IP Flow mask: Full Flow
Configured flow mask is Destination flow
Active IP MLS entries = 0
Netflow Data Export version: 8
Netflow Data Export disabled
Netflow Data Export port/host is not configured
Total packets exported = 0
```

```
MSFC ID   Module   XTAG   MAC                 Vlans
-------   ------   ----   ---                 -----
52.0.03   15       1      01-10-29-8a-0c-00   1,10,123,434,121
                                              222,666,959
```

To display all entries in the MLS cache, enter the following command:

```
Console> (enable) show mls entry

Destination IP      Source IP    Port  DstPrt SrcPrt Destination Mac
--------------      ---------    ----  ------ ------ ---------------
MLS-RP 192.168.1.2:
192.168.6.2         192.168.26.9 UDP   6009   69     00-10-0b-16-98-00
192.168.26.9        192.168.6.2  UDP   6002   69     00-00-00-00-00-09

Vlan  Port
----  ----
250   1/1-2
26    4/7
```

To display MLS entries for a specific destination IP address, enter the following command:

```
Console> (enable) show mls entry destination 192.168.1.2/24

Destination IP     Source IP    Port DstPrt SrcPrt Destination Mac
--------------     ---------    ---- ------ ------ ---------------
MLS-RP 192.168.1.2:
172.20.22.14       192.168.1.10 TCP  6001   Telnet 00-60-70-6c-fc-224

Vlan  Port
----  ----
      2/1
```

Chapter Summary

In this chapter, we have discussed Multilayer Switching (MLS) technology and how it is implemented in a Cisco environment. MLS provides the same Layer 3 functionality as traditional routers do, but the actual Layer 3 switching functions occur on an ASIC module rather than on a router's processor.

MLS works by identifying network flows on a network. These flows are unidirectional conversations from a source host to a network destination. By using the network and transport layer information in the packet headers and then forwarding the packets via dedicated ASICs, MLS provides a tremendous performance improvement over traditional forms of routing.

MLS comprises three components:

- *MLS Switching Engine (MLS-SE)*—Available on the Catalyst 5000 and 6000 Series of switches with the NetFlow Feature Card (NFFC) or the latest Supervisor Engines with the NFFC functionality built in. The Catalyst 2926G, 2948G-L3, and 4908G-L3 switches also provide MLS-SE features.
- *MLS Route Processor (MLS-RP)*—Can be an internal routing blade, such as the RSM or RSFC in a Catalyst 5000, or an MSM or MSFC in a Catalyst 6000. The MLS-RP can also be one of the Cisco routers that support MLS.
- *MLS Switching Protocol (MLSP)*—Runs between the MLS-SE and the MLS-RP.

In effect, MLS emulates the same techniques as traditional routers, without having to send the packets to the router to resolve Layer 3 addresses. The MLS-RP and the MLS-SE know of each other through MLSP hello messages. When a router interface gets the bits from a network stream, the router does what it has always done: It checks for a valid packet, examines the routing table to determine where to send the packet, builds a new header with the router's MAC address as the source address, and sends the packet to the destination out the destination interface.

When the switch gets this packet, it notices the source destination is from the MLS-RP, because the switch has received MLSP messages with the router's MAC address. So, it builds a cache table for the network flow and substitutes its MAC address for the source address. In this manner, any successive packets in that flow are multilayer-switched by the MLS-SE without having to use the router.

The MLS cache maintains flow information for all active flows. The state and identity of the flows are maintained as long as packet traffic for that flow is active. MLS builds the MLS cache based upon information it has learned in the packet header.

A flow mask specifies how the MLS entry is created based on the source, destination, and transport port information in the header. This information is sent by the MLS-RP to all MLS-SEs using the MLSP. Only the most specific flow mask is used by the MLS-SE. There are three types of flow masks: destination-IP, source-destination IP, and IP-flow.

Some Cisco IOS features have negative effects on MLS, and should be avoided—for example, actions such as clearing the IP routing table, using header compression, or applying security. Some IOS features, such as data encryption, network address translation, and IP accounting, can also have an effect on MLS. In addition, IP access lists can impact MLS. Any interface to which MLS is applied cannot have an input access list applied to it. On the other hand, input access lists can be modified to be outbound access lists, which are executed at wire speed.

Configuring MLS involves tasks on the MLS-RP and the MLS-SE. If you are using an internal router on the Catalyst 5000, the only tasks necessary are to enable MLS on each interface. You must do so only if MLS has been disabled, because the interfaces are MLS-enabled by default. You also need to make sure the interfaces are in the same VTP domain. On a Catalyst 6000, the tasks are even easier: No configuration is needed unless you have disabled MLS.

If you are using an external router, you need to configure it to use MLS. If your switch has been defined to be in a VTP domain, the MLS-RP must be in the same domain or no MLS will occur. You must configure each interface acting as an MLS-RP for MLS. At least one interface must be configured as the MLS management interface. Finally, if the router is connected via non-trunk links to the switch, you need to configure a VLAN ID for each link.

On the MLS-SE, you will need to configure the switch to know the IP destination of the MLS-RP if it is an external router. If it is an internal MLS-RP, no configuration tasks are needed. The default behavior of IP is to maintain a cache entry for each destination IP address. This entry can be modified either to a source-destination pair or to a more specific IP flow.

The processing of the MLS cache entries may cause performance problems on your switch, so monitoring the IP cache is a good practice. The MLS cache is limited to a maximum size of 128K, so packets are regularly dropped from the cache. The pruning mechanism can be modified. You can modify the MLS cache flows with the aging time process, which limits how long the MLSP waits before flushing cache entries. At the end of the aging time interval, if no other traffic flow has occurred, the entry is flushed.

Another good method for keeping the size of the cache more manageable is to have the MLS cache prune entries that are no longer needed. This type of pruning is known as fast aging time. This method deals with the types of connections that are used by IP hosts for a single connection but are never used again—for instance, DNS lookups or Trivial File Transfer Protocol (TFTP) transfers. Once these types of connections are completed, there is no need to maintain a cache entry for the traffic flow, because the traffic flow is over.

Review Questions

1. Which of the following switches does not support MLS?
   a. Catalyst 4908G-L3
   b. Catalyst 2948G-L3
   c. Catalyst 5000 with Supervisor IIG
   d. Catalyst 6000 with Supervisor IA

2. How often does MLSP send out hello messages?
   a. Every 10 seconds
   b. Every 15 seconds
   c. Every 30 seconds
   d. When the router powers up
3. Which identifier does an MLS-SE insert to distinguish MLS-RP?
   a. XTAG
   b. VLAN ID
   c. Netflow ID
   d. RP ID
4. What is the first packet received in a network flow, which makes a partial entry in the MLS cache?
   a. Enabler packet
   b. Candidate packet
   c. Initial packet
   d. MLS header packet
5. What is the packet received in a network flow that completes the MLS cache entry for a network flow?
   a. Enabler packet
   b. Candidate packet
   c. Final packet
   d. MLS end packet
6. What is the maximum size of the MLS cache?
   a. 32K
   b. 64K
   c. 128K
   d. 256K
7. Which of the following flow masks are used with MLS?
   a. Destination-IP
   b. Source-destination-IP
   c. IP-flow
   d. All of the above

8. MLS is disabled if Network Address Translation is used.
   a. True
   b. False
9. Which type of access list cannot be used with MLS?
   a. Input access list
   b. Output access list
   c. Standard access list
   d. Extended access list
10. Which command enables MLSP on an MLS-RP?
   a. **mls rp ip**
   b. **mls ip rp**
   c. **set mls ip**
   d. **mls rp**
11. Which command is used to see the MLS-RPs configured for a switch?
   a. **show mls rp ip-addr**
   b. **show mls rp**
   c. **show mls include**
   d. All of the above
12. In which VTP domain should an MLS-RP be placed?
   a. A unique VTP domain.
   b. The same domain as the MLS-SE.
   c. The NULL domain.
   d. There is no requirement for the MLS-RP.
13. Which domain is the MLS-RP placed in if it is not explicitly placed in a VTP domain?
   a. The default VTP domain
   b. The same domain as the switch
   c. The NULL domain
   d. VTP domain 1
14. On which part of a router should MLS be configured?
   a. Globally
   b. Any interface that participates in MLS
   c. Both a and b
   d. Neither a nor b

15. MLS is enabled by default on all switches.
    a. True
    b. False
16. An MLS-RP must be configured for which of the following switches?
    a. Catalyst 2926G
    b. Catalyst 2948G-L3
    c. 4908G-L3
    d. All of the above
    e. Both a and b
17. How long after a candidate entry has been seen must an enabler packet be seen before the entry is dropped from the MLS cache?
    a. 5 seconds
    b. 15 seconds
    c. 30 seconds
    d. No time requirement
18. Which command changes the amount of time an entry is kept in an MLS cache?
    a. **set aging time**
    b. **set age time**
    c. **set agingtime**
    d. **set threshold**
19. What is the range in which the aging time can be configured?
    a. 1 to 1,024 seconds
    b. 8 to 246 seconds
    c. 8 to 2,032 seconds
    d. 32 to 128 seconds
20. What size does Cisco recommend the MLS cache be kept below?
    a. 32K
    b. 64K
    c. 128K
    d. 256K

Real-World Projects

Joe Snow has just completed a major upgrade to his Catalyst 5000 and added new modules that give him many additional features. He has purchased a new Supervisor Engine III module to upgrade his Supervisor II—it will give him much more processing power and other benefits. In addition, he has purchased a Route Switch Feature Card (RSFC) to give him an internal router blade on the switch. He has also purchased a NetFlow Feature Card (NFFC) daughter card for his Supervisor Engine. He wants to set up MLS on his switch to take advantage of the wire-speed capabilities of the MLS process.

Project 11.1

To configure MLS on a route processor, perform the following:

1. Globally enable MLS with this command:

```
Router(config) mls rp ip
```

2. In order to place the VLANs in the same VTP domain, the MLS interface must agree:

```
Router(config) Interface vlan 100
Router(config-if)ip address 192.138.1.2 255.255.255.0
Router(config-if)mls rp ip
Router(config-if)mls rp vtp-domain coriolis
```

3. Set up one of the interfaces as the MLS management interface:

```
Router(config-if)interface vlan 110
Router(config-if)ip address 192.168.2.1 255.255.255.0
Router(config-if)mls rp ip
Router(config-if)mls rp management-interface
```

4. To see if MLS has been configured correctly, issue the following command:

```
Router# show mls rp
multilayer switching is globally enabled
mls id is 0006.7c71.8600
mls ip address 192.168.1.2
mls flow mask is destination-ip
```

11

```
number of domains configured for mls 1
vlan domain name: coriolis
   current flow mask: destination-ip
   current sequence number: 82078006
   current/maximum retry count: 0/10
   current domain state: no-change
   current/next global purge: false/false
   current/next purge count: 0/0
   domain uptime: 02:54:21
   keepalive timer expires in 11 seconds
   retry timer not running
   change timer not running

   1 management interface(s) currently defined:
      vlan 1 on Vlan110

   2 mac-vlan(s) configured for multi-layer switching:

      mac 0006.7c71.8600
         vlan id(s)
         1    3

   router currently aware of following 1 switch(es):
      switch id 00e0.fe4a.aeff
```

Everything looks good here. Now, Joe goes to his switch to do some work.

Project 11.2

To enable and configure MLS on a switch, perform the following:

1. Enable MLS on the switch:

```
Console> (enable) set mls enable
```

2. To make sure MLS cache entries do not stay too long after they're no longer needed, modify the aging time value:

```
Console> (enable) set mls agingtime 512
Multilayer switching aging time set to 512
Console> (enable)

Console> (enable) set mls agingtime fast 32 0
Multilayer switching fast aging time set to 32 seconds for entries
with no more than 0 packets switched.
Console> (enable)
```

3. Issue the **show mls** command to verify the MLS operation:

```
Console> (enable) show mls
Multilayer switching enabled
Multilayer switching aging time = 512 seconds
Multilayer switching fast aging time = 32 seconds, packet threshold = 1
Destination-ip flow
Total packets switched = 101892
Active entries = 2153
Total packets exported = 20

MLS-RP IP      MLS-RP ID      Xtag   MLS-RP             MAC-Vlans
---------      ----------     ----   ------             ---------
192.168.1.2    0000808cece0    2     00-00-80-8c-ec-e0   100

192.168.2.1    0000808c1214    3     00-00-80-8c-12-14   110
```

Chapter Twelve

Hot Standby Routing Protocol

After completing this chapter, you will be able to:

- ✓ Identify problems using a default gateway
- ✓ Identify problems using a proxy ARP
- ✓ Identify problems using RIP
- ✓ Identify problems using IRDP
- ✓ Identify the HSRP groups
- ✓ Identify HSRP group member types
- ✓ Identify the virtual MAC and IP addresses
- ✓ Configure HSRP groups
- ✓ Understand the HSRP message fields
- ✓ Explain the difference between active and standby routers
- ✓ List the HSRP interface states
- ✓ Configure internal route processors for HSRP
- ✓ Configure optional settings for HSRP

When administrators design a network, their goal is to build in redundancy as best they can. In a true Cisco Switched Campus Model, every device has a backup device standing by in case of a failure. Route processor devices such as internal cards in multilayer switches and routers have traditionally been among the hardest devices to configure for fast convergence redundancy. Several techniques and special uses of protocols have been devised by different administrators to overcome this IP-based problem—all of which, before Hot Standby Routing Protocol (HSRP), have had certain problems to overcome.

The Cisco Switched Campus Model builds redundancy into the Layer 2 switch block level devices. HSRP was designed to build in redundancy in the Layer 3 routing devices found in the core layer of the network. It provides convergence in seconds without manual intervention from a system administrator—while remaining transparent to the interfaces on the network. It can be applied to almost any LAN type, which is a great asset to this protocol.

Problems to Overcome

In a standard LAN environment, end-user workstations, servers, and other peripherals lack the ability to exchange routing information to other segments. They may be able to assign a Layer 3 destination address to the header of a data packet and route that packet to a default gateway, but they can't route that data out of the local LAN segment.

Note: *The default gateway is the protocol address for the route processor to which data packets containing a destination address outside of the local segment are sent.*

In order to route information out of the local LAN segment, a host uses a preconfigured or Dynamic Host Configuration Protocol (DHCP) assigned default gateway. In the event that the Layer 3 routing device assigned as the default gateway fails, all the devices on the local LAN can communicate only with each other. The local collision or broadcast domain becomes the entire network in the eyes of each device. You can place another default gateway on the network, but there is no clear way of providing a secondary configuration to another default route without manual configuration by an administrator.

The time involved in restoring Layer 3 connectivity without considerable delay exceeds the tolerance of most network users—especially in large network segments. Let's look at some ways that administrators and engineers have devised to overcome the problem of an assigned default gateway and the associated benefits and difficulties for each technique. The protocols we'll look at are as follows:

- Proxy Address Resolution Protocol (Proxy ARP)
- Routing Information Protocol (RIP)
- ICMP Router Discovery Protocol (IRDP)

Proxy ARP

One solution to creating redundancy for Layer 3 is to use Proxy Address Resolution Protocol (Proxy ARP). The Proxy ARP broadcasts an IP ARP request for the Media Access Control (MAC) address of the router. The router replies with the MAC address of the requesting node.

If there is a failure, however, the node configured for the default gateway has two options. Either the node must be rebooted or it must wait for the ARP protocol update and for the flush period of the ARP entry to expire. This delay creates a very high convergence period.

Routing Information Protocol

Another solution designed to inject Layer 3 routing redundancy allows nodes utilizing IP to use Routing Information Protocol (RIP) to discover secondary routers located on the network. This method allows the end-user node to maintain a routing table that determines the shortest path by calculating the number of hops and using the router with the fewest hops.

However, RIP has a very slow convergence time when a change in the network topology occurs. It may take up to three times the interval set in the update interval setting before RIP chooses another default route from the table.

ICMP Router Discovery Protocol

ICMP Router Discovery Protocol (IRDP) is probably one of the longest protocol names to come along. It is another solution to the redundant secondary router problem. IRDP is one of the most commonly used solutions for locating a redundant router in the event of failure when HSRP is not implemented in the network.

IRDP is an extension of the Internet Control Message Protocol (ICMP) that is used to allow network administrators to ping and trace the routes of other interfaces in the network as they troubleshoot network problems. ICMP provides the mechanisms that allow routers to advertise the default routes available in the network.

This protocol has far more features than RIP and Proxy ARP for discovering the addresses of the neighboring routers. It requires no manual configuration by an administrator, and the host interfaces don't need to understand any routing protocols.

Hosts that use IRDP listen for a hello multicast message from the default router. Each hello multicast message—also known as an *IRDP advertisement*—is valid for a predefined value included in the header of the IRDP advertisement and applies to all addresses in the packet. In the event that the host interface does not receive another IRDP advertisement during the predefined value—sometimes referred to as the *lifetime value*—the host interface considers the default route void.

One of the problems with IRDP is its high convergence time in the event of a failure. The default lifetime of the default route is 30 minutes, and advertisements are sent every 7 to 10 minutes. The router controls the interval at which the advertisement messages are sent. IRDP requires you to configure two separate intervals on the router: the minimum advertising interval and the maximum advertising interval. All advertisements are sent during that window of time. A change in the network topology can go unnoticed for almost 30 minutes. A solution to all these problems faced by network administrators was needed.

THE SOLUTION

The Hot Standby Routing Protocol (HSRP) is a proprietary protocol from Cisco that provides a Layer 3 redundant route processor solution. HSRP is very similar to the Virtual Router Redundancy Protocol (VRRP), which is an IETF standard.

HSRP uses a priority scheme to determine which HSRP-configured router is to be the default active router. To configure a router as the active router, you assign a default priority to the standby interface that is higher than the priority of all the other HSRP-configured route processor interfaces.

HSRP works by exchanging multicast messages that advertise priority among HSRP-configured route processor interfaces. When the active router fails to send a hello message within the configurable period of time, the standby router with the highest priority becomes the active router. (Hello messages will be covered later in this chapter.)

HSRP defines a group of routers working together as one virtual router. It enables host interfaces to continue communicating outside the local segment even if the host interface's default route fails. With HSRP, a group of routers works in tandem to provide fault tolerance.

HSRP assigns the group of routers to a virtual IP address and a MAC address. Because the routers in the group route packets to a virtual IP address, packets are still routed through the network even when their destination router is pushed off a shelf in your wiring closet and suffers from Humpty-Dumpty syndrome—you can't put it back together again. Routers can fail for many reasons, most of which relate to electrical and component issues.

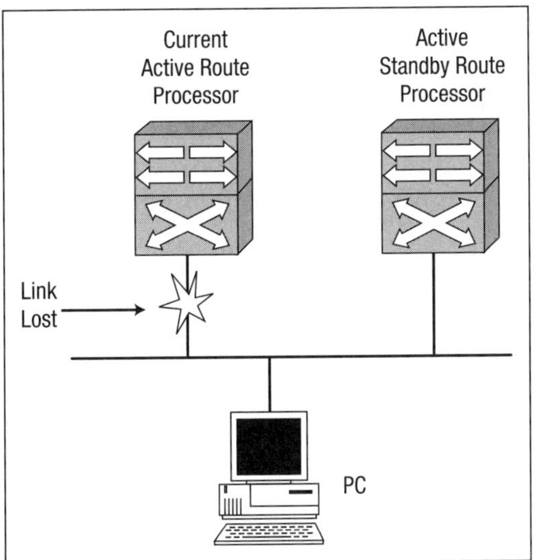

Figure 12.1 Two routers and a link failure. The standby route processor assumes the failed default route processor's position in the network.

HSRP is one of the best solutions when host interfaces on a local LAN segment require continuous access to the network resources. As shown in Figure 12.1, when a failure does occur, HSRP automatically lets the elected standby route processor assume the role and function of the offline router.

HSRP classifies each route processor on the network into standby groups. More than one standby group can be assigned to each route processor. The number of standby groups that can be assigned is limited by the physical topology being used. Table 12.1 shows the number of standby groups that can be configured on each type of physical LAN topology. Each group contains a route processor in each of the following roles:

- Active route processor
- Standby route processor
- Virtual route processor

All other route processors fall into the "other route processor" category.

Table 12.1 The maximum number of standby groups that can be assigned to a route processor based on the physical topology.

Topology	Standby Groups
Ethernet	255
FDDI	255
Token Ring	3

Warning: By increasing the number of standby groups on a route processor, you decrease the route processor's performance and increase latency. You would primarily increase the number of standby groups to facilitate load sharing.

In the standby group, the route processor with the highest priority becomes the active router or the default gateway. In later sections, you will learn how to configure the standby priority. If it is not manually assigned, the priority is 100. But what if none of the route processors has a group priority assigned? In the case of equal priority between more than one route processor in the group, the route processor with the highest IP address for the respective group will be elected as the active route processor. In addition, the route processor with the second highest IP address will become the standby route processor. All the other route processors will be placed in a listen state (discussed in the next section).

The standby router will take over once three hello messages are not received by the route processor that is currently active for the group. The actual convergence time is contingent upon the HSRP timers for the group. The HSRP **hellotime** timer defaults to 3, and the **holdtime** timer defaults to 10. An interesting feature of HSRP is that the standby route processor will take over even if the active router's LAN interface state is displaying the message "interface up line protocol down."

HSRP Message Format

All route processors in the HSRP standby group send and receive HSRP messages to and from one another. The messages are used to determine the roles of each route processor in the group. User Datagram Protocol (UDP) utilizing TCP port 1985 encapsulates the data in the data portion of the UDP packet. The packet is then sent to an all-router multicast address with a time to live (TTL) of one hop.

The fields contained in the HSRP message are as follows:

- **Version**—Indicates the HSRP version.
- **Op Code**—Describes the type of message contained in the packet. There are three types of messages:
  - **Hello**—The first and most common is a hello message, which is sent to indicate that a route processor in the standby group is functioning in the group.
  - **Coup**—The coup message is used when a route processor wants to become the active route processor.
  - **Resign**—The resign message is used to notify the other standby group members that a route processor no longer can or will participate as the active route processor.

- **State**—Indicates the current state of the route processor sending the message.
- **Hellotime**—Indicates the time period in seconds between hello messages that the sending route processor sends. The default is three seconds.
- **Holdtime**—Used when sending hello messages. This field indicates the length of time in seconds that the message should be considered valid. The **holdtime** should be at least three times that assigned to the **hellotime**. The default time is 10 seconds.
- **Priority**—Used to elect the active and standby route processors. The route processor with the highest priority in the HSRP group wins the election and becomes the active route processor.
- **Group**—Indicates the standby group number. The valid numbers are 0 to 255; 255 groups can be configured as valid HSRP groups.
- **Authentication data**—Contains an eight-character clear text password that is continuously reused.
- **Virtual address**—Contains the IP address of the router that is used by the HSRP group.

Once the standby route processor becomes active, it will respond to any end station sending packets to the virtual MAC address. When an IP host interface sends an ARP request with the virtual route processor's address, the route processor will respond with the address of the virtual route processor's MAC address—not its own. This virtual MAC address is the well-known MAC address of 0000.0c07.ac11, where 11 is the HSRP group identifier, 0000.0c is the vendor code, and 07.ac is the HSRP well-known MAC address.

To find the current IP address of the virtual router, you can use the **show ip arp** command and look for the virtual route processor IP and hardware MAC address. You can also use the **show standby** command.

Route processors using HSRP can provide redundant backup for the default gateway as well as load-sharing in order to balance traffic across VLANs and IP subnets. A separate HSRP standby group is configured for each VLAN. Because route processors can be assigned as members of multiple HSRP standby groups, each standby group can have its own priority and its own active route processor. As shown in Figure 12.2, the active route processor for standby group 1 assigned to VLAN 1 uses route processor A. VLAN 2 using standby group 2 uses route processor B. In the event of a failure, the standby group would begin to use the other route processor. In this situation, load sharing would take place until there was a failure.

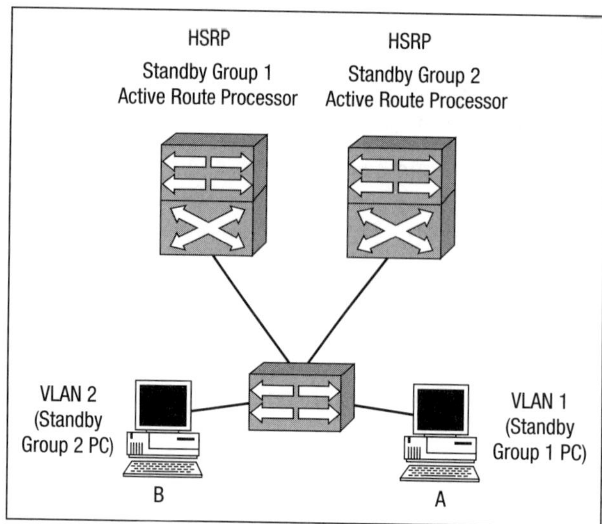

Figure 12.2 VLAN 1 and VLAN 2 utilize load balancing across multiple route processors. In the event that one route processor fails, the other will take over.

Each standby group contains an IP address and a well-known MAC address assigned to the group. The IP address for the standby group is within the range of IP addresses belonging to the subnet or VLAN to which the route processor is providing services. The IP address cannot be assigned to any other device in the network except the standby group interfaces operating in the standby group.

Inter-Switch Link (ISL) links are used to transport VLAN information across the links to the different route processors used in each standby group. In order to pass HSRP standby group information between links for multiple VLANs, the interfaces in the group must be configured with ISL. The encapsulation format must be defined and an IP address must be assigned to an interface.

Note: *Refer to Chapter 8 for information on configuring ISL encapsulation and assigning an IP address to an interface.*

Just as in Spanning Tree Protocol, a route processor goes through different states before it becomes fully functional. In the next section, we'll look at these different states and how skipping one or more of the states affects the HSRP.

The HSRP States

A route processor such as a router can transition through six HSRP states. Let's take a look at the definition of the different states, which are listed here in detail:

- *Initial state*—All route processors begin in this state. This is the starting state in which HSRP is not running. The route processor can be found in this state after a power cycling or if there is a configuration change applied to the route processor.

- *Learn state*—The route processor transitions to this state and remains here until it receives a hello message from the current active router. The hello message allows the route processor to learn the virtual IP address of the current virtual router.
- *Listen state*—In this state, the route processor has learned the IP address of the virtual router and is listening for more updated information through hello messages. The route processor is neither active nor standing by. It is basically a transitional state from the Learn state to the Speak state.
- *Speak state*—In this state, the route processor begins to forward its own periodic hello messages and to notify the other route processors that it is an active participant in the voting process to become an active or standby route processor. From here, it will forward to either the Active state or the Standby state.
- *Standby state*—In the HSRP, there must be at least one standby route processor. If there is more than one, the route processor becomes what is known as a *standby candidate route processor*. The route processor with the highest standby priority will enter the Active state in the event of a failure.
- *Active state*—The route processor in the Active state acts as the default gateway for the IP address assigned to the virtual router. It forwards any packets received for the virtual IP address or MAC address sent from any of the HSRP group's host interfaces. It also continues to send hello messages to the other route processors to verify that it holds this function.

Configuring HSRP

In the following section we will walk through multiple configuration examples. More than one HSRP group can be configured on a Route Switch Feature Card (RSFC) VLAN interface to provide a transparent route processor backup for the network. Every VLAN interface in an HSRP group shares a virtual IP and MAC address. By configuring the end users' interfaces to use the HSRP virtual IP address as the default gateway, in the event of a failure of any route processor, there will be no interruption in Layer 3 routing to the end users.

You can configure HSRP on a number of different types of Cisco route processors, including routers. The Switching exam focuses on those route processors that are included on the Catalyst line of switches, particularly the 5000 and 6000 families. In the first example of configuring HSRP, we will use a Cisco Catalyst 5009 with an RSFC. You can configure multiple route processors on the same switch with interfaces for the same HSRP group. You can also configure multiple groups with multiple interfaces on the same route processor.

***Note:** Remember that the RSM, Multilayer Switch Feature Card (MSFC), and RSFC command sets are virtually identical.*

Basic Configuration of HSRP

In order to configure HSRP on the first RSFC, you must start a session from the switch IOS. To start a session on the RSM located in the switch as module 3, use the following command from Privileged Mode on the switch IOS:

```
COR5000>(enable) session 3
Trying Router-3...
Connected to Router-3
COR5000RSM>
```

Once you have started a configuration session, you need to enter Configuration Mode for the VLAN interface that needs to be identified. To configure the interface for VLAN 3, use the following commands:

```
COR5000RSM>enable
COR5000RSM#configure terminal
Enter configuration commands, one per line. End with CNTL/Z.
COR5000RSM(config)#interface vlan 3
COR5000RSM(config-if)#
```

The next step is to enable HSRP and specify the HSRP IP address by using the following command:

```
standby 3 ip 38.187.127.254
```

The group number is 3 and the virtual IP address is 38.187.127.254. If you do not specify a group number, then group 0 is used by default. This is the virtual IP address of the default gateway that you would assign manually or by DHCP to the end stations operating in this VLAN.

Next you need to specify the priority for the HSRP interface, using the following command:

```
standby 3 priority 160
```

You should increase the priority of the interface in the HSRP group that you would like to be active by default. The interface with the highest priority becomes the active route processor for the HSRP group. Again, 3 refers to the HSRP group number corresponding to the VLAN interface number. The number 160 is the new priority for the HSRP group.

Disabling ICMP Redirects

It is important to disable all protocols that enable the host interfaces to discover the real MAC address of an HSRP standby group route processor interface. When enabling HSRP, ICMP redirects are automatically disabled. When you use the **show running-configuration** command under each VLAN interface configured for HSRP, a line will appear stating *no ip redirects*. This line indicates that ICMP redirects have been disabled. To remove an interface from an HSRP standby group, in Interface Configuration Mode enter the command **no standby**, followed by the group number.

Note: *If no priority is configured, the interface priority defaults to 100.*

The next example shows how to configure two RSFC interfaces as part of HSRP group 200 using all the required and optional commands we've discussed. Notice that on both route processors, the same virtual IP address is used for both groups.

Here is the configuration of the first RSFC for the HSRP standby group 200:

```
CORIOLIS5000RSFC#configure terminal
Enter configuration commands, one per line. End with CNTL/Z.
CORIOLIS5000RSFC(config)#interface vlan200
CORIOLIS5000RSFC(config-if)#standby 200 ip 68.187.127.30
CORIOLIS5000RSFC(config-if)#standby 200 priority 150
CORIOLIS5000RSFC(config-if)#standby 200 preempt
CORIOLIS5000RSFC(config-if)#standby 200 timers 5 15
CORIOLIS5000RSFC(config-if)#standby 200 authentication password
CORIOLIS5000RSFC(config-if)#^Z
CORIOLIS5000RSFC#
```

12

The following is the configuration of the second RSFC. The priority setting here is lower than that of the first RSFC, making the first one the active route processor and this one the standby route processor for the group:

```
CORIOLIS5000RSFC2#configure terminal
Enter configuration commands, one per line. End with CNTL/Z.
CORIOLIS5000RSFC2(config)#interface vlan200
CORIOLIS5000RSFC2(config-if)#standby 200 ip 68.187.127.30
CORIOLIS5000RSFC2(config-if)#standby 200 priority 100
CORIOLIS5000RSFC2(config-if)#standby 200 preempt
CORIOLIS5000RSFC2(config-if)#standby 200 timers 5 15
CORIOLIS5000RSFC2(config-if)#standby 200 authentication password
CORIOLIS5000RSFC2(config-if)#^Z
CORIOLIS5000RSFC#
```

Optional Settings

Right here in the configuration, you can make another optional configuration for the VLAN interface. Doing so allows the interface to preempt the current active HSRP interface and become active if the interface priority is higher than the priority of the current active interface. You can assign the standby group 3 a preempt delay of 10 with the command **standby 3 preempt delay 10**. To remove the route processor from preempt status for group number 3, use the command **no standby 3 preempt**.

You can also set the HSRP hello and hold timers manually for each interface. The default values are 3 seconds for the hello timer and 10 seconds for the hold timer. All of the interfaces in the HSRP group should use the same timer values on all member route processors in the group. To set the hello time to 5 seconds and the hold time to 15 seconds for HSRP group 3, use the command **standby 3 timers 5 15**. To remove the manual settings and return the settings to the default timers for the HSRP group 3, use the command **no standby 3 timers**.

You can also specify a clear-text password for the HSRP authentication string for the interface. All interfaces in the HSRP group use the same authentication string. To set the HSRP group 3 with the password *bookmark*, use the command **standby 3 authentication bookmark**.

Enabling HSRP Interface Tracking

Interface tracking enables a standby group route processor to automatically adjust the priority levels based on the availability of the route processor. If a tracked interface becomes unavailable, the HSRP priority of the route processor is automatically decreased. When a route processor with HSRP tracking fails, it reduces the likelihood that a route processor with an unavailable interface will remain the active route processor for the standby group.

If the route processor fails, it automatically decrements its priority on that interface and stops transmitting hello messages out the interface. The standby route processor assumes the active router role when no hello messages are detected for the specified holdtime period.

To configure tracking on the HSRP route processor interface, in Interface Configuration Mode, enter the following command on the interface that will be tracking:

```
standby 3 track 7 20
```

The 3 indicates the HSRP standby group number, 7 indicates the VLAN interface being tracked, and 20 indicates the priority amount to decrease. This setting means that if the route processor's priority was 150 and it were to fail, the tracking interface would decrease its priority by 20 to a value of 130.

Tip: You can use the same command on an external route processor, as well. If you were in Interface Configuration Mode for interface E1 and wanted to track the interface S1 for the same HSRP standby group, and with the same priority reduction setting, you would use the command **standby 3 track s1 20**.

show standby Command

To view the standby status of an HSRP interface, use the following command in EXEC Mode (the **vlan3** command indicates the VLAN and **3** indicates the HSRP standby group):

```
show standby vlan3 3
```

The output should look similar to this:

```
CORIOLIS5000RSFC# show standby vlan3 3

Vlan3 - Group 3
   local state is Active, priority 160, may preempt
   Hellotime 5 holdtime 15
   Next hello sent in 00:00:02.922
   Hot standby IP address is 68.187.127.254 configured
   Active router is local
   Standby router is 68.187.127.1 expires in 00:00:05
   Standby virtual mac address is 0000.0c07.ac03
```

12

Note: *To get a brief output of all the configured interfaces, you can use the* ***show standby brief*** *command.*

debug Command

The Cisco IOS supports the use of the HSRP **debug** command. By enabling the **debug** command, you can display the HSRP as the state changes and see debugging information regarding the sending and receiving of HSRP packets. To enable HSRP debugging, enter the following command in Privileged EXEC mode:

```
debug standby
```

Warning: The debugging feature is automatically assigned a high priority on the CPU, so this command can have a big impact on the route processor's performance.

The output will look similar to this:

```
3wld : %STANDBY-6-STATECHANGE: Standby: 0: Vlan3 state Init -> Listen
3wld : %STANDBY-6-SUMMM: Standby: 0: Vlan3 state Listen   -> Speak
3wld : SBO:Vlan3 Hello out 68.187.127.254 Speak pri 160 hel 5 hol 15
 ip 68.187.127.1
3wld : SBO:Vlan3 Hello out 68.187.127.254 Speak pri 160 hel 5 hol 15
 ip 68.187.127.1
3wld : SBO:Vlan3 Hello out 68.187.127.254 Speak pri 160 hel 5 hol 15
 ip 68.187.127.1
```

***Note:** To disable the debugging feature, enter either the **no debug standby** command and the standby group number or the **no debug** command.*

Chapter Summary

In this chapter, you learned the different methods used before HSRP to provide redundancy at Layer 3 for the route processors to provide a redundant default gateway for end-user interfaces. HSRP uses a priority scheme to determine which HSRP-configured router is to be the default active router. To configure a route processor as the active route processor for the standby group, assign a priority that is higher than the priority of all the other HSRP-configured route processor interfaces. The default priority is 100, so if you configure a standby group interface on a route processor with a higher priority, that route processor will become the default active router.

HSRP works by exchanging multicast messages that advertise priority among HSRP-configured route processor standby groups. When the active router fails to send a hello message within a configurable period of time, the standby router with the highest priority becomes the active router. HSRP-configured routers exchange three types of multicast messages:

- *Hello*—Tells the other HSRP route processors the HSRP priority and state information. By default, an HSRP route processor sends hello messages every three seconds.
- *Coup*—When a standby route processor assumes the function of the active route, it sends a coup message to notify the other route processors of the change.
- *Resign*—A route processor that is the active route processor sends this message when it is about to shut down or when a route processor that has a higher priority sends a hello message.

Some key things to remember about HSRP are:

- Member route processors in an HSRP standby group provide an illusion to the host interfaces in a VLAN or segment that a single route processor is operating.
- Standby group route processors use multicast messages to communicate with one another.
- Although there are multiple route processors in a standby group, only one is active and forwarding packets for group members and host interfaces.
- The standby route processor assumes the responsibilities of the active route processor in the event of a failure.
- Any protocol that informs interfaces of the real MAC address of the route processors such as ICMP redirects need to be disabled.

Review Questions

1. Which virtual identifiers are used in HSRP? [Choose the two best answers]
   a. Virtual MSM
   b. Virtual IP address
   c. Virtual MAC
   d. Virtual serial number

2. HSRP is designed to create redundancy for which network components?
   a. Hubs
   b. Bridges
   c. Route processors
   d. Host interfaces
3. HSRP provides services at which layer of the OSI Model?
   a. Layer 1—physical layer
   b. Layer 2—data link layer
   c. Layer 3—network layer
   d. Layer 6—presentation layer
4. HSRP can be used on which physical LAN type(s)?
   a. Token Ring
   b. FDDI
   c. Ethernet
   d. All of the above

5. Which protocols were used before HSRP to resolve the router redundancy issues? [Choose the three best answers]
   a. SAP
   b. Proxy ARP
   c. IRDP
   d. RIP
6. How many standby groups can be configured on a single route processor with FDDI or Ethernet?
   a. 255
   b. 3
   c. 64
   d. 100
7. What is the range of numbers that can be assigned to a standby group on an internal route processor?
   a. 100 to 200
   b. 0 to 64
   c. 1 to 255
   d. 0 to 255
8. Which of the following fields are included in an HSRP message?
   a. State
   b. Priority
   c. Version
   d. All of the above
9. In which HSRP state does a route processor begin to send its own hello messages?
   a. Listen state
   b. Standby state
   c. Active state
   d. Speak state
10. Which state does an HSRP interface transition to and remain in until it receives a hello message from the current active route processor?
    a. Initial state
    b. Listen state
    c. Learn state
    d. Standby state

11. Which command properly formats a manually configured hello timer to 6 seconds and the hold time to 18 seconds for standby group 4?
    a. **standby 4 preempt 6 18**
    b. **standby 4 timers 18 6**
    c. **standby 18 timers 4 6**
    d. **standby 4 timers 6 18**

12. To set a clear-text password for the standby group 3 to the word *hsrp1*, which command would you use?
    a. **standby authentication 3 hsrp1**
    b. **standby 3 authentication hsrp1**
    c. **standby 3 password hsrp1**
    d. **standby password 3 hsrp1**

13. Which protocols can be used with HSRP?
    a. IP
    b. IPX
    c. AppleTalk
    d. SAP

14. Which command can be used when you need to identify the virtual IP or virtual MAC address of the active route processor?
    a. **show ipx**
    b. **show virtual ip**
    c. **show ip arp**
    d. **show vmac vip**

15. To assign a priority of 170 to a route processor interface for standby group 6, which command is properly formatted?
    a. **standby 6 priority 170**
    b. **priority 6 170**
    c. **set priority 170 for standby 6**
    d. **set standby 6 priority 170**

12

Real-World Projects

The Coriolis Group has just gotten over a problem in which the route processor located on one of its Cisco Catalyst 5000 Series switches failed. Unfortunately, no redundant route processor was in place. This situation had catastrophic results—the editorial staff were unable to do their jobs without access to FTP,

Internet services, or email for two days until the route processor card was replaced.

The sales representative has just returned from meeting with The Coriolis Group to discuss and decide on its options. The final decision was to use the Route Switch Module and to add a Route Switch Feature Card.

Trusted technical consultant Joe Snow has the two RSFCs in stock and is being sent to Coriolis to install the cards. Once it is installed, Joe will need to configure both cards with an HSRP.

Project 12.1

To configure an RSM with HSRP, perform the following:

1. Access a session on the RSM by using the following command on the Catalyst switch:

```
CORIOLIS5000>(enable) session 3
Trying Router-3...
Connected to Router-3.
COR5000RSM#
```

2. Enter Configuration Mode on the RSM:

```
COR5000RSM#configure terminal
Enter configuration commands, one per line. End with CNTL/Z.
COR5000RSM(config)#
```

3. Enter the VLAN Interface Configuration Mode on which you wish to enable HSRP:

```
COR5000RSM(config)#interface vlan1
COR5000RSM(config-if)#
```

4. Enter the virtual IP address for the standby group:

```
COR5000RSM(config-if)#standby 1 ip 68.187.127.254
COR5000RSM(config-if)#
```

5. Set this interface to be the active route processor with a priority of 110:

```
COR5000RSM(config-if)#standby 1 priority 110
```

6. Configure the hello timer to 5 seconds and the hold timer to 15 seconds:

```
COR5000RSM(config-if)#standby 1 timers 5 15
```

7. Set the clear-text password to *bookpass*:

```
COR5000RSM(config-if)#standby 1 authentication bookpass
```

8. Exit the interface:

```
COR5000RSM(config-if)#^Z
```

9. Don't forget to save your configuration:

```
COR5000RSM# copy running-config startup-config
```

Project 12.2

To configure the second RSM with HSRP, perform the following:

1. Access a session on the RSM by using the following command on the Catalyst switch:

```
CORIOLIS5000>(enable) session 5
Trying Router-5...
Connected to Router-5.
COR5000RSM#
```


2. Enter Configuration Mode on the RSFC:

```
COR5000RSFC#configure terminal
Enter configuration commands, one per line. End with CNTL/Z.
COR5000RSFC(config)#
```

3. Enter the VLAN Interface Configuration Mode on which you wish to enable HSRP:

```
COR5000RSFC(config)#interface vlan1
COR5000RSFC(config-if)#
```

4. This is a new route processor installed on the Catalyst 5000, so Joe needs to configure the interface with a real-life IP address, routing protocol, and network information. Use the following commands:

```
COR5000RSFC(config)#ip routing
COR5000RSFC(config)#router rip
COR5000RSFC(config-router)#network 68.187.127.0
COR5000RSFC(config-router)#interface vlan1
COR5000RSFC(config-if)#ip address 68.187.127.5 255.255.255.0
```

5. Enter the virtual IP address for the standby group:

```
COR5000RSFC(config-if)#standby 1 ip 68.187.127.254
COR5000RSFC(config-if)#
```

6. Set this interface to be the active route processor with a priority of 110:

```
COR5000RSFC(config-if)#standby 1 priority 110
```

7. Configure the hello timer to 5 seconds and the hold timer to 15 seconds:

```
COR5000RSFC(config-if)#standby 1 timers 5 15
```

8. Set the clear-text password to *bookpass*:

```
COR5000RSFC(config-if)#standby 1 authentication bookpass
```

9. Exit the interface:

```
COR5000RSFC(config-if)#^Z
```

10. Don't forget to save your configuration:

```
COR5000RSFC# copy running-config startup-config
```

CHAPTER THIRTEEN

13

ATM AND LANE

After completing this chapter, you will be able to:

- ✓ Understand ATM technology and terms
- ✓ Describe LANE technology
- ✓ Identify the components of LANE
- ✓ Describe the functions of the LECS, LES, BUS, and LEC
- ✓ Configure LANE on a Catalyst switch

Asynchronous Transfer Mode (ATM) is a standard developed by the International Telecommunication Union Telecommunication Standardization Sector (ITU-T). ATM is based on the switching and multiplexing techniques proposed by the ITU for Broadband Integrated Services Digital Network (B-ISDN) access. ATM is a cell-based networking technology that was designed to be an extremely efficient method of supporting multiple types of traffic—such as voice, data, or video—at very high speeds.

ATM has many unique characteristics that allow it to effectively support today's networking requirements. The ATM protocols have been designed specifically to support high-speed networks at speeds ranging up to many gigabits per second. Although some other protocols, such as Gigabit Ethernet, also provide high-speed networking and work very well in LAN environments, only ATM can handle network traffic in both LAN and WAN environments without regard to the type of physical medium.

In addition, ATM has built-in support for Quality of Service (QoS) that guarantees a level of service for network services such as bandwidth utilization, network throughput, or delay. This is an especially critical area when you're dealing with technologies such as voice or video services.

Despite these advantages, ATM is fundamentally different from the traditional methods used to transport network data. Traditional methods use either character- or frame-based modes to transfer data. ATM, on the other hand, is a cell-based switching technology that is a mixture of circuit switching and frame switching technologies. As a result, it provides the benefits of both types of technologies and is more efficient than the traditional networking methods in transporting data. In order to use ATM, though, you need to understand how it works and some of the terms and concepts associated with it.

The goal of this chapter is to provide you with an understanding of how the ATM technology functions. We will show you the structure of the ATM cells, explain the concepts behind virtual circuits, and introduce you to the different layers of ATM. We will explain what Local Area Network Emulation (LANE) is and how it is done. Last, we will show you how to configure ATM on Cisco Catalyst switches.

Overview of ATM Technology

ATM transports network data in fixed-sized units commonly called *cells*. Each cell is 53 bytes in length and is divided into a 5-byte header and 48 bytes of data. The 53-byte size of the cells is a compromise between the default sizes wanted by the voice, data, and video advocates. This cell size is a good example of how standards are implemented. One side wanted small cells (32); another wanted large packets (64). Therefore, they added 32 and 64 to get 96, and divided by 2, yielding 48-byte ATM cells (plus the 5-byte header). The fixed size of the cells provides the following benefits:

- Hardware implementation is simplified.
- Bandwidth is used more efficiently because applications can share the bandwidth more fairly.
- Bursty applications can be accommodated more easily.
- Data loss can be handled more efficiently.

An ATM network contains two types of devices: an ATM switch and ATM endpoints. ATM endpoints are devices that have an ATM network interface adapter—such as a computer, router, Data Service Unit (DSU), or LAN switch—and that transmit data to an ATM switch. An ATM switch is responsible for receiving this data, updating the header information, and switching the data out the proper interface to its destination.

An ATM interface can connect an endpoint to a switch, in which case it is known as a User to Network Interface (UNI); or, it can connect two ATM switches, in which case it is known as a Network to Network Interface (NNI). The two types of connections can be further divided into private and public networks. As the name implies, a private network connects an ATM endpoint to a private network, whereas a public network connects an ATM endpoint to a public switch, such as one owned by a telco.

ATM Cell Header

ATM cell headers use one of two formats, depending on whether the endpoints are a UNI or an NNI connection. The main differences between the two formats are that the NNI header does not contain a Generic Flow Control (GFC) field and in an NNI header, the Virtual Path Identifier (VPI) occupies the entire first 12 bits. A cell header for a UNI cell is shown in Figure 13.1.

The following definitions apply to the cell header fields:

- *Generic Flow Control (GFC)*—This 8-bit field is used to provide local functions, such as identifying multiple stations that share a single ATM interface. GFC is typically not used.
- *Virtual Path Identifier (VPI)*—This 8-bit field is used with the VCI to identify the next destination of a cell as it passes through a series of ATM switches on its way to its destination.
- *Virtual Channel Identifier (VCI)*—This 8-bit field is used in conjunction with the VPI to identify the next destination.

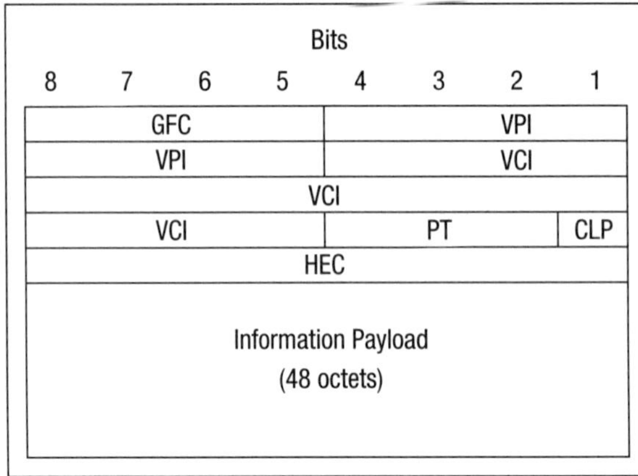

Figure 13.1 An ATM UNI cell header.

- *Payload Type (PT)*—This 3-bit field indicates whether the cell contains user data or control data. If the cell contains user data, the second bit indicates congestion and the third bit indicates whether the cell is the last in a series of cells that represents a single ATM adaptation layer 5 (AAL5) frame.
- *Congestion Loss Priority (CLP)*—This 1-bit field indicates whether the cell should be discarded if it encounters extreme congestion as it moves through the network.
- *Header Error Control (HEC)*—This 8-bit field indicates a checksum calculated only on the header itself.

ATM Reference Model

ATM uses a logical reference model to describe the functions it supports. It is the same concept as the OSI Reference Model. The ATM Reference Model is composed of several layers:

- Physical layer
- ATM layer
- ATM adaptation layer (AAL)

The ATM layer and the ATM adaptation layers are roughly equivalent to the data link layer of the OSI Reference Model, and the ATM physical layer is similar to the physical layer of the OSI Reference Model.

As shown in Figure 13.2, the ATM Reference Model also contains three management planes, which cover all layers of the model. The control plane is responsible for the generation and management of signaling requests. The user plane is responsible for the management of the transfer of data. Above the ATM adaptation layer are higher-layer protocols representing traditional transports and applications.

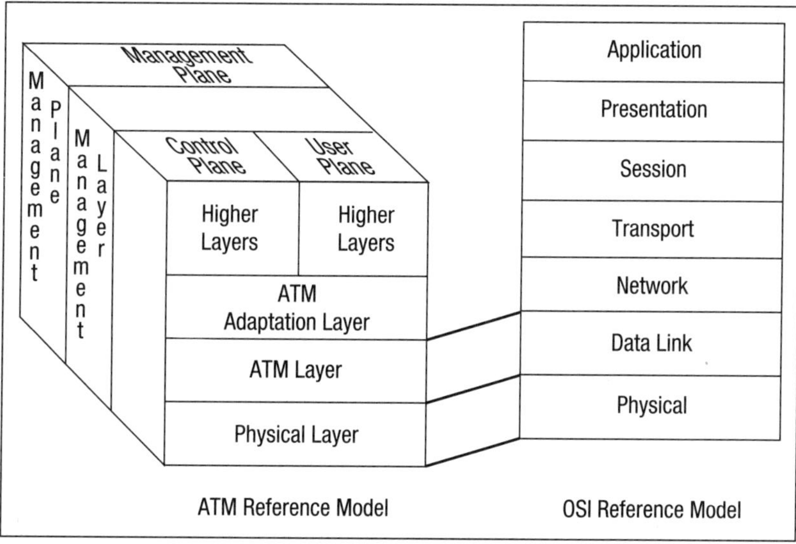

Figure 13.2 The ATM Reference Model.

ATM Physical Layer

The ATM physical layer controls transmission and receipt of bits on the physical medium. It also keeps track of ATM cell boundaries and packages cells into the appropriate type of frame for the physical medium being used. The ATM physical layer is divided into two parts: the physical medium dependent (PMD) sublayer and the transmission convergence (TC) sublayer.

The PMD sublayer is responsible for sending and receiving a continuous flow of bits with associated timing information to synchronize the transmission and reception of data. ATM can use any physical medium capable of carrying ATM cells. Some of the existing standards that can carry ATM cells are Synchronous Optical Network (SONET), DS-3/E3, 100Mbps local fiber, 155Mbps local fiber, and 155Mbps over shielded twisted pair.

The TC sublayer maintains ATM cell boundaries, ensures valid data, maintains synchronization of the data, and packages the ATM cells into a format that is appropriate for the physical medium.

ATM Layer

The ATM layer is responsible for establishing connections and passing cells through the ATM network. To do this, it uses the information contained in the header of each ATM cell. ATM switches use the VPI and VCI fields of the cell header to identify the next network segment that a cell needs to transit on its way to its final destination. A *virtual channel* is equivalent to a *virtual circuit* in that both terms describe a logical connection between the two ends of a communications connection. A *virtual path* is a logical grouping of virtual circuits that allows an ATM switch to perform operations on groups of virtual circuits.

ATM Adaptation Layer

The ATM adaptation layer (AAL) translates between the different types of network traffic—such as video streams, data packets, and voice packets—of upper-layer processes and ATM cells. In other words, the AAL receives packets from upper-level protocols and breaks them into the 48-byte segments that form the payload field of an ATM cell. Several types of AAL standards are defined for this layer. Which AAL you use will largely depend on the type of traffic and what you are trying to do with that traffic. The characteristics of each AAL are as follows:

- *AAL1*—A connection-oriented service that provides end-to-end timing provisions. It maintains a constant data transfer rate. It is appropriate to use to transport voice traffic and video traffic or other timing-sensitive data, such as System Network Architecture/Synchronous Data Link Control (SNA/SDLC). It requires timing synchronization between the source and destination; so, you need to use a medium that supports clocking, such as SONET.
- *AAL2*—Reserved for data traffic that requires variable bit rates (VBR) and timing sensitivity. This layer is not currently defined and is an incomplete standard.
- *AAL3/4*—Support both connection and connectionless data. AAL3 and AAL4 were designed to be used by network service providers and are closely aligned with Switched Multimegabit Data Service (SMDS). AAL3/4 is used to transmit SMDS packets over an ATM network. It is suitable for use in environments that send or receive large files. AAL3 is identical to AAL4, except that AAL3 is connection-oriented and AAL4 is connectionless-oriented.
- *AAL5*—The primary AAL used for non-SMDS data. It supports both connection-oriented and connectionless data. It is used for such applications as classical IP over ATM (CLIP) and LAN Emulation (LANE). This layer is the one that Catalyst switches use to provide LANE services.

ATM Addressing

For an ATM device to be able to connect to other ATM devices, it must have a unique ATM address associated with it. In addition, the device must also know the address to your device. ATM uses private and public types of addresses. Because the ATM standard has adopted the subnetwork model of addressing, the ATM layer is responsible for mapping network layer addresses to ATM addresses.

Currently, two types of ATM addressing plans identify ATM UNI addresses. The first standard is a telephony-based format defined by ITU-T; this standard uses telephony-like E.164 addresses. This is the format used to connect an endpoint to a carrier's network. Unfortunately, E.164 addresses are available only to monopoly carriers, which prevents the addresses from being assigned to competitors or to other private businesses.

A second format, defined by the ISO, uses a data-oriented network service access point (NSAP) format. This is the format used to connect an endpoint to a private network. The ATM Forum has included a method to incorporate the E.164 address of the public network a customer is attached to in its NSAP addresses. The forum is also working on a method for the carriers to use NSAP-based addressing on their networks.

NSAP addresses consist of the following three fields:

- *Authority and Format Identifier (AFI)*—Indicates which standard is being used for the address. An AFI of 47 indicates a British Standards Institute address (Cisco uses this on all its ATM devices); an AFI of 39 indicates an ISO address; and an AFI of 39 indicates an E.164 address.
- *Initial Domain Identifier (IDI)*—Indicates the address allocation and administrative authority.
- *Domain Specific Part (DSP)*—Contains the actual routing information.

Figure 13.3 shows the format of an ATM NSAP address.

Local Area Network Emulation (LANE)

In a LAN environment, broadcast support is an inherent part of the networking technology. Legacy networks have native broadcast support to resolve address mapping and resolution. ATM networks, in contrast, are non-broadcast multiple access (NBMA) networks with no such support. The LANE standard was created by the ATM Forum in 1994 to provide connectivity for ATM networks to legacy Ethernet and Token Ring networks.

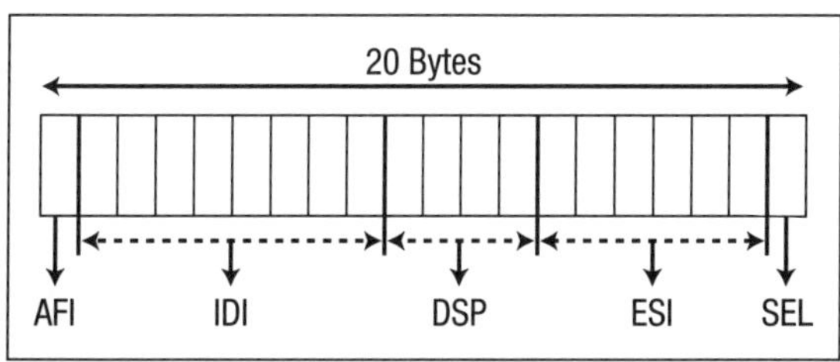

Figure 13.3 ATM address formats.

LANE provides these services by making an ATM interface look like an Ethernet or Token Ring interface. The ATM devices have Media Access Control (MAC) addresses, just like Ethernet or Token Ring devices. Because the ATM interfaces can use the same frame format as legacy devices, LAN-based applications can run without changing their network-layer drivers.

This approach allows the benefits of the LAN environment, such as backward compatibility with existing LANs, broadcasting support, and best-effort delivery, but also prevents the use of ATM-specific benefits such as QoS, service levels, and flexible bandwidth allocation. In this respect, you should probably look at LANE as an interim step for the incremental introduction of ATM to the networking environment.

LANE Components

ATM LANE uses a client/server architecture to create an emulated LAN (ELAN). As in a VLAN, an ELAN contains local broadcasts and multicasts to the devices assigned to it. A router is required to connect to other devices outside of the ELAN. An ATM network can support multiple ELANs, and membership in an ELAN is independent of the physical location of the end system. ELAN names must be unique on an interface. If two interfaces participate in LANE, the second interface might be in a different switch cloud.

LANE devices can be either clients or servers. The following sections describe the components that make up the LAN Emulation service (LE service).

LAN Emulation Client

The LAN Emulation Client (LEC) resides in every ATM end system and provides a LAN interface to higher-layer protocols and applications. A LEC forwards data to other LANE components in the ELAN and performs control functions. Each LEC is a member of only one ELAN. For this reason, an Ethernet switch may have multiple LECs for each VLAN. Examples of LEC implementations can be servers, routers, switches, or other network hosts. The LEC has the following functions:

- Address resolution of MACs
- Data transfer
- Address caching
- Interfacing with other LANE components
- Interface driver support

LAN Emulation Server

The LAN Emulation Server (LES) for an ELAN is the central piece of LANE and gives the LECs the information they need to establish ATM connections to other LECs in their ELAN. A single LES is responsible for address registry and resolution for an ELAN. When an LEC joins an ELAN, it forms a connection with the LES. The LEC registers its MAC and ATM address with the LES. The LES has the following functions:

- LECs support
- Address registration from LECs
- Address resolution from LECs
- Interfacing to LEC, LECS, and BUS

Broadcast-and-Unknown Server

The Broadcast-and-Unknown Server (BUS) provides broadcasting support for an ELAN. The BUS distributes multicast data, sends or distributes unicast data, and interfaces with the other LANE components. When the destination address of an Ethernet or Token Ring frame contains a local broadcast or a multicast address, the LEC forwards the traffic to the BUS, which forwards it to all the other LECs in the ELAN. At least one combined LES and BUS is required per ELAN. The BUS has the following functions:

- Distributing multicast data
- Sending or distributing unicast data
- Interfacing to LEC and LES

LAN Emulation Configuration Server (LECS)

The LAN Emulation Configuration Server (LECS) contains a database of ATM addresses of LES/BUS pairs for configured ELANs. An LEC consults the LECS to determine the LES's ATM address when it first joins an ELAN. The LECS returns the ATM address of the LES for that ELAN.

Note: *At least one LECS is required per ATM LANE switch cloud.*

The LECS has the following functions:

- Registration of LECS ATM addresses to supply to LECs
- Configuration support for LECS to provide LES addresses to LECs
- Interfacing to LEC and LES

Integrated Local Management Interface

The Integrated Local Management Interface (ILMI) protocol was defined by the ATM Forum and is used to aid in initialization and configuration of ATM LECs. ILMI uses the Simple Network Management Protocol (SNMP) to share information between an ATM client and an ATM switch. ILMI works in conjunction with the ATM signaling AAL (**qsaal**) by setting up virtual channels (VCs) to two well-known ATM addresses. The first of these VCs is to the **qsaal** and uses the VPI=0 and VCI=5. This Private Virtual Circuit (PVC) sets up the signaling required for ATM to set up and tear down Switched Virtual Circuits (SVCs). The second VC enables ILMI and allows the LANE card to share management information with the ATM switch via the LECS. ILMI is set up for the well-known PVC address of VPI=0 and VCI=16.

The basic functions of ILMI are to enable the LEC to discover the ATM address of the LECS and to allow the LEC to tear down virtual circuits when they are no longer in use. ILMI provides the ability of the ATM switch to share its ATM prefix with the LECs, which lets the LECs share the same initial 13 bytes of the switch's 20-byte ATM address. This scheme makes it easier to route traffic between switches, because the switch only needs to look at the first 13 bytes to determine which ATM switch has the end-station. ILMI is an extremely popular way to resolve addressing in ATM networks.

LANE Guidelines

When setting up LANE components, you should consider the following guidelines:

- The LECS should always be assigned to the major interface.
- If the LES/BUS and the LEC are on the same ELAN, they can be configured on the same subinterface. LECs for two separate ELANs cannot be configured on the same subinterface.
- LESs/BUSs for different ELANs cannot be configured on the same subinterface.
- The operating LECSs must use exactly the same configuration database. You can create identical databases by configuring a LECS database on one device and copying it to the other devices—for example, by using the **config net** command.
- The LANE subsystem can support up to 16 LECS addresses.
- An unlimited number of LESs/BUSs can be defined per ELAN.
- A LEC will consider itself to be the master LEC until a higher-level LEC takes priority.

- If multiple LES/BUS pairs are configured for an ELAN, the priority of a given LES/BUS pair is determined by the order in which it was entered in the LECS database. When a higher-priority LES/BUS pair comes online, it takes over the functions of the current LES/BUS on the ELAN.
- It may take up to one minute for changes made to the list of LECS addresses to propagate through the network. Changes made to the configuration database regarding LES/BUS addresses take effect almost immediately.
- If no designated LECS is operational or reachable on an ELAN, the ATM Forum-defined well-known LECS address is used.

How LANE Works

Earlier, we discussed how the different LANE components interact with each other to support the LAN emulation services. A LEC goes through three stages to join an ELAN:

- Initialization and configuration
- Joining and registering with the LES
- Finding and joining the BUS

Let's step through the process. Suppose you're working on an ELAN and you want to access a file stored on a server that is located on a physically separate LAN. The steps are as follows:

1. You send the file request. Your LEC determines if it knows the ATM address of its LES.
2. If your LEC does not know this address, the client queries the LECS and asks for the ATM address of the LES.
3. After your LEC receives the correct address, it queries the LES for the ATM address of the LES where the file is located.
4. If the LES knows this address, it sends the address to your LEC. If the LES does not know this address, it queries the LANE BUS. The LANE BUS, in turn, asks all the LECs on the ELAN for their ATM addresses. The LANE BUS returns the correct address to the LES, which returns the address to your LEC.
5. Your LEC establishes a virtual circuit to the server on which the file is stored. Then, the LEC converts its Ethernet or Token Ring frames into cells and sends these cells over the virtual circuit to the server.

Configuring LANE

The steps in configuring LANE are identical for both the Catalyst 5000 and 6000 switch families, because they involve connecting to a separate ATM module that has its own subset of the IOS command set. To configure the ATM module, you need to connect to the ATM LANE module using the **session** command. You can determine the ATM LANE module number by issuing a **show module** command.

Because the ATM LANE module is an IOS-based switch, you need to be in Privileged EXEC mode and enter Configuration Mode to enter commands. As with all IOS-based machines, it is necessary to save to memory whatever configuration changes you make, if you wish to keep them. An example of accessing the ATM module located in slot 5 of a Catalyst 6500 is as follows:

```
Console> (enable) session 5
Trying ATM-5...
Connected to ATM-5.
Escape character is '^]'.
```

Determining the Default Addresses

ATM addresses are 40 digits long. As we mentioned earlier, ATM uses the ILMI protocol to provide the ATM prefix address of the switch for the LECs. This process configures the initial 26 digits of the ATM address, which are identical for each LEC. The next 12 digits of the ATM address are known as the End System Identifier (ESI). To provide this part of the ATM address, Cisco includes a pool of 16 MAC addresses for each ATM module, although only 4 are used. The following are assigned to the LANE components:

- The prefix fields are the same for all LANE components and indicate the identity of the ATM switch.
- All LECSs are assigned an ESI field value from the first pool of MAC addresses assigned to the interface.
- All LESs are assigned an ESI field value from the second pool of MAC addresses.
- The BUS is assigned an ESI value from the third pool of MAC addresses.
- The LECS is assigned an ESI value from the fourth pool.

Cisco assigns the remaining two digits of the ATM address (known as the *selector field*) based on the subinterface in which the LANE component resides. Because the LECS must reside on the major interface, its selector value is always 00. To find the default ATM addresses the ATM LANE module has assigned, use the

show lane default-atm-addresses command. An example of this command and the related output follows:

```
ATM#show lane default-atm-addresses
interface ATM0:
LANE Client:        47.00918100000000E04FACB401.00E04FACB070.**
LANE Server:        47.00918100000000E04FACB401.00E04FACB071.**
LANE Bus:           47.00918100000000E04FACB401.00E04FACB072.**
LANE Config Server: 47.00918100000000E04FACB401.00E04FACB073.00
```

***Note:** The asterisks in this display indicate that the addresses are in hexadecimal. The ATM LANE module does not list these addresses with this command.*

Configuring the LES/BUS

An LES and a BUS need to be configured for each ELAN. As we mentioned before, the LES is the component responsible for resolving MAC addresses to ATM addresses. The BUS is the component responsible for servicing Ethernet and Token Ring local broadcasts and multicast. The LES and the BUS must be configured in the same end-station in Cisco's implementation of LANE.

To do this on an ATM LANE module, you need to use subinterfaces. Depending on the level of traffic you expect, you may want to place different LES/BUS components throughout your network to prevent a bottleneck from forming. When you configure a LES or BUS, you must specify the name of the ELAN for which it is responsible. To configure a LES or BUS, you need to complete the following tasks:

1. Enter Configuration Mode.
2. Specify the subinterface for the ELAN and what the link type will be (Ethernet or Token Ring).
3. Enable the LES/BUS for an ELAN.
4. Repeat for all LESs/BUSs.

13

The following is an example of how to configure a LES/BUS for two ELANS, the default ELAN, and the TEST_ELAN:

```
ATM#configure terminal
Enter configuration commands, one per line.  End with CNTL/Z.
ATM(config)#interface atm0.1
ATM(config-subif)#lane server-bus ethernet default
ATM(config-subif)#interface atm0.2
ATM(config-subif)#lane server-bus ethernet TEST_ELAN
ATM(config-subif)#end
```

To verify the configuration, issue the following command:

```
ATM#show lane server
LE Server ATM0.1  ELAN name: default  Admin: up  State: operational
type: ethernet         Max Frame Size: 1516
ATM address: 47.00918100000000E04FACB401.00100DAACC41.01
LECS used: 47.007900000000000000000000.00A03E000001.00 NOT yet connected

LE Server ATM0.2  ELAN name: TEST_ELAN  Admin: up  State: operational
type: ethernet         Max Frame Size: 1516
ATM address: 47.00918100000000E04FACB401.00100DAACC41.02
LECS used: 47.007900000000000000000000.00A03E000001.00 NOT yet connected
```

Note: *Don't forget to issue the command* ***copy running-config startup-config***.

Configuring a LEC for an ELAN

It is the job of a LEC to pass traffic between separate VLANs on the Catalyst switches and the ELANs on the ATM switch. You can configure multiple LECs for one or more ELANs on the ATM modules, up to a maximum of 255. Prior to setting up a LEC on the ATM module, a VLAN must be configured on the switch and the LES/BUS for an ELAN must be configured on an ATM module subinterface.

When you configure a LEC on the ATM module, you map a VLAN on the Catalyst 5000 or 6000 switch to an ATM ELAN. Because each LEC represents a different VLAN, each LEC must be configured on separate subinterfaces. As with the LES/BUS configuration, you must specify the type of emulation used as well as the ELAN name on the ATM side. An example of configuring two LECS on two subinterfaces follows:

```
ATM#configure terminal
Enter configuration commands, one per line.  End with CNTL/Z.
ATM(config)#interface atm0.1
ATM(config-subif)#lane client ethernet 1 default
ATM(config-subif)#interface atm0.2
ATM(config-subif)#lane client ethernet 2 TEST_ELAN
ATM(config-subif)#end
ATM#
```

To verify the operation, issue the following command:

```
ATM#show lane client
LE Client ATM0.1  ELAN name: default  Admin: up  State: initialState
Client ID: unassigned        Next join attempt in 0 seconds
```

```
Join Attempt: 4
Last Fail Reason: Config VC being released
HW Address: 0010.0daa.cc40   Type: ethernet        Max Frame Size: 1516
        VLANID: 1
ATM Address: 47.00918100000000E04FACB401.00100DAACC40.01

VCD  rxFrames  txFrames  Type        ATM Address
  0         0         0  configure   47.007900000000000000000000
.00A03E000001.00
  0         0         0  direct      00.000000000000000000000000
.000000000000.00
  0         0         0  distribute  00.000000000000000000000000
.000000000000.00
  0         0         0  send        00.000000000000000000000000
.000000000000.00
  0         0         0  forward     00.000000000000000000000000
.000000000000.00

LE Client ATM0.2  ELAN name: TEST_ELAN  Admin: up  State: initialState
Client ID: unassigned        Next join attempt in 1 seconds
Join Attempt: 2
Last Fail Reason: Config VC being released
HW Address: 0010.0daa.cc40   Type: ethernet        Max Frame Size: 1516
        VLANID: 2
ATM Address: 47.00918100000000E04FACB401.00100DAACC40.02

VCD  rxFrames  txFrames  Type        ATM Address
  0         0         0  configure   47.007900000000000000000000
.00A03E000001.00
VCD  rxFrames  txFrames  Type        ATM Address
  0         0         0  direct      00.000000000000000000000000
.000000000000.00
  0         0         0  distribute  00.000000000000000000000000
.000000000000.00
  0         0         0  send        00.000000000000000000000000
.000000000000.00
  0         0         0  forward     00.000000000000000000000000
.000000000000.00
```

In this example, the state is **initialState**. This state indicates that the LEC is not yet a member of the ELAN. The zeroes in the ATM address columns indicate that the LECS database has not yet been configured. This is normal—LECS will not come up until the LES/BUS is configured and the LECS database has been configured.

13

Configuring the LECS

The LECS database contains the information about the LANE components. Included in this database is information regarding the address of each LES/BUS and the name of the ELAN it controls. The name of the default ELAN, if needed, is also included. At least one LECS database must be present in the ATM LANE network. Multiple LECS can be configured, but databases with the same name must be identical. A default ELAN allows any LEC that wishes to join it to do so. Restricted ELANs can be set up that require you to list each LEC that is eligible to join.

Prior to configuring the LECS, you will need to go to each LES and get its ATM address. This address can be gathered with the following command:

```
ATM#show lane server
LE Server ATM0.1  ELAN name: default  Admin: up  State: operational
type: ethernet          Max Frame Size: 1516
ATM address: 47.00918100000000E04FACB401.00100DAACC41.01
LECS used: 47.007900000000000000000000.00A03E000001.00 NOT yet connected
```

Make a note of the address following the **ATM address:** label. To set up this LEC in a default unrestricted ELAN, perform the following commands:

```
ATM#configure terminal
Enter configuration commands, one per line.  End with CNTL/Z.

ATM(config)#lane database LANE_Backbone
ATM(lane-config-database)#name default server-atm-address
 47.00918100000000E04FACB401.00100DAACC41.01ATM(lane-config-database)
 #default-name default
ATM(lane-config-database)#end
```

To see the results of this operation, issue the following command:

```
ATM#show lane database

LANE Config Server database table 'LANE_Backbone'
default elan: default
elan 'default': un-restricted
  server 47.00918100000000E04FACB401.00100DAACC41.01 (prio 0)
```

Setting Up a Restricted ELAN

The process of setting up a restricted ELAN is similar to the previous procedure in that you create database entries that link the name of each ELAN to the ATM address of its server. However, with a restricted ELAN, only those clients specified in the database can join the ELAN. When you create a restricted ELAN, you need to specify where each of the LANE clients is located by linking the client's

ATM address with the name of the ELAN. A good practice is to set up a default ELAN for LANE clients that are not explicitly placed in an ELAN. To set up the configuration server for emulated LANs with restricted membership, follow these steps:

```
ATM#configure terminal
Enter configuration commands, one per line.  End with CNTL/Z.
ATM(config)#lane database LANE_Backbone
ATM(lane-config-database)#name mgr_ELAN server-atm-address
47.00918100000000E04FACB401.00100DAACC41.02 restricted
ATM(lane-config-database)#default-name default
#lane database LANE_Backbone
ATM(lan-config-database)client-atm-address
47.00918100000000E04FACB401.00100DAACC40.02 name mgr_ELAN
ATM(lane-config-database)#end
```

Activating the LECS

After you have completed configuring the LECS database, you configure the LECS address and bind it to the interface. The following is an example:

```
ATM#configure terminal
Enter configuration commands, one per line.  End with CNTL/Z.
ATM(config)#interface atm0
ATM(config-if)#lane config auto-config-atm-address
ATM(config-if)#lane config database LANE_Backbone
ATM(config-if)#end
```

13

Verify the proper setup with the following command:

```
ATM#show lane config
LE Config Server ATM0 config table: LANE_Backbone
Admin: up  State: operational
LECS Mastership State: active master
list of global LECS addresses (58 seconds to update):
47.00918100000000E04FACB401.00100DAACC43.00  <-------- me
ATM Address of this LECS: 47.00918100000000E04FACB401
.00100DAACC43.00 (auto)
 vcd  rxCnt  txCnt  callingParty
  11      1      1  47.00918100000000E04FACB401
.00100DAACC41.01 LES default 0
active
cumulative total number of unrecognized packets received so far: 0
cumulative total number of config requests received so far: 3
cumulative total number of config failures so far: 1
    cause of last failure: no configuration
    culprit for the last failure: 47.00918100000000E04FACB401
    .00E04FACB070.04
```

Chapter Summary

In this chapter, we covered Asynchronous Transfer Mode. The ITU-T standards body developed ATM as a technology that could handle the demands of an integrated data, voice, and video network.

ATM is a difficult subject for most people because they rarely are exposed to it on a day-to-day basis like Ethernet or Token Ring. In today's networking environment, however, increased emphasis is being put on integrating data, voice, and video in networks, and ATM is a driving force. The ability of ATM to ensure timely delivery of packets based on their type is something no other protocol has today. In addition, ATM can be used on both LANs and WANs on almost any type of media with speeds that can scale up to many gigabits per second.

ATM is a cell-based technology, which differs widely from the packet-based networks like Ethernet and Token Ring. Each ATM cell is 53 bytes in length: 5 bytes for the header and 48 bytes for the data payload. Although a fixed-length 53-byte cell may seem small in comparison to packet-based technology, it offers some benefits and efficiencies, such as easier hardware implementation and the ability to handle data loss much more efficiently.

An ATM network contains two types of devices: ATM switches and ATM endpoints. There are two types of ATM interfaces: a User to Network Interface (UNI) that connects an ATM device to a switch and a Network to Network Interface (NNI) that connects an ATM to an ATM switch.

The ATM standard uses a reference model to describe the functions of the protocol. The ATM Reference Model includes four layers, which roughly correspond to the OSI Model, and three management planes. The ATM physical layer is similar to the physical layer of the OSI chart, and the ATM layer and the ATM adaptation layer are similar to the data link layer of the OSI chart.

The ATM physical layer controls the transmission and receipt of bits on the physical medium. The ATM layer is responsible for establishing connections and passing cells through the ATM network.

The different types of network traffic are translated in the ATM adaptation layer. Four AALs are defined, but only three are actively in use. These are the AAL1 service, which is used to transport timing-dependent traffic (such as voice); AAL3/4, which is used by network service providers in SMDS networks; and AA5, which is the primary AAL used for non-SMDS traffic that doesn't require the pacing AAL1 would provide.

There are two types of ATM addressing plans. The first, defined by the ITU-T, uses E.164 telephony-like addresses and is used to connect to the public networks of large carriers. The second is the NSAP format originated by the IOS, which is used to connect to private networks.

Another important topic we covered in this chapter was Local Area Network Emulation (LANE). Because ATM is a non-broadcast medium, LANE provides backward compatibility to legacy Ethernet and Token Ring networks. LANE makes an ATM interface look like an Ethernet or Token Ring network interface, so no modifications to existing network drivers or applications need to be made to support ATM environments.

ATM LANE works with a client/server architecture to create an emulated LAN (ELAN). An ELAN is very similar to a VLAN in that it also limits local broadcasts and multicast traffic to the ELAN. LANE devices can be either clients or servers. The LAN Emulation service (LE service) consists of several different components.

The LAN Emulation Client (LEC) resides in every ATM device and provides a LAN interface to higher-layer protocols. The LAN Emulation Server (LES) is the centerpiece of the LANE architecture. A single LES is responsible for address registry and resolution for an ELAN. The Broadcast-and-Unknown Server (BUS) is the means by which ATM provides broadcasting support for an ELAN. The LAN Emulation Configuration Server (LECS) contains the database of LES/BUS pairs for all the configured ELANs.

The LANE guidelines suggested by Cisco were included in this chapter, as well as a description of how LANE works in operation. Finally, we covered the steps to configure LANE on a Catalyst ATM LANE module.

Review Questions

1. The ATM standard was developed by which standards body?
   a. IOS
   b. OSI
   c. ITU-T
   d. BISDN

2. On which of the following are ATM data units based?
   a. Packet-based
   b. Cell-based
   c. Circuit-switched
   d. Frame-switched

3. What is the length of the ATM cell?
   a. 53 bits
   b. 48 bytes
   c. 53 bytes
   d. 64 bytes
4. When an ATM endpoint connects to an ATM switch, which type of ATM interface is used?
   a. NNI
   b. CCI
   c. UNI
   d. Direct
5. When an ATM endpoint connects an ATM switch to another ATM switch, it uses which type of interface?
   a. CCI
   b. UNI
   c. NNI
   d. Indirect
6. What does ATM identify using the combination of the VPI and VCI fields?
   a. The size of the cell
   b. The payload type
   c. The checksum of the cell
   d. The next destination of the cell through a series of switches
7. In the ATM Reference Model, the ATM layer and the ATM adaptation layer are similar to which OSI layer?
   a. Physical layer
   b. Link layer
   c. Data layer
   d. Data link layer
8. What is the chief function of the ATM physical layer?
   a. To establish connections and pass cells through the ATM network
   b. To maintain a constant data rate
   c. To control transmission and receipt of the bits

9. What is the chief function of the ATM layer?
    a. Maintaining a constant data rate
    b. Establishing connections and passing cells through an ATM network
    c. Identifying the next destination of a cell through a switch
    d. Connecting an ATM endpoint to a switch
10. Which adaptation layer is chiefly designed for transporting video or voice traffic?
    a. AAL1
    b. AAL2
    c. AAL3/4
    d. AAL5
11. Which adaptation layer was designed for use as a network service provider?
    a. AAL1
    b. AAL2
    c. AAL3/4
    d. AAL5
12. Which ATM addressing plan is used to connect to a carrier's ATM network?
    a. NNI
    b. E.164
    c. NSAP
    d. ISO
13. Which ATM addressing plan developed by ISO is used to connect to a private ATM network?
    a. NSAP
    b. NNI
    c. UNI
    d. E.164
14. Pick three characteristics of an ATM ELAN.
    a. Contains local broadcasts
    b. Must be unique on an interface
    c. Only one ELAN on an ATM network
    d. Independent of the physical network

15. Which ATM LANE component forwards data to other LANE components?
    a. LEC
    b. LECS
    c. LES
    d. BUS
16. Which ATM LANE component provides broadcasting support?
    a. LES
    b. BUS
    c. LECS
    d. LEC
17. The database of the LES/BUS ATM addresses is stored in which LANE component?
    a. LES
    b. LECS
    c. BUS
    d. LEC
18. What is the chief purpose of the ILMI protocol?
    a. Aiding in the initialization and configuration of ATM LECs
    b. Remote management
    c. Distributing multicast traffic
    d. Address resolution for LECS
19. The ILMI provides the ability to share the ATM prefix of which ATM device?
    a. LEC
    b. Catalyst switch
    c. End-station
    d. ATM switch
20. Which ATM component must be defined on a major interface?
    a. LEC
    b. LECS
    c. BUS
    d. LES

21. Which ATM component would a LANE client query to determine an end-station's ATM address?
    a. LEC
    b. LECS
    c. LES
    d. BUS

22. Which command is used to access an ATM module in a Catalyst 5000 located in slot 5?
    a. **connect 5**
    b. **session 5**
    c. **module 5**
    d. **telnet 5**

23. The first 12 bytes of the ATM address are known by what term?
    a. End System Identifier
    b. Equipment System Identifier
    c. Selector field
    d. ATM MAC address

24. The last two digits of the ATM address are known by what term?
    a. ESI
    b. Selector field
    c. End selector field
    d. 00

25. What is the maximum number of LECs that can be configured on an ATM module?
    a. 10
    b. 1024
    c. 255
    d. 2

Real-World Projects

When our faithful consultant, Joe Snow, gets into his office, the message-waiting light is blinking on his desk phone. As he retrieves his voice messages, one in particular catches his attention: It is an urgent message from his boss to come see him about an exciting new project. After stopping by the coffee machine to freshen up his cup, he enters his boss's office.

During the meeting, Joe's boss explains that he has been to a week-long seminar on new trends in networking. He has decided to network all of the company's branch offices and to start a remote conferencing system. The system will be an ATM network so that voice, video, and some data will be able to be on the same network. It will be a turnkey solution, so nothing will need to be done on the ATM switches or the network routers. However, he is concerned that the existing Ethernet network at the corporate office will not be able to see the ATM applications. He wants Joe to set up the network so everyone can access the applications on this network. Joe explains to him that this can be done by enabling Local Area Network Emulation services on the Catalyst 6500 he just installed.

Project 13.1

To complete this job, Joe will need to perform the following tasks on the Catalyst LANE module:

- Set up the ATM signaling on the major interface to be able to find the ATM switch
- Build a LEC server for the domain
- Start up the LAN Emulation Server (LES) and the Broadcast-and-Unknown Server (BUS)
- Start up the LAN Emulation Client (LEC)

1. Set up ATM signaling and ILMI Private Virtual Circuit (PVC) on the Catalyst ATM LANE module. Use the well-known PVCs for **qsaal** (VPI=0,VPC=5) and ILMI (VPI=0,VPC=16):

```
Console> (enable) session 5
Trying ATM-5...
Connected to ATM-5.
Escape character is '^]'

ATM> enable
ATM# configure terminal
ATM#(config) int atm 0
ATM#(config) atm pvc 1 0 5 qsaal
ATM#(config) atm pvc 2 0 16 ilmi
```

2. Build an LECS. One LECS must be present per domain and it must be defined on the main interface. For now, set up an unrestricted ELAN that any ATM LEC can join:

```
ATM(config)# lane database Corporate_Backbone
ATM(lane-config-database)# name default server-atm-address
 47.00918100000000E04FACB401.00100DAACC41.01
ATM(lane-config-database)#default-name default
ATM(lane-config-database)#end
```

3. Start the LECS:

```
ATM#(config) int atm 0
ATM#(config) lane config database Corporate_Backbone
ATM#(config) lane config auto-config-atm-address
```

4. Start the LES and BUS. One of these must exist for each ELAN. They also must be on a subinterface on the same device:

```
ATM#(config) int atm 0.1 multipoint
ATM#(config) lane server-bus ethernet default
```

5. Start the LEC:

```
int atm 0.1 multipoint
lane client ethernet1 default
```


As time goes by, the ATM solution that Joe put in is working like a charm. People are able to run voice, video, and data traffic over his ATM backbone and all is well. Lately, however, there has been some concern that the ATM setup is unrestricted and anyone can join the network. One of the applications that is used on this LAN is an executive videoconference. This videoconference is a critical function for Joe's boss, so to make sure that other host traffic doesn't interfere with it, Joe's management wants to add another ELAN to support it. For performance and security concerns, it has been decided to make it a restricted ELAN, limited to those clients that are authorized to use it.

Joe's process for setting up a restricted ELAN is similar to how he would set up an unrestricted ELAN. Because the first task done in Project 13.1 was to set up ATM signaling, and ILMI has been done, it is not necessary to do this step.

Project 13.2

Joe will need to do the following tasks to complete his project:

- Create a database for the LANE configuration server
- Bind the ELAN to the ATM address of the LANE server

- Specify a default ELAN
- Add an entry in the database for each client in the restricted ELAN

1. Create a LANE database for the LANE configuration server:

```
ATM(config)# lane database Corporate_Backbone
```

2. Bind the name of the ELAN to the ATM address of the LANE server. Include the restricted parameter to make this a restricted-membership ELAN:

```
ATM(lane-config-database)# name eng server-atm-address
47.00918100000000E04FACB401.00100DAACC41.01 restricted
```

3. Create a default ELAN so clients that aren't explicitly bound to the restricted ELAN can connect:

```
ATM(lane-config-database)# name default server-atm-address
47.00918100000000E04FACB401.00100DAACC41.01
ATM(lane-config-database)#default-name default
```

4. Add a database entry for each client of the associated restricted ELAN:

```
ATM(lane-config-database)# client-atm-address
47.00918100000000E04FACB401.0800200c3000.02 name mgr
ATM(lane-config-database)# client-atm-address
47.00918100000000E04FACB401.0800200c3001.02 name mgr
ATM(lane-config-database)# client-atm-address
47.00918100000000E04FACB401.0800200c3002.02 name mgr
```

CHAPTER FOURTEEN

14

IP MULTICAST

After completing this chapter, you will be able to:

- ✓ Identify the three IP multicast traffic types
- ✓ Understand the addressing scheme of the IP multicast protocol
- ✓ Explain how MAC addresses map to Class D addresses
- ✓ Understand the differences between IGMPv1 and IGMPv2
- ✓ Understand the protocols that IGMP supports
- ✓ Identify Cisco's CGMP features
- ✓ Configure IP multicasting

In the past, the majority of network traffic consisted of a single conversation between one sender and one receiver. Although that still remains the case in most environments, today's networks have seen a large increase in data traffic—including high-bandwidth applications, such as messaging applications, voice traffic, multimedia, distance learning, and (of course) the Internet. In many cases, this type of traffic involves one server sending a data stream to multiple devices. Some good examples are video conferencing and software updates over an intranet.

This type of traffic can be very demanding in terms of data usage. For example, if 100 people want a 1.5MB file, that translates into a demand of more than 150MB of data-link usage. Ouch! Even on a T3, that's a lot of simultaneous use. What's more, this calculation doesn't take into account the rest of the users' applications and data requirements.

We need a better way to send and receive data. The objective is to receive the data once and have it be copied from the destination router or switch to all the recipients who need the data. This ability is what *IP multicasting* offers. IP multicasting is based on the concept that the end receivers join a multicast group. Traffic is then delivered to all members of that group by the network infrastructure. The sender of the data does not need to know anything about the receivers. In this manner, only one copy of a multicast message will pass over any link in the network, and copies of the message will be made only where paths diverge at a router. This is a much more effective method of delivering traffic destined for multiple locations, and it provides significant performance improvements for the network.

In this chapter, we will explain the concepts behind IP multicasting. We will cover the types of multicast traffic and introduce you to the way multimedia traffic types are routed on a network. Finally, we will look at the methods to configure IP routing on your Catalyst switches and how to manage the resulting multicast traffic. We will begin with a discussion of the different types of multicast traffic.

IP Multicasting Overview

IP multicasting is an extension to the standard IP protocol and is described in RFC 1112, "Host Extensions for IP Multicasting." IP multicasting is the transmission of an IP datagram to a group of hosts identified by a single IP destination address. A multicast datagram is delivered to all members of its destination host group with the same reliability as regular unicast IP datagrams. There is no restriction on membership in these groups—hosts may be members of multiple groups, and they may join or leave at any time.

IP multicast datagrams are handled by multicast routers. A host transmits an IP multicast datagram as a local network multicast that reaches all the members of the destination host group. The multicast router will examine the packet and, if it is destined for other networks, will take responsibility for forwarding it to all other networks that have members of the destination group.

To really get to know the advantages of IP multicasting, let's examine how IP multicast traffic can be sent over networks.

Multimedia Traffic Types

IP multicast traffic can be sent through the network using one of three types of transmission methods. They are:

- Broadcast
- Unicast
- Multicast

Let's look at each of these types and see how they affect the network.

Broadcasts

In a typical broadcast network, broadcasts are stopped at the route processor. Broadcasts can be set to forward to every device on the network; however, this setup is not very efficient, because every PC in the network must process every piece of data that flows through the network. This process not only slows down the network, but the CPUs inside the users' PCs must process the data, which in turn takes away from the processing power of the PC for other uses such as data applications. Data broadcasts are typically small frames sent across the network—so, the performance effect is negligible, unless there is a broadcast storm.

Multimedia broadcasts, in contrast, can be huge packets several megabits in size. Processing these types of broadcasts can quickly use up all the available bandwidth in the network and bring the end workstations to a crawl. This is particularly true if you are in a shared 10BaseT environment. Figure 14.1 shows the traffic flow in a broadcast environment.

Unicasts

Unicast applications send one copy of each packet to each member of the multipoint group. This technique is simple to implement, but it has significant scaling restrictions if the group is too large. With unicasts, the broadcasts are not limited to a particular VLAN or subnet, and they can be used in wide area networks (WANs). As the number of users grows larger, so does the number of transmissions to the multiple clients. Due to the large size of audio and video

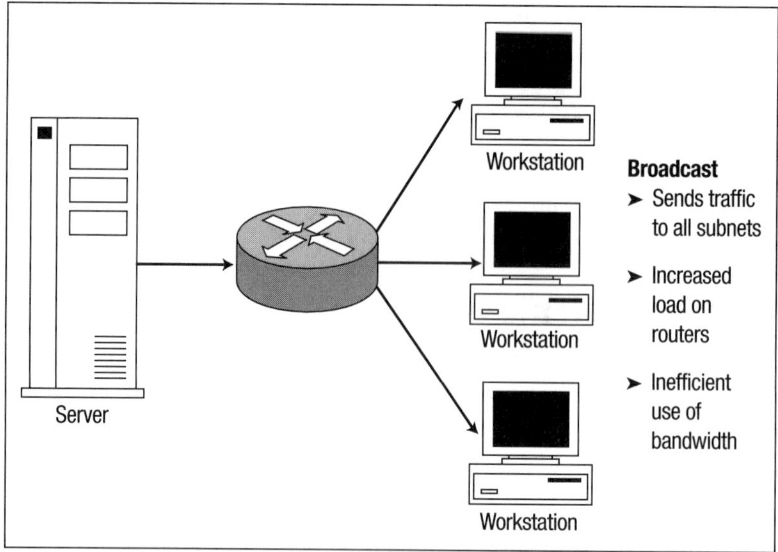

Figure 14.1 Broadcast traffic flow.

transmissions, network designers grow particularly concerned when such transmissions are obtained using unicast transmissions. Unicast traffic flow is shown in Figure 14.2.

Because a separate unicast data stream must be sent to each individual client on the network, bandwidth can be used up incredibly quickly. A network utilizing

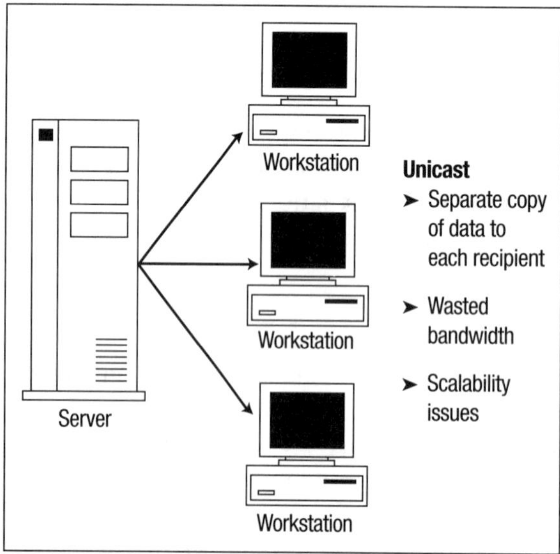

Figure 14.2 Unicast traffic flow.

Table 14.1 Number of users that can successfully utilize full-screen, full-motion video on each type of link from server to clients.

Link Type	Connections Supported
10Mbps	6 to 7 connections
100Mbps	50 to 60 connections
1,000Mbps	250 to 300 connections

10Mbps links can support only six or seven full-screen, full-motion video streams if each stream uses approximately 1.5Mbps of server-to-client bandwidth. This limitation is shown in Table 14.1.

Multicasts

IP multicasting is by far the best solution for transmitting multimedia over wide area and local links. In a multicast environment, the server needs to send only a single copy of the data on a single data stream to multiple clients utilizing group membership. Multicasting eliminates redundant transmissions, which saves bandwidth and reduces network host processing. Instead of transmitting to an individual host, it transmits to an identified group. Host groups support dynamic group membership without any regard to the location or number of clients. A single interface can be a member of multiple host groups. Multicast traffic flow is shown in Figure 14.3.

IP multicasting uses Class D IP network addresses to route data to different groups and hosts. In all likelihood, your basic networking classes probably covered IP network address Classes A, B, and C, but they may not have said much about Classes D and E. Maybe you were told that they are used for experimental purposes only and not to worry about them. Well, as you will see in the next few sections, things have changed.

IP Multicasting Addresses

IP multicasting uses a variation of a Class D network address to route multicast data streams. A Class D address is in the address range from 224.0.0.0 to 239.255.255.255. The IP multicast address is a variation or combination of the Media Access Control (MAC) address and the destination IP. Due to the nature of multicast addresses, they are frequently referred to as *multicast groups*. In addition, certain *well-known groups* have been identified by the Internet Assigned Numbers Authority (IANA). These are detailed in RFC 2365, and are known as *administrative scopes*. We will learn about the most well-known Cisco related addresses later in this section.

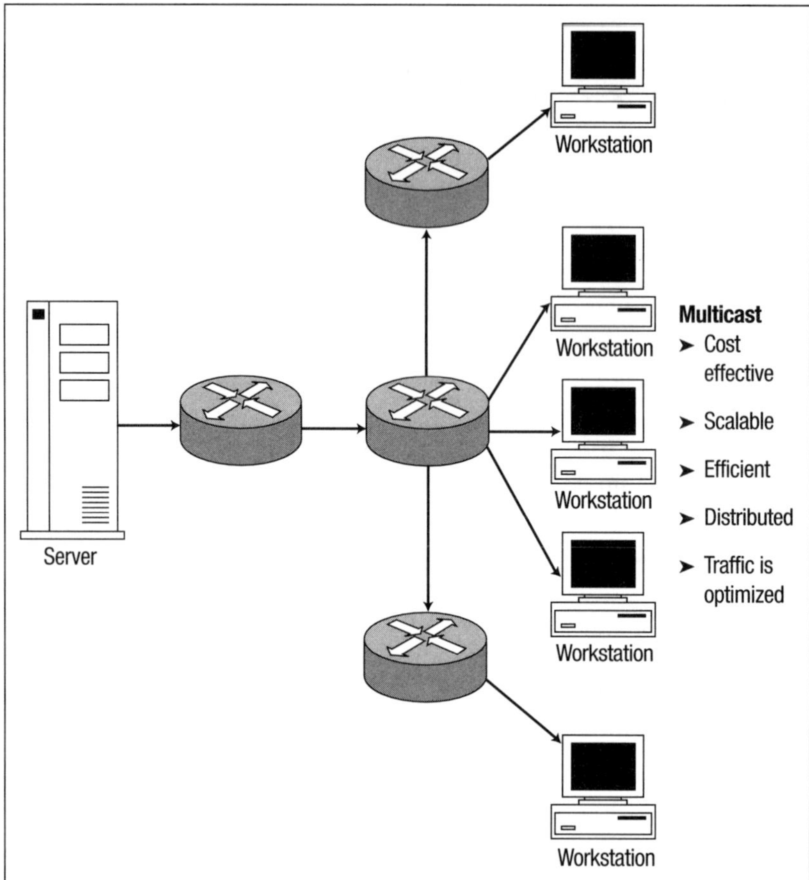

Figure 14.3 Multicast traffic flow.

The Multicast IP Structure

An IP multicast frame contains a single IP address. The host group is also identified by a single IP address. An IP multicast datagram combines a MAC address and a destination IP address to form a unique address. Let's look at how this is done by examining Figure 14.4.

A Class D address is a 32-bit IP address for IP multicasting that sets the first 4 high-order bits in the first octet address to 1110 or 224. The remaining 28 bits are used for the group address. Several well-known statically set IP addresses are set by the IANA, as shown in Table 14.2.

Static Class D Addresses

Two ranges of static IP addresses are reserved in the Class D series. The range from 224.0.0.0 to 224.255.255.255 is reserved for well-known addresses and local administrative purposes. Cisco routers by default do not forward IP multicast frames that arrive for any address beginning with 224.

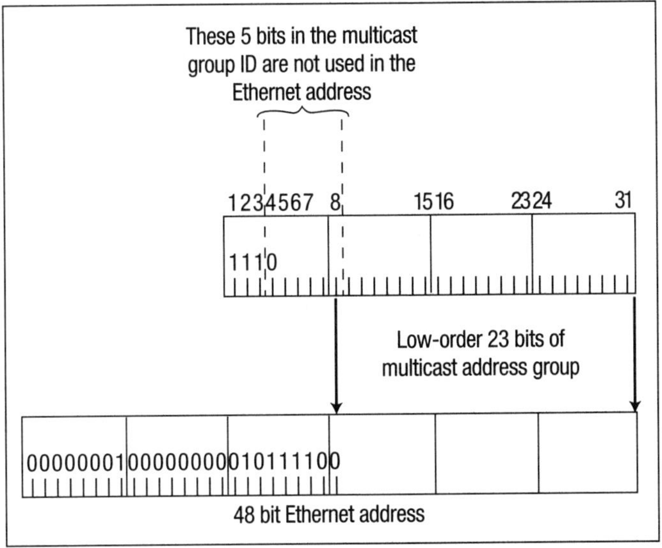

Figure 14.4 The IP multicast address structure.

The range from 239.0.0.0 to 239.255.255.255 is reserved for administrative scoping. When an administrative scope zone has been configured between route processors encircling a region in the network, these routers can be configured to deny multicast traffic for a certain address range from coming or going. This denial can be configured for networks that keep certain high-bandwidth traffic available for designated areas of the network.

Other addresses and ranges have been reserved for applications; for example, the range from 224.0.13.000 to 224.0.13.255 is reserved for Net News. For an updated list of reserved addresses and ranges, refer to Appendix D.

Table 14.2 Well-known static Cisco multicast addresses or permanent host groups, which work similarly to TCP UDP ports.

Well-Known Address	Destination
224.0.0.0	All subnet hosts
224.0.0.1	All subnet route processors
224.0.0.2	Not defined
224.0.0.3	Distance vector routing protocols
224.0.0.4	Open Shortest Path First (OSPF) route processors
224.0.0.5	Open Shortest Path First (OSPF) designated route processors
224.0.0.9	Routing Information Protocol (RIP)
224.0.0.13	Protocol Independent Multicast (PIM) route processors

Dynamic Class D Addresses

Multicast addresses can also be dynamically assigned on an on-demand basis.

Mapping Addresses in an IP Multicast Environment

IANA has been allocated a reserved portion of the IEEE-802 MAC-layer multicast address space. All of the addresses in IANA's reserved block begin with 01-00-5E (hex). A simple procedure was developed to map Class D addresses to this reserved address block; this procedure allows IP multicasting to take advantage of the hardware-level multicasting supported by network interface cards.

Ethernet frames have a 48-bit destination address field. The mapping between a Class D IP address and an Ethernet multicast address is obtained by placing the low-order 23 bits of the Class D address into the low-order 23 bits of the addresses reserved by IANA for multicasting. Because the IP multicast groups are 28 bits long, there is no one-to-one mapping; so, only the least significant bits are mapped. For example, a multicast address of 224.12.8.5 would map to an Ethernet MAC address of 01-00-5E-0C-08-05.

The fact that the upper 5 bits are ignored may cause some problems with duplicate addresses, because up to 32 different IP groups could be placed into the same Ethernet address. For example, the multicast addresses 224.138.8.5 (E0-8A-08-05) and 225.10.8.5 (E1-0A-08-05) would be mapped to the same Ethernet address (01-00-5E-0A-08-05). This situation does present a possibility, however slight, of collisions occurring in the network.

When choosing which multicast group your application should send to, you should consider that the mapping is not unique and the interface card can receive multicast frames in which multiple addresses may occur. For instance, 225.0.0.1 is a valid IP multicast address, but its MAC layer address will be the same as 224.0.0.1. This is also true for 224.128.0.1. If you use these addresses for your multicast application, you may have problems in your network.

Delivery of Multicast Datagrams

When the sender and receivers are members of the same subnet, delivery of multicast frames is a simple matter. The source station addresses the IP packet to the multicast group, the network interface card maps the Class D address to the multicast address, and the frame is sent. Receivers that want to capture the frame notify their IP layer that they want to receive datagrams addressed to the group.

When the sender is on one subnet and the receivers are on different subnets, the routers need to use a multicast routing protocol that permits the construction of multicast delivery trees and supports multicast data packet forwarding. That protocol is the Internet Group Management Protocol (IGMP).

Internet Group Management Protocol

The Internet Group Management Protocol (IGMP) is a method used to control the creation of multicast groups. An individual host uses IGMP to join a multicast group by informing its local router of a specific multicast group from which it wishes to receive data transmissions. Based on the group membership information learned from IGMP, multicast routers periodically query the network to determine if known group members are still active. There are two versions of IGMP: version 1 (IGMPv1), which was defined in RFC 1112; and version 2 (IGMPv2), which was defined in RFC 2236.

The Join Process

In both versions of IGMP, the join process is similar. If more than one router on the network is using IP multicasting, one of the routers will be designated to send out *Host Membership Query* messages to the all-hosts multicast address of 224.0.0.1. This query will determine which groups are active on the network. The router sets the time to live (TTL) field of the message to 1, which ensures that the query message is not forwarded beyond the routers.

When a host receives a query message, it responds with a *Host Membership Report* for each host group to which it belongs. A host does not need to wait for a query—it can send an unsolicited Host Membership Report to the multicast address 224.1.1.1, which is the all-routers address. Doing so will ensure that the host will receive the data if it is the only member of the group present on the network. If the router does not receive a report for a particular group after a number of queries, the router assumes that group members are no longer present on the interface, and the group is removed from the list of group memberships for the directly attached subnetwork.

IGMP Version 2

IGMPv2 includes additional functionality to reduce some problems associated with IGMPv1. One change is the method that IGMPv2 uses to elect a multicast *querier* that services multicast requests from hosts. In IGMPv1, the querier election was determined by the multicast routing protocol. This process frequently caused problems, because each multicast routing protocol used a different method for determining the multicast querier. In IGMPv2, the router with the lowest IP address on the LAN is elected the multicast querier.

Other changes between IGMPv1 and IGMPv2 are the addition of two new message types:

- *Group-Specific Query messages*—Allow a router to transmit a query to a specific multicast group rather than to all groups residing on a directly attached subnetwork.

- *Leave Group messages*—The last host in a group transmits a Leave Group message to the all-routers group (224.0.0.2) with the group field set to the group it has left. This method lowers the latency involved in leaving multicast groups.

Time to Live

An important topic with IGMP is the use of the IP time to live (TTL) field. The TTL field is a value in an IP packet that tells a network router whether the packet has been in the network too long and should be discarded. A multicast datagram with a TTL of 0 is allowed only on the same host. A TTL of 1, which is the default value, is allowed only on the local subnet. If a higher TTL is set, the router is allowed to forward the packet.

By increasing the TTL value, a multicast application can look farther and farther from its origin for a server. This process works in the following manner: The host first sends a multicast message with a TTL of 1. If it doesn't receive a response, it sends a multicast message with a TTL of 2, then 3, and so on, until it reaches its limit. In this manner, the application can locate the nearest server that can be reached.

IGMP Protocols

In order to build multicast routes for each multicast group, routers communicate with each other via one of the following protocols:

- Distance Vector Multicast Routing Protocol (DVMRP)
- Multicast Open Shortest Path First (MOSPF)
- Protocol Independent Multicast (PIM)

The following sections discuss these protocols.

Distance Vector Multicast Routing Protocol

DVMRP uses a technique known as *reverse path flooding* when a router receives a packet addressed to a multicast group. The router looks to see if this is the first time it has seen this particular packet or whether it has seen the packet before. If this is the first time it's seen a packet from the source, the router forwards the packet on all interfaces except the one on which it arrived. This forwarding helps ensure that the multicast packet reaches all routers in the network. If the router has seen the packet before, the packet is simply discarded.

Reverse path flooding is easy to implement, because a router only needs to keep track of the most recently seen packets. However, because it generates duplicate packets and doesn't have any consideration for the path it takes, it doesn't scale very well. Despite these limitations, DVMRP is widely used on the Internet and is the basis for the Internet Multicast Backbone (MBONE). The MBONE is used primarily to transmit desktop video conferencing and—due to the use of DVMRP as its protocol—it has been responsible for several Internet meltdowns when the volume of traffic is overwhelming.

Multicast Open Shortest Path First

The MOSPF protocol, in contrast, requires the routers in a multicasting environment to be aware of all the possible connections in the network. MOSPF is an extension of the OSPF protocols, so OSPF must be running in the network. OSPF is a link-state routing protocol that allows a network to be split into multiple areas. The OSPF link-state database provides the complete map of an area at each router. MOSPF works by including the multicasting information in the OSPF link-state advertisements.

By adding a new type of link-state advertisement (LSA) called the Group-Membership Link State Advertisement, the information about the location of members of multicast groups can be obtained and put in the database. Using the OSPF link-state information, the shortest-path delivery trees rooted at the source nodes can be constructed. Then, group membership information is used to prune those links that don't lead to a group member. As in the OSPF protocol, each router maintains a complete database of the entire network's topology. As such, MOSPF is usually suitable only for smaller environments with stable connections.

Protocol Independent Multicast

The Protocol Independent Multicast (PIM) routing protocol is a standard currently under development by the IETF. PIM is intended to be a standard multicast routing protocol that can provide scalable interdomain multicast routing across the Internet. As its name implies, PIM is not dependent on any routing protocol to perform its functions; however, this independence does not eliminate the use of a routing protocol to provide routing information and to adapt to topology changes.

PIM operates in two modes: Dense Mode (DM) and Sparse Mode (SM). DM is designed to operate in an environment where bandwidth is plentiful and the multicast traffic is destined for all LANs. DM is suitable for environments where there are a small number of senders and many receivers. DM is also a good choice in high-traffic networks with a constant stream of multicast traffic. PIM DM-enabled routers that have no local members of a group will prune themselves from that group with prune messages sent to neighboring IP multicast routers. The neighbors that receive the prune messages stop sending multicast messages and start a timer. When this timer has expired, they begin sending multicast messages to the pruned group again. This process is known as the *broadcast and prune cycle*.

SM is designed to operate in environments where group members are distributed across many regions of the Internet and where bandwidth is not necessarily widely available. SM does not imply that the group has few members, just that they are widely dispersed across the Internet. The objective behind SM is to prevent the likelihood that a relatively small number of devices wanting to participate in a multicast environment will cause the multicast traffic to overwhelm the network. SM is designed to limit multicast traffic so that only those routers interested in receiving traffic for a particular group participate in it.

PIM SM uses the concept of a *rendezvous point (RP)*. Each sender of data selects an RP and a small ordered set of alternative RPs. In each multicast group, there is only one active RP. A receiver wishing to join a multicast group contacts its directly attached router, which in turn joins the multicast distribution tree by sending an explicit join message to the group's primary RP. A source uses the RP to announce its presence and to find a path to members that have joined the group. Once the data stream begins, the routers in the network path find the best route to use. When SM is used, only hosts that have requested to join the group will receive the traffic.

***Note:** Cisco routers use PIM Sparse Mode. They can receive and forward messages to DVMRP neighbors, but they do not actually implement DVMRP in their networks.*

Cisco Group Management Protocol

Cisco Group Management Protocol (CGMP) was developed for the Catalyst 5000 because the hardware (Enhanced Address Recognition Logic [EARL]) cannot distinguish between IP multicast data packets and IGMP report messages that are addressed to the same MAC address. Other platforms (Catalyst 1900, 2820, and 3000) have adopted CGMP for this feature. CGMP allows switches to perform tasks similar to those performed by IGMP. Cisco equipment uses a combination of CGMP, PIM, and IGMP software components.

A Cisco switch uses CGMP exclusively and requires a connection to a router that is also configured to use CGMP. A router that has been configured to use both CGMP and IGMP to route multicast messages sees all IGMP packets and informs the switches of requests to join or leave IP multicast groups from hosts via CGMP. CGMP automatically detects which of the switch ports have CGMP-capable routers attached to them, but the switch ports that support CGMP also can be hard-coded into the switch configuration.

Cisco routers use the PIM protocol for routing multicast traffic to and from other sources in the network, and they use CGMP to send those requests to Catalyst switches. Each router interface that supports multicast traffic needs to be enabled to use PIM. When an IGMP control packet is received on a CGMP/IGMP-capable router, the router creates a CGMP or IGMP packet that contains the join or leave request type, the multicast group address, and the MAC address of the host. The router sends the packet to a well-known address that the switches listen to.

When a switch receives the packet, the Supervisor Engine module interprets the packet and searches its EARL table to determine whether it contains the MAC address of the host asking to join the multicast group. If the EARL has the MAC address in its table, a multicast forwarding entry is created in the EARL forwarding table. The host associated with that port receives multicast traffic for that multicast group. In this way, the EARL automatically learns the MAC addresses and port numbers of the IP multicast hosts. If the EARL table doesn't have an entry for the MAC address, the switch updates its forwarding table.

Queries are sent from the IGMP/CGMP router on a regular basis to the multicast groups. If a host wishes to remain in the group, it responds to the query. If it wishes to leave the group, it does not respond. After the host has failed to respond to several of these queries, the router sends a CGMP/IGMP command to the switch, instructing it to remove the multicast group from its forwarding table.

On Catalyst 6500s and the Catalyst 5000 with Supervisor Module III software release 4.1 or above, you can enable IGMP Snooping. IGMP Snooping watches for client IGMP join requests and builds the multicast groups in the Carrier Access Module (CAM) without the need for the router to inform the switch of the multicast groups. Cisco didn't use IGMP Snooping before, because the hardware could not detect if the packet was an IGMP packet. However, with the NetFlow Feature Card (NFFC), the hardware can now perform this detection.

In contrast to IGMP Snooping, CGMP operation does not adversely affect Layer 2 forwarding performance. Without CGMP, multicast traffic is flooded to the entire Layer 2 switch fabric. The upstream router prevents the multicast traffic from hitting the campus backbone, but does nothing to control the traffic in the switch fabric. With CGMP, however, the multicast traffic can be controlled—not only in the Catalyst 5000 switch directly connected to the router, but also in the downstream Catalyst switches. CGMP results in the ability to deliver multicast traffic at over 1 million packets per second and is the preferred method for implementing IP multicasting on Catalyst switches.

Configuring IP Multicast Routing

IP multicasting in a Cisco environment uses a combination of all the technologies we've mentioned. The following list summarizes where Cisco supports the protocols needed to implement IP multicast routing:

- IGMP is used between hosts and routers on a network to control multicast groups of which the hosts are members.

- PIM is used between routers to control which multicast packets to forward.
- DVMRP is used on the MBONE. Cisco IOS software supports PIM-to-DVMRP interaction.
- CGMP is used on routers connected to Cisco Catalyst switches to perform tasks similar to those performed by IGMP.

Implementing IP multicast support involves configuring a variety of devices and components. You must carry out careful planning and configuration to ensure the components are properly configured to support the IP multicast environment. To implement IP multicasting in a Cisco environment, you need to perform the following tasks:

1. Enable IP multicasting on a Cisco router
2. Enable PIM on the router interface
3. Configure IGMP on the router
4. Enable CGMP on the router
5. Enable CGMP on the switch
6. Perform miscellaneous tasks

Let's walk through these steps in more detail.

Enable IP Multicasting on a Cisco Router

By default, IP multicasting is not enabled on Cisco routers. To enable IP multicasting, enter the following command in Global Configuration Mode:

```
Router (config)# ip multicast-routing
```

Enable PIM on the Router Interface

The previous command configures IP multicasting on a global basis. However, routers forward multicast traffic on an interface-by-interface basis, so whatever multicast protocol you use must be applied to every interface to which you want to forward multicast traffic. As we stated before, Cisco routers use the PIM protocol, so PIM needs to be enabled on the interface you want to use. Enabling PIM on an interface also enables IGMP operation on that interface.

You can configure an interface to use Dense Mode, Sparse Mode, or Sparse-Dense Mode. The way you configure PIM also affects how the router builds its multicast routing table. For example, DM interfaces are always added to the table, but SM interfaces are added only when join messages are received from downstream routers, or if there is a directly connected member on the interface.

To configure PIM on an interface to be in Dense Mode, use the following command in Interface Configuration Mode:

```
Router (config)# int vlan 1
Router (config-if) ip pim dense-mode
```

To configure PIM on an interface to be in Sparse Mode, use the following command in Interface Configuration Mode:

```
Router (config)# int vlan 1
Router (config-if) ip pim sparse-mode
```

When you're using SM operation, if an RP is known for the group, the multicast packets are sent to the RP. When no RP is known, the packet is flooded in a DM fashion. An RP can be manually configured, or the multicast router can be configured to use Auto-RP. Auto-RP is a Cisco proprietary mechanism that automates the sparse-group-to-RP mappings in a network. This automation can be very handy in a large network. A multicast router can serve as an RP for several groups, and a group can have more than one RP. To manually set a multicast router to be an RP, use the following command in Global Configuration Mode:

```
Router (config)# ip pim rp-address 192.168.1.2
```

After you have configured Auto-RP, you need to configure the multicast router to announce itself as a candidate RP for a range of multicast group addresses. To do this, use the following command:

```
Router (config)# ip pim send-rp-announce ethernet0
```


The final part of this process is to define the *RP mapping agent*, which is the multicast router that tells the other routers which group-to-RP mapping to use. This information helps to prevent mapping conflicts. An RP mapping agent should be configured on a multicast router whose network connection is stable. All routers within TTL number of hops (as defined by the **scope** parameter) from the source multicast router receive the Auto-RP discovery messages.

To assign the role of RP mapping agent in the router, use the following command in Global Configuration Mode:

```
Router (config)# ip pim send-rp-discovery scope 16
```

In these examples, the multicast router at 192.168.1.2 will act as an Auto-RP, will announce that status to the other multicast routers, and will serve as an RP mapping agent for up to 16 hops.

To monitor your network, you can use the **show ip pim** commands. To display information about interfaces configured for PIM, use the following EXEC Mode command:

```
cs> show ip pim interface
Address         Interface        Mode     Neighbor  Query      DR
                                          Count     Interval
192.168.1.2     Ethernet0        Dense    2         30         192.168.1.2
```

To display information about the RPs configured in your network, enter the following command:

```
cs# show ip pim rp
Group: 224.1.1.1, number of RPs: 1
  RP address: 192.168.1.2, state: Up, next RP-reachable in 0:01:01
```

To display information about who is configured for PIM on your network, enter the following command:

```
cs> show ip pim neighbor
PIM Neighbor Table
Neighbor Address  Interface          Uptime    Expires
192.168.1.1       Ethernet0          17:38:16  0:01:25
192.168.1.30      Ethernet0          17:33:20  0:01:05   (DR)
```

Configure IGMP on the Router

The first task in the implementation of IGMP is to define which of the multicast groups your multicast router is to be a member of. Once a multicast router has been configured as a member of a multicast group, it will respond to IGMP echo requests that are addressed to that group. At this point, if you ping the multicast group address, all hosts present will respond to the query. Enable the multicast router to become a member of a multicast group with the following command:

```
Router (config) int vlan 1
Router (config-int) ip igmp join-group 224.1.1.1
```

By default, a Cisco multicast router supports IGMPv2. Some versions of the Cisco IOS detect IGMPv1 packets, but that feature is not supported on the latest releases of the IOS. All hosts on the network must support the same version. If you need to modify the IGMP version—for example, to version 1—use the following command:

```
Router (config-if) ip igmp version 1
```

If you want the multicast messages to go beyond your local subnet, you need to change the TTL value. Only multicast packets with a TTL greater than the interface TTL threshold are forwarded on the interface. The default value is 0, which means that all multicast packets are forwarded on the interface.

Enable CGMP

CGMP must be enabled on the multicast router to which a switch is connected and on the switch itself. CGMP should be enabled only on routers connected to Catalyst switches. When CGMP is enabled on a Cisco router, it triggers a CGMP join message. To enable CGMP for IP multicasting on a Cisco router, use the following command in Interface Configuration Mode:

```
Router (config-if) ip cgmp
```

To enable CGMP for IP multicasting on Catalyst switches, enter the following command:

```
Console> (enable) set cgmp enable
CGMP support for IP multicast enabled.
```

To enable CGMP fast-leave processing, enter the following command:

```
Console> (enable) set cgmp leave enable
CGMP leave processing enabled.
Console> (enable)
```

To show the CGMP leave statistics, enter the following command:

```
Console> (enable) show cgmp leave

CGMP:       enabled
CGMP leave: enabled
Console> (enable)
```

To show the CGMP switch statistics, enter the following command:

```
Console> (enable) show cgmp statistics 1
CGMP enabled

CGMP statistics for vlan 1:
valid rx pkts received          511715
invalid rx pkts received        0
valid cgmp joins received       511829
valid cgmp leaves received      175
valid igmp leaves received      0
```

```
valid igmp queries received      3412
igmp gs queries transmitted      0
igmp leaves transmitted          0
failures to add GDA to EARL      0
topology notifications received  60
number of CGMP packets dropped   1032227
```

CHAPTER SUMMARY

IP multicasting is a routing technique that allows IP traffic to be sent from one source or multiple sources and delivered to multiple destinations. Instead of sending individual packets to each destination, as in unicast technology, a single packet is sent to a multicast group, which is identified by a single IP destination group address. IP multicast routing arose because unicast and broadcast techniques do not handle the requirements of new applications very well.

At the heart of IP multicasting is the Internet Group Management Protocol (IGMP). IGMP is defined by RFC 1112 and relies on the use of Class D IP addresses for the creation of multicast groups. IGMP is used to dynamically register individual hosts in a multicast group.

Hosts identify group memberships by sending IGMP messages, and traffic is sent to all members of that multicast group. Under IGMP, routers listen to IGMP messages and periodically send out queries to discover which groups are active or inactive on particular LANs. Routers communicate with each other by using one or more protocols to build multicast routes for each group.

Several routing protocols are used to discover multicast groups and to build routes for each group. These include Protocol Independent Multicast (PIM), Distance Vector Multicast Routing Protocol (DVMRP), and Multicast Open Shortest Path First (MOSPF).

PIM includes two different modes of behavior for dense and sparse traffic environments: *Dense Mode* and *Sparse Mode*. The PIM Dense Mode uses a process of reverse path flooding that is similar to the DVMRP. Differences exist, however, between Dense Mode PIM and DVMRP. PIM, for example, does not require a particular unicast protocol to determine which interface leads back to the source of a data stream. DVMRP employs its own unicast protocol, whereas PIM uses whatever unicast protocol the internetwork is using. PIM Sparse Mode is optimized for networks with many data streams but relatively few LANs. It defines a rendezvous point that is then used as a registration point to facilitate the proper routing of packets.

DVMRP is used as the basis for the Internet's Multicast Backbone (MBONE) and is well known for not scaling well. DVMRP involves a multicast router sending a copy of a packet out to all paths (except the path back to the origin) upon the packet's receipt. Routers then send a prune message back to the source to stop a data stream if the multicast router is attached to a LAN that does not want to receive messages from a particular multicast group.

MOSPF is an extension of OSPF. In general, MOSPF employs a unicast routing protocol that requires each multicast router in a network to be aware of all available links. An MOSPF multicast router calculates routes from the source to all possible group members for a particular multicast group. MOSPF routers include multicast information in OSPF link states. MOSPF calculates the routes for each source/multicast group pair when the multicast router receives traffic for that pair, and routes are cached until a topology change occurs. MOSPF then recalculates the topology. MOSPF works only in networks that use OSPF as their routing protocol. In addition, MOSPF is best suited for environments with relatively few active source/group pairs. MOSPF can take up significant multicast router CPU bandwidth in environments that have many active source/group pairs or that are unstable.

Cisco Catalyst switches use a protocol known as Cisco Group Management Protocol (CGMP). CGMP was originally developed for the Catalyst 5000 because the hardware could not distinguish between IP multicast data packets and IGMP report messages that are addressed to the same MAC address. Newer models of the Catalyst 5000 and 6500 support IGMP Snooping, but CGMP remains the method of choice for most Catalyst users. Implementing CGMP is a simple act of entering the **set cgmp enable** command. CGMP automatically detects which switch ports have CGMP-capable routers attached to them.

Cisco implements IP multicasting by utilizing separate IP multicast protocols on different platforms:

- IGMP is used between hosts and routers on a network to control multicast groups of which the hosts are members.
- PIM is used between routers to control which multicast packets to forward.
- DVMRP is used on the MBONE.
- Cisco IOS software supports PIM-to-DVMRP interaction.
- CGMP is used on routers connected to Cisco Catalyst switches to perform tasks similar to those performed by IGMP.

Review Questions

1. IP multicast is described in which of the following RFCs?
   a. RFC 1577
   b. RFC 1112
   c. RFC 1111
   d. RFC 1812
2. A network broadcast sends data to which devices on a network?
   a. Every device on the network
   b. Only the end user's machine
   c. The switch only
   d. The multicast router only
3. Which of the following best describes how unicast will send a broadcast to multiple addresses?
   a. One copy to multiple clients
   b. One copy to each device in a multipoint group
   c. One copy to multiple devices in a group
   d. All the devices on a network
4. Which of the following best describes how multicast will send a broadcast to multiple addresses?
   a. One copy to multiple clients
   b. One copy to each device in a multipoint group
   c. One copy to multiple devices in a group
   d. All the devices on a network
5. IP multicasts use which class of IP network addresses?
   a. Class A
   b. Class B
   c. Class C
   d. Class D
6. Class D addresses are in which address range?
   a. 224.1.1.0 to 224.255.255.255
   b. 224.0.0.1 to 224.255.255.255
   c. 224.0.0.0 to 239.255.255.255
   d. 224.0.0.0 to 239.255.55.255

7. What well-known IP multicast address is used for sending distance vector routing protocol information?
   a. 224.0.0.1
   b. 224.0.0.3
   c. 224.0.0.4
   d. 224.0.0.5
8. What is the reserved block of MAC addresses used for IP multicasting?
   a. 08-00-00
   b. 01-00-5E
   c. 01-00-00
   d. 224.0.0.1
9. Which protocol is used to control the creation of multicast groups?
   a. IP
   b. PIM
   c. ICMP
   d. IGMP
10. The multicast address 224.1.1.1 is used for what purpose?
   a. Time to live
   b. To send a Host query to all devices
   c. To send a Host Membership Query to all multicast routers
   d. To send a Host Membership Report to all multicast routers
11. In IGMPv2, which multicast router is designated as the querier?
   a. The multicast router with the highest IP address.
   b. The multicast router with the lowest IP address.
   c. It is randomly selected.
   d. The multicast protocol determines the querier.
12. A TTL of 1 allows multicast protocols to be forwarded to which destination?
   a. All subnets
   b. The host only
   c. The local subnet
   d. One hop

13. MBONE uses which type of multicast routing protocol?
    a. DVMRP
    b. RIP
    c. PIM
    d. MSOSPF
14. Which modes does PIM support? [Choose the two best answers]
    a. Dense Mode
    b. Scant Mode
    c. Sparse Mode
    d. Stream Mode
15. Each IP multicast group can have up to how many RPs defined?
    a. No limit
    b. Only 1
    c. Many, but only 1 is active
    d. 2
16. CGMP is used on Cisco switches to provide which functions?
    a. EARL
    b. IGMP
    c. PIM
    d. MAC layer
17. Which protocol is used between Cisco routers to exchange IP multicast messages?
    a. IGMP
    b. DVMRP
    c. PIM
    d. CGMP
18. IP multicasting is enabled on Cisco routers by default.
    a. True
    b. False
19. Where is the PIM function configured?
    a. On a multicast router in Global Configuration Mode
    b. Per interface
    c. On a Catalyst switch
    d. On a Catalyst module

20. To implement IGMP on a multicast router, you must first perform what task?
    a. Join a multicast group
    b. Start CGMP on a switch
    c. Connect to the Internet
    d. Configure an RP

Real-World Projects

Joe Snow is quite pleased with the work he has done on his network, and for the most part it has operated at very high performance. Lately, though, he has seen some issues pop up on the network. About a month ago, his department installed a new video conferencing system. This system allows his company to provide remote access to meetings people can't attend in person. It also allows remote training capabilities, and the HR department has used it to train employees.

Joe has noticed that occasionally, when the video applications are running, the response time on his network crawls to a halt. After investigation, he has determined that a dozen or more people sometimes access the system at the same time. He has done some reading about video technology and believes that if he implements IP multicasting, he will be able to dramatically improve network performance.

Joe also has noticed an increase in the number of Internet video applications being used at his site. Soon, he will deal with the configuration steps needed to manage DVMRP traffic more efficiently. For the moment, however, he will configure the RSM module in his Catalyst 5000 to work in IP PIM Sparse Mode; he will also enable his switch for CGMP.

Project 14.1

To configure an RSM module to work in PIM Sparse Mode, perform the following:

1. Connect to the RSM of the switch to configure it as a multicast router:

```
Switch1>(enable) session 3
Trying Router-1...
Connected to Router-1
Router1>
```

2. Join a multicast group on interface VLAN1:

```
Router1> enable
Router1# configure terminal
Enter configuration commands, one per line. End with CNTL/Z.
Router1(config)# interface vlan 1
Router1(config-if)# ip igmp join-group 224.10.1.2
```

3. Verify which IGMP end-stations have joined the multicast group by entering the following command:

```
Console> (enable) show multicast router
IGMP enabled

Port       Vlan
----       ----
1/1        1
2/1        2,99,255

Total Number of Entries = 2
'*' - Configured
Console> (enable)
```

4. Select the IGMP version that the multicast router uses:

```
Router1(config-if) ip igmp version 2
```

5. Enable IP multicast routing in Global Mode:

```
Router1 (config)ip multicast-routing
```

6. Enable an IP multicast routing protocol. In this case, because there will be relatively few members in the multicast group, use Sparse Mode PIM on the interface:

```
Router1(config-if) ip pim sparse-mode
```

Project 14.2

To enable the switch for CGMP, do the following:

1. Exit the RSM session and enable CGMP on the Catalyst switch:

```
Switch1> (enable) set cgmp enable
CGMP support for IP multicast enabled.
```

2. To show CGMP statistics, enter the following command:

```
Console> (enable) show cgmp statistics 1
CGMP enabled

CGMP statistics for vlan 1:
valid rx pkts received          211915
invalid rx pkts received        0
valid cgmp joins received       211729
valid cgmp leaves received      186
valid igmp leaves received      0
valid igmp queries received     3122
igmp gs queries transmitted     0
igmp leaves transmitted         0
failures to add GDA to EARL     0
topology notifications received 80
number of CGMP packets dropped  2032227
Console> (enable)
```

3. Enable CGMP leave processing:

```
Switch1> (enable) set cgmp leave enable
CGMP leave processing enabled.
```

4. To show CGMP statistics, use the following command:

```
Console> (enable) show cgmp leave

CGMP:       enabled
CGMP leave: enabled
```

Chapter Fifteen

15

Policy Networking

After completing this chapter, you will be able to:

- ✓ Identify the security features of each layer of the network
- ✓ Know the definition of an access policy
- ✓ Identify and implement a security policy
- ✓ Manage network device security policies
- ✓ Implement security in the access layer
- ✓ Implement security in the distribution layer
- ✓ Create and apply access lists
- ✓ Know the limitations of implementing security in the core layer

The objectives of this book to this point have focused on the reasons for implementing switching, the switches themselves, switch components, configuring switches, configuring components, switching protocols, and identifying the different topologies. This chapter focuses on the creation of access policies and how to implement those policies.

Security is one of the most important functions of today's networks. Without security, competitors have free access to information; information is open to hackers and others who should not have it; your network is subject to terrorism; and you can never count on data integrity. Security must start at the physical device and extend throughout the entire network. The security features that can be applied with the Internetwork Operating System (IOS) software running on a switch or router is not enough to protect your network. All these areas—including security policies, management policies, and device security—should be included in your access policy.

After the access policies are created, it's a great advantage for you—as the administrator of your network—to know how to implement those policies at the core, distribution, and access layers of the campus network. The following sections will cover all this material in depth and explain how it relates to IP switching and routing.

Chapter Terms

The following are terms you should know when reading the rest of this chapter:

- *Distribution list*—Allows you to filter inbound or outbound routing updates at the distribution layer.
- *In-band management*—Refers to the type of management used when Trivial File Transfer Protocol (TFTP) servers, network management software, and virtual terminal ports are used to manage the switch or router.
- *Out-of-band management*—Refers to the type of management used when the Console 0 and Auxiliary 0 ports are used for switch or router management.
- *Route summarization*—Provides the ability to summarize multiple subnets within a few subnets, thereby reducing the size of the routing table.
- *Virtual terminal (VTY) ports*—Used in out-of-band management to Telnet in to the switch. By default, five VTY ports can be configured so that five simultaneous connections can be made to the switch or router.

Note: *Pay attention to these terms, because they show up in most Cisco CCNA, CCDA, and CCNP tests.*

Creating an Access Security Policy

An *access security policy* is designed to secure the network and prevent unwanted network access. Creating a documented access policy for your business or entity allows the network administrator to provide a service-level agreement based on a set of defined traffic and security standards.

An access security policy should define the following:

- The physical security of all the devices in the network
- Control of user access to the network through the implementation of virtual LANs (VLANs) and port security
- What traffic should be allowed in and out of the network
- Route filters to determine the data that should be sent through the network and what route filters should be applied at the core layer
- User groups that have access to each area of the network
- Types of access each user group should have to the network

Each layer of the network has a different function and applies policies differently. Figure 15.1 shows the policies and switches found at each layer of the network.

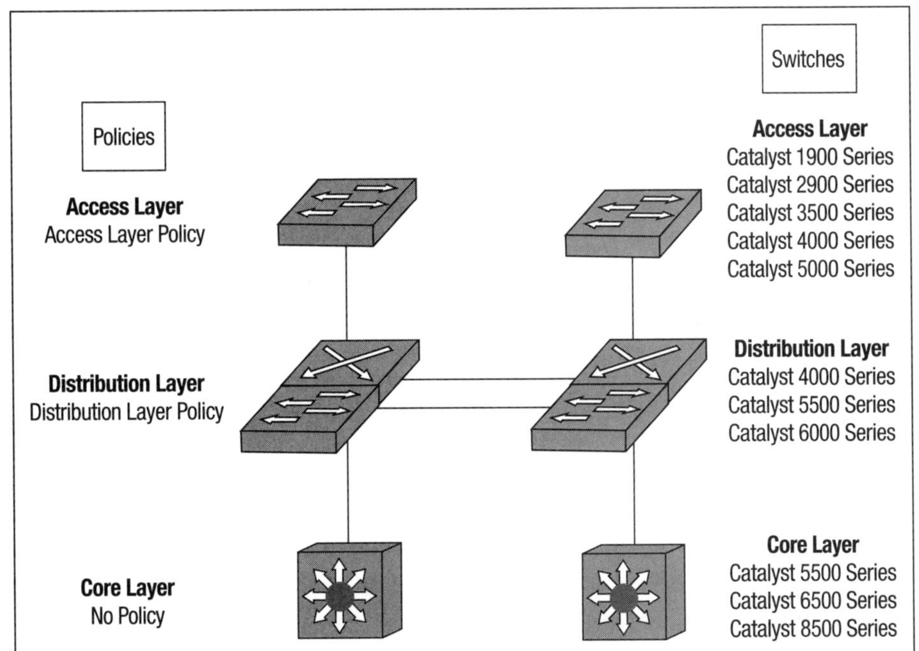

Figure 15.1 The policies and switches found at each layer of the switched network.

Policies defined in the access security policy need to be applied to all the devices in your network. In the following sections, we will address how security should be applied at each individual layer of the network.

Policies at the Core Layer

By implementing security policies at the core layer, you increase the latency at this layer. The job of the core layer is to pass traffic as quickly as possible. Policies should be applied at the access and distribution layers before the data reaches this level. The core layer should rely on the other two layers to provide security policies and to block traffic. Route summarization and distribution lists implemented at the distribution layer can greatly reduce the latency at this layer.

Tip: The only policies at the core layer should relate to Quality of Service (QoS), to aid in congestion management or congestion avoidance.

Policies at the Distribution Layer

The distribution layer is the primary layer for implementing your security and access policies. Implementation at this layer can be as simple as applying policies blocking a certain workgroup, or as complex as defining which path certain types of data should take through the network. This layer is also responsible for advertising correct routes, blocking identified traffic, and limiting the amount of data sent to the core layer.

In this section we will cover the following issues relating to the distribution layer of the network:

- Distribution layer policies
- Access and distribution lists
- Managing virtual terminal access
- Managing HTTP access

Distribution Layer Policies

The distribution layer is the demarcation point between the access and core layers. Thus it is the perfect point in the network in which to place policies and to administer most of your network policies. The distribution layer should define which resources and routes are sent to the core layer, as well as what traffic should be allowed in or out of the switch block.

A good policy at this layer ensures that no unnecessary traffic or incorrect routes are advertised to the core layer switch blocks. A good distribution layer policy should define the following:

- The user traffic that can span different VLANs. This can be defined by applying access lists to identified interfaces to permit or deny certain data traffic.
- The routes that should be seen by the core switch block. They can be defined by applying distribution lists.
- The services that will ultimately be advertised to the rest of the network. These services include the Domain Name Service (DNS) and Dynamic Host Configuration Protocol (DHCP).

Access Lists

Access lists are lists of conditions that control access to the switch, router, or route processor. An access list is like an imaginary policeman who controls access from or to different segments of the network. Let's pretend that the input port and the output port have a police officer to stop or direct traffic in and out of a port or interface. Once an access list has been applied to an interface, an implied "no access" appears at the end of each access list. This means that the police officer guarding the interface has orders to deny all traffic unless other orders permit the data to pass through.

The Internet Protocol (IP) and Internetwork Packet Exchange (IPX) protocol access lists work about the same way. They both filter packets by comparing an identified value and acting upon a permit or deny statement. Once you build an access list, your policeman (access list) can be applied to an inbound interface or an outbound interface. As soon as the access list is applied to an interface, your data traffic policeman starts to look at each packet of data flowing through the interface. The policeman compares the frame's receiving information (such as the source address) to the values in your access list. If a match is made, the officer follows the order to permit or deny the data. If he denies the data, an Internet Control Message Protocol (ICMP) message is sent to the source address listed in the packet header, notifying it of the denial.

15

In Figure 15.2, the source address of 38.187.128.6 is trying to send a data packet to 38.187.128.10. There is no permit statement for the source address; so, the access list automatically denies the packet.

Several times in this chapter, you will be reminded that an implicit "deny all" statement appears at the end of each access list. Before you apply the access list to the currently used management station using a console port or virtual terminal line, always remember to check that you have a permit statement near the top

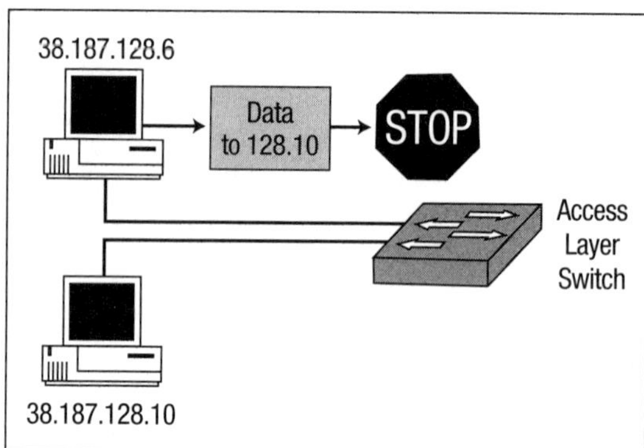

Figure 15.2 The data encounters an access list with no permit statement applied to the interface to allow a frame from the source address 38.187.128.6 to send data to the destination address.

of your access list for the management station you are using. You won't believe how many times we have had to deal with an administrator who is unfamiliar with access lists and who has locked himself out of his own switch or route processor.

It is important to remember that an access list is read in the order that it is configured. You can't permit a subnet or range of addresses and then deny an address in that range in a deny statement later in the list. Once the access list finds a match, it follows the rules to that match and then stops looking for another match. Let's look at an analogy. Suppose you're walking down a lane in a parking lot, looking for your car. Once you find your car, you don't continue looking. It is the same with access lists—if the access list makes a match, it does not continue looking for further instructions.

Standard and Extended Access Lists

There are two types of access lists: *standard* and *extended*. Both types of access lists permit or deny based on certain criteria. The standard access list allows a permit or deny statement based only on the source address. The extended access list is a bit more complex—it allows you to permit or deny based on the source address, destination address, protocol type, application type, or port number of the packet.

Standard IP and IPX addresses are the easiest to configure. The configuration statement requires an access list number, a permit or deny statement, and then the source address. This statement allows packets originating from the identified source address to be permitted or denied through the interface to which the access list is applied. Let's take a look at an example of permitting the source address from Figure 15.2 on access list 2:

```
5000RSM (config)# access-list 2 permit 38.187.128.6
```

To identify a subnet in one statement, you can use a wildcard value after the IP address. Without a wildcard value, the source address must match completely. The wildcard value looks a lot like a subnet mask. A 0 in the wildcard string indicates that the value must match exactly in the same octet of the IP address. A value of 255 means that any number in that corresponding octet of the IP address can be used. Let's look at the following access list string as an example:

```
access-list 2 permit 193.5.5.10 0.0.0.255 log
```

Tip: An octet is the 8-bit value between each dot in an IP address. Let's say we are using the IP address 38.187.128.6. The first octet is 38, and the fourth or last octet is 6.

The 0.0.0 of the wildcard address means that the first three octets of the source interface's IP address must exactly match the first three octets of the network portion of the Class C IP address: 193.5.5. Because the last octet is 255, the last octet of the source interface of received data can be any host address value. This statement means that any host address with the network ID 193.5.5 will be permitted.

Based on your IP scheme, you may be using variable-length subnet masks (VLSM). To identify the IP addresses that can be used with your chosen subnet mask, you must use the correct inverse address to identify those addresses. The inverse wildcard address allows you to specify only a small range of hosts. This is sometimes referred to as a *block size*. You have to specify the range of values in a block size of eight. In other words, you can't choose to specify 25 networks. So for this example, the range could be 24 or 32, but not 25.

Let's say that you want to block access to part of network that is in the range from 200.1.8.0 through 200.1.15.0. That is a block size of 8. Your network number would be 172.16.8.0, and the wildcard would be 0.0.7.255. Why is that? The 7.255 is what the router uses to determine the block size. The network and inverse wildcard addresses tell the IOS to start at 200.1.8.0 and go up a block size of eight addresses to network 200.1.15.0.

We won't go into a lengthy discussion on binary math, but actually all you need to do is remember that the wildcard is always one number less than the block size. In the previous example, the wildcard would be 7 because our block size is 8. If you used a block size of 16, the wildcard would be 15. Table 15.1 shows the possible wildcard inverse addresses that can be matched to the subnet mask.

The type of access list defined is identified by the number you assign to the access list. Table 15.2 identifies the types of access lists that can be configured, along with the associated string of numbers that can be used with each type.

Table 15.1 Possible wildcard inverse addresses.

Mask	Wildcard Inverse Address
255	0
254	1
252	3
248	7
240	15
224	31
192	63
128	127
0	255

Table 15.2 The available access list numbers and the associated access list types.

Available Numbers	Access List Type
1 through 99	IP standard
100 through 199	IP extended
200 through 299	Protocol-Type-Code
300 through 399	DECnet
600 through 699	AppleTalk
700 through 799	48-Bit Media Access Control (MAC) address
800 through 899	IPX standard
900 through 999	IPX extended
1000 through 1099	IPX Service Advertising Protocol (SAP)
1100 through 1199	Extended 48-bit MAC address
1200 through 1299	IPX summary address

Extended access lists use many of the same configuration rules as standard access lists. An extended access list allows filtering based on source address, destination address, protocol type, application, or TCP port number. Just as in standard access lists, an implied "deny all" exists at the end of each list.

The IP extended access list command is more complex than the standard access list command and offers many more options. The IP extended access list syntax is shown here:

```
access-list access-list-number {deny | permit} {protocol type}
source-address source-wildcard destination-address destination-wildcard
[protocol specific options|operator] [log]
```

Tip: You can use the syntax **any** to replace the source or destination address. The **any** syntax implies all addresses.

Let's take a look at the syntax elements for the IP extended access list that are not included in the standard access lists:

- ***access-list-number***—For an IP extended access list, the range of possible numbers is 100 to 199.
- **deny | permit**—A **permit** indicates whether the source will be allowed in or out of an interface. A **deny** indicates that the data will be dropped and an ICMP message will be sent to the source address.
- ***protocol type***—This syntax element indicates the protocol to match. Possible options include **eigrp**, **icmp**, **igrp**, **ip**, **nos**, **ospf**, **tcp**, **udp**, or any number from 0 to 255.

Tip: The protocol type **ip** indicates all protocol types.

- ***operator***—This syntax element compares source or destination ports. Possible syntaxes include **lt** (less than), **gt** (greater than), **eq** (equal), **neq** (not equal), and **range** (inclusive range).
- **log**—This syntax enables logging of information about packets that match access list entries.

Warning: The **log** command is optional and logs information about all packets that match the access list entry. Enabling this feature uses considerable processing power. You should use it for troubleshooting purposes only.

Let's take a look at the **any** syntax:

```
5000RSM(config)# access-list 199 permit tcp 0.0.0.0 255.255.255.255
    0.0.0.0 255.255.255.255 gt 255

5000RSM(config)# access-list 199 permit tcp any any gt 255
```

15

The first line permits any incoming IP address to any destination using any TCP port greater than port 255. The second line does the same thing, but replaces the source, destination, and wildcard addresses with the **any** command.

Now, let's examine how well-known TCP ports can work:

```
access-list 199 permit tcp any any eq 25

5000RSM(config)# access-list 199 permit tcp any any eq smtp
```

The first line indicates that access list 199 permits any address to enter the interface for TCP port 25, which is the well-known TCP port for Simple Mail Transfer Protocol (SMTP). The second line does the same thing, but instead of using the TCP port number, it uses the acronym.

The host syntax indicates a single host, as shown in the source address in this example:

```
5000RSM(config)# access-list 199 permit tcp host
   38.187.128.6 any eq smtp
```

The following is an example of configuring your access list to allow ICMP echo and echo reply. Echo and echo reply are used in troubleshooting with the IP **ping** and **tracert** commands:

```
5000RSM(config)# access-list 199 permit icmp any any echo

5000RSM(config)# access-list 199 permit icmp any any echo-reply
```

Warning: By permitting all ICMP traffic, this command allows the router to pass spoofed ICMP packets, which could lead to a systems failure or unwanted network access. Use caution when permitting certain types of data traffic.

The following example permits User Datagram Protocol (UDP) packets with a DNS name as the destination:

```
5000RSM(config)# access-list 199 permit udp any eq domain any
```

You can add a message in your access list by using the **remark** command. This command can help you identify lines in your access list. The following is an example of using the **remark** command:

```
5000RSM(config)# access-list 1 remark Sean's IP Address
5000RSM(config)# access-list 1 permit 38.187.128.52
5000RSM(config)# access-list 1 remark Joe Snow's IP Address
5000RSM(config)# access-list 1 deny 38.187.128.53
```

To remove a remark, use a command like the following:

```
5000RSM(config)# no access-list 5 remark Doug's IP address
5000RSM(config)#
```

Applying Access Lists

Access lists can be created by a variety of means. Once the access lists are created, different commands allow you to apply an access list to different types of interfaces. Access lists can be applied on the interface where the data enters the switch. To keep the data from flowing through the fabric and exiting out any interface or port, use the **in** syntax. If you would like this data to flow through the switch but not exit out a certain interface or port, use the **out** syntax on the outbound interface. The following list shows the different commands and the types of interfaces associated with each command:

- **access-class**—Applies the access list to an interface for security purposes. This command identifies users who may access specified virtual terminal (VTY) lines.
- **access-group**—Allows you to apply an access list to an interface or port to manage data traffic for an identified protocol. For example, with the IP protocol (which includes all the associated IP protocols), to apply access list 2 for the interface where data you wish to filter will enter, use the command **ip access-list 2 in** while in Interface Configuration Mode.
- **distribute-list**—Identifies the routing update information that applies rules to allow the switch to learn new routes or advertise known routes to other routers or route processors.
- **ipx output-sap-filter**—Allows the applied access list to determine what IPX protocol services will be advertised in or out of an interface.

Applying Filters to Virtual Terminal Lines

The **access-class** command allows you to apply an access list to a line interface to control access to VTY lines. By default, five VTY lines come in to your Cisco IOS or router. Because you do not know which one you will be using when you Telnet into your switch or router, you must apply the same access list to all the interfaces.

15

First, let's create an access list that allows Telnet access to the switch from the IP address 38.187.128.18 (the IP address of the only PC you will be using to Telnet into your switch). To do this, use the following command:

```
5000RSM (config)# access-list 5 permit 38.187.128.18
```

Next, you need to enter Line Configuration Mode for all five VTY lines with the following command:

```
5000RSM (config)# line vty 0 4
5000RSM (config-line)#
```

Finally, use the **access-class** command to apply the access list to an inbound interface with the following command:

```
5000RSM (config-line)# access-class 5 in
5000RSM (config-line)#
```

If you need to apply the access list to an outbound interface, use the following command:

```
5000RSM (config-line)# access-class 5 out
5000RSM (config-line)#
```

Applying Filters to HTTP Access

Starting with the release of version 11.0(6) of the Cisco IOS, Cisco included the Hypertext Transfer Protocol (HTTP) server software, which allows you to manage the Cisco IOS from a Web browser. This software makes managing your switches easier—but opens a giant security hole.

By default, access through HTTP is disabled. To enable access through HTTP, use the following command:

```
5000RSM(config)# ip http server
```

An access list can be configured to allow you to choose the IP address of the network device that can be used to access the switch. For example, use the following command to allow a PC with the IP address 38.187.28.12 for access list 2:

```
5000RSM(config)# access-list 2 permit 38.187.28.12
```

Suppose this is the only statement in the access list using the HTTP Switch Manager with Web browser access. Because of the implied "deny all," once this access list is applied, only a PC with IP address 38.187.28.12 will be able to manage the switch. Before this access list will take effect, however, you must still apply the access list, state the authentication type, and configure the username and password. The following shows an example of applying access list 2, which was created in the previous example:

```
5000RSM(config)# ip http access-class 2
```

You can apply four different types of authentication to HTTP access on a switch or router. Table 15.3 describes each of the four types of authentication.

To apply the authentication type, use the following command:

```
5000RSM(config)# ip http authentication local
```

Table 15.3 The four HTTP authentication types for a switch route processor or router.

Syntax	Description
aaa	Allows authentication, authorization, and accounting (AAA) to be used for authentication
enable	Allows the enable password method; the default method of HTTP server user authentication
local	Allows the local user database on the Cisco router, route processor, or access server to be used for authentication
tacacs	Allows the Terminal Area Security Access Control (TACACS) or Extended TACACS (XTACACS) server to be used for authentication

***Note:** You can use the **no ip authentication** command to disable the configured authentication type.*

To configure the username Sean and the password book1, use the following command:

```
5000RSM(config)# username sean password book1
```

You can provide an added layer of protection. Normally, the Cisco IOS ClickStart software or the Cisco Web browser interface uses the standard TCP port 80. However, you can configure another port for access from a Web browser. To set the TCP port to 50, use the following command:

```
5000RSM(config)# ip http port 50
```

You can reset the HTTP TCP port configuration to 80 by using the following command:

```
5000RSM(config)# no ip http 80
```

15

Applying Access Lists to Route Filtering

By controlling the routing tables in the core layer devices of the network, you can limit the size of the tables. Doing so allows the switches to process more quickly, prevents users from getting to networks that do not have a default or static route, and maintains routing information integrity.

One way to do this is to apply an access list using the **distribute-list** command. After creating a standard access list, you can apply it to an inbound or outbound interface. The following is the **distribute-list** command and the syntax for an inbound interface:

```
distribute-list {access-list number|name} in [type number]
```

The following is the syntax for the **distribute-list** to allow you to apply an access list to an outbound interface:

```
distribute-list {access-list number|name} out
[interface name|routing process|autonomous system number]
```

Figure 15.3 shows a standard Class B network in which two subnets intersect at the distribution layer switch. Subnet 128 belongs to our production network, and subnet 129 is used only for testing and development of new LAN topologies. We want subnet 128 to be permitted through to the core layer on our Gigabit Ethernet port g0/0, which connects to the core layer switch. The second network is used for testing purposes only, so our access list should block any traffic from that subnet from reaching the core layer switches. For this scenario, we will assume there are no other subnets in our switch block to contend with.

Let's create an access list that allows traffic from network 38.128.0.0 but denies traffic from interface 38.129.0.0. Use the following command, keeping in mind that an implied "deny all" exists at the end of our access list:

```
access-list 1 permit 38.128.0.0 0.0.255.255
```

Next, you must specify a routing protocol: in this case, Enhanced Interior Gateway Routing Protocol (EIGRP). To do so, use the following command:

```
router eigrp 1
```

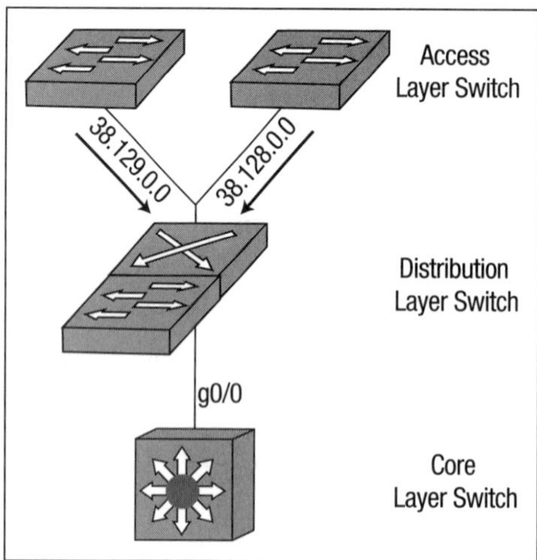

Figure 15.3 Two Class B IP subnets connected from the access layer to the distribution layer switch. The distribution layer switch connects to the core layer switch using Gigabit Ethernet 0/0 (g0/0).

The last step is to apply the configured access list. Use the **distribute-list** command for interface g0/0 to filter outbound traffic from network 38.129.0.0:

```
distribute-list 1 out g0/0
```

Security at the Access Layer

The access layer should have little policy. The switches at this layer should rely on port-level security and passwords required on the network interfaces.

The access layer policy controls physical access to the components of the network. Physical access involves the following:

- Configuring users and passwords on the physical devices
- Limiting Telnet access
- Limiting access to network switches by implementing privilege levels
- Configuring banner messages
- Physical device security
- Port security
- VLAN management

Configuring Passwords

Passwords can be configured on every access method to a Cisco Catalyst switch. Passwords can be applied to the console port, auxiliary (AUX) port, and VTY lines. We covered password configuration in Chapter 5.

Limiting Telnet Access

VTY access can be secured with a password. However, when a careless administrator walks away from a logged-in Telnet session, the door is open with full access to the entire network. This situation allows anyone with access to that terminal to make changes and attack the network.

A solution is to add another layer of security. You can do this by applying a time-out condition to unused VTY sessions. The Cisco IOSs calculate unused sessions in seconds or minutes, depending on the IOS version. Should the session not receive a character input from the administrator's session within the configured amount of time, the session is closed, and the administrator using the session is logged out.

To configure a timeout value for Cisco IOS command-based switches, use the following command. The timeout value is set to five minutes, using seconds:

```
2924XL (config)# line console
2924XL (config)# time-out 300
```

Tip: You can use the **lock** command to lock an unused Telnet session. After you issue the **lock** command, the system will ask you to enter and verify an unlocking password.

To configure a Set/Clear command-based switch to five minutes, use the following syntax:

```
5009 (enable) set logout 5
```

To configure the timeout value to five minutes on the console port of an IOS-based route processor or router, use the following syntax:

```
5000RSM (config)# line console 0
5000RSM (config-line)# exec-timeout 5
```

To configure the timeout value to five minutes on the VTY lines of an IOS-based route processor or router, use the following syntax:

```
5000RSM (config)# line vty 0 4
5000RSM (config-line)# exec-timeout 5
```

Tip: To configure seconds beyond a minute, you can add an additional value to the command. For example, if you want the **exec-timeout** to be 5 minutes and 10 seconds, the command is **exec-timeout 5 10**.

Implementing Privilege Levels

Privilege levels can be assigned to limit switch users' ability to perform certain commands or types of commands. You can configure two types of levels in the IOS: user levels and privilege levels. A user level allows a user to perform a subset of commands that does not allow for configuration changes or debug functions. A privilege level, on the other hand, allows the user to use all the available commands, including configuration change commands.

You can assign a user 16 different levels, from level 0 to level 15. Level 1 is set to User EXEC Mode by default. This level gives the user very limited access, primarily to **show** commands. Level 15 defaults to the Privileged EXEC mode, which gives the user full access to all configuration commands in the IOS (including the **debug** command).

Privilege level 0 is a special level that allows the user to use a more specific defined set of commands. As an example, you could allow a certain user to use only the **show arp** command. This command is useful when a third party is using a sniffer on your network and needs to match a MAC address to an IP address and vice versa.

Using the **privilege level** command allows you to assign a better-defined set of commands for a selected user. Let's walk through how to do this. First, you need to select a user and associate that user with a privilege level. User Ted Moore has the login name tmoore; let's assign him a privilege level of 3. To do this, use the following command in Global Configuration Mode:

```
5000RSM (config)# privilege configure level 3 tmoore
5000RSM (config)#
```

You should assign a password for each configured privilege level. To assign the password ted1 to privilege level 3, use the following command:

```
5000RSM (config)# enable secret level 3 ted1
```

When Ted wants to log in to the switch, he will use the following command:

```
5000RSM (config)# username tmoore password ted1
```

This setup allows the user tmoore to use certain **show** commands by default, but gives him no access to the **debug** or configuration commands. To allow the user to use all the **debug** commands in privilege level 3, use the following command:

15

```
5000RSM (config)#  privilege exec level 3 debug
5000RSM (config)#
```

To allow users with privilege level 3 a certain command syntax for **debug**, such as **debug ip**, use the following command:

```
5000RSM1 (config)#  privilege exec level 3 debug ip
5000RSM1 (config)#
```

Note: *Privilege level 0 includes five commands associated with the privilege level:**disable**, **enable**, **exit**, **help**, and **logout**.*

Configuring Banner Messages

In studying for Cisco exams (such as CCNP and CCNA), you are instructed on creating banner messages in almost every class. In fact, you have probably messed around on a non-production router or switch and inserted your own saying or name. In a production environment, your switch or router greets potential threats to your network with a banner message.

Although this task seems miniscule, it is very important to your security. Many times, a hacker has gotten away with his crime and a district attorney has decided not to pursue hacking charges, because the greeting welcomed intruders into the network. Never use the word *welcome* in your banner messages!

To configure a Message of the Day (MOTD) banner on a Set/Clear command-based switch, use the following command from a Privileged Mode prompt:

```
CAT5000(enable) set banner motd 'We Prosecute Unauthorized Access!'
```

To configure an MOTD banner on a Cisco IOS command-based switch or route processor, use the following command from a Global Configuration Mode prompt:

```
CAT5000RSM (config)# banner login 'We Prosecute Unauthorized Access!'
```

Physical Device Security

Physical access to all devices in your network—not just switches—should be included in your access policy. Protecting the physical access to a machine on your network is very important. Passwords can be applied to all access points from the network to the switch, but backdoor methods are always available. A person with physical access and the right knowledge can apply those techniques to the device to gain entry.

You can create and apply a control policy in your network. Make sure that you provide a policy that includes all the physical devices and their links at all the layers of your network. It's just as easy to attack your network from the access layer as from the core layer.

You should provide a proper physical environment that allows for locking the room where devices are kept, locking device racks, and securing backup power sources and physical links. You should also verify that passwords are applied at all levels, and you should disable unused or unnecessary ports (including AUX ports) in your network.

Tip: Make sure that your room provides proper ventilation and temperature controls while providing the listed security.

Port Security

The Cisco IOS provides a feature called *port security* that lets you limit the MAC addresses that are allowed to use the ports on the switch. MAC addresses come pre-configured on a Network Interface Card (NIC), and because of applied industrywide standards, no two NIC cards have the same MAC address. By configuring certain MAC addresses to use the switch, you greatly increase control over which PCs can access the switch.

When port security is enabled on a switch, the switch ports are configured to accept only traffic from an identified MAC address or addresses. When a port on the switch receives a data frame, it compares the source MAC address of the frame to the secure source address learned or configured on the port. If the port receives data from a MAC address that has not been previously identified, the switch locks and disables the port. The light on a Cisco switch that has been locked down and disabled turns orange, indicating that the port is disabled.

Note: *If SNMP is configured, a trap link down message will automatically be sent to the SNMP manager.*

You should know a couple of points before trying to apply port security:

- Do not apply port security to trunk links, because they carry data from multiple VLANs and MAC addresses.
- Port security cannot be enabled on a Switched Port Analyzer (SPAN) source or destination port.
- You cannot configure dynamic or static content addressable memory (CAM) entries on a secure port.
- After you enable port security on any switch port, any static or dynamic CAM entries associated with the port are cleared and any currently configured permanent CAM entries are treated as secure MAC addresses.
- Not all Cisco switches support port security. Check Cisco Connection Online (CCO) at **www.cisco.com** to see if your hardware and IOS version support port security.

The default settings of a switch allow all MAC addresses the right to access all ports on a switch. If you enable port security, immediately only those MAC addresses explicitly identified can send data to the switch ports. You can configure ports with a static MAC address assignment or a dynamic MAC address assignment.

Static MAC Assignment vs. Dynamic MAC Assignment

Dynamic MAC address assignment allows the administrator to do basically nothing. Once port security is enabled, the first interface to broadcast its MAC address on the port becomes the port's secure MAC address. If another machine broadcasts a frame over the physical wire to the switch port with another MAC address, the port will automatically go into a locked-down, disabled mode.

Static MAC address assignment requires the network administrator to physically assign a MAC address to a port. This is the most secure way of creating the list, but it requires a lot of time and effort to manage. For smaller networks, this might be a good solution; in bigger networks, it is not easily implemented.

To enable dynamic port security on a Set/Clear command-based switch for module 1 port 3, use the following command:

```
2926G>(enable) set port security 1/3 enable
Port 1/3 port security enabled with the learned mac address.
Trunking disabled for Port 1/3 due to Security Mode
```

To show a port configuration for port security, use the following **show** command:

```
2926G> (enable) show port 1/3
```

The output should look similar to this:

```
Port  Name  Status     Vlan  Level   Duplex  Speed  Type
----  ----  ------     ----  -----   ------  -----  ----
1/3         connected     2  normal  half    100    100BaseTX

Port Security Secure-Src-Addr   Last-Src-Addr     Shutdown Trap IfIndex
---- -------- ---------------   -------------     -------- ---- -------
1/3  enabled  00-30-19-4c-80-a6 00-30-19-4c-80-a6

Port   Broadcast-Limit   Broadcast-Drop
----   ---------------   --------------
1/3                  -                0

Port  Align-Err  FCS-Err  Xmit-Err  Rcv-Err  UnderSize
----  ---------  -------  --------  -------  ---------
1/3           0        0         0        0          0

Port Single-Col Multi-Coll Late-Coll Excess-Col Carri-Sen Runts Giants
---- ---------- ---------- --------- ---------- --------- ----- ------
1/3           0          0         0          0         0     0      0
```

```
Last-Time-Cleared
-----------------
Fri Dec 22 2000, 19:53:38
```

To enable static port security for module 1 port 3, manually specify the secure MAC address of the attached interface 00-30-19-4c-80-a6 using the following command:

```
2926G> (enable) set port security 1/3 enable 00-30-19-4c-80-a6
Port 2/1 port security enabled with 00-30-19-4c-80-a6
as the secure mac address
Trunking disabled for Port 1/3 due to Security Mode
2926G> (enable)
```

On a Cisco IOS command-based switch, you can use the **port secure** interface configuration command to enable addressing security. In Interface Configuration Mode, to assign a port to allow only one MAC address, use the following command:

```
2924XL(config-if)# port secure max-mac-count 1
```

Tip: You can assign **max-mac-count** a value between 1 and 132.

Use the **show mac-address-table** command from Privileged EXEC Mode to display the MAC address table. Here is the command and syntax placement—Table 15.4 shows the description of each syntax element:

```
show mac-address-table [static | dynamic | secure | self |
  aging-time | count]
[address hw-addr] [interface interface] [atm slot/port][vlan vlan-id]
```

15

Table 15.4 The **show mac-address-table** command optional syntax descriptions.

Syntax	Description
static	Displays the static addresses
dynamic	Displays the dynamic addresses
secure	Displays the secure addresses
self	Displays addresses added by the switch itself
aging-time	Displays aging time for dynamic addresses for all VLANs
count	Displays a count for different kinds of MAC addresses
address	Displays information for a specific MAC address
hw-addr	Displays information for the given MAC address
interface	Displays addresses for the specific port

(continued)

Table 15.4 The **show mac-address-table** command optional syntax descriptions *(continued)*.

Syntax	Description
atm	Adds dynamic addresses to an ATM module slot/port
slot	Associates the dynamic address with a slot (1 or 2) port
port	Adds dynamic addresses to a port (the port number is always 0 for ATM interfaces)
vlan	Displays addresses for a specified VLAN
vlan-id	Displays addresses for the VLAN

To show the MAC table in Privileged Mode, use the following command:

```
2924XL# show mac-address-table
```

The output from the **show mac-address-table** command looks like the following:

```
Dynamic Addresses Count:                5
Secure Addresses (User-defined) Count: 0
Static Addresses (User-defined) Count: 0
System Self Addresses Count:            12
Total MAC addresses:                    8

Non-static Address Table:

Destination Address   Address Type   VLAN   Destination Port
-------------------   ------------   ----   ----------------
00-30-19-4c-80-a6     Dynamic           3   FastEthernet0/6
00-30-19-4c-80-a5     Dynamic           1   FastEthernet0/4
00-30-19-4c-80-b3     Dynamic           1   FastEthernet0/4
00-30-19-4c-80-13     Dynamic           3   FastEthernet0/6
00-30-19-4c-80-c4     Dynamic           3   FastEthernet0/6
```

Tip: You can use the **no port secure** command to disable addressing security or to set the maximum number of addresses allowed on the interface to the default value of 132.

VLAN Management

When you first provide the switch with an IOS, all the ports on the switch are assigned to VLAN1. In a typical environment, VLAN1 is also kept as the management VLAN. This means that anyone entering the network on VLAN1, where the ports were not configured or were reset to their defaults, would be in the management VLAN. Cisco recommends that the management VLAN be moved to a VLAN other than the default VLAN1 to prevent the types of problems just described.

Note: *We cover VLAN configuration in Chapters 8 and 10.*

Chapter Summary

In this chapter, we covered the wide array of policy decisions that must be made regarding the creation of an access security policy. Each different layer of your network must be included to form a complete policy. Physical security needs to be considered to make sure that untrusted individuals with internal access will not be able to apply well-known techniques of physical access.

In addition, this chapter provided an outline of policies that should be implemented on each layer of the network, including physical access. For each layer of the network, we discussed the policies that should be implemented, gave an in-depth discussion on implementing each policy, and included a step-by-step example of how to configure each policy.

You should go back to the sections that discuss the access layer and the distribution layer as many times as necessary until you have a complete understanding of this material. The test covers these sections in great detail.

One other item we would like to note is that when applying an access list, you are creating a policy by which you can ban yourself from accessing the switch. The Cisco IOS will apply an access list without warning you that your configuration session will be terminated because you failed to enter a permit statement for yourself. You can literally lock yourself out of your own switch.

Remember just a few things before applying your access list to an interface you use for managing the switch:

- Always check that the access list includes a permit statement for yourself.
- Check all the lines in your access list above your permit statement to verify that no deny statement appears ahead of your permit statement. Remember, the statements are processed in the order they are configured.

When applying the access list to a switch—especially to one in your distribution layer, where it can affect many people—back up your configuration so that you can easily reinstall the old configuration in the event of a problem. If you don't run a 24-hour-a-day, 7-day-a-week business, schedule implementation of your access lists during a scheduled down time and test your configuration thoroughly. If your configuration uses more than one switch block, don't forget to test whether access is available from each switch block to another according to the rules in your access list.

By following these safety precautions, you can save your users and yourself large doses of headache medicine.

Review Questions

1. Which information should be included in an access security policy?
   a. Control of user access to the network
   b. Types of route filtering to determine routes that should be seen by the core block
   c. Physical security of network devices
   d. All of the above
2. Which wildcard address specifies all the nodes in a Class C network?
   a. 0.0.0.0
   b. 0.0.0.255
   c. 0.0.255.255
   d. 0.0.255.0
3. Which command would permit only the address 38.187.128.7?
   a. **access-list 1 permit any any**
   b. **access-list 38.187.128.7**
   c. **access-list 1 permit 38.187.128.7**
   d. **access-list 1 permit 38.187.128.7 0.0.0.255**
4. Which command would identify an IP extended access list?
   a. **access-list 800**
   b. **access-list 9**
   c. **access-list 201**
   d. **access-list 101**
5. Which command would apply an access list to a virtual terminal line?
   a. **access-group**
   b. **distribution-list**
   c. **access-class**
   d. **ipx output-sap-filter**

6. Which command would allow you to enable HTTP access to the Cisco IOS on a switch?
   a. **ip http authentication local**
   b. **ip http server**
   c. **no ip http**
   d. **http server**
7. Which of the following is not an authentication type that can be applied to the HTTP access for switch management?
   a. Enable password method
   b. Local
   c. TACACS
   d. access-class
8. Which methods apply security to virtual terminal lines? [Choose the two best answers]
   a. Applying a timeout value to all virtual terminal lines
   b. Applying a password to the console port
   c. Applying a password to the virtual terminal lines
   d. Applying a password to the AUX 0 port
9. Which of the following is the default privilege level for the Privileged EXEC Mode on an IOS-based switch?
   a. 0
   b. 15
   c. 1
   d. 16
10. Which of the following can be used with in-band management? [Choose the two best answers]
   a. Console 0
   b. Virtual terminal lines
   c. AUX 0
   d. TFTP

11. With port security on an IOS command-based switch, what is the maximum **max-mac-count** value that can be assigned to a port?
    a. 1005
    b. 255
    c. 1
    d. 132
12. On a port with port security configured, what color will the port light change to when the port receives data from an unknown MAC address?
    a. Yellow
    b. Green
    c. Orange
    d. Red
13. Which commands will allow you to configure a login message on a Cisco switch? [Choose the two best answers]
    a. **set banner motd**
    b. **banner login**
    c. **banner login motd**
    d. **config login banner**
14. Which command displays the port security configuration?
    a. **show ?**
    b. **show module**
    c. **show port**
    d. **show all**
15. Which string of numbers is available for a 48-bit MAC address access list?
    a. 300 through 399
    b. 700 through 799
    c. 800 through 899
    d. 900 through 999
16. The Cisco IOS can provide all the security a network needs.
    a. True
    b. False
17. An access list has an implied "permit all" at the end.
    a. True
    b. False

18. Which of the following would be the inverse wildcard mask for an octet in the subnet mask of 224?
    a. 31
    b. 1
    c. 0
    d. 63
19. Port security on a switch port compares which of the following addresses to incoming frames to verify authenticity?
    a. IP address
    b. MAC address
    c. IPX address
    d. Gateway address
20. Which of the following wildcard masks would indicate all nodes in a standard Class B IP network?
    a. 0.255.255.255
    b. 0.0.0.255
    c. 0.0.255.255
    d. 0.0.0.0

Real-World Projects

Joe Snow has been called out to do some security consulting for a large manufacturing company. Recently, the two owners of the company came to an agreement to split the company in half and go their separate ways. One owner has discovered that IT staff now working for the other owner have been using FTP to gain access to the network. In addition, they are gaining access to the company's confidential assets.

The owner would like Joe to ensure that all FTP access—including FTP passwords and all unnecessary login accounts—are eliminated. To go one step further, Joe is to make sure that no access goes past the route processor interface to FTP.

The owner has added another complication: FTP is used by his advertising company to upload ads for overview and verification. The company uses a Class C IP address scheme from 193.5.5.0 to 193.5.5.254. These should be the only addresses allowed. Let's take a look at the servers located on the access layers and determine where Joe should apply an access list, as depicted in Figure 15.4.

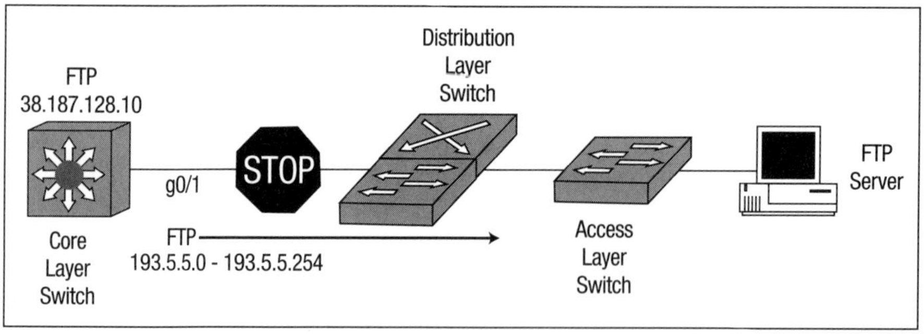

Figure 15.4 The FTP server located on the company's access layer switch, the FTP traffic that should be allowed, and the FTP traffic that should be denied.

Project 15.1

To create the access list, perform the following:

1. Because the access list will be read in order, you first need to permit the addresses that can access the FTP server. FTP uses both ports 20 and 21, so it should be configured like this:

```
RSM(config)# access-list 100 permit tcp 193.5.5.0 0.0.0.255 any eq 20
RSM(config)# access-list 100 permit tcp 193.5.5.0 0.0.0.255 any eq 21
```

TIP: For an added level of security, you can identify the individual hosts' IP addresses that are trying to access your network.

2. The following commands will deny all the other traffic on ports 20 and 21:

```
RSM(config)# access-list 100 deny tcp any any eq 20
RSM(config)# access-list 100 deny tcp any any eq 21
```

3. Because the access list has an implied "deny all" at the end, you need to apply a rule that any other traffic can pass through. The **ip** indicates that all IP protocols are being identified:

```
RSM(config)# access-list 100 permit ip any any
```

This command statement looks like you are giving access to FTP again. However, by the time IP traffic reaches this statement in the access list, it already will have filtered and denied all port 20 and 21 traffic.

Project 15.2

Joe does not want to apply the access list to the outbound interface, because then the FTP packets would span the switch fabric and use up bandwidth and processing power. He wants to apply the access list immediately to the inbound interface of the company's distribution layer switch.

To apply the access lists to an interface, perform the following:

1. Access the interface to be configured. In this case, from Global Configuration Mode, use the following command:

   ```
   interface gigabit0/1
   ```

2. Apply the access list to the interface to block access to inbound packets using the following command:

   ```
   ip access-group 100 in
   ```

That's it! Unless the packets for FTP are coming from the advertising company, no one else will be able to access the FTP server using FTP.

CHAPTER SIXTEEN

16

MANAGING CISCO SWITCHES

After completing this chapter, you will be able to:

- ✓ Provide an overview of network management
- ✓ Describe the methods used to manage a Cisco switched environment
- ✓ Describe the operations of the Cisco Discovery Protocol
- ✓ Understand the components of CiscoWorks2000
- ✓ Understand the functionality of CiscoWorks for Windows

As networks grow increasingly vital to business operations, the process of managing these networks has become a critical component of the network infrastructure. Network management software has evolved to provide an administrator with the capabilities to install, configure, troubleshoot, diagnose, and monitor network components.

All of the Cisco switches support two types of management: in-band and out-of-band. *In-band management* uses the IP protocol to access one of the switch's LAN or WAN ports. *Out-of-band management* uses the console port to access the device. This method is not reliant on the network to manage the switch and is particularly helpful for accessing the device if the network is down.

In addition, all Catalyst switches support the Simple Network Management Protocol (SNMP). The switches also support four embedded Remote Network Monitoring (RMON) groups and provide the capability to use a Switched Port Analyzer (SPAN) for in-band traffic monitoring. By default, the Cisco Discovery Protocol (CDP) runs on all Catalyst switches. Many Cisco products use CDP to provide information about the devices in your network.

This chapter will cover the basics of network management. We will discuss the functional areas of network management as defined by the International Organization for Standardization/Open System Interconnection (ISO/OSI) standards body and examine what each of these areas includes. In addition, we will discuss SNMP, RMON, and CDP. We will also cover Cisco's network management product offerings, including CiscoWorks2000 and CiscoWorks for Windows. Both products provide network administrators with a variety of tools to monitor, control, and manage the network.

We will begin with an overview of what network management is all about.

Overview of Network Management

There are numerous ways to describe the function of network management systems. The ISO divides the management of networks into OSI management functional areas. The acronym FCAPS is used to represent these five elements of the ISO definition:

- *Fault/problem management*—Concerns detecting, diagnosing, and correcting network and system faults. It accomplishes this by handling alerts, managing events, and providing diagnostic tools and corrective or alternative actions.
- *Configuration management*—Deals with the installation, identification, removal, and configuration of hardware, software, and services. Configuration management concerns itself with the ability to administer changes to a managed

object, as well as the ability to detect changes in a device's status. Some of the applications within the configuration management functional area are software management, change control, and inventory management.

- *Accounting management*—Concerns allocating costs associated with billing for time and services rendered by the service provider. Users, applications, and other resources, and billing for that utilization, are also concerns of this area.
- *Performance management*—Involves measurement and analysis of short- and long-term network and system statistics. This area is related to the usage, response time, availability, and error rates of the network and network applications. Performance management deals primarily with providing an efficient use of resources and not with the detection of problems in the network. Performance data is used proactively to prevent failures, as a planning and design aid, and as a performance-tuning advisor for improving network and systems efficiency. Performance baselines can be used as a tool in fault isolation.
- *Security management*—Concerns managing security for the communications network and the network management infrastructure. This area includes user access rights, data privacy, alarms and audit trails of security attacks/breaches, and the management of security mechanisms and password distribution.

Goals of Network Management

Successful deployment of a network management system depends on defining policies for the operation and performance of network resources based on the benefits to the business. These policies are then translated into measurable operational goals. The following list is an example of operational goals:

- Maintain and improve business user productivity through improvements in service levels
- Facilitate the introduction of new and more efficient technologies
- Allow for continual network growth and change in a distributed environment
- Improve productivity and service by providing a reliable network infrastructure for business system software
- Provide a centralized site for network operations
- Make efficient use of network technology skill
- Create proactive and reactive network management policies
- Establish baseline performance levels for the network

Components of Network Management

A network management architecture has three principle components, as follows:

- *Managing entity or network manager*—An application running in a network management station (NMS) located somewhere in the network, typically in the network operations center of the organization. The managing entity is a central point for network management activities. It is responsible for collecting, processing, analyzing, and displaying network management information. It provides the applications to configure, monitor, analyze, and control the various components that comprise the network.
- *Managed devices*—Network equipment installed on the network. A managed device could be a host, router, bridge, hub, printer, or any other type of device on a network. A managed device can consist of several *managed objects*. These managed objects can be either hardware located within the managed device, such as the network interface card; or software, such as the routing protocol on the device. These managed objects are collected into a *Management Information Base* (MIB). There is a standard definition of an MIB for every device. Each of the managed devices also has a *network management agent* that communicates with the managing entity.
- *Network Management Protocol (NMP)*—A protocol that runs between the managing entity and the managed devices. The NMP allows the managing entity to query the status of managed devices via its *agents*. The agents use the NMP to inform the manager of events that occur on the network, such as hardware failures or down links. This protocol is typically the Simple Network Management Protocol (SNMP).

SNMP

SNMP is a communication protocol that has gained wide acceptance as a way of managing network devices. It is an agreed-upon standard created by the Internet Engineering Task Force (IETF) and is applicable to many types of networks, although its broadest use is in TCP/IP networks.

SNMP's biggest advantage is its widespread use in networks. SNMP agents are available for virtually every type of network device, from mainframe computers to routers and, yes, switches.

As we mentioned in the previous section, SNMP defines a client/server relationship. The client program (the managing entity) makes virtual connections to a server program (the agent) that resides on a remote network device, and serves information back to the manager regarding the device's status. The managing entity monitors and updates the values in the MIB, via the agent.

SNMP functions as a request-response protocol. The network management system issues a request, and managed devices return responses. SNMP provides four main functions to retrieve information, set device values, and receive notification of network events:

- **Get**—Used by the NMS to retrieve the value of one or more object instances from an agent
- **GetNext**—Used by the NMS to retrieve the value of the next object available within an agent
- **Set**—Used by the NMS to set the values of objects within an agent
- **Trap**—Used by agents to inform the NMS of a significant event

In order to use most network management software on Cisco switches, it is necessary to set up SNMP on your switches if you have not already done so. The following commands will enable SNMP to set a trap receiver to receive SNMP messages:

```
Console> (enable) set snmp community read-only readme
SNMP read-only community string set to 'readme'.
Console> (enable) set snmp community read-write not4every1
SNMP read-write community string set to 'not4every1'.
Console> (enable) set snmp community read-write-all rooter
SNMP read-write-all community string set to 'rooter'.
Console> (enable) set snmp trap 192.168.1.2 read-write
SNMP trap receiver added.
Console> (enable) set snmp trap enable all
All SNMP traps enabled.
```

Remote Network Monitoring (RMON)

RMON is a subset of SNMP. An RMON device collects data on the network and periodically sends the data to a central management station. RMON collects information regarding which hosts are attached to the LAN, how much they talk, and the conversation flow between hosts. The management station collects knowledge about all the traffic on the network, not just the device that the station is running on. RMON can filter and capture packets as well as automatically collect network traffic data, compare the data to thresholds you have set up, and send traps to your management station when events occur in the network.

RMON includes nine groups of SNMP variables:

- *Statistics group*—Information measured for each monitored interface, including port usage and error statistics.
- *History group*—Statistical samples over a period of time.

- *Alarm group*—Statistical samples that are compared to thresholds you have set. An *event* is generated when a threshold is crossed (discussed later).
- *Event group*—Lets you monitor logging events you have defined.
- *Host group*—Statistics for each host.
- *HostTopN group*—The top *N* hosts.
- *Matrix group*—A list of the conversations between pairs of hosts, and statistics about those conversations.
- *Filter group*—A pattern to match against the network traffic.
- *Packet Capture group*—Provides the ability to capture packets.

All Catalyst switches support the first four RMON groups. This support is known as Mini-RMON. An external device is needed in order to access more than Mini-RMON.

To enable RMON (if it isn't already enabled), enter the following commands:

```
Console> (enable) set snmp rmon enable
SNMP RMON support enabled.
```

To see the status of RMON, you must use the **show snmp** command, as follows:

```
Console> (enable) show snmp
RMON:                        Enabled
Extended RMON:               Extended RMON module is not present
Traps Enabled:
Port,Module,Chassis,Bridge,Repeater,Vtp,Auth,ippermit,Vmps,config,
     entity,stpx
Port Traps Enabled: 1/1-2,4/1-48,5/1
Community-Access     Community-String
----------------     ----------------
read-only            readme
read-write           not4everl
read-write-all       rooter
Trap-Rec-Address                                 Trap-Rec-Community
----------------                                 ------------------
192.168.1.2                                      read-write
192.168.1.2                                      read-write-all
```

Switched Port Analyzer (SPAN)

As we mentioned earlier, Catalyst switches monitor only the first four layers of RMON. This is due to the overhead involved in maintaining all nine layers of the RMON stack—it would quickly swamp even the most robust Cisco switch. In order to get all nine layers of RMON, you will need to use an external probe such as one from the Cisco SwitchProbe series or an RMON probe (available from a variety of vendors).

Because switches have a one-to-one dedicated path from a host to a switch port, in order to monitor the traffic on different ports it is necessary to mirror the traffic from one port to that of another port. This is done via the SPAN port.

The following example shows how to configure SPAN so that both transmitted and received traffic on port 1/1 (the source) is mirrored on port 1/2 (where the probe would be located):

```
Console> (enable) set span 1/1 1/2
Enabled monitoring of Port 1/1 transmit/receive traffic by Port 2/1
Console> (enable) show span
Status          : enabled
Admin Source    : Port 1/1
Oper Source     : Port 1/1
Destination     : Port 1/2
Direction       : transmit/receive
Incoming Packets: disabled
Console> (enable)
```

You can also span an entire virtual LAN (VLAN), as this example shows:

```
Console> (enable) set span 100 1/2
Enabled monitoring of VLAN 100 transmit/receive traffic by Port 2/1
Console> (enable) show span
Status          : enabled
Admin Source    : VLAN 100
Oper Source     : Port 1/1-4
Destination     : Port 1/2
Direction       : transmit/receive
Incoming Packets: disabled
Console> (enable)
```


To disable the SPAN port, enter the following command:

```
Console> (enable) set span disable
Disabled monitoring of VLAN 100 transmit traffic by Port 1/2
```

Cisco Switch Management

Cisco offers a variety of ways to manage its switches. Managing Catalyst switches fall into the following categories:

- **show** commands
- Cisco Discovery Protocol
- CiscoWorks2000
- CiscoWorks for Windows

In the following sections we'll examine each of these management categories.

show Commands

Probably the simplest way to manage your switches is to Telnet to the switch. Once you are there, you can configure and maintain the switches interactively. A wealth of information is available via the **show** commands. If you are using an IOS-based switch, a number of **debug** commands also can show what is occurring on the switch.

One of the biggest problems with using this method is the large number of **show** commands. For example, a Catalyst 6000 switch includes more than 140 **show** commands. This approach requires an administrator to be very comfortable with the command set. Actually, depending on the models of switches in your network, you may need to be familiar with several command sets.

Some of the more useful **show** commands for monitoring your switch via a console or Telnet session let you perform these tasks:

- Check system status
- Check module status
- Check port status and capabilities
- Check network status

Let's look at specific commands in these areas.

Checking System Status

To show the overall status of the switch, use the **show system** command. This command will show you the status of the power supplies and the fan. It will let you know how long the switch has been up and will tell you the current and peak traffic load on the switch's backplane. It also tells when the peak traffic load was experienced, to further help you isolate a performance problem. To show the system status, perform this task in Privileged Mode:

```
Console> (enable) show system
PS1-Status PS2-Status Fan-Status Temp-Alarm Sys-Status Uptime     Logout
                                                       d,h:m:s
---------- ---------- ---------- ---------- ---------- -------    ------
ok         none       ok         off        ok         2,19:43:11 20 min

PS1-Type PS2-Type Modem    Baud  Traffic  Peak  Peak-Time
-------- -------- -----    ----  -------  ----  ---------
WS-C4008 none     disable 9600  5%       15%   Fri Apr 29 2000, 18:54:17

System Name        System Location        System Contact
-----------        ---------------        --------------
Cat4000            Network Ops center     root@yourcorp.com
```

Checking Module Status

The **show module** command will tell you what modules are installed on a switch, their status, their MAC addresses, and what software versions are installed on them. This command's **Status** column will show you whether a module has failed. An example of the output from **show module** is shown here:

```
Console> (enable) show module
Mod  Slot  Ports  Module-Type            Model              Status
---  ----  -----  -----------            -----              ------
1    1     2      1000BaseX Supervisor   WS-X6K-SUP1-2GE    ok

Mod    Module-Name    Serial-Num
---    -----------    ----------
1                     SAD03041234

Mod  MAC-Address(es)                          Hw     Fw        Sw
---  ---------------                          --     --        --
1    00-50-f0-a8-26-c8 to 00-50-f0-a8-26-c9   1.4    5.1(1)    5.2(1)CSX
     00-50-f0-a8-26-c6 to 00-50-f0-a8-26-c7
```

Checking Port Status

Another useful command is **show port**. The **show port** command helps you track down cabling problems. It is especially useful for auto-negotiation problems, if you are using full-duplexing. If the two sides of the connection do not agree on how to negotiate, it is unlikely that you will be able to form a connection using auto-negotiation—you may need to hard-code a speed and duplex setting that the two sides will accept. The output from a **show port** command is shown here:

```
Console> (enable) show port 1/1
Port     Name      Status        Vlan     Duplex     Speed     Type
----     ----      ------        ----     ------     -----     ----
 1/1               connected     1        full       1000      1000BaseSX

Port  Security Secure-Src-Addr  Last-Src-Addr Shutdown Trap      IfIndex
----  -------- ---------------  ------------- -------- ----      -------
 1/1  disabled                                No       disabled 4

Port      Broadcast-Limit     Broadcast-Drop
----      ---------------     --------------
 1/1                    -                  0

Port   Send     FlowControl    Receive    FlowControl    RxPause     TxPause
       admin    oper           admin      oper
----   -----    -----------    -------    -----------    -------     -------
 1/1   desired   off           off        off            0           0

Port   Status      Channel    Admin    Ch    Neighbor    Neighbor
                   Mode       Group    Id    Device      Port
----   ------      -------    -----    --    --------    --------
 1/1  connected    auto       10        0

Port   Align-Err    FCS-Err    Xmit-Err    Rcv-Err    UnderSize
----   ---------    -------    --------    -------    ---------
 1/1           0          0           0          0            0

Port  Single-Col Multi-Coll Late-Coll Excess-Col Carri-Sen Runts Giants
----  ---------- ---------- --------- ---------- --------- ----- ------
 1/1           0          0         0          0         0     0      0

Last-Time-Cleared
-----------------
Tue May 1 2000, 11:01:45
```

You can display the capabilities of any port in a switch using the **show port capabilities** command, as follows:

```
Console> (enable) show port capabilities 1/1
Model                    WS-X6K-SUP1-2GE
Port                     1/1
Type                     1000BaseSX
Speed                    1000
Duplex                   full
```

```
Trunk encap type          802.1Q,ISL
Trunk mode                on,off,desirable,auto,nonegotiate
Channel                   yes
Broadcast suppression     percentage(0-100)
Flow control              receive-(off,on,desired),send-(off,on,desired)
Security                  yes
Membership                static
Portfast                  yes
QOS                       rx-(1q4t),tx-(2q2t)
Rewrite                   no
UDLD                      Capable
```

Checking Network Connectivity

You can check the status of network connections by using the **ping** and **traceroute** commands.

Using the **ping** command is pretty straightforward—you simply ping the remote device's IP address. The **ping** command will return one of the following responses:

- *Normal response*—If the remote device responds, you get a *hostname is alive* message.
- *Destination does not respond*—If the host fails to respond, a *no answer* message is returned.
- *Unknown host*—An *unknown host* message is returned if the host does not exist.
- *Destination unreachable*—A *destination unreachable* message is returned if your default network cannot access the remote network.
- *Network or host unreachable*—An *unreachable* message is returned if no entry is present in the route table for the host or network.

The following example shows how to use the **ping** command:


```
Console> (enable) ping 192.168.1.1
192.168.1.1 is alive
```

The **traceroute** command is used to discover the path that a packet takes to reach a remote destination. It shows the Layer 3 information of every hop the packet takes through the network. An example of this command is as follows:

```
Console> (enable) traceroute 192.168.1.100
traceroute to 192.168.1.100(192.168.1.100),30 hops max,40 byte packets
 1 192.168.1.1 (192.168.1.1)  1 ms  2 ms  1 ms
 2 192.168.1.100 (192.168.1.100)  2 ms  2 ms  2 ms
Console> (enable)
```

Cisco Discovery Protocol (CDP)

CDP is a Cisco proprietary protocol that runs on all Cisco devices. It is a Layer 2 protocol, so it does not matter what protocols are running on the device. Cisco devices use CDP to discover basic information about their neighboring network devices by sending out multicast messages every 60 seconds. CDP devices do not forward CDP broadcasts they receive. CDP runs on all media that support Subnetwork Access Protocol (SNAP), including Ethernet and Token Ring networks, serial links, Fiber Distributed Data Interface (FDDI), and Frame Relay.

CDP listens to neighboring devices and exchanges information about the physical interface, IP address, chassis type, and software versions on each device. By default, all ports are enabled for CDP, although it can be disabled for the entire device or on a per-port basis. For example, to disable CDP for module 2 ports 1 through 5, enter the following command:

```
Console> (enable) set cdp disable 2/1-5
CDP disabled on ports 2/1-5.
```

To find out which CDP neighbors are seen by a switch, enter the following command:

```
Console> (enable) show cdp neighbors
* - indicates vlan mismatch.
# - indicates duplex mismatch.
Port      Device-ID              Port-ID     Platform
----      ---------              -------     --------
 2/2      CAB012307H1(2948)      2/3         WS-C2948
 3/1      CAB012306JR(4003)      2/2         WS-C4003
```

To get information about a specific port, use the following command:

```
Console> (enable) show cdp neighbors 2/2 detail
Port (Our Port): 2/2
Device-ID: CAB012307H1(2948)
Device Addresses:
  IP Address: 192.168.1.2
Holdtime: 180 sec
Capabilities: TRANSPARENT_BRIDGE SWITCH
Version:
  WS-C2948 Software, Version McpSW: 5.1(57) NmpSW: 5.1(1)
  Copyright (c) 1995-1999 by Cisco Systems, Inc.
Platform: WS-C2948
Port-ID (Port on Neighbors's Device): 2/3
VTP Management Domain: Engr_LAN
```

```
Native VLAN: 100
Duplex: full
Console> (enable)
```

In this example, CDP gives you the name and platform of the device connected to port 2/2 of your switch. It displays the IP address of the switch and the software version running on it. Also included in this display is the Virtual Trunking Protocol (VTP) domain the switch is in and its VLAN information.

The **cdp** command is very useful for troubleshooting problems, because it does not rely on a Layer 3 protocol to communicate. By using this command, you can verify that two devices are communicating with each other and eliminate the network physical layer as the likely culprit.

CiscoWorks2000

CiscoWorks2000 is a family of products used to provide a single source for managing Cisco's switches, routers, and remote access gear. It features a Web-based interface and a streamlined way to set up and maintain virtual and emulated LANs. CiscoWorks2000 is really a combination of many different application packages.

The LAN version of CiscoWorks2000 includes the following applications:

- Resource Manager Essentials (RME)
- Campus Manager; also known as CiscoWorks for Switched Internetworks (CWSI)
- TrafficDirector
- CiscoView

The WAN version of CiscoWorks2000 provides the following products:

- Resource Manager Essentials (RME)
- TrafficDirector
- CiscoView
- Internet Performance Monitor (IPM)
- Access Control List (ACL)

Resource Manager Essentials

Resource Manager Essentials is a collection of Web-based applications that provide network administrators with the tools to manage Cisco switches, access servers, and routers. RME simplifies the gathering of information critical to maintaining network uptime; it also simplifies time-consuming administrative tasks.

RME includes the following applications to help you manage Cisco devices:

- Configuration Manager—Maintains a collection of device configuration files. It keeps an archive of these files and provides the ability to search for specific configuration values. It also allows you to compare the contents of different configuration files in side-by-side windows.
- Syslog Analyzer—Collects system logging messages from Cisco devices. It categorizes the errors by device or severity and identifies the probable cause. It also suggests some appropriate actions that may correct the problem.
- Inventory Manager—Gives detailed, in-depth reports on the hardware and software characteristics of Cisco routers and switches.
- Software Image Manager—Helps to automate the upgrading of system images on switches and routers. It can be set up to acquire the appropriate images from the Cisco Web site, to test that all prerequisites are met, and to download the images to selected devices. RME maintains a central database of Cisco IOS and Catalyst image software. This utility also allows you to schedule batch updates to groups of routers using Trivial File Transfer Protocol (TFTP). You can schedule the updates at a time you choose and even have the Software Image Manager email you when the job is done.
- Cisco Management Connection—Allows other Cisco products and other vendors to link to the CiscoWorks2000 system.
- Change Audit Manager—Lets you view what network changes were made by whom and when. It also lets you know whether the changes were made from a command-line interface (CLI) or a CiscoWorks2000 application.
- Availability Manager—Provides statistics about the reachability status and response times for Cisco devices in your network. It also tracks and analyzes reloads of devices and why they occurred.

Campus Manager

Campus Manager provides tools for network discovery and mapping your Cisco devices. It has functions that allow you to configure Asynchronous Transfer Mode (ATM) and LAN Emulation (LANE) components, track users, manage your network traffic, and enhance your network performance. It supports Cisco's GUI-based management tool—CiscoView—which displays the Cisco devices in a graphical view.

Administrators can use Campus Manager to change, monitor, and control network devices in a centralized location much more easily than you can do on an individual basis. Some of the Campus Manager features are as follows:

- Network discovery and display of Cisco networks accessible through Web-based maps

- Configuration ofVLAN, LANE, and ATM services and assignment of switch ports to those services
- Display of link status
- Configuration discrepancy detection
- Diagnostic tools for connection issues between network devices
- User tracking functions that enable you to locate users by MAC address, IP address, Windows NT login, Novell Directory Service (NDS) login, or Unix hostname, with their physical connections to the switched network

TrafficDirector

TrafficDirector uses RMON to gather, monitor, and record information about network devices. With TrafficDirector, you can track device usage, RMON events, and trends regarding network traffic. In addition, TrafficDirector allows you to identify network problems and isolate many fault conditions that occur in data communication networks.

TrafficDirector consists of a GUI-based application that you can either run as a standalone application or launch from within CiscoView. It uses external RMON agents to collect the information about the network and report it back to the application. The main TrafficDirector window is shown in Figure 16.1.

In a network that has multiple segments, a combination of agents can report data back to the TrafficDirector application. The Mini-RMON in every switch can

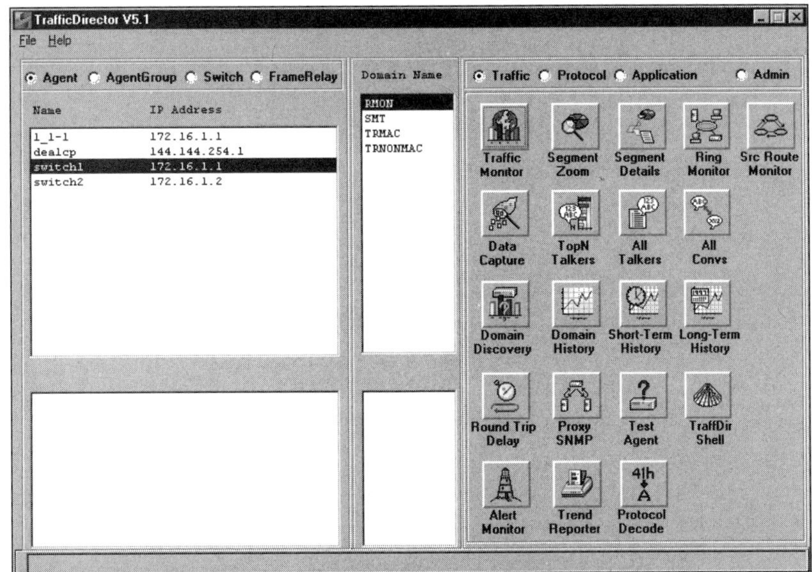

Figure 16.1 The main window of TrafficDirector.

report, as can multiple SwitchProbe devices or the Network Analysis Modules (NAM) in Catalyst 5000 and 6000 Series switches. At intervals that you can define, the agents upload their data to the TrafficDirector management station, which aggregates the data and reformats it for display and reporting.

You can also establish thresholds based upon events that occur on the network. The RMON device will listen to the network traffic and create alarms and events based on the threshold you have defined. When the event happens, a trap is sent to the TrafficDirector application.

In addition, you can define trap messages that occur for both rising and falling thresholds. The messages are sent to the management console when a threshold has been reached. The trap messages can be very useful, because they help to isolate the source of the problem for switch ports.

TrafficDirector includes another application called Trend Reporter that will run standard reports at regular intervals to help keep you appraised of the status of your network. These reports can be used for troubleshooting purposes, to create or maintain a network baseline, or to forecast network growth. The reports are stored in a SQL Server database so you can retrieve the information later.

TrafficDirector also provides a packet decode utility, which enables you to capture and display network traffic data.

CiscoView

CiscoView lets you monitor Cisco routers and switches using a GUI-based device-management application. Information provided by CiscoView can be helpful in resolving some network problems. Using CiscoView, you can view a Cisco device's front or back panel to determine the device's status, view statistics, and perform comprehensive configuration of Cisco switches and routers. A pictorial view of a Cisco Catalyst 5000 is shown in Figure 16.2.

The Threshold Manager application of CiscoView lets you define normal operational boundaries that, if crossed, will alert you of a potential problem. Threshold Manager allows you to set thresholds and retrieve event information via RMON; it provides an easy interface to access device-specific threshold settings. Using Threshold Manager, you can set thresholds for network devices using either predefined default policies or policies that you define. These policies can be applied automatically to target devices.

VlanDirector

VlanDirector helps to simplify the task of creating, modifying, and managing VLANs. With VlanDirector, you can make configuration changes using drag-and-drop mouse clicks. VlanDirector allows you to manage your VLANs from a central application, thereby reducing the amount of time spent planning and managing additions, moves, and changes in your network.

Figure 16.2 A graphical view of the Catalyst 5000 as shown by CiscoView.

When you first launch VlanDirector, it performs a discovery of your network. After it has mapped your network, you can view the existing VLANs and make any changes to them, or create new VLANs if you wish. VlanDirector also includes CiscoView to display Cisco devices. You can use the CiscoView application to drag and drop ports from the CiscoView window into a new or existing VLAN.

Tip: VlanDirector uses CDP to discover the physical connectivity of the devices in the known network. VlanDirector cannot manage devices that do not run CDP.

Internetwork Performance Monitor

Internetwork Performance Monitor (IPM) allows you to monitor the performance of IP and System Network Architecture (SNA) in a network. IPM was designed to measure the response time between hosts on a router-to-router basis in the network. IPM uses the Response Time Reporter (RTR) feature that is available in IOS-based devices.

Using this feature, IPM determines the paths used between two devices and measures and displays the response time for each router hop in the path, as well as the performance for the IP and SNA sessions. You can set thresholds for these measurements, and SNMP traps can be sent if thresholds are violated. IPM can store this information to aid in long term planning, analysis, and problem determination.

ACL Manager

The Access Control List (ACL) Manager helps you manage access lists on Cisco devices running IOS-based software. By using an easy-to-understand Windows Explorer-type interface, the ACL Manager simplifies the task of creating and maintaining these lists—you can concentrate on meeting the security requirements of your network without having to learn the IOS syntax. ACL Manager allows users to create, modify, and deploy ACLs to multiple devices in the network.

An ACL consists of one or more access control entries (ACEs) that define what the network traffic profile should consist of. This profile can be used by other IOS features such as traffic filtering, Telnet access, and custom queuing. ACL Manager provides inventory and change audit features that ease the job of setting up and changing device configurations.

The ACL Manager works with the RME Configuration Management and Inventory Manager applications. It uses device information from the Inventory Manager, and reads the configuration in the Configuration Management to create the ACL model used in the ACL Manager.

CiscoWorks for Windows

CiscoWorks for Windows (CWW) is Cisco's network management solution targeted for smaller organizations that don't need all the features of a full-blown network management application (and the costs that come with them). CWW provides a set of tools for monitoring and configuring Cisco switches, routers, and other devices. CWW can also be used to monitor other non-Cisco devices such as printers, workstations, and servers, unlike the full-blown version of CiscoWorks2000.

CWW uses the WhatsUp Gold package (from Ipswitch, Inc.) as its underlying network management software. Included in CWW are the following components:

- *CiscoView*—Provides graphical views of Cisco devices, which are similar to the Unix and Windows NT versions of CiscoView. With CiscoView, you can determine a device's status and monitor interfaces, ports, or modules. You can also perform diagnostics on devices, configure device setups, and manage a set of individual devices.
- *Threshold Manager*—Allows the administrator to set thresholds on Cisco devices.
- *StackMaker*—Provides the ability to combine multiple Cisco devices of specific types into a single stack and manage them as a single device. The StackMaker window displays all devices in the stack in the order they are installed. By default, the seed device (the starting point of the stack) is noted with an asterisk.

- *Show Commands*—Gives switch and router system and protocol information. The Show Commands application creates a Telnet session, executes the command in the device, collects the output of the command, and displays the output information in the Show Commands window. This feature helps to reduce the complexity of the switching command-line interface.

Chapter Summary

In this chapter, we covered some of the methods you can use to monitor your Catalyst switches to improve performance and reliability. As networks have become more business critical, network management software has been developed by Cisco and many other vendors to provide administrators with the tools to install software and components, configure devices, troubleshoot and diagnose problems, and monitor vital network components.

All of the Cisco switches support both in-band and out-of-band management: You can access them in-band through the network or out-of-band through the console port (in the event of network failure). In addition, Catalyst switches provide support for SNMP and RMON so network applications can access them.

In this chapter, we provided an overview of network management. According to the ISO/OSI model, there are five functional areas of network management: fault, configuration, accounting, performance, and security (FCAPS):

- Fault management deals with detecting, diagnosing, and correcting network and system faults.
- Configuration management handles the installation, identification, removal, and configuration of hardware, software, and services.
- Accounting management deals with the costs of providing these services.
- Performance management deals primarily with providing an efficient use of resources in a network.
- Security management controls securing the network recourses.

We discussed some of the goals of network management, which are based on providing the business with tangible benefits that can be translated into measurable operational goals.

In addition, we discussed the three components of network management: the network manager (or managing entity), a managed device, and the Network Management Protocol. The network manager is the overseer of the whole process and is responsible for collecting the various pieces of information on the devices in the network. A managed device is a network device with one or more managed objects. These objects are collected into a Management Information Base (MIB) that is accessed by a network agent that communicates to the network manager via the NMP.

The NMP is almost always the Simple Network Management Protocol (SNMP), which has become the method of choice for network management, owing primarily to its almost universal acceptance by the networking community. SNMP works in a request-response mode. The network manager requests information from a managed object, and the device returns a response. SNMP is enabled by default on Catalyst switches.

Remote Network Monitoring (RMON) is a subset of SNMP and is also enabled by default on all Catalyst switches. RMON has nine groups that gather information about the devices they support: Statistics, History, Alarm, Event, Host, HostTop*N*, Matrix, Filter, and Packet Capture. The first four groups make up a subset called Mini-RMON, which all switches support. To get full RMON support, you will need to enable a Switched Port Analyzer (SPAN) port and mirror one or more ports to a port that has an external probe or protocol analyzer attached to it.

In this chapter we also discussed the various methods used to monitor and control your network. These methods range from simply Telnetting to the switch and issuing **show** commands to using more complex network management products.

Some of the more important **show** commands can display system, port, or module status. These commands will tell you if the modules are functioning correctly, or whether a port has been disabled or has logged errors. However, relying upon these types of commands to monitor your switch forces you to react to problems as they occur and does very little to prevent problems or to give you a heads-up about possible future problems. For that purpose, you need to get a more robust tool, such as CiscoWorks2000 or CiscoWorks for Windows.

CiscoWorks2000 is a family of products used to provide a single source for managing Cisco's switches, routers, and remote access gear. It has a Web-based interface that makes the tasks of setting up and maintaining virtual and emulated LANs a little easier—especially for administrators who are not familiar with the switches' command-line interface. CiscoWorks2000 is a combination of application packages: Resource Manager Essentials (RME), Campus Manager (also known as CiscoWorks for Switched Internetworks [CWSI]), CiscoView, and TrafficDirector. For the WAN version of CiscoWorks2000, the Internet Performance Manager and the Access Control List Manager are included in the package.

RME is further composed of other applications that simplify gathering information critical to maintaining network uptime and that also simplify time-consuming administrative tasks. These other applications include Configuration Management, Syslog Analyzer, Inventory Manager, Software Image Manager, Cisco Management Connection, Change Audit Manager, and Availability Manager.

Campus Manager provides additional tools for discovering your network and helping to map your Cisco devices. It allows you to configure ATM and LANE components, track users, manage your network traffic, and enhance your network performance, all from a central management station. It supports Cisco's GUI-based management tool—CiscoView—which displays the Cisco devices in a graphical view.

REVIEW QUESTIONS

1. Which types of management do Cisco devices support? [Choose the two best answers]
   a. In-band
   b. Outband
   c. Out-of-band
   d. Internal
2. In-band management requires which type of connection to a switch?
   a. Layer 3 access
   b. Console access
   c. Modem
   d. All of the above
3. Out-of-band management requires which type of connection to a switch?
   a. Layer 3 access
   b. Console access
   c. Modem
   d. All of the above
4. Which functional area of network management concerns itself with network usage and response time?
   a. Fault
   b. Configuration
   c. Accounting
   d. Performance
   e. Security

5. A network manager performs what type of network management function?
   a. Collects and analyzes network information
   b. Manages network objects
   c. Informs network devices of events that occur on the network
   d. Manages entities on the network
6. A collection of managed objects is known by what term?
   a. MIB
   b. Agent
   c. Managing entity
   d. Managed device
7. Which networking component does the network manager query to determine a network device's status?
   a. MIB
   b. Agent
   c. Managing entity
   d. Managed device
8. Without any additional devices, how many RMON groups are supported on the Catalyst IOS?
   a. 1
   b. 2
   c. 3
   d. 4
9. Agents inform the NMS of an event through what operation?
   a. SNMP **Get**
   b. SNMP **Set**
   c. SNMP **Send**
   d. SNMP **Trap**
10. Which of the following groups is not a member of Mini-RMON?
    a. Statistics
    b. History
    c. Alarm
    d. Host

11. Which SNMP group is used to gather statistics about network hosts?
    a. Host *N*
    b. Host
    c. Statistics
    d. History
12. Which of the following commands would you use to see the RMON status on a switch?
    a. **show rmon**
    b. **show rmon status**
    c. **show snmp**
    d. **show snmp rmon**
13. What is the term used to describe the mirroring of data from one port to another?
    a. RMON
    b. SPAN
    c. Mirror
    d. SwitchProbe
14. Which command shows the overall condition of a switch?
    a. **show status**
    b. **show switch**
    c. **show system**
    d. **show statistics**
15. What response is received from a **ping** command if no entry for the remote device is in the switch's routing table?
    a. Destination does not respond
    b. Unknown host
    c. Destination unreachable
    d. Network or host unreachable
16. Which CiscoWorks2000 application allows you to maintain a database of system images and perform scheduled updates on devices?
    a. Configuration Manager
    b. Inventory Manager
    c. Change Manager
    d. Software Image Manager

17. Which CiscoWorks2000 application gives you network discovery tools and the ability to map your network?
    a. RME
    b. CDP
    c. RMON
    d. Campus Manager
18. Which CiscoWorks2000 application allows you to set RMON thresholds on network devices?
    a. CiscoView
    b. RME
    c. NAM
    d. TrafficDirector
19. VlanDirector uses which protocol to discover your network?
    a. SNMP
    b. RMON
    c. CDP
    d. All of the above
20. CiscoWorks for Windows uses which management application as the underlying network management software?
    a. Ipswitch
    b. TrafficDirector
    c. WhatsUp Gold
    d. SNMP

Real-World Projects

Joe Snow, our faithful technical guru, needs to implement RMON on a 2912 XL switch and a 2926G switch that he has just installed at The Coriolis Group. The 2912 XL uses the Cisco IOS command-line interface that closely resembles that of the routers, and the 2926G uses a Set/Clear command-line interface.

Project 16.1

Enabling SNMP on a Cisco command-line interface:

1. To enable SNMP and allow read-only access to hosts using the "public" SNMP string, use the following command in Configuration Mode:

```
snmp-server community public
```

2. After enabling SNMP, you must define a host IP address to send SNMP Trap messages for the "public" group. Here is an example:

```
snmp server host 38.187.128.6 public
```

3. To verify the configuration and that RMON is running, use the following command in EXEC Mode:

```
show rmon
```

Project 16.2

Configuring RMON on a Set/Clear-based interface:

1. Configure the read-only SNMP community of "public" by using the following command:

```
set snmp community read-only public
```

This command correlates to the following command string:

```
set snmp community {read-only|read-write|read-write-all}
  [community string]
```

2. Assign the SNMP log server responsible for receiving traps with the following command:

```
set snmp trap 38.187.128.6 community public
```

This command correlates to the following command string:

```
set snmp trap [host IP address] [community string]
```

3. Enable RMON with the following command:

```
Console> (enable) set snmp rmon enable
SNMP RMON support enabled.
```

4. To verify the configuration of RMON use the following command:

```
Console> (enable) show snmp
RMON:                         Enabled
Extended RMON:                Extended RMON module is not present
Traps Enabled:
Port,Module,Chassis,Bridge,Repeater,Vtp,Auth,ippermit,Vmps,config,
  entity,stpx
Port Traps Enabled: 1/1-2,3/1-8
Community-Access     Community-String
----------------     ----------------
read-only            Everyone
read-write           Administrators
read-write-all       Root
Trap-Rec-Address                          Trap-Rec-Community
----------------                          ------------------
38.187.128.4                              read-only
38.187.128.6                              read-only
Console> (enable)
```

Chapter Seventeen

Sample Test

Question 1

Which of the following are benefits of implementing virtual LANs?

❍ a. Efficient bandwidth utilization

❍ b. Load balancing among multiple paths

❍ c. Isolation between problem components

❍ d. All of the above

Question 2

In the process of selecting a root bridge, which bridge will become the root bridge?

❍ a. The bridge with the highest IP address

❍ b. The bridge with the lowest bridge identifier

❍ c. The bridge with the highest bridge identifier

❍ d. None of the above

Question 3

A Spanning Tree Bridge ID is made up of which two components? [Choose the two best answers]

❑ a. 32-byte IP address

❑ b. 2-byte priority

❑ c. 6-byte MAC address of the switch

❑ d. None of the above

Question 4

On an IOS command-line interface-based switch, which command would be used to show the configuration of Fast EtherChannel?

❍ a. **show ip config**

❍ b. **show fec**

❍ c. **show port channel**

❍ d. None of the above

Question 5

In order to decrease the time it takes for a querier to realize that a host has discontinued participating in a multicast group, which feature was added to IGMPv2?

❍ a. Drop Messages

❍ b. Leave Groups

❍ c. Reduced Latency Notification Messages

❍ d. None of the above.

Question 6

Spanning Tree Protocol is defined in which IEEE standard?

❍ a. 802.1D

❍ b. 802.1Q

❍ c. 802.5

❍ d. None of the above

Question 7

When a bridge receives a frame known as an *unknown unicast*, where does the bridge forward the frame?

❍ a. To the route processor acting as a querier

❍ b. To the local default gateway address

❍ c. Out all ports on the bridge except the receiving port

❍ d. None of the above

Question 8

Which best represents the functioning of a transparent bridge?

❍ a. A bridge that modifies frames it forwards

❍ b. A bridge that learns of interfaces connected to it by listening

❍ c. A bridge that only collects IP addresses of packets received

❍ d. A bridge that operates at the Layer 3 network layer

Question 9

What is the main function of Spanning Tree Protocol (STP)?

❍ a. To assign VLAN ports in a tree fashion

❍ b. To block VLAN ports configured with the same VLAN

❍ c. To block redundant links in the network

❍ d. To forward multiple VLAN frames on a trunk

Question 10

Which of the following is the maximum effective cable distance from the wiring closet to the end-user interface for 2-pair Category 5 100BaseTX and 4-pair Category 5 1000BaseT?

❍ a. 25 meters

❍ b. 260 meters

❍ c. 100 meters

❍ d. Up to 10 kilometers

❍ e. 400 meters

Question 11

An All Routes Explorer (ARE) packet is marked by each bridge in which data field?

❍ a. Source Address field

❍ b. Routing Information field

❍ c. Destination Address field

❍ d. Time-To-Live (TTL) field

Question 12

When a 1 is specified in the Type field of an IGMPv1 packet, which type of packet is being received?

❍ a. Multicast packet query

❍ b. Host membership report

❍ c. Dynamic host configuration query

❍ d. Host membership query

Question 13

Which of the following bridging types can be found in a Token Ring and Ethernet network?

❍ a. Source Route Transparent Bridging (SRT)

❍ b. Transparent Bridging (TB)

❍ c. Source Route Switching (SRS)

❍ d. Source Route Bridging (SRB)

Question 14

What is the theoretical maximum throughput of an Ethernet link configured for half duplex?

❍ a. 200 percent

❍ b. 90 to 100 percent

❍ c. 40 to 50 percent

❍ d. 5 to 10 percent

Question 15

Which of the following is a challenge of flat network topologies?

❍ a. Every device processes every packet sent through the network

❍ b. No way to provide network security

❍ c. Does not allow for redundant links

❍ d. All of the above

Question 16

On an IOS-based command-line interface switch, the port cost can be configured between which two numeric values?

❍ a. 0 and 255

❍ b. 0 and 1005

❍ c. 1 and 65,535

❍ d. 10 and 100

Question 17

If there are four route processors on the network with the following IP addresses, which route processor will become the multicast designated querier?

❍ a. 68.168.126.3

❍ b. 68.168.122.1

❍ c. 68.168.130.9

❍ d. 168.68.127.4

Question 18

Which of the following is supported in Cisco switches?

❍ a. Fiber Distributed Data Interface (FDDI)

❍ b. Asynchronous Transfer Mode (ATM)

❍ c. Hot Standby Routing Protocol (HSRP)

❍ d. All of the above

Question 19

What is the effective maximum cable distance for 1000BaseCX using copper shielded twisted pair (STP)?

❍ a. 25 meters

❍ b. 260 meters

❍ c. 100 meters

❍ d. Up to 10 kilometers

❍ e. 400 meters

Question 20

To enter Privileged EXEC Mode from User EXEC Mode, which of the following commands would you use?

❍ a. **secret**

❍ b. **enable**

❍ c. **start**

❍ d. **config**

Question 21

Which type of Protocol Data Unit (PDU) is used with Layer 3 route processors?

❍ a. Frames

❍ b. Packets

❍ c. TCP segments

❍ d. Bits

Question 22

When a host using IGMPv1 wants to join a multicast group, the host sends a host membership report to which of the following Class D addresses?

❍ a. 224.1.1.1

❍ b. 224.0.0.1

❍ c. 255.255.255.255

❍ d. 239.0.0.0

Question 23

Which of the following is not a valid Virtual Trunking Protocol (VTP) management mode?

❍ a. Server Mode

❍ b. Help Mode

❍ c. Client Mode

❍ d. Transparent Mode

Question 24

Which of the following are true of FDDI? [Choose the two best answers]

- ❑ a. Provides speeds of 2Gbps or more
- ❑ b. Provides speeds of up to 100Mbps
- ❑ c. Provides redundancy in the event of a link failure
- ❑ d. Can be installed more easily than UTP Category 5 cable

Question 25

100BaseT4 has an effective maximum cable distance of 100 meters using which cable types?

- ❍ a. 4-pair Category 3 UTP
- ❍ b. 4-pair Category 4 UTP
- ❍ c. 4-pair Category 5 UTP
- ❍ d. All of the above

Question 26

Periodically, bridges create a special multicast frame. What is the frame referred to as?

- ❍ a. ARP Message
- ❍ b. Multicast Frame
- ❍ c. Bridge Protocol Data Unit
- ❍ d. Reverse ARP message

Question 27

Which VTP management domain mode allows you to create, delete, and modify VLANs?

- ❍ a. Server Mode
- ❍ b. Change Mode
- ❍ c. Client Mode
- ❍ d. Transparent Mode

Question 28

A bridge generates which type of frame to determine whether a destination is local?

❍ a. ARP frame

❍ b. Test frame

❍ c. RIP frame

❍ d. Broadcast

Question 29

What are the basic methods for implementing VLAN boundaries? [Choose the two best answers]

❑ a. WAN topology

❑ b. End-to-end

❑ c. Local VLANs

❑ d. LAN wire speeds

Question 30

Which of the following best describes a trunk link?

❍ a. A link that enables access to the Internet

❍ b. A link that allows FTP and HTTP to flow together

❍ c. A link that can carry traffic for multiple VLANs

❍ d. A link that is used only in Token Ring environments

Question 31

How do excessive broadcasts decrease PC system performance?

❍ a. Increase system interrupts

❍ b. Increase CPU usage to process received frames

❍ c. Increase latency in the PC's processing of its own frames and applications

❍ d. All of the above

Question 32

Transparent bridges use which type of address to make forwarding decisions?

❍ a. Logical address

❍ b. MAC address

❍ c. IP address

❍ d. Multicast address

Question 33

Host membership query messages to discover which host groups have members are assigned which time to live (TTL) value?

❍ a. None

❍ b. 1

❍ c. 2

❍ d. 3

Question 34

Which of the following is not a LANE component?

❍ a. LEC

❍ b. BUS

❍ c. LES

❍ d. EBC

Question 35

Which VTP management mode would you configure your switch for if you did not want to participate in a VTP management domain?

❍ a. Server Mode

❍ b. Change Mode

❍ c. Client Mode

❍ d. Transparent Mode

Question 36

Which of the following best describes an ASIC?

❍ a. Easily upgraded

❍ b. A processor or CPU

❍ c. Specialized circuit that handles limited tasks

❍ d. Used only in Cisco products

Question 37

How many slots can be found on a Cisco Catalyst 5500 Series switch?

❍ a. 1

❍ b. 8

❍ c. 13

❍ d. None

Question 38

100BaseFX utilizing a 62.5 microfiber-optic core and a 125 micron outer cladding has what maximum effective cable distance?

❍ a. 25 meters

❍ b. 260 meters

❍ c. 100 meters

❍ d. Up to 10 kilometers

❍ e. 400 meters

Question 39

Which IEEE standard deals with bus networks utilizing CSMA/CD?

❍ a. 802.10

❍ b. 802.3

❍ c. 802.5

❍ d. 802.12

Question 40

No decision making and high-speed data transfer are both characteristics of which layer of the Cisco Switched Campus Model?

❍ a. Transport layer

❍ b. Core layer

❍ c. Access layer

❍ d. Distribution layer

Question 41

Which type of device is used to communicate between VLANs?

❍ a. Layer 2 switch

❍ b. Route processor

❍ c. Hub

❍ d. Token Ring MAU

Question 42

In a hierarchical network, each layer is responsible for which of the following tasks?

❍ a. Hand-shaking between layers

❍ b. Providing flow control

❍ c. Segmentation and reassembly of data

❍ d. Error control

❍ e. None of the above

❍ f. All of the above

Question 43

Early network designers tried to design networks around which of the following rules?

❍ a. 60/30 rule

❍ b. 40/60 rule

❍ c. 80/20 rule

❍ d. 50/50 rule

Question 44

Which of the following best describes Spanning Tree Protocol's main responsibility?

❍ a. Assigning VLAN numbers to ports

❍ b. Detecting as well as eliminating network data loops

❍ c. Discovering new devices on the network

❍ d. Monitoring port costs between links

Question 45

Which of the following is not a feature of the Cisco Catalyst 5000 Series switches?

❍ a. The IOS is a Set/Clear-based command set.

❍ b. Uses a menu-driven interface.

❍ c. Uses a Supervisor I, II, or III Engine.

❍ d. Runs diagnostics when power is cycled.

Question 46

Which type of Protocol Data Unit (PDU) is used with Layer 2 bridges and switches?

❍ a. Frames

❍ b. Packets

❍ c. TCP segments

❍ d. None of the above

Question 47

Which of the following is true about Spanning Tree Protocol (STP)?

❍ a. STP is used for hardware diagnostics on the switch.

❍ b. Inter-Switch Link (ISL) allows a unique spanning tree on each VLAN.

❍ c. You cannot implement STP and VLANs on the same switch.

❍ d. STP aids in electing route processor queriers.

Question 48

An IGMPv1 countdown timer is set to a randomly selected number between which two values?

❍ a. 0 and 5

❍ b. 0 and 20

❍ c. 0 and 10

❍ d. 0 and 255

Question 49

Which of the following are the goals of a good network designer?

❍ a. Considering the needs of the customer

❍ b. Developing a solution that meets a project need

❍ c. Testing and deploying a design

❍ d. All of the above

❍ e. None of the above

Question 50

Which of the following is true of Cisco Discovery Protocol (CDP)?

❍ a. CDP is a Layer 4 protocol.

❍ b. CDP does not support Token Ring.

❍ c. CDP is supported on all Cisco devices, including hubs.

❍ d. CDP cannot be used to aid in troubleshooting network issues.

❍ e. All of the above.

Question 51

Which of the following is not a configurable mode for Virtual Trunking Protocol (VTP)?

❍ a. Transparent Mode

❍ b. Client Mode

❍ c. Host Mode

❍ d. Server Mode

Question 52

Which of the following is the default VLAN port configuration for the Catalyst 5000 Series?

❍ a. Ports are set to VLAN 255.

❍ b. Ports are set to VLAN 100.

❍ c. Ports are set to VLAN 1.

❍ d. Ports do not belong to a VLAN.

Question 53

When multiple route processors reside on a network, which feature is used in deciding the elected multicast querier?

❍ a. A well-known IP address

❍ b. The highest MAC address

❍ c. The highest IP address

❍ d. The lowest IP address

Question 54

Which statement best describes FIFO?

❍ a. The switch forwards the packet as soon as it determines the destination address from the header.

❍ b. Packets are forwarded in the order they arrive.

❍ c. It allows higher priority packets to be forwarded first.

❍ d. None of the above.

Question 55

The user's point of access into the network switch block takes place at what layer of the Cisco Switched Campus Model?

❍ a. Transport layer

❍ b. Core layer

❍ c. Access layer

❍ d. Distribution layer

Question 56

Which of the following is not true of Cisco Group Management Protocol (CGMP)?

❍ a. Cisco route processors aid switches in receiving updates concerning MAC addresses and multicast applications.

❍ b. You must enter the multicast address for each client participating in a multicast group.

❍ c. CGMP is used to intelligently forward multicast frames.

❍ d. CGMP is used to dynamically discover end stations using multicast applications.

Question 57

In Cisco switches and routers, a color refers to what entity?

❍ a. A switch

❍ b. A VLAN or subnet

❍ c. A router

❍ d. A server

Question 58

When does a switch run the POST feature?

❍ a. When powering down

❍ b. When power is cycled on the switch

❍ c. Automatically every 30 seconds

❍ d. When a manual instruction is given

Question 59

To view the route processor that has been elected as the multicast querier for interface E0, which of the following commands would be used?

❍ a. **show ip int e0**

❍ b. **show ip igmp interface e0**

❍ c. **show ip route**

❍ d. **show ?**

Question 60

The Master Communication Processor (MCP) is a feature of which switching component?

❍ a. Network Management Processor (NMP)

❍ b. Multilayer Switching Module (MSM)

❍ c. Supervisor Engine

❍ d. LAN Module ASIC (LMA)

Question 61

Local Target Logic (LTL) is responsible for aiding which ASIC in locating the destination port for frame forwarding?

❍ a. SAMBA ASIC

❍ b. EARL ASIC

❍ c. SAINT ASIC

❍ d. CEF ASIC

Question 62

Which of the following best describe a local VLAN?

❑ a. A VLAN that spans a WAN to multiple locations

❑ b. A VLAN that encompasses only one core layer switch

❑ c. A VLAN centralized to a common geographical location

❑ d. None of the above

Question 63

Which command allows you to save configuration changes to a Trivial File Transfer Protocol (TFTP) server on a Cisco Catalyst 5000?

❍ a. **download**

❍ b. **write terminal**

❍ c. Saves automatically every 30 seconds

❍ d. **save config TFTP**

Question 64

Which is not a quality of an end-to-end VLAN?

❍ a. Users are grouped into VLANs regardless of physical location.

❍ b. VLANs are restricted to one geographical location.

❍ c. Users are in the same VLAN when moved around the network.

❍ d. Each VLAN uses a common set of security requirements.

Question 65

Which of the following is not true of Fast EtherChannel?

❍ a. Ports in the same bundle can be set to different wire speeds.

❍ b. Multiple VLANs can use a single trunk link.

❍ c. All ports in a channel must have security disabled.

❍ d. All ports must use the same duplex.

Question 66

Which of the following devices allow you to route between VLANs?

❍ a. An external route processor

❍ b. A Route Switch Module (RSM)

❍ c. A Route Switch Feature Card (RSFM)

❍ d. All of the above

Question 67

Which is not a feature of Virtual Trunking Protocol (VTP)?

❍ a. VTP requires a management domain.

❍ b. VTP is a group of switches that share VLAN information.

❍ c. Each management domain must use a unique name.

❍ d. A switch can belong to multiple VTP management domains.

Question 68

Which best describes a single static VLAN?

❍ a. A port is assigned to a VLAN.

❍ b. VLANs can be configured by CiscoWorks software.

❍ c. Ports change VLANs based on MAC address.

❍ d. None of the above.

Question 69

Which switching method can switch to store-and-forward after a predetermined number of errors in frames received?

❍ a. Cut-through

❍ b. Fast-forward

❍ c. Fragment-free or runtless

❍ d. EtherFast

Question 70

A LAN switch is considered which of the following?

❍ a. A Layer 2 multiport bridge

❍ b. A Layer 3 mutliport bridge

❍ c. A Layer 2 multiport hub

❍ d. A Layer 2 multiport repeater

Question 71

What is the maximum effective distance of a Cisco switch or router with 1000BaseLX cable using single-mode fiber with a 9-micron core and a 1300 nanometer laser?

❍ a. 25 meters

❍ b. 260 meters

❍ c. 100 meters

❍ d. From 3 kilometers to 10 kilometers

❍ e. 400 meters

Question 72

Which is not a benefit of switching?

❍ a. Smaller collision domains

❍ b. Decreased collisions

❍ c. Increased number of interfaces in each broadcast domain

❍ d. Smaller broadcast domains

Question 73

On a Set/Clear-based switch, which of the following commands would allow you to assign VLAN 3 to port 3 on module 1?

❍ a. **set vlan 1 3/3**

❍ b. **set module 1 to vlan 3 all**

❍ c. **set vlan 3 1/3**

❍ d. All of the above

Question 74

Ethernet uses which type of bridging?

❍ a. Source Route Bridging

❍ b. Transfer Bridging

❍ c. Transparent Bridging

❍ d. Source Route Switching

Question 75

To view the elected multicast querier on a specified interface, which command modes can be used on the switch IOS? [Choose the two best answers]

❑ a. Global Configuration Mode

❑ b. Privileged EXEC Mode

❑ c. User EXEC Mode

❑ d. Interface Configuration Mode

Question 76

Which of the following are requirements of implementing MLS in a Cisco Catalyst 5000 Series switch?

❍ a. NFFC or NFFC II

❍ b. Supervisor Engine III or III F

❍ c. RSM or RSFC

❍ d. Supervisor Engine software release 4.1(1) or later

❍ e. Cisco IOS Release 12.0W5 or later

❍ f. All of the above

Question 77

On a non-switched Ethernet segment, how many devices will see data transmitted on the wire?

❍ a. All

❍ b. One

❍ c. Up to 10

❍ d. Only the devices that the data addresses

Question 78

To verify your VLAN configuration on your Set/Clear-based command switch, in which command mode would you use the **show vlan** command?

❍ a. Global Configuration Mode

❍ b. Privileged EXEC Mode

❍ c. User EXEC Mode

❍ d. Interface Configuration Mode

Chapter Eighteen

Answer Key

1. d
2. b
3. b, c
4. c
5. b
6. a
7. c
8. b
9. c
10. c
11. b
12. d
13. a
14. c
15. d
16. c
17. b
18. d
19. a
20. b
21. b
22. a
23. b
24. b, c
25. d
26. c
27. a
28. b
29. b, c
30. c
31. d
32. b
33. b
34. d
35. d
36. c
37. c
38. e
39. b
40. b
41. b
42. f
43. c
44. b
45. b
46. a
47. b
48. c
49. d
50. c
51. c
52. c
53. d
54. b
55. c
56. b
57. b
58. b
59. b
60. c
61. b
62. b, c
63. b
64. b
65. a
66. d
67. d
68. a
69. c
70. a
71. d
72. c
73. c
74. c
75. b, c
76. f
77. a
78. b

Question 1

The correct answer is d. The benefits of virtual LANs include efficient bandwidth utilization, load balancing among multiple paths, and isolation between problem components.

Question 2

The correct answer is b. In the process of selecting a root bridge, the lowest bridge identifier is the factor that determines which bridge will become the root bridge.

Question 3

The correct answers are b and c. A Spanning Tree Bridge ID is made up of a 2-byte priority and a 6-byte MAC address. A 32-byte IP address is used in Layer 3 logical addressing for the IP protocol. Therefore, answer a is incorrect.

Question 4

The correct answer is c. On an IOS command-line interface-based switch, the command that shows the configuration of Fast EtherChannel is **show port channel**. **show ip config** and **show fec** are not real commands. Therefore, answers a and c are incorrect.

Question 5

The correct answer is b. In order to decrease the time it takes for a querier to realize that a host has discontinued participating in a multicast group, Leave Groups were added to IGMPv2. They broadcast a message to the all-routers group with the well-known IP address of 224.0.0.2. Drop Messages and Reduced Latency Notification Messages do not exist. Therefore, answers a and c are incorrect.

Question 6

The correct answer is a. Spanning Tree Protocol is defined by the IEEE 802.1D standard to prevent bridging loops from forming in the network. The IEEE 802.1Q defines frame tagging for VLANs. Therefore, answer b is incorrect. IEEE 802.5 defines standards for Token Ring. Therefore, answer c is incorrect.

Question 7

The correct answer is c. When a bridge receives a frame known as an *unknown unicast*, it forwards the frame out all the ports on the bridge except the port that received the frame. A route processor acting as a querier is used in IP multicast. Therefore, answer a is incorrect. The local default gateway address is a Layer 3 solution that prevents broadcasts such as those a bridge will make. Therefore, answer b is incorrect.

Question 8

The correct answer is b. A transparent bridge learns of interfaces connected to it by listening. Bridges use Layer 2 MAC addresses and reside transparently in the network without modifying frames. Therefore, answers a, c, and d are incorrect.

Question 9

The correct answer is c. The main function of STP is to block redundant links in the network. It takes no part in the VLAN assignment, VLAN forwarding, or blocking. Therefore, answers a, b, and d are incorrect.

Question 10

The correct answer is c. The maximum effective cable distance from the wiring closet to the end-user interface for 2-pair Category 5 100BaseTX and 4-pair Category 5 1000BaseT is 100 meters. The maximum distance for 1000BaseCX is 25 meters. Therefore, answer a is incorrect. The maximum distance for 1000BaseSX is 260 meters. Therefore, answer b is incorrect. The maximum distance for 1000BaseLX is up to 10 kilometers. Therefore, answer d is incorrect. The maximum distance for 100BaseFX is 400 meters. Therefore, answer e is incorrect.

Question 11

The correct answer is b. An ARE packet is marked by each bridge in the Routing Information field if the destination is not found on the local segment in a Token Ring network. The Source Address field contains the sending interface's address. Therefore, answer a is incorrect. The Destination Address field contains the destination interface address for the packet. Therefore, answer c is incorrect. The TTL field is used to assign a maximum number of hops or the time period in which a packet could live (in seconds). Therefore, answer d is incorrect.

Question 12

The correct answer is d. When a 1 is specified in the Type field of an IGMPv1 packet, the type of packet being received is a host membership query. The other answers are fictitious. Therefore, answers a, b, and c are incorrect.

Question 13

The correct answer is a. SRT can use an Ethernet MAC or a Token Ring RIF. TB is used only in Ethernet networks. Therefore, answer b is incorrect. SRS and SRB use a RIF and are used only in Token Ring. Therefore, answers c and d are incorrect.

Question 14

The correct answer is c. Due to collisions and other perils, the theoretical maximum throughput of an Ethernet link configured for half duplex is 40 to 50 percent. Because you can configure traffic in only one direction in full duplex, collisions are almost eliminated, making the theoretical maximum throughput nearly 200 percent. Therefore, answer a is incorrect. Answers b and d are both invalid answers.

Question 15

The correct answer is d. Every device processes every packet sent through a flat topology network. There is no way to provide network security through network links, leaving the network open to man-in-the-middle attacks. Because every frame travels every link, there cannot be more than one link to the destination. Frames would traverse the network in a continuous loop.

Question 16

The correct answer is c. On an IOS-based command-line interface, the switch port cost value can be configured between 1 and 65,535. An octet of an IP address can be configured from 0 to 255. Therefore, answer a is incorrect. The other values are not valid. Therefore, answers b and d are incorrect.

Question 17

The correct answer is b. If more than one route processor exists on the network, the IP-designated querier is the route processor with the lowest IP address.

Question 18

The correct answer is d. Cisco switches support all of the listed answers. FDDI is used at the physical layer to route data through FDDI rings. ATM and LAN Emulation (LANE) are very efficient data routing protocols. HSRP allows a redundant route processor to be standing by on the network in case of a failure.

Question 19

The correct answer is a. The maximum effective cable distance from the wiring closet to the end-user interface for 1000BaseCX is 25 meters. The maximum distance for 1000BaseSX is 260 meters. Therefore, answer b is incorrect. The maximum distance for 2-pair Category 5 100BaseTX and 4-pair Category 5 1000BaseT is 100 meters. Therefore, answer c is incorrect. The maximum distance for 1000BaseLX is up to 10 kilometers. Therefore, answer d is incorrect. The maximum distance for 100BaseFX is 400 meters. Therefore, answer e is incorrect.

Question 20

The correct answer is b. To enter Privileged EXEC Mode from User EXEC Mode, you would use the **enable** command from the User EXEC Mode prompt. This command will allow you to increase the number of commands available to configure a router or switch. Use **help** or **?** to list the available commands for the currently selected mode.

Question 21

The correct answer is b. The PDUs used at Layer 3 to route data through the network are packets. Frames are used at Layer 2. Therefore, answer a is incorrect. TCP ports are used at Layer 4. Therefore, answer c is incorrect. Bits are used at the physical layer or Layer 1. Therefore, answer d is incorrect.

Question 22

The correct answer is a. A host using IGMPv1 joins a multicast group by sending a host membership report to the Class D address 224.1.1.1. The address 224.0.0.1 is a Class D address, but it signifies the multicast all hosts address. Therefore, answer b is incorrect. The address 255.255.255.255 signifies that the packet is an IP broadcast to all hosts on a subnet. Therefore, answer c is incorrect. The address 239.0.0.0 is a Class D address that starts the address series used for multicast administrative scoping. Therefore, answer d is incorrect.

Question 23

The correct answer is b. Help Mode is not a valid VTP management mode. Server Mode, which is configured by default, allows a switch to create, modify, and delete VLANs for the VTP management domain. Therefore, answer a is incorrect. In Client Mode, the switch has the same functionality as in Server Mode, with the exception that it cannot change any VLAN information. Therefore, answer c is incorrect. In Transparent Mode, switches can be configured not to accept VTP information. Transparent Mode switches will still send VTP information and advertisements, but they will not update their databases nor send out information on VLANs or topology changes. Therefore, answer d is incorrect.

Question 24

The correct answers are b and c. FDDI operates at the physical layer in rings. It can reach throughput speeds of up to 100Mbps. Because FDDI uses a dual set of rings, if one ring is lost, another ring can continue forwarding data. FDDI uses fiber optic cable in which the inner core is made of glass and projects light. The inner core is fragile and has a very intolerant bend radius, making it harder to install and implement.

Question 25

The correct answer is d. Because 100BaseT4 uses multiple cable pairs to send data to reach an effective throughput, it has an effective maximum cable distance of 100 meters on all three types of cable listed.

Question 26

The correct answer is c. Periodically, bridges create a special multicast frame referred to as a Bridge Protocol Data Unit. IP Address Resolution Protocol (ARP) and Reverse Address Resolution Protocol (RARP) messages are sent on the network to aid in matching MAC and IP addresses. Therefore, answers a and d are incorrect. There is no such thing as a Multicast Frame. Therefore, answer c is incorrect.

Question 27

The correct answer is a. The VTP management domain mode that allows you to create, delete, and modify VLANs is Server Mode. There is no such mode as Change Mode. Therefore, answer b is incorrect. In Client Mode, the switch has the same functions as in Server Mode, with the exception that it cannot change any VLAN information. Therefore, answer c is incorrect. In Transparent Mode, switches can be configured not to accept VTP information. Transparent Mode switches will still send VTP information and advertisements, but will not update their databases or send out information on VLANs or topology changes. Therefore, answer d is incorrect.

Question 28

The correct answer is b. A bridge generates a test frame to determine whether a destination address is local. ARP is used in IP to match IP addresses to MAC addresses. Therefore, answer a is incorrect. RIP is used in Token Ring. Therefore, answer c is incorrect. A broadcast is a frame that is filtered, blocked, or forwarded by a switch depending on the configuration. Therefore, answer d is incorrect.

Question 29

The correct answers are b and c. The two basic methods for describing VLAN boundaries are by using end-to-end VLANs or local VLANs. A local VLAN is a VLAN that encompasses only one small local geographical area. An end-to-end VLAN encompasses more than one geographical area. LAN wire speeds and WAN topologies affect VLANs but are not used in describing VLAN boundaries. Therefore, answers a and d are incorrect.

Question 30

The correct answer is c. A trunk link can carry traffic from multiple VLANs from a switch to a router, a router to router, a switch to switch, or a switch to a server configured with a compatible Network Interface Card (NIC). There are no links that will enable access to just the Internet, control FTP and HTTP flows, or be restricted to Token Ring environments. Therefore, answers a, b, and d are incorrect.

Question 31

The correct answer is d. Excessive broadcasts decrease PC system performance by increasing system interrupts, dramatically increasing CPU usage to process received frames, and increasing latency in the time it takes the PC to process frames containing the host's destination address as well as applications running on the PC.

Question 32

The correct answer is b.Transparent bridges use the physical or MAC address to make forwarding decisions.A logical address is used in Layer 3 devices. IP addresses are a good example of a logical address.Therefore, answers a and d are incorrect.You cannot use a multicast or a home address on a bridge.Therefore, answer d is incorrect.

Question 33

The correct answer is b. Host membership query messages used to discover which host groups have members are assigned a TTL value of 1.This means that they can traverse the network only one hop before being discarded.

Question 34

The correct answer is d.The Ethernet Bundle Controller (EBC) is used in EtherChannel. Should one link in the bundle fail, the EBC informs the Enhanced Address Recognition Logic (EARL) ASIC of the failure, and the EARL in turn ages out all addresses learned on that link.The EBC and the EARL then recalculate in the hardware, sending queries to the other switches and learning the destination link based on the responses.The LEC resides in every ATM end system and provides a LAN interface to higher-layer protocols and applications.

The LES is a central piece of LANE and gives the LECs the information they need to establish ATM connections to other LECs.Therefore, answers a and c are incorrect.The BUS provides broadcasting support for an ELAN. It distributes multicast data, sends or distributes unicast data, and interfaces with the other LANE components.Therefore, answer b is incorrect.

Question 35

The correct answer is d.You would configure your switch for Transparent Mode if you did not want to participate in a VTP management domain. Transparent Mode allows a switch to process and forward VTP advertisements but make no database updates. Server Mode, which is configured by default, allows you to create, modify, and delete VLANs for the management domain. Therefore, answer a is incorrect. Change Mode is not a valid option.Therefore, answer b is incorrect. In Client Mode, the switch has the same functions as in Server Mode, with the exception that it cannot change any VLAN information. Therefore, answer c is incorrect.

Question 36

The correct answer is c. ASICs are most accurately characterized as specialized circuits that handles limited tasks. ASICs are part of the hardware and are not easily upgraded, they are not processors or CPUs, and they are used in many components by other vendors. Therefore, answers a, b, and d are incorrect.

Question 37

The correct answer is c. Thirteen slots are available on the Cisco Catalyst 5500 Series switches. Slot 1 is used for a Supervisor Engine and slot 2 can be used for a redundant Supervisor Engine. If a redundant Supervisor Engine is not used, slot 2 can be used for any line module.

Question 38

The correct answer is e. The maximum effective cable distance from the wiring closet to the end-user interface for 100BaseFX utilizing a 62.5 microfiber-optic core and a 125 micron outer cladding is 400 meters. The maximum cable distance for 1000BaseCX is 25 meters. Therefore, answer a is incorrect. The maximum distance for 1000BaseSX is 260 meters. Therefore, answer b is incorrect. The maximum distance for 2-pair Category 5 100BaseTX and 4-pair Category 5 1000BaseT is 100 meters. Therefore, answer c is incorrect. The maximum distance for 1000BaseLX is up to 10 kilometers. Therefore, answer d is incorrect.

Question 39

The correct answer is b. The IEEE standard that deals with bus networks utilizing CSMA/CD is 802.3. The IEEE 802.10 standard is a Cisco proprietary protocol, used primarily to transport VLAN information over Fiber Distributed Data Interface (FDDI). Therefore, answer a is incorrect. The IEEE 802.5 standard is used to define Token Ring. However, it does not specify a particular topology or transmission medium. Therefore, answer c is incorrect. The IEEE 802.12 standard defines 100BaseVG/AnyLAN, which uses a 1000Mbps signaling rate and a special media-access method, allowing 100Mbps data traffic over voice-grade cable. Therefore, answer d is incorrect.

Question 40

The correct answer is b. No decision making and high-speed data transfer are both characteristics of the core layer of the Cisco Switched Campus Model. The transport layer is part of the OSI Reference Model. Therefore, answer a is incorrect. The access layer is the layer at which the user's interface connects to the network. Therefore, answer c is incorrect. The distribution layer is where most policy decisions and media translations occur. Therefore, answer d is incorrect.

Question 41

The correct answer is b. Bridges and switches operate at Layer 2 and cannot route VLAN or subnet traffic. That is the job of an internal route processor or an external router. Therefore, answer a is incorrect. A hub makes no routing decisions and merely forwards data received out all of its ports. Therefore, answer c is incorrect. A Token Ring Multistation Access Unit (MAU) allows access for Token Ring stations on the network and has nothing to do with routing VLAN traffic. Therefore, answer d is incorrect.

Question 42

The correct answer is f. In a hierarchical network, each layer is responsible for hand-shaking between layers, providing flow control, segmentation of data, reassembly of data, and error control. The Cisco Switched Campus Network has three layers: the core layer, the distribution layer, and the access layer.

Question 43

The correct answer is c. Early network designers tried to design networks around the 80/20 rule. They tried to keep 80 percent of the network traffic localized and send only 20 percent of the traffic across the WAN or other network segments to conserve high-cost bandwidth.

Question 44

The correct answer is b. STP's main responsibility is detecting as well as eliminating network data loops. It is not to assign VLAN numbers to ports, discover new devices on the network, or monitor port costs between links. Therefore, answers a, c, and d are incorrect.

Question 45

The correct answer is b. The Cisco Catalyst 1900, 2820, and 3000, not the 5000, uses a menu-driven interface. The Cisco Catalyst 5000 Series uses a Set/Clear-based command set in its IOS, supports a Supervisor I, II, or III Engine, and runs the Power-On Self Test (POST) diagnostic system on boot up. Therefore, answers a, c, and d are incorrect.

Question 46

The correct answer is a. The PDUs used with Layer 2 bridges and switches are frames. Layer 3 uses packets and Layer 4 uses TCP segments and TCP ports. Therefore, answers b, c, and d are incorrect.

Question 47

The correct answer is b. STP uses ISL to allow a unique spanning tree on each VLAN. STP is not used for hardware diagnostics on the switch. Therefore, answer a is incorrect. You can implement STP and VLANs on the same switch. Therefore, answer c is incorrect. STP does not aid IP multicast in electing route processor queriers. Therefore, answer d is incorrect.

Question 48

The correct answer is c. An IGMPv1 countdown timer is set to a randomly selected number of seconds between 0 and 10.

Question 49

The correct answer is d. Goals of a good network designer are keeping in mind the needs of the customer, developing solutions that meet the needs of a project, and testing and deploying the network design.

Question 50

The correct answer is c. CDP is supported on all Cisco devices, including hubs. CDP is not a Layer 4 protocol; it operates at the lower layers; and it is compatible with most media types including Ethernet, FDDI, serial, and Token Ring. Therefore, answers a and b are incorrect. CDP can be used for troubleshooting many network issues. Therefore, answer d is incorrect.

Question 51

The correct answer is c. Host Mode is not a configurable mode for VTP. Transparent Mode allows a switch to process and forward VTP advertisements but make no database updates. Server Mode, which is configured by default, allows you to create, modify, and delete VLANs for the management domain. In Client Mode, the switch has the same functions as in Server Mode, with the exception that it cannot change any VLAN information.

Question 52

The correct answer is c. The default VLAN port configuration for the Catalyst 5000 Series places all ports in VLAN 1. Ports must belong to a VLAN and they are not set to VLANs 255 or 100 by default. Therefore, answers a, b, and d are incorrect.

Question 53

The correct answer is d. If there is more than one route processor on the network, the IP designated querier is the route processor with the lowest IP address. A well-known IP address is used in designating multicast groups. Therefore, answer a is incorrect. The highest IP address and MAC address have no bearing on the election of the querier. Therefore, answers b and c are incorrect.

Question 54

The correct answer is b. First in, first out (FIFO) means that packets are guaranteed to be forwarded out the destination port in the same order that they arrived. FIFO does not handle priority or custom queuing. Therefore, answers a, c, and d are incorrect.

Question 55

The correct answer is c. The access layer is the user's point of access into the network switch block where the physical cable from the user's interface connects to the switch block in the Cisco Switched Campus Model. The transport layer refers to the OSI layers. Therefore, answer a is incorrect. The core layer is the highest level of the Cisco Switched Campus Model; it requires high availability and switches data as quickly as possible without applying policies. Therefore, answer b is incorrect. The distribution layer handles inter-VLAN routing and applies policy decisions. Therefore, answer d is incorrect.

Question 56

The correct answer is b. Addresses are dynamically assigned when using CGMP with multicast clients. Cisco route processors aid switches in receiving updates concerning MAC addresses and multicast applications; CGMP is used to intelligently forward multicast frames; and CGMP is used to dynamically discover end stations using multicast applications. Therefore, answers a, c, and d are incorrect.

Question 57

The correct answer is b. In Cisco switches and routers, a color is used to help identify a VLAN or subnet. A switch, a router, or a server is not referred to as a color even if it is the only device in a particular subnet or VLAN. Therefore, answers a, c, and d are incorrect.

Question 58

The correct answer is b. The switch runs the Power-On Self Test (POST) when the power is cycled on the switch, to test the switching components to verify that they are functioning properly. The switch does not run the post when powering down, automatically, or when any manual instruction is given. Therefore, answers a, c, and d are incorrect.

Question 59

The correct answer is b. To view the route processor that has been elected as the multicast querier for interface E0, use the command **show ip igmp interface e0**. The **show ip int e0** command shows IP statistics for the Ethernet 0 port. Therefore, answer a is incorrect. The **show ip route** command is used in troubleshooting IP. Therefore, answer c is incorrect. The **show ?** command would display options available for the **show** command. Therefore, answer d is incorrect.

Question 60

The correct answer is c. The MCP is a feature of the Supervisor Engine. The Supervisor Engine is literally the brains of the switch. It handles almost all higher-layer functions as well as data packet arbitration and forwarding decisions. The NMP is a feature of the Supervisor Engine that is responsible for general control and some management functions of the switch. Therefore, answer a is incorrect. The MSM is a route processor for the Cisco Catalyst 6000 family of switches. Therefore, answer b is incorrect. The LMA is an ASIC part of the Cisco Catalyst 3000 Series switch that provides frame buffering, address learning, bus arbitration, and switching decisions for Ethernet ports. Therefore, answer d is incorrect.

Question 61

The correct answer is b. The Enhanced Address Recognition Logic (EARL) is responsible for looking at all the frames as they arrive on the bus. The EARL then makes a switching decision based on the destination MAC address after determining which virtual local area network (VLAN) the frame arrived from. The Synergy Advanced Multipurpose Bus Arbiter (SAMBA) and the EARL work together to allow port access to the bus, thereby letting frames be forwarded correctly. Therefore, answer a is incorrect. The Synergy Advanced Interface and Network Termination (SAINT) ASIC is responsible for half-duplex and full-duplex Ethernet support. Therefore, answer c is incorrect. The Cisco Express Forwarding (CEF) ASIC is Cisco's newest ASIC; it uses an adjacency table and a Forwarding Information Base (FIB) to make high-speed forwarding decisions. Therefore, answer d is incorrect.

Question 62

The correct answers are b and c. A local VLAN is a VLAN centralized to a common geographical location and encompasses only one core layer switch, unless a redundant core layer switch is used for redundancy or link failure. It does not span multiple locations. Therefore, answer a is incorrect. The other type of VLAN that is not located in a single geographical location is an end-to-end VLAN.

Question 63

The correct answer is b. The **write terminal** command saves configuration changes to a TFTP server on a Cisco Catalyst 5000, which uses a Set/Clear command set. The **download**, automatically saving every 30 seconds, and **save config TFTP** options are all incorrect and are designed to confuse you, just like the real test. You can use the **write ?** command to view the syntaxes available for the command.

Question 64

The correct answer is b. In end-to-end VLANs, the VLANs are not restricted to one geographical location. However, end-to-end VLAN users can be grouped into VLANs regardless of physical location. Therefore, answer a is incorrect. Users are in the same VLAN when moved around the network. Therefore, answer c is incorrect. Each VLAN has a common set of security requirements. Therefore, answer d is incorrect.

Question 65

The correct answer is a. Ports in the same bundle cannot be set to different wire speeds in a Fast EtherChannel bundle. Multiple VLANs can use a single EtherChannel trunk link. Therefore, answer b is incorrect. All ports in a channel must have security disabled. Therefore, answer c is incorrect. All ports in a bundle must use the same duplex. Therefore, answer d is incorrect.

Question 66

The correct answer is d. An external route processor (also known as a router), an RSM, and an RSFM all allow you to route traffic between virtual LANs.

Question 67

The correct answer is d. A switch can be a member of only one VTP management domain. A switch running VTP requires a management domain to be configured. Therefore, answer a is incorrect. VTP is a group of switches that share VLAN information. Therefore, answer b is incorrect. Each management domain must share a unique name. Therefore, answer c is incorrect.

Question 68

The correct answer is a. A static VLAN is a VLAN assigned to a particular port. Any interface using that port is automatically a member of that VLAN. Dynamic VLANs can be configured by CiscoWorks software to associate a MAC address to a VLAN. Therefore, answer b is incorrect. Ports changing VLANs based on the MAC address is also a feature of dynamic VLANs, not static VLANs. Therefore, answer c is incorrect.

Question 69

The correct answer is c. Fragment-free or runtless switching can switch to store-and-forward after a predetermined number of errors in frames received. Fragment-free is a fast packet-switching method that reads the first 64 bytes of the frame to determine if the frame is corrupted. If this first part is intact, then the frame is forwarded. If frame errors pass a predetermined threshold, the switching method switches to store-and-forward.

Cut-through packet switching is a method that does not copy the entire packet into the switch buffers. Instead, the destination address is placed in buffers, the route to the destination node is determined, and the packet is quickly sent out the corresponding port without error checking. Therefore, answer a is incorrect. Fast-forward and EtherFast are not switching methods. Therefore, answers b and d are incorrect.

Question 70

The correct answer is a. A LAN switch is considered a Layer 2 multiport bridge. Bridges and switches operate at Layer 2, filtering broadcasts and decreasing the size of collision domains, and hubs and repeaters increase the collision domain size. Therefore, answers b, c, and d are incorrect.

Question 71

The correct answer is d. The maximum effective cable distance from the wiring closet to the end-user interface for 1000BaseLX cable using single mode fiber with a 9-micron core and a 1300 nanometer laser is 3 to 10 kilometers using Cisco switches. The other answers represent distance lengths for other types of cabling. Therefore, answers a, b, c, and e are incorrect.

Question 72

The correct answer is c. An increased number of interfaces in each broadcast domain is not a feature of switches. Making smaller broadcast domains, making smaller collision domains, and decreasing data collisions in the network are all benefits of switches. Therefore, answers a, b, and d are incorrect.

Question 73

The correct answer is c. On a Set/Clear-based switch, the command that allows you to assign VLAN 3 to port 3 on module 1 is **set vlan 3 1/3**.

Question 74

The correct answer is c. Ethernet uses Transparent Bridging as its primary bridging. Source Route Bridging (SRB) is used to segment Token Ring networks; it requires all rings and bridges to have a unique number. Therefore, answer a is incorrect. Source-Route Switching (SRS) is a type of bridging that combines SRB and SRT. It was developed to allow more physical rings on the network, and it allows for growing bandwidth needs while preserving the benefits of SRB. Therefore, answer b is incorrect. Transfer Bridging is not a valid bridging type. Therefore, answer d is incorrect.

Question 75

The correct answers are b and c. To view the route processor that has been elected as the multicast querier for interface E0, use the command **show ip igmp interface e0**. You can use this command in either Privileged EXEC or User Exec Mode. Global Configuration Mode and Interface Configuration Mode cannot be used. Therefore, answers a and d are incorrect.

Question 76

The correct answer is f. The NFFC or NFFC II, Supervisor Engine III or III F, RSM or RSFC, Supervisor Engine software release 4.1(1) or later, and Cisco IOS Release 12.0W5 or later are all requirements of implementing MLS in a Cisco Catalyst 5000 Series switch.

Question 77

The correct answer is a. On a non-switched Ethernet segment, every interface is in the same broadcast domain, so every interface will see any piece of data transmitted on the wire. The end-user interface must process every packet or frame to determine if it is the interface of destination. This processing can cause congestion on the network, slowing traffic and requiring switches to be implemented to split the broadcast domain into smaller broadcast domains.

Question 78

The correct answer is b. To verify your VLAN configuration for a particular VLAN on your Set/Clear-based command set switch, in Privileged EXEC Mode, use the command **show vlan** followed by the VLAN number for which you want to view. To view all the VLANs configured, use the **show vlan** command without a VLAN number. To view trunks, use the **show trunk** command. Global Configuration Mode, User EXEC Mode, and Interface Configuration Mode cannot be used. Therefore, answers a, c, and d are incorrect.

APPENDIX A

ANSWERS TO REVIEW QUESTIONS

CHAPTER 1 SOLUTIONS

1. **d.** Store-and-forward, cut-through, and fragment-free are all methods of switching used in Cisco switches.
2. **d.** Full duplex uses both transmission and receive pairs of wires at the same time. With half duplex, Ethernet stations could either transmit or receive, but not do both at the same time. Full duplex allows simultaneous conversation in both directions.
3. **b.** Bridges operate at the data link layer.
4. **c.** Routers operate at the network layer.
5. **b.** CSMA/CD is the mechanism that Ethernet uses to avoid collisions.
6. **a, b, d.** Switches reduce network bottlenecks, allow scalable growth, and reduce broadcasts on networks.
7. **c.** *Latency* is the term used to describe the length of time from the moment a packet enters the input port on the switch until the time that the bridge forwards the packet out the exit port.
8. **b, d.** Increased network traffic and retransmissions of data are problems commonly associated with cut-through switching. These problems are primarily due to the lack of error checking.
9. **a.** A network broadcast storm is something that occurs on the network that causes all devices on the network to respond to that error.
10. **b, d, e.** Catalyst 1900, 2820, and 3000 class switches are the only ones that support both these methods of switching.
11. **c.** Store-and-forward devices must examine the entire header and are therefore slower than the other types of switching.
12. **c.** A backbone is a high-capacity infrastructure that provides optimal transport of data at very high speeds.

13. **b, c.** Excessive collisions and poor response times are indicators of a saturated shared environment.
14. **b.** IEEE 802.3 is commonly referred to as the *Ethernet Standard*.
15. **b, d.** The ability to have dedicated data paths and cut-through switching allowed maximum utilization of the network port and reduced the latency associated with bridging.
16. **a.** True.
17. **b.** A source-route bridge knows the entire path from source to destination.
18. **d.** *Flooding* is the term for when a bridge transmits a packet to all network segments except the source segment. This occurs when a packet is received on a bridge that has an unknown address.
19. **a.** *Latency* is the term for the delay introduced as a result of bridging.
20. **d.** Ethernet is overwhelmingly the protocol of choice on today's networks.
21. **c.** *Frame* is the term used to describe the unit a network station transmits or receives.
22. **d.** A hub that connects other hubs in a multi-tiered fashion is typically called a *backbone hub*.
23. **a.** The fact that all stations on a hub share the same bandwidth is the biggest issue with using hubs.
24. **b, d.** The chief duties of a bridge are filtering packets and forwarding them to the proper port.
25. **d.** Routers typically do not improve throughput in a network.

Chapter 2 Solutions

1. **c.** Although the other four are all design factors, only scalability deals with network growth.
2. **d.** In the Cisco Switched Campus Model relating to Catalyst switches, you will find the Cisco 5500, 6000, 6500 and the 8500 series switches in the core layer.
3. **d.** In the core layer you will find high-speed switches such as the 5500, 6500, and 8500 Catalyst Family switches. In the core you might also find some other types of switches such as the IGX 8400 Series, BPX 8600 Series, MGX 8800 Series, and 12000 GSR series.

4. **c, d.** In the access layer you will find the 1900, 2900, 3500, 4000, and 5000 series switches.

5. **c.** Hubs and bridges are typically found in the data link layer.

6. **d.** LAN protocols operate at the physical and data link layers.

7. **a.** Routing protocols are used for path determination.

8. **c.** The network layer is where packets are routed between segments. Typically, some switches and most routers operate at the network layer

9. **c.** Accessing the Internet requires a router and a gateway located at Layer 3, so that would not be a benefit of Layer 2 switching.

10. **c.** Sending a print job to a local printer in your local segment or collision domain uses no Layer 3 intervention.

11. **d.** Forwarding based on TCP/IP address is handled at Layer 3.

12. **e.** Although printers are part of the whole equation, they are not a design factor category.

13. **c.** IEEE 802.5 covers the standards for Token Ring Source Route Bridging. It does not cover Transparent Bridging (TB).

14. **b.** Early network designers tried to follow the 80/20 rule, keeping 80 percent of network traffic on the local segment.

15. **a, c, d.** The needs of the customer, satisfying the company's needs, and testing the design are all things a good network designer should keep in mind when designing the network.

16. **e.** Handshaking between layers, flow control, segmentation, reassembly, and error control are all responsibilities of each layer.

17. **b.** The core layer should not be making any policy decisions. Its only function should be to summarize the data and forward it as quickly as possible.

18. **c.** The users' point of access to the network is at the access layer switch in the switch block.

19. **b.** The IEEE standard responsible for standardizing bus networks with CSMA/CD is the IEEE 802.3 standard.

20. **b.** The entity that provides communication to the peer layers in the OSI Model is the Service Access Point (SAP).

Chapter 3 Solutions

1. **d.** CEFA is Cisco's newest ASIC. It uses a very fast algorithm to calculate the route for a particular destination. It works with the Forwarding Information Base and the adjacency table to efficiently process switching information in Cisco's higher end switches, such as the Cisco 8500 and 12000 Series.

2. **b.** Only Token Ring uses Source Route Translational Bridging (SR/TLB). One of SR/TLB's main functions is to allow conversion on Token Ring to another physical media type.

3. **a.** Source Route Bridging and Source Route Transparent Bridging make up Source Route Switching. It is designed to overcome the limitations of SRB.

4. **d.** SRS is the best switching method in this situation because it is the most efficient method of bridging over multiple rings.

5. **b, e.** Only Transparent Bridging and Source Route Translational Bridging are found in both Token Ring and Ethernet environments.

6. **d.** The Routing Information Field (RIF) is marked in All Routes Explored packets.

7. **a.** Source Route Transparent bridging (SRT) has an advantage over SRB and TB. It combines TB and SRB to address the different methods of Token Ring addressing.

8. **c.** If you answered anything other than c, you might as well pack up the switch and send it back for repair. Always remember to be very careful with the types of cables you are using and the source they are connected to. Connecting a live wire into the back of your switch can destroy the switch.

9. **a.** The Phoenix ASIC is a special component of the Supervisor III Engine that provides gigabit switching between buses.

10. **c.** The adjacency table maintains one-to-one correspondence with the Forwarding Information Base.

11. **b, c.** The Content Addressable Memory (CAM) table can hold 16,000 or 64,000 entries, depending on the chosen configuration.

12. **b.** You can use the **ip cef accounting per-prefix** command in Global Configuration Mode to set Network Accounting for CEF to collect the numbers of packets and bytes. To collect the numbers of packets express-forwarded through a destination, you can also use the command **ip cef accounting non-recursive** in Global Configuration Mode.

13. **c.** The Internet Engineering Task Force (IETF) is the organization responsible for the RMON standards.
14. **d.** RMON supports the MAC-layer Statistics Group, Promiscuous Statistics Group, Ring Station Group, and the Ring Station Order Group. There is no group called the Data Link Layer Group.
15. **a.** Color Blocking Logic (CBL) is a feature of the SAMBA ASIC that is used to help the EARL make forwarding decisions. It also makes sure that a tagged frame that comes from a particular VLAN does not exit through a port belonging to another VLAN.

Chapter 4 Solutions

1. **c.** The Cisco Catalyst 5509 would work best in the core layer of the network.
2. **b.** Fixed configuration switches are switches without modular ports.
3. **c, d.** The Catalyst 3900 Series and the Catalyst 5000 Series are the two series of Cisco switches that provide for support of Token Ring.
4. **a, c.** The Catalyst Switch Matrix can be used to stack up to eight switches from the Catalyst 3000 Series and the 3900 Series.
5. **d.** The Route Switch Module (RSM), Multilayer Switch Module (MSM), and Route Switch Feature Card (RSFC) are all route processors that can provide Layer 3 routing in Cisco Catalyst switches.
6. **c.** The Cisco Catalyst 2924 XL with 10/100 is the most appropriate device for the access layer.
7. **a.** The Catalyst 4000 with a 6-port Gigabit Ethernet Module is the switch that would work best in the distribution layer.
8. **b.** Over-subscription occurs when the total bandwidth of the ports is greater than the capacity of the switching fabric.
9. **c.** The Catalyst 6000 Series switch supports the FlexWAN Module.
10. **b.** The switching fabric is the "highway" that data takes to get from the port of entry to the exit port.
11. **a.** The Cisco Catalyst 1924 would work best in the access layer of the network.
12. **a.** The backplane is the series of electric traces located on the back of the switch chassis.

13. **c.** The Catalyst 3000 Series of switches uses a menu-driven interface.
14. **a.** The Catalyst 2924 XL does not use a Cisco IOS using the Set/Clear command set.
15. **b.** False. Only two ports on a Catalyst 1912 can be configured to use 100BaseT.
16. **a.** The primary Supervisor Engine should be placed in Slot 1. The redundant Supervisor Engine should be placed in Slot 2.
17. **c.** The 5500 switch chassis contains 13 slots for additional line cards or modules.
18. **d.** The Catalyst 5000 family of switches can use either a Supervisor Engine I, II, or III.
19. **c.** There is no supported RMON group called the Policy Group.
20. **b.** The Cisco Catalyst 3900 is Cisco's Token Ring switch for the access layer.

Chapter 5 Solutions

1. **a.** The maximum length for a 100BaseT Ethernet link is 200 meters from the hub to the destination interface without some other device intervening to boost or re-create the signal.
2. **b.** Utilizing Fast Ethernet 62.5-micron fiber, data can span 400 meters between two devices without help from any other device.
3. **a, b.** Today's network backbones require the highest speed possible and utilize faster technologies such as FDDI and Gigabit Ethernet.
4. **a, b.** Two standards merged to create Gigabit Ethernet. Those were the ANSI X3T11 standard and the IEEE 802.3 standard.
5. **b, c.** The two fiber types that are supported by Gigabit Ethernet are 50-millimeter and 62.5-micron fiber.
6. **c.** Because FDDI or fiber utilizes light, it is impervious to the effects of electrical magnetic interference.
7. **b, d.** The two types of RJ-45 cabling are straight and rolled.
8. **c, d.** The two types of RJ-45 to DB-25 connectors used by Cisco switches are the DCE and DTE.
9. **a, c.** The 4000 and 5000 Series are not IOS-based switches and use the Set/Clear command line interface.

10. **c.** In the default configuration, all VLANs are assigned to VLAN1, not VLAN10.
11. **c.** The **set password** command allows you to set a Privileged Mode password. For instance, if you wanted to set the password to book1234, you would use the command **set password book1234**.
12. **b.** The correct command to set the system location to Coriolis is **set system location Coriolis.** The list of possible answers included one other real command: **set system name Coriolis** would set the system name, not the location.
13. **a.** The mode you first enter when logging on to a Cisco switch is the EXEC Mode. EXEC Mode is a small subset of the commands available in Privileged Mode.
14. **c.** The command **enable password level 15** would grant privileged access to an IOS-based switch. The command **enable password** would also grant this access.
15. **b.** The maximum length of a 10BaseFL segment is 2000 meters.
16. **a.** The key sequence !! on an IOS-based machine would recall the previous command. The up arrow would do the same thing.
17. **c.** By default, no password is configured on a switch. In addition, even if a password is configured, it does not take effect for 30 seconds after the switch boots up.
18. **c.** The command **set ip route default 192.168.1.2** will set up a default route.
19. **b.** The serial line interface protocol (SLIP) is used to set up PPP access to a console port.
20. **c.** To set a default route on an IOS-based switch you would use the command **ip route 0.0.0.0 0.0.0.0 192.168.1.2**. In this command, the first set of **0.0.0.0** refers to the network (all 0s means all numbers) and the second set refers to the netmask.

Chapter 6 Solutions

1. **c.** A Catalyst 5000 with a Supervisor Engine III can store two configuration files, called cfg1 and cfg2.
2. **b.** A configuration file on a Catalyst 5000 can be up to 256K.
3. **a, b.** The two types of images you can use on a Set/Clear device are Supervisor Engine and Intelligent Module.

4. **a.** The correct command to copy a configuration file to Flash memory on a Set/Clear switch is **copy config cfg1**.
5. **a.** The correct command is **write network**. After you press Enter, the system will prompt for the network location.
6. **b.** A Catalyst 5000 can hold up to 1,024 messages in its log file. After it has reached this limit, it will discard the earliest entry.
7. **c.** Up to three log servers can be configured on a Set/Clear switch.
8. **a.** Severity level 0 refers to emergency messages or below.
9. **b.** NTP uses coordinated universal time, also known as Greenwich mean time.
10. **b.** This command sets up the pacific standard time time zone on a Set/Clear switch. The -8 means this time zone is eight hours behind UCT.
11. **a.** This command is used to configure a switch to use a primary DNS server on IP address 192.168.1.2. If you leave off the **primary**, the first entry is it.
12. **a.** This command prevents the possibility of damaging your modem or console port.
13. **a.** By default, local authentication is used. If you configure TACACS+ or RADIUS and then remove it, the switch will return to local authentication.
14. **a.** This command enables TACACS+ authorization to IP address 192.168.1.2 on a Set/Clear switch.
15. **a.** The current configuration of the switch is held in memory in the startup configuration.
16. **d.** Note the use of the URL-based file convention. On some machines, you may need to specify the directory after the address.
17. **b.** The **show version** command will also give you this information.
18. **c.** This command is needed if you are not on the console port.
19. **b.** To forward logging messages to a syslog server located at IP address 192.168.1.2, use the **logging** command.
20. **a.** This command tells NTP where to get the time.
21. **d.** PST is eight hours behind UCT.
22. **c.** When you use MD5 encryption, only NTP servers with the same key will peer.

23. **c.** You can configure up to six DNS servers. The switch will go through the list until it finds one available.

24. **d.** DNS is one of the IP services you can configure on an IOS-based switch.

25. **c.** The RJ-45 to DB-25 DTE male connector that came with your switch has the letters *MODEM* written on it.

26. **a.** This command sets up TACACS+ authentication for login purposes. It will still use the local enable password.

Chapter 7 Solutions

1. **c.** The Mode button on the front of the switch allows for diagnostic testing of the switch.

2. **b.** The Exception Statistics Report shows the errors on an individual port.

3. **d.** The Modify Password option is available from the Console Settings menu and not from the System Configuration menu.

4. **a, c, d.** You can upgrade the firmware on the 1900 or 2820 Series switch with TFTP client, TFTP server, and XMODEM. Kermit is supported on other Cisco switches but not on the Cisco Catalyst 1900 or 2820 Series of switches.

5. **b.** The first port of an expansion module is identified by an A1.

6. **b.** The Network Management menu's IP Configuration option allows you to configure the IP address on a switch.

7. **c.** The G option from the RS-232 Interface menu allows you to activate changes. A configures auto answer, I initializes a modem string, and C cancels and restores the previous settings.

8. **a.** The switch automatically saves each configuration change.

9. **b.** The IP address on the IP Configuration menu is the only option on the menu that does not require a reboot to take effect.

10. **c.** The suspended-not-present port status indicates that the switch cannot detect a link at the other end of the cable.

11. **a.** The suspended-jabber port status indicates that the switch has received multiple undecipherable frames.

12. **b.** You can assign a description or name to a port using the Port Configuration menu.

13. **b.** The address table can contain a maximum of 132 MAC addresses on the Cisco Catalyst 1900 and 2820 Series of switches.
14. **b.** The default baud rate on the RS-232 interface on the Cisco Catalyst 1900 or 2820 Series of switches is 9600.
15. **d.** The baud rate of 36000 is not valid on the RS-232 interface on the Cisco Catalyst 1900 or 2820 Series of switches.
16. **b.** The Standard Edition IOS 1900 and 2820 switches cannot use the Cisco command-line interface. That feature is an option on the Enterprise Edition.
17. **a.** Token Ring ports are not found on any of the 1900 Series switches.
18. **b.** The 1900 Series switch does not have a power switch for cycling the power. You must unplug the switch to turn off the power.
19. **b.** Port Configuration is not found on the Standard Edition User Interface menu.
20. **c.** PortFast allows ports, including those on the 1900 and 2820 Series switches, to enter forwarding mode almost immediately. This would be used on ports where a server or single workstation resides.

Chapter 8 Solutions

1. **a.** A native VLAN is the VLAN a port would be assigned to if it were not participating in a trunk.
2. **b, c.** ISL uses a two-level tagging scheme with a 26-byte header and a 4-byte checksum. It also implements processing in the hardware ASICs to provide wire-speed performance.
3. **b, c.** VLANs address the problems of adding Layer 3 network management, scalability problems of a flat network, the addition of QoS at Layer 2, and security.
4. **c.** If you did not need to add, delete, or modify VLANs for VTP, you would choose to make it a Client Mode switch. In this mode, the switch acts just like a server with the exception of adding, modifying, or deleting VLANs.
5. **b, c, d.** You can configure a VLAN by port, user-defined value, or protocol.
6. **d.** The sole function of VTP is to map together trunked ports for either two switches or a switch and a router.
7. **c.** This is the correct way of mapping VLAN 20 to module 2, port 3.

8. **b.** This command allows you to configure the switch VTP domain to coriolis.

9. **d.** VLANs using Spanning Tree Protocol operate at Layer 2. This is sort of a trick question if you don't keep in mind that VLANs are a Layer 2 solution to routing data traffic.

10. **b, c, d.** All devices in a VLAN are part of the same broadcast domain and are considered a logical segment. They can be defined by port or protocol, or they can be user defined, such as by MAC address.

11. **b.** The switch will merely ignore the message. It will act only upon messages that it receives within its own VTP domain.

12. **e.** Factors that should determine the number of VLANs in your switch block or LAN are data traffic patterns of the network, application types that are running on the network, network management needs, and user commonalities.

13. **a, b.** The two types of VLANs are local VLANs and End-to-End VLANs.

14. **c.** To configure a VTP management domain in secure mode configure a management domain password.

15. **a.** VLAN tags are not removed when tagged frames are sent out trunk ports. The end-user interface does not know what the tagging information means and considers the frame as corrupted.

Chapter 9 Solutions

1. **b.** A redundant link is known as a secondary or alternate path to a network destination.

2. **c.** Overcoming transparent bridging problems inspired the IEEE 802 Internetworking Committee to create the Spanning Tree Protocol specification.

3. **a, b, c, e.** Determining the location of loops in the network, electing a root bridge, monitoring the state of the spanning tree, and notifying the other switches of changes are all responsibilities of BPDUs.

4. **c.** VLAN 1 carries BPDUs for the spanning tree when CST is implemented. PVST+ would allow for BPDUs to be sent on a separate port for each VLAN.

5. **d.** Per-VLAN Spanning Tree (PVST) provides an alternative to CST for use on larger-scale switched networks to allow a separate instance of

Spanning Tree Protocol to be used on each individual VLAN. Although PVST+ also provides the same features and additional interpretabilities, it was not listed as a choice.

6. **c.** The correct command to configure a backup root bridge is **set spantree secondary**.
7. **d.** STP can be configured on only 64 VLANs. You can have up to 1,005 VLANs, but STP must be disabled on all but 64. By default, STP is enabled on VLANs 1 through 64.
8. **b.** The correct way to change the VLAN port priority to 16 is **spantree priority 16**.
9. **a.** Although all the possible answers are ASICs, the EARL ASIC is the ASIC notified when there are link bundle failures.
10. **c.** A VLAN port priority can be a numerical value between 0 and 63.
11. **d.** Only static type ports can be configured by Port Aggregation Protocol (PAgP) to form a bundle. Ports configured with different duplex speed and those set to dynamically assign VLANs cannot be bundled.
12. **c.** PortFast allows for ports with a server or workstation to transition to a forwarding state almost immediately after startup of the switch.
13. **a.** STP would refer to the Port ID using the lower of the Port IDs as the tiebreaker.
14. **b.** The default bridge priority value of a secondary root switch or bridge is a value of 16,384. The value of the root bridge would be 8,192.
15. **a.** Fast EtherChannel provides line speeds of 200Mbps to 800Mbps in full duplex mode.

Chapter 10 Solutions

1. **b.** Throughput is measured in terms of the amount of data that can be put through a network without experiencing packet loss or excessive collisions.
2. **a.** Forwarding rate is measured in the number of packets per second that can be transmitted on the physical wire.
3. **d.** A device that provides resources to the network is known as a resource node.
4. **b.** A device that makes requests of resource nodes is a demand node.
5. **d.** A collision domain is formed by all the nodes on a port of a bridge or switch.

6. **c.** All the nodes that reside on a specific VLAN make up the broadcast domain.
7. **c.** A utilization rate of 35 to 40 percent is considered in the average range. Anything more than that should be looked at more closely.
8. **c.** A switch is considered to be a blocking switch when it is unable to handle the throughput of all the connected devices.
9. **c.** A Route Switch Module provides Layer 3 functionality for a Catalyst 5000.
10. **c.** IGMP helps control multicast traffic.
11. **c.** Use the **show module** command to see what modules are installed on your switch.
12. **b.** Use the **session 3** command to access an RSM located on module 3.
13. **c.** In order to Telnet to a switch, you must set a password on the VTY line.
14. **c.** Protocol filtering is not supported on an ISL trunk.
15. **b.** False. Throughput is the measure most commonly used, but it is not the only measure.
16. **a.** The NetFlow Feature Cards I and II Route Switch Processor provides the ability to filter based on Layer 4 information.
17. **b.** The NetFlow Feature Card II enables a switch to achieve wire-speed capabilities for multicast operations.
18. **b.** False. A NetFlow Feature Card does require either an internal or external router to provide Layer 3 or 4 functionality.
19. **c.** There are 13 slots available.
20. **b.** A Supervisor Engine must go into slot 1 or 2 on a Catalyst switch.
21. **d.** A Route Switch Module can support 256 VLANs.
22. **c.** A Catalyst 4000 is not a modular switch.
23. **b.** The command **show running-config** displays the working configuration of a Catalyst 5000 RSM. This configuration can also be seen using the command **write terminal**.
24. **a.** For the VLAN interface to become active, you must issue the interface command **no shutdown**.
25. **c, d.** The VINES protocol is not supported on the Catalyst 2948G and the Catalyst 4000.

CHAPTER 11 SOLUTIONS

1. **d.** A Catalyst 6000 with Supervisor IA has the integrated NFFC functions and doesn't require a separate daughtercard.
2. **b.** MLSP sends out a multicast hello message every 15 seconds.
3. **a.** For all nontrunked MLS-RPs, the MLS-SE will insert an XTAG to distinguish the MLS-RP.
4. **b.** The first packet in a potential network flow is called a candidate packet.
5. **a.** The second packet in a network flow that completes an MLS entry is called an enabler packet.
6. **c.** The maximum size of the MLS cache is 128K.
7. **d.** All of these flow masks are used with MLS.
8. **a.** MLS is disabled if Network Address Translation is used.
9. **a.** An input access list cannot be used with MLS.
10. **a.** The command **mls rp ip** enables MLS on an MLS-RP.
11. **d.** All of the commands will show the MLS-RPs configured for a switch.
12. **b.** The MLS-RP should be placed in the same domain as the MLS-SE, or it will not participate in MLS.
13. **c.** The MLS-RP is placed in the NULL domain if it is not explicitly placed in a VTP domain.
14. **c.** MLS should be configured globally for the router and also on each interface that participates in MLS.
15. **a.** MLS is enabled by default on all switches.
16. **d.** An MLS-RP must be configured for all of these switches, because they do not have an internal route processor.
17. **a.** An MLS-SE must hear from an enabler packet within five seconds after receiving a candidate packet, or the entry is dropped from the MLS cache.
18. **c.** The **set agingtime** command changes the amount of time an entry is kept in an MLS cache.
19. **c.** The aging time can be configured for 8 to 2,032 seconds.
20. **a.** Cisco recommends the MLS cache be kept below 32K in size.

Chapter 12 Solutions

1. **b, c.** The two virtual identifiers are the administrator-assigned virtual IP address and the HSRP-assigned, well-known virtual MAC address.
2. **c.** HSRP was designed to create a transparent redundant default gateway for end users. Because the default gateway IP address is the address of the route processor, route processors is the correct answer.
3. **c.** HSRP provides services for the layer on which a router or route processor would be found. Therefore, Layer 3, the network layer, is correct.
4. **d.** HSRP supports virtually any LAN type. Token Ring, FDDI, and Ethernet are all supported by HSRP.
5. **b, c, d.** Proxy ARP, IRDP, and RIP were all solutions used prior to HSRP to resolve Layer 3 route processor redundancy issues.
6. **a.** FDDI and Ethernet both support up to 255 HSRP standby groups on a route processor. Token Ring supports only three.
7. **d.** The possible range of numbers that can be assigned to an HSRP standby group on an MSM, RSM, RSFC, or MSFC is 0 to 255.
8. **d.** All the fields listed as possible answers can be found in the HSRP multicast message.
9. **d.** Although messages are sent in other states, the key word here is *begin*. The Speak state is the first state in which an HSRP interface begins to forward its own hello messages.
10. **c.** If there is an active route processor on the network forwarding HSRP hello messages, the HSRP interface will remain in the Learn state until it receives a hello message containing the virtual IP and virtual MAC addresses.
11. **d.** The command **standby 4 timers 6 18** properly formats an HSRP timer.
12. **b.** The command **standby 3 authentication hsrp1** properly formats an HSRP clear-text password.
13. **a.** This was sort of a trick question, but it's one you might see on the test. HSRP is an IP-only protocol.
14. **c.** The **show ip arp** command can be used to see the virtual MAC and virtual IP addresses.
15. **a.** The command **standby 6 priority 170** properly formats an HSRP priority.

Chapter 13 Solutions

1. **c.** The International Telecommunications Union Telecommunications Standardization Sector (ITU-T) developed the ATM standard.
2. **b.** ATM is a cell-based technology and uses 53-byte cells or data units to pass data through the network.
3. **c.** An ATM cell is 53 bytes in length: 5 for the header, 48 for the payload.
4. **c.** A connection from an ATM endpoint to an ATM switch is a User to Network Interface (UNI).
5. **c.** A connection between two ATM switches is a Network to Network Interface (NNI).
6. **d.** The VPI and VCI fields are used by ATM to identify the destination of the data.
7. **d.** The ATM layer and the AAL are similar to the data link layer of the OSI Model.
8. **c.** Control and transmission of the bits of data is the job of the ATM physical layer.
9. **b.** The chief job of the ATM layer is to establish connections and pass the cells to the network
10. **a.** AAL1 is the most appropriate layer to use for video.
11. **c.** AAL3/4 is the layer NSPs use to pass traffic.
12. **b.** The E.164 addressing plan is used to connect to carrier networks.
13. **a.** The NSAP addressing scheme is used to connect to a private network.
14. **a, b, d.** Multiple ELANs can be assigned on an ATM network.
15. **a.** A LANE emulation client is responsible for forwarding the data to other end systems.
16. **b.** The Broadcast and Unknown Server handles broadcasting support for ATM LANE.
17. **b.** The LECS contains the database of LANE ATM addresses.
18. **a.** The ILMI helps initialize and configure ATM LECs.
19. **d.** ILMI allows an ATM client to share the first 13 bytes of the ATM switch it is connected to.
20. **b.** A LECS must be configured on a major interface.

21. **c.** The LES is the component queried for an ATM address.
22. **b.** The **session** command is used to access an ATM LANE module.
23. **a.** The first 12 digits are known as the End System Identifier (ESI).
24. **b.** The last two digits are known as the selector field.
25. **c.** A maximum of 255 LECs can be configured on an ATM LANE module.

CHAPTER 14 SOLUTIONS

1. **b.** Multicasting is described in RFC 1112,"Host Extensions for IP Multicasting."
2. **a.** A network broadcast is sent to every device on the network.
3. **b.** A unicast sends one copy of each packet to each member of the multipoint group.
4. **c.** A multicast sends a single copy to multiple devices in a group.
5. **d.** IP multicasts use a Class D network address.
6. **c.** Class D addresses are in the address range from 224.0.0.0 to 239.255.255.255.
7. **b.** 224.0.0.3 is used for distance vector protocols such as EIGRP. RIP has its own multicast address.
8. **b.** The reserved block of MAC addresses used for IP multicasting is 01-00-5E.
9. **d.** IGMP is used to control creation of multicast groups.
10. **d.** 224.1.1.1 is the all-routers address. It is used to send unsolicited Host Membership Reports.
11. **b.** IGMPv2 designates the router with the lowest IP address as the querier.
12. **c.** A TTL of 1 will allow multicast protocols on the local subnet only.
13. **a.** The MBONE uses the Distance Vector Multicast Routing Protocol (DVMRP).
14. **a, c.** PIM supports Dense Mode and Sparse Mode multicasts.
15. **c.** Multiple RPs can be defined, but only one is active.
16. **b.** CGMP is used on Cisco switches to provide the functions that IGMP would normally provide.

17. **c.** PIM is the protocol used by Cisco routers to exchange IP multicast messages.

18. **b.** False. IP multicasting is disabled on Cisco routers by default.

19. **b.** PIM is enabled only on the interfaces on which you configure it.

20. **a.** To implement IGMP, you must first join a multicast group.

Chapter 15 Solutions

1. **d.** An access security policy should define the control of user access to the network, route filtering to determine routes that should be seen by the core block, and the physical security of all network devices.

2. **b.** The wildcard address 0.0.0.255 specifies all the nodes in a Class C network.

3. **c.** Because an implied "deny all" exists at the end of each access list, the **access-list 1 permit 38.187.128.7** command would permit only the address 38.187.128.7.

4. **d.** An IP extended access list is defined with a number in the range of 100 to 199, making the command **access-list 101** correct.

5. **c.** The **access-class** command would apply an access list to a virtual terminal line.

6. **b.** The **ip http server** command would allow you to enable HTTP access to the Cisco IOS on a switch.

7. **d.** The **access-class** command is not a security method for HTTP. The enable password method, local method, and TACACS are all configurable security methods that can be applied to HTTP IOS configuration access.

8. **a, c.** You can apply security to virtual terminal ports by applying a timeout value and by applying a password to all virtual terminal lines.

9. **b.** The default privilege level for the Privileged EXEC Mode is 15 on an IOS-based switch.

10. **b, d.** In-band management includes management from virtual terminal lines and TFTP. The console and AUX ports are used in out-of-band management.

11. **d.** With port security on an IOS command-based switch, the maximum **max-mac-count** value that can be assigned to a port is 132.

12. **c.** On a port with port security configured, the light will change to an orange color when the port receives data from an unknown MAC address, indicating the port has been disabled.

13. **a, b.** Depending on the IOS being used, the **set banner motd** and **banner login** commands allow you to configure a login message on a Cisco switch.

14. **c.** The **show port** command displays the port security configuration on an interface.

15. **b.** A 48-bit MAC address access list can be identified by the access list numbers 700 through 799.

16. **b.** The Cisco IOS cannot provide all the security a network needs. Physical and management access need to be addressed as well.

17. **b.** An access list has an implied "deny all" at the end of the list. When an access list is created, permit statements need to be placed in the access list to filter out any data traffic you do not want.

18. **a.** The inverse wildcard mask for an octet with the subnet mask of 224 would be 31.

19. **b.** The source address, which is a 48-bit MAC address, is compared to incoming frames to verify authenticity. When port security is configured, the port automatically disables any frame that contains a non-matching MAC address, and the port light will show an orange color, indicating that the port is disabled.

20. **c.** The wildcard mask of 0.0.255.255 indicates all nodes in a Class B network.

Chapter 16 Solutions

1. **a, c.** Cisco devices support both in-band and out-of-band management connections.

2. **a.** In-band management requires network access and a Layer 3 protocol such as IP to connect to a switch.

3. **b.** Out-of-band management requires console access.

4. **d.** The performance area of network management deals with network usage and response time.

5. **a.** A network manager collects and analyzes network information received from network devices.

6. **a.** A collection of managed objects is known as a Management Information Base (MIB).
7. **b.** A network manager queries an agent to determine a network device's status.
8. **d.** Catalyst switches support four of the nine RMON groups without a WAN probe or other such device.
9. **d.** An SNMP Trap message is sent to a network manager when an event occurs on a managed object.
10. **d.** The Host group is not a member of Mini-RMON.
11. **b.** The Host group gathers statistics about network hosts.
12. **c.** The **show snmp** command shows the RMON's status on the switch.
13. **b.** SPAN is the term used to describe the mirroring of data from one port to another.
14. **c.** The **show system** command displays the overall condition of a switch.
15. **d.** If no entry exists for the remote device in the routing, the ICMP request will be directed to the default gateway. If no ICMP reply is received, a *Network or host unreachable* message is displayed.
16. **c.** Change Manager keeps a database of software images you can use to perform updates.
17. **d.** Campus Manager presents a graphical view of your network.
18. **d.** TrafficDirector allows you to set RMON thresholds on network devices.
19. **c.** VlanDirector uses CDP to discover your network.
20. **c.** CiscoWorks for Windows uses WhatsUp Gold as the underlying network management software.

APPENDIX B

STUDY RESOURCES

BOOKS

Cisco Systems, *Cisco IOS 12.0 Switching Services*, Cisco Press, Indianapolis, Ind., 1999. ISBN: 1-57870-157-0. Consult this book for information on the Cisco IOS 12.0 and how the Cisco IOS adapts to Cisco switching.

McDysan, David E. and Darren L. Spohn, *ATM Theory and Applications*, McGraw-Hill, New York, 1998. ISBN: 0-07045-346-2. This book is a great resource on Asynchronous Transfer Mode (ATM) and LAN Emulation (LANE).

Smith, Marina. *Virtual LANs*, McGraw-Hill, New York, 1998. ISBN: 0-07-913623-0. A good resource book on VLANs.

ONLINE RESOURCES

Many documents are available on the Web, but the best place for information is the Cisco Web site. Cisco is one of the best companies at providing documentation on its products. You can find the Cisco Web site at **www.cisco.com**.

Asynchronous Transfer Mode

- *Configuring ATM accounting and ATM RMON*—**www.cisco.com/univercd/cc/td/doc/product/dsl_prod/6260/swcnfg/cnfatm.htm**
- *Configuring ATM signaling*—**www.cisco.com/univercd/cc/td/doc/product/dsl_prod/6260/swcnfg/cnfs.htm**
- *Configuring ATM interfaces*—**www.cisco.com/univercd/cc/td/doc/product/dsl_prod/6260/swcnfg/conatm.htm**
- *Configuring ATM routing on a Cisco 6000 DSLAM*—**www.cisco.com/univercd/cc/td/doc/product/dsl_prod/6260/swcnfg/pnni.htm**
- *ATM fundamentals information on an 8500 Series switch*—**www.cisco.com/univercd/cc/td/doc/product/atm/c8540/wa5/12_0/3a_11/atm_tech/basics.htm**

- *A good overview of ATM*—**www.cisco.com/univercd/cc/td/doc/product/wanbu/9_3/bpx/bpxiappc.htm**

Cisco IOS

- *The Cisco IOS Easy IP*—**www.cisco.com/warp/public/cc/cisco/mkt/ios/nat/tech/ezip1_wp.htm**
- *IOS troubleshooting commands*—**www.cisco.com/univercd/cc/td/doc/product/software/ios113ed/113ed_cr/fun_r/frprt4/frtroubl.htm**

Hot Standby Routing Protocol

- *Frequently asked questions and solutions*—**www.cisco.com/warp/public/619/3.html**
- *Sample configuration of HSRP*—**www.cisco.com/warp/public/619/1.html**
- *Basic HSRP diagram and operation questions and answers*—**www.combinet.com/warp/public/619/2.html**

Inter-Switch Link

- *ISL Functional Specification*—**www.cisco.com/warp/public/741/4.html**
- *ISL trunking on the Catalyst 5000 and 6000 families of switches*—**www.cisco.com/warp/public/793/lan_switching/2.html**

IP Multicast

- *Higher-level protocols used with multicast*—**www.ipmulticast.com/community/whitepapers/highprot.html**
- *Simple Multicast Routing Protocol*—**www.cisco.com/univercd/cc/td/doc/cisintwk/ito_doc/smrp.htm**
- *Multicast commands*—**www.cisco.com/univercd/cc/td/doc/product/software/ios121/121cgcr/ip_r/iprprt3/1rdmulti.htm**

Multilayer Switching

- *Overview of multilayer switching*—**www.cisco.com/univercd/cc/td/doc/product/software/ios120/12cgcr/switch_c/xcprt5/xcmls.htm**
- *Configuring multilayer multicast switching*—**www.cisco.com/univercd/cc/td/doc/product/software/ios121/121cgcr/switch_c/xcprt5/xcdmmsc.htm**

- *Configuring IP multilayer switching for IOS 12.1*—**www.cisco.com/univercd/cc/td/doc/product/software/ios121/121cgcr/switch_c/xcprt5/xcdmsc.htm**
- *Configuring IPX multilayer switching*—**www.cisco.com/univercd/cc/td/doc/product/software/ios121/121cgcr/switch_c/xcprt5/xcdmsipx.htm**

Quality of Service

- *Quality of service overview*—**www.cisco.com/univercd/cc/td/doc/product/software/ios121/121cgcr/qos_c/qcdintro.htm**
- *Configuring QoS on a Cisco Catalyst 6000*—**www.cisco.com/univercd/cc/td/doc/product/lan/cat6000/sw_5_4/config/qos.htm**
- *Configuring IOS QoS solutions on the Catalyst 6000*—**www.cisco.com/univercd/cc/td/doc/product/lan/cat6000/ios127xe/qos.htm**
- *Tag switching*—**www.cisco.com/warp/public/732/Tech/tag**

Spanning Tree Protocol

- *Configuring STP on a Cisco Catalyst 2900*—**www.cisco.com/univercd/cc/td/doc/product/lan/c2900xl/29_35sa6/olhelp/stphelp.htm**
- *Configuring STP on a Cisco Catalyst 6000*—**www.cisco.com/univercd/cc/td/doc/product/lan/cat6000/sw_5_3/cofigide/spantree.htm**

TACACS+

- *Configuring TACACS+ on the Catalyst 5000, 5500, 4000, and 2900 Series*—**www.cisco.com/warp/public/473/cat_tacacs_plus.html**
- *Configuration examples using TACACS+*—**www.cisco.com/univercd/cc/td/doc/product/software/ios121/121cgcr/secur_c/scprt1/scdathor.htm**

VLANs

- *Comprehensive Products for Switched Internetworking (also known as Cisco's VLAN Roadmap)*—**www.cisco.com/warp/public/538/7.html**
- *VLAN and router technical tips*—**www.cisco.com/warp/public/741/10.html**
- *IEEE 802.10 VLAN encapsulation information*—**www.cisco.com/warp/public/741/3.html**

- *VLAN configuration issues on the Catalyst 5000*—**www.cisco.com/warp/public/741/9.html**

Standards Organizations

- *American National Standards Institute (ANSI)*—This organization coordinates many specialized standards organizations and technical committees. ANSI's Web site can be found at **www.ansi.org**.
- *Electronic Industries Association (EIA)*—This is the parent organization for a number of standards groups, including the Telecommunications Industry Association (TIA). TIA/EIA standards relate mostly to cabling. The TIA members are providers of communications and information technology products and services. The TIA/EIA Web site can be found at **www.tiaonline.org**.
- *Gigabit Ethernet Association*—This group was formed to promote industry cooperation in developing Gigabit Ethernet. You can find this group's Web site at **www.gigabit-ethernet.org**.
- *High Speed Token Ring Association*—This group was formed by Token Ring vendors to establish high-speed solutions for Token Ring. Its Web site can be found at **www.hstra.com**.
- *Institute of Electrical and Electronics Engineers (IEEE)*—This standards organization creates and publishes standards related to electronic technologies. It is best known for its 802 committee, which has produced a series of documents that describe LAN protocols and physical transmission topology standards. The IEEE's Web site can be found at **www.ieee.org**.
- *International Organization for Standardization (ISO)*—This organization is best known for the Open System Interconnection (OSI) Model. It creates and publishes standards that cover a wide range of topics. The ISO Web site can be found at **www.iso.ch**.
- *International Telecommunications Union Telecommunication Standardization Sector (ITU-T)*—This organization is responsible for the networking standards relating to Asynchronous Transfer Mode (ATM). The ITU-T Web site can be found at **www.itu.int**.
- *Internet Engineering Task Force (IETF)*—This organization is responsible for TCP/IP, Simple Network Management Protocol (SNMP), and Internet standards. A lot of its work relates to upgrading and enlarging the TCP/IP protocol suite and networks utilizing that protocol. The IETF Web site can be found at **www.ietf.org**.

- *National Committee for Information Technology Standards (NCITS)*—This organization was formed to produce market condition standards for storage devices, multimedia, programming languages, and security. The T11 committee is responsible for fiber channel standards. You can find the NCITS T11 Web site at **www.t11.org**.

Cisco Group Study and Users Groups

Some of the best resources for Cisco information are Cisco users groups and group study Web sites. Most major cities have one or both. Joining a group is a great way to keep up on technical information and gain a network of friends off of whom you can bounce troubleshooting questions. The following are some of the best sites we have found for Cisco users groups:

- *Capital District Cisco Users Group, Albany, New York*—**www.cdcug.org**
- *Cisco Users Group for Central Iowa*—**http://cisco.knis.com**
- *Colorado Springs Cisco Users Group, Colorado*—**http://cug.atsgroup.com**
- *Dallas/Ft. Worth Cisco Users Group, Texas*—**http://dfw.cisco-users.org**
- *Denver Cisco Users Group, Colorado*—**www.twpm.com/dcug/**
- *Groupstudy.Com*—**www.groupstudy.com**
- *Kansas City Cisco Users Group, Kansas*—**www.cugkansas.com/home.cfm**
- *New England Cisco Users Group*—**www.ciscousers.com**
- *Northern California Cisco Users Group, Sacramento, California*—**www.csecnet.com/cisco/index.htm**
- *Omaha Cisco Users Group, Omaha, Nebraska*—**www.teklnk.com**
- *Sacramento/Placer County, California Cisco Study Group*—**www.cisco-cert.org**
- *San Diego Cisco Users Group, California*—**www.sdvar.com/SDCUG/**
- *South Carolina Cisco Users Group*—**www.angelfire.com/sc/cisco/**
- *Southern California Cisco Users Group*—**www.sccug.org**

Live Cisco Training/Internet-Based Labs

- *Certification Solutions, author Sean Odom's Web site*—Meet Joe Snow, and get valuable updates to this book at **www.thequestforcertification.com**.
- *CertificationZone.com*—This is a great site for whitepapers, labs, and practice questions related to the CCNA and CCIE certifications. Watch for upcoming whitepapers from the authors of this *Exam Prep* at **www.certificationzone.com**.

- *Fatkid.com*—This company claims to have the lowest prices on Cisco educational material, as well as a virtual rack. Go to **www.fatkid.com**.
- *GroupStudy.com*—This study group on the Web uses email to interact with others. There is a Cisco study group and a CCIE study group for more advanced students. If you subscribe, you can expect to receive up to 300 emails per day, but it is a great resource for questions and answers. You'll find it at **www.groupstudy.com**.
- *MentorLabs.com*—For online Cisco labs and equipment, check out **www.mentorlabs.com**.

APPENDIX C

HEXADECIMAL CONVERSION

If you know how to perform basic binary conversion, hexadecimal conversion is somewhat easy. It takes the eight binary bits of a decimal value into a pair of four-bit numbers called *nibbles*. The nibbles are then converted into hexadecimal numbers in the range 0 through F, as shown in Table C.1.

Let's take a look at the decimal value 177 using its binary value of 10110001. The total binary value contains 8 bits. Each bit represents a value in the power of 2, which increases a power of 1 from right to left. The following shows an 8-bit binary string with the bit values turned on to equal the binary value of 177:

1	0	1	1	0	0	0	1
128	64	32	16	8	4	2	1

Table C.1 The hexadecimal values 0 through F.

Decimal Value	Hexadecimal Value	Nibble Value
0	00	0000
1	01	0001
2	02	0010
3	03	0011
4	04	0100
5	05	0101
6	06	0110
7	07	0111
8	08	1000
9	09	1001
10	0A	1010
11	0B	1011
12	0C	1100
13	0D	1101
14	0E	1110
15	0F	1111

The first line shows the binary numbers totaling 177. Notice that in the second line, starting with the 128 bit being turned on (the 1 represents a turned-on bit), all the bits in the string from right to left can be used without going over the desired value. If you total the turned-on bits, 128+32+16+1 you reach the value of 177.

To get the hexadecimal value, you would first split the 8-bit number into two 4-bit numbers (nibbles). The first nibble (1011) breaks down into

```
8(1) + 4(0) + 2(1) + 1(1)
```

which equals the decimal value 11. In turn, 11 equals the hexadecimal value B.

The second nibble (0001) breaks down to

```
8(0) + 4(0) + 2(0) + 1(1)
```

which equals the decimal value 1. So, the binary 10110001 is equal to B1.

The binary and hexadecimal values are important in many segments of switching, routing, and networking, including the well-known MAC addresses in multicast, network interface card MAC addresses, and IPX addresses. Table C.2 lists the 8-bit binary and hexadecimal addresses for the decimal values from 0 through 255.

Table C.2 The decimal conversions to hexadecimal and binary values.

Decimal Value	Hex Value	Binary Value
0	00	00000000
1	01	00000001
2	02	00000010
3	03	00000011
4	04	00000100
5	05	00000101
6	06	00000110
7	07	00000111
8	08	00001000
9	09	00001001
10	OA	00001010
11	OB	00001011
12	OC	00001100
13	OD	00001101
14	OE	00001110

(continued)

Table C.2 The decimal conversions to hexadecimal and binary values *(continued)*.

Decimal Value	Hex Value	Binary Value
15	OF	00001111
16	10	00010000
17	11	00010001
18	12	00010010
19	13	00010011
20	14	00010100
21	15	00010101
22	16	00010110
23	17	00010111
24	18	00011000
25	19	00011001
26	1A	00011010
27	1B	00011011
28	1C	00011100
29	1D	00011101
30	1E	00011110
31	1F	00011111
32	20	00100000
33	21	00100001
34	22	00100010
35	23	00100011
36	24	00100100
37	25	00100101
38	26	00100110
39	27	00100111
40	28	00101000
41	29	00101001
42	2A	00101010
43	2B	00101011
44	2C	00101100
45	2D	00101101
46	2E	00101110
47	2F	00101111
48	30	00110000
49	31	00110001
50	32	00110010
51	33	00110011
52	34	00110100

(continued)

Table C.2 The decimal conversions to hexadecimal and binary values *(continued)*.

Decimal Value	Hex Value	Binary Value
53	35	00110101
54	36	00110110
55	37	00110111
56	38	00111000
57	39	00111001
58	3A	00111010
59	3B	00111011
60	3C	00111100
61	3D	00111101
62	3E	00111110
63	3F	00111111
64	40	01000000
65	41	01000001
66	42	01000010
67	43	01000011
68	44	01000100
69	45	01000101
70	46	01000110
71	47	01000111
72	48	01001000
73	49	01001001
74	4A	01001010
75	4B	01001011
76	4C	01001100
77	4D	01001101
78	4E	01001110
79	4F	01001111
80	50	01010000
81	51	01010001
82	52	01010010
83	53	01010011
84	54	01010100
85	55	01010101
86	56	01010110
87	57	01010111
88	58	01011000
89	59	01011001
90	5A	01011010

(continued)

Table C.2 The decimal conversions to hexadecimal and binary values *(continued)*.

Decimal Value	Hex Value	Binary Value
91	5B	01011011
92	5C	01011100
93	5D	01011101
94	5E	01011110
95	5F	01011111
96	60	01100000
97	61	01100001
98	62	01100010
99	63	01100011
100	64	01100100
101	65	01100101
102	66	01100110
103	67	01100111
104	68	01101000
105	69	01101001
106	6A	01101010
107	6B	01101011
108	6C	01101100
109	6D	01101101
110	6E	01101110
111	6F	01101111
112	70	01110000
113	71	01110001
114	72	01110010
115	73	01110011
116	74	01110100
117	75	01110101
118	76	01110110
119	77	01110111
120	78	01111000
121	79	01111001
122	7A	01111010
123	7B	01111011
124	7C	01111100
125	7D	01111101
126	7E	01111110
127	7F	01111111
128	80	10000000

(continued)

Table C.2 The decimal conversions to hexadecimal and binary values *(continued)*.

Decimal Value	Hex Value	Binary Value
129	81	10000001
130	82	10000010
131	83	10000011
132	84	10000100
133	85	10000101
134	86	10000110
135	87	10000111
136	88	10001000
137	89	10001001
138	8A	10001010
139	8B	10001011
140	8C	10001100
141	8D	10001101
142	8E	10001110
143	8F	10001111
144	90	10010000
145	91	10010001
146	92	10010010
147	93	10010011
148	94	10010100
149	95	10010101
150	96	10010110
151	97	10010111
152	98	10011000
153	99	10011001
154	9A	10011010
155	9B	10011011
156	9C	10011100
157	9D	10011101
158	9E	10011110
159	9F	10011111
160	A0	10100000
161	A1	10100001
162	A2	10100010
163	A3	10100011
164	A4	10100100
165	A5	10100101
166	A6	10100110

(continued)

Table C.2 The decimal conversions to hexadecimal and binary values *(continued)*.

Decimal Value	Hex Value	Binary Value
167	A7	10100111
168	A8	10101000
169	A9	10101001
170	AA	10101010
171	AB	10101011
172	AC	10101100
173	AD	10101101
174	AE	10101110
175	AF	10101111
176	B0	10110000
177	B1	10110001
178	B2	10110010
179	B3	10110011
180	B4	10110100
181	B5	10110101
182	B6	10110110
183	B7	10110111
184	B8	10111000
185	B9	10111001
186	BA	10111010
187	BB	10111011
188	BC	10111100
189	BD	10111101
190	BE	10111110
191	BF	10111111
192	C0	11000000
193	C1	11000001
194	C2	11000010
195	C3	11000011
196	C4	11000100
197	C5	11000101
198	C6	11000110
199	C7	11000111
200	C8	11001000
201	C9	11001001
202	CA	11001010
203	CB	11001011
204	CC	11001100

(continued)

Table C.2 The decimal conversions to hexadecimal and binary values *(continued)*.

Decimal Value	Hex Value	Binary Value
205	CD	11001101
206	CE	11001110
207	CF	11001111
208	D0	11010000
209	D1	11010001
210	D2	11010010
211	D3	11010011
212	D4	11010100
213	D5	11010101
214	D6	11010110
215	D7	11010111
216	D8	11011000
217	D9	11011001
218	DA	11011010
219	DB	11011011
220	DC	11011100
221	DD	11011101
222	DE	11011110
223	DF	11011111
224	E0	11100000
225	E1	11100001
226	E2	11100010
227	E3	11100011
228	E4	11100100
229	E5	11100101
230	E6	11100110
231	E7	11100111
232	E8	11101000
233	E9	11101001
234	EA	11101010
235	EB	11101011
236	EC	11101100
237	ED	11101101
238	EE	11101110
239	EF	11101111
240	F0	11110000
241	F1	11110001
242	F2	11110010

(continued)

Table C.2 The decimal conversions to hexadecimal and binary values *(continued)*.

Decimal Value	Hex Value	Binary Value
243	F3	11110011
244	F4	11110100
245	F5	11110101
246	F6	11110110
247	F7	11110111
248	F8	11111000
249	F9	11111001
250	FA	11111010
251	FB	11111011
252	FC	11111100
253	FD	11111101
254	FE	11111110
255	FF	11111111

APPENDIX D

INTERNET MULTICAST ADDRESSES

Certain Class D IP network addresses in the range of 224.0.0.0 through 239.255.255.255 are used for host extensions for IP Multicast as specified in the Request For Comment (RFC) 1112 standard created by the Internet Engineering Task Force (IETF). The well-known addresses are assigned and maintained by the Internet Assigned Numbers Authority (IANA). This list specifies the extensions required of a host implementation of the Internet Protocol (IP) to support multicasting.

In troubleshooting your network, you may find the multicast addresses shown in Table D.1 flowing through your network. The handy guide provided by the tables in this appendix will help you see which addresses are well-known addresses assigned by RFCs, which routing protocols use which multicast address, and which addresses are used by private organizations. This information will be of great benefit when you're troubleshooting and deciding which addresses to deny into your network to conserve bandwidth.

Table D.1 lists the addresses, their purpose, and the RFC or contact acronym. For those that do not have both a contact name and email address, the email address is listed. Table D.2 lists the multicast group assignments. Table D.3 lists the titles of the RFCs from Table D.1. Table D.4 lists the contact acronyms from Tables D.1 and D.2, the contact for the assigned address, and the supplied email address of the contact.

This appendix uses many acronyms. The most important found in the well-known addresses are listed here:

- *DVMRP*—Distance Vector Multicast Routing Protocol
- *DHCP*—Dynamic Host Configuration Protocol
- *OSPF*—Open Shortest Path First
- *RIP*—Routing Information Protocol
- *RP*—Route Processor
- *PIM*—Protocol Independent Multicast

Warning: These addresses are subject to change. If you cannot find an address listed here that appears to be assigned, refer to the following location: **ftp://ftp.isi.edu/in-notes/iana/assignments/**.

Table D.1 Address, purpose, and RFC or contact acronym. See Table D.4 for the name and email address of the contact.

Address	Purpose	Reference/Contact Acronym
224.0.0.0	Base address (Reserved)	RFC1112/JBP
224.0.0.1	All systems on this subnet	RFC1112/JBP
224.0.0.2	All routers on this subnet	JBP
224.0.0.3	Unassigned	JBP
224.0.0.4	DVMRP routers	RFC1075/JBP
224.0.0.5	OSPFIGP all routers	RFC2328/JXM1
224.0.0.6	OSPFIGP designated routers	RFC2328/JXM1
224.0.0.7	ST routers	RFC1190/KS14
224.0.0.8	ST hosts	RFC1190/KS14
224.0.0.9	RIP2 routers	RFC1723/GSM11
224.0.0.10	IGRP routers	Farinacci
224.0.0.11	Mobile-agents	Simpson
224.0.0.12	DHCP server/relay agent	RFC1884
224.0.0.13	All PIM routers	Farinacci
224.0.0.14	RSVP-ENCAPSULATION	Braden
224.0.0.15	All-cbt-routers	Ballardie
224.0.0.16	Designated-sbm	Baker
224.0.0.17	All-sbms	Baker
224.0.0.18	VRRP	Hinden
224.0.0.19	IP all L1Iss	Przygienda
224.0.0.20	IP all L2Iss	Przygienda
224.0.0.21	IP all intermediate systems	Przygienda
224.0.0.22	IGMP	Deering
224.0.0.23	GLOBECAST-ID	Scannell
224.0.0.24	Unassigned	JBP
224.0.0.25	Router-to-switch	Wu
224.0.0.26	Unassigned	JBP
224.0.0.27	All MPP	Martinicky
224.0.0.28	ETC control	Zmudzinski
224.0.0.251	mDNS	Cheshire
224.0.1.0	VMTP Managers Group	RFC1045/DRC3
224.0.1.1	NTP Network Time Protocol	RFC1119/DLM1
224.0.1.2	SGI-Dogfight	AXC

(continued)

Table D.1 Address, purpose, and RFC or contact acronym. See Table D.4 for the name and email address of the contact *(continued)*.

Address	Purpose	Reference/Contact Acronym
224.0.1.3	Rwhod	SXD
224.0.1.4	VNP	DRC3
224.0.1.5	Artificial Horizons-Aviator	BXF
224.0.1.6	NSS-Name Service Server	BXS2
224.0.1.7	AUDIONEWS-Audio News Multicast	MXF2
224.0.1.8	SUN NIS+ Information Service	CXM3
224.0.1.9	MTP Multicast Transport Protocol	SXA
224.0.1.10	IETF-1-LOW-AUDIO	SC3
224.0.1.11	IETF-1-AUDIO	SC3
224.0.1.12	IETF-1-VIDEO	SC3
224.0.1.13	IETF-2-LOW-AUDIO	SC3
224.0.1.14	IETF-2-AUDIO	SC3
224.0.1.15	IETF-2-VIDEO	SC3
224.0.1.16	MUSIC-SERVICE	Guido Van Rossum
224.0.1.17	SEANET-TELEMETRY	Andrew Maffei
224.0.1.18	SEANET-IMAGE	Andrew Maffei
224.0.1.19	MLOADD	Braden
224.0.1.20	Any private experiment	JBP
224.0.1.21	DVMRP on MOSPF	John Moy
224.0.1.22	SVRLOC	Veizades
224.0.1.23	XINGTV	Gordon
224.0.1.24	Microsoft-DS	**arnoldm@microsoft.com**
224.0.1.25	NBC-PRO	**bloomer@birch.crd.ge.com**
224.0.1.26	NBC-PFN	**bloomer@birch.crd.ge.com**
224.0.1.31	Ampr-info	Janssen
224.0.1.32	Mtrace	Casner
224.0.1.33	RSVP-encap-1	Braden
224.0.1.34	RSVP-encap-2	Braden
224.0.1.35	SVRLOC-DA	Veizades
224.0.1.36	RLN-server	Kean
224.0.1.37	Proshare-mc	Lewis
224.0.1.38	Dantz	Yackle
224.0.1.39	Cisco-rp-announce	Farinacci
224.0.1.40	Cisco-rp-discovery	Farinacci
224.0.1.41	Gatekeeper	Toga
224.0.1.42	Iberiagames	Marocho
224.0.1.43	NWN-Discovery	Zwemmer
224.0.1.44	NWN-Adaptor	Zwemmer

(continued)

Table D.1 Address, purpose, and RFC or contact acronym. See Table D.4 for the name and email address of the contact *(continued)*.

Address	Purpose	Reference/Contact Acronym
224.0.1.45	ISMA-1	Dunne
224.0.1.46	ISMA-2	Dunne
224.0.1.47	Telerate	Peng
224.0.1.48	Ciena	Rodbell
224.0.1.49	DCAP-servers	RFC2114
224.0.1.50	DCAP-clients	RFC2114
224.0.1.51	MCNTP-directory	Rupp
224.0.1.52	MBONE-VCR-directory	Holfelder
224.0.1.53	Heartbeat	Mamakos
224.0.1.54	Sun-mc-grp	DeMoney
224.0.1.55	Extended-sys	Poole
224.0.1.56	Pdrncs	Wissenbach
224.0.1.57	TNS-adv-multi	Albin
224.0.1.58	Vcals-dmu	Shindoh
224.0.1.59	Zuba	Jackson
224.0.1.60	Hp-device-disc	Albright
224.0.1.61	TMS-production	Gilani
224.0.1.62	Sunscalar	Gibson
224.0.1.63	MMTP-poll	Costales
224.0.1.64	Compaq-peer	Volpe
224.0.1.65	IAPP	Meier
224.0.1.66	Multihasc-com	Brockbank
224.0.1.67	Serv-Discovery	Honton
224.0.1.68	Mdhcpdisover	RFC2730
224.0.1.69	MMP-bundle-Discovery1	Malkin
224.0.1.70	MMP-bundle-Discovery2	Malkin
224.0.1.71	XYPOINT DGPS Data Feed	Green
224.0.1.72	GilatSkySurfer	Gal
224.0.1.73	SharesLive	Rowatt
224.0.1.74	NorthernData	Sheers
224.0.1.75	SIP	Schulzrinne
224.0.1.76	IAPP	Moelard
224.0.1.77	AGENTVIEW	Iyer
224.0.1.78	Tibco Multicast1	Shum
224.0.1.79	Tibco Multicast2	Shum
224.0.1.80	MSP	Caves
224.0.1.81	OTT (One-way Trip Time)	Schwartz
224.0.1.82	TRACKTICKER	Novick

(continued)

Table D.1 Address, purpose, and RFC or contact acronym. See Table D.4 for the name and email address of the contact *(continued)*.

Address	Purpose	Reference/Contact Acronym
224.0.1.83	DTN-mc	Gaddie
224.0.1.84	Jini-announcement	Scheifler
224.0.1.85	Jini-request	Scheifler
224.0.1.86	SDE-Discovery	Aronson
224.0.1.87	DirecPC-SI	Dillon
224.0.1.88	B1Rmonitor	Purkiss
224.0.1.89	3Com-AMP3 dRMON	Banthia
224.0.1.90	ImFtmSvc	Bhatti
224.0.1.91	NQDS4	Flynn
224.0.1.92	NQDS5	Flynn
224.0.1.93	NQDS6	Flynn
224.0.1.94	NLVL12	Flynn
224.0.1.95	NTDS1	Flynn
224.0.1.96	NTDS2	Flynn
224.0.1.97	NODSA	Flynn
224.0.1.98	NODSB	Flynn
224.0.1.99	NODSC	Flynn
224.0.1.100	NODSD	Flynn
224.0.1.101	NQDS4R	Flynn
224.0.1.102	NQDS5R	Flynn
224.0.1.103	NQDS6R	Flynn
224.0.1.104	NLVL12R	Flynn
224.0.1.105	NTDS1R	Flynn
224.0.1.106	NTDS2R	Flynn
224.0.1.107	NODSAR	Flynn
224.0.1.108	NODSBR	Flynn
224.0.1.109	NODSCR	Flynn
224.0.1.110	NODSDR	Flynn
224.0.1.111	MRM	Wei
224.0.1.112	TVE-FILE	Blackketter
224.0.1.113	TVE-ANNOUNCE	Blackketter
224.0.1.114	Mac Srv Loc	Woodcock
224.0.1.115	Simple Multicast	Crowcroft
224.0.1.116	SpectraLinkGW	Hamilton
224.0.1.117	Dieboldmcast	Marsh
224.0.1.118	Tivoli Systems	Gabriel
224.0.1.119	PQ-Lic-mcast	Sledge
224.0.1.120	HYPERFEED	Kreutzjans

(continued)

Appendix D

Table D.1 Address, purpose, and RFC or contact acronym. See Table D.4 for the name and email address of the contact *(continued)*.

Address	Purpose	Reference/Contact Acronym
224.0.1.121	Pipesplatform	Dissett
224.0.1.122	LiebDevMgmg-DM	Velten
224.0.1.123	TRIBALVOICE	Thompson
224.0.1.124	UDLR-DTCP	Cipiere
224.0.1.125	PolyCom Relay1	Coutiere
224.0.1.126	Infront Multi1	Lindeman
224.0.1.127	XRX DEVICE DISC	Wang
224.0.1.128	CNN	Lynch
224.0.1.129	PTP-primary	Eidson
224.0.1.130	PTP-alternate1	Eidson
224.0.1.131	PTP-alternate2	Eidson
224.0.1.132	PTP-alternate3	Eidson
224.0.1.133	ProCast	Revzen
224.0.1.134	3Com Discp	White
224.0.1.135	CS-Multicasting	Stanev
224.0.1.136	TS-MC-1	Sveistrup
224.0.1.137	Make Source	Daga
224.0.1.138	Teleborsa	Strazzera
224.0.1.139	SUMAConfig	Wallach
224.0.1.140	Unassigned	
224.0.1.141	DHCP-SERVERS	Hall
224.0.1.142	CN Router-LL	Armitage
224.0.1.143	EMWIN	Querubin
224.0.1.144	Alchemy Cluster	O'Rourke
224.0.1.145	Satcast One	Nevell
224.0.1.146	Satcast Two	Nevell
224.0.1.147	Satcast Three	Nevell
224.0.1.148	Intline	Sliwinski
224.0.1.149	8x8 Multicast	Roper
224.0.1.150	Unassigned	JBP
224.0.1.166	Marratech-cc	Parnes
224.0.1.167	EMS-InterDev	Lyda
224.0.1.168	Itb301	Rueskamp
224.0.2.1	"RWHO" Group (BSD) (unofficial)	JBP
224.0.2.2	SUN RPC PMAPPROC_CALLIT	BXE1
224.2.127.254	SAPv1 announcements	SC3
224.2.127.255	SAPv0 announcements	SC3

Table D.2 The multicast group assignments for Class D IP addresses.

Address Range	Group Assignment	Reference
224.0.0.0 through 224.0.0.255	Routing Protocols	
224.0.1.27 through 224.0.1.30	Lmsc-Calren-1 to 4	Uang
224.0.1.151 through 224.0.1.165	Intline 1 to15	Sliwinski
224.0.1.169 through 224.0.1.255	Unassigned	JBP
224.0.2.064 through 224.0.2.095	SIAC MDD service	Tse
224.0.2.096 through 224.0.2.127	CoolCast	Ballister
224.0.2.128 through 224.0.2.191	WOZ-Garage	Marquardt
224.0.2.192 through 224.0.2.255	SIAC MDD market service	Lamberg
224.0.3.000 through 224.0.3.255	RFE generic service	DXS3
224.0.4.000 through 224.0.4.255	RFE individual conferences	DXS3
224.0.5.000 through 224.0.5.127	CDPD groups	Bob Brenner
224.0.5.128 through 224.0.5.191	SIAC market service	Cho
224.0.5.192 through 224.0.5.255	Unassigned	IANA
224.0.6.000 through 224.0.6.127	Cornell ISIS Project	Tim Clark
224.0.6.128 through 224.0.6.255	Unassigned	IANA
224.0.7.000 through 224.0.7.255	Where-Are-You	Simpson
224.0.8.000 through 224.0.8.255	INTV	Tynan
224.0.9.000 through 224.0.9.255	Invisible Worlds	Malamud
224.0.10.000 through 224.0.10.255	DLSw froups	Lee
224.0.11.000 through 224.0.11.255	NCC.NET audio	Rubin
224.0.12.000 through 224.0.12.063	Microsoft and MSNBC	Blank
224.0.13.000 through 224.0.13.255	UUNET PIPEX Net News	Barber
224.0.14.000 through 224.0.14.255	NLANR	Wessels
224.0.15.000 through 224.0.15.255	Hewlett Packard	Van Der Meulen
224.0.16.000 through 224.0.16.255	XingNet	Uusitalo
224.0.17.000 through 224.0.17.031	Mercantile & Commodity Exchange	Gilani
224.0.17.032 through 224.0.17.063	NDQMD1	Nelson
224.0.17.064 through 224.0.17.127	ODN-DTV	Hodges
224.0.18.000 through 224.0.18.255	Dow Jones	Peng
224.0.19.000 through 224.0.19.063	Walt Disney Company	Watson
224.0.19.064 through 224.0.19.095	Cal Multicast	Moran
224.0.19.096 through 224.0.19.127	SIAC Market Service	Roy
224.0.19.128 through 224.0.19.191	IIG Multicast	Carr
224.0.19.192 through 224.0.19.207	Metropol	Crawford
224.0.19.208 through 224.0.19.239	Xenoscience, Inc.	Timm
224.0.19.240 through 224.0.19.255	HYPERFEED	Felix
224.0.20.000 through 224.0.20.063	MS-IP/TV	Wong
224.0.20.064 through 224.0.20.127	Reliable Network Solutions	Vogels
224.0.20.128 through 224.0.20.143	TRACKTICKER Group	Novick

(continued)

Table D.2 The multicast group assignments for Class D IP addresses *(continued)*.

Address Range	Group Assignment	Reference
224.0.20.144 through 224.0.20.207	CNR Rebroadcast MCA	Sautter
224.0.21.000 through 224.0.21.127	Talarian MCAST	Mendal
224.0.22.000 through 224.0.22.255	WORLD MCAST	Stewart
224.0.252.000 through 224.0.252.255	Domain Scoped Group	Fenner
224.0.253.000 through 224.0.253.255	Report Group	Fenner
224.0.254.000 through 224.0.254.255	Query Group	Fenner
224.0.255.000 through 224.0.255.255	Border Routers	Fenner
224.1.0.0 through 224.1.255.255	ST multicast groups	RFC1190/KS14
224.2.0.0 through 224.2.127.253	Multimedia conference calls	SC3
224.2.128.0 through 224.2.255.255	SAP Dynamic assignments	SC3
224.252.0.0 through 224.255.255.255	DIS transient groups	Joel Snyder
225.0.0.0 through 225.255.255.255	MALLOC	Handley
232.0.0.0 through 232.255.255.255	VMTP transient groups	DRC3
233.0.0.0 through 233.255.255.255	Static allocations	Meyer2
239.000.000.000 through 239.255.255.255	Administratively scoped	IANA/RFC2365
239.000.000.000 through 239.063.255.255	Reserved	IANA
239.064.000.000 through 239.127.255.255	Reserved	IANA
239.128.000.000 through 239.191.255.255	Reserved	IANA
239.192.000.000 through 239.251.255.255	Organization-Local Scope	Meyer/RFC2365
239.252.000.000 through 239.252.255.255	Site-Local Scope	Meyer/RFC2365
239.253.000.000 through 239.253.255.255	Site-Local Scope	Meyer/RFC2365
239.254.000.000 through 239.254.255.255	Site-Local Scope	Meyer/RFC2365
239.255.000.000 through 239.255.255.255	Site-Local Scope	Meyer/RFC2365

Table D.3 Titles of RFCs.

Reference RFC	RFC Title
RFC1045	VMTP: Versatile Message Transaction Protocol Specification
RFC1075	Distance Vector Multicast Routing Protocol
RFC1112	Host Extensions for IP Multicasting
RFC1119	Network Time Protocol (Version 1), Specification and Implementation
RFC1190	Experimental Internet Stream Protocol, Version 2 (ST-II)
RFC2328	OSPF Version 2
RFC1723	RIP Version 2: Carrying Additional Information
RFC1884	IP Version 6 Addressing Architecture
RFC2114	Data Link Switching Client Access Protocol
RFC2365	Administratively Scoped IP Multicast
RFC2730	Multicast Address Dynamic Client Allocation Protocol (MADCAP)

Table D.4 Contact acronyms, including the contact name for the assigned multicast addresses and the supplied email address of the contact.

Contact Abbreviation	Contact Name	Email Address
Albin	Jerome Albin	albin@taec.enet.dec.com
Albright	Shivaun Albright	shivaun_albright@hp.com
Armitage	Ian Armitage	ian@coactive.com
Aronson	Peter Aronson	paronson@esri.com
AXC	Andrew Cherenson	arc@SGI.COM
Baker	Fred Baker	fred@cisco.com
Ballardie	Tony Ballardie	a.ballardie@cs.ucl.ac.uk
Ballister	Tom Ballister	tballister@starguidedigital.com
Banthia	Prakash Banthia	prakash_banthia@3com.com
Barber	Tony Barber	tonyb@pipex.com
Bhatti	Zia Bhatti	zia@netright.com
Blackketter	Dean Blackketter	dean@corp.webtv.net
Blank	Tom Blank	tomblank@microsoft.com
Braden	Bob Braden	braden@isi.edu
Bob Brenner	No contact information	
Brockbank	Darcy Brockbank	darcy@hasc.com
BXE1	Brendan Eic	brendan@illyria.wpd.sgi.com
BXF	Bruce Factor	ahi!bigapple!bruce@uunet.UU.NET
BXS2	Bill Schilit	schilit@parc.xerox.com
Carr	Wayne Carr	Wayne_Carr@ccm.intel.com
Casner	Steve Casner	casner@isi.edu
Caves	Evan Caves	evan@acc.com
Cheshire	Stuart Cheshire	cheshire@apple.com
Chiang	Steve Chiang	schiang@cisco.com
Cho	Joan Cho	jcho@siac.com
Cipiere	Patrick Cipiere	Patrick.Cipiere@sophia.inria.fr
Tim Clark	No contact information	
Costales	Bryan Costales	bcx@infobeat.com
Crawford	James Crawford	jcrawford@metropol.net
Crowcroft	Jon Crowcroft	jon@hocus.cs.ucl.ac.uk
CXM3	Chuck McManis	cmcmanis@sun.com
Daga	Anthony Daga	anthony@mksrc.com
Deering	Steve Deering	deering@cisco.com
DeMoney	Michael DeMoney	demoney@eng.sun.com
Dillon	Doug Dillon	dillon@hns.com
Dissett	Daniel Dissett	ddissett@peerlogic.com
DLM1	David Mills	Mills@huey.udel.edu
DRC3	Dave Cheriton	cheriton@dsg.stanford.edu

(continued)

Table D.4 Contact acronyms, including the contact name for the assigned multicast addresses and the supplied email address of the contact *(continued)*.

Contact Abbreviation	Contact Name	Email Address
Dunne	Stephen Dunne	**sdun@isma.co.uk**
DXS3	Daniel Steinberg	**daniel.steinberg@eng.sun.com**
Eidson	John Eidson	**eidson@hpl.hp.com**
Farinacci	Dino Farinacci	**dino@cisco.com**
Felix	Ken Felix	**kfelix@pcquote.com**
Fenner	Bill Fenner	**fenner@parc.xerox.com**
Flynn	Edward Flynn	**flynne@nasdaq.com**
Gabriel	Jon Gabriel	**grabriel@tivoli.com**
Gaddie	Bob Gaddie	**bobg@dtn.com**
Gal	Yossi Gal	**yossi@gilat.com**
Gibson	Terry Gibson	**terry.gibson@sun.com**
Gilani	Asad Gilani	**agilani@nymex.com**
Goland	Yaron Goland	**yarong@microsoft.com**
Gordon	Howard Gordon	**hgordon@xingtech.com**
Green	Cliff Green	**cgreen@xypoint.com**
GSM11	Gary S. Malkin	**gmalkin@xylogics.com**
Guttman	Erik Guttman	**erik.guttman@eng.sun.com**
Hall	Eric Hall	**ehall@ntrg.com**
Hamilton	Mark Hamilton	**mah@spectralink.com**
Handley	Mark Handley	**mjh@ISI.EDU**
Hinden	Bob Hinden	**hinden@Ipsilon.com**
Hodges	Richard Hodges	**rh@source.net**
Holfelder	Wieland Holdfelder	**whd@pi4.informatik.uni-mannheim.de**
Honton	Chas Honton	**chas@secant.com**
IANA	IANA	**iana@iana.org**
Iyer	Ram Iyer	**ram@aaccorp.com**
Jackson	Dan Jackson	**jdan@us.ibm.com**
Janssen	Rob Janssen	**rob@pe1chl.ampr.org**
JBP	Jon Postel	**postel@isi.edu**
JXM1	Jim Miner	**miner@star.com**
Kean	Brian Kean	**bkean@dca.com**
Kreutzjans	Michael Kreutzjans	**mike@pcquote.com**
KS14	Karen Seo	**kseo@bbn.com**
Lamberg	Mike Lamberg	**mlamberg@siac.com**
Lee	Choon Lee	**cwl@nsd.3com.com**
Lewis	Mark Lewis	**Mark_Lewis@ccm.jf.intel.com**
Lindeman	Morten Lindeman	**Morten.Lindeman@os.telia.no**

(continued)

Table D.4 Contact acronyms, including the contact name for the assigned multicast addresses and the supplied email address of the contact *(continued)*.

Contact Abbreviation	Contact Name	Email Address
Lyda	Stephen T. Lyda	**slyda@emsg.com**
Lynch	Joel Lynch	**joel.lynch@cnn.com**
Malamud	Carl Malamud	**carl@invisible.net**
Malkin	Gary Scott Malkin	**gmalkin@baynetworks.com**
Mamakos	Louis Mamakos	**louie@uu.net**
Manning	Bill Manning	**bmanning@isi.edu**
Marocho	Jose Luis Marocho	**73374.313@compuserve.com**
Marquardt	Douglas Marquardt	**dmarquar@woz.org**
Marsh	Gene Marsh	**MarshM@diebold.com**
Martinicky	Brian Martinicky	**Brian_Martinicky@automationintelligence.com**
Meier	Bob Meier	**meierb@norand.com**
Mendal	Geoff Mendal	**mendal@talarian.com**
Meyer	David Meyer	**meyer@ns.uoregon.edu**
Meyer2	David Meyer	**dmm@cisco.com**
Moelard	Henri Moelard	**hmoelard@wcnd.nl.lucent.com**
Moran	Ed Moran	**admin@cruzjazz.com**
John Moy	John Moy	**jmoy@casc.com**
MXF2	Martin Forssen	**maf@dtek.chalmers.se**
Nelson	Gunnar Nelson	**nelsong@nasd.com**
Nevell	Julian Nevell	**jnevell@vbs.bt.co.uk**
Novick	Alan Novick	**anovick@tdc.com**
O'Rourke	Stacey O'Rourke	**stacey@network-alchemy.com**
Parnes	Peter Parnes	**peppar@marratech.com**
Peng	Wenjie Peng	**wpeng@tts.telerate.com**
Poole	David Poole	**davep@extendsys.com**
Przygienda	Tony Przygienda	**prz@siara.com**
Purkiss	Ed Purkiss	**epurkiss@wdmacodi.com**
Querubin	Antonio Querubin	**tony@lava.net**
Revzen	Shai Revzen	**shrevz@nmcfast.com**
Rodbell	Mike Rodbell	**mrodbell@ciena.com**
Roper	Mike Roper	**mroper@8x8.com**
Guido Van Rossum	No contact information	
Rowatt	Shane Rowatt	**shane.rowatt@star.com.au**
Roy	George Roy/Bill Owens	**owens@appliedtheory.com**
Rubin	David Rubin	**drubin@ncc.net**
Rueskamp	Bodo Rueskamp	**br@itchigo.com**

(continued)

Appendix D

Table D.4 Contact acronyms, including the contact name for the assigned multicast addresses and the supplied email address of the contact *(continued)*.

Contact Abbreviation	Contact Name	Email Address
Rupp	Heiko Rupp	**hwr@xlink.net**
Sautter	Robert Sautter	**rsautter@acdnj.itt.com**
SC3	Steve Casner	**casner@precept.com**
Scannell	Piers Scannell	**piers@globecastne.com**
Scheifler	Bob Scheifler	**bob.scheifler@sun.com**
Schwartz	Beverly Schwartz	**bschwart@bbn.com**
Shindoh	Masato Shindoh	**jl11456@yamato.ibm.co.jp**
Shum	Raymond Shum	**rshum@ms.com**
Simpson	Bill Simpson	**bill.simpson@um.cc.umich.edu**
Sledge	Bob Sledge	**bob@pqsystems.com**
Sliwinski	Robert Sliwinski	**sliwinre@mail1st.com**
Stanev	Nedelcho Stanev	**nstanev@csoft.bg**
Stewart	Ian Stewart	**iandbige@yahoo.com**
Strazzera	Paolo Strazzera	**p.strazzera@telematica.it**
Sveistrup	Darrell Sveistrup	**darrells@truesolutions.net**
SXA	Susie Armstrong	**armstrong.wbst128@xerox.com**
SXD	Steve Deering	**deering@parc.xerox.com**
Thaler	Dave Thaler	**dthaler@microsoft.com**
Thompson	Nigel Thompson	**nigelt@tribal.com**
Timm	Mary Timm	**mary@xenoscience.com**
Toga	Jim Toga	**jtoga@ibeam.jf.intel.com**
Tse	Geordie Tse	**gtse@siac.com**
Tynan	Dermot Tynan	**dtynan@claddagh.ie**
Uang	Yea Uang	**uang@force.decnet.lockheed.com**
Uusitalo	Mika Uusitalo	**msu@xingtech.com**
Van Der Muelen	Ron van der Muelen	**ronv@lsid.hp.com**
Veizades	John Veizades	**veizades@tgv.com**
Velten	Mike Velten	**mike_velten@liebert.com**
Vogels	Werner Vogels	**vogels@rnets.com**
Volpe	Victor Volpe	**vvolpe@smtp.microcom.com**
Wallach	Walter Wallach	**walt@sumatech.com**
Wang	Michael Wang	**michael.wang@usa.xerox.com**
Watson	Scott Watson	**scott@disney.com**
Wei	Liming Wei	**lwei@cisco.com**
Wessels	Duane Wessels	**wessels@nlanr.net**
White	Peter White	**peter_white@3com.com**
Wissenbach	Paul Wissenbach	**paulwi@vnd.tek.com**
Wong	Tony Wong	**wongt@ms.com**

(continued)

Table D.4 Contact acronyms, including the contact name for the assigned multicast addresses and the supplied email address of the contact *(continued)*.

Contact Abbreviation	Contact Name	Email Address
Woodcock	Bill Woodcock	**woody@zocalo.net**
Wu	Ishan Wu	**iwu@cisco.com**
Yackle	Dotty Yackle	**ditty_yackle@dantz.com**
Zmudzinski	Krystof Zmudzinski	**kzmudzinski@etcconnect.com**
Zwemmer	Arnoud Zwemmer	**arnoud@nwn.nl**

Glossary of Acronyms

AAL
ATM Adaptation Layer

ABR
Available Bit Rate (used in ATM)

ACL
Access Control List

AMP
Active Monitor Present (used in Token Ring)

ANSI
American National Standards Institute

APaRT
Automated Packet Recognition and Translation

ARE
All Routes Explorer

ARP
Address Resolution Protocol

ASIC
Application-Specific Integrated Circuit

ASP
ATM System Processor

ATM
Asynchronous Transfer Mode

ATS
Asynchronous Transmission Synchronization

AUI
attachment unit interface (used in Ethernet)

AUX
auxiliary port

B-ICI
Broadband Interexchange Carrier Interconnect (used in ATM)

BNC Connector
Bayonet Neil-Concelman Connector

BOOTP
Bootstrap Protocol

BPDU
Bridge Protocol Data Unit

BPS
bits per second

BRI
Basic Rate Interface

BUS
broadcast and unknown server (used in LANE)

BVI
Bridged Virtual Interface

CAM
Carrier Access Module or Content Addressable Memory

CAU
Controlled Access Unit (used in Token Ring)

CBL
Color Blocking Logic

CBR
Constant Bit Rate (used in ATM)

CDDI
Copper Distributed Data Interface

CDP
Cisco Discovery Protocol

CEF
Cisco Express Forwarding (used in ASIC)

CES
Circuit Emulation Services

CFI
canonical format indicator (used in VLANs)

CGMP
Cisco Group Management Protocol

CIDR
classless interdomain routing

CRC
Cyclical Redundancy Check

CRS
Configuration Report Server (used in Token Ring)

CSMA/CA
Carrier Sense Multiple Access Collision Avoidance

CSMA/CD
Carrier Sense Multiple Access Collision Detection

CSU
Channel Service Unit

DA
destination address

DAS
Dual Attached Stations (used in FDDI)

DCE
Data Communications Equipment

dCEF
Distributed Cisco Express Forwarding (used in ASIC)

DHCP
Dynamic Host Configuration Protocol

DRD
Destination Route Descriptor (used in Token Ring)

DSAP
Destination Service Access Point

DSL
Digital Subscriber Line

DSU
Data Service Unit

DTE
Data Terminal Equipment

DTP
Dynamic Trunk Protocol/Dynamic Trunk Link Protocol

DTR
Dedicated Token Ring

EARL
Enhanced Address Recognition Logic (used in ASIC)

ECU
Embedded Control Unit

EIA
Electronic Industries Association

EISA
Extended Industry Standard Architecture

ELAN
emulated LAN

ELFEXT
Equal Level Far End Crosstalk

EMI
electromagnetic interference

E-RIF
Embedded Routing Information Field

FC
Fibre Channel

FCS
frame check sequence

FDDI
Fiber Distributed Data Interface

FDM
frequency division multiplexing

FE
Forwarding Engine

FIFO
first in, first out

FMI
Fiber optic Medium Interface (used in Token Ring)

FTP
File Transfer Protocol

Gb
gigabit

GBIC
Gigabit Interface Converter

Gbps
gigabits per second

GE
Gigabit Ethernet

GNS
Get Nearest Server

HDLC
High-level Data Link Control

HSRP
Hot Standby Routing Protocol

HSSDC
High-Speed Serial Data Connector

HSSI
High Speed Serial Interface

HSTR
High Speed Token Ring

HTTP
Hypertext Transfer Protocol

IANA
Internet Assigned Numbers Authority

ICMP
Internet Control Message Protocol

ICV
Integrity Check Value

IDB
Interface Descriptor Block

IEC
International Electrotechnical Commission

IEEE
Institute of Electrical and Electronics Engineers

IETF
Internet Engineering Task Force

IGMP
Internet Group Management Protocol

IGRP
Interior Gateway Routing Protocol

ILMI
Integrated Local Management Interface (used in ATM)

InterNIC
Internet Network Information Center

I/O
input/output

IOS
Internetwork Operating System (used by Cisco)

IP
Internet Protocol

IPX
Internetwork Packet Exchange

IPX/SPX
Internetwork Packet Exchange/Sequenced Packet Exchange

IRTF
Internet Research Task Force

ISA
Industry Standards Architecture

ISDN
Integrated Services Digital Network

ISL
Inter-Switch Link

ISO
International Organization for Standardization

IVL
Independent VLAN Learning

K
kilobyte

Kb
kilobit

L2F
Layer 2 Forwarding Protocol

L2TP
Layer 2 Tunneling Protocol

LACP
Link Aggregation Control Protocol

LACPDU
Link Aggregation Control Protocol Data Unit

LAG
Link Aggregation Group

LAN
local area network

LANE
LAN Emulation

LAT
Local Area Transport

LB-LAN
locally bridged local area network

LCP
Line Module Communication Processor

LEC
LAN emulation client or Local Exchange Carrier

LECID
LAN emulation client ID

LECS
LAN emulation configuration server

LES
LAN emulation server

LLC
Logical Link Control

LMA
LAN Module ASIC

LSAP
Link Service Access Point

LTL
Local Target Logic

MAC
Media Access Control

MAN
metropolitan area network

MAU
Media Access Unit (used in Ethernet) or Multistation Access Unit (used in Token Ring)

Mb
megabit (One million bits)

Mbps
megabit(s) per second

MCP
Master Communication Processor

MIB
Management Information Base (used in SNMP)

MIC
Medium Interface Connector

MLS
Multilayer Switching

MLSP
Multilayer Switching Protocol

MMF
Multimode Fiber

MPOA
Multiprotocol Over ATM

MSAU
Multistation Access Unit (used in Token Ring)

MSDU
MAC Service Data Unit

MSM
Multilayer Switch Module

NAA
Network Address Authority

NCITS
National Committee for Information Technology Standards

NCP
NetWare Core Protocol

NDIS
Network Driver Interface Specification

NDS
Novell Directory Services

NFFC
Netflow Feature Card

NIC
Network Interface Card

NLM
NetWare Loadable Module

NMP
Network Management Processor

NNI
Network to Network Interface

NOS
network operating system

NTP
Network Time Protocol

NVRAM
Non-Volatile RAM

OSI
Open System Interconnection

OSPF
Open Shortest Path First

PAgP
Port Aggregation Protocol

PDU
Protocol Data Unit

PFPA
Proprietary Fat Pipe ASIC

PIM
Protocol Independent Multicast

PING
Packet Internet Groper

PMA
physical medium attachment

PMD
physical medium dependent

PMI
physical medium independent

POST
Power-On Self Test

POTS
Plain Old Telephone System

PPP
Point-to-Point Protocol

PPTP
Point-To-Point Tunneling Protocol

PRI
Primary Rate Interface

PS
power supply

PSTN
Public Switched Telephone Network

PVC
permanent virtual circuit

PVI
Port VLAN Identifier

QoS
Quality of Service

RARP
Reverse Address Resolution Protocol

RB
remote bridge

RD
route descriptor (used in Bridging)

RFC
Request For Comments (used by IETF)

RI
ring in

RIF
Routing Information Field

RIP
Routing Information Protocol

RMON
Remote Network Monitoring

RO
ring out

RP
Route Processor

RSFC
Route Switch Feature Card

RSM
router switching module

SA
source address

SAID
Secure Association Identifier

SAP
service access point or Service Advertising Protocol

SAP Agent
Service Advertising Protocol Agent

SAS
Single Attached Station (used in FDDI)

SDE
Secure Data Exchange (used in PDU)

SE
Switch Engine

SFD
Start Frame Delimiter

SMA
Sub Miniature Type A

SMDS
Switched Multimegabit Data Service

SMF
Single-mode fiber

SMF-IR
Single-mode fiber—intermediate range

SMF-LR
Single-mode fiber—long range

SMI
Structure of Management Information (used in SNMP)

SMIB
Security Management Information Base

SMP
Standby Monitor Present (used in Token Ring)

SMS
Selective Multicast Service

SMT
Station Management (used in FDDI)

SNA
System Network Architecture

SNAP
Subnetwork Access Protocol

SNMP
Simple Network Management Protocol

SP
Switch Processor

SPAN
Switched Port Analyzer

SPX
Sequenced Packet Exchange

SRB
Source Route Bridging

SRS
Source Route Switching

SRT
Source Route Transparent

SR/TLB
Source Route Translational Bridging

SSAP
Source Service Access Point

SSD
Start-of-Stream Delimiter

SSL
Secure Sockets Layer

SSRP
Simple Server Redundancy Protocol

ST
Straight Tip (FDDI connector)

STA
Spanning Tree Algorithm

STE
Spanning Tree Explorer

STP
shielded twisted-pair or Spanning Tree Protocol

SVC
Switched Virtual Circuit

SVL
Shared VLAN Learning

TB
Transparent Bridging

Tbps
terabits (1000 billion bits) per second

TCI
tag control information

TCP
Transmission Control Protocol

TCU
Trunk Coupling Unit (used in Token Ring)

TDR
Time Domain Reflectometer

TFTP
Trivial File Transfer Protocol

TIA
Telecommunications Industry Association

TPID
tag protocol identifier

TTRT
Target Token Rotation Timeout (used in FDDI)

UBR
Unspecified Bit Rate (used in ATM)

UDP
User Datagram Protocol

UNI
User to Network Interface

UTP
Unshielded Twisted Pair

VCI
Virtual Channel Identifier (used in ATM)

VID
VLAN identifier

VLAN
virtual LAN

VPI
Virtual Path Identifier (used in ATM)

VRRP
Virtual Router Redundancy Protocol

VTP
Virtual Trunk Protocol/Virtual Trunking Protocol

WAN
wide area network

GLOSSARY OF TERMS

10Base2
The IEEE 802.3 standard for running Ethernet at 10Mbps over a thinnet coaxial cable. The maximum length for a 10Base2 segment is 185 meters, or 607 feet.

10Base5
The IEEE 802.3 standard for running Ethernet at 10Mbps over a thicknet coaxial cable. The maximum length for a 10Base5 segment is 500 meters, or 1,640 feet.

10BaseT
The IEEE 802.3 standard for running Ethernet at 10Mbps over shielded or unshielded twisted-pair wiring. The maximum length for a 10BaseT segment is 100 meters, or 328 feet.

100BaseFX
An IEEE standard for running Fast Ethernet over fiber-optic cable.

100BaseT
The IEEE 802.3u standard for running Ethernet at 100Mbps over a shielded or unshielded twisted-pair cable. Also known as *Fast Ethernet*.

100BaseT4
A technology that allows the use of Fast Ethernet technology over existing Category 3 and Category 4 wiring, utilizing all four pairs of wires.

100BaseVG(Voice Grade)/AnyLAN
The IEEE 802.12 standard that allows data transmissions of 100Mbps over Category 3 or data-grade wiring, which utilizes all sets of wires.

1000BaseX
The IEEE 802.3z standard that defines standards for data transmissions of 1,000Mbps. Also known as *Gigabit Ethernet*.

access layer
In the Campus Hierarchical Model, the layer where the workstation connects to the network. This is where hubs or switches reside and where workgroups access the network.

access lists
A security feature used with the Cisco IOS to filter traffic types as part of data routing. Access lists are also used to filter traffic between different VLAN numbers.

address
A set of numbers, usually expressed in binary format, used to identify and locate a resource or device on a network.

address filter
A way of using Layer 2 MAC addresses or switching ports to filter traffic. This process allows you to filter traffic and restrict access without the use of VLANs. This is a feature of the Cisco Catalyst 3000 Series. It uses a process similar to access lists on the Cisco IOS. However, you can apply multiple address filters to the same interface.

Address Resolution Protocol (ARP)
The protocol used to map the IP address to the MAC address.

Adjacency Table
Works with the FIB and the CEF ASIC to keep a table of nodes that are adjacent or within a single hop from the switch. CEF uses the adjacency table to prepend Layer 2 addressing table information.

administrator
A person responsible for the control and security of the user accounts, resources, and data flow on the network.

All Routes Explorer (ARE)
On a Token Ring network, if the node of destination is not found on the local network segment, an ARE frame is sent to all the bridges. Each bridge receiving an ARE updates the frame with a RIF and then forwards the frame out all the ports.

American National Standards Institute (ANSI)
The organization that publishes standards for communications, programming languages, and networking.

ANDing
The process of comparing the bits of an IP address with the bits in a subnet mask to determine how a packet will be handled.

anycast address
An address used in ATM for shared multiple-end systems. An anycast address allows a frame to be sent to specific groups of hosts.

application layer
The layer of the OSI model that provides support for end users and for application programs using network resources.

Application Specific Integrated Circuit (ASIC)
A feature of many LAN controllers. ASICs are internal to the switch. They work in conjunction with the internal processor to make Layer 2 forwarding decisions. However, they lack the ability to make flexible software-implemented forwarding decisions. Their ability to perform small tasks quickly and inexpensively makes them a key in the switching process. ASICs used in Cisco switches and routers are the Phoenix, FE, LMA, PFPA, SAMBA, SAGE, SAINT, and CEF.

Asymmetric Digital Subscriber Line (ADSL)
A service that transmits digital voice and data over existing (analog) phone lines.

Asynchronous Transfer Mode (ATM)
International standard originally developed by the ITU-T that is used in high-speed transmission media such as E3, SONET, and T3 for cell relay. It can be used in multiple service types such as voice, video, or data and sent in fixed-length, 53-byte cells. ATM has become common on the corporate networks of today. It guarantees throughput and minimizes delay. It can provide scalability up to multi-gigabit per second speeds.

Asynchronous Transmission Synchronization (ATS)
A process used in serial data transfer in which a start bit and a stop bit are added so the receiving station can know when a particular bit has been transferred. Also known as *bit synchronization*.

ATM adaptation layer (AAL)
The ATM layer that adapts data to the ATM 48-byte payload. There are a number of adaptations to this layer, such as AAL1, AAL2, AAL3/4, and AAL5. AAL5 is by far the most common in today's networks. AAL5 defines how data from a node on the network such as a PC or server handles ATM cells. AAL5 is also used by Cisco Catalyst switches with LANE to perform segmentation and reassembly of ATM frames into cells and cells into frames.

ATM System Processor (ASP)
A Cisco ATM cell-switching processing card, located on the Cisco Catalyst 5500 chassis or slot 2 on the LS1010 chassis.

attachment unit interface (AUI)
IEEE 802.3 specification used between a Multistation Access Unit (MAU) and an Ethernet network interface card. MAUs are typically associated with Token Ring networks and AUI ports are specific to Ethernet. It connects an AUI port on the Ethernet access card to an Ethernet 10Base2, 10Base5, or 10BaseFL transceiver.

attachment unit interface (AUI) connector
A 15-pin D-type connector sometimes used with Ethernet connections.

attenuation
The loss of signal that is experienced as data is transmitted across network media.

Automated Packet Recognition and Translation (APaRT)
A FDDI line module feature found on Cisco Catalyst 2820 and 5000 Series switches that allows for the automatic detection of frame types with translational bridging. It uses the CAM table to get the frame-type information for all end nodes.

backbone
A high-capacity infrastructure system that provides optimal transport on a LAN. Typically in a LAN, the data running from router to router, switch to switch, or switch to router is transported through a faster physical topology than the rest of the local area or virtual LAN devices. The physical cable is called the backbone.

BackboneFast
Initiated when a root port or blocked port receives an inferior BPDU from its designated bridge. It allows the secondary or backup port to immediately begin forwarding after a link fault with the root link. It bypasses the MaxAge timer.

backplane
Similar to the motherboard in a PC. The primary data/control bus located on a Cisco Catalyst switch. It interconnects all the modules inside the switch chassis.

bandwidth
The rated throughput capacity of a given network protocol or medium.

base bandwidth
The difference between the lowest and highest frequencies available for network signals. The term is also used to describe the rated throughput capacity of a given network protocol or medium.

Basic Rate Interface (BRI)
An ISDN digital communications line that consists of three independent channels: two Bearer (or B) channels, each at 64Kbps; and one Data (or D) channel at 16Kbps. ISDN BRI is often referred to as 2B+D.

baud rate
Named after a French telegraphy expert named J. M. Baudot, this term is used to define the throughput speed or rate of signal transfer.

binary
A Base 2 numbering system used in digital signaling, characterized by 1s and 0s.

binding
The process of associating a protocol and a network interface card (NIC).

bit
An electronic digit used in the binary numbering system.

blocking architecture
A condition in which the total bandwidth of the ports is greater than the capacity of the switching fabric.

bridge
A device that connects and passes packets between two network segments that use

the same communications protocol. Bridges operate at the data link layer of the OSI Reference Model. A bridge filters, forwards, or floods an incoming frame based on the MAC address of that frame.

Bridge Protocol Data Unit (BPDU)
A multicast frame generated by the switch that carries information about itself and changes in the network topology.

bridging address table
A list of MAC addresses kept by bridges and used when packets are received to determine which segment the destination address is on before sending the packet to the next interface or dropping the packet if it is on the same segment as the sending node.

broadband
A communications strategy that uses analog signaling over multiple communications channels.

Broadband Interexchange Carrier Interconnect (B-ICI)
An interface that connects between two ATM carriers.

broadcast
A packet delivery system in which a copy of a packet is given to all hosts attached to the network.

broadcast domain
In a non-switched network, a broadcast domain is all the devices that can receive a broadcast from one machine in the network sent on the physical wire. A segment not separated by a Layer 3 device or Layer 2 device that can filter broadcasts is the broadcast domain. On a switched network using VLANs, your broadcast domain is all the ports or collision domains that belong to the same VLAN.

broadcast storm
Occurs when broadcasts throughout the LAN become so numerous that they use up all the available bandwidth on a LAN, thus grinding the network to a halt.

brouter
A device that can be used to combine the benefits of both routers and bridges. Its common usage is to route routable protocols at the network layer and to bridge nonroutable protocols at the data link layer.

brownout
A short-term decrease in the voltage level, usually caused by the startup demands of other electrical devices.

bus
A path used by electrical signals to travel between the CPU and the attached hardware.

bus mastering
A bus accessing method in which the network interface card takes control of the bus in order to send data through the bus directly to the system memory, bypassing the CPU.

bus topology
A linear LAN architecture that uses a common cable with multipoint connections for the flow of data in a serial progression to all nodes on that network segment.

byte
A set of bits (usually 8) operating as a unit to signify a character.

cable modem
A modem that provides Internet access over cable television lines.

campus
A group of buildings in a fixed geographical location, owned and controlled by the organization.

Carrier Access Module (CAM)
A module attaching to the ATM cell switching bus. A CAM can support two

port-adapter modules to provide physical ATM line ports used by end nodes. A CAM can be placed in the Cisco Catalyst 5500 in slot 9, 10, 11, or 12. It can also be placed in the LS1010 in slot 0, 1, 3, or 4.

Carrier Sense Multiple Access with Collision Avoidance (CSMA/CA)
A media-access method that uses collision avoidance techniques.

Carrier Sense Multiple Access with Collision Detection (CSMA/CD)
A media-access method that uses collision detection and that listens to the network to see if it is in use. If the network is clear, data is transmitted. If a collision occurs, both stations will retransmit their data.

change control
A process in which a detailed record of every change made to the network is documented.

channel
A communications path used for data transmission.

Channel Service Unit (CSU)
A network communications device used to connect to the digital equipment lines of the common carrier, usually over a dedicated line or Frame Relay. Used in conjunction with a Data Service Unit (DSU).

Circuit Emulation Services (CES)
A PAM module that allows none ATM devices utilizing either T1 or E1 interfaces to attach to an ATM switch backplane. This module can be used to connect PBX, video conferencing, and none ATM routers to the network backbone.

Cisco Discovery Protocol (CDP)
A Cisco protocol that gathers and stores information about other neighboring devices on the network. It can be used in Ethernet, Token Ring, Serial, and FDDI media types. All Cisco devices including hubs support CDP.

Cisco Express Forwarding (CEF)
Cisco's newest ASIC, which utilizes the Forwarding Information Base and an Adjacency Table to route Layer 2 and Layer 3 addresses with very high performance.

Cisco Group Management Protocol (CGMP)
A Cisco protocol used by the Catalyst switch to forward multicast frames intelligently. CGMP dynamically discovers end-user stations participating in multicast applications. When receiving a multicast, it forwards the multicast directly to the end users instead of broadcasting the multicast throughout the network.

Class A network
A TCP/IP network that uses addresses starting between 1 and 126 and supports up to 126 subnets with 16,777,214 unique hosts each.

Class B network
A TCP/IP network that uses addresses starting between 128 and 191 and supports up to 16,384 subnets with 65,534 unique hosts each.

Class C network
A TCP/IP network that uses addresses starting between 192 and 223 and supports up to 2,097,152 subnets with 254 unique hosts each.

Class D network
A TCP/IP network that uses addresses starting between 224 and 240. Typically reserved for experimental uses and not found in production networks.

Class E network
A TCP/IP network that uses addresses starting between 241 and 254. Typically reserved for experimental uses and not found in production networks.

classless interdomain routing (CIDR)
A technique that allows multiple addresses to be consolidated into a single entry.

Clear Header
A field (part of the 802.10 header) that copies the encrypted Protected Header for security purposes to help guarantee against tampering with the frame. Also known as the *Secure Data Exchange (SDE) Protocol Data Unit.*

ClearChannel Architecture
The switching architecture found in the Cisco Catalyst Series 1900 and 2820 switches. The architecture is made up of the 1Gbps Packet Exchange Bus, Forwarding Engine, Embedded Control Unit, a management interface, and a 3MB shared memory buffer.

client
A node that requests a service from another node on a network.

client/server networking
Networking architecture utilizing front-end demand nodes that request and process data stored by the back end or resource node.

coaxial cable
Data cable, commonly referred to as *coax*, made of a solid copper core, which is insulated and surrounded by braided metal and covered with a thick plastic or rubber covering. This is the standard cable used in cable TV and in older bus topology networks.

collision
The result of two frames transmitting simultaneously in an Ethernet network and colliding, thereby destroying both frames.

collision domain
All the interfaces on a single segment that can send data on the same physical wire. In a hub, all the interfaces connected to all the hub ports are in their own collision domain. In the case of a switch, all the nodes connected to each individual port are in their own collision domain.

Color Blocking Logic (CBL)
A feature of the SAMBA ASIC used to force the EARL to make forwarding decisions. It also makes sure that a tagged frame that comes from a particular VLAN does not exit through a port belonging to another VLAN. CBL also assists in placing ports in one of four different modes for Spanning Tree Protocol: blocking, learning, listening, or forwarding.

common carrier
Supplier of communications utilities, such as phone lines, to the general public.

communication
The transfer of information between nodes on a network.

connectionless-oriented communication
Packet transfer in which the delivery is not guaranteed.

connection-oriented communication
Packet transfer in which the delivery is guaranteed.

connectivity
The linking of nodes on a network in order for communication to take place.

Content Addressable Memory (CAM)
A table used by a bridge to make forwarding and filtering decisions. The CAM table contains MAC addresses with port addresses leading to the physical interfaces. The CAM table uses a specialized interface that is faster than RAM to make forwarding and filtering decisions. The CAM table updates information by examining frames it receives from a segment and then updating the table with the source MAC address from the frame.

control plane
Functions that dictate how data actually flows through the switch fabric.

Copper Distributed Data Interface (CDDI)
The implementation of the FDDI standard using electrical cable rather than optical cable.

core block
End point for networks; requires fast access and no policy implementation.

core layer
In the OSI Hierarchical Model, the backbone of the network; designed for high-speed data transmission.

crosstalk
Electronic interference caused when two wires get too close to each other.

cut-through packet switching
A switching method that does not copy the entire packet into the switch buffers. Instead, the destination address is placed in buffers, the route to the destination node is determined, and the packet is quickly sent out the corresponding port. The switch begins forwarding the frame as soon as the first 13 bytes and MAC address are received. It relies on the receiving device to discard the frame if there is corruption. Cut-through packet switching maintains a low latency.

Cyclical Redundancy Check (CRC)
A method used to check for errors in packets that have been transferred across a network. A computation bit is added to the packet and recalculated at the destination to determine if the entire packet contents have been transferred correctly.

D connectors
Connectors shaped like a "D" that use pins and sockets to establish connections between peripheral devices using serial or parallel ports. The number that follows is the number of pins the connector uses for connectivity. For example, a DB-9 connector has 9 pins, and a DB-25 has 25 pins.

DAC
A device connected to the FDDI counter-rotating rings. The DAC serves as a hub to provide passive connections to the rings for peripheral devices.

data field
In a frame, the field or section that contains the data.

data plane
Functions applied directly against the actual data being directed in and out of the switching fabric.

data link layer
This is Layer 2 of the OSI Reference Model. The data link layer is above the physical layer. Data comes off the cable, through the physical layer, and into the data link layer.

Data Service Unit (DSU)
Formats and controls data for transmission over digital lines. Used in conjunction with a Channel Service Unit (CSU).

data terminal equipment
A device—at the user end of a user-network interface—that serves as a data source, a destination, or both. These devices include computers, protocol translators, and multiplexers.

datagram
Information groupings that are transmitted as a unit at the network layer.

DB-9
A connector that has 9 pins and is used for serial-port or parallel-port connection between PCs and peripheral devices.

DB-25
A connector that has 25 pins and is used for serial-port or parallel-port connection between PCs and peripheral devices.

dedicated line
Generally used in WANs to provide a constant connection between two points.

default gateway
Normally a router or a multihomed computer to which packets are sent when they are destined for a host that is not on their segment of the network.

demand node
Any end user or interface that requests and accesses network resources such as servers or printers.

destination address
The network address where the frame is being sent. In a packet, this address is encapsulated in a field of the packet so all nodes know where the frame is being sent.

Destination Service Access Point (DSAP)
A one-byte field in the frame that combines with the service access point (SAP) to inform the receiving host of the identity of the destination host.

dialed number identification service
The method for delivery of automatic number identification using out-of-band signaling.

diameter
A unit of measurement between the root switch and child switches, calculated from the root bridge, with the root bridge counting as the first switch. Each subsequent child switch out from the root bridge is added to come up with the diameter number.

dial-up networking
The connection of a remote node to a network using POTS or PSTN.

Digital Subscriber Line (DSL)
A public network technology that delivers high bandwidth over conventional copper wiring at limited distances.

Distributed Switching
An implementation in which switching decisions are made at the local port or the line module.

distribution layer
In the Hierarchical Model, this layer functions as the separation point between the core and access layers of the network. The devices in the distribution layer implement the policies that define how packets are to be distributed to the groups within the network.

domain
A logical grouping of interfaces in a network or intranet to identify a controlled network of nodes that are grouped as an administrative unit.

Dual Attached Stations (DAS)
A connection that allows a device to connect to both FDDI counter-rotating rings.

dual-homed
A FDDI end station attached to two DACs for redundancy.

dumb terminal
An end-user station that can access another computer or switch but cannot provide any processing at the local level.

Dynamic Host Configuration Protocol (DHCP)
A protocol that provides an IP address to requesting demand nodes on the network.

Dynamic ISL
A protocol that performs trunking negotiation. It also verifies that two connected ports can become trunk links. A Dynamic ISL port can be configured in one of four modes: On, Off, Desirable, or Auto.

dynamic VLAN port
A VLAN number assigned to a certain MAC address. The node attaching to any

dynamic port on the switch is a member of the VLAN assigned to the MAC address. Dynamically assigned VLANs are configured by using CiscoWorks 2000 or CiscoWorks for Switched Internetworks software.

dynamic window
A mechanism that prevents the sender of data from overwhelming the receiver. The amount of data that can be buffered in a dynamic window can vary.

electromagnetic interference (EMI)
External interference from electromagnetic signals that causes reduction of data integrity and increased error rates in a transmission medium.

Electronics Industries Association (EIA)
A group that specifies electrical transmission standards.

Embedded Control Unit (ECU)
A component of the ClearChannel Architecture that handles frame switching on the Cisco Catalyst Series 1900 and 2820 switches in software. The ECU is an Intel 486 processor, flash memory module, and a 512K DRAM. It is also used in initializing the switch, using STP on a per-VLAN basis, controlling the LEDs on the chassis, maintaining RMON statistics, and handling in-band and out-of-band management of the switch.

Emulated LAN (ELAN)
A feature used by ATM LANE to perform the basic functionality of a VLAN in Token Ring or Ethernet environments. ELANs, like VLANs, require a route processor such as a router to route frames between ELANs.

encapsulation
The technique used by layered protocols in which a layer adds header information to the Protocol Data Unit (PDU) from the layer above.

Enhanced Address Recognition Logic (EARL) ASIC
An ASIC located on the Catalyst 5000 family of switches that sees all the frames that cross the bus. Performs a task similar to that of the CAM. The ASIC is responsible for making switching decisions based on the MAC address and the source VLAN. It is also responsible for updating the address table.

encryption
The modification of data for security purposes prior to transmission so that it is not comprehensible without the decoding method.

Enterprise Services
Services that involve crossing the backbone to achieve access. These services are typically located on a separate subnet than the rest of the network devices.

EtherChannel
A connection used on the Catalyst 3000 family or Kalpana switches. It allows as many as seven Ethernet links to be bundled and load-balanced frame by frame to provide up to 140Mbps of bandwidth. It can utilize half-duplex or full-duplex links.

Extended Industry Standard Architecture (EISA)
The successor to the ISA standard; provides a 32-bit bus interface used in PCs.

Fast EtherChannel
A connection used on the Catalyst 5000 family of switches. It allows as many as seven Ethernet links to be bundled and load-balanced frame by frame to provide up to 800Mbps of bandwidth. It can utilize half-duplex or full-duplex links.

Fast Ethernet
IEEE 802.3 specification for data transfers of up to 100Mbps.

fault tolerance
A theoretical concept defined as a resistance to failure. It is not an absolute and can be defined only in degrees.

fiber channel or fibre channel
A technology that defines full gigabit-per-second data transfer over fiber-optic cable.

Fiber Distributed Data Interface (FDDI)
A high-speed data-transfer technology designed to extend the capabilities of existing local area networks using a dual-rotating ring technology similar to Token Ring.

fiber-optic cable
Also known as fiber optics or optical fiber. A physical medium capable of conducting modulated light transmissions. Compared with other transmission media, fiber-optic cable is more expensive, but is not susceptible to electromagnetic interference and is capable of higher data rates.

File Transfer Protocol (FTP)
The set of standards or protocols that allows you to transfer complete files between different computer hosts.

flash memory
A type of memory that keeps its contents (usually the operating system) when the power is cycled.

flow control
A method used to control the amount of data that is transmitted within a given period of time. There are different types of flow control. See also *dynamic window* and *static window*.

Forwarding Engine (FE)
A major component of ASIC; part of the ClearChannel Architecture on the Cisco Catalyst Series 1900 and 2820 switches. It is responsible for learning addresses, allocating buffer space in the shared memory space, queuing frames, forwarding decisions, and maintaining statistics.

Forwarding Information Based Switching (FIB)
A mirror image of the IP routing table's routing information, similar to a routing table or information base. It updates routing information when routing or topology changes occur in the network and recalculates the next-hop information. FIB maintains a list of all known routes and eliminates the need for route cache maintenance associated with fast switching or optimum switching. FIB is used with the CEF ASIC.

fragment-free
A fast packet-switching method that reads the first 64 bytes of the frame to determine if the frame is corrupted. If this first part is intact, then the frame is forwarded. Also known as *runtless switching*.

frame
Grouping of information transmitted as a unit across the network at the data link layer.

Frame Check Sequence field
This field performs a cyclic redundancy check (CRC) to ensure that all of the frame's data arrives intact.

frame filtering
A process useful for VLANs that utilizes a filtering table to drop frames based on a certain value contained in any one of the many fields in the data frame, such as the source or destination address. As part of normal operations, switches share filter tables. The frame's contents are compared to the filter table in the switch, thereby increasing the latency of the switch. Frame filtering is not used in the Cisco Catalyst 5000 or 6000 family of switches to implement VLANs.

Frame Length field
In a data frame, the field that specifies the length of a frame. The maximum length for an 802.3 frame is 1,518 bytes.

Frame Relay
A data-link–layer switching protocol used across multiple virtual circuits of a common carrier, giving the end user the appearance of a dedicated line.

frame tagging
A VLAN implementation method used to add VLAN information to data frames. As a frame enters the switch, it is tagged with VLAN information. It retains this information through the switch fabric; the tagging is removed before the frame exits the switch port with the attached destination interface. The process is transparent to the sending and receiving interfaces.

Frame Type Field
In a data frame, the field that names the protocol that is being sent in the frame.

frequency division multiplexing (FDM)
A technology that divides the output channel into multiple, smaller-bandwidth channels, each using a different frequency range.

full backup
A backup method in which every file on the hard drive is copied.

full duplex
Transmission method in which the sending and receiving (Rx and Tx) channels are separate; therefore, collisions cannot occur. Data is transmitted in two directions simultaneously on separate physical wires.

gateway
A hardware and software solution that enables communication between two dissimilar networking systems or protocols. Gateways usually operate at the upper layers of the OSI protocol stack, above the transport layer.

gigabit (Gb)
One billion bits or one thousand megabits.

Gigabit Ethernet
IEEE specification for transfer rates up to one gigabit per second.

guaranteed flow control
A method of flow control in which the sending and receiving hosts agree upon a rate of data transmission. After they agree on a rate, the communication will take place at the guaranteed rate until the sender is finished. No buffering takes place at the receiver.

half duplex
A circuit designed for data transmission in both directions, but not simultaneously.

head-of-line blocking
Situation in which congestion on an outbound port limits throughput to uncongested ports. It is completely different from oversubscription. Physical data from another source device blocks the data of the sending device.

High Speed Serial Interface (HSSI)
The network standard for high-speed serial communications over WAN links. It includes Frame Relay, T1, T3, E1, and ISDN.

host
Any system on a network. In the Unix world, any device that is assigned an IP address.

host ID
A unique identifier for a client or resource on a network.

hostname
The NetBIOS name of the computer or node, given to the first element of the Internet domain name. It must be unique on your network.

Hot Standby Routing Protocol (HSRP)
A Cisco protocol that provides redundancy. Should a link fail, another can be configured to take its place.

hub
A hardware device that connects multiple independent nodes. Also known as a *concentrator* or *multiport repeater.*

Hypertext Transfer Protocol (HTTP)
A protocol used by Web browsers to transfer pages and files from the remote node to your computer.

IEEE
See *Institute of Electrical and Electronics Engineers*.

IEEE 802.1
Standard that defines the OSI model's physical and data link layers. This standard allows two IEEE LAN stations to communicate over a LAN or WAN and is often referred to as the *internetworking standard*. It also includes the Spanning Tree Algorithm specifications.

IEEE 802.2
Standard that defines the LLC sublayer for the entire series of protocols covered by the 802.x standards. This standard specifies the adding of header fields, which tell the receiving host which upper layer sent the information. It also defines specifications for the implementation of the Logical Link Control (LLC) sublayer of the data link layer.

IEEE 802.3
Standard that specifies physical-layer attributes—such as signaling types, data rates, and topologies—and the media-access method used. It also defines specifications for the implementation of the physical layer and the MAC sublayer of the data link layer, using CSMA/CD. This standard also includes the original specifications for Fast Ethernet.

IEEE 802.4
Standard that defines how production machines should communicate and establishes a common protocol for use in connecting these machines. It also defines specifications for the implementation of the physical layer and the MAC sublayer of the data link layer using token access over a bus topology.

IEEE 802.5
Standard often used to define Token Ring. However, it does not specify a particular topology or transmission medium. It provides specifications for the implementation of the physical layer and the MAC sublayer of the data link layer using a token-passing media-access method over a ring topology.

IEEE 802.6
Standard that defines the distributed queue dual bus (DQDB) technology to transfer high-speed data between nodes. It provides specifications for the implementation of metropolitan area networks (MANs).

IEEE 802.7
Standard that defines the design, installation, and testing of broadband-based communications and related physical media connectivity.

IEEE 802.8
Standard that defines a group of people who advise the other 802-standard committees on various fiber-optic technologies and standards. This advisory group is called the Fiber Optic Technical Advisory Group.

IEEE 802.9
Standard that defines the integration of voice and data transmissions using isochronous Ethernet (IsoEnet).

IEEE 802.10
Another Cisco adopted protocol, used primarily to transport VLAN information over Fiber Distributed Data Interface

(FDDI). You will find this protocol primarily used in FDDI backbones to transport VLAN information and data.

IEEE 802.11
Standard that defines the implementation of wireless technologies, such as infrared and spread-spectrum radio.

IEEE 802.12
Standard that defines 100BaseVG/AnyLAN, which uses a 1000Mbps signaling rate and a special media-access method allowing 100Mbps data traffic over voice-grade cable.

IEEE 802.1D
The standard that defines the Spanning Tree Protocol and Spanning Tree Algorithm.

IEEE 802.1Q
Standard for inserting a frame tag VLAN identifier in the frame header. As a frame enters the switch fabric, it is tagged with additional information regarding the VLAN properties. The tag remains in the frame as it is forwarded between switches and is removed prior to exiting the access link to the destination interface. This process is completely transparent to the end user.

Industry Standards Architecture (ISA)
The standard of the older, more common 8-bit and 16-bit bus and card architectures.

input/output (I/O)
Any operation in which data either enters a node or is sent out of a node.

Institute of Electrical and Electronics Engineers (IEEE)
A professional organization that develops standards for networking and communications.

Integrated Local Management Interface
A protocol created by the ATM forum to allow any ATM switch and ATM device to communicate using Simple Network Management Protocol (SNMP).

Integrated Services Digital Network (ISDN)
An internationally adopted standard for end-to-end digital communications over Public Switched Telephone Network (PSTN) that permits telephone networks to carry data, voice, and other source traffic.

intelligent hubs
Hubs that contain some management or monitoring capability.

interface
A device, such as a card or a plug, that connects pieces of hardware with the computer so that information can be moved from place to place (for example, between computers and printers, hard disks, and other devices, or between two or more nodes on a network).

internal IPX address
A unique 8-digit number that is used to identify a server. Usually generated at random when the server is installed.

internal loopback address
Used for testing with TCP/IP. This address—127.0.0.1—allows a test packet to reflect back into the sending adapter to determine if it is functioning properly.

International Standards Organization (ISO)
A voluntary organization founded in 1946, responsible for creating international standards in many areas, including communications and computers.

Internet Assigned Numbers Authority (IANA)
The organization responsible for Internet protocol addresses, domain names, and protocol parameters.

Internet Control Message Protocol (ICMP)
Network-layer Internet protocol, documented in RFC 792, that reports errors and provides other information relevant to IP packet processing.

Internet Engineering Task Force (IETF)
A group of research volunteers responsible for specifying the protocols used on the Internet and for specifying the architecture of the Internet.

Internet Group Management Protocol (IGMP)
Protocol responsible for managing and reporting IP multicast group memberships.

Internet layer
In the TCP/IP architectural model, this layer is responsible for the addressing, packaging, and routing functions. Protocols operating at this layer of the model are responsible for encapsulating packets into Internet datagrams. All necessary routing algorithms are run here.

Internet Network Information Center (InterNIC)
The group that provides Internet services, such as domain registration and information, directory, and database services.

Internet Protocol (IP)
Network-layer protocol, documented in RFC 791, that offers a connectionless internetwork service. IP provides features for addressing, packet fragmentation and reassembly, type-of-service specification, and security.

Internet Research Task Force (IRTF)
The research arm of the Internet Architecture Board. This group performs research in areas of Internet protocols, applications, architecture, and technology.

internetwork
A group of networks that are connected by routers or other connectivity devices so that the networks function as one network.

Internetwork Operating System
Cisco's proprietary operating system used in its routers and switches.

Internetwork Packet Exchange (IPX)
The network-layer protocol generally used by Novell's NetWare network operating system. IPX provides connectionless communication, supporting packet sizes up to 64K.

Internetwork Packet Exchange/Sequenced Packet Exchange (IPX/SPX)
Default protocol used in NetWare networks. A combination of the IPX protocol to provide addressing and SPX to provide guaranteed delivery for IPX. Similar in nature to its counterpart, TCP/IP.

Inter-Switch Link (ISL)
A special Cisco proprietary Ethernet protocol that assigns a 26-byte header to an encapsulated frame and a 4-byte checksum, sometimes referred to as the FCS or the CRC.

IPSec
A protocol designed for virtual private networks (VPNs). Used to provide strong security standards for encryption and authentication.

IPX address
The unique address used to identify a node in the network.

kilobit (Kb)
One thousand bits.

kilobyte (K)
One thousand bytes.

LAN Emulation (LANE)
A standard created by the ATM forum to govern the connections of ATM endstations to either Ethernet or Token Ring devices.

LAN Module ASIC (LMA)
An ASIC part of the Cisco Catalyst 3000 Series switch that provides frame buffering, address learning, bus arbitration, and switching decisions for Ethernet ports.

latency
The time used to forward a packet in and out of a device. Commonly used in reference to routing and switching.

Layer 2 Forwarding Protocol (L2F)
A dial-up VPN protocol designed to work in conjunction with PPP to support authentication standards, such as TACACS+ and RADIUS, for secure transmissions over the Internet.

Layer 2 Tunneling Protocol (L2TP)
A dial-up VPN protocol that defines its own tunneling protocol and works with the advanced security methods of IPSec. L2TP allows PPP sessions to be tunneled across an arbitrary medium to a *home gateway* at an ISP or corporation.

learning bridge
A bridge that builds its own bridging address table, rather than requiring you to enter information manually.

Line Module Communication Processor (LCP)
Located on each line module; it is the responsibility of the LCP to provide communications for the MCP located on the Supervisor Engine.

local area network (LAN)
A group of connected computers that are located in a geographic area, usually a building or campus, and that share data and services.

local broadcast
A broadcast on the local network, looking for the IP address of the destination host.

local services
Services where the device supplying the services resides on the same subnet as the device requesting the services.

Local Target Logic (LTL)
A feature of some line modules that assists the EARL in making forwarding decisions.

local VLAN
Beneficial for networks whose resources are centralized and in one geographical location. The VLAN can span one switch or many switches within the same floor or building.

logical addressing scheme
The addressing method used in providing manually assigned node addressing.

Logical Link Control (LLC)
Sublayer of the data link layer of the OSI Reference Model. Provides an interface for the network-layer protocols and the Media Access Control (MAC) sublayer; also part of the data link layer.

loop
A continuous circle that a packet takes through a series of nodes in a network until it eventually times out. Without a protocol such as STP to detect loops, if no life cycle is assigned to the packet, the data could continuously encircle the network.

loopback plug
A device used for loopback testing.

loopback testing
A troubleshooting method in which the output and input wires are crossed or shorted in a manner that allows all outgoing data to be routed back into the card.

management
Fault, capacity, accounting, performance, and security control for a network.

Master Communication Processor (MCP)
A feature of the Supervisor Engine that takes commands from the Network Management Processor (NMP) and forwards them to the correct Line Module Communication Processor (LCP). MCP is also responsible for testing and configuring the local ports, and controlling the ports using LTL and CBL. It also performs diagnostics on the memory, SAINT ASICs, LTL, and CBL. MCP also is responsible for downloading software to the line modules.

Media Access Control (MAC) address
A six-octet number that uniquely identifies a host on a network. It is a unique number that is burned into the network interface card, so it cannot be changed.

Media Access Control (MAC) layer
In the OSI model, the lower of the two sublayers of the data link layer. Defined by the IEEE as responsible for interaction with the physical layer.

Media Access Unit (MAU)
IEEE 802.3 specification referring to a transceiver. Not to be confused with a Token Ring MAU (Multistation Access Unit), which is sometimes abbreviated MSAU.

megabit (Mb or Mbit)
One million bits. Term used to rate transmission transfer speeds (not to be confused with megabyte).

megabyte (MB)
One million bytes. Usually refers to file size.

message
A portion of information that is sent from one node to another. Messages are created at the upper layers of the OSI Reference Model.

microsegmentation
The process of using switches to divide a network into smaller segments.

microwaves
Very short radio waves used to transmit data over 890MHz (megahertz).

modem
A device used to modulate and demodulate the signals that pass through it. It converts the direct current pulses of the serial digital code from the controller into the analog signal that is compatible with the telephone network.

multicast
A single packet transmission from one sender to a specific group of destination nodes.

multilayer switches
A combination of Layers 2, 3, and 4 switches that use the concept of route once, switch many.

multiprocessor
Support for multiple processors in a single machine.

Multiprotocol Over ATM (MPOA)
An ATM forum standard that includes enhancements to LANE and adds Layer 3 switching capabilities to ATM switches.

Multistation Access Unit (MAU or MSAU)
A concentrator or hub used in a Token Ring network. It organizes the connected nodes into an internal ring and uses the RI (ring in) and RO (ring out) connectors to expand to other MAUs on the network.

NetFlow Switching
A feature incorporated into the MSM, NFFC, and NFFC II that was originally instituted and developed for Cisco's Enterprise Routers. NetFlow allows for

transparent switching in hardware, incorporating QoS features including security, multicast forwarding, multilayer switching, NetFlow data exporting, and packet filtering at Layer 3 and Layer 4 application ports.

NetWare Core Protocol (NCP)
NetWare protocol that provides a method for hosts to make calls to a NetWare server for services and network resources.

NetWare Loadable Module (NLM)
A service or process running on a NetWare server.

network down
Situation in which the clients are unable to utilize the services of the network. This can be administrative scheduled downtime for upgrades or maintenance, or it can be the result of a serious error.

Network Driver Interface Specification (NDIS)
Microsoft proprietary specification or standard for a protocol-independent device driver. These drivers allow the NIC (network interface card) to bind multiple protocols to the same NIC, allowing the card to be used by multiple operating systems. Similar to Open Data-Link Interface (ODI).

network ID
The part of the TCP/IP address that specifies the network portion of the IP address. It is determined by the class of the address, which is determined by the subnet mask used.

network interface card (NIC)
Also known as a *network adapter*. The hardware component that serves as the interface, or connecting component, between your network and the node. It has a transceiver, a MAC address, and a physical connector for the network cable.

network interface layer
The bottom layer of the TCP/IP architectural model. Responsible for sending and receiving frames.

network layer
The third layer of the OSI Reference Model, where routing based on node addresses (IP or IPX addresses) occurs.

Network Management Processor (NMP)
A feature of the Catalyst Supervisor Engine that is responsible for general control and some management functions of the switch. It is responsible for executing the system's configuration changes, the CLI, and running diagnostics on boot components as well as new additional components.

Network Time Protocol (NTP)
A protocol that allows all network equipment to synchronize the date and time on the private or internetwork environment.

Network to Network Interface (NNI)
An interface that provides connectivity between two ATM switches.

non-blocking
A condition in which the fabric contains more bandwidth than the sum total of all the ports' bandwidth combined.

Non-Volatile RAM (NVRAM)
Static memory similar to that of the flash. Memory stored in NVRAM does not get lost when the power is cycled on the device. On a switch, the NVRAM stores the VLAN configuration, system configuration, SNMP parameters, STP configuration, and configuration of each port.

Novell Directory Services (NDS)
The user, group, and security information database of network resources utilized in a NetWare 4.x and/or NetWare 5.x internetwork.

Open Systems Interconnection (OSI) Model
A seven-layer model created by the ISO to standardize and explain the interactions of networking protocols.

over subscription
A condition in which the total bandwidth of the ports is greater than the capacity of the switching fabric. Also referred to as a *blocking architecture*.

Packet Internet Groper (PING)
A TCP/IP protocol-stack utility that works with Internet Control Message Protocol and uses an echo request and reply to test connectivity to other systems.

password
A set of characters used with a username to authenticate a user on the network and to provide the user with rights and permissions to files and resources.

patch panel
A device where the wiring used in coaxial or twisted-pair networks converges in a central location and is then connected to the back of the panel.

peer-to-peer networking
A network environment without dedicated servers, where communication occurs between similarly capable network nodes that act as both client and server.

permanent virtual circuit (PVC)
A logical path established in packet-switching networks between two locations. Similar to a dedicated leased line. Also known as a *permanent virtual connection* in ATM terminology. (Not to be confused with Private Virtual Circuit, also known as a PVC.)

permissions
Authorization provided to users, allowing them to access objects on the network. The network administrators generally assign permissions. Slightly different from but often used with *rights*.

physical addressing scheme
Refers to the MAC address on every network card manufactured. Cannot be changed.

physical layer
Bottom layer (Layer 1) of the OSI Reference Model, where all physical connectivity is defined.

Plain Old Telephone System (POTS)
The current analog public telephone system. Also known as the PSTN.

Plug and Play
Architecture designed to allow hardware devices to be detected by the operating system and for the driver to be automatically loaded.

Point-To-Point Protocol (PPP)
A common dial-up networking protocol that includes provisions for security and protocol negotiation and provides host-to-network and switch-to-switch connections for one or more user sessions. The common modem connection used for Internet dial-up.

Point-To-Point Tunneling Protocol (PPTP)
A protocol that encapsulates private network data in IP packets. These packets are transmitted over synchronous and asynchronous circuits to hide the underlying routing and switching infrastructure of the Internet from both senders and receivers.

polling
The media-access method for transmitting data, in which a controlling device is used to contact each node to determine if it has data to send.

Port Adapter Modules
Modules attached to the Carrier Access Modules on the LS1010 ATM and Catalyst 5500 Series ATM bus that provide physical ATM line ports for the end-user stations.

Port Aggregation Protocol (PAgP)
Manages the Fast EtherChannel bundles and aids in the automatic creation of Fast EtherChannel links.

PortFast
A protocol that forces an STP port to enter the forwarding state immediately after startup for a single workstation or server connected to a switch port.

Power On SelfTest (POST)
A series of tests run on a Cisco Catalyst switch when the power is turned on. POST tests the hardware, memory, processors, ports, and ASICs to verify they are functioning properly.

presentation layer
Layer 6 of the OSI Reference Model. Prepares information to be used by the application layer.

Primary Rate Interface (PRI)
A higher-level network interface standard for use with ISDN. Defined at the rate of 1.544Mbps, it consists of a single 64Kbps D channel plus 23 (T1) or 30 (E1) B channels for voice or data.

Private Virtual Circuit (PVC)
A logical connection between locations through a Frame Relay and ATM cloud. When a company has three branch offices, and each location physically connects to the Frame Relay provider's network cloud through a series of switches, it appears to the end users as if the three branch offices are directly connected to the local network. (Not to be confused with Permanent Virtual Circuit, also known as a PVC.)

proprietary
A standard or specification that is created by a manufacturer, vendor, or other private enterprise and is not always a recognized standard.

Proprietary Fat Pipe ASIC (PFPA)
An ASIC utilized on the Catalyst 3000 Series switches that use none 10BaseT ports such as Fast Ethernet, 100VG/AnyLAN, ATM, or the Stackport of the Stack Port Matrix. Functionally, the PFPA is the same as the LMA.

protocol
A set of rules that govern network communications between networks, computers, peripherals, and operating systems.

Protocol Identification field
In a frame, a five-byte field used to identify to the destination node what protocol is being used in the data transmission.

protocol stack
Two or more protocols that work together, such as TCP and IP or IPX and SPX. Also known as a *protocol suite.*

Public Switched Telephone Network (PSTN)
All the telephone networks and services in the world. The same as POTS, PSTN refers to the world's collection of interconnected public telephone networks that are both commercial and government owned. PSTN is a digital network, with the exception of the connection between local exchanges and customers, which remains analog.

Quality of Service (QoS)
A guarantee of a particular level of service for a connection. QoS uses queuing and other methods to guarantee that bandwidth is available for a certain protocol, application, or address. QoS is important for implementing applications such as voice and video.

queuing
A way of providing QoS by using buffering and priority control mechanisms to control data congestion on the network.

read/writes
The counting of packets on the ingress (read) as well as the egress (write) from the switching fabric.

Remote Network Monitoring (RMON)
An Internet Engineering Task Force (IETF) standard that defines how devices gather and share network monitoring information used to send information gathered to an SNMP Management Station. RMON gathers Layer 2 information concerning bandwidth use, collisions, and errors. Catalyst switches can gather four of the nine different information types: Statistics, History, Alarms, and Event. The other five groups can be monitored using a SPAN port and an attached protocol analyzer or probe.

remote node
A node or computer that is connected to the network through a dial-up connection. Dialing in to the Internet from home is a perfect example of the remote node concept.

remote services
Services where the device supplying the services resides on a separate subnet from the device requesting the services.

repeater
A device that regenerates and retransmits the signal on a network. Generally used to strengthen signals going long distances.

Request For Comments (RFC)
Method used to post documents regarding networking or Internet-related standards or ideas. Some have been adopted and accepted by the Internet Architecture Board as standards.

resource node
An interface on the network that provides a service for a demand node. Resource nodes can be such items as servers and printers. Incorrect placement of your resource networks can have terrible effects on your network.

rights
Authorization provided to users, allowing them to perform certain tasks. The network administrators generally assign rights. Slightly different from but often used with *permissions*.

ring in (RI)
A connector used in an IBM Token-Ring network on a Multistation Access Unit (MAU) to expand to other MAUs on the network. Counterpart to the RO (ring out), the RI connector on the MAU connects to the media to accept the token from the ring.

ring out (RO)
A connector used in an IBM Token-Ring network on a Multistation Access Unit (MAU) to expand to other MAUs on the network. Counterpart to the RI (ring in), the RO connector on the MAU connects to the media to send the token out to the ring.

RJ-11 connector
Used with telephone systems; can have either four or six conductors. A red/green pair of wires is used for voice and data; a black/white pair is used for low-voltage signals.

RJ-45 connector
An Ethernet cable connector used with twisted-pair cable, which can support eight conductors for four pairs of wires.

Routing Information Field (RIF)
A field on Source Route Bridge Token Ring frames that contains information

about the rings and bridges that the frame must travel to the destination interface.

Routing Information Protocol (RIP)
Protocol that uses hop counts as a routing metric to control the direction and flow of packets between routers and switches on an internetwork.

runtless switching
A switching method where the switch reads the first 64 bytes to verify that there is no corruption of the packet. If there is corruption, a preset maximum of errors changes the switching type from cut-through switching to store-and-forward switching. Also known as *fragment-free switching*.

Secure Data Exchange (SDE) Protocol Data Unit
A field (part of the 802.10 header) that copies the encrypted Protected Header for security purposes to help guarantee against tampering with the frame. Also known as the *Clear Header*.

Security Association Identifier (SAID)
One of the three values that make up a Clear Header on the FDDI frame type. It is used for security for the Clear Header. The Clear Header contains a SAID, LSAP, and the Management Defined Field (MDF).

Sequenced Packet Exchange (SPX)
Protocol used in conjunction with IPX when connection-oriented delivery is required. It is used mainly in NetWare network environments.

server
A resource node that fulfills service requests for demand nodes. Usually referred to by the type of service it performs, such as file server, email server, or print server.

service access point (SAP)
A field in a frame that tells the receiving host which protocol the frame is intended for.

Service Advertising Protocol (SAP)
NetWare protocol used on IPX networks. SAP maintains server information tables, listing each service that has been advertised to it, and provides this information to any nodes attempting to locate a service.

Service Advertising Protocol (SAP) agent
Router or other node on an IPX network that maintains a server information table. This table lists each service that has been advertised to it and provides this information to any nodes attempting to locate a service.

session
The dialogue that exists between two computers.

session layer
The fifth layer of the OSI Reference Model, which establishes, manages, and terminates sessions between applications on different nodes.

shared systems
The infrastructure component routed directly into the backbone of an internetwork for optimal systems access. Provides connectivity to servers and other shared systems.

shielded twisted-pair (STP)
Twisted-pair network cable that has shielding to insulate the cable from electromagnetic interference.

Simple Network Management Protocol (SNMP)
A protocol used in TCP/IP networks to provide network devices with a method to monitor and control network devices. It is used to manage configurations, statistics

collection, performance, and security, and to report network management information to a management console that is a member of the same community.

Simple Network Management Protocol (SNMP) trap
An SNMP protocol utility that sends out an alarm in an identified community notifying members of the community that some network activity differs from the established threshold, as defined by the administrator.

Simple Server Redundancy Protocol (SSRP)
A Cisco protocol that provides redundancy for all LANE server components.

Single Attached Station (SAS)
A FDDI device that has only a single connection to a single DAC.

smart bridge
A bridge that builds its own bridging address table—no manual configuration or intervention is required. Also known as a *learning bridge*.

socket
A logical interprocess communications mechanism through which a program communicates with another program or with a network.

socket identifier
An 8-bit number used to identify the socket. Developers and designers of services and protocols usually assign socket identifiers. Also known as a *socket number*.

source address
The address of the host who sent the frame. It is contained in the frame so the destination node knows who sent the data.

Source Route Bridging (SRB)
A type of bridging used to segment Token Ring networks that requires all rings and bridges to have a unique number.

Source Route Switching (SRS)
A type of bridging that combines SRB and SRT. Developed to allow more physical rings on the network. It allows for growing bandwidth needs while preserving the benefits of SRB.

Source Route Translational Bridging (SR/TLB)
A type of bridging that bridges a Token Ring segment to another physical media type such as Ethernet or FDDI. It is transparent to the source and destination interfaces.

Source Route Transparent Bridging (SRT)
A type of bridging that combines SRB and TB. Using SRT, the bridge places a RIF into a frame traveling from the TB to the SRB side. It then strips the RIF when the frame travels from the SRB port to the TB port.

Source Service Access Point (SSAP)
A one-byte field in the frame that combines with the SAP to tell the receiving host the identity of the source or sending host.

Spanning Tree Algorithm (STA)
Defined by IEEE 802.1 as part of the Spanning Tree Protocol to eliminate loops in an internetwork with multiple paths. The Spanning Tree Algorithm is responsible for performing Spanning Tree Protocol topology recalculations when a switch is powered up and when a topology change occurs.

Spanning Tree Protocol (STP)
Protocol developed to eliminate the loops caused by the multiple paths in an internetwork. Defined by IEEE 802.1. The Spanning Tree Protocol communicates topology changes from switch to switch with the use of Bridge Protocol Data Units (BPDUs).

static IP addresses
IP addresses that are assigned to each network device individually; often referred to as *hard-coded*.

static VLAN port
A port on a switch manually assigned a VLAN number. Any node or interface connected to the port automatically becomes a member of the assigned VLAN.

static window
A mechanism used in flow control that prevents the sender of data from overwhelming the receiver. Only a set amount of data can be buffered in a static window.

station IPX address
A 12-digit number that is used to uniquely identify each device on an IPX network.

storage area network
A subnetwork of storage devices, usually found on high-speed networks and shared by all servers on the network.

store-and-forward
A fast packet-switching method that produces a higher latency than other switching methods. The switch waits for the entire packet to arrive before checking the CRC. It then forwards or discards the packet.

StreetTalk
A global naming service created by Banyan and included with the Banyan VINES network operating system.

subnet mask
A 32-bit address that is used to mask or "screen" a portion of the IP address to differentiate the part of the address that designates the network and the part that designates the host.

subnetting
The process of dividing your assigned IP address range into smaller clusters of hosts.

Subnetwork Access Protocol (SNAP)
An Internet protocol that specifies a standard method of encapsulating IP datagrams and ARP messages on a network.

supernetting
Aggregating IP network addresses and advertising them as a single classless network address.

switch
A Layer 2 networking device that forwards frames based on destination addresses.

switch block
Switching devices located in wiring closets, requiring high-speed uplinks and redundancy.

Switched Multimegabit Data Service (SMDS)
Defined by IEEE 802.6; the physical-layer implementation for data transmission over public lines at speeds between 1.544Mbps (T1) and 44.736Mbps using cell relay and fixed-length cells.

Switched Port Analyzer (SPAN)
A port at which traffic from another port or group of ports is attached to a protocol analyzer or probe device. The SPAN aids in the diagnoses of problems related to traffic patterns on the network.

switched virtual circuit
A virtual circuit that is established dynamically on demand to form a dedicated link and is then broken when transmission is complete. Also known as a *switched virtual connection* in ATM terminology.

switching fabric
A term used to describe the "highway" the data takes to get from the input port on a switch to the output port.

synchronous transmission
Digital signal transmission method using a precise clocking method and a predefined number of bits sent at a constant rate.

syslog
Messages sent to a remote machine regarding the switch system configuration, such as software and configuration changes.

T1
Digital WAN carrier facility that transmits DS-1–formatted data at 1.544Mbps through the telephone switching network, using AMI or B8ZS coding.

TACACS+
A security feature that uses an MD5 encrypted algorithm to enforce strict authentication controls. It requires both a user name and password, allowing administrators to better track network usage and changes based on user accounts.

TCP/IP
See *Transmission Control Protocol/Internet Protocol.*

Telecommunications Industry Association (TIA)
An organization that develops standards—with the Electronics Industries Association (EIA)—for telecommunications technologies.

Telnet
Standard terminal-emulation protocol in the TCP/IP protocol stack. It is used to perform terminal emulation over TCP/IP via remote terminal connections, enabling users to log in to remote systems and use resources as if they were connected to a local system.

thicknet coax
Thick cable most commonly found in the backbone of a coaxial network. Usually about .375 inch in diameter.

thinnet coax
Cable that is thinner than thicknet; about .25 inch in diameter. It is commonly used in older bus topologies to connect the nodes to the network.

token
A frame that provides controlling information. In a Token Ring network, the node that possesses the token is the one that is allowed to transmit next.

Token Ring
An IBM proprietary token-passing LAN topology defined by the IEEE 802.5 standard. It operates at either 4 or 16Mbps in a star topology.

Token Ring adapters
Traditional ISA or Microchannel devices with 4 or 16Mbps transfer capability, used to connect nodes to a Token Ring network.

topology
The shape or layout of a physical network and the flow of data through the network.

Transmission Control Protocol (TCP)
Part of the TCP/IP protocol stack. A connection-oriented, reliable data-transmission communication service that operates at the OSI transport layer.

Transmission Control Protocol/ Internet Protocol (TCP/IP)
The suite of protocols combining TCP and IP, developed to support the construction of worldwide internetworks. See *Transmission Control Protocol* and *Internet Protocol.*

Transmission Control Protocol/ Internet Protocol (TCP/IP) socket
A socket, or connection to an endpoint, used in TCP/IP communication transmissions.

transmit
The process of sending data using light, electronic, or electric signals. In networking, this is usually done in the form of digital signals composed of bits.

Transparent Bridging (TB)
A bridging type that uses the MAC address to make forwarding and filtering decisions transparent to the sender and receiver interfaces. Used in Ethernet.

transport layer
Layer 4 of the OSI Reference Model; controls the flow of information.

Trivial File Transfer Protocol (TFTP)
A simplified version of FTP, allowing files to be transferred over a network from one computer to another. Also used to install the Cisco IOS on an IOS-based switch, router, or GSR.

trunk link
A special type of VLAN connection. Unlike a user port, trunk links expect the device at the other end of the connection to understand the inserted frame tags. Standard Ethernet and Token Ring cards do not understand frame tags.

twisted-pair
A type of cable that uses multiple twisted pairs of copper wire.

unicast
A frame in which the destination MAC address specifies the single computer of destination. Summarized as direct network traffic between two individual nodes.

unshielded twisted-pair (UTP)
A type of cable that uses multiple twisted pairs of copper wire in a casing that does not provide much protection from EMI. The most common network cable in Ethernet networks, it is rated in five categories.

UplinkFast
Provides fast convergence after an STP topology change and achieves load balancing between redundant links.

User Datagram Protocol (UDP)
A communications protocol that provides connectionless, unreliable communications services and operates at the transport layer of the OSI model. It requires a transmission protocol such as IP to guide it to the destination host.

User to Network Interface (UNI)
An interface that provides a connection between an ATM end-station interface and an ATM switch interface.

virtual LAN (VLAN)
Allows a network administrator to divide a bridged network into several broadcast domains. Each VLAN is considered its own separate subnet, and Layer 3 routing is still required to route between VLANs. VLANs can be based on the port identifier of the switch, the MAC address, Layer 3 addressing, directory information, or application information. VLANs can be implemented on different media types such as Ethernet, FDDI, Token Ring, or ATM. The benefits of VLANs are limited broadcast domains, added security, and redundancy.

virtual private network (VPN)
A network that uses a public network such as the Internet as a backbone to connect two or more private networks. Provides users with the equivalent of a private network in terms of security.

VLAN Trunking Protocol (VTP)
A protocol used to enhance and configure the extension of broadcast domains across multiple switches. VTP dynamically reports the addition of VLANs throughout the switched network, in turn creating a consistent switched network.

VLAN Trunking Protocol (VTP) pruning
A protocol used to reduce the number of switches participating in VTP by removing switches from the database that do not have certain VLANs assigned to numbered ports. For example, if switch 1 and switch 2 have ports belonging to VLAN 6 and switch 3 does not, switch 2 will not forward VLAN 6 traffic on the trunk link to switch 3 unless switch 3 is a gateway to another switch that has VLAN 6 member ports. If VTP pruning were not enabled on a trunk port, all VLAN traffic would travel through the trunk links to all the switches whether they had destination ports or not.

wide area network (WAN)
Data communications network that serves users across a broad geographical area. Often uses transmission devices such as modems and Channel Service Units/Data Service Units (CSU/DSU) to carry signals over leased lines or common carrier lines.

window flow control
A flow-control method in which the receiving host buffers the data it receives and holds it in the buffer until it can be processed. After it is processed, an acknowledgment is sent to the sender.

INDEX

B

C

F

I

K

L

N

Q

R

T

U

V

W

X

What's on the CD-ROM

The *CCNP Switching Exam Prep* companion CD-ROM contains elements specifically selected to enhance the usefulness of this book, including:

- *One 100-question practice exam*—The practice exam questions simulate the interface and format of the actual certification exams. You can choose from numerous testing formats, including Fixed-Length, Random, Test All, and Review. You also have the option to save a test and go back to it later so you can take the same test over, or so you can review the questions you got wrong.
- *Getting Excited About Switching!*—A basic overview PowerPoint slide presentation of switching and related concepts to help explain the benefits of switching, basic terms, and switch architectures.

System Requirements

Software

- *For the CD questions*—Your operating system must be Windows 95, 98, NT 4, 2000, or higher.
- *For the Getting Excited About Switching! PowerPoint slide presentation*—Use Microsoft PowerPoint 97 or Microsoft PowerPoint 2000.

If you do not have Microsoft PowerPoint, you can use the Microsoft PowerPoint Viewer available for free from the Microsoft Web site at **http://support.microsoft.com/support/kb/articles/Q110/8/41.ASP**.

There are two versions of Microsoft PowerPoint Viewer: The 16-bit PowerPoint Viewer (Pptvw16.exe) can be used with Windows 3.1, Windows NT 3.51, or Windows 95. The 32-bit PowerPoint Viewer (Pptvw32.exe) can be used with Windows NT 3.51/4.0, Windows 95/98, or Windows 2000.

Hardware

- An Intel (or equivalent) Pentium 100MHz processor is the minimum platform required; an Intel (or equivalent) Pentium 133MHz processor is recommended.
- 32MB of RAM is the minimum requirement.
- Available disk storage space of at least 10MB is recommended.
- A color monitor (256 colors) is recommended.